THE NEW ILLUSTRATED
ENCYCLOPEDIA OF
MOTORCYCLES

THE NEW ILLUSTRATED
ENCYCLOPEDIA OF
MOTORCYCLES

Edited by Erwin Tragatsch
Revised by Brian Woolley

THE WELLFLEET PRESS
WELLFLEET

A QUARTO BOOK

Published by Wellfleet Press
114 Northfield Avenue
Edison, New Jersey 08837

ISBN 1-55521-809-1

Reprinted 1994

This book was designed and produced by
Quarto Inc
The Old Brewery
6 Blundell Street
London N7 9BH

Original edition edited and written by the late
Erwin Tragatsch, with additional text by David
Minton and Graeme Ewens. New and revised text
for this edition by Brian Woolley. Original
photography from the collection of the late
Erwin Tragatsch, Classic Bike and EMAP.

Typeset in Britain by QV Typesetting, London
Manufactured in Hong Kong
by Regent Publishing Services Limited
Printed in China
by Leefung-Asco Printers Limited

CONTENTS

INTRODUCTION

The author, on a 498cc four-cylinder Gilera works racing machine.

THIS ENCYCLOPEDIA lists in alphabetical sequence more than 2,500 makes of motorcycle, produced in at least 30 countries, from 1894 to the present day. The companies' commercial and sporting histories and their ranges of models, whether great or small, are discussed. Facts, figures, dates and technical details are provided. Many of the entries are illustrated, sometimes with hitherto-unpublished photographs.

Some of the early firms listed were very small, and assembled their machines entirely from bought-in parts, but all of them made production motorcycles. Companies which produced only 'one-offs', or which were merely workshops or dealers, are not included. The principal engines used by each manufacturer are detailed, and there are additional lists of important proprietary engines. There are also separate lists showing the major models of motorcycle produced throughout the world during interesting periods in the history of the industry.

I believe this to be the most comprehensive book of its kind, and I hope that it will be interesting not only to the motorcycle technician, dealer and sportsman but also to the collector, owner (past or present) or simply the enthusiast. When I began to compile my previous book *The World's Motorcycles, 1894–1963*, some of my friends in the industry suggested that I had engaged myself in an impossible task. When the

book was published, it became a best-seller, filling a gap in the bookshelves of many a motorcycle enthusiast. That success led to the compilation of a much bigger book, with its extensive illustration. This latest edition has been completely updated, new photographs have been included and some existing ones superseded by better illustrations.

My involvement with motorcycles has been life-long. I have worked within the industry itself, in the motorcycle trade, in motor-sport, and in the motoring Press. My own experience, and widespread international research over a long period, have helped me fill the pages which follow. I have been helped by veteran riders, designers, manufacturers and their employees, many of them personal friends. Some of them have provided from memory details of machines which were built many decades ago.

Acquaintanceships have been renewed, and pleasant times recalled. It may have been 'impossible', but it was thoroughly enjoyable. I hope you enjoy it, too.

Erwin Tragatsch

Erwin Tragatsch

THE PIONEER YEARS

IN THE SECOND half of the 19th century, both in Europe and in the USA, there were a good many attempts to build a practical steam bicycle. None was truly successful. Reducing engine and steam system to a manageable size and weight almost inevitably compromised power output and reliability, but the real drawback was the speed with which any steam engine evaporated its water. Topping-up the boiler feed water tank every ten or 15 miles was hardly convenient, or indeed always possible, while carrying a reserve supply was no answer at all. Few people did more to further the cause of the light steam-powered vehicle than the famous Count de Dion, yet his first sight of a very early petrol-engined car was enough to convince him that here lay the future. For all his success hitherto with steam, it was to the internal combustion engine that he immediately turned.

The internal combustion engine itself went through a considerable period of development and refinement. The earliest gas engines had no compression stroke and so were extremely inefficient. Etienne Lenoir's commercially successful workshop engine of 1860 drew in gas and air for half of one stroke, whereupon it was ignited, the subsequent expansion providing what power there was. Exhaust took place on the return stroke. The engine was 'double acting' — ignition took place on both sides of the piston. The four-stroke cycle of induction, compression, expansion and exhaust, proposed by French railway engineer Alphonse Beau de Rochas in 1862, was first attempted — and patented — by Nikolaus Otto of the Deutz gas engine works in Germany in 1876. Nine years later,

Otto's one-time colleagues, Gottlieb Daimler and Paul Maybach, tested a liquid-fuelled four stroke engine in a two wheeled chassis they called the 'Einspur'. Often spoken of as the world's first motorcycle, the Einspur, of course, was intended to test only the engine, but, in fact, it was a remarkably well thought-out and practical vehicle for its time.

Daimler's engine was astonishingly well adapted to automotive use. Light and self-contained, it was of 270cc, with the flywheel assembly enclosed in a cast aluminium crankcase, with a fan-cooled cast iron cylinder and cylinder head. The inlet valve opened automatically, while the exhaust valve was push-rod operated from a camtrack in the face of one of the flywheels. The 'benzene' (petrol) fuel was vaporised by passing air over its surface in a carburettor. Mistrusting electrical ignition, the inventors used a 'hot tube' of platinum, heated externally by a petrol-fuelled burner. The engine ran at the then remarkable speed of 800rpm, and produced something like half a horsepower.

That Europe was indeed ready for the automotive engine in 1885 is shown by the almost simultaneous appearance of petrol engined tricars from Karl Benz in Germany and Edward Butler in England. Of the two, Butler's was in its later, developed form far the more sophisticated, but repressive British traffic laws, not repealed until 1896, prevented it ever reaching commercial production. Butler's engine was fitted with rotary valves, a sort of primitive 'magneto' (actually dependent on the generation of static electricity rather than magnetic flux) and a spray carburettor, rather than a surface vaporiser.

Butler's patent on the carburettor prevented later inventors from obtaining a monopoly.

Count Albert De Dion and his partner Georges Bouton of the firm of De Dion, Bouton, probably did as much — and more — than anyone else to further the cause of the early motorcycle. They themselves concentrated in the 1890s on petrol-engined tricycles rather than on two wheelers, but their single-cylinder engine was suitable for both. In 1897 De Dion, Bouton offered these engines for sale to all comers, thus enabling scores of experimenters to copy — and improve upon — the remarkably successful machine popularised by the Werner brothers. As a result, the De Dion engine was copied — with and without acknowledgement — and made under licence all over the world, In its early form, the De Dion was of 70mm × 70mm 270cc, which was very soon uprated to 86mm × 86mm 500cc. As an indication of the De Dion's outstanding penetration of the market, it was significant that these were the engine dimensions chosen by Britain's newly formed Auto Cycle Club in 1903, when it came to standardise capacity classes for competition.

The engine was entirely conventional with air cooling, automatic inlet valve, surface carburettor and battery and coil ignition. However, it set new standards in precision engineering and provided a bench mark for power and reliability by which all other contemporary engines were judged. Needless to say, it soon had many rivals, of which the Belgian Minerva and the French Clement were the most popular, while inventors were quick to improve on the basic concept. As early as

Germany's Hildebrand and Wolfmuller Motorrad (left, top), the world's first production motor cycle. By the 1920s, BMW was leading the German industry, with its methodical production approach (left, bottom).

Infinitely variable ratio belt drive as used by Rudge (left, bottom). The pulleys expanded and contracted in sympathy to keep the belt adjusted. The 550cc side-valve Triumph, in the three-speed Sturmey Archer countershaft gearbox, was introduced in 1915 (right, bottom).

1898 in Britain, Coventry's Percy Riley, later to become a famous car maker, built an engine with a mechanically operated inlet valve, and went on to develop (and patent) 'overlap' valve timing. There were spray carburettors in profusion, one of the best of which was the British Amac of 1903. The hated and unreliable battery and coil ignition system was gradually superseded by the magneto, perfected through the work of Frederick Simms in England and Robert Bosch in Stuttgart in collaboration, first as a low-tension system and, then in 1902 as a high-tension one with rotating armature. (As a result of Bosch's developments, high tension magnetos became a virtual German monopoly, which led to some practical difficulties on the outbreak of the First World War in 1914).

Early development of the motorcycle seemed best advanced when it was left to the instincts of 'practical men' — gifted amateurs and superior blacksmiths, rather than formal engineers. This is no doubt a gross oversimplification, but certainly the purpose-designed Hildebrand and Wolfmuller Motorrad of 1894 was a failure, as was the equally impressive four-cylinder motor cycle designed by Colonel Holden — later to design the Brooklands track — a few years later. Both employed direct drive via the exposed connecting rods to crank axles on the rear spindle, which naturally severely limited engine speed and flywheel effect. In point of fact, the Motorrad had a capacity of no less than 1490cc, and made about 2hp at 380 rpm — at which engine speed of about 25mph was attained. All that bulk, weight and complication produced a performance that was put to shame by the Werner brothers' crude Motocyclette.

From time to time, other engineers took a look at the motorcycle of their day and decided that they could do better. In 1908, for instance T W Badgery of the James Cycle Co commissioned a design from the well thought of consulting engineer P L Renouf, which was the sensation of that year's London Motor Cycle Show. The 'Safety James' had a tubular chassis on car lines, centre-hub steering, quickly detachable wheels on single sided stub axles, and internal expanding brakes fore and aft. It had a 500cc single cylinder SV engine of James' own make, and belt drive, with an engine-pulley clutch. Alas, it was a monumental flop, and the James company rapidly turned to more orthodox designs. The response to the four-cylinder air-cooled 680cc Wilkinson TAC and later 850cc water-cooled TMC models was also disappointing. For 1910 and 1912, these offered truly advanced and luxurious specifications, but failed to sell in realistic numbers.

It seemed as though motor cycle design had to advance a bit at a time, not too precipitately and never too boldly. To be sure, Alfred Scott's radical two stroke twin of 1909 (1908 if you count six prototypes built by Jowett Brothers for development) found a market — but never a large one, even after Scott's TT wins in 1912 and 1913. And, in retrospect, the wonder is that the Scott sold at all, for not only was the two-stroke engine virtually unheard of, but this one was a twin and was partly — very soon fully — watercooled. The straight-tube triangulated frame, and the cylindrical fuel tank embracing the saddle tube must also have looked very strange to the average motor cyclist of 1909.

One of the Scott's most striking features was that it had a kickstarter — the first ever offered — and so the engine could be started at rest, and the machine moved off by engaging the lower of two 'gears' — actually two separate primary chains driving two sprockets on a countershaft with expanding clutches. The kickstart apart, there was nothing new about this. P & M, for one, had long since offered such a gear, as had many of the large V twin 'tricars' that were popular between about 1904 and 1909. What riders were demanding at about the same time as the Scott made its appearance, was a 'free engine' or clutch, and it was a big selling point for Triumph when they fitted a multi-plate clutch in the rear hub in 1909. There were, of course, even then, numerous proprietary clutches, usually incorporated in a special belt pulley.

Sprung front forks started to become really popular in about 1907. Again, many were proprietary fittings designed for use on older machines, though, for example, Quadrant had had such a front fork since 1903, while Rex had fitted them as standard since 1906.

Some of the early designs look downright dangerous to modern eyes, and probably were! Once again, the Scott of 1909 had perhaps the best design of all, with a true telescopic action. The famous Druid front fork, with parallel lever action controlled by coil springs first appeared in 1906, and became very popular — almost standard wear on British bikes and in successively modified form — setting a fashion that was to last for 30 odd years and more.

Spring frames were the subject of many an invention in the early years, though very few of them had much merit. Curiously, those that enjoyed a certain success, such as the BAT, the Zenette and the much later Edmund, were not really spring frames at all, but sprung sub-frames, whereby the saddle and footrests were isolated together from road shocks. Such systems did absolutely nothing to help to

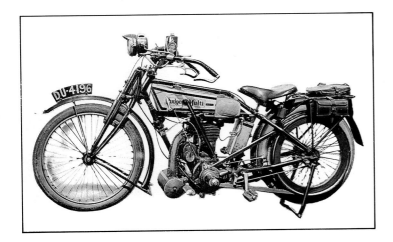

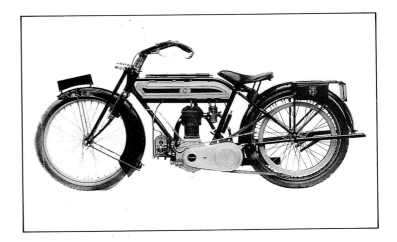

keep the rear wheel in contact with the road.

Lighting remained an afterthought. Few people rode at night in any case, and very few motor cycles were sold with lights of any sort. At first, cycle oil lamps were used, and sturdier versions were soon made. But from an early date, acetylene gas lighting became available and was soon accepted as standard. It might be messy and demand considerable looking after, but it was comparatively reliable and cheap.

As for brakes, the less said the better! Even so meticulous an engineer as Alfred Scott could at that time see no further than a cycle type stirrup at the front, and a shoe bearing on the inside of a drum formed in the rear chain sprocket. Front brakes were in any case regarded as mere 'bobby dodgers' not to be used — in the first place because they damaged the paint and plating of the front rim, but also because of the firm conviction that front brakes were dangerous. This superstition was a long time a-dying. As late as the 1960s a national survey in Britain found that over 40% of motor cyclists never used the front brake!

Change speed gears were a fruitful field for inventors in those early years. The 'adjustable pulley' was an early development, usually sold as a proprietary item and a not terribly satisfactory one at that. Early competition riders would carry two belts — one for use on the level, with the pulley flanges screwed close together to give a high ratio. When a freak hill had to be climbed, the pulley flanges were screwed apart and a slightly shorter belt fitted. The once famous Zenith Gradua and Rudge Multi systems were extensions of this idea. These took mechanical control of the driving pulley and, in the case of Zenith, actually automatically extended, or shortened, the wheelbase of the motor cycle to keep the belt taut. The Rudge Multi's rear pully flanges moved in and out in reverse sympathy with those on the engine pulley.

Quite a few simple two speed epicyclic gears — notably the NSU — made an early appearance, and eventually migrated to the rear hub in bicycle fashion. Such three-speed Armstong hubs featured strongly in the results of the 1911 Junior TT, held for the first time on the Mountain circuit in the Isle of

Early days in France and Germany. **Above left: The first Daimler and Maybach two-wheeler. Left: The De Dion-Bouton three-wheeler. Above: Road conditions contrasted infavourably with those of the track. Right: Tessler tweaks a speed record on a British BAT in 1903.**

12

THOSE MAGNIFICENT MEN ON THEIR CYCLING MACHINES

A steam engine, fired by petrol, powered this von Sauerbronn-Davis velocipede, 1883

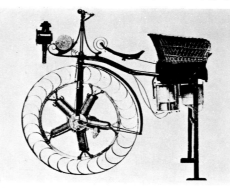

The 1887 Millet prototype had a radial engine similar to those later used in aircraft

Propellor power . . . a chitty, chitty, bang bike by Anzani had its test flight in 1906

Look, no pedals! An ordinary bicycle gets a shove from an auxiliary engine . . . Italy, 1893

'Luxurious, high-powered, all-weather car-ette' . . . twin engined Quadrant, made in Britain, 1905

Where to put the engine? Above the front wheel, perhaps? That (1) was Werner's solution, in 1899. Enfield placed the engine in the same place, but to drive the rear wheel

Strange layouts abounded at the turn of the century . . . Singer positioned the engine in the hub of the front wheel (2). Further variations came from British Excelsior (3), Phelon and Moore (4), Hildebrand and Wolfmüller (5), Beeston (6), Ormonde (7), Singer again (8) and Humber (9).

In Czechoslovakia, Laurin & Klement produced the elegant single-cylinder B–D in 1903 (top), and more sporting versions such as the V-twin CCR (below). Bottom: Ludwig Opel with a 2¾ hp Opel motorcycle on army manoeuvres in 1905.

Man. But the Indians that finished 1-2-3 in the Senior race that year, used countershaft gearboxes, and these made a big impression. Development of such gearboxes was rapid, and their wide acceptance really dated from the use by the Triumph company of the superb Sturmey Archer gearbox and clutch in their late Veteran masterpiece, the 550cc model H of despatch rider fame in the war years between 1914 and 1918.

Throughout the era, the side-valve engine reigned supreme. The ohv layout occasionally appeared for racing, but showed no great superiority. The theoretical advantages of overhead valves were, with compression ratios of about 4-1, more apparent than real, and valve steels being what they then were, the ohv layout was widely mistrusted for its threat of mechanical carnage from a 'dropped' valve. Pistons were universally of cast iron, though racing pistons were painstakingly (and expensively) machined from steel.

Ball and roller bearings were coming into use, especially for racing, but phosphor bronze bushes were still widely used, almost always lubricated by 'spit and hope' total loss systems. These depended upon a simple hand-operated pump transferring oil into the crankcase, whence it was distributed by 'splash'.

Two major companies — JAP, founded in 1903 and Precision dominated the engine scene, as far as Britain was concerned. Though the latter did not start making engines until 1910, their wares rapidly gained a fine reputation. The Stevens brothers of Wolverhampton had made engines of various sizes before settling for making the 350cc AJS motor cycle, while Dalton & Wade, Blumfeld and half a dozen others, long forgotten, also competed for a place. Of imported engines, the MAG, made by Motosacoche of Geneva, was by far and away the most successful.

Nor were these engines the 'longstrokes' beloved of ill-informed myth, but were mostly near-square in their bore and stroke configuration. Towards the end of the period, small capacity V twins became popular, and did well in competitions.

The 'Lightweight' — 250cc — class was hardly established before 1914. By that year, the weak and feeble machines, virtually motorised bicycles, that had struggled for a foothold in 1900, had become sturdy, powerful and reliable motorcycles that had, in the words of a contemporary writer, 'attained a state very close to perfection'. Such complacency invites mockery, but there is no doubt

An early Scott two-stroke with water-cooled cylinder heads and air-cooled cylinders, telescopic front forks and all-chain drive (below) Acetylene powered this early headlamp (bottom).

that, looking back a mere 14 or 15 years, there was some excuse for it. The motor cycle, indeed, had come a long, long way. Few people realised how much further it still had to travel on the road to 'perfection'.

The notorious Devil's Elbow on the T.T. circuit (main picture) and the start of the first-ever T.T. race in 1908 (inset) with its winner, Harry Reed, on his D.O.T. (inset). An Indian came second the following year, having led for half the race.

THE AMERICAN STORY

A STEAM-POWERED bicycle built by Sylvanus Roper in 1870 is still preserved in the Smithsonian Museum in Washington DC, the real involvement of the USA in the story of the motorcycle dates from the importation of a De Dion tricycle in 1898 by Hiram Maxim who, at the time, was — among his many other activities — consulting engineer to Colonel A A Pope's Columbia bicycle manufacturing concern. Columbia, in fact, were the first company to offer a motorcycle for sale in the country in 1900; within months, they had a dozen competitors, none of whom offered much more than the crudest of specifications.

In early 1901, however, the Indian, designed by Springfield bicycle maker, George M Hendee, and toolmaker Oscar Hedstrom, made its first appearance. Its strengthened bicycle frame, retaining the pedalling gear, incorporated the single cylinder engine as part of the seat tube, and thus inclined rearwards. It had an automatic inlet valve and an ingenious spray carburettor of Hedstrom's own design, but the engine itself, though designed by Hedstrom was made by the Thor Manufacturing Co, as were all Indian engines until 1905.

From the start, Indian used chain drive to the rear wheel as did most of their rivals. Curiously, one of the few makes to use belt drive — and to persist with it until 1912 — was the Harley Davidson, first produced for sale in 1904. Though Indian sales were modest at first — 143 machines in 1902 — success came quickly, after good showings in early endurance events, and Hendee and Hedstrom

pursued a policy of innovation and improvement. In 1907, when sales were in the thousands, a V twin engine of 600cc was introduced, built by Indian themselves, with the 'Hedstrom motor' cast into the crankcase. One such machine, with twistgrip throttle control and a sprung front fork, was shipped to Britain, where it took part in the ACC's 1000-mile trial, winning a gold medal. Indian were already extremely alive to the possibilities of export to Europe, and especially to Britain.

In 1909, expatriate American W H Wells was made British concessionaire, and entered himself and George Lee Evans in the Senior TT in the Isle of Man. Sensationally, Evans led the race for half its distance, finishing a close second to Matchless rider Harry Collier. In 1910, Indian introduced a two-speed countershaft gearbox and clutch. Already successful at home in pure speed events on board tracks, they now provided Wells' English agency with racing machines that competed with spectacular success at Brooklands. And for the 1911 Senior TT, run for the first time on the famous Mountain circuit, Indian visited in force, with George Hendee himself, Oscar Hedstrom, ace rider Jake de Rosier, and a full compliment of machinery and race mechanics. They meant to win — and win they did, with their British riders taking the first three places. In 1912, Indian's sales reached 20,000.

Not that Indian had it entirely their own way in America in the first decade of the new century. In racing, and especially in board track

...ey Davidson favoured belt drive (bottom right), but ...f their competitors followed.

One of the all-conquering Indians in the 1911 Senior T.T., seen here at Union Mills. The rider, C.B. Franklyn, was later a leading designer for Springfield.

racing, they had serious rivals in Excelsior, Merkel and Cyclone. Harley Davidson, who made their first V twin in 1909, did not race themselves, but were happy to advertise the success of private owners. And by about 1912, there were at least 30 well-established makes that almost had the status of household names, in US motorcycle manufacturing.

By that time a pattern had been established. Roads that were atrocious by European standards demanded sturdier frames. Front forks were usually of the bottom link pattern and again very robust. Twist grips were common for controls, with the throttle usually on the left, and piano wires were used rather than the Bowden cable that was ubiquitous in Europe.

Brakes were, if anything, ahead of those in Europe, a popular system being a contracting band and expanding shoes using the same drum on the rear wheel. Similarly, American carburettors, such as the Holley, Schebler and Hedstrom, were definitely ahead of their European counterparts. Much attention was paid to comfort, with large and elaborately suspended saddles and sturdy metal footboards. Spring frames were not common, but when offered, as by Pope, they were of sound design. Europeans found American controls difficult. As noted above, the throttle was usually controlled by the left hand, but so were the gears if any and, often, even the clutch — this might have a lever alongside the left hand side of the tank as well as a foot pedal, also on the left.

Lighting and electrical equipment was generally excellent. The US manufacturers did not make the mistake of depending on Germany for magnetos, and offered electric lighting as standard, long before it was thought of in Europe. Indian, indeed, scored a notable 'first' in 1914 with the all electric 'Hendee special' featuring electric starting! Though this innovation was a failure, costing the company a good deal of money, it illustrates Indian's forward-looking attitude.

As early as 1914, however, economic forces were at work that could not be denied. Quite a few of the pioneer names had already disappeared in the face of determined marketing by Indian, Harley Davidson and Excelsior. Now the appearance of incredibly cheap cars, such as Ford's Model T, was to eat into the sales of motorcycles, so it was no coincidence that, between 1915 and 1918, such well thought of companies as Pope, Yale, Iver Johnson, Cyclone, Thor and Peerless ceased production along with many others. Of those 'household names' a mere half dozen survived into the 1920s and only Indian, Harley Davidson and Excelsior lasted out the decade.

Excelsior — sold in Europe as 'the American X' — had sprung from Ignatz Schwin's bicycle manufacturing company in Chicago in 1908 and during the war years had absorbed the Detroit-built four-cylinder in-line Henderson, which Excelsior were to sell in vastly improved form post-war. In-line fours, indeed, became something of a cult in the USA. They had their origin in the Pierce Arrow of 1909, a free-hand copy of an imported Belgian FN. The Pierce lasted just long enough to inspire the Henderson, first made in 1912. Post war, the Henderson brothers left Excelsior to make the Ace, which, when Bill Henderson was killed in a road accident, passed in due course to Indian. As the Indian Four, it remained in production until the USA entered the Second World War in 1941.

The USA's other highly respected in-line four was the Cleveland, made from 1925 to 1929. All of these were extremely powerful luxurious motorcycles with tireless performance. As much as anything, they exemplified a general US trend in the 1920s towards a super sporting performance that no car — cheap or otherwise — could provide. With a power-to-weight ratio at least three times better than that of a powerful car, US V twins and fours were used in large numbers by the police, the armed forces and, to a lesser extent, by public utilities. They also sold to sporting enthusiasts, the V twins forming the backbone of

Class C Amateur racing in the 1930s. The demands of off-road competition, hill climbing, and long distances on the vastly improved roads of that era resulted in motorcycles that, to European eyes, soon became grotesquely over-engineered.

Excelsior had dropped out of contention in 1931 to concentrate on bicycles and, for most of the 1930s, Indian and Harley Davidson were on a fairly equal footing in almost every respect. There was one vital difference, however. George Hendee had retired from his Indian company in 1916. Harley Davidson remained firmly in the hands of the families who had started it back in the pioneer days of the 1900s.

The 1930s saw a general stagnation in design, confirmed rather than otherwise by Class C competition, which limited amateur racing to side-valve engines of 750cc. An afterthought in the regulations allowed over-head-valve engines of 500cc, though this remained academic, until Canadian rider Billy Matthews won the 1941 Daytona 200 mile race on a Norton International! The overwhelming popularity of British motor cycles in the USA after the Second World War was a phenomenon that the local industry could never have foreseen. Harley Davidson retrenched — and bought out the Italian Aermacchi company between 1956 and 1960. Indian, however, tried to meet the invasion head on with a totally new European-type range, the so-called 'Torque' models, the 220cc (later 250cc) and 440cc (later 500cc) single-cylinder Arrow and vertical twin Scout. A 1000cc in-line four was also planned. At this point, the British company J Brockhouse & Co provided a massive capital injection that gave them control, not only of the Indian Sales Corporation, but of manufacturing at Springfield. Losses on the

During the First World War, the American Forces ordered 70,000 Harleys, some rigged as armed outfits (above). Britain had a Clyno-Vickers machine-gun outfit (below).

The fust Yank and Harley to enter Germany 11/12/18

Torque range forced Brockhouse to suspend manufacture in 1953 and subsequent 'Indians' sold in America were thinly-disguised British models. Indian's long and honourable history was over.

Harley Davidson took a different view of the US market. Arguing that, though lightweights might be popular, there would always be sales for the traditionally rugged style of native motorcycle, they re-designed and updated their big V twins and elevated their ownership into a cult. They were able to use their Italian connection to satisfy the consid-

Historic border-crossing (left) by Harley-Davidson on Armistice Day, 1918. British dispatch-riders used machines by Phelan and Moore, Douglas, BSA, Triumph and others.

erable demand for cheaper and lighter models with at least an American name, meanwhile doggedly improving their bigger and better V twins. The Aermacchi connection was severed in the late 1970s. By that time, persistance, determination and excellence of management had once again made Harley Davidson a force to be reckoned with in the US market. They had survived the British invasion, the subsequent flooding of the market by the Japanese and the brief era of Spanish imports. In the 1980s, indeed, Japanese manufacturers paid Harley Davidson the ultimate compliment of blatantly copying their layout and styling! Harley Davidson's survival — and survival in good health and on their own terms — is one of the most fascinating episodes in motor cycling's long and honourable history.

Small-town America, 1910. A Sunday morning gathering of enthusiasts in Nebraska, about to set off for a 150-mile jaunt.

The mid-1930s Harley Davidson (left) and Indian (right), both the product of Class C amateur racing.

THE 1920s...THE GOLDEN AGE

GOLDEN AGES BECOME so only in retrospect, so no doubt motor cyclists everywhere grumbled just as much about their grievances in the years between the wars as they ever did before, or have done since. Those years, however, definitely saw enormous changes for the better, both in the economic circumstances of the average enthusiast — this was the first time ordinary wage earners found themselves able to afford to buy and run a motor cycle — and in the way motor cycles were designed.

If the average motor cycle of 1939 is compared with that of 1919, the average enthusiast would marvel not so much at the differences but at the improvements. Side valves have given way to overhead versions, which are fully enclosed at that, quietened by a copious circulation of oil that, as a bonus, carries away excessive heat from the cylinder head. The lubrication system itself is vastly improved, with, instead of the arbitrary injection of oil by a simple hand-operated pump, automatic engine-driven pumps circulating it to every vital part and allowing it to cool by returning it to the oil tank. Dubious three-speed gearboxes with clumsy hand change have given way to foolproof four-speed varieties, operated by a foot pedal. Brakes have improved beyond belief. So have tyres, which are now wired onto the rims rather than held on by air pressure. No longer does a deflated tyre roll off the rim in lethal fashion. Transmission belts have been replaced by chains. Even the cheapest lightweight two-stroke has electric lighting, usually with a battery and automatic control that ensures correct charging by the built-in dynamo.

The motor cycle of 1939, therefore, is altogether a more practical affair than its 1919 ancestor. It is easier to clean, too, with lavish user of untarnishable, durable chromium plating in place of nickel, which, unless laboriously polished, dulled to a dirty grey within weeks. Performance has been transformed as well. Between the first post-war Senior TT of 1920 and that of 1939, the speed had risen from the 51.48mph of Tommy de la Hay's side-valve Sunbeam to the staggering 89.38mph of Georg Meier's supercharged double ohc BMW twin.

Such was the universal appeal of motor cycling in these years that, despite local influences and accidents that shaped the designs of one national industry along other lines to those of another, progress was constant, in Europe at any rate. That the same was not true of the USA was not the fault of the US motorcycle industry.

In fact, the best American motor cycles of 1919 were considerably in advance of most of their European contemporaries. Pre war, the US industry had already standardised the use of countershaft gearboxes, while, in Europe flimsy epicyclic hub gears had been all the rage. Similarly, the USA had gone over to chain drive, while Europe stuck to the belt. The motor cycles themselves were handsome, powerful and robustly made. The factories were superbly equipped, taking advantage of the most up-to-date production methods, which meant that US machines could be shipped across the Atlantic and still sell at competitive prices. They did so in sufficient quantities to panic the British and European domestic industries into demanding that tariff barriers should be erected to half this penetration. This came to pass. For all their vision and efficiency, US manufacturers were abruptly denied access to an export market that had become vital to them, because cheap cars, a menace before the war, now threatened the very existence of the domestic American motor cycle.

The industry shrank and retrenched, with many of the companies that had survived until now disappearing. The 'big three' — Indian, Harley Davidson and Excelsior (makers of big V twins as well as the superb Henderson four) — were forced to depend on what export markets were left to them, and on sales to the police, the armed forces, pubic utilities, and sportsmen. Excelsior stopped manufacture in the face of the depression in 1931, leaving Indian and Harley Davidson to fight out their bitter rivalry.

The USA's vanishing motor cycle industry was saved in the 1930s by the introduction of Class C Amateur racing, whose regulations specified little more than basically standard production machines with 750cc side-valve engines should be used. Events comprised a strange mix of road racing, enduro runs, TT racing, flat track and speedway contents. TT racing was on a dirt surface, with gradients and left and right turns. Flat track was on loose-surfaced tracks of up to half a mile, while speedway racing took place on longer tracks with steeply banked turns.

Class C was an instant success. After 1937, when Daytona Beach became its focal point, a genuine revival of interest in motor cycles and motorcycling resulted. On the other hand, however, the somewhat restrictive formula and the need for one motor cycle to fulfill so many functions led to stagnation and moved the US motor cycle far away from the concepts of European design.

There was another facet of the US scene, particularly in urban California, that is often forgotten. This was the motor scooter, which cropped up over and over again in the years between the wars. It was one such scooter, an American Autoped, owned by a prominent English member of parliament, that found its way into an article in early 1919 in the *Daily News* and started a craze in Britain that amounted to a mania. The newspaper was swamped with letters, literally by the sackful. A rumour that one London store had Autopeds in stock saw people queuing half way down Oxford Street. The interest spilled over into the motor cycle magazines though, to give them their due, the editorial staff showed little enthusiasm. Every week saw dozens of projected designs, most of them crude and impractical. Many small under-capitalised firms were set up to build scooters and a few actually staggered into production, by which time the mania had subsided. This left concerns such as ABC Skootamota, Kenilworth and Autoglider — high and dry. No wonder that British manufacturers hesitated when Italian and German scooters appeared on the market 30 odd years later.

Curiously, though the craze for scooters did not reach the same height in Germany, it

The post-war years saw a short-lived craze for the scooter (left). The unorthodox 5-cylinder Megola was raced by Toni Bauhofer and reached speeds up to 140 km/h.

lasted longer, and DKW made scooters that at least sold in reasonable numbers. Expatriate Danish engineer J S Rasmussen had founded his DKW company at Zschopan near Chemnitz in Saxony to build steam lorries — Dampe Kraft Wagen — but quickly switched after 1919 to making clip-on auxiliary engines for bicycles, scooters and ultra lightweight motor cycles, all powered by simple two-stroke engines designed by Herman Weber. These engines were also widely sold in Germany to other makers. Though DKW did make larger

machines, favourable tax concessions meant that the vast majority were of 200cc and less.

Somehow, the company managed to survive the appalling hyper-inflation of 1923 that killed off so many other concerns and indeed flourished mightily. They began racing in the 175cc and later 250cc classes with Hugo Ruppe-designed engines, utilising his patented Ladepumpe charging piston below the crankcase. Soon these 'blown' DKWs demanded water cooling to cope with their power. They were extremely successful

in road racing and in the long-distance hill climbs so popular in Germany. However, in Grand Prix racing they were not really a match for the British four-strokes, or, for that matter, the Austrian Puchs, which used a split-single two-stroke engine, also pump-charged.

So soundly were DKW beaten by Puch in the 1930 and 1931 seasons that they called in designer Arnold Zoller, who laid out split-single racing engines — still using the charging piston — that were gradually developed into

'Lawrence of Arabia' (big picture)
owned no less than eight Brough-
Superior machines. In the bottom
picture, from the left, designer
and manufacturer George Brough,
racer Eddy Meyer and works manager
Ike Webb outside the factory in 1927.

the most powerful two-strokes that the world had ever seen. As a result, DKW won the 250cc European championship in 1934, 1935 and 1938 and both the 250cc and 350cc championships in 1939. Perhaps their finest achievement was Ewald Kluge's 1938 Lightweight TT win at over 80mph, a result that convinced even the most sceptical.

Germany's other most celebrated and successful motor cycle between the wars was the BMW, first seen at the Paris Salon of 1923. Originally war-time aircraft engine makers, BMW had embarked on a number of enterprises before starting to manufacture a proprietary flat-twin motor cycle engine. They then decided to make a motor cycle of their own, with shaft drive, so that a transverse engine layout and unit gearbox were natural features to incorporate. Like DKW, BMW raced from an early date with great success and adopted supercharging wholeheartedly. Rider Ernst Herne held the world's fastest record no less than six times in the 1930s, BMW won the 500cc European championship of 1938, and in 1939, riders Georg Meier and Jock West finished first and second in the Senior TT.

Innovative and superbly crafted, the big BMW bikes were very expensive as befitted what were probably the best motor cycles in the world in those years. They did make smaller, somewhat less expensive single-cylinder models of between 200cc and 400cc — still with shaft drive — but exclusivity was BMW's trademark. Next to Britain's, the German industry between the wars was probably the busiest in Europe, despite economically troubled times. Strangely, many firms, by no means obscure concerns, used British engines, gearboxes and other proprietary components. To some extent, this was a tribute to the efficiency of the British industry and its resulting low prices, but it also reflected the esteem in which British motor cycles were held on the continent. JAP, Blackburne, Sturmey Archer (Raleigh) and Python (Rudge) engines were widely used, as were the Bradshaw oil-cooled engine and the remarkable Barr & Stroud sleeve valve. It was a considerable loss to Britain when Adolf Hitler came to power and put an end to this widespread dependence on imported compoents. No less was it a source of embarressment to those German firms left high and dry.

As in Germany, France saw an upsurge of interest in motor cycling immediately after the First World War and a number of imaginative and advanced designs were produced.

Aircraft makers Bleriot and engine manufacturers Gnome et Rhone both saw the mass production of motor cycles as the solution for factories suddenly made idle. The former showed interesting vertical twins, while the latter chose to build the British ABC under licence. Somehow, however, French enthusiasm was short-lived, though the native industry tried hard to keep up with the latest technological developments, this soon became little more than a prestige exercise at the annual Paris Salon. What did sell, and in numbers that kept the industry alive if not exactly flourishing, was the 100cc Velomo-

teur that was untaxed and could be ridden without even the formality of a driving licence.

Nor was there the sporting interest in France that so sustained motor cycling in Germany. The French Grand Prix turned into an ill-supported and even worse attended farce. The magnificent racing complex built at Montlhery, 20 miles from Paris, never paid its way — though the 1.7-mile banked track was popular for record breaking. Yet, strangely, the 'speed week' at Arpajon, held on a narrow tree-lined stretch of road with a four mile undulating straight, attracted entrants from all over Europe, while the Bol d'Or, an extraordinary 24-hour race with no change of rider, that started in 1924 on a public road circuit in the forest of St Germain near Paris, survived for the next 15 years. The first race was won by an 500cc ohv Sunbeam, victory in it remaining a British preserve, which makes its survival all the more surprising.

Italy was a late comer to motor cycle manufacture, but, as the 1920s wore on, made up for it in full measure. Garelli and Moto Guzzi joined Gilera and Frera as sporting makers, as did Benelli and Bianchi. Italian designers were early and enthusiastic advocates of ohv and ohc engines and the use of light alloy components and soon developed a sense of style that they have never lost.

Racing — especially long-distance open road racing from town to town — became an Italian institution. With the supercharged Rondine — later Gilera — the Italians could justly have claimed to have begun the trend to four-cylinder racing machines. Dorino Serafini's European title on the 500cc Gilera in 1939 was a taste of things to come. Moto Guzzi first raced in the TT in 1926, and in 1935 were rewarded when Stanley Woods won both Lightweight and Senior races. And in 1937 on a Moto Guzzi Omobono Tenni won the Lightweight TT — the first foreign rider ever to win a TT.

Yet, for all their excellence and sporting pedigree, Italian motor cycles were virtually unknown elsewhere in Europe. Given their reputation in racing and in the International Six Days Trial, why the Italians made no attempt to export is hard to understand. Perhaps it was because, as in Germany, taxation encouraged smaller engines, so many of those exquisite Italian ohc models were of 250cc and below.

Without doubt, however, it was the British industry that dominated European motor cycling between the wars. To some extent, this was because it enjoyed a virtually 'captive' colonial export market, particularly in Australia, but there was naturally more to it than that. The concentration of diverse skills and experience in the British Midlands, the intense competition between not only motor cycle manufacturers, but also the makers of proprietary equipment, and the part played by an unsensational and responsible specialist press all played their parts.

Though British design ws perhaps conservative, this may have been no bad thing — evolution is better than revolution, as history seems to show. In addition, many British designers were only too aware of the strange story of the post-war ABC. This wonder motor cycle, with its 400cc ohv flat twin engine set transversely across the frame, unit construction car-type gearbox with gate change by hand lever, self-dumping leaf-spring suspension fore and aft, internal expanding brakes, ingenious frame design and electric lighting with built-in dynamo, embodied everything that a motor cyclist could wish, including generous weather protection.

Designed by the young Granville Bradshaw, the ABC truly appeared to be ten — even 20 — years ahead of its time when it was revealed in prototype form early in 1919. The machine was to be made by the Sopwith aviation and engineering company in a purpose-equipped factory, with a production target of 10,000 a year, but despite the brilliance of the overall concept and Sopwith's money, the ABC was a damaging fiasco. It took 15 months to reach production, only for Sopwith to go into voluntary liquidation after fewer than 2,500 motor cycles had been made. A disappointed British public turned to the next best, which might not be all that much ahead of the times, but which did at least live up to its maker's claims and its reputation.

Such British marques as Sunbeam, Norton,

By the late 1930s, the German BMW, with oil-damped telescopic front forks, was probably the most luxurious motor cycle.

25

Shown here with his 996cc Zenith, designer and rider Bert le Vack broke many records. Bottom picture: Swiss MAG-engined German Standard machines in the 1928 ADAC five-country trial. The riders are (from left) Pail Rüttchen and Eugen Gerlach.

AJS, Scott, BSA and Triumph sold world wide. British bikes won the TT year after year and the European Grand Prix races as well. Britain's dominance of the market extended beyond the super-sports mould into other areas as well. There were plenty of companies using the 270cc Villiers two-stroke engine, or the small side-valve engines made by JAP or Blackburne. As in Germany, there were many 'manufacturers' who made little themselves, assembling their motor cycles almost entirely from bought-in components. This could be an expensive method, especially for the smaller firms who could not bargain quantity against prices, as could a larger company, such as, say, OK Supreme. Many small firms, and quite a few larger ones were under capitalised, and so did not survive the depression of the early 1930s. Some, however, flourished. New Imperial, for instance, began to make their own engines in the mid 1920s and went on to introduce their own range of unit construction engines and gearboxes and their own cantilever spring frames in the 1930s. Vincent HRD became their own engine makers in the 1930s, as did Excelsior with the famous Manxman ohc engines, which they took over when Blackburne stopped making motorcycle engines.

The king of the assemblers was the incomparable George Brough, who, working from his small Nottingham factory, advertised his Brough Superiors as 'The Rolls Royce of motor cycles'. Brough always insisted on the best, was his own head tester and rode his own machinery in trials and speed events with great success.

Brough Superiors really were hand-made. Having ordered one and paid a deposit, customers were encouraged to visit the factory several times to check on progress. On each visit they were expected to pay a further installment — a procedure that, on the one hand, mad the eventual settling of a the final bill less painful, and, on the other, gave Brough a healthy cash flow.

Most of Brough's machines used big V twin JAP (and in later years Matchless) engines, though he built several 'show stoppers' — a transverse engined V twin, a narrow angle V four and an in-line air-cooled four-in-line, it is doubtful if he had any serious intention of making any of them. However, he did make a dozen or so outfits with an 800cc water-cooled Austin 7 engine, gearbox and shaft drive, with the final drive unit between closely two-strokes — entered the market with a set twin rear wheels. Unfortunately, the outbreak of war in 1939, stopped the develop-

ment of another model that Brough certainly intended to make. This was the ill-fated 1000cc transverse flat four Golden Dream, with contra-rotating crankshafts, unit gearbox and shaft drive. It had been the sensation of the 1938 Motor Cycle Show. If 1920s were the years of development, the 1930s were those of consolidation. The depression of the early 1930s that eliminated many small companies — and brought changes of ownership to several larger ones — only confirmed the conviction that sales depended upon value for money. The resilience of the motor cycle industry was quite remarkable. The years between the wars culminated with the birth of — not a new motor cycle, but a new style of motor cycle — Edward Turner's 500cc Triumph twin. Nothing new in itself, the Speed Twin and its super sports version, the Tiger 100, opened up a whole new prospect. To have been young, to have been able to buy and run a Triumph Twin in 1937 must have been exciting indeed! Little did those lucky few realise what lay ahead not so far in the future. But that is the way of the world, and we cannot blame those who experienced those days — and indeed those who only read about them — from regarding the years between the wars as a Golden Age.

This superb 750cc four-cylinder Moto-became dates from the late 1930s; the average Frenchman in the inter-war years, however, was more likely to be riding the 100cc Velomoteur.

THE STORY OF AN INDUSTRY

THE HISTORY OF ANY long-lived enterprise is shaped by more forces than we usually believe, and the history of the motorcycle industry — and of motorcycles — is no exception.

Foremost — without which there would be no story — was the work of countless individuals. Many of them are now forgotten, though some are remembered, while a few have become legends, but all of them, in whichever country and at whatever time, had to contend with the changing world around them.

Advances in technology, improved materials, new inventions, all had to be taken on board. So did fluctuations in prosperity and the rise and fall of different markets. Changing prices of raw materials — and of petrol — were important. Taxes and tariffs — on imports or exports — could be altered at the stroke of a pen. And industrial strife and unrest could play a major part. These and a thousand other factors over a span of more than 90 years, explain many apparent anomalies.

Early improvements to motorcycles included spray carburettors and high tension magneto ignition, both of which improved reliability beyond belief. Throttle and ignition controls were moved from the tank top to the handlebars and operated by Bowden cables. Automatic inlet valves gave way to mechanical operation. By about 1907, spring front forks were becoming common. Engines were almost all of about 500cc with side valves; larger V twins of up to 1000cc were usually used when a sidecar was to be pulled.

There had been two speed transmissions from a very early date, notabl that designed by Richard Moore of P & M in 1904, but early engines were enormously flexible, and fixed ratio single speed transmission with V belt drive lasted a long time. A belt was light, cheap and gave wonderfully smooth drive without an expensive shock absorber or cush drive. While they might slip in wet weather, belts did not rapidly wear out, from the mud and grit thrown up from water-bound Macadam roads as did exposed chains. Various 'free engine' clutches and variable ratio pulleys were offered from an early date as proprietary fittings; the ingenious Zenith Gradua and Rudge Multi systems of 'infinitely variable' drive prolonged the life of belt drive up to and beyond the First World War.

Brakes in early days were crude. At the front, there was simply a cycle-type stirrup, which nobody used for fear of a front wheel skid on the loose surfaced roads. At the rear,

The scene outside the Rudge depot at the 1911 T.T. Victor Surridge (nearest camera) was killed during a crash in practice shortly after this — the first T.T. fatality.

there was a shoe that wedged into the belt drive rim. But except in cities, traffic was almost unbelievably sparse.

Such was the general state of the motorcycle in Britain and Europe in about 1907. In that year, there were two innovations that were to affect the British industry enormously and help to make it the strongest in Europe by 1914. the 2¾-mile banked track at Brooklands was opened. Subsequently, this was to prove a testing ground that played a valuable role for over 30 years until it was closed for ever by the outbreak of war in 1939. Of even more importance was the Tourist Trophy race in the Isle of Man. Racing in Europe had lost its way since open road events had been banned after the catastrophic Paris-Madrid race of 1903. The main European event, the International Cup, was an ill conceived farce that was not even spectacular, for only three entries were allowed from each country.

Nor did International Cup regulations do anything to spur development of real motorcycles, for engines of unlimited size were allowed with no fuel consumption limits, whilst at the same time, total weight had to be under 110 lb. Cheating, too, was endemic. British riders, disgusted by the 1906 fiasco, approached the Auto Cycle Club of Britian, and the result was the TT.

The Auto Cycle Union, as it had become by 1907, framed regulations year by year that really did 'improve the breed'. Run at first on the 14-odd mile St John course, the race proved a real test and speeds and reliability improved year by year.

The winning speed rose from 38mph in 1907 to over 50mph in 1910. The ACU then — to encourage development of change speed gears — moved the race to the 37½ mile Mountain circuit, which, slightly altered in 1920 to 37¾ miles and improved beyond belief over many years, is still in use today. European manufacturers took part from the start, while, by 1911, such was the TT's prestige that Indian came all the way from the USA to compete — and were rewarded by a 1-2-3 Senior win. This was a shock to British pride, but it was to be a further 24 years before there was another foreign victory.

The outbreak of war in 1914 had little influence on either the industry or on design, though the drying-up of German supplies meant that the making of magnetos had to developed. A few radical post-First World War designs, notably the transverse twin ABC, excited much interest, but the ABC died of slapdash hasty design and the ineptitude of its sponsors — the wartime airframe makers, Sopwith.

Countershaft gearboxes and chain drive — both pioneered by Indian (and made acceptable by their TT win) took over in the early 1920s and gearbox manufacture became another speciality.

Proprietary engine makers fought each

other to a standstill that soon left JAP and Blackburne the survivors with some opposition from the oil-cooled Bradshaw and the unique sleeve valve Barr & Stroud. 'Assembled' motor cycles flourished, their builders making nothing themselves, but buying in engines, frames, gearboxes, wheels, tanks, saddles and other components from the huge infrastructure that had developed. Villiers of Wolverhampton became suppliers of proprietary two-stroke engines to the world. Nor were British exports confined to its empire. Germany became so dependent upon the British industry that by 1930, purchases of engines, gearboxes and other components reached a value exceeded only by exports of complete motor cycles to Australia.

Italy too, was a good customer, for the Italian industry was a late starter. Sunbeam, Norton, AJS and other sporting British machines had a ready sale there. So, too, was France, where the native industry took an easy option, largely making a living from 'Velomoteurs' of 100cc that sold for not much more than the price of a bicycle and needed no road tax, licence or insurance.

Between the wars, the motorcycling world believed that British was best, even though good, even great motorcycles were being made elsewhere. Germany's BMW and DKW, Belgium's FN and Switzerland's Motosacoche, Italy's Gilera and Moto Guzzi, were all excellent makes as were many more. But between the wars, Britain undoubtedly led the world. America's early promise had faded with the success of Henry Ford's Model T. With the Tin Lizzie costing less than a good

motorcycle, only the market for heavy, large capacity high performances bikes was left, exemplified by Indian and Harley Davidson. As American design became introverted and the machines ever bigger and heavier, it lost its appeal in other markets.

After the Second World War, a policy of austerity and petrol rationing at home meant that the British bought mainly utility 125cc and 197cc two-strokes, but the industry set to with a will to sell, to America sporting 500cc and later 600cc and 650cc machines modelled on Triumph's successful pre-war Speed Twin. However, unknowingly, the British industry had entered an era of stagnation. For the moment, it was too easy. Even the dreary little two-strokes found export buyers in their tens of thousands, but, over the next dozen years or so, these markets, most of them in 'empire' countries, were to contract and disappear behind trade barriers favourable to them, but not to the British. Eventually, the only real overseas market left was the USA. The actual home market shrank too — far too much to support the whole industry. A second-hand car rather than a sidecar outfit became the working man's transport. With the appearance of the Austin Morris Mini, the ordinary motor cycle was doomed.

The British industry, with its eye on the USA, seemed particularly inept over the one area that was left in the home market. The appearance of 50cc mopeds from Germany and Italy produced no response. BSA had made a dreadful job of the clever, but flawed, BSA Dandy, while their 75cc Beagle and the 50cc Ariel Pixie scarcely saw production.

Thus, the Japanese — in particular Honda — from a vast and protected home market, were able to penetrate Britain at a level that the domestic manufacturers hardly acknowledged as existing.

When Honda launched their four cylinder 750cc CB750 in the USA in 1969, it gave the British a mortal blow. In an era of high taxation and dreadful labour relations, the BSA company made some terrible blunders and with the ill fated 350cc BSA Fury and Triumph Bandit twins, missed the market entirely for the 1972 season. The Japanese moved in for the kill, and the rest is history.

When the late Erwin Tragatsch first compiled this monumental work, he lamented the still recent facts. 'The saddest story of all', he called the death of the British industry with which he had been so well acquainted. He blamed bad management — of which in later years there had been more than enough. But he also blamed bad government — a point often overlooked by commentators with no experience of business. Yet could anything have saved British motor cycles? Probably not, in view of the shrinking home market, except protectionist policies which no British government would countenance. Germany's proud and confident industry largely collapsed in the late 1950s because of overproduction, rising domestic affluence, the

Inside the machine shop of an early motor cycle factory. Though the actual bikes have changed dramatically, manufacturing methods have not altered that substantially; contrast this picture of a modern Japanese plant with the previous one, which dates from the turn of the century.

The Honda CB750 four-cylinder 'superbike' (below) ended the dominance of large British machines in America. Bottom: Two motorcycling milestones — the 50cc NSU Quickly moped (left) and the tiny Honda 'stepthrough' (right) that emerged a decade later.

appearance of cheap cars and failure to export. Italy's industry was horribly weakened at the same time by labour troubles and, though the Italians did adopt a protectionist attitude, much of what is left of their industry has entered the 1990s in very indifferent health.

It is easy to forget that for roughly 25 years there was a flourishing Spanish industry with quite remarkable export sales to the USA. It was hampered — and yet at the same time protected — by the Franco regime's insistence on self sufficiency, and export successes were largely based on the low Spanish labour costs of the time. But when Spain again became part of the European community, its industry was as vulnerable as any to the Japanese.

Worldwide, sales of motor cycles have dropped to such a low total figure that the output of one vigorous and extremely efficient industry, the Japanese, can satisfy the entire demand. In fact it can more than satisfy it, and signs are that even the Japanese industry is suffering from over-production.

Attempts both in Britain and elsewhere to establish a sort of 'bespoke' motor cycle industry — selling expensive hand made machines of individualistic design have met with various difficulties. A few have been minimally successful. Some more ambitious ventures, such as Hesketh, have been failures. It would be unfair and premature to apply that epithet to the rotary engined Norton, but that company has had an uphill struggle. John Bloor's brave attempt to revive Triumph is too young to be judged.

In Britain at any rate, successive legislation has, in the 1990s, made it harder and harder to become a motor cyclist at all, and at the end of 1991, draconian rises in the cost of insurance look like accelerating motor cycling's decline.

In astonishing contrast is the interest of Britain and Europe in the 'classic movement' which was focussed by the publication in the late 1970s of the magazine *Classic Bike* and which has gathered momentum ever since. A whole new industry has arisen to service this interest. Perhaps one day from this will come a new motorcycle industry — who knows? Stranger things have happened as the 20th century enters its last decade.

Many different manufacturers supplied machines for military use. American M.P.s used the Harley-Davidson; BMW supplied their R35 (below) and R75 (right). Bottom: BSA were one of the major British suppliers, making both 350 and 500cc models. The Indian soldier is reclining on a Matchless G3/L, a 350cc ohv machine.

THE GREAT DESIGNERS

PERHAPS the first really famous design, if only because it was so bold, was Paul Kelecom's FN four-cylinder-in-line of 1904. At first of only 400cc, it had shaft drive but neither clutch nor gears. It was rapidly improved and enlarged, gained a clutch and gears and not only sold extensively in its native Belgium, but was exported to England and America. The first American 'in-line-four', the Pierce Arrow, was an acknowledged copy of an imported FN and started a tradition that embraced Henderson, ACE, Excelsior, Cleveland and Indian. The FN 4, latterly of 750cc and with chain final drive, was made until 1926. Nor was this Kelecom's only successful design.

In England, Alfred Scott virtually re-invented the Day-cycle (crankcase compression) two-stroke engine, developing it over several years into a small twin suitable for a motorcycle. First offered for sale in 1909, the 'two speed, two cylinder, two stroke' Scott was a design of remarkable integrity that sold steadily until the end of the 1920s. Indeed the engine layout lasted into the 1960s.

The air-cooled single-cylinder Levis two-stroke, designed by Howard (Bob) Newey and the Butterfield half-brothers, was the first downright practical and uncomplicated light-weight. It first appeared in 1911, became enormously successful and was the basis of Levis two-strokes until 1939. It was also very widely imitated and made under licence. The German Zundapp company paid it a wonderful compliment in 1921 when they copied it to the smallest detail — without acknowledgement. They subsequently copied Levis model changes year by year until 1926.

No such copying was involved in the Velocette two-stroke of 1913, designed by Percy Goodman. Velocette, too, continued to make excellent two-strokes until the Second World War. Goodman also designed the immortal overhead camshaft K series of Velocettes, which first appeared in 1925, and later, the 'high camshaft' series of MOV, MAC and MSS — 250cc, 350cc and 500cc. The 500cc Velocetter 'Thruxton' was still in production in 1970 — a design life of 37 years.

Other long-lived designs include the horizontal single-cylinder layout of Carlo Guzzi's Moto Guzzi of 1921, Adalberto Garelli's side-by-side split-single two-stroke of 1933 and Giovanni Marcellino's fore-and-aft split single Puch (with asymmetrical port timings) that stayed in production in one model or another from 1923 until the late 1960s.

However, very rarely is a design really and truly 'original'. Edward Turner is often credited with having 'invented' the even-firing vertical twin with his Triumph Speed Twin of 1937. This is nonsense. There had been dozens of such twins in the past, while Triumph themselves had made the 650cc Val Page designed 6/1 twin since 1933, and even that was probably inspired by designs by Herman Reeb that Horex in Germany had launched a year earlier as 600cc and 800cc ohc models for sidecar use. But Turner's 1937 design, though in no way radical, was so remarkably neat and compact, so simple to produce, and had such a good all-round performance, that it set a style that was to be copied by all. Development of Turner's design in its various versions, lasted for more than 40 years.

Turner, in fact, had earlier been responsible for another design that really did show originality — the 500cc overhead camshaft Ariel Square Four that was the sensation of the 1930 Motor Cycle Show. Its unique cylinder layout and coupled contra-rotating crankshafts were never copied in its lifetime, its production life spanning nearly thirty years. Its capacity was raised to 600cc and then, with a complete redesign, to 1000cc. Brilliant designer as he was, Turner proved an even greater success as a manager at Triumph, where his career was legendary.

Nothing like so flamboyant as Turner, though equally deserving of being remembered as a designer, was Val Page, who joined JAP in 1914 and, after the war, revitalised their range of engines before leaving in 1925 to join Ariel. Once again he laid down a series of designs that put Ariel on a par with any other manufacturer of the time. He helped Turner with the square four and then went to Triumph. There, he designed the 250cc, 350cc and 500cc range of ohv singles later restyled by Turner as the Tiger 70, Tiger 80 and Tiger 90 models. As earlier mentioned, he also designed the 650cc 6/1 twin. In 1936, Page moved to BSA, where again he drew up a range of eminently modern single cylinder engines, which included the original M23 Gold Star. He moved back to Ariel in 1939. His last design for them was the brilliant all-enclosed 250cc twin-cylinder Ariel Leader two-stroke and its sporting version, the Arrow. Very few designers in any country can have been so prolific and successful.

In 1919, J S Rasmussen's DKW factory in Saxony set Germany on the road to supremecy in the manufacture of two strokes between the wars. Original designs by Hugo Ruppe were developed and then superseded by those of Herman Weber. In 1931, the Swiss-born designer Arnold Zoller was called in to develop split-single DKW racing

Three great designers — Val Page (left), Bert Hopwood (right) and Edward Turner (centre) — photographed at Triumph in 1937.

George William Patchett (left) of McEvoy, FN and Jawa and Walter William Moore of Douglas, Norton and NSU.

machines with water cooling and piston-pump assisted (blown) induction. With patient development by August Prussing, the 'blown' DKW became insuperable in the 250cc class in European road racing in the 1930s.

Unlike Puch, whose Marcellino designed and developed racers had inspired DKW to call in Arnold Zoller, DKW did not sell split-single two-strokes for road use. Instead, they became the first in the world to market 'flat-top piston' two-strokes, using the Schnurle patents. Herman Weber was again the designer. His RT125 of 1937 set entirely new standards of two-stroke performance.

However, the RT125's extraordinary claim to fame was that its design was copied post-war by BSA for their 125cc Bantam, by Harley Davidson, by JL0, by Yamaha, by Suzuki and by at least another half dozen firms in Russia and Eastern Europe. It even formed the basis of post war DKW and MZ racing machinery when Germany was re-admitted to international competition. Under the control of race chief Walter Kaaden, MZ went on to develop the first two-strokes to equal and then to surpass the specific power outputs of four-stroke engines. Today's all conquering racing two-strokes all derive from Kaaden's work at MZ.

Walter Moore designed a 500cc ohc racing engine for Norton, which won the 1927 Senior TT on its first outing. Thereafter, though, it proved disappointing, so when Moore left to join NSU in Germany and to design a similar engine for them, Norton's Joe Craig breathed over young Arthur Carroll's shoulder as he designed a new engine for 1931 — with which Tim Hunt that year 'did the double', winning both Junior and Senior TTs. So was born the Manx Norton, which in the next 18 seasons, was to win 28 TTs, not to mention uncounted Grand Prix races, quite apart from its myriad successes in the hands of private owners right into the 1960s and even beyond.

In post-war Italy, Giulio Carcano attained legendary stature with his designs and development for the Moto Guzzi racing team between 1948 and 1957, his masterpiece being the celebrated 500cc V8. But one Moto Guzzi design of that era, the 500cc in-line watercooled four-cylinder with shaft drive, raced in 1953 and 1954, was designed not by Carcano, but by Carlo Giannini. He, together with Pietro Remor, had been involved long before the war with the four-cylinder design that became the watercooled supercharged Rondine, later taken over by Gilera for the 1937 season.

Post war, Remor was to design first the 1947 air cooled 500cc four-cylinder Gilera, and then in 1950, the very similar four-cylinder MV. Credit for developing the Gilera must go to Franco Pasoni, and that for the MV to Arturo Magni. Remor left MV in 1953 and joined the obscure company Motom. But between 1958 and 1974, MV won the 500cc world championship no less than 17 times.

One cannot leave Italian designers without mentioning Moto Guzzi's Antonio Miccuchi, while Fabio Taglioni of Ducati will always be remembered for his desmodromic valve gear, first used in 1958. Until very recently, his advanced designs kept Ducati right at the forefront of the field with medium-to-large-capacity sporting twins.

Remor (left) with Gilera

Joe Craig supervises a Manx Norton engine test. He was the architect of Norton's racing success for 25 years.

Fabio Taglioni (above) designed the Ducati desmodromic valve gear in the early 1960s. The system is still in use. Right: Giulio Carcano with Moto-Guzzi Junior TT winner in 1956.

Jack Williams, chief development engineer on the AJS 7R, with son-in-law Tom Herron, of Yamaha

Pioneer Max Friz . . . he made aircraft engines, then the first BMW motorcycle

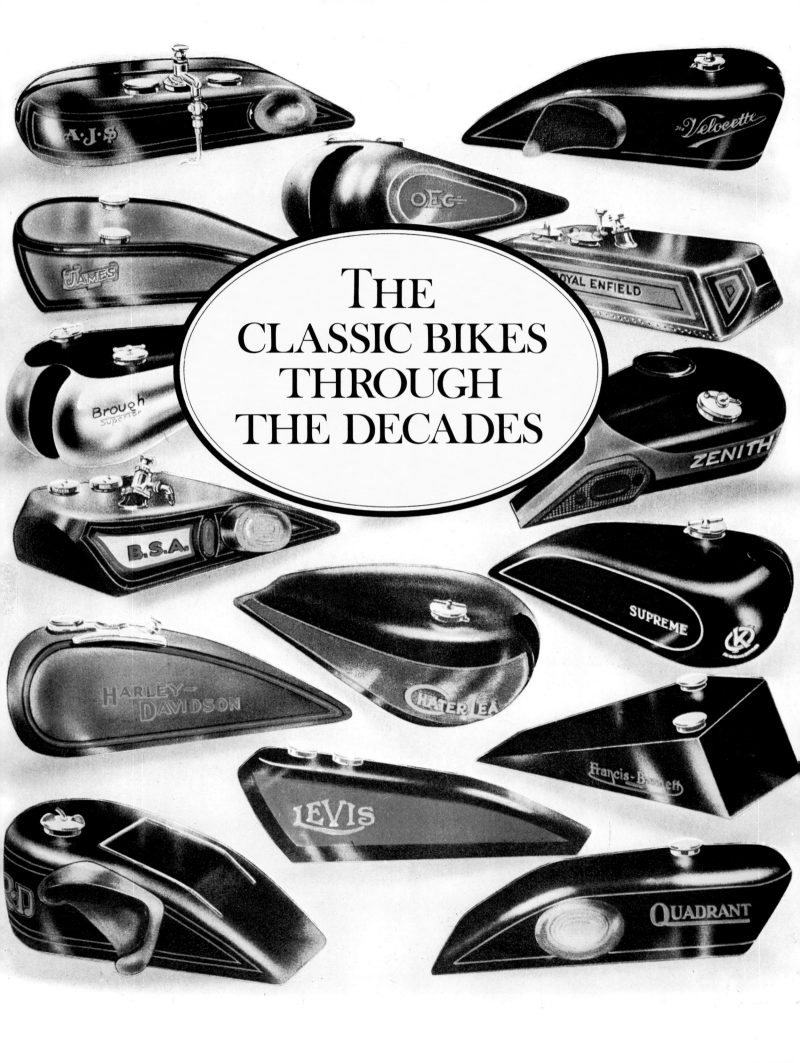

The CLASSIC BIKES THROUGH THE DECADES

NO FOUR-CYLINDER MOTORCYCLE has achieved such pre-eminence in its own time as the Henderson. It provided riders in the early years of motorcycling with simple starting, smoothness, silence, oil tightness, reliability and generous power to a degree unmatched elsewhere. The model shown here is that of 1912, the first year of production. The original 7 hp model was soon further developed, with a multi-speed gearbox, improved power, and more robust construction. Sales rose accordingly, and the model achieved greater popularity than any comparable machine in the United States. Finally, Ignaz Schwinn's Excelsior Company bought the firm in 1917, initially retaining the services of founders William and Tom

Henderson. After that, the Henderson big four also incorporated the name Excelsior on the tank. Two years later, William and Tom Henderson left Excelsior, unhappy with the new business arrangement. William founded his own motorcycle company, under the name of Ace. He was soon manufacturing an Ace four, and challenging the Henderson's reputation for quality. After many successful years Ace ran into financial troubles, and was bought by Indian.

THE NAME SCOTT is central to the history of the motorcycle. Alfred Scott was an inventor and engine-designer who played a leading part in the development of the two-stroke machine. Scott built his first motorised bicycle in Yorkshire as early as 1898, using a twin-cylinder two-stroke. The engine was fitted to a heavy pedal-cycle, and transmission was by friction roller. By 1903, he had built a machine with rear-wheel power, and a year later Scott was granted British patent rights on a two-stroke vertical-twin engine. Scott's first true production motorcycle was manufactured in 1908. Its engine was built to the Scott design by the nearby Jowett car factory, another Yorkshire concern famous in automotive history. This 333cc engine had a bore and stroke of 58 × 63mm, and the entire unit weighed only 371 lbs. The cylinder heads were water-cooled through a thermosiphon system, but the barrels were air-cooled. By 1914, Scott had settled the design of his machines, and was using a wholly water-cooled engine. The two-speed machine had standard gear-ratios of 3:1 and 4:1, and the unusual "open" frame design which characterised the marque. This frame design was popular with women motorcyclists, whose dignity it helped preserve. Telescopic front forks were used from the very first, and a disc-valve induction and exhaust system was introduced at an early stage. Other machines could match the Scott's 55 mph top speed, but none of its contemporaries offered the same handling qualities. It was this characteristic in particular which afforded Scott such great racing success. Like most unconventional machines, the Scott was the creature of its designer. Alfred Scott himself left the company after the First World War, and died in 1923; within four or five years, the marque had lost much of its shine. Production since a takeover in 1950 has been limited to small-scale revivals. The Scott shown here is a 486cc model specially reconstructed for vintage racing.

INDIAN WAS WITHOUT DOUBT one of the foremost names in the development of the modern motorcycle. In 1905, the factory became one of the first to put a V-twin into commercial manufacture. The first V engine was little more than a doubling up of two Indian 1·75 hp singles, but improved and enlarged versions soon followed. These ultimately provided the basis for the very advanced motorcycles produced under the aegis of the factory's founder, George Hendee, and the great designer Oskar Hedström. After they had left the company, Charlie Gustafson became Indian's chief designer in 1915. He established the side-valve style which became a tradition of the factory and of the American motorcycle industry. His great machine

was the 7 hp 998 cc Power Plus shown here. This sophisticated and speedy motorcycle included such advanced equipment as leaf-spring suspended pivoted fork rear suspension, all chain drive, electric lighting, electric starting and a proper kick-start.

Indian

AS THE ORIGINAL William Brough motorcycle company entered the last year of its life, the son's rival firm launched the most famous machine to bear the family name. The Brough Superior SS100, introduced in 1925 was more popular than any other prestige sports roadster before or since. The SS100, shown here, was an overhead-valve V-twin. It became one of the two mainstays of Brough Superior's 19-year production period, along with its predecessor, the SS80 side-valve V-twin. As with all engines of its type, the side-valve twin was less durable at speed than the ohv. The '100' and '80' model designations referred to the machines' guaranteed top speed. Brough Superior was also known for a proliferation of multi-cylindered exotica.

Brough Superior

The machines were largely assembled from proprietary components — the engines were principally JAP or Matchless units, and even the famous Castle forks were originally a Harley Davidson design. This philosophy was the Achilles' heel of Brough Superior.

The company tried unsuccessfully to develop its own power-units, and the cost of buying-in specially-manufactured engines in small quantities eventually proved to be crippling. The company stopped motorcycle production in 1940.

SUNBEAM

THE SUNBEAM MODEL 90, shown on the right in its traditional black-and-gold livery, is probably the finest example of British single-cylinder engineering. It used simple, proven designs, with meticulous finish. The machine was conceived in 1923 as a sports roadster, and successfully adapted as a works racer. It was produced in both 350 and 500cc ohv versions. Production standards dropped after the factory was bought in 1930 by ICI (Imperial Chemical Industries). Sunbeam was later owned by Associated Motorcycles and BSA.

Douglas

ALTHOUGH DOUGLAS did sometimes use other engine layouts, the marque was always known for its horizontally-opposed twins. Today, Douglas is usually remembered for its post-war series of transverse-engined 350cc machines, but these were only made in the company's last seven years. In its earlier days, and for more than three decades, Douglas found its fame and fortune in exceptionally well-planned twins with a fore-and-aft arrangement. The success of these machines owed much to the work of the company's chief development rider, Freddie Dixon, during the middle and late 1920s. Fate also played a part. When the Douglas EW series of 350sv racers began to find the competition tough, Douglas had planned a new ohc model, but a fire at the works destroyed the blueprints and set back the company's work. The new engine was abandoned, and the company chose instead to give a new life to its old ohv twins, with considerable development work by Dixon. By happy chance, these machines proved most successful in the newly-arrived sport of speedway. Some of their success was due to a freak of design which led the frame to flex during broadsliding, but their achievements on the cinder track boosted all aspects of the Douglas reputation. During this period, the classic Douglas machine was the model FW, which was produced in 500cc and 600cc versions. The road-racing version is shown here. The road-racing models were capable of 90 mph and 95 mph respectively. In 1929 alone, 1300 machines were sold.

Rudge

SOME OF THE BEST British production bikes were replicas of their makers' works racing models. A fine example was the 1929 Rudge-Whitworth Ulster, which came from a factory famous for its advanced approach. The machine was introduced to celebrate Graham Walker's win in the Ulster Grand Prix, and it proved to be exceptionally fast and reliable. It had a four-speed positive-stop, foot-change gearbox, dry sump lubrication with a mechanical pump, and a four-valve cylinder head in a penthouse combustion chamber.

THE BRITISH EXCELSIOR company is re-membered with affection for a 250cc single which was popularly known as the "Mechanical Marvel," but this four-valve ohv machine suffered from its own com-plexity. Undaunted, Excelsior continued along the same development path with an improved four-valver, the famous Manxman, shown here. This machine had a single overhead camshaft, and each inlet valve was fed by its own Amal RN carburettor. The bronze head, as shown, improved thermal efficiency in the days before aluminium had come into common use. The Manxman shown is a 250, but a 350 was also produced. Valve gear and carburettor tune still proved "very pernickerty" according to Excelsior's managing director Eric Walker, and in 1938 the firm introduced two-valve engines. These were equally fast, but wholly reliable. They had sprung frames, and proved so successful that they continued to be raced in private hands into the early 1950s.

Velocette

OTHER SINGLE-CYLINDER machines may have exemplified a particular aspect of engineering or of performance, but those produced by Velocette demonstrated the full range of attributes. This was best accomplished by the KTT (left), a racing replica of the works' own grand prix machinery, which was also notable as the first model to sport the Velocette-perfected foot gear-change system. This was an ohc

single of 350cc, sold with a guaranteed top speed of 85 mph. As an option, Velocette offered a 100 mph dope-tuned model sporting a 9:1 compression ratio. The range ran from the 1929 Mk 1 illustrated here to the 1949 Mk VIII. In 1956, Velocette demonstrated its skills with a quite different range of well-remembered singles. These were ohv sports roadsters. First came the 499cc Venom, shown above, with a "square" (86 × 86mm) engine, then the smaller 349cc Viper. The Venom engine developed 36 bhp at 6,200 rpm, giving the machine a top speed of 95 mph. After 12 and 24-hour records had been set at Montlhéry, a highly-tuned version was produced as a clubman racer. This was the Thruxton (right), which had a top speed of approximately 120 mph.

BSA

FOR MOST OF ITS LIFE, the BSA marque was known primarily for singles of simple and inexpensive design, made for everyday transport. The motorcycles in the small picture are examples: a 250cc machine from 1925 (background) and the 1928 "Sloper". In later years, the same qualities of durability and reliability were showcased in a much more exotic motorcycle, the Gold Star. No clubman racer has ever enjoyed the success or reputation of the "Goldie". The range was produced in trial, scramble, touring and racing versions, and a 1959 model of the latter is shown here. The 500cc engine developed up to 40 bhp at just over 7,000 rpm, through a close ratio gearbox. Top speed was around 120 mph in full clubman trim.

HARLEY–DAVIDSON

THE HARLEY-DAVIDSON Electra-Glide has its origins in the SV 74 twin of 1922, although its more recent and direct ancestor is the first ohv 1200 of 1941. These early machines displayed the familiar styling features of most American motorcycles: leading link front forks, solid rear wheel mounting, pan saddles, footboards, high, wide handle-bars, and a V-twin engine, all of which produce comfort at low cruising speeds. Over the years, the range has been modernised and renamed, but the essential concept has remained the same. In 1949, the Hydra-Glide was introduced with a telescopic front fork. The next model, with pivoted-fork rear suspension, produced in 1959, was the Duo-Glide. With the addition of a starter motor in 1965 came the name Electra-Glide. Since then, little has changed except the adoption of cast alloy wheels, although numerous Japanese components, such as forks and carburettor, have been adopted. The Electra-Glide is the heaviest mass-produced motorcycle ever built, weighing 800 lbs fully equipped. The 45°, 1207cc V-twin has hydraulically-activated push-rods and produces 62 bhp at 5,200 rpm, and 70ft/lbs of torque at 4,000 rpm. The XLCR (below, kitted out for the track) has similarly won cult status among the world's army of Harley fanatics. The classic sporting Harley, the XLCR was launched in 1976; it is the fastest production bike Harley-Davidson have ever built, with a flat out top speed of a good 120mph. What this, and subsequent Harleys are about — currently the regular 1340cc Evolution series engines are fitted to a range of 17 different bikes — is big vee-twin power, image and style.

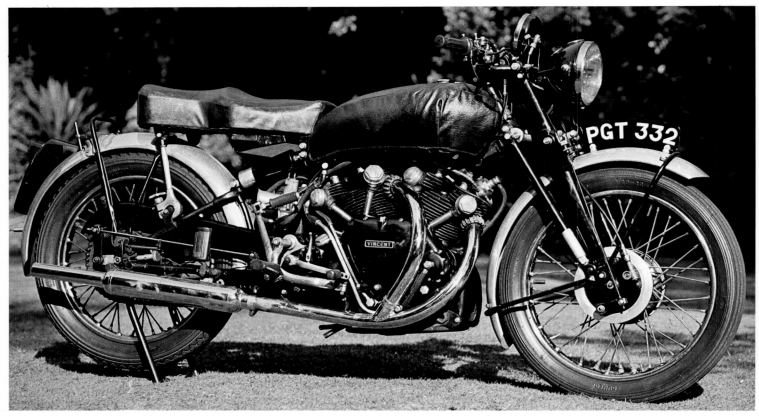

THERE ARE MANY REASONS for celebrating the famous marque founded by Howard R. Davies (hence its original name, HRD) and bought shortly afterwards by Philip Vincent. Modern motorcycle manufacturers have still barely caught up with the progressive chassis-group designs produced by Vincent 35 years ago, though the marque is more commonly remembered for its spree of speedy achievement during the 1950s. Perhaps these sporting feats were the inspiration for the unusually-large and ambitious speedo which was fitted to Vincent motorcycles. Factory and private riders captured national and world speed and sprint records by the

handful on the competition model of the period, the Black Lightning. The word "Black" featured in the names of several famous Vincent machines. One unsupercharged Black Lightning achieved a speed of 185·15 mph in the hands of Russell Wright, a New Zealander, in 1955. Sadly, this was also the last year of full production.

The firm went out in a blaze of glory, with the announcement of the semi-streamlined Series D models, but few were actually made. In design, these machines were the natural successors to the Series C Rapides, which had been launched in 1949, with 50-degree 998cc V-twin engines. The Series C standard touring machine provided a top speed of approximately 105/110 mph, and its sporting counterpart the Black Shadow (shown here) went to 110/120 mph, reaching 56 mph in only six seconds. These machines were in turn developed from the Series A Rapides, which were launched in 1937, had 47-degree engines, and had a web of external pipes.

ARIEL was in every sense an historic British marque. Established since 1898, the firm exhibited all the characteristics of British motorcycle manufacture. The products were well made, even sporty, but initially of conventional design. In 1929, a much more sophisticated machine made a considerable break with tradition. This was a 500cc four with a highly-unusual "square" cylinder configuration and single overhead camshaft. This distinctive engine layout became so identifiable with the marque that the nickname "Squariel" passed into the language of motorcycling. Like the later Triumph Speed Twin, another pace-setting machine, the Square

Four was designed by Edward Turner. It had an all ball-and-roller bearing engine and horizontally-split crankcase. In 1931, the engine was bored out from 51 to 56 mm, thus increasing capacity to 600cc. Although some modest success was achieved in competition, such as the Bickel

brothers' supercharged 111·42 lap at Brooklands in 1934, the machine was really a sporting tourer. In 1936, Ariel launched a 1,000cc Square Four of quite new engine design. This model had a pushrod power-unit, with plain bearings, and it also utilised a unique trailing-link rear-suspension system. It remained in production in various roadster forms until the late 1950s, by which time it boasted four individual exhaust-pipes ports and an all-aluminium engine. The 1956 luxury roadster shown here develops 42 bhp at 5,800 rpm, providing a top speed of 105 mph. It has a bore and stroke of 65 × 75 mm. The machine's kerb-weight is 495 lbs.

TRIUMPH

TRIUMPH WILL ALWAYS be associated with the vertical-twin engine-layout. This classic design was introduced in 1938, in the 498cc Speed Twin, which was the forerunner of many famous motorcycles. A memorable example was the larger Thunderbird (above), introduced in 1949. This 649cc tourer produced 34 bhp at 6,000 rpm on a compression ratio of 7:1. Three standard models averaged 101·06 mph between them for 500 miles at Montlhéry. A total break with the vertical-twin layout came in the 1960s with the transverse three-cylinder Trident (left). The T160 had a 740cc engine of 67 × 70 mm bore and stroke, giving 58 bhp at 7,250 rpm to reach a top speed of around 120 mph. Production ended in the mid-1970s.

Norton

IT WAS THE GREAT racing success of the Norton marque which created the need for an improved frame in the 1940s. The need was met by the McCandless brothers' Featherbed frame, which in turn influenced motorcycle design almost everywhere. After being introduced on the Manx racers, the Featherbed frame was modified for road use in the existing 497cc tourer, which became the Dominator in 1952. The example shown above is a Manx built in 1958. Ten years after its launch, the Dominator had grown to 647cc, with a maximum road speed of 112 mph. In 1965, Norton launched the 745cc Atlas, but a more significant development came two years later. The same engine was fitted, with rubber mountings, into a new duplex frame. This new model, the Commando, was subsequently increased in size to 828cc. With a top speed of 120 mph, the Commando (bottom) is the most powerful road-going Norton ever produced.

LIKE THE LAMBORGHINI CAR, the equally exotic Laverda is the product of an Italian agricultural engineering group. With its race-bred frame and sleek styling, the 130 mph RGS 1000 (below) is Laverda's flagship. It is derived from the Laverda Jota, which with a top speed of 150 mph verified in independent tests, was the fastest production roadster ever built. The RGS 1000 is powered by a 981cc three-cylinder motor which features 120° crankshaft and gives 80 bhp.

THE MV AGUSTA AMERICA is arguably the finest sports roadster in production, and without doubt a classic among the multicylindered big bikes. The entire power-unit is a development of the company's racing 500cc four of the 1950s. MV was the last European marque to dominate the Grand Prix circuits, and retired solely for commercial reasons, but it took several attempts before the factory's sporting experience could be translated into a successful roadster. The 788cc dohc America develops 75 bhp at 8,500 rpm, and its top speed is approximately 135 mph.

MOTO GUZZI

WHILE JAPANESE motorcycles have become increasingly sophisticated, the largest of the Italian manufacturers has responded by offering machines of comparable performance but robust simplicity. The V 850 GT of 1972 typifies Moto Guzzi's approach. The transverse twin turns out 64·5 bhp at a mere 6,500 rpm, providing a top speed of 115 mph. In 1975, the entire range was expanded to include the revolutionary V 1,000, with hydraulic torque converter.

DUCATI

IT WAS BUILT for its high-speed handling, apparently with no other priority in mind, and in this respect the Ducati Desmo 864cc of 1975 has no serious rival. Its top speed is 135 mph, its kerb weight a mere 428 lbs, and it is a remarkably stable motorcycle. The machine also benefits from the efficiency and reliability of the desmodromic valve system. Only Ducati has used this system with total success. The technique was employed to great effect in the 1972 750 SS clubman racer, after being first introduced by the factory's chief engineer, Fabioni Taglioni, in the successful Grand Prix period which was during the late 1950s.

BMW PREACHED THE virtues of conservatism in motorcycle design for decades, preferring to rely on tried and tested engineering, rather than embark on innovation for innovation's sake. The flat twin concept, for long favoured by the company, dated back to the 1930s, for instance; the R100RS (main picture), the classic BMW of the mid-1970s onwards, changed relatively little over the years. Though aerodynamically the machine was very advanced — the result of concentrated fairing development involving elaborated wind tunnel testing — the engine was a practical and simple horizontally-opposed 980cc ohv twin, producing 70bhp at 7,000 rpm and a top speed of around 125mph. Contrast this with the revolutionary K1 (inset), which BMW launched in 1989. This striking, sensa-

tional looking machine was designed to meet and beat the Japanese competition. Its distinctive bodywork is designed for absolute aerodynamic efficiency, while its engine is an improved 16-valve version of the four-cylinder K100 engine of 1984. The combustion chambers were reworked and the crankshaft, con rods and pistons lightened, so the unit revved harder, while the machine also utilises the Bosch Motoronic digital engine management system, as fitted to BMW cars. Top speed is 149mph.

THE CBR1000 (main picture) is Honda's flagship sports roadster. Launched in 1987, the machine triumphantly fulfills the brief Honda gave its designers — to produce a 1000cc open class sports bike for the road rider that was powerful, comfortable and smooth to ride and sophisticated in appearance. The CBR1000's success underlines Honda's decades of experience in building in-line fours. The bike exudes confidence, balance and completeness. It is a road rider's machine par excellence, with an excellent riding position, plenty of room for a pillion and luggage and, between your legs, a short stroke, 16 valve in-line four that will pull top gear from 2000rpm. The power output is smooth, with no discernible vibration except at the top of the rev range, where there is a real top end rev

thrust. The ST1100 Pan-European (inset) is another Honda beauty. What distinguishes it from its stablemates is that, although built in Japan, it was the first Honda to be designed and styled in Europe. Launched in 1990, it is every inch a sports-touring flagship. It comes with a large, spacious saddle, a big full fairing and windscreen, an ample fuel tank, a comfortable riding position and a large 1084cc vee-four engine, specially built for long distance reliability.

YAMAHA'S 1989 FZR-750R (OWO1) (top picture) looks exactly what it is — a mean racing machine. It is available for road use only because the factory had to build over 1000 examples to qualify the bike to compete in World Super-Bike racing. It built on the success of the established FZR1000 (above), which, since its launch in 1987 has become an industry classic. The design is an object lesson in the mating of a hugely powerful engine to a

strong, yet fairly light and fast-responding, chassis, the result being a bike that, although undeniably a pure sports machine, is one of the very best road bikes available, as worldwide sales confirm. Top speed of the 1989 Exup variant is an official 172mph.

⚡ SUZUKI

SUKUKI'S ENTRY INTO the four-stroke super-bike arena started back in 1977 with the GS750; the line continued with the GSX1100E Katana (main picture). The company also dominated the two-stroke scene with their RG500, which, in its heyday, took the manufacturer's championship for seven consecutive seasons. Suzuki's current two-stroke contender is the RGV500 (right), a trim-looking Vee 4 that was launched in 1987 and has been steadily refined and improved ever since. Experts claim its biggest asset is its quick handling, achieved by taking weight off the front wheel and shifting the compact engine rearwards in the frame. The engine design, however, has posed problems; the RGV has suffered from ignition, crankshaft and piston failures though Suzuki is confident that these problems will be resolved sooner rather than later.

KAWASAKI

KAWASAKI'S QUEST FOR speed made it the first manufacturer in the world to offer fuel-injection as a production standard, as in the GPZ1100 (top); today, the ZZ-R1100 (above) is the only mass-production motor cycle with a top speed genuinely in excess of 170mph. Launched in 1990, it currently dominates the super—bike scene, one reason for this being the use of a ram-air intake system, based on Formula One car technology. The faster the machine goes, the more air it rams in, with more airflow, power and speed as a result. Its stable-mate, the ZXR750 (right), was launched in 1989 as a race replica for the road. It features a proven roadster engine, itself extensively revised in 1990, in a race-orientated chassis. The result — a very fine sports roadster.

THE A-Z
OF THE WORLD'S
MOTORCYCLES

Key to abbreviations:
TS = Two-stroke
sv = Side-valve
ohv = Overhead-valve
hc = High camshafts
ohc = Overhead camshafts
dohc = Double overhead camshafts
ioe = Inlet over exhaust

DEFINITIONS:

Horsepower = bhp
33,000 ft-lb per min or 550 ft-lb per second = 1·01387 cv (764·08 watts).

Kilogramme (kg) =
Metric standard unit of mass = 2·20462 lb.

Litre (1) =
The volume occupied by 1 kg of distilled water at 4°C and 760mm of mercury pressure.

Mile =
1760 yards (5280 ft) = 1609·344 m.

Millimetre (mm) =
1/1000 metre = 0·0393701 ins.

TABLE OF RAC HORSEPOWER RATINGS:

Cylinder-Diameter in mm:	1 Cyl:	2 Cyl:	Cylinder-Diameter in mm:	1 Cyl:	2 Cyl:
50	1·54	3·1	67	2·78	5·6
51	1·61	3·2	68	2·87	5·7
52	1·67	3·34	69	2·95	5·9
53	1·74	3·48	70	2·04	6·1
54	1·80	3·6	71	3·12	6·2
55	1·87	3·7	72	3·21	6·4
56	1·94	3·98	73	3·30	6·6
57	2·01	4·0	74	3·39	6·8
58	2·08	4·16	75	3·49	6·98
59	2·15	4·3	76	3·58	7·2
60	2·23	4·5	77	3·67	7·3
61	2·30	4·6	78	3·77	7·5
62	2·38	4·8	79	3·87	7·7
63	2·46	4·9	80	3·97	7·9
64	2·54	5·1	85	4·48	8·96
65	2·61	5·2	90	5·02	10·0
66	2·70	5·4			

RAC RATING FORMULAE:

$$\frac{\text{Bore (squared} \times \text{No of cylinders)}}{2 \cdot 5} = \text{Power at flywheel}$$

For power at road wheels divide by 3 (cylinder dimensions in inches). If taken in mm, divide by 1613 instead of 2·5 for power at flywheel.

This formula used mainly before WWII

CYLINDER DISPLACEMENT

Multiply the bore with the bore
Multiply the result with the stroke
Multiply this result with 0·785 and
Multiply with number of cylinders.

Sample: Moto Guzzi V 1000:
88mm × 88mm = 7744
7744 × 78mm = 60,4032
6040 × 0·785 = 47,4140
474 × 2 = 948cc

MILES = KILOMETRES:

10	=	16
15	=	24
20	=	32
30	=	48
40	=	64
50	=	80
100	=	160
200	=	320
300	=	480

CONVERSION FACTORS:

Multiply:	By:	To obtain:	Multiply:	By:	To obtain:
Centimetres	0·0328084	Feet	Kilometres per hour	0·621371	Miles per hour
Centimetres	0·393701	Inches	Kilometres per litre	2·82473	Miles per Imp. gal.
Centimetres per second	0·036	Kilometres per hour	Litres	1000·028	Cubic centimetres
Cubic centimetres	0·0610237	Cubic inches	Litres	61·0255	Cubic inches
Cubic inches	16·3871	Cubic centimetres	Litres	0·264178	Gallons (US)
Feet	30·48	Centimetres	Litres	0·219976	Gallons (Imperial)
Feet	12	Inches	Litres	1·7598	Pints (Imperial)
Gallons (Imperial)	4·54596	Litres	Litres per kilometre	0·354016	Gal. (Imp.) per mile
Gallons (United States)	0·832680	Gallons (Imperial)	Litres per kilometre	0·425153	Gal. (US) per mile
Gallons (United States)	3·78533	Litres	Miles (also mph)	1·609344	Kilometres (also kph)
Horsepower (British)	745·7	Watts	Millimetres	0·0393701	Inches
Horsepower (Metric)	0·986320	Horsepower (British)	Pounds	0·45359237	Kilogrammes
Inches	2·54	Centimetres	Square centimetres	0·15500	Square inches
Inches	25·4	Millimetres	Square inches	6·4516	Square centimetres
Kilogrammes	35·274	Ounces	Square inches	645·16	Square millimetres
Kilogrammes	2·20462	Pounds	United States gallons	0·83268	Imperial gallons
Kilometres	0·621371	Miles	United States gallons	3·78533	Litres
Kilometres	1093·61	Yards	Yards	0·9144	Metres

A

ABAKO / *Germany 1923–1925*
Small 129cc single-cylinder machines with own two-stroke deflector-type three-port engines, two and three-speed Sturmey-Archer gearboxes and chain drive to the rear wheel.

ABBOTSFORD / *England 1919–1920*
Scooter-like lightweights with 1·5 hp ohv power units. Limited production.

ABC / *England 1913–1914*

Designed by Granville Bradshaw for the All British (Engine) Company, this 496cc ioe flat twin was the first motorcycle created by Bradshaw. Some of these engines were supplied to W. Brough.
1914–1919 The reorganised ABC Motors Ltd, originally at Brooklands, Byfleet, moved to Walton-on-Thames and produced mainly war material and motorcycle engines for the military.
1920–1922 Another reorganisation, which took place at Walton-on-Thames. Production centred around spare parts and the development of new designs, but there were no new motorcycles put on the market. Bradshaw's policy was to sell his designs to a manufacturing concern.
1919–1922 This was the *real* ABC, built by The Sopwith Aviation & Engineering Co. Ltd at Kingston-on-Thames, a company which built aircraft during the war and which afterwards took over Bradshaw's newest creation. This was a transverse-mounted 398cc flat twin with ohv, 4-speed gearbox, all chain drive, spring frame and forks, automatic lubrication etc. Often regarded as the predecessor of the first BMW, the Sopwith-ABC was an advanced but underdeveloped design when Sopwith put it on the market. The valve gear was unreliable, the lubrication bad and although they could sell more than they were able to produce, the ABC failed and by 1921 Sopwith were in liquidation, mainly because failures of the design led to too many

guarantee claims. The price for the Standard Model was £98, the Lucas Dynamo Model was offered at £118.
France 1920–1924 Made under licence from Sopwith by a branch factory of the French Gnome & Rhone aero-engine and motorcycle company, the French ABC lasted longer than the English original. Cpt. Bartlett, who headed the production in France, used modified cylinder heads for his machines and supplied in addition to the 348cc ABC a 493cc machine. Together with Naas, he competed in races and other sporting events with great success.

ABC Skootamota / *England 1919—22*
Granville Bradshaw designed and Gilbert Campling made and sold this scooter, with 'half an ABC industrial engine' driving the rear wheel by chain. Tubular welded frame, no suspension. Best of a bad bunch!

ABC / *England 1920–1924*
Built by J. Barwell at Birmingham, this ABC had no connection with Bradshaw's ABC designs. It was an assembled machine with 296cc and afterwards 247cc Villiers two-stroke proprietary engines.

ABC / *Germany 1922–1925*
Another, but little known ABC built in Berlin. The engine was a deflector-type 149cc two-stroke of the company's own design and manufacture.

ABENDSONNE / *Germany 1933–1934*
Designed by Georg Weissbinder, who coupled two 98cc Villiers engines together. Few of these machines were actually made.

ABERDALE / *England 1946–1959*
London-built 48cc autocycles and lightweight motorcycles with 98cc and 123cc Villiers and Sachs two-stroke power units. Bown, another

398cc ABC (ohv flat-twin) 1921

manufacturer of such machines, took over Aberdale production in 1959.

ABE-STAR / *Japan 1951–1959*
One of the many Japanese motorcycle factories of the 1950s. Top model was a 148cc four-stroke with the company's own ohv engine.

ABINGDON / *England 1903–1925*
Early models had MMC, Minerva Kerry and Fafnir engines; later ones used Abingdon's own 3·5 hp singles and 5–6 hp V-twins. After 1918 the range consisted of 348cc singles, 496cc and 796cc V-twins with Abingdon sv engines. A 624cc single was built for a short period. The producer, Abingdon-King-Dick, a well-known tool factory at Birmingham, after 1925 renamed the machines AKD and concentrated on singles up to 346cc. Abingdon motorcycles were of sturdy design and many were sold in the colonies.

ABJ / *England 1950–1954*
Lightweights with 48cc, 98cc and 123cc Villiers two-stroke engines, made by a bicycle factory. The 48cc Auto-Minor was sold for £41 15s.

ABRA / *Italy 1923–1927*
Assembled motorcycles with German 146cc DKW two-stroke engines. From 1924 onwards also used their own 132cc engines. Small production.

ACCOSSATO / *Italy 1976–*
Manufacturer of 49, 79, and 124cc moto-cross, trial and enduro two-strokes with Minarelli and Hiro engines.

ACE / *America 1919–1929*
William 'Bill' Henderson sold his famous four-cylinder Henderson design in 1917 to the Chicago-based Schwinn company and in 1919 founded the ACE Motor Corporation in Philadelphia. There he once more built four-cylinder air-cooled in-line unit-design motorcycles with 1168cc, later 1229cc and 1266cc engines. He was killed in 1922 in an accident while testing a new model and another famous designer, Arthur Lemon, took over design and development. All engines had ioe valves, light-alloy pistons and Schebler carburettors. The engines developed between 20 and 25 bhp. In 1927 Indian took over the ACE, which ran into commercial difficulties, and moved production to Springfield, Massachusetts. It was renamed Indian 4 after 1929.

ACHILLES / *Czechoslovakia 1906–1912*
Built by a bicycle factory in what is now Czechoslovakia, Achilles motorcycles had 3·5 hp single-

cylinder and 5 hp V-twin proprietary engines made by Fafnir and Zeus.

ACHILLES / *Germany 1953–1957*
Scooter-like machines with 98cc and 123cc Sachs engines and also sporting 48cc mopeds. The same company built motorcycles in the Austro-Hungarian Empire before WWI. When they closed down in 1957 in Germany, the English Norman motorcycle factory bought the production equipment.

ACMA / *France 1948–early 1960s*
Licensed production of Italian 123cc, 147cc and 173cc Vespa scooters. The factory was at Fourchambault.

ACME / *England 1902–1922*
Built motorcycles with 2 hp Minerva and 2·5 hp Automoto engines. After 1918, 293cc JAP, their own 348cc sv singles and 997cc sv V-twins came into production. In 1922 Acme amalgamated with Rex at Coventry. The result was Rex-Acme motorcycles, which became famous when Walter Handley won races on Blackburne-engined racing models. *See also* Rex-Acme.

293cc Acme (sv-JAP) 1922

ADER / *France 1901–1906*
Pioneer manufacturer, who also built cars.

Motorcycles built by Clément Ader had 2 hp single-cylinder and transverse-mounted V-twin 4 hp engines.

246cc Adler (TS twin) 1953

ADLER / *Germany 1901—1957*
Originally bicycle makers, who first fitted De Dion engines, then made their own singles and twins until 1907, when the concern switched from bikes to cars. In 1949 motorcycle production resumed with the superb 100cc (later 125cc) M series two-strokes. An advanced and luxurious 200cc and 250cc two-stroke twin range was soon developed — later copied in Japan by Yamaha and Suzuki. The final Adler offering was a scooter, though the water-cooled RS250 racer, developed by privateer Helmut Hallmeier, did well in German events. Adler eventually abandoned motor cycles to become highly successful makers of typewriters and office equipment.

ADMA / *Germany 1924–1926*
Interesting 169cc two-strokes with internal flywheels. Own design, limited production.

1229cc ACE (ioe four-in-line) 1923

ADONIS / *France 1949–1952*
Small Vap-engined 48cc and 75cc scooters of simple design.

ADRIA / *Germany 1912–1928*
Sturdy sv singles of 276cc, 282cc, 294cc and 346cc capacity. Adria also built proprietary engines for cars and boats, but motorcycle manufacture was on a limited scale only.

ADS / *Belgium 1949–1954*
Small assembler of 98cc machines with Sachs and Ilo two-stroke engines.

ADVANCE / *England 1906–1912*
Once a well-known make with own 3 hp, 3·5 hp and V-twin 6 hp power units. Compared to other makes of that period, Advance motorcycles had very low frames.

AEL / *England 1919–1924*
A motorcycle and accessories dealer in Coventry who fitted various 147cc to 348cc proprietary engines made by Villiers, JAP and Blackburne. The frames were probably built by Hobart in Coventry.

AEOLUS / *England 1903–1905*
Interesting 492cc single-cylinder design with shaft drive to the rear wheel. Production was on a limited scale.

AEOLUS / *England 1914–1916*
Had no connection with the first London-made Aeolus. This Aeolus was fitted with its own 269cc two-stroke engines. The company — Bowns Ltd. — produced Bown lightweight machines after 1945.

AER / *England 1938–1940*
Scott motorcycle specialist A. E. Reynolds produced from 1927 onwards modified 498cc and 598cc Scott machines, called Reynolds Special. In the late 1930s, modern 246cc single-cylinder and 346cc vertical twin two-strokes of his own design and manufacture came into being. WWII stopped production.

AERO-CAPRONI / *Italy 1948–1964*
Once a famous aircraft factory at Trento, Aero-Caproni built after the war motorcycles of their own design with 73cc, 124cc and 148cc ohv and partly face-cam ohc engines. Some had tubular, others pressed steel frames, 48cc machines were also built and there was a 149cc model with a transverse-mounted ohv flat-twin unit-design engine in a pressed steel frame. This model had 7·5 bhp at 6000 rpm and a 60 mph top speed. Small two-stroke models assembled by Aero Caproni (Capriolo) had NSU engines.

AERMACCHI / *Italy 1950—1978*
Famous aircraft manufacturers, Aermacchi made a scooter before, in 1956, it launched Alfredo Bianchi's all-enclosed 'Chimera' with horizontal single cylinder ohv 175cc engine and unit 4-speed gearbox. The Chimera did not sell and the engine was enlarged to 250cc for a more conventional sports model, which did well in production racing. Later came genuine racing machines of first 250cc, then 350cc, which, though outclassed at Grand Prix level, enjoyed great success in racing in Britain and Europe until about 1970. Aermacchi riders won the 1966 Lightweight Manx Grand Prix, the Junior race in 1967, 1970 and 1972 and finished second in the Junior TT in 1969 and 1970. Taken over in 1960 by America's Harley Davidson, Aermacchi also made a line of lightweights, directed at the US market. In the early 1970s, two-strokes for both the road and for racing appeared, with famous Italian rider Renzo Pasolini riding the racing versions in the 250cc and 350cc classes. He was tragically killed in the accident at Monza in 1973 that also claimed Finnish rider Jarno Saarinen.

Though the road machines still sold freely in the USA, they eventually fell victim to the anti-pollution legislation that outlawed two-strokes there. By the late 1970s, Harley Davidson had re-established the big vee twins in the US market.

In July 1978 Harley Davidson sold Aermacchi at Varese to a new company called Cagiva and a famous name came to an end.

AEROS / *Czechoslovakia 1927–1929*
Designed by Franz Brezina, the Aeros had a BMW-like frame with a leaf spring fork and German 347cc and 497cc Küchen three-valve ohc proprietary single-cylinder engines.

AETOS / *Italy 1912–1914*
Produced one model only, a 492cc V-twin 3·5 hp machine.

AFW / *Germany 1923–1925*
Limited manufacture of 246cc ohv machines with engines supplied by the Bielefeld-based Hansa factory.

AGF / *France 1948–1956*
Well-known as producer of scooters and motorcycles with 123cc and 173cc Ydral proprietary engines.

AGON / *Germany 1924–1928*
The Benninger-designed machines had different engines, including the 197cc Paqué, 346cc Bradshaw, 498cc Küchen and JAP units from 173cc to 996cc. 746cc and 996cc JAP-engined Agons were V-twins.

AGRATI / *Italy 1958—*
Agrati made bicycle frames and, post war, mopeds and scooters, from 50cc up to 150cc. The engines were supplied by Garelli to whom Agrati supplied frames in turn. In 1961 the two companies were merged to their mutual benefit. *See also Garelli.*

AGS / *The Netherlands 1971–*
Moto-cross machines with 123cc two-stroke engines supplied by Sachs, Puch, Zündapp and other makers.

AIGLON / *France 1908–1953*
Zurcher, Minerva, Mirus, Peugeot, AMC, FMC and others supplied engines for many years to Aiglon. Debarelle's last models had 123cc and

346cc AER (TS twin) 1953

174cc ohv AMC engines and FMC-built 248cc two-strokes.

AIM / *Italy 1974–*
Producer of sports machines, especially moto-cross versions with 49cc and 124cc Franco-Morini two-stroke engines.

AIROLITE / *England 1921–1923*
Lightweight machines with 110cc Simplex two-stroke engines.

AJAX / *England 1923–1924*
Cheaply assembled machines with open frames. These housed 147cc, 247cc and 269cc Villiers two-stroke and 346cc Blackburne sv engines.

AJR / *Scotland 1925–1926*
One of the few Scottish makes, A. J. Robertson of Edinburgh built machines which housed 346cc and 490cc single-cylinder ohv engines made by JAP in London. Robertson rode them in many sporting events.

AJS / *England 1911—1969*
The Stevens brothers, Harry, George, Jack and Joe, experimented with petrol engines as early as 1897 at their father's engineering works in Wolver-hampton. They went on to make excellent air- and water-cooled engines for early motor cycles, tricars and light four wheelers. In 1909, using Jack's initials, (Albert John Stevens), they formed the AJS company and in 1914 entered the Junior TT with 350cc side valve engines bikes with all chain drive, two-speed gearboxes and two-speed 'overdrive'. Riders Eric and Cyril Williams finished 1-2, Eric Williams making the fastest lap time at over 47mph. With a new trendsetting ohv machine, Cyril Williams won the 1920 Junior, and in 1921 Eric Williams and H R Davies again scored 1-2. Sensationally, Davies went on to win the Senior race — on his 350cc AJS !

In 1922 came yet another 1-2 in the Junior TT, but there was no further TT victory for AJS until 1930, when Jimmy Guthrie sprang a surprise in the Lightweight class. For 1926, AJS introduced chain-driven ohc racers and, throughout the 1920s, were renowned for their excellent sports models, including the celebrated ohv 350cc 'Big Port'.

However the Stevens brothers overreached themselves with ventures into cars, trucks, buses and even radios, and had to sell out to the Collier brothers, makers of Matchless motorcycles, in 1931. As Associated Motor Cycles Ltd (AMC) the Matchless and AJS ranges were rationalised in the 1930s, but AMC continued to make the ohc sports and racing AJS models. They also showed an ohc Vee 4 at Olympia in 1935, which appeared as a 'blown' 500cc racer in 1936, but without success. It reappeared again with water-cooling in 1938, but, though this version was blisteringly fast, its handling was atrocious. Walter Rusk lapped at 100mph on one in the 1939 Ulster Grand Prix before retiring.

Post war, AJS launched new 350 and 500 singles, with 'Teledraulic' front forks and soon with swinging arm rear suspension. The concern also offered up-to-date 500cc vertical twins, followed by 550cc, 600cc and 650cc versions, notable for their use of a three-bearing crankshaft. AJS also raced a brand new horizontal engined parallel twin — the dohc 500cc 'Porcupine' — on which Les Graham won the first 500cc World Championship

498cc AJS (H10) 1927

996cc AJS (sv V-twin) 1930

496cc AJS (ohc V-four Prototype) 1935

495cc AJS (supercharged ohc V-four) 1939

in 1948. The next year, he had all but won the 1949 Senior TT when his magneto broke two minutes from the chequered flag! The factory continued racing the Porcupines until 1954 with considerable success. Though they also raced the single-cylinder 350cc chain driven ohc 7R (Rod Colman winning the 1954 Junior on a special three-valve version),

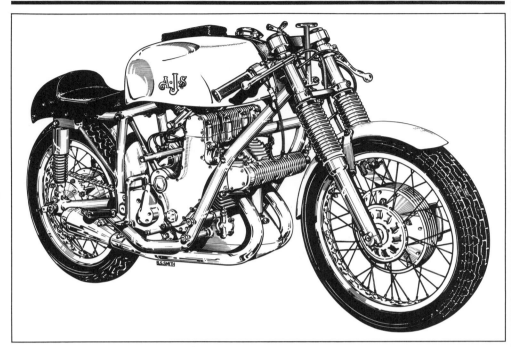

498cc AJS (ohc twin Porcupine) 1953

348cc AJS (ohc 'Boy's Racer') 1948

348cc AJS (3 ohc 3-valve works racer) 1953

this machine won its fame in the hands of scores of private owners and was the mainstay of the Junior class in Britain and Europe for many years.

AJS riders won the Junior Manx Grand Prix ten times between 1950 and 1965. In trials and motocross, 350cc and 500cc AJS machines performed as well as any others; indeed, although often considered 'conservative' in retrospect, the post-war AJS models exactly suited the taste and temper of the times — and they sold for export as freely as they did at home.

Despite new 'Lightweight' 250cc and 350cc models for 1958, AMC sales declined in the 1960s and so did profits, largely due to bad management. The company collapsed in 1967 and was sold to Manganese Bronze Holdings. They attempted to keep alive the name AJS on Villiers-engined motocross machines, but finally gave up to concentrate on another AMC make, Norton. So ended nearly 60 years of a world-famous marque. Celebrated riders associated with AJS as well as those men-

tioned include: Jimmy Simpson, Walter Handley, Frank Longman, Bert Denly, Jock West, Hugh Viney, George Rowley, Bob McIntyre and Alistair King. Though production of AJS largely ceased in 1967, two-strokes based on the Villiers Starmaker engine were made for some years, while today the name is still owned by Fluff Brown's Andover based company.

AJW / England 1926–1977

Designed by A. J. Wheaton as a machine to oppose George Brough's Brough-Superior motorcycles, the AJW had at first big V-twin sv and ohv JAP and British-Anzani engines with 678cc and 996cc capacity. Beautifully made with

678cc AJW (ohv JAP) 1929

saddle tanks and a very low saddle position, Sturmey-Archer gearboxes. Pilgrim oil-pumps, Binks and Amal carburetters etc. they were expensive. This led to smaller models with 172cc

490cc AJW (ohv JAP) 1952

and 247cc Villiers engines. During the 1930s, most AJW machines had 496cc single-cylinder ohv power units made by Python (Rudge), JAP and Stevens (the Stevens brothers, former owners of the AJS factory). After 1945 the reorganised AJW factory, now owned by J. O. Ball, built beautiful 498cc vertical twins with JAP sv engines. Limited production of these engines forced AJW to stop manufacture of these machines. Assisted by Ball's son Alan, only 49cc mopeds with Sachs and Franco Morini engines appeared on the market until AJW folded in 1977.

AKD / England 1926–1933

Successor to Abingdon motorcycles. The factory still exists as manufacturer of tools. The range of

173cc AKD (ohv Sport) 1929

models included 147cc, 173cc and 198cc ohv singles and 298cc and 346cc sv singles of AKD's own design and manufacture. 173cc super-sports models were successful around 1930 at races.

AKKENS / *England 1919–1922*
Made by a small company, Akkens motorcycles had 292cc Union two-stroke engines with deflector-type pistons.

ALATO / *Italy 1923–1925*
Made by the Gosio brothers at Turin, Alato machines had own 131cc two-stroke engines.

ALBA / *Germany 1919–1924*
A good four-stroke machine with 198cc and 247cc sv engines. The last model was a unit-design 249cc ohv version. Alba at Stettin (now Poland), owned by Alfred Baruch, also built delivery three-wheelers and supplied motorcycle engines to other factories including Huy and Teco. Although they stopped motorcycle manufacture in the mid-1920s, a company headed by Alfred Baruch's son Manfred supplied spares until the mid-1930s.

249cc Alba (ohv) 1924

ALBERT / *Germany 1922–1924*
Built during the inflation period in Germany 183cc two-strokes with own engines in limited quantities.

ALBERTUS / *Germany 1922–1924*
Was the original manufacturer of motorcycles with the Julius Löwy-designed crude-oil two-stroke engines of 113cc, 142cc and 176cc. While the engines were made at the Königsberg works, complete Albertus motorcycles came from Achern in Badonia.

ALCYON / *France 1902–late 1960s*
Once a leading motorcycle producer. Bought during the years other French makes including Labor, Thomann, Amor and Olympique. Already built in pre-1914 days potent V-twins and vertical twins, and when Alcyon competed in

142cc Albertus (TS crude-oil engine) 1922

1912 in the Isle of Man TT races, they had 348cc ohv singles with two inlet valves and two exhaust valves. These engines were designed by Zurcher. Between the wars, most Alcyon models had 98cc to 248cc two-stroke and 173cc to 498cc four-stroke sv and ohv engines. Some bigger versions already had shaft drive around 1930, and some had pressed-steel frames. 173cc Alcyon racing models, ridden by Joly and Lemasson, won many races in the late 1920s and early 1930s. After 1945 Alcyon produced two- and four-strokes up to 248cc with AMC, Zurcher, Vap and other engines and concentrated on 48cc mopeds and similar designs.

ALDBERT / *Italy 1953–1959*
Well-designed typical Italian machines with 49cc to 173cc two-stroke and 173cc to 246cc four-stroke ohv engines. The Razzo model had a 174cc 60mm × 61mm bore/stroke ohv unit-design 4-speed engine and a 93 mph top speed.

ALECTO / *England 1919–1924*
Had own 295cc and 345cc two-stroke deflector-type three-port engines and belt drive to the rear wheel. An all-chain 345cc model was made 1923–1924. It had 76mm bore and 76mm stroke.

ALERT / *England 1903–1906*
Made by Smith & Molesworth at Coventry, these machines had 2·35 hp, 2·75 hp and 3·25 hp Sarolea engines.

ALEU / *Spain 1953–1956*
Conventional design with 198cc and 247cc two-stroke engines of Spanish manufacture.

ALFA / *Germany 1925–1928*
Designed by the former BMW chief development engineer Alexander von Falkenhausen, the Alfa had 172cc Villiers engines; some later models had bigger ones including a 344cc vertical twin.

ALFA / *Italy 1923–1926*
Assembled machines with English 170cc ohv Norman and 346cc ohv Bradshaw and Blackburne engines. Limited production.

ALFA-GNOM / *Austria 1926–1928*
Made by Franz & Anton Rumpler, manufacturers of FAR motorcycles, the ·598cc Alfa-Gnom had a single-cylinder ohc engine.

ALGE / *Germany 1923–1931*
Produced 173cc to 498cc single-cylinder sv and ohv machines of conventional design and also transport three-wheelers with motorcycle engines. Owned by Alfred Geissler, Alge also fitted from 1928 onwards 173cc and 347cc Villiers engines and 497cc sv Blackburne engines.

ALIPRANDI / *Italy 1925–1930*
Beautiful 123cc and 173cc machines with Swiss Moser ohv engines. Other models made by the Aliprandi brothers had 173cc to 498cc sv and ohv power units by JAP and Sturmey-Archer.

ALKO / *Austria 1927–1930*
Assembled motorcycles with sv and ohv JAP and MAG engines, with capacities from 490 to 996cc. The last ones were V-twins.

ALLDAYS/*England 1903–1915*
Built as early as 1898 De Dion-engined three wheelers, later cars and motorcycles. These had their own 499cc single-cylinder and 539cc V-twin sv engines. Concentrated afterwards on Allon motorcycles.

ALLEGRO/*Switzerland 1925–early 1960s*
Well-known make which won many races in the 175cc class with Marcel Bourquin and the manufacturer Arnold Grandjean in the saddle. These machines had 172cc Villiers Brooklands two-stroke racing engines. In 1929 Grandjean built a 344cc racer for his own use in races, which had two such engines coupled together in tandem. Production versions had engines up to 348cc, supplied by Villiers, MAG and Sturmey-Archer. Allegro supplied mopeds in later years.

ALLON/*England 1915–1924*
Already mentioned with Alldays, the Allon housed its own 292cc deflector-type two-stroke engine. The second model, supplied 1923–1924, had a 346cc sv engine made by JAP.

ALLRIGHT/*Germany 1901–1927*
Known in England as Vindec-Special and VS, the Allright was also sold in other countries under the Tiger and Roland trademark. Early models had Belgian Kelecom, Minerva and FN, from 1905 onwards German Fafnir engines and Belgian Truffault forks (swinging arms). The German Cito works amalgamated in 1922 with Allright with the result that Allright also produced the famous KG (Krieger-Gnädig) motorcycle. This was a 503cc, later 498cc ohv unit-design single with shaft-drive to the rear wheel. The range also included 149cc two-strokes of the company's design and 248cc to 996cc sv and ohv JAP engines. Some models had MAG and Blackburne engines. All were of orthodox 'English design' and also had many English components. Chief designer Rudi Albert in the mid-1920s modified the 1919 KG design, which now received a horizontal shaft to the rear wheel and also the improved ohv engine. Allright motorcycle production stopped when they decided to concentrate on the manufacture of Tiger forks, hubs and other accessories. Paul Henkel, a former KG technician, took over the production of these machines until his death in 1932. Among successful Allright and Allright-KG riders were Zündorf, Soenius, Ehrlenbruch, Kniebecke, Roggenbuck, Fast, and Karsch.

ALLSTATE/*Austria 1953–1963*
This is the name of Austrian Puch machines sold in the USA since about 1953 by Sears-Roebuck of Chicago through their nationwide branches. Allstate is a Sears trademark, also applied to car parts, insurance etc.

ALMA/*France 1949–1959*
Producers of mopeds, scooters and lightweight machines from 49cc to 149cc with their own engines and also proprietary engines made by Le Paulin and Ydral.

ALMORA/*Germany 1924–1925*
Interesting but not very successful design. Used Julius Löwy-developed 113cc, 138cc and 176cc two-stroke engines which ran on crude oil after they had been 'hotted up' on petrol. They failed because they didn't develop enough power and proved unreliable.

ALP/*English 1912–1917*
Was originally an English branch of the Swiss Moto-Rêve motorcycle factory. Produced models with 3 hp and 3·5 hp V-twins, with vertical twin-cylinder engines and as a bread-and-butter model a 199cc machine with an English Precision proprietary engine. The last Alp had a 348cc two-stroke engine.

ALPHONSE THOMANN/*France 1908–1923*
Once a well-known make, which was not the same as Thomann. Main production concentrated around 98cc to 173cc two-strokes.

ALPINO/*Italy 1948–1962*
Typical Italian post-war machines from 48cc to 174cc with two- and four-stroke ohv engines. 48cc models broke world records with Tamarozzi, Pennati, Pasini and Sozzani.

ALTA/*Wales 1968–1971*
Trials models with 50cc, 80cc and 125cc Suzuki engines, made by the son of Geoffrey Taylor, famous for his pre- and post-war Alta Sports and racing cars.

ALTEA/*Italy 1939–1941*
Designed by former MAS boss Alberico Seilig for the famous Max Türkheimer motorcycle company at Milan, the modern Altea had a 198cc unit-design engine with vertical overhead valves among its interesting features. Türkheimer, since 1897 Ariel importer and once even shareholder of the English Ariel works, also built Astra motorcycles.

ALTENA/*Holland 1900–1906*
Dutch Pioneer from Heemstede-Harlem, fitted De Dion and own engines with 2 hp and 3 hp.

ALTER/*France 1955–1956*
Small French manufacturer of 49cc machines with various two-stroke engines.

AMAG/*Germany 1924–1925*
Another small producer of lightweight machines. These had 149cc Bekamo two-stroke engines which used a pumping cylinder in the crankcase.

AMBAG/*Germany 1923*
Fitted 155cc Gruhn sv single-cylinder engines into their own frames.

AMBASSADOR/*England 1947–1964*
Owned by ex-motorcycle, car and motor-boat racing driver Kaye Don, the Ascot-based company was also importer of German Zündapp motorcycles and American Pontiac cars. All Ambassador motorcycles housed 147cc to 248cc two-stroke Villiers engines. When he retired in

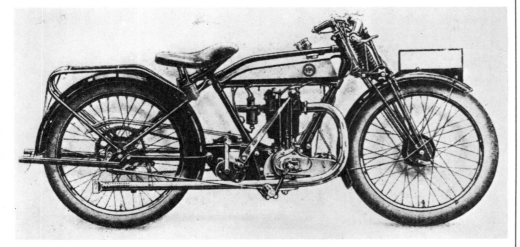

346cc Allright (ohv JAP) 1924

1964, everything connected with Ambassador manufacture was sold to the DMW factory.

AMC / USA 1912–1915

There was no conection between the Allied Motor Corporation of Chicago and either Associated Motor Cycles Ltd of London or the French AMC proprietary engine concern. The American AMC was a typically sturdy big V twin with a 980cc i.o.e. engine and bottom-link front forks.

AMERICAN / America 1911–1914

It is possible that this make was identical with the above AMC, although the address reads American Motorcycle Co. of Chicago. Manufacture consisted of a 4 hp single with 550cc power unit.

AMERICAN / America 1978–1979

A 748cc with vertical ohv twin power units, designed by the former Triumph (Coventry) technician Jack Wilkes.

AMERICAN-X / America 1910–1930

Made by Ignaz Schwinn's Excelsior Company at Chicago, this was really a 996cc Excelsior ioe V-twin, exported to England. As there was already an English Excelsior factory, the American product was renamed American-X.

AMI / Germany 1921–1925

A 49cc ohv engine for bicycles designed by Heinrich Hillebrand, late of Hillebrand & Wolfmüller motorcycle-pioneering fame. A similar engine was made by the Columbus engine factory (later Horex) and called Gnom. Both had to be fitted in front of the pedalling gear. This started a fight between Ami and Gnom which lasted a long time in the courts.

AMI / Switzerland 1950–1954

Designed by Jaroslav Frei, former boss of the Czech Jawa factory, the Ami was a scooter with 98cc and later 123cc two-stroke engines.

AMMON / Germany 1923–1925

Interesting frame design, which consisted partly of tubes and partly of pressed steel. Used various proprietary engines which included DKW, Baumi and Bekamo two-strokes and the 123cc Paqué ohv engine.

AMO / Germany 1921–1924

Simple design of 146cc two-stroke lightweight machines.

AMR / Italy 1979–

Specialises in moto-cross, trial and enduro machines with German Sachs two-stroke engines from 123 to 400cc.

AMO / Germany 1950–1954

Mopeds with own 48cc two-stroke engines made by Westendarp & Pieper, a company which built TX motorcycles in the mid-1920s. The factory was at Berlin.

AMS / Spain 1954–1965

Assembled two-stroke motorcycles with 124cc, 198cc and 247cc Hispano-Villiers engines. They also built 248cc vertical twins.

ANCILOTTI / Italy 1967–1985

Makers of moto cross, enduro and one day trials models, using Sachs, Hiro and Franco Morini engines of 50cc and 125cc. Later produced a 246cc model. Well through of in their day, but production ceased in 1985.

124cc Ancilotti (TS Sachs Trial) 1974

ANCORA / Italy 1923–1939

Fitted for many years 147cc to 347cc Villiers engines and won many races during the late 1920s when the late Raffaele Alberti rode a 172cc Brooklands Villiers-engined Ancora in competitions. Umberto Dei bought the factory in the

early 1930s and built 60cc, 74cc and 98 cc models; after 1945 Dei supplied more light-weights, this time with the Garelli-built 39cc Mosquito bicycle engine.

ANDREES / Germany 1923–1929

Assembled good machines with oilcooled 346cc and 496cc flat twin Bradshaw engines and also used after 1925 proprietary units made by MAG and Blackburne. These included 346cc single-cylinder and 498cc and 598cc V-twin MAG motors with ioe valves. Among successful Andrees riders were Heinz Kürten and Franz Sieder. The end came in 1929, when H. W. Andrees built a new factory for the mass-production of 198cc single-cylinder two-stroke motorcycles and engines. The commercial depression at that period wrote the finish to his ambitions.

ANGLIAN / England 1903–1912

Anglian, of Beccles, Suffolk, made motor cycles and forecars with De Dion and, later, other proprietary engines. Featured two speeds and chain drive. Well regarded and successful in early long distance trials.

ANGLO-DANE / Denmark 1912–1914

Built in Copenhagen by Fredricksen Motors, the Anglo-Dane was made from English components and with different engines of JAP and Villiers manufacture. The production was on a limited scale.

ANKER / Germany 1949–1958

A once famous German bicycle factory which built Ilo and Sachs-engined two-stroke mopeds and motorcycles from 48cc to 244cc. Afterwards they concentrated on business machines including cash registers, but closed down early in 1976. The actual motorcycle production was transferred in 1952 to a branch factory at Paderborn. The main works were at Bielefeld.

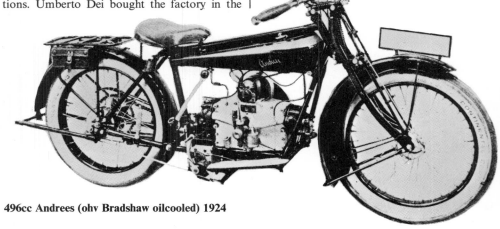

496cc Andrees (ohv Bradshaw oilcooled) 1924

ANTOINE/*Belgium 1900–1910*
A pioneer company which first fitted Kelecom engines and afterward produced 3, 3·5 and 4 hp singles and 4·5 and 5 hp V-twins. They also supplied engines to other motorcycle manufacturers. Other Antoine products included car and aero engines.

APACHE/*America 1907–1911*
Made by Brown & Beck at Denver, Colorado, the Apache had a rearward-facing 597cc single-cylinder ioe engine of their own manufacture.

APEX/*Germany 1925–1926*
Assembled sporting machines at Cologne with 247cc and 347cc ohv Blackburne single-cylinder engines. The production was on a small scale.

APOLLO/*Sweden 1951–*
Now part of the Volvo-controlled MCB group, Apollo motorcycles had among others 123cc Villiers and 198cc Zündapp engines. Production now concentrates on 49cc mopeds.

APRILIA/*Italy 1960–*
Bicycle makers, who first marketed a moped, then from 1975, moto cross machines with Sachs, Hiro and latterly Rotax engines. Very successful in moto cross, road racing and sales of 'replicas'. Excellent export record in Europe. In 1991 Aprilia were an ambitious and still expanding company.

AQUILA/*Italy 1927–1935*
The Turin-built Aquila was originally a 174cc two-stroke and later ohv machine. Made by a small company, during the 1930s they used English Rudge-built Python 248cc, 348cc and 498cc four-valve, single-cylinder ohv engines.

Other models had the 497cc Küchen sv single-cylinder and the Italian OBM engine.

AQUILA/*Italy 1953–1958*
The Rome-built Aquila had no connection with the older machine of the same name. The range of models included 48cc, 123cc and 158cc two-strokes and 98cc and 174cc ohv four-strokes of sound design and finish.

ARAB/*England 1923–1926*
Simple lightweight machines with 147cc Villiers engines.

ARBINET/*France 1927–1934*
Used exclusively their own two-stroke engines of 98cc, 173cc, 198cc, 347cc and 497cc capacity in conventional frames.

ARC/*Spain 1954–1956*
Hispano-Villiers-engined 123cc two-strokes of simple design.

ARCO/*Germany 1922–1931*
Watercooled 248cc and 348cc ohv single-cylinder machines and from 1929 onwards also a water-

499cc Arco (ohc watercooled) 1929

cooled 498cc ohc single formed the range of Speyer/Rhine-built Arco models. From 1927 onwards, the make was owned by an Amsterdam finance group.

ARDEA/*Italy 1928–1933*
A Moto-Guzzi-like design with a flat single-cylinder 173cc and later also 248cc ioe and ohv engine. Competed successfully in trials with Silvio Vailati, Virginio Fieschi and Bruno Martelli.

ARDEN/*England 1912–1920*
Small but versatile company which built small cars and also motorcycles with 269cc two-stroke Villiers as well as their own engines. These were supplied also to other producers, including Priory.

ARDENT/*France 1950–1957*
Mini-scooters and motorcycles with 49cc and 64cc Vap and Le Paulin engines.

ARDIE/*Germany 1919–1958*
Founded by ex-Premier technician Arno Dietrich, the first Ardie machines had their own 305cc and 348cc two-stroke deflector-type engines. After 1925 Ardie— since Dietrich's fatal

305cc Ardie (TS) 1924

accident in 1922 owned by the Bendit family— used exclusively JAP engines from 246cc to 996cc. Bestseller was the 490cc single-cylinder sv machine, but there were even V-twins with the 45 hp and 55 hp ohv JAP racing engines. Frames made from Duralumin were used in the early 1930s. Bark, Küchen, Sturmey-Archer and Sachs afterwards supplied to Ardie proprietary engines up to 598cc. Tubular frames· were used again and in 1938 Richard Küchen designed an interesting 348cc V-twin ohv machine with the engine transversely mounted. It never went into quantity production. After the war, Noack created new crossflow two-strokes with flat pistons from 124cc to 346cc. The last ones were

346cc Arco (ohv watercooled) 1927

vertical twins. The Nuremberg factory was at that time owned by the Barthel-controlled Dürkopp works at Bielefeld. Ardie was a successful make in races during the 1920s and early 1930s. Besides the Thumshirn team — Hans, Konrad and Georg — they had excellent riders in Franz Islinger, Karl Dobberkau, Gerd in der Elst, Josef Schörg and Karl Dobler and won many events, including TT races in Austria and Hungary.

490cc Ardie (sv JAP) 1928

246cc Ardie (TS twin) 1954

ARDITO / *Italy 1951–1954*
A small producer with a big production programme of various two-strokes from 48cc to 98cc and ohv four-strokes from 123cc to 173cc.

ARGENTRE / *France 1927–1932*
Assembled machines with many English components. Built 247cc and 347cc two-strokes with their own engines and also 348cc sv and ohv models with JAP engines.

ARGEO / *Germany 1924–1927*
Berlin-built two-strokes with own 198cc and 246cc deflector-type engines.

ARGUL / *Germany 1923–1926*
Limited production of two-strokes from 146cc to 198cc with engines supplied by DKW and Bubi and of four-stroke machines with Alba power units.

ARI / *Germany 1924–1925*
Another small producer of 146cc two-stroke motorcycles with DKW engines.

ARIEL / *England 1902–1970*
Built De Dion-engined three-wheelers at Birmingham in 1898 and four years later began the manufacture of motorcycles with 3·5 hp single-cylinder White & Poppe engines. In later

years, Ariel built them under licence. When the 1914 war broke out, the Ariel range consisted of 498cc sv singles and 998cc ioe V-twins. Other models had 348cc and 669cc V-twin power units, which were superseded by 794cc V-twins. In 1921 a 586cc single with 86·4mm bore and 100mm stroke came on the market, followed in 1922 by a 664cc single with 92mm bore and 100mm stroke. Another new model was a MAG-engined 992cc V-twin which was sold for £125 solo and £160 with sidecar. The price for the 499cc sv single was then £95. By 1924 the Ariel range consisted of a 247cc sv Blackburne-engined machine, 498cc sv and ohv models and a 993cc ioe V-twin.

Ariel, then owned by Jack Sangster, was joined in 1927 by the young technician Edward Turner. Chief designer was Val Page, who designed new 498cc ohv and 557cc sv singles, which proved to be bestsellers. In charge of publicity was Vic Mole, and of competitions the famous Harold Perrey. New 248cc and 348cc machines appeared

557cc Ariel (sv) 1929

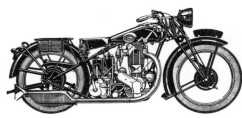

497cc Ariel (ohv) 1930

498cc Ariel (ohc Square Four) 1931

596cc Ariel (ohc Square Four) from a 1934 brochure

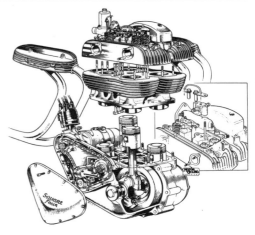

997cc Ariel (ohv 4-cylinder) 1959. Right: The famous Square Four engine.

248cc Ariel (ohv Red Hunter) 1936

198cc Ariel (TS-twin 'Arrow') 1962

soon afterwards and 1931 saw the introduction of the well-known 498cc Square-Four, with the four aircooled cylinders set in a square formation and the ohv gear operated by a chain-driven camshaft. This machine was designed by Edward Turner. Redesigned Square-Fours with 596cc and 996cc followed during the 1930s, and also models with forward inclined engines (slopers) and some very nice sports models, the 248cc, 348cc and 498cc ohv Red Hunter range. The big sv single now had 598cc and on the big Square Fours the ohc valve gear was superseded by pushrods.

In 1936 Edward Turner left to become boss of Triumph in Coventry, after Jack Sangster bought that factory. During the war, many 347cc ohv Ariel machines were used by the Forces. Main Ariel production after the war concentrated around 347cc and 497cc ohv Red Hunter singles including competition models, 498cc ohv vertical twins, a 598cc sv single and the 997cc Square Four. This machine sold in 1952 for £287 10s. On the other end of the scale, the 197cc Colt, an ohv single selling for £134, came into production and also the twin-cylinder Huntmaster range, including 646cc ohv versions. Jack Sangster, also head of BSA at Birmingham since the early fifties, moved Ariel nearer to Armoury Road. Many BSA and Ariel parts were identical. Edward Turner moved from Meriden (Triumph) to Armoury Road (BSA). He was also responsible for Ariel — which eventually moved from Selly Oak (Birmingham) into the BSA factory — and created in the early 1960s the 49cc Pixie, an ohv single, which did not gain much fame. In contrast, the famous 247cc vertical twin two-strokes, the Leader and the Arrow which were designed once more by Val Page, proved to be excellent machines. A 197cc version was the last real Ariel machine to be built. By 1970 the name Ariel was unfortunately no more on a two-wheel machine. All that are left are memories of success in trials and of famous trials riders, including Harold Perrey, Fred Povey, Ted Ray, Ron Langston and the famous Sammy Miller.

614cc Aristos (sv flat-twin watercooled) 1923

ARISTOS / *Germany 1923–1924*
Designed by Johannes Pässler, the 614cc Aristos was a very unorthodox machine with a water-cooled flat twin sv engine. The Mars-like frame was made of welded steel plates and allowed a low seat position. The Berlin-based company never developed this machine to the full. This led to more reorganisations and also to two more trade names for the Aristos inside of three years: Menos and Sterna. The differences between the three makes were small; they included, besides different tank transfers, the colour and the fork design.

ARLIGUE / *France 1950–1953*
Small assembler of motorcycles with AMC and Ydral proprietary engines from 98cc to 248cc.

ARMAC / *America 1911–1913*
Produced 14 different models with their own 4 hp single-cylinder and 7 hp V-twin engines.

ARMIS / *English 1920–1923*
Well-made machines with 269cc Precision two-stroke, 293cc and 348cc JAP, 346cc and 538cc Blackburne and 654cc V-twin ioe MAG engines.

ARMOR / *France 1910–1934*
Once a popular make and since the 1920s part of Alcyon. Produced two-strokes from 98cc and four-strokes from 173cc upwards. These included 498cc ohv and ohc unit-design singles, some with shaft-drive to the rear wheel.

ARMSTRONG / *England 1902–1905*
Assembled machines with 211cc Minerva engines and frames supplied by Chater-Lea.

ARMSTRONG / *England 1913–1914*
Only a single model with a 269cc Villiers engine was made before WWI stopped manufacture.

ARMSTRONG / *England 1980–1987*
An industrial group, which took over CCM and Cotton. Produced mainly competition machines with Rotax engines, and bitg four strokes for the British army.

ARNO / *England 1906–1914*
Coventry-made machines with 249cc, 348cc and 498cc sv engines. Limited production.

ARROW / *England 1913–1917*
Birmingham-built 211cc two-stroke machines with engines supplied by Levis and Precision.

ARROW / *America 1909–1914*
Lightweight motorcycles with 1 hp engines of own manufacture.

ASAHI / *Japan 1953–1965*
Old arms factory which already built in 1909 prototypes of motorcycles. When they went into quantity production in 1953, most models had 123cc and 173cc two-stroke engines of own design and manufacture.

ASCOT / *England 1905–1906*
Assembler of motorcycles with Minerva and Antoine engines.

ASCOT-PULLIN / *England 1928–1930*
Cyril Pullin's most advanced motorcycle design, the 498cc Ascot-Pullin, was built at Letchworth. It had 82mm bore, 94mm stroke, a flat single-cylinder ohv engine with alu-pistons, dry-sump lubrication, 3-speed gearbox, fully enclosed chains, hydraulically operated brakes, quickly detachable and interchangeable wheels, handle-bars of pressed steel with a range of built-in instruments, leg-shields, windscreen etc. Despite the comparatively low price of £75, the Ascot-Pullin failed to gain much popularity.

ASHFORD / *England 1905*
Assembled machines with 3.5 hp engines supplied by Minerva and Fafnir.

ASL / *England 1907–1915*
A company formed to publicise and exploit Professor Archibald Sharpe's pneumatic suspension units — hence Air Springs Ltd. Used mainly single cylinder and Vee twin JAP engines in large luxurious frames with air springing fore and aft. A very clever idea and well made machines, but before their time.

496cc ASL (sv JAP) 1909

ASPES / *Italy 1967–1982*
Though Aspes used Franco Morini and Minarelli engines in some of their machines, they mainly relied on their own 125cc two-stroke unit, with five- and six-speed gearbox. The RCC Moto Cross and Juma sports road bike (the later capable of 85mph) both used this engine, while a full road race version was also offered in the late 1970s. The 125cc Aspes moto-cross model was particularly popular in Britain in schoolboy scambling.

ASSO / *Italy 1927–1931*
Sporting lightweights with own 174cc unit-design ohv engines.

ASTER / *French 1898–1910*
Originally a producer of proprietary engines during the pioneering period, Aster also built three-wheelers, cars and motorcycles. Most Aster engines had horizontally-split crankcases made of bronze. One of the most popular models was a 355cc single, which was also supplied to the Orient motorcycle factory in the USA.

492cc Astra (ohv) 1939 (I)

ASTON / *England 1923–1924*
Was a 142cc two-stroke machine not unlike the Atlas. It had a deflector-type three-port engine with outside flywheel and was supplied with one, two and three-speed gearboxes and belt drive. Only the last versions could be supplied with belt-cum-chain drive.

ASTORIA / *Germany 1923–1925*
Built 289cc two-stroke machines on a limited scale. Nestoria, another Nuremberg factory, took over Astoria when they ran into difficulties.

ASTORIA / *Italy 1950–1957*
Designed and produced by ex-racer Virginio Fieschi, Astoria of Milano built nice two-strokes and ohv singles from 124 to 246cc. The range also included a fast 174cc production racer with an ohc engine of own manufacture.

ASTRA / *Germany 1923–1925*
The first Astra had 293cc Bosch-Douglas flat twin engines; from 1924 onwards they fitted also 348cc and 490cc (496cc) sv and ohv JAP and Blackburne single-cylinder engines into low frames. Ernst Henne, who later broke world records for BMW, in 1924–1925 rode an Astra machine with a 348cc ohv Blackburne engine. SMW at Munich built the Bosch-Douglas flat twins under licence.

ASTRA / *Italy 1931–1951*
A famous former Italian motorcycle importer, Max Türkheimer & Co. at Milan was since 1898 closely connected with Components Ltd. (Ariel) at Birmingham and shareholder of Charles Sangster's company. This arrangement continued when Jack Sangster took over from his father. Türkheimer used many Ariel-made parts,

especially frames, for his Astra machines; many 248cc and 498cc Astra sv and ohv singles used Ariel engine parts. Other models had 123cc, 174cc and 220cc. In pre-1914 days, Otav and other motorcycles were also made by the Türkheimer group.

ASTRAL / *France 1919–1923*
Concentrated on 98cc and 122cc two-strokes and was part of the Austral group which was again part of the Alcyon combine.

ATALA / *Italy 1925–1934*
An assembled machine which used mainly English components. Among them were the 174cc to 496cc sv and ohv engines made by JAP and Blackburne.

ATALA / *Italy 1954–1977*
Accessory manufacturers, who also built 50cc, 70cc 100cc and 125cc mopeds and lightweights with their own two-stroke engine. Also made scooters. Production was considerable, but spasmodic.

ATLANTA-DUO / *England 1935–1937*
Made by OEC at Portsmouth, Hants., these machines had duplex steering, rear springing, foot boards, leg-shields and a low position (19 inches from ground) and Dunloppilo seats for two. The JAP engines used were 248cc and 490cc ohv singles and 746cc sv V-twins.

ATLANTIC / *France 1929–1932*
Limited manufacture of 98cc two-strokes and 347cc and 497cc ohv and ohc engines made by Chaise, Blackburne and other suppliers of proprietary engines. At a Paris show, Atlantic exhibited a motorcycle equipped with a fully enclosed engine.

ATLANTIC / *Germany 1923–1925*
Small producer of 193cc sv single-cylinder motorcycles with engines supplied by the former Hansa factory at Bielefeld.

ATLANTIK / *Germany 1925–1926*
Built on a limited scale 173cc two-stroke machines.

ATLANTIS / *Germany 1926–1932*
Made by a small company, the first models had own 348cc and 398cc single-cylinder two-stroke engines. From 1927 onwards, 497cc ohc Küchen, 498cc sv JAP, 598cc sv Blackburne and 498cc, 746cc and 990cc ioe MAG engines came into production. All MAG engines were V-twins.

ATLAS / *England 1913–1914*
Also a small company. Used 492cc JAP and 496cc sv single-cylinder Blumfield proprietary engines.

ATLAS / *England 1922–1925*
Birmingham-built 142cc two-stroke of simple design with forward-facing carburettor and belt drive to the rear wheel. Used one and two-speed gearboxes. Price with 2-speed gearbox: £30/9.

142cc Atlas (TS) 1924 (GB)

ATLAS / *Germany 1924–1929*
Fitted own 248cc and 348cc single-cylinder two-stroke engines. Designer/manufacturer Schleif rode these machines with success in hill-climbs.

248cc Atlas (TS) 1925 (D)

ATTOLINI / *Italy 1920–1923*
Equipped with rear suspension, the Attolini housed a 269cc Villiers two-stroke engine.

AUGUSTA / *Italy 1924—1931*
Designed by Angelo Blatto, the Augusta was launched with an advanced 350cc overhead camshaft engine. Later models had 125cc and 175cc engines still with overhead camshafts. Earned a sporting reputation, being fast, but they were also unreliable. Like many small companies, probably lacked the resources to develop a design advanced for its day.

AURORA / *England 1902—1907*
Used a variety of proprietary engines from 2·25 hp to 3·25 hp. Engine suppliers included MMC, Coronet, Whitley, Coventry-built Condor and other makes.

AURORA / *Isle of Man 1919—1921*
Built in Douglas—the Aurora was a machine with a 318cc two-stroke engine made by Dalm. The other Isle of Man-built motorcycle was the Peters.

AUSTEN / *England 1903—1906*
Small assembler who fitted 2·25 hp Kelecom engines, among others.

AUSTRAL / *France 1908—1932*
Old established factory. Produced for many years 211cc two-strokes, after 1918 ones with 246cc capacity. The range also included machines with 246cc and 346cc sv and ohv JAP and Zurcher engines. Austral was also part of the Alcyon group of companies.

AUSTRIA / *Austria 1903—1907*
Was one of the first producers of bicycle attachments. The engine, designed by Josef Mezera, had 0·8 hp. His son Rudolf Mezera was with the Austro-Motorette factory during the 1920s and also raced in the Austrian TT of 1926.

AUSTRIA / *Austria 1930—1933*
The Lamperts-owned Austria motorcycle factory—housed in the former DSH works at Trautmannsdorf—built 246cc and 347cc machines with frames made from Duralumin and actually built by Ardie in Nuremberg. The range of engines included watercooled Villiers and aircooled Villiers, as well as the 347cc sv single made by Sturmey-Archer in Nottingham. Designer at the Austria factory was Hauler.

AUSTRIA-ALPHA / *Austria 1933—1952*
Formerly with the Werner-MAG factory and a successful racing motorcyclist, Josef V. Illichmann designed first various racing machines including a 248cc narrow-angle ohc V-twin and a 498cc ohv single. After the war he built mainly models with 248cc double-piston Puch two-stroke engines and 244cc Ilo vertical twin two-strokes. Afterwards he concentrated on the manufacture of foot gear-changes, rear suspensions, full-width hubs, forks and other parts. Now he owns one of the largest foundries in Austria.

AUSTRO-ILO / *Austria 1938*
Only a few of these 120cc Ilo-engined two-strokes had been built when Hitler occupied Austria and stopped this company from further manufacture of motorcycles.

AUSTRO-MOTORETTE / *Austria 1924—1927*
Built first 82cc two-stroke bicycle engines, afterwards Karl Schüber-designed 144cc vertical-twin two-stroke motorcycles. Interesting were the 173cc Austro-Motorette racing machines of 1926 with vertical-twin double-ohc engines, raced in the Austrian TT by Rudolf Mezera and Ladislaus Hajos-Hihalom. They proved very fast, but did not finish.

144cc Austro-Motorette (TS twin) 1927

AUSTRO-OMEGA / *Austria 1932—1939*
Superbly finished and well made 348cc, 490cc and 746cc machines with sv and ohv JAP engines and other English components. A few racing models had 348cc Sturmey-Archer ohv power units. Ridden by Hermann Deimel, Rudi Hunger and Franz Behrendt, they won many races. Martin Schneeweiss used in 1934—1935 a JAP-engined 498cc Austro-Omega ohv racing single.

490cc Austro Omega (ohv JAP) 1932

198cc Autinag (TS) 1925

AUTINAG / *Germany 1924—1925*
Limited production of 127cc and 198cc two-strokes and of a MAG-engined 496cc single-cylinder machine with ioe valves.

AUTO-BI / *America 1902—1912*
Produced motorcycles and scooter-like machines with enclosed engines. Supplier of engines with 1·5 hp and 2·5 hp was E. R. Thomas.

347cc Austria (TS Villiers) 1931

AUTO-BIT/*Japan 1952–1962*
Produced 249cc single-cylinder machines on typical English lines.

AUTO-ELL/*Germany 1924–1926*
Designed by racing motorcyclist Max Ell, these lightweight machines had 142cc Grade two-stroke power units.

AUTOFLUG/*Germany 1921–1923*
Scooter-like machines with a long wheelbase and small wheels, designed by Egon Weitzel for a former aircraft manufacturer. The normal Auto-flug motorcycle had identical 129cc and 146cc Bekamo engines to the scooter-like machines. The Ruppe-designed Bekamo engine was a two-stroke with a pumping cylinder in the bottom of the crankcase.

122cc Autoflug (TS Bekamo) 1922

AUTOGLIDER/*England 1919–1922*
Another scooter-like machine with a 292cc Union two-stroke engine above the small front wheel.

AUTOMOTO/*France 1901–1962*
A pioneer make which built for many years very sturdy—and quite heavy—motor cycles with engines up to 499cc. Used engines made by Zurcher, Chaise, JAP, Villiers; after 1945 mainly AMC ohv engines up to 248cc. Never regarded as a very sporty machine, the Automoto of pre-1939 days was a typical 'farmers machine' of great durability. During the concentration of the French motorcycle industry, Automoto joined the Peugeot group, which already included the Terrot-Magnat Debon combine.

490cc Automoto (ohv Chaise) 1929

AUTOPED/*America 1915–1921*
Once a well-known scooter with a 155cc four-stroke engine above the small front wheel. Krupp in Germany and CAS in Czechoslovakia built the Autoped under licence.

AUTOSCO/*England 1920–1921*
Another early scooter, which failed to become popular. The engine had 180cc.

AVADA/*The Netherlands 1953–late 1950s*
Small moped manufacturer who used 49cc two-stroke engines.

AVELLO/*Spain 1976–*
Lightweights from 49 to 79cc built by a branch factory of the big Austrian Puch works.

AVENIR/*Belgium 1956–*
Another mofa and moped manufacturer who built two-strokes of 49cc capacity.

AVIS-CELER/*Germany 1925–1931*
Hanover-based Avis-Celer built machines with Villiers engines from 172cc to 346cc and—from 1928 onwards—also bigger models with 347cc and 497cc ioe and ohv single-cylinder MAG engines. Leading rider was Hermann Wiedemann, whose 248cc, 348cc and 498cc racing versions housed engines made by JAP.

AVON/*England 1919–1920*
Limited production of motorcycles with 347cc Villiers single-cylinder two-stroke engines.

AWD/*Germany 1921–1959*
AWD & Wurring motor cycles used such proprietary engines as DKW, Blackburne, JAP, Kuchen, Sachs, Villiers and Ilo over the years. Pre war, August Wurring was known for building special

racing motor cycles to order. In post-war years, a similar operation was again set up, using proprietary engines of between 100cc and 250cc. The last models made use of a 250cc twin Ilo two-stroke engine.

248cc AWO (ohv shaft-driven racer) 1953

AWO/*East Germany 1949–1957*
Built at the former Simson-Supra car factory at Suhl in Thuringia, the AWO was a 246cc single-cylinder ohv machine with unit-design engine and shaft drive to the rear wheel. Special works racing models had 248cc vertical twin-cylinder single and double ohc power units with chain, bevel and gear-driven ohc and also single-cylinder engines with overhead camshafts. During the 1950s, the name changed to Simson.

AYRES-LEYLAND/*England 1920*
Flat twins with 688cc Coventry Victor sv engine, own gearbox and spring frame.

AZA/*Czechoslovakia 1924–1926*
Light-weight machines with 147cc engines. The same Prague factory also built the big 996cc JAP-engined MC V-twin machines.

AZZARITI/*Italy 1933–1934*
Designed by Vincenzo Azzariti, these 173cc and 348cc ohc machines had twin-cylinder engines, some of which had desmodromic valve gear, in which the valve is opened by a cam and then closed by another cam, rather than by a spring.

496cc AWD (sv Columbus) 1936

B

BAC/*England 1951–1953*
The Gazelle, made by this Blackpool-based aircraft company, was one of the first British scooters after WWII. It was supplied with 98cc and 123cc Villiers engines. The BAC lightweight motorcycle also had the 98cc Villiers engine.

BADGER/*America 1920–1921*
Unconventional design with the 163cc four-stroke engine built into the rear wheel.

BAF/*Czechoslovakia 1927–1930*
Designed by B. A. Frisek, the Prague-built BAF motorcycles had Bekamo two-stroke 173cc and 246cc 'pumping-piston', 346cc ohv Kühne and 496cc Chaise unit-design ohc single-cylinder.

BAIER/*Germany 1924–1930*
One of the many two-stroke motorcycle factories which existed during the 1920s in Berlin. The first models were 173, 198 and 248cc singles with some unit-design engines. From 1927 onwards the only model in production, a design by Willy and Karl Baier, was a 492cc two-piston one-cylinder machine with a BMW-like triangular frame.

487cc Baier (TS double-piston single) 1928

BAILEUL/*France 1904–1910*
Small producer who fitted Peugeot and Buchet engines into his machines.

BAJAJ/*India 1960–*
Originally an Italian Lambretta scooter built under licence from Piaggio & Co., the new 124cc, 5·8 bhp Bajaj is now being exported into Europe under the 'Chetak' trade mark.

BAKER/*England 1927–30*
Frank Baker worked for the American firm Cleveland before making Precision proprietary engines in Britain. After the crash of the post-WWII Beard-

more Precision company, Baker designed stylish Villiers-engined lightweights of 150cc-250cc, the 175cc 'racer' being especially popular. The company was taken over by James in 1930.

BALALUWA/*Germany 1924–1925*
The Balaluwa was a nice 346cc ohv single-cylinder machine of very advanced design. Like other German factories of that period, it probably had insufficient finances to carry on.

BALKAN/*Bulgaria 1958–1975*
Built Jawa-like 246cc single-cylinder two-strokes and concentrated afterward on various models —including mopeds—with 49cc and 73cc two-stroke engines of own manufacture.

BAM/*Germany 1933–1937*
The 'Germany' in this case refers mainly to the transfer, i.e. the 'BAM', on the tank. Reason for BAM 'production' was Adolf Hitler, who made import of foreign motorcycles nearly impossible. The Belgian FN works had an assembly plant at Aachen and a sales office at Berlin; as they were not able to send their own motorcycles via Aachen to Germany, they created a new name which stood for 'Berlin-Aachener-Motorradwerke'. Apart from the name, everything was original FN. The range included 198cc two-stroke singles, 346cc sv and 497cc sv and ohv models. This arrangement satisfied the Hitler Government.

BAMAR/*Germany 1923–1925*
Assembler of lightweight motorcycles with 149cc and 198cc engines made by DKW, Gruhn, Baumi, Alba and other engine suppliers. Limited production.

BAMO/*Germany 1923–1925*
Another small German make. Used 148cc and 173cc DKW proprietary engines.

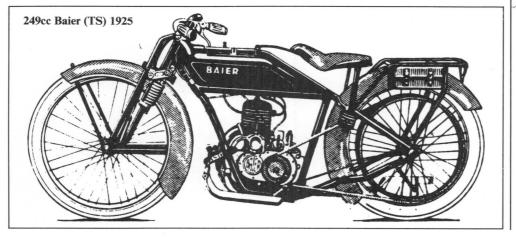

249cc Baier (TS) 1925

BANSHEE / *England 1921–1924*
Produced machines with 269cc Villiers engines and was among the first to fit the 347cc Barr & Stroud sleeve-valve engine. Other models had oilcooled 346cc Bradshaw and 347cc and 497cc Blackburne sv and ohv engines.

BARDONE / *Italy 1938–1939*
Once a well-known producer of delivery three-wheelers, Bardone also built heavy 499cc motorcycles with their own unit-design ohv single-cylinder engines.

BARNES / *England 1904*
A little-known make which fitted various proprietary engines, including the MMC and 211cc Minerva.

BARON / *England 1920–1921*
Concentrated on assembling motorcycles with 292cc Union and 348cc Blackburne sv engines.

BARRY / *Czechoslovakia 1932–1939*
The first models were 248cc ohv racing singles, designed by Friedrich Drkosch. A 98cc two-stroke of up-to-date design was ready for production when WWII broke out.

BARTALI / *Italy 1953–1961*
Named after a famous bicycle racer, Gino Bartali, these good-looking motorcycles had 48cc, 124cc and 158cc two-stroke and 123cc, 174cc and 198cc ohv engines. The 158cc Marziano was a super-sport model.

BARTER / *England 1902–1905*
Unusual single-cylinder machines with rear-wheel drive taken directly from the camshafts.

The designer W. J. Barter afterwards created the Fairy (Fee) motorcycles with flat-twin engines which were the forerunners of Douglas machines.

BARTISCH / *Austria 1925–1929*
Franz Bartisch designed in 1925 a 348cc single-cylinder machine with chain-driven ohc and added in 1928 a 498cc model with bevel-driven ohc. This machine had no outside oil pipes and was of very clean design. Lack of finance prevented the manufacture of large numbers of these excellent machines.

BASTERT / *Germany 1949–1955*
Still well-known company which produced Sachs and Ilo-engined motorcycles from 49cc to 247cc and also various mopeds and scooters.

BAT / *England 1902–1926*
Designed by the famous pioneer competition rider T H Tessier and made by his family firm. BAT ('Best after test') were early users of cylinder and V twin JAP engines, with a range of capacities from 500cc to 1000cc. The BATs featured a magneto at petrol tank level driven by bevels and shaft and also a spring sub-frame, often mistakenly called a 'spring frame'. Very sporting.

BATAVUS / *Holland 1911–*
Factory known for 49cc mofas, mopeds and lightweight motorcycles which also produced in earlier years motorcycles up to 198cc with Ilo, Villiers and Sachs engines.

BAUDO / *Italy 1920–1928*
Produced at Turin JAP-engined V-twins with 474cc, 668cc and 972cc. After 1924 the range included models with 248cc Train engines (two-

strokes), 348cc Barr & Stroud sleeve-valve singles, 173cc Moser ohv motors and also JAP-engined versions of 173cc, 246cc and 346cc.

BAUER / *Germany 1936–1954*
Well-known bicycle factory. Produced in pre-1939 days mopeds with 74cc and 98cc Sachs engines, after 1945 motorcycles with 123cc, 147cc and 173cc Sachs and Ilo two-strokes. A new 247cc machine, introduced in 1952, led to technical and resulting commercial difficulties. This machine had an ohv single-cylinder engine with the carburettor in front and the exhaust valve on the rear of the engine. This arrangement led to overheating and a comparatively low output. Bauer carried on bicycle production, but withdrew completely from the manufacture of motorcycles in 1954.

BAUGHAN / *England 1930–1936*
Built by an experienced trials man who later as ACU official was in charge of big trials including the International. Most Baughan machines were made for cross-country events and his sidecars had their own drive. The engines used were 247cc 347cc and 497cc sv and ohv Blackburne.

BAYERLAND / *Germany 1924–1930*
A 996cc V-twin with a JAP ohv racing engine, ridden by Sepp Giggenbach, won the Grand Prix of Europe in 1927 in the 1000cc class. Bayerland machines had 248cc, 348cc and 490cc sv and ohv JAP engines. Designer of Bayerland motorcycles was Anton Bayerlein.

BAYERN / *Germany 1923–1926*
The first models had 293cc Bosch-Douglas flat twin engines, built under licence by SMW of Stockdorf, near Munich. After 1924 new versions with 498cc, 746cc and 988cc V-twin MAG engines came into being. The production of these machines was not large.

746cc Bayern (ioe MAG V-twin) 1926

BAYLEY-FLYER / *America 1914–1917*
Very unorthodox design with a flat 3·5 hp twin-cylinder engine, shaft drive, automatic gear change and hand starter. Despite these features, not many Bayley-Flyers reached the market.

8½ hp BAT single, 1903

BB / *Germany 1923–1925*
Assembled machines with 197cc Alba sv single-cylinder engines.

BB / *Italy 1925–1927*
Small 123cc two-strokes with a horizontal cylinder. Designer-manufacturer of these nice lightweights was Ugo Bocchi.

BCR / *France 1923–1930*
Raynal's motorcycles were among the first to use rear springing. He was also manufacturer of Poinard machines. Most models had 98cc and 174cc two-stroke engines, others were fitted with sv and ohv JAP engines of 248cc, 348cc and 498cc.

BD / *Czechoslovakia 1927–1929*
Superb J. F. Koch-designed 490cc unit-design ohc touring-sport single-cylinder machines, made by the Breitfeld-Daněk machine factory at Prague. When Praga, the well-known car makers, took over this factory, they continued the manufacture of motorcycles under the Praga trade-mark. Koch also joined Praga.

490cc BD (dohc) 1928

BEARDMORE PRECISION *England 1921–1924*
Giant Scottish industrial group Beardmore (ships, locomotives, cars, aircraft engines) took over Frank Baker's Precision company to produce an advanced, but ugly, motor cycle with leaf springing fore and aft, integral petrol tank and band brakes. The marque generally used Precision engines, though one model was fitted with the sleeve-valve Barr & Stroud. Beardmore themselves built a disastrous ohc engine with twin carburettors for the

346cc Beardmore-Precision (sleeve-valve B&S) 1923

1¾ hp Beeston (De Dion engine) 1897

1924 Junior TT. In the event 250cc engines with leaf valve springs were hastily substituted, but failed. Beardmore then closed the operation.

BEAUFORT / *England 1923–1926*
Producer of Argson invalid threewheelers, Beaufort also produced a 170cc single-cylinder two-stroke motorcycle.

BEAU-IDEAL / *England 1905–1906*
Assembled motorcycles with Clement, Minerva and JAP engines.

BEAUMONT / *England 1921–1922*
Designed by Monty Beaumont, these machines had 269cc Wall two-stroke engines and also 348cc Blackburne sv motors. Beaumont became better known in the 1940s when he designed the ill-fated Kendall 'people-car' with a three-cylinder radial engine.

BE-BE / *Germany 1923–1927*
Small 117cc two-stroke made by a small iron-producing company.

BECCARIA / *Italy 1925–1928*
Motorcycles assembled from mainly English components. These included 346cc Villiers and 348cc sv and ohv Blackburne engines.

BECKER / *Germany 1903–1906*
Limited production of machines with their own and with Fafnir single-cylinder and V-twin engines.

BECO / *Germany 1923–1925*
Motorcycle assembler who fitted 149cc DKW two-stroke proprietary engines into simple frames of own production.

BEESTON / *England 1898–1910*
Owned by the motor pioneer Harry John Lawson, Beeston was one of the oldest makes in the trade. They produced at and around Coventry in different factories three-wheelers, motorcycles and cars. Beeston motorcycles had strengthened bicycle frames and the 1·75 hp engine housed between the pedalling gear and the rear wheel. The engine was of De Dion design, of which H. J. Lawson had all patent and production rights for England. The capacity of the engine used in Beeston motorcycles was 346cc.

BEFAG / *Germany 1922–1924*
Used the Julius Löwy-designed 113cc and 176cc crude-oil engines in conventional frames.

BEHAG / *Germany 1924–1926*
Simple design with open frames. Fitted own 218cc two-stroke and JAP engines of 348cc and 490cc with side-valves.

BEKAMO / *Germany 1922–1925*
Famous two-stroke machines with a pumping piston at the bottom of the crankcase. Designed by Hugo Ruppe, the first models had wooden frames, from 1923 onwards they had orthodox tubular frames. The powerful 129cc engines won many races and were also sold to other motorcycle producers as proprietary power units. Other factories produced Bekamo engines under licence. Among them were Windhoff, MFZ,

129cc Bekamo (TS) 1924 (D)

Eichler, TX and Böhme. Leading Bekamo riders were Sepp Thevis, Max Hucke, Paul Lüdtke, Karl Jurisch, Kurt Pohle, Gerhard Ahrens, Otto Heller and others.

173cc Bekamo (TS) 1927 (CS)

BEKAMO / *Czechoslovakia 1923–1930*
The first Czechoslovakian Bekamo machines were made at the Berlin Bekamo works. For tax reasons they had the two-stroke pumping-piston engines reduced to 124cc and while the German factory still used wooden frames, the Czechoslovakian Bekamo works at Rumburk fitted these power units into equally unorthodox TX frames. These had a top tube of 8-inch diameter which acted as the petrol/oil tank. The Rumburk factory was until 1925 an assembly plant for Bekamo machines supplied to Czechoslovakia, but when the German factory at Berlin closed down, everything was transferred to Rumburk. A 174cc model was added in 1927 and in 1929 a 248cc Bekamo with an orthodox tubular frame, made at the Aeros factory, came into being. Leading riders on Czechoslovakian Bekamos were Heller, Franz Olbrich and Josef Kosinka.

BENELLI / *Italy 1919–1989*
Established in 1911 as engineers, Benelli, owned by the six Benelli brothers, made a 98cc 'clip-on' engine in 1919, but their first 98cc and later 150cc two-stroke motor cycles were launched in 1921. Tonino, the youngest brother, raced a 150cc successfully until 1927, when Giovanni and Giuseppe created the first 175cc ohc model. This soon became a dohc, and Tonino and other riders Baschieri, Aldrigheti and Serafini made it famous on the continent, along with the larger 250cc version. Tonino was killed in a road accident in 1937, by which time Benelli were one of Italy's 'big five' manufacturers.

In the late 1930s, Benelli experimented with supercharging, building a superb transverse blown water-cooled 250cc four that was never raced.

248cc Benelli (ohc) 1939

However, Ted Mellors used an ordinary dohc 250cc Benelli for the 1939 Lightweight TT. Post war, Dario Ambrosini won many 250cc races, becoming world champion in 1950. When he was

248cc Benelli (dohc works-racer) 1952

killed early in 1951, Benelli gave up racing.

For the road, Benelli made two- and four-strokes, mostly under 250cc. In the 1960s, the company re-entered racing with a 250cc four ridden by Silvio Grosetti, Tarquinio Provini and Renzo Pasolini. After the Japanese withdrew, Kel Carruthers won the world championship in 1969, but sales subsequently declined and in 1971 Benelli were bought by Alesandro de Tomaso.

New 125cc and 250cc two stroke twins were launched, but were overshadowed by grandiose announcements of a 750cc (later 900cc) six cylinder and 500cc and 250cc fours! In the event, few were made and it was sales of mopeds and scooters that kept the company afloat in the 1980s. Production of the four strokes ended late in 1987 and a new range of fashionably styled 125cc two strokes was introduced at the Milan Show. However, these were not enough to revive the company's flagging fortunes, since, for one thing, they were far too

906cc Benelli (ohc 900 Sei) 1982

605cc Benelli (ohc four Sport) 1982

expensive to compete with Japanese competition. In 1989 Alessandro de Tomaso saw the red light and sold the Benelli factory. The new owners assembled a few mopeds, but essentially, 60 odd years of glorious history was ended.

231cc Benelli (TS twin) 1977

BENOTTO / *Italy 1953–1957*
One of the many small factories of the 1950s Benotto fitted German Ilo two-strokes from 48cc to 198cc and also ohv engines to 198cc.

BERCLEY / *Belgium 1905–1909*
Designed by Gustave Kindermann, the Bercley was one of the first vertical twins in quantity production. The sv engine had 616cc and was of advanced design.

BERESA / *Germany 1923–1925*
Produced motorcycles with 198cc sv engines on a limited scale.

BERGFEX / *Germany 1904–1909*
Berlin-built single and V-twin machines with

their own and also with Aachen-built Fafnir proprietary engines.

BERGO / *Germany 1924*
Assembled machines with 145cc DKW two-stroke power units.

BERINI / *The Netherlands late 1950s*
Well-known manufacturer of mopeds etc. with 49cc two-stroke rotary-valve engines.

BERLIN / *East Germany 1958–1965*
Scooter, equipped with 148cc MZ two-stroke engines.

BERNARDET / *France 1930–1934*
Chaise and Train proprietary engines from 98cc to 498cc drove these machines, which were in limited production.

BERNARDET / *France 1949–1957*
Another business founded and owned by the three Bernardet brothers — René, Robert and Roger — produced exclusively scooters, which in the 1950s were among the leaders in France.

616cc Bercley (sv twin) 1905

They had 123cc and 246cc Ydral two-stroke engines.

BERNEG / *Italy 1954–1961*
Beautiful small 159cc and 174cc vertical-twin machines, designed by Alfonso Drusiani. They had their own ohc engines and were built to the highest standards.

BERO / *Germany 1924–1925*
Light-weight machines with 145cc DKW two-stroke engines. Limited production.

BERTIN / *France 1955–1958*
Manufacturer of small machines with 49cc engines.

BERWICK / *England 1929–1930*
The only English make which fitted shaft drive to the rear wheel at that time. The engines used were 246cc and 346cc single-cylinder Villiers.

BETA / *Italy 1948–*
Beta was founded in 1948 by Giuseppe Bianchi and soon produced an impressive range of two-strokes and ohv four-strokes of between 125cc and 200cc. They made a 175cc sports racing two-stroke — the MT (Milan-Taranto), which was well regarded. The four-strokes gave way to an all two-stroke range; in recent years, Beta has followed the usual trend of off-road styling with genuine trials and moto-cross machines as well as imitation ones. Beta still make nicely styled small road bikes.

BEUKER / *Germany 1921–1929*
Two-stroke machines with 145cc, 173cc, 198cc, 231cc and 246cc engines of own design and manufacture. The Beuker engines were of the deflector-type and had three ports.

BEZDĚZ / *Czechoslovakia 1923–1926*
Produced bicycle engines and also complete machines with these 145cc sv power units.

BH / *Spain 1956–1960*
Small moped manufacturer, who used 49cc two-stroke engines.

B & H / *England 1923*
Engine producer who also built 996cc V-twin sv machines on a limited scale and for a limited period. These machines were made at the once-famous Napier Works.

BIANCHI / *Italy 1897–1967*

Edoardo Bianchi was one of the great pioneers in Italy. His first motorised bicycle was made in 1897, his first car in 1900. By 1903 he fitted engines in the centres of strengthened bicycle frames; by 1905 he used Truffault leading-link forks and by 1910 a superb 498cc single made Bianchi a very successful make. A 650cc V-twin was built in 1916 and in 1920 enlarged to 741cc. A smaller, 598cc V-twin came into production in 1921 and there was also a new all chain-drive 498cc single. It was followed in 1923 by a 348cc sv single and two V-twin models with 498cc and 598cc; in 1924 by 173cc ohv single-cylinder machines. 1925 saw the introduction of the 348cc ohv single and of the famous 348cc double ohc works racing machines designed by Bianchi chief engineer Albino Baldi. Ridden by Tazio Nuvolari, Amilcare Moretti, Mario Ghersi, Karl Kodric, Gino Zanchetta, Luigi Arcangeli and others, these Bianchi 'doubleknockers' were until 1931 the most successful Italian racing 350s. In addition, they were probably the fastest of their kind in the world. Bianchi also built during the 1930s Baldi-designed 498cc single-cylinder ohc racing machines. Ridden by Giordano Aldrighetti, Aldo Pigorini, Terzo Bandini, Dorino Serafini, Guido Cerato, Alberto Ascari and others, they too were successful. A new 1938-built 498cc four-cylinder double-ohc machine with supercharger was never fully developed. After 1945 Bianchi returned to racing with 123cc and 248cc single-cylinder ohc machines, and—during the late 1950s—with new 248cc and 348cc twin-cylinder double-ohc models, designed by Colombo and Tonti. Among the riders was Ernesto Brambilla and there were also a few bored-out models for the 500cc class. Production versions of Bianchi machines included many 49cc, 122cc and 173cc two-strokes and also the Tonale, with its own 173cc ohc engine, which had the camshaft driven by chain. Some 49cc two-strokes had engines built under Puch licence. Bianchi had given up car manufacture many years ago and it was a sad day in 1967 when this once great company also stopped the production of motorcycles.

348cc Bianchi (dohc works-racer) 1925

500cc Bianchi dohc early 1950s

173cc ohc Bianchi Sportster 1962

173cc Bianchi (ohv Sport) 1939

BICHRONE / *France 1902–1907*

One of the first producers of motorcycles with two-stroke engines of 2·25 hp, 2·50 hp and 2·75 hp, also supplied to other factories.

BIM / *Japan 1956–1961*

Was one of the small Japanese factories which built BMW-like sv twin machines without great commercial or sporting successes. Models included 248cc, 348cc, 498cc and 598cc machines.

BIMM / *Italy 1972–1980*

Younger Italian producer of trials and motocross machines with 49cc and 123cc Minarelli two-stroke engines.

BIMOFA / *Germany 1922–1925*

Designed by Gustav Kunstmann, German Bimofa 1·8 hp and 2·5 hp machines had sv engines made by Hansa.

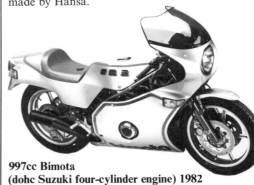

997cc Bimota
(dohc Suzuki four-cylinder engine) 1982

BIMOTA / *Italy 1975–*

Specialist frame builders, who are manufacturers in their own right as well, using Japanese and Italian large capacity multi-cylinder engines. Very successful in road racing. Now a vital part of the Cagiva group.

BINKS / *England 1903–1906*

Charles Binks, who later became famous as a producer of carburettors, was one of the pioneers of four-cylinder motorcycle manufacture. His 'fours' had aircooled in-line engines of 385cc. Some models had them transverse mounted.

385cc Binks (sv four) 1905

BINZ/*Germany 1954–1958*
Simple scooter with 49cc Sachs and Ilo engines.

BIRCH/*England 1902–1905*
The first Birch was already made in 1901. The designer J. J. Birch of Nuneaton near Coventry, had the single cylinder built into the rear wheel. This design was sold to the Coventry Singer Company. The conventional Birch motorcycles had a triangular frame, which included a built-in crankcase and bottom bracket casting. Bradbury built such machines under Birch licence. Birch engines were of 2, 2·5 and 3·5 hp. All had direct belt drive to the rear wheel.

BIRMA/*France 1949–late 1950s*
Lightweight machines of 98cc with Aubier-Dunne two-stroke engines.

BISMARCK/*Germany 1904–1956*
Produced big V-twins up to 1300cc with engines supplied by Minerva, Anzani and Fafnir. Around 1908 they stopped motorcycle manufacture and resumed in 1931 with motorised bicycles of 75cc

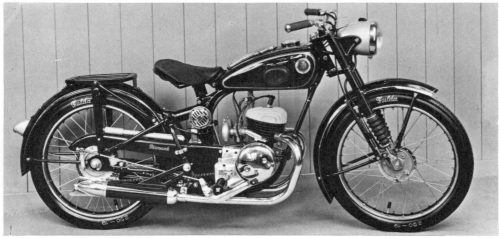

123cc Bismarck (TS Ilo) 1953

and 98cc. Emil Fischer designed after 1945 well-made two-stroke motorcycles of 98cc, 147cc and 173cc capacity. Sachs and Ilo supplied the engines.

BISMARCK/*Germany 1921–1923*
Yet another small German company which used this trade mark for small bicycle attachments and afterwards for 148cc 1·5 bhp single-cylinder sv machines.

BISON/*Austria 1924–1926*
Designed by Oskar Hacker, who later became chief designer of the Austro-Daimler car factory, Bison motorcycles always had flat twin-cylinder engines. Among them were the 293cc Bosch-Douglas, the 493cc BMW and the Coventry-built 678cc Coventry-Victor. Limited production.

493cc Bison (sv BMW flat-twin) 1925

BITRI/*The Netherlands 1955–1957*
Small producer of scooters with 147cc engines.

BJR/*Spain 1953–early 1960s*
Produced 123cc and 174cc machines with two-stroke engines.

BLACKBURNE/*England 1908–1921*
Cecil and Alick Burney were pioneers of the British motorcycle industry. Originally con-

448cc Blackburne (sv) 1921

nected with Geoffrey De Havilland, they designed engines, later complete motorcycles of 3·5 and 4 hp (singles) and 8 hp (twins). They eventually left the company and concentrated on the manufacture of proprietary power units. In 1921 Osborn Engineering Company (OEC) took over the manufacture of Blackburne motorcycles.

BLACKFORD/*England 1902–1904*
Designed by Frank Blackford, these machines had 211cc Minerva engines.

BLACK-PRINCE/*England 1919–1920*
E. W. Cameron's design was more a black sheep than a prince. It had a 497cc flat-twin two-stroke engine with one plug only and a pressed steel frame with rear suspension. It is unlikely that this engine was ever fully developed. When Cameron closed down, the production concentrated on a more orthodox model with a tubular frame and 292cc Union two-stroke engine.

174cc Bleha (TS) 1924

BLEHA/*Germany 1923–1926*
Not a big factory, which fitted 247cc DKW two-stroke and 247cc sv engines of own design and manufacture.

BLÉRIOT/*France 1920–1923*
There was a certain similarity between Sopwith in England and Blériot. Both aircraft factories turned to motorcycle production after WWI, Sopwith with the ABC, Blériot with 498cc vertical twins. Blériot's were built with sv and with ohv, but proved to be a failure, like the ABC, because they were not fully developed.

498cc Blériot (sv twin) 1920

BLOTTO / *France 1951–1955*
Limited production of two-stroke machines with proprietary engines from 123cc to 348cc.

BLUMFIELD / *England 1908–1914*
T. W. Blumfield became the creator of Blumfield motorcycles and engines. Some versions had watercooled engines and competed in TT races.

48cc BM (dohc) 1956

BM / *Italy 1950–1972*
Mario Bonviccini used Ilo and Franco Morini two-stroke engines of between 125cc and 175cc to launch his range, but soon devised his own superb ohc engines of 50cc, 65cc and 125cc. A dohc racer was produced in 1956, while later machines included a range of nicely styled 80cc two-strokes, for the road and also for off-road riding.

BM / *Italy 1928–1931*
Meldi's BM motorcycles, built in limited numbers, had 490cc single-cylinder sv and ohv JAP engines.

BMA / *Italy 1978–*
Small manufacturer of competition machines with 124cc and 248cc two-stroke engines. The Rome based factory also sells outside Italy.

BMG / *Hungary 1939–1944*
Lightweight machines with their own 98cc two-stroke engines.

BMP / *Italy 1920–1925*
Two-stroke machines with their own 240cc engines and four-speed gearboxes.

BMW / *Germany 1923–*
BMW started out as an aircraft engine factory in Munich, Bavaria — hence the name Bayerische Motoren Werke — in 1916. After WWT, BMW made wood-working machinery, before switching to concentrate on motor cycle engine manufacture, with the 500cc side valve flat twin M2B15 unit designed by Max Friz, which was supplied to Victoria, SMW, SDB, Bison and other smaller companies. It was also fitted to the Helios that BMW made in their factory for another concern in 1921 and 1922. BMW management felt that they could do better and the result was the 500cc side valve R32 BMW, designed by Max Friz and first seen at the Paris show in 1923. The R32 utilised the transverse flat twin engine, engine-speed clutch, unit gearbox and shaft transmission that still characterize BMW flat twins nearly 70 years later. It had a leaf spring front fork with trailing link action very much like the Indian. In 1924 Rudolph Schleicher designed a sports model, the 500cc ohv R37, which made 16bhp at 4000rpm — a lot for the time — and was extensively raced in Germany. Between 1925 and 1967 BMW also made vertically-engined single-cylinder motor cycles from time to time, usually 250cc, but, in the early 1930s, 300cc, 350cc and 400cc as well.

In 1929 came the 733cc side valve R62, followed by the ohv R63 of similar capacity. BMW introduced pressed steel frames in 1930 and used them

until 1935, when a considerable redesign took place. Tubular frames were reintroduced, together with the first oil-damped telescopic front forks, a major contribution to motorcycle technology. Telescopic rear suspension followed in 1938.

BMWs had always been raced in Germany, and the factory first took the world's speed record in 1929 with a super-charged 750cc twin ridden by Ernst Henne. Henne was to break the record no less than seven times between 1929 and 1937, latterly with a fully streamlined supercharged 500cc model, which recorded 173.67mph. On the continent, supercharged 500cc BMW racers ridden by Tony Bauhofer Karl Gall, Otto Ley and latterly Georg Meier challenged and sometimes beat the British in Grand Prix events. BMW entered the Senior TT in 1937 and 1938 and in 1939 won the race with a bike ridden by Georg Meier, with British rider Jock West second. Meier had won the 500cc European championship in 1938; in 1939, he finished runner up.

493cc BMW (sv R-32) 1923

733cc BMW (ohv supercharged works-racer) 1929

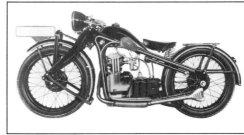

198cc BMW (ohv R-2) 1931

Post-war, when Germany was re-admitted to the FIM, BMW built a batch of ohc racers (the RS500 of 1953), with Earles front forks and swinging arm rear suspension. Works rider Walter Zeller did well with one of these, and BMW briefly supported Geoff Duke, Dickie Dale and Fergus Anderson,

246cc BMW (ohv R-25) 1950

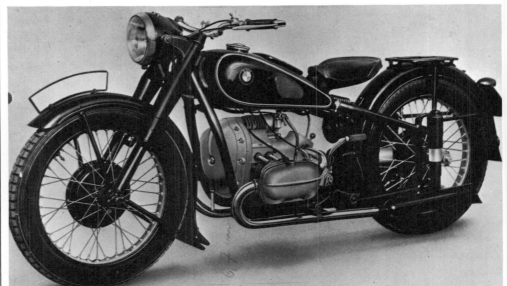

496cc BMW (ohv R-51) 1938

but financial troubles with the BMW car factory limited their efforts, which ceased in late 1957. However, the RS500 engine became the mainstay of sidecar racing for the next 20 years, BMW winning the world championship an incredible 13 times in succession between 1954 and 1966 — and many times more in later years.

Post-war, the first road model was the R24 single of 1949; the first new twins, the 500cc R51/2 and the 600cc R67, followed in 1950 and 1951 respectively. Both had telescopic front forks and rear suspension. In 1954 Earles front forks were introduced, with swinging arm at the rear for the 500cc

496cc BMW (ohc Racer) 1954

746cc BMW (ohv R-75 Army model) 1941

R50 and 600cc R60 models; these remained in use until 1969, when telescopic front forks were re-introduced on the 500cc R50/5, 600cc R60/5 and 750cc R75/5. Thereafter BMW developed and refined their superb twins, going to 800cc, 900cc and 1000cc capacity.

Much speculation about a four-cylinder BMW to compete with the Japanese was silenced in 1983 when the radically different K100 design by Stefan Pechernegg was first shown. It had its dohc in-line engine laid on its side with the crankshaft in line with the frame, a unit gearbox and shaft drive. In 1985 the K100 was supplemented by the K75, a similarly laid-out 750cc three-cylinder model. In various specifications the K100 and K75 have since found very ready general acceptance. They were expected to supercede the flat twin — but nearly 70 years after its inception, the latter is still being made, though only in 1000cc form. BMW

596cc BMW (ohv R168) 1955

can claim to be one of the oldest motor cycle companies in existence, and, with their transverse-engined flat twins, to have fostered the most long lived design ever.

599cc BMW (ohv R60/6) 1974

800cc BMW (ohv R80 ST) 1983

980cc BMW (ohv R100 RT) 1982

980cc BMW (ohv R100RS) 1982

473cc BMW (ohv R45) 1980

BNF / *Germany 1903–1907*
Bielefeld based, the company produced mainly machines with 2·75 hp single and 3·5 hp V-twin Fafnir engines.

BOCK & HOLLÄNDER / *Austria 1905–1911*
Produced in 1898 four-wheeled vehicles with engines, afterwards a real car, the Regent. On the motorcycle side, 3·5 hp and 6 hp machines with V-twin engines came into being. When WAF — a car factory—took over Bock & Holländer at Vienna, no more motorcycles were built.

BODO / *Germany 1924–1925*
Small assembler who used 147cc DKW two-stroke engines.

246cc Boge (sv) 1924

BOGE / *Germany 1923–1927*
The well-known manufacturer of shock-absorbers built 246cc and 346cc sv machines with their own engines; a very successful 246cc Boge had an ohv Blackburne single-cylinder engine and was ridden in races by Curt Wemhöner.

BÖHME / *Germany 1925–1930*
Designed by two-stroke expert Martin Böhme, these watercooled 123cc, 129cc, 173cc and 246cc

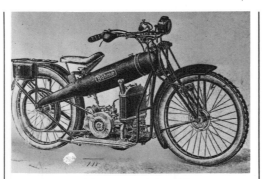
129cc Böhme (TS watercooled) 1925

single-cylinder machines had also Dunelt-like double-diameter pistons and horizontal cylinders.

598cc Böhmerland (ohv 'Touring') 1927

BÖHMERLAND / *Czechoslovakia 1925–1939*
Very unconventional motorcycles which were also supplied with the name Čechie instead of Böhmerland on the tank. Designed by Albin Liebisch, they had a very long wheelbase, a very strong frame and fork and disc wheels made of cast light alloy. Some extra-long models had

three 'officially permitted' seats and two petrol tanks, mounted on each side of the rear wheel. There was also a racing-model with a shorter wheelbase, which was used in hill climbs. All models had the ohv single-cylinder 598cc Liebisch engine and even the last machines made just before WWII had engines with open pushrods and valve-gears—not dissimilar to the ones designed in 1925 by Liebisch. A new 348cc two-stroke single-cylinder Böhmerland with a lighter but still unconventional frame was built in 1938. As a result of the war, only a few were made.

BOLIDE / *France 1902–1910*
Made at Pantin, these machines had own 1·5 hp power units.

BOND / *England 1949–1955*
The first Bond product was a 98cc Minibike with a pressed steel frame. More orthodox motor-cycles with tubular frames had 98cc and 123cc Villiers and 123cc JAP two-stroke engines.

BOOTH / *England 1901–1903*
London-built motorcycles with 2·75 hp, 3·50 hp and 4 hp engines made by De Dion and Minerva.

BORD / *England 1902–1906*
Another London-built machine with a 1·5 hp engine.

BORGHI / *Italy 1951–1963*
Assembler of lightweight machines with 38cc Mosquito and 49cc Cucciolo engines. The 123cc Olympia had a BSA Bantam two-stroke engine.

598cc Böhmerland (ohv 'Long-Touring') 1935

BORGO / *Italy 1906–1926*
Once a famous factory, founded by A. B. Borgo and his brother Carlo. Built fast 497cc singles with ioe valves, and afterwards singles with 453cc, 493cc, 693cc and even 827cc. Another Borgo – Edmondo Michele — designed bicycle engines and built at his Turin factory in 1915 a 996cc V-twin with belt drive to the rear wheel. A 477cc ohv V-twin was built in 1921. It reached up to 6000 rpm. With four-valve heads, these machines won many events. The last Moto-Borgo was a 496cc V-twin with ohv and a two-speed gearbox in unit with the engine. It had chain drive and a very low saddle position. The top speed was around 80 mph. After 1926 Borgo concentrated mainly on making pistons.

BORHAM / *England 1902–1905*
Minerva 2 hp and 2·5 hp engines were fitted to these primitive machines.

BOUCHET / *France 1902–1905*
Not much is known about these machines, which used acetylene instead of petrol.

BOUGERY / *France 1896–1902*
One of the first French makes. The engine was mounted between the pedalling gear and the rear wheel.

BOUNDS-JAP / *England 1909–1912*
Assembled motorcycles with 345cc single-cylinder and 492cc V-twin JAP proprietary engines.

BOVY / *Belgium c1906–1932*
Albert Bovy built transport vehicles in 1902 and also cars in limited numbers. His motorcycles were of typical English design and of sturdy appearance. They had 98cc to 996cc proprietary engines made by JAP, MAG, Python, Blackburne, Aubier-Dunne and others.

BOWDEN / *England 1902–1905*
Frank Bowden, who eventually became Sir Frank, fitted 2 hp and 2·5 hp engines made by FN and also by his own works into his motorcycles. He was also the founder of the Raleigh-Sturmey-Archer Company at Nottingham.

BOWN / *England 1922–1924*
Small assembler of machines with 147cc Villiers and 248cc and 348cc JAP and Blackburne engines.

BOWN / *England 1950–1958*
Originally known under the Aberdale trade

123cc Brand (TS Bekamo) 1923

mark, Bown autocycles were built in different versions with 98cc Villiers engines. Motorcycles made by this company had 98cc and 123cc Villiers engines, but from 1955 onward manufacture concentrated around 49cc Sachs-engined mopeds.

BPR / *Switzerland 1929–1932*
Founded by former Moto-Rêve and Motosacoche employees — Buratti, Ponti and Roch — BPR fitted 347cc and 497cc single-cylinder Moser and Motosacoche engines into well-made frames. They had also a branch in France.

BPS / *France 1973–1978*
Young French producer of trials and motocross machines with engines of 49cc to 123cc supplied by Franco-Morini, Sachs, Aspes and Minarelli. Good and successful design.

BRAAK / *Germany 1923–1925*
Assembled machines with 129cc and 198cc Heilo and Namapo engines with frames, which were supplied by Gruhn of Berlin.

BRADBURY / *England 1901–1925*
Once a leading British motorcycle factory at Oldham. Built under Birch patent, the first single-

554cc sv Bradbury 1914

cylinder models had 2 hp and 2·5 hp. When WWI broke out, the range of models included 554cc singles, 749cc V-twins and 499cc flat twin versions. Improved machines followed after the war and before Bradbury stopped cycle production, there was a 349cc sv single.

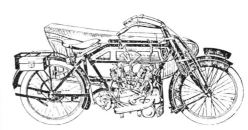
788cc Bradbury (sv V-twin) 1921

BRAND / *Germany 1925–1930*
Small factory which built two-stroke machines with flat single-cylinder Bekamo licence engines of 123cc, 147cc and 173cc. These Hugo Ruppe designed engines had a pumping cylinder at the bottom of the crankcase.

BRAVIS / *Germany 1924–1926*
A famous German rider, Franz Seelos of Munich, rode these 148cc two-strokes and 293cc flat-twins with Bosch-Douglas licence engines successfully in many events, mainly in the Bavarian part of Germany.

BREDA / *Italy 1946–1951*
Like Macchi and Caproni, Breda was originally a leading aircraft factory. After the war the firm built motorised bicycles with their own 65cc two-stroke engine.

BRÉE / *Austria 1902–1904*
Of French origin, Théodor Brée built at Vienna lightweight machines with 1·5 hp single-cylinder,

two-stroke engines of his own design and manufacture.

BRENNABOR / *Germany 1902–1940*
There were two periods when the firm built motorcycles. The first was until 1912, when they fitted 3·5hp, 4hp and 6hp engines of Zedel, Fafnir and of their own manufacture into sturdy frames. Afterwards they concentrated on bicycles and cars, but when they stopped car manufacture in 1933, production at the Brandenburg/Havel factory included motorised bicycles with 73cc and 98cc Sachs and Ilo engines.

BREUIL / *France 1903–1908*
Fitted different proprietary engines from 4hp to 6hp into their own frames. The engines were mainly Peugeot, Aster and Zurcher.

BRIDGESTONE / *Japan 1952–early 1970s*
Was part of the famous Bridgestone tyre factory and commenced manufacture of motorised two-wheelers with 49cc two-stroke mopeds. Later they built first class motorcycles, mainly 98cc singles and 173cc, 247cc and 348cc vertical twins; all two strokes with rotary-disc engines of their own manufacture. Among the models were many special versions for the USA market, which was of great importance for Bridgestone as they were not interested in the home market, because of the opposition of Honda, Yamaha, Suzuki and Kawasaki, which were among the best customers of Bridgestone tyres. To keep such big tyre customers, Bridgestone decided eventually to pull out of the manufacture of motorcycles.

BRILANT-ALCYON / *Czechoslovakia 1932*
Built by a well-known bicycle factory — Fuchs & Co. at Zuckmantel — the Brilant-Alcyon (Alcyon licence) had a 98cc two-stroke engine and was intended to become a 'people's motorcycle'. Only few of these machines were made.

BRILLANT / *France 1903–1904*
Small assembler of motorcycles which used Peugeot and Zurcher engines.

BRITAX / *England 1954–1956*
Produced mini-scooters with 48cc Ducati ohv engines and were also the first in England to build 49cc racing machines, called Hurricane. They were powered by Cucciolo ohv engines. Britax is still a leading producer of accessories.

BRITISH-RADIAL / *England 1920–1922*
Interesting and unorthodox motorcycles with 369cc three-cylinder radial sv engines, designed

497cc Brondoit (ohv MAG) 1928

by J. E. Manes. The engines were made by C. B. Redrup; Chater-Lea supplied the frames. The 120 degree three had a vaned outside flywheel, detachable heads, enclosed valves etc. Production was on a limited scale.

BRITISH-STANDARD / *England 1919–1923*
A wide range of 147cc to 548cc engines made by Villiers, TDC, JAP, Bradshaw, Blackburne and Barr & Stroud, powered these 'perfectly standard' motorcycles.

BRM / *Italy 1955–1957*
Produced small 48cc two-stroke machines and had no connection with the once famous British BRM racing car firm at Bourne.

BROCKHOUSE / *England 1948–1955*
Famous engineering company and one time producer of 98cc Corgi Mini-scooters which could be folded up. Eventually bought the Indian motorcycle factory at Springfield, Massachusetts in the USA and produced for them at the English factory the 248cc Indian Brave, which had its own sv single-cylinder unit-design engine.

Some other firms, including OEC and DOT, fitted it also into their frames. Brockhouse afterwards sold Indian to Associated Motor Cycles Ltd. in London.

BRONDOIT / *Belgium 1924–1929*
Paul de Bussy's Brondoit (Brondoit-Herstal) factory produced 248cc and 348cc two-stroke machines with outside flywheel engines and also from 1928 onward a sporting 498cc model with the Swiss single-cylinder double-port ohv engine, made by MAG (Motosacoche).

BROUGH / *England 1908–1926*
This was the machine designed and built by W. E. Brough, George Brough's father. The range consisted first of singles and V-twins, but soon William Brough became a flat-twin devotee. With Granville Bradshaw on friendly terms, he used first Bradshaw's 496cc ABC engines, afterwards his own 496cc ohv and 692cc as well as 810cc sv engines. All were flat twins, a design which was not favoured by his son George Brough, who eventually left his father's works and founded his own motorcycle factory at Haydn Road, Nottingham in 1921.

497cc Brough (ohv flat-twin) 1919

BROUGH-SUPERIOR / *England 1921–1940*
Known as the 'Rolls-Royce among motorcycles', Brough-Superior motorcycles were built regardless of costs by George Brough, son of W. E. Brough. He was a famous technician and since his youth a very successful competitor in sporting events, first with his father's Brough machines, then with his own Brough-Superiors, which were mainly built with V-twin engines. These included

998cc Brough-Superior (sv JAP SS80) 1930

models with 678cc, 746cc, 980cc, 996cc and 1150cc engines, made by JAP, MAG and Matchless; in some cases especially for Brough-Superior, in other cases with special parts for this make. There was also a 498cc ohv V-twin with a JAP engine in 1930 and in 1932 a 796cc four-in-line with a watercooled and modified Austin car engine. This model, destined for sidecar work, had two rear wheels, which were only a few inches apart and fitted in the centre. Most famous were George Brough's SS100 ohv and SS80 sv V-twins and there were also many interesting one-off prototypes, ie machines which never came into quantity production. These included aircooled 996cc V-fours, aircooled 990cc fours-in-line and also the famous Dream of 1938, which had a transverse-mounted flat four-cylinder 996cc engine and shaft drive. It was not yet fully developed when the war broke out. Brough intended to produce motorcycles again after 1945, but as there were no suitable engines available, he eventually had to give up. Famous Brough-Superior personalities included Harold 'Oily' Karslake, works manager Icke Webb and T. E. Lawrence of Arabia, who owned seven BS machines during the years. Among the leading racing men were Brough himself, Eric Fernihough, Freddy Dixon, E. C. E. Baragwanath, Bert le Vack, Joe Wright, Eddy Meyer, Kpt. Vladimir Kučka, Ernst Zündorf, Otokar Weinhara, Bob Berry and Lucky Schmied.

998cc Brough-Superior (ohv Matchless SS100) 1938

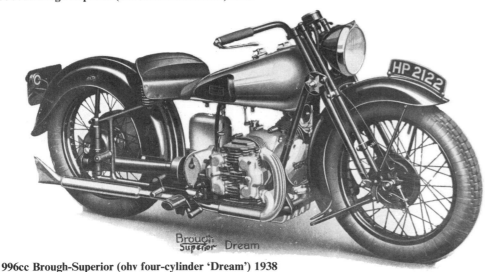

996cc Brough-Superior (ohv four-cylinder 'Dream') 1938

1150cc Brough-Superior (sv BS 1150) 1938

BROWN / *England 1902–1919*
Brown motorcycles had 348cc and 498cc single-cylinder and 498cc V-twin sv engines. After 1919 they used the name Vindec, but had no connection with the former German Allright motorcycles of the same name, Vindec-Special (VS). These names were used by Allright only for machines exported to England.

BROWN-BICAR / *England (USA) 1907–1913*
Equipped with 3 hp single-cylinder and 5 hp V-twin engines, the Brown-Bicar was an unusual motorcycle design with enclosed engines. It was also built in the USA under licence, but was not a commercial success.

BRUNEAU / *France 1903–1910*
The first versions had Zedel proprietary engines, but around 1905 Bruneau built 498cc vertical-twin machines of his own design. They were among the first vertical-twins ever made.

BSA / *England 1906–1971*

Years before BSA (Birmingham Small Arms) produced complete motorcycles, they supplied most British and foreign factories with cycle parts of the highest calibre. The first complete machines were motorized bicycles. Afterwards, single-cylinder sv models with their own engines were built. These were 498cc (85mm × 88mm bore/stroke, 3·5 hp) and 555cc (85mm × 98mm bore/stroke, 4·5 hp) designs. The first sv V-twin had 770cc and was built in 1921. The following year another V-twin with 986cc made its first appearance. Other models built during the 1920s and early 1930s included the famous round-tank 249cc version, 349cc sv and ohv singles and similar 498cc models. There were also 174cc two-strokes, and in the late 1920s 493cc singles including the famous Slopers with sv and especially ohv engines. The 1930 range included 249cc sv and 249cc double-port ohv singles, 349cc sv and ohv singles and also 493cc versions with (as always) BSA's own sv and ohv power units. Most models were supplied with vertical or inclined engines, the ohv versions with one or, if required, two exhaust pipes. The V-twins had 770cc and 986cc engines. The 174cc two-stroke was superseded by a 149cc ohv single during the 1930s. Other models in these pre-war days had 249cc sv and ohv and similar 348cc and 499cc single-cylinder engines. Then came 498cc and 748cc ohv V-twins and a 595cc sv single. The prices in

246cc BSA (sv 'Roundtank') 1924

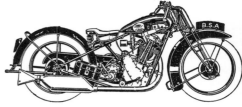

497cc BSA (ohv 'Sloper') 1928

493cc ohv BSA Empire Star 1938

497cc BSA (ohv 'Gold Star') 1960

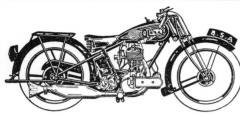
493cc BSA (sv) 1929

1936: 149cc ohv £31/7s./6d., 499cc sv £56/10s., 748cc ohv V-twin £75 and the same for the 986cc sv V-twin. Although BSA never competed officially in races, in the late 1930s they produced very sporting singles. Walter Handley won a Gold Star in June 1937 at Brooklands (riding a tuned 493cc ohv Empire Star), an award made to all riders who lapped the track at over 100 mph. This led in 1938 to the first 'Gold Star' BSA model, which — also with 348cc engine — was built for many years and after WWII was one of the most popular sports machines ever built in England, especially among clubmen, as these machines were not only fast and reliable, but also comparatively cheap and of simple design. Among many other events, they won clubman's TT races and also showed great reliability and high speeds in the 'pure' TT events. New 123cc, 148cc and 174cc two-stroke singles, the Bantam models, were introduced after the war, in which 493cc sv singles were among the leading machines of the Forces.

Among the post-war BSA models were the single-cylinder 249cc and 343cc ohv Star versions new 497cc and 646cc vertical ohv twins and also different single-cylinder trials and scrambles models. During the late 1960s they had 441cc single-cylinder Victor and twin-cylinder Royal Star versions with 499cc (65·5mm × 74mm bore/stroke) engines as well as 654cc (75mm × 74mm bore/stroke) twins, which included the Thunderbolt, Lightning, Hornet and Spitfire models. In the early 1970s BSA produced 173cc Bantam two-strokes, 247cc and 441cc Starfires and Shooting Stars with ohv single-cylinder engines, 654cc Thunderbolt ohv twins, the very popular 654cc Lightning ohv twin and the Firebird, a 654cc twin-cylinder 55 bhp scrambler. New was the 740cc Rocket, a three-cylinder ohv machine with a transverse mounted engine. This machine had 58 bhp at 7250 rpm and a top speed of over 120 mph. Later models had 64 bhp at 7500 rpm. In addition, there was also a new Gold Star, the 500SS, with a 499cc single-cylinder ohv engine. Once England's leading motorcycle factory, BSA ceased production in 1971,

A reconstructed BSA Co Ltd was formed to make lightweights for export with Italian and Japanese engines. Ken Sprayson of Reynolds Tubes fame also produced replica Manx Norton frames at BSA until very recently.

646cc BSA (ohv 'Lightning Clubman' twin) 1965

249cc BSA (ohv 'Star') 1967

173cc BSA (TS 'Bantam Sports') 1967

B & S / *Germany 1925–1930*
Identical to Brand two-stroke machines with 123cc, 147cc and 173cc pumping cylinder Bekamo engines. The B&S stood for Brand & Söhne of Berlin.

BUBI / *Germany 1921–1924*
Small bicycle producer who built 1·5 hp two-stroke engines into strengthened bicycle frames.

BUCHER / *Italy 1911–1920*
Known also as Bucher-Zeda, the once prominent factory built singles and V-twin cylinder machines of 342cc, 499cc and 568cc with their own ohv engines.

BUCHET / *France 1900–1911*
Better known as producer of proprietary engines and cars, Buchet also built motorcycles in limited numbers and even some unusual three-wheelers; one—a racing version in 1903—had a vertical twin-cylinder engine of 4245cc.

BÜCKER / *Germany 1922–1958*
Was a leading assembler of motorcycles from 98cc to 996cc in Germany. The proprietary engines used included the makes Cockerell, Rinne, Columbus, MAG, JAP, Blackburne and Bark. After 1945 all Bücker machines had Ilo or Sachs two-stroke engines, including 244cc twin-cylinder versions. In the late 1940s, a pre-war 248cc Bücker with an ohv JAP engine, ridden by Friedl Schön, won the 250cc road-championship of Germany.

BULLDOG / *England 1920*
Small assembler of orthodox lightweight machines. Used 269cc Villiers two-stroke engines.

BULLO / *Germany 1924–1926*
Unconventional electric motorcycle made at Bremen. The power unit was mounted in the steering centre and supplied via a 120-Ah-Battery 0·7 hp. Only a limited number were built.

BÜLOW / *Germany 1923–1925*
Produced 2, 2·5 and 3 hp machines with own two-stroke engines.

BULTACO / *Spain 1958—mid-1980s*
Founded by Francesco X. Bulto, previously co-founder of Montesa, and early successful in

244cc Bultaco (TS 'Metralla') 1971

Spanish racing. Later, modestly successful in Grand Prix, but better known for its sales of 125cc, 250cc and later 350cc racers to private owners. Later still, Bultaco turned successfully to moto-cross and especially to trials, enlisting held from Sammy Miller who became the premier trials rider. Bultaco two-strokes sold well in the USA as road and trail bikes in the 1960s and 1970s, but their sales declined with new clean air laws. Bultaco turned to 50cc road racing in 1976 and won the world title four times between then and 1981. However, the company was in financial trouble by then and, despite government intervention and talks of merger with Montesa and Ossa, failed in the mid-1980s.

BURFORD / *England 1914–1915*
The war prevented any larger production of these 496cc single-cylinder sv and 269cc two-stroke Villiers-engined machines.

BURGERS-ENR / *The Netherlands 1897–1961*
Once a leading Dutch make which for a long period fitted engines of their own design; afterwards 497cc Blackburne single-cylinder and 676cc JAP V-twin engines. There was also a 246cc two-stroke with the Vitesse engine.

BURKHARDTIA / *Germany 1904–1908*
Early two-stroke machines with 165cc single-cylinder and 244cc twin-cylinder engines, made by the famous Grade works at Magdeburg. The twin-cylinder versions had vertical cylinders.

BURNEY / *England 1923–1925*
Designed by Cecil Burney, formerly of Burney & Blackburne fame, these 497cc machines had their own sv engines with an outside flywheel. Cpt. Baldwin, the well-known rider, was commercially connected with this make. Burney also built a very limited number of 679cc sv V-twins.

BUSI / *Italy 1950–1953*
Sporting two-stroke machines of typical Italian design. The range included 123cc, 160cc, 173cc and 198cc versions.

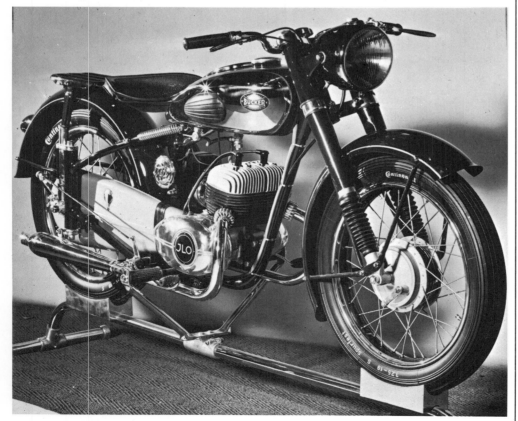

244cc Bücker (TS Ilo twin) 1953

BUSSE/*Germany 1922–1926*
Well-designed and sturdy machines with 143cc Grade and 147cc and 173cc DKW two-stroke proprietary engines. There was also a 198cc model with the ohv Paqué engine and other versions with power units of their own design and manufacture.

BUYDENS/*Belgium 1950–1955*
Produced two-stroke machines with Ydral and

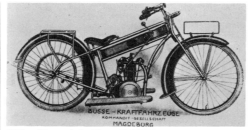
198cc Busse (ohv Paqué) 1925

Sachs engines from 123cc to 248cc. The production was on a limited scale.

BV/*Czechoslovakia 1923–1930*
Made by a small factory, the BV—Balzer & Vemola—were fitted with the company's own engines. These included 173cc two-strokes, 346cc and 746cc sv, as well as 496cc ohv versions. The biggest model was a V-twin. Julius Vemola himself raced a 496cc single with ohc in 1925.

C

CABRERA/*Italy 1979–*
Produces on a small scale 124 and 158cc two-stroke trial machines.

CABTON/*Japan 1954–1961*
Was a leading manufacturer. The machines, built much on typical English lines were 123cc to 246cc two-strokes and — mainly — ohv vertical-twins from 248cc to 648cc.

CAESAR/*England 1922–1923*
Small assembler of lightweights with 269cc Villiers two-stroke engines.

124cc Cagiva (watercooled moto-cross T/S) 1982

CAGIVA /*Italy 1979—*
The Castiglioni brothers, owners of a huge metal pressing business, bought Aermacchi from Harley Davidson, and showing brilliant business skills, revived the company. (Cagiva is an amalgam of Castiglioni and Varese). So successful were they that during the 1980s, they successively bought out Ducati, Bimota, Husqvarna and Morini. The company now markets a bewildering variety of machines under these names and their own, mixing the various specialist technologies and skills.

CALCOTT/*England 1910–1915*
Built by a well-known car-factory at Coventry. White & Poppe proprietary engines of 292cc and also their own 249cc and 292cc singles powered these machines.

CALTHORPE/*England 1911–1939*
Founded by George Hands, Calthorpe had a very mixed story with many ups and even more downs, but they built some very nice machines at reasonable prices. The first machines had 211cc two-stroke engines, others four-stroke Precision and JAP power units. During the 1920s, various 147cc to 498cc single-cylinder Villiers, JAP and Blackburne engines powered Calthorpes. From 1925 onward, new 348cc ohv and 498cc ohc single-cylinder models of their own manufacture

493cc Calthorpe (ohc) 1926

496cc Calthorpe (ohv Matchless) 1939

came into being. From 1929, the Ivory range of new 348cc ohv machines, later also 248cc and 498cc versions—all with ohv double-port engines—headed Calthorpe production. Prices were comparatively low and just before the Birmingham factory closed down in 1938, official prices for the fully equipped machines were as follows: 248cc £47, 348cc £52 10s. and

498cc £54 10s. When the receiver sold the works, Bruce Douglas of Bristol, who was a nephew of the founder of the Douglas motorcycle factory and who owned a firm producing parts for aircraft engines, bought the Calthorpe production equipment and moved it to Bristol. There he built new models with 347cc and 497cc ohv Matchless single-cylinder engines. Only a few were finished when the war broke out. After 1945 he did not return to motorcycle manufacture and eventually sold the equipment to the DMW factory. Calthorpe was never a leading producer of successful racing machines, but had some successes with Stanley Gill and the Austrian Rudi Hunger.

CALVERT / *England 1899–1904*
Motorcycle pioneer, who used Minerva engines as well as their own 2·25, 2·75 and 3·25 hp motors.

CAMBER / *England 1920–1921*
Built by a motorcycle dealer, these machines had 492cc sv Precision engines.

CAMBRA / *Germany 1921–1926*
The Berlin-built Cambra was (unlike most other Berlin-made motorcycles of that period) a four-stroke, with 180cc and 198cc and had their own sv engines.

CAMILLE-FAUCEAUX / *France 1952–1954*
Producer of mini-scooters with 65cc engines.

CAMPION / *England 1901–1926*
Was a well-known bicycle factory at Nottingham, which used a variety of proprietary engines when they produced motorcycles. These had capacities from 147cc to 996cc. Engine suppliers were Minerva, MMC, Fafnir, Precision, Villiers, Blackburne and JAP. The big models with the

494cc Can-Am (Rotax ohc 4-valve single) 1982

V-twin JAP engines had Brough-Superior-like petrol tanks. Campion also supplied frames to other firms and when Jock Porter's New Gerrard factory at Edinburgh could not cope with production, from 1924 to 1926 they had New Gerrards built at the Campion works.

CAN-AM / *Canada 1973–1987*
The Canadian Bombardier Snowmobile Group also owns the Austrian engine manufacturer Rotax, famous for their two-stroke twins (with disc valves, contra-rotating tandem crankshafts and water cooling), as well as their larger single-cylinder four-stroke engines. Can-am were big in moto-cross and employed the famous ex-BSA team rider Jeff Smith for many years. Clean air legislation in the US market limited the scope of the two strokes and, in 1987, manufacture of the Can

Am motorcycle was halted and efforts switched to snowmobiles and boats, produced under the Bombardier name. Rotax engines, however, are still made.

CAPPONI / *Italy 1924–1926*
Two-stroke machines with own 173cc three-port engines. Limited production.

CAPRIOLO / *Italy 1948–1963*
Former aircraft factory, which produced 73cc ohv machines with pressed steel frames and unit-design engines. Later models also included 123cc ohv versions with tubular frames. There were also NSU-engined two-strokes and some interesting face-cam ohc machines with capacities up to 123cc. Another interesting Trento-built Capriolo design was a 149cc flat twin with a transverse-mounted unit-design ohv engine and a pressed steel frame. Capriolo also built transport three-wheelers with 75cc and 150cc engines.

CAPRONI-VIZZOLA / *Italy 1953–1959*
Sturdily built machines with—mainly—engines supplied by NSU of Germany. The range included the 198cc Cavilux, as well as the 173cc and 248cc ohv singles. The last one was based on the NSU Max and was called Cavimax. This engine developed 17 bhp at 6500 rpm.

CARABELA / *Mexico 1971–*
Mainly built for the USA market, the Mexican Carabela shows typical Italian lines. The range

198cc Cambra (sv) 1925

149cc Capriolo (ohv flat-twin) 1955

includes two-strokes of 102, 123, 173, 193 and 245cc for moto-cross, trials (enduro) and also use on normal roads. Earlier models used European engines, partly even Jawa and Villa.

CARDAN/*France 1902–1908*
Motorcycles with De Dion engines and shaft drive ('Cardan-drive') to the rear wheel.

CARFIELD/*England 1919–1924*
Equipped with spring frames, Carfield motorcycles had 247cc and 269cc Villiers two-stroke and 347cc Blackburne sv single-cylinder engines. Another model used the Coventry-Victor 688cc sv flat twin engine.

CARLEY/*France 1950–1953*
Mini-scooter with a flat 49cc two-stroke engine.

CARLTON/*England 1913–1940*
Bicycle factory, which is now part of the Raleigh group. Owned in the 1930s by former tuning wizard and racing motorcyclist Don R. O'Donovan who was also motorcycle designer at Raleigh (Sturmey-Archer), Carlton produced 123cc two-strokes with Villiers engines and also supplied similar machines under a different name to a leading motorcycle dealer at London.

CARLTON/*Scotland 1922*
Orthodox lightweight machines with 269cc Villiers engines, built in limited numbers.

CARNIELLI/*Italy 1951–*
Producer of the well-known 48cc Graziella folding mofa, Carnielli built during the years many different lightweights. These included 73cc two-strokes and also models with 98cc ohv NSU engines. There was also a co-operation with the German Victoria factory which supplied 48cc two-stroke and other engines.

CARPATI/*Rumania 1960–*
Leading moped producer in Rumania. Builds its own 65cc two-stroke engines.

CARPIO/*France 1930–1935*
Lightweight machines with 98cc and 124cc Aubier-Dunne and Stainless two-stroke engines.

CARREAU–*France c1903*
Produced motorcycles with 1·5 hp engines.

CAS/*Czechoslovakia 1921—1924*
Designed by J. Reichziegal, the CAS scooter closely resembled the British ABC Skootamota, but used a flat twin 4-stroke engine of 130cc and then 150cc.
CAS also made lightweight motor cycles, with 175cc and 225cc two stroke engines.

CASAL/*Portugal 1964–*
The first Casal machines had Zündapp engines and also a Zündapp-like appearance. Afterwards they fitted their own two-stroke engines

from 49cc to 248cc and also produced a water-cooled 49cc machine. Other versions included 74cc machines and various trials and moto-cross models. A 248cc trials model has a 27 bhp motor.

CASALINI/*Italy 1958–1963*
Mini-scooter producer who switched to the manufacture of a wide range of 48cc mopeds.

CASOLI/*Italy 1928–1933*
Sporting 172cc machines with Villiers and own two-stroke engines. Limited production.

CASTADOT/*Belgium 1900–1901*
Only few of these machines—which had 1·5 hp Zedel engines—were built.

CASTELL/*England 1903*
Assembler who fitted Minerva and Sarolea engines into their own frames.

CASWELL/*England 1904–1905*
Strengthened bicycle frames with 2·5, 2·75 and 3·5 hp Minerva engines.

CAYENNE /*England 1912—1913*
An obscure firm which may have been of continental origin, that entered a water-cooled ohv single in the 1913 Senior TT.

CAZALEX/*France 1951–1955*
Lightweight machines with two-stroke engines from 49cc to 124cc.

CAZANAVE/*France 1955–1957*
Producer of 49cc mopeds and lightweight machines.

CBR/*Italy 1912–1914*
Turin-built machines. The range included two-strokes, a 225cc sv machine and also bigger models with 3, 5 and 8 hp engines.

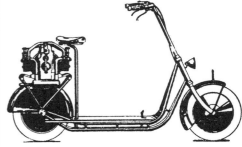

248cc CAS (sv flat-twin) 1922

746cc CEMEC (sv flat-twin) 1954

CC / *England 1921–1924*
The initials 'CC' were those of Charles Chamberlain, a small producer in Bispham, Blackpool, Lancashire. CC machines were offered in capacities ranging from 147cc to 996cc, but it is not certain what went into production. Engines included a 269cc Villiers, and Blackburnes of 347 and 497cc.

CCM / *England 1971–*
Makers of trials and moto-cross machines originally based on BSA engines, later extensively developed by founder Alan Clews. Many famous riders, such as Nick Jeffries, John Banks and Norman Barrow, rode CCMs. CCM was absorbed by Armstrong in 1980 and sold back to Clews in 1987.

CECCATO / *Italy 1950–1963*
Produced a wide range of two-strokes from 49cc to 173cc and also ohv — partly even ohc — models from 73cc to 123cc. The 73cc ohc Super Sport had 8 bhp at 11,000 rpm, the 98cc version 11 bhp at 10,500 rpm. The single ohc was driven by a train of gears; the top speed of these machines was 71·5 and 77·5 mph respectively.

CEDOS / *England 1919–1929*
Well-made 211cc and 249cc two-strokes which were also delivered with open frames for use by ladies. From 1924 onwards, the range included also 348cc ohv models with Bradshaw and Blackburne engines, a 348cc sv Blackburne-engined version and a 990cc V-twin with an sv JAP engine and Brough-Superior-like petrol tank.

CEMEC / *France 1948–1955*
Predecessor of Ratier and successor to CMR, CEMEC built mainly BMW-like 746cc transverse-mounted flat twins with sv engines, and a limited number of 746cc and 493cc ohv models

on similar lines. All had plunger rear suspension and telescopic forks.

CENTAUR / *Germany 1924–1925*
Small assembler of lightweight machines with 1·5 hp sv engines supplied by Gruhn of Berlin.

CENTAUR / *England 1901–1915*
Once a well-known make and also a technically interesting design. Among the models were 348cc V-twins and a 492cc sv single, which originally had the silencer inside the front downtube. Later Centaur models used square cylinder cooling fins.

CENTER / *Japan 1950–1962*
Sporting 149cc ohv singles with own unit-design engines.

CENTURY / *England 1902–1905*
A long forgotten make which used Minerva and MMC engines.

CF / *Italy 1928–1971*
Designed by Catelli and Fiorani, these were potent 173cc and 248cc ohc singles, which won many Italian races. Fusi, closely connected with Belgian FN, bought the CF factory in 1937. After an interruption, a reorganised company built 49cc two-stroke machines from the late 1960s onwards.

CFC / *France 1903–1906*
Strengthened bicycle frames with 1·5 hp engines.

CHAMPION / *America 1911–1913*
Made by Peerless at St. Louis, the aircooled 1261cc four-in-line Champion had a car-like frame built under Militaire licence and idler wheels on both sides. The ioe engine had ball gear-change and shaft drive to the rear wheel. Both wheels had wooden spokes. Production of these unconventional motorcycles was on a limited basis.

Champion

CHAMPION / *Japan 1960–1967*
These machines, made by Bridgestone Tyre Co., had two-stroke engines from 49cc to 123cc.

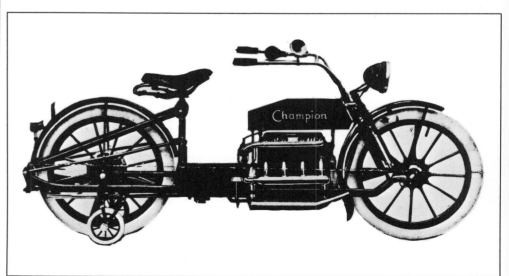

1306cc Champion (ioe Militaire-Patents four-cylinder) 1917

CHARLETT / *Germany 1921–1924*
Lightweight machines with their own 195cc sv single-cylinder engines.

CHARLKRON / *Germany 1925*
Small producer of 348cc and 498cc single-cylinder machines with 3-valve ohc 'K' (Küchen) proprietary engines.

CHARLTON / *England 1904–1908*
These motorcycles were equipped with 402cc Buchet engines, which were originally made in France.

CHASE / *England 1902–1906*
Made by the Chase brothers, of London, then leading bicycle racers. Chase motorcycles had various engines made by Minerva, MMC and Precision.

CHATER LEA / *England 1900—1937*
Chater — soon Chater Lea — at first supplied components, such as frame lugs, forgings and castings and special gears, to the trade; they survived as general engineers for 50 years after they stopped making motorcycles. In later years, they made only a 550cc S.V. Blackburne-engined sidecar outfit, most of which were supplied to the AA for road patrol use. Manufacture ceased when Blackburne stopped making engines.

Earlier, Chater Lea had used a very wide range of engines, including MAG, JAP and Villiers as well as Blackburne. They also made their own 350cc ohc engine in the 1920s and had some success with it, especially on the continent. This was actually a 'face cam' engine, not to be confused with the true ohc modified Blackburne 350cc engine.

With that, in a Chater Lea frame, Doug Marchant exceeded 100mph — first time for a 350cc machine — over a flying kilometre at Brooklands in 1924.

CHELL / *England 1939*
Lightweight machines with 123cc Villiers engines, made in limited numbers only.

CHIORDA / *Italy 1954—1956*
Produced 48cc ohv machines; afterwards mainly 49cc two-strokes with Franco Morini engines, including moto-cross versions.

CHRISTOPHE / *France 1920s*
Identical production to Automoto with two-strokes up to 248cc and sv models up to 498cc. The range also included 498cc double-port ohc models with unit-design engines.

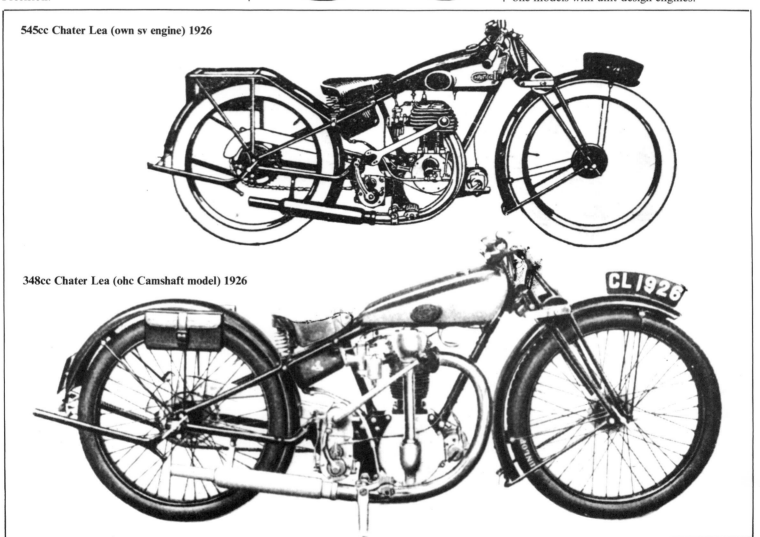

545cc Chater Lea (own sv engine) 1926

348cc Chater Lea (ohc Camshaft model) 1926

CIE/*Belgium 1900–1905*
Pioneer in the motorcycle game with 3 hp and 4 hp machines designed by M. Coutourier and the famous Paul Kelecom, who also built proprietary engines and became technical director at the FN works at Herstal.

CIMA/*Italy 1924–1927*
Assembler of sporting motorcycles with 247cc and 347cc sv and ohv Blackburne engines. Limited production.

CIMATTI/*Italy 1949—1984*
A cycle maker, who began making mopeds and lightweights soon after WWII and steadily built up this business, refusing to move to larger machines. Engines included Franco Morini, Minarell, Demm, HWM and FBM. Despite Cimatti's apparent success (50,000 units in 1977), the company collapsed in 1984.

CITA/*Belgium 1922–1925*
Motorcycles with triangular frames and own 173cc, 198cc and 348cc ohv engines.

CITO/*Germany 1905–1927*
Old established bicycle factory. Produced first singles and V-twins with Fafnir engines and in the early 1920s a 346cc two-stroke with its own three-port engine. These machines were made at the branch factory of Cito-Cologne, at Suhl in Thuringia, now part of the DDR. At Suhl was also the Krieger-Gnädig (KG) motorcycle factory, which built 503cc and later 499cc singles of advanced design with shaft drive to the rear wheel. As the demand rose for these machines Cito took over the KG production, but in 1923

Cito became part of the Cologne-based Allright works. Allright was a motorcycle producer in its own right, but they continued with the manufacture of KG motorcycles until 1927 at the Suhl works, partly also at Cologne. And even when Allright ceased building motorcycles to concentrate on bicycles, forks, brake-hubs and other parts, the KG was not dead; production moved to the Paul Henkel bicycle factory at Mäbendorf near Suhl and continued until 1932.

CITYFIX/*Germany 1949–1953*
Produced mini-scooters and lightweight machines with 58cc Lutz and 98cc Sachs two-stroke engines.

CL/*Germany 1951*
Offered mini-scooters with 34cc engines. Production was very small.

CLAES/*Germany 1904–1908*
Made by a once well-known bicycle factory, Claes motorcycles with 3·5 hp and 5 hp Fafnir engines were also known with the Pfeil badge on the tank.

CLARENDON/*England 1901–1911*
Coventry-based bicycle and car producer, whose motorcycles had not only own 3 hp engines, but also proprietary engines made by Scout, Birch, Hamilton, Whitley and Coronet. Clarendon machines were of sturdy design and had an excellent finish.

CLAUDE DELAGE/*France 1925*
Small company which produced motorcycles

and cars on a limited scale, but had no connection with the famous Delage car factory.

CLEMENT/*France 1897–1905*
Famous French motorcycle and car pioneer. Built singles and V-twins, in 1920 even a 998cc ohc racing V-twin. The last model built by the Louis Clement works — which still had the name Adolphe Clement on the door and which were at Levallo, Mézières — was a 63cc machine with an ohv unit-design engine.

142cc Clement-Garrard 1902

CLEMENT-GARRARD/*England 1902–1911*
Clement-Garrard was connected with the French factory of Adolphe Clement. Their English importer was Charles Garrard who called the imported motorcycles Clement-Garrard. He was also connected with James Lansdowne Norton, who produced frames for him until Norton founded his own motorcycle factory and used these Clement-Gerrard 1·5 hp and 2 hp single and 3 hp V-twins which had very large outside flywheels and very small crankcases.

CLEMENT-GLADIATOR/*France 1901–1935*
Produced large cars until they built motorcycles too. Became successful in the 1920s when some potent 248cc JAP-engined ohv machines left the old works on the Seine. Clement-Gladiator was also a pioneer of good rear suspensions, which they used with triangular frames during the late 1920s and Andreino won many races on these machines. The range of models included machines from 98cc to 498cc with two-stroke sv and ohv engines.

CLESS & PLESSING/*Austria 1903–1906*
This Graz-built motorcycle had its own 2·75 hp and 3·5 hp single-cylinder and 5 hp V-twin engines. In the Czech parts of the old Austro-Hungarian Empire, the Cless & Plessing was known as the Noricum.

CLEVELAND/*America 1915–1929*
Made by the once famous Cleveland car factory, the Cleveland motorcycle was of very sound design. The first machine was a 269cc two-stroke;

346cc Cito (TS) 1922

269cc Cleveland (TS) 1918

346cc Cleveland (ohv) 1925

996cc Cleveland (ioe four-in-line) 1929

746cc Cleveland (ioe four-in-line) 1926

in 1924 came a 347cc single with an ioe engine and soon afterwards a 746cc four-in-line with air-cooling was built. The last Cleveland, built from 1928 onward, was an improved and modernised version of the 746cc Four with a 996cc capacity.

CLEVELAND / *England 1911–1914*
Freddie Dixon, the famous rider, was closely connected with this Middlesbrough-based producer. The models included 2·75 hp and 3·5 hp singles with Precision engines.

CLUA / *Spain 1952–1964*
Connected with the Italian Alpino factory, Clua built two-strokes with 74cc, 98cc, 123cc and 173cc engines.

CLYDE / *England 1898–1912*
G. H. Wait of Leicester, designer and manufacturer of these superb machines, died in the 1950s. He was a pioneer who also built cars and

three-wheelers. His machines had 2·75, 6·5 and 8 hp engines of JAP and also of his own manufacture. Some models already had watercooled engines in 1903.

CLYNO / *England 1911–1924*
Another factory which built motorcycles and cars. Motorcycles had 5, 6 and 8 hp engines made partly by the Stevens brothers, who owned the AJS works at Wolverhampton, where the Clyno was built too. A reorganisation after WWI led to new 269cc two-strokes and 925cc V-twin sv models. When in 1924 demand for Clyno cars increased, it was decided to drop motorcycle manufacture.

CM / *Italy 1930–1957*
Created by two famous riders and technicians Oreste Drusiani and Mario Cavedagna, the first CM was a 173cc ohc machine. Other models included 248cc, 348cc and 496cc ohc and also 496cc ohv singles. Headed now by Salvia, CM also built in the mid-1930s very fast 348cc ohc racing machines which were ridden by Guglielmo Sandri. After the war, all CM machines had 123cc, 158cc and 173cc single-cylinder and 248cc twin-cylinder two-stroke engines. In addition, there was the Francolino, a very sporting 173cc ohc machine built in the mid-1950s. This engine had 9·5 bhp at 6500 rpm.

CM / *Germany 1921–1923*
The Munich-built CM had a 110cc Cockerell two-stroke engine and was in limited production only.

CMM / *England 1919–1921*
Small producer who fitted 292cc Union two-stroke engines into their own frames.

CMP / *Italy 1953–1956*
Fitted 48cc, 73cc, 98cc and 123cc Ceccato two-stroke engines and also 48cc Sachs two-strokes into modern frames of their own manufacture. Another model had the 123cc Ceccato ohv engine.

CMR / *France 1945–1948*
Produced after the war from existing and partly new parts BMW models R12 and R71 in France. These flat twins had 745cc and were, of course, transverse mounted.

110cc Cockerell (TS) 1922

COCKERELL/*Germany 1919–1924*
Designed by Fritz Cockerell, who also created the 5-cylinder Megola, these lightweight machines had his own flat single-cylinder two-stroke engines of 110cc, 145cc and 169·5cc capacity. Sporting versions had watercooled power units. Cockerell also designed 38cc bicycle attachments and created many other engines in the late 1920s including a watercooled four-cylinder motorcycle and Diesel and two-stroke engines. In addition, he created four and six-cylinder two-stroke cars and other power units. Cockerell motorcycles were fast, economical and reliable and in 1924 his riders on watercooled 145cc racing machines — Karl Adam and Hans Letnar — won the Championship of Germany in the 150cc class.

CODRIDEX/*France 1952–1956*
Manufacturers of mopeds with 49cc and 65cc engines.

COFERSA/*Spain 1953–1960*
Assembler of two-stroke machines with engines from 98cc to 198cc.

COLIBRI/*Austria 1952–1954*
Scooters with 123cc two-stroke Auto-Union (DKW) engines. Limited production.

COLOMB/*France 1950–1954*
Small assembler of scooters and lightweight motorcycles.

COLONIAL/*England 1911–1913*
The Carter-designed single-cylinder machine had its own 450cc two-stroke engine.

COLUMBIA/*America 1900–1905*
Built at the Pope works, the Columbia had Pope-built single-cylinder and V-twin engines.

COLUMBIA/*France 1922–1926*
Sv singles of 197cc and 247cc capacity in simple and open frames.

745cc Cockerell (TS 4-cylinder Prototype w/c) 1927

COLUMBUS/*Germany 1923–1924*
Built good bicycle attachment engines and a 248cc ohv machine, which became the first Horex motorcycle when the Kleemann family bought the Columbus engine factory.

COM/*Italy 1926–1928*
One of the many small Italian producers of 123cc and 173cc machines.

COMERY/*England 1919–1922*
A factory owned by racing motorcyclist Archie Cook. Produced motorcycles with 269cc Villiers two-stroke engines.

COMET/*England 1902–1907*
Fitted Minerva engines of 2·75 and 3·5 hp into own frames made from BSA cycle parts.

COMET/*Italy 1953–1957*
Superb, but quite expensive 173cc ohv and 173cc as well as 246cc vertical twin ohc machines designed by Alfonso Drusiani and built in his own works.

COMMANDER/*England 1952–1953*
Made at the last pre-war Rudge factory at Hayes, the R. W. Dennis-designed Commander was an unorthodox design. It had a frame made from

123cc Commander (TS Villiers Prototype) 1952

square tubes and a partly enclosed engine. This was a 98cc or 197cc Villiers two-stroke. The factory belonging to the General Steel group never went into quantity production.

CONDOR / *England 1907–1914*
Built proprietary engines and complete motor-cycles. Unique was a single-cylinder model with 96mm bore and 122mm stroke. At 810cc this was probably the biggest single in commercial production.

CONDOR / *Switzerland 1901–*
Next to Motosacoche, Switzerland's leading motorcycle manufacturer. Fitted in early years Zedel, afterwards mainly MAG (Motosacoche) engines from 246cc to 746cc with ioe and partly ohv engines. Small models had 147cc to 198cc Villiers motors. After 1945, a 346cc two-stroke

497cc Condor (ohv MAG) 1931

twin was built but main production concentrated on 678cc flat twins with their own transverse-mounted sv engines and shaft drive to the rear wheel. Another Condor had its own 247cc ohv engine as well as shaft drive. Together with the twin, these machines were built mainly for the Swiss forces. There was also a 248cc machine which had an ohc engine, supplied by Ducati. Condor was a very active competitor in races and during the late 1920s and early 1930s when they used 248cc, 348cc and 498cc Marchant-designed

ohc Motosacoche racing engines they were very successful. Among leading Condor riders were Georges Cordey, Ernst Hänny, Léon Divorne, Paul Wuillemin, Armin Bättig and Paul Dinkel.

CONDOR / *Germany 1953–1954*
Scooter-like motorcycles with 48cc two-stroke engines.

346cc Connaught (sv JAP) 1927

CONNAUGHT / *England 1910–1927*
Producer of excellent 293cc and 347cc two-stroke singles with belt and chain drive to the rear wheel. The range of models became larger when Connaught introduced 1925 models with 348cc sv and ohv Blackburne and ohv Bradshaw (oil-cooled) engines. Bert Perrigo, who afterwards went to BSA, and Jack Sprosen were among leading Connaught riders. The Birmingham-based factory bought in 1924 the JES motor-cycle production which was at Gloucester.

CONSUL / *England 1916–1922*
Small assembler, who produced Villiers-engined 269cc and 247cc models with orthodox frames.

COOPER / *America 1972–*
Made in Mexico by Islo at Salfillol for the American importer, Cooper machines are equip-

ped with 246cc single-cylinder two-stroke engines. There are different models for trials (enduro) and moto-cross.

CORAH / *England 1905–1914*
Superbly made 498cc single-cylinder sv machines and 746cc ohv V-twin JAP engined models. The small factory fitted upon request other proprietary engines as well.

CORGI / *England 1946—1952*
The tiny Corgi folding scooter was made by Brock-house Engineering of Southport and was derived from the Excelsior Wellbike, designed to be dropped alongside airborne troops in wartime. The Corgi had a 98cc Excelsior Sprite engine whereas the Wellbike, confusingly, had used a Villiers engine.

CORONA / *England 1901–1904*
Small producer of machines with 1·5 hp Minerva, 2 hp Clement and British 2·5 hp proprietary engines.

CORONA / *Germany 1902–1924*
The first Corona motorcycles had single-cylinder and V-twin engines mounted between the saddle

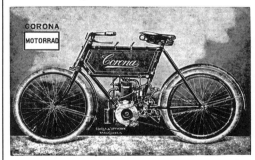

2½ hp Corona (sv) 1904

tube and the rear wheel. Zedel and Fafnir supplied the engines. Afterwards they had a more orthodox design. Motorcycle production stopped in 1907, but was taken up again in 1922, when Corona announced 346cc sv singles and 493cc flat twins. The later ones had BMW sv engines.

CORONA-JUNIOR / *England 1919–1923*
Concentrated manufacture on a 447cc single-cylinder sv machine which in 1919 was sold for £85 and in 1923 for £75.

CORRE / *France 1901–1910*
Better known as a car manufacturer which eventually was bought by La Licorne, Corre built also a range of motorcycles with Zurcher, Peugeot and Zedel engines.

678cc Condor (sv flat-twin) 1955

CORYDON / *England 1904–1908*
Produced 2·5 hp single-cylinder and 3 hp as well as 4·5 hp V-twin machines of good quality.

COSMOS / *Switzerland 1904–1907*
Fitted 3 hp and 4 hp Zedel and Fafnir engines into strengthened bicycle frames.

COSSACK / *Russia 1973–*
Name for Russian-built motorcycles in some foreign countries. The Russian state-owned factories produce the 174cc Voskhod and 346cc Ish-Planeta single cylinder two-strokes, the 347cc Ish-Jupiter two-stroke twin, the BMW-like 650cc Ural flat twin with a transverse-mounted ohv engine and the Dneipr, which is a modernised version of the Ural, although both models have 32 bhp only.

650cc Cossack (D model) 1977

COTTEREAU / *France 1903–1909*
One of the first car producers in France. Cottereau motorcycles had Minerva, Peugeot and also their own engines from 2 hp to 6 hp. From 1911 onward, Cottereau cars became known as CID cars.

COTTON / *England 1919—1980*
FW Cotton designed and patented a frame with tri-angulated straight tubes and set up business in Gloucester to make motorcycles with Villiers two-strokes and ohv Blackburne engines. Stanley Woods first rode for Cotton in the 1922 Junior TT finishing fifth, but won easily the following year. Thereafter Cotton-Blackburnes became very popular and were raced successfully.

Cotton also used JAP Python and Villiers engines, but the company was run down by 1939. Post war, it was brought by accountant Monty Denley and engineer Pat Onions. To a completely fresh design, they made Villiers-engined road, scramblers and trials machines. These, and Villiers 250cc Starmaker-engined road racers, were successful in the 1960s, a period when Derek Minter and Bill Ivy raced for Cotton. Later, shortage of Villiers engines dictated the use of Italian Minarellis. Denley and Onions sold out and the new management concentrated on Austrian Rotax engines mainly for road racing, though some machines were made for the police. Production came to a halt in 1980.

COULSON / *England 1919–1924*
Built 347cc and 497cc sv singles and also 497cc ohv V-twins with JAP engines. The last Coulson-B had a 346cc ohv Bradshaw engine with oil-cooling. Most models used a spring frame and Eric Longden gained many successes with F. Aslett Coulson-designed machines. Originally made at Kings Cross, London, the factory was

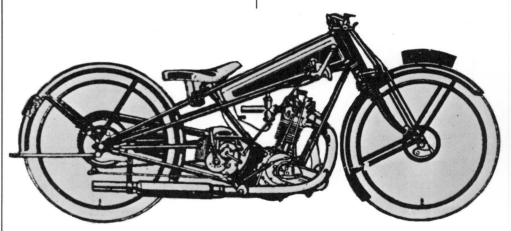

346cc Cotton (ohv Blackburne) 1923

490cc Cotton (ohv JAP) 1938

afterwards bought by A. W. Wall and eventually H. R. Backhouse & Co. Ltd. of Birmingham.

COVENTRY-B&D / *England 1923–1925*
Barbary and Downes were ex-employees of the defunct Hobart motorcycle factory and founders of this make. They also built 170cc Wee-McGregor two-stroke machines. The Coventry-B&D was built with JAP engines from 346cc to 996cc and with the 346cc Barr & Stroud sleeve-valve engine. The production was on a limited scale.

COVENTRY-CHALLENGE / *England 1903–1911*
A bicycle dealer who fitted into strengthened frames engines made by Fafnir, Minerva and other makes. Designer-manufacturer was Edward O'Brien.

248cc Coventry-Eagle (ohv Blackburne) 1936

497cc Coventry-Eagle (ohv Sturmey-Archer) 1929

172cc Coventry-Eagle (TS Villiers) 1931

497cc Coventry-Eagle (ohv Matchless) 1937

COVENTRY-EAGLE / *England 1901–1939*
Well-known assembler of superb machines. Owned by the Mayo family, Coventry-Eagle was originally a bicycle factory which built over the years motorcycles with engines from 98cc to 996cc They used Villiers, JAP, Sturmey-Archer, Blackburne and Matchless engines. During the 1920s they had Brough-Superior-like petrol tanks and the Flying 8 was a popular model with the big 996cc V-twin sv JAP engine. Among the racing versions, the JAP-engined 248cc single, ridden by Mita Vychodil of Czechoslovakia and Martin Schneeweiss of Austria, won many events. At Brooklands a 996cc ohv JAP-engined V-twin broke records and when Bert Le Vack in 1922–1924 raced new ohc JAP engines, he used Coventry-Eagle frames too. An interesting frame was introduced in 1928. It was a pressed steel, channel section frame, which over the years housed various Villiers engines. Mammut of Germany built this frame under licence. Another sensation was the Pullmann, introduced in 1935 with a chassis-like pressed steel frame and rear suspension. The rear wheel was enclosed by deeply valanced mudguards. Engines for the Pullmann were the 247cc Villiers deflector-type, the 247cc Villiers flat-top and the 246cc ohv Blackburne. The last Coventry-Eagle motorcycles had tubular frames with 123cc Villiers engines and 247cc, 347cc and 497cc ohv single-cylinder power-units made by Matchless in London. Production ceased with the outbreak of World War II.

COVENTRY-MASCOT / *England 1922–1924*
Produced exclusively motorcycles with 348cc engines. Blackburne supplied sv versions, Bradshaw the oilcooled ohv motor and Barr & Stroud delivered their sleeve-valve power units to this small factory.

COVENTRY-MOTETTE / *England 1899–1903*
Improved Bollée design with a 2·5 hp engine, designed by Turrell.

COVENTRY-STAR / *England 1919–1921*
Assembled machines with 269cc Liberty and Villiers engines.

COVENTRY-VICTOR / *England 1919–1936*
England's leading producer of opposed twin-cylinder engines of 499cc, 688cc and 749cc capacity and of complete motorcycles with these engines. From 1926 onwards there was also a three-wheeler in production; in 1929 Coventry-Victor also produced Speedway machines with 499cc ohv flat twins. McKechnie, Bison, Jeecy-Vea, Socovel and others used C-V power units.

CP-ROLEO / *France 1924–1939*
Interesting design, which used frames made from pressed steel and partly cast iron. These frames included the petrol and oil reservoir. Some

models had normal tubular frames. Engines used were 247cc to 498cc sv and ohv JAP, Voisin, LMC and Chaise.

CR / Germany 1926–1930
Assembled machines with 172cc Villiers two-stroke engines.

CRESCENT / Sweden 1954—late 1970s
Like Monark and NV, Crescent were members of the Swedish MCB group. They concentrated mainly on small proprietary engined two-stroke motor cycles, although in their main activity as outboard boat engine makers, they had their own designs. One of these, a three cylinder 500cc water-cooled two-stroke, was often used in solo and sidecar racing by amateur constructors in the 1970s. Rudi Kurth indeed built such a solo for the Monark factory, but it was not successful.

CREST / England 1923
Assembled machines with 346cc Barr & Stroud sleeve-valve and 347cc Villiers two-stroke engines.

CROCKER / American 1936—1941
Albert Crocker, with minimal facilities, built his 998cc ohv vee twins in a small Los Angeles workshop. Highly regarded by those who knew them, they rivalled and sometimes beat Harleys and Indians.

CROFT / England 1923–1926
Known also as Croft-Anzani, as most Croft machines housed 996cc four and eight-valve V-twin Anzani ohv engines, designed by the famous Hubert Hagens. A few Croft machines had the 1078cc Anzani engine and all had the Brough-Superior-like petrol tank. The production was on a limited scale.

CROWNFIELD / England 1903–1904
These Jack Perkins-designed machines had open frames. Engines fitted were the 1·75 hp and 2·25 hp Kerry and Givaudan.

CRT / Italy 1925–1929
Designed and built at Treviso by Cavasini and Romin, the CRT was a sporting 248cc and 348cc machine with Blackburne ohv engines.

CRYPTO / England 1902–1908
Leading make during the period. Designed by W. G. James, most Crypto machines had 2·5 hp and 3 hp Peugeot and Coronet proprietary engines.

CSEPEL / Hungary 1932–1951
Once the leading Hungarian motorcycle factory, which was part of the great Manfred Weiss steel works at Budapest. The Laszlo Sagi-designed two-strokes had 98cc, 123cc and 146cc engines. During a reorganisation, the state-owned factory dropped the Czepel transfer in 1952 and the new models got the Pannonia and Danuvia transfers on the petrol tank.

CUDELL / Germany 1898–1905
Pioneer which first built three-wheelers and afterwards 402cc and 510cc motorcycles with De Dion engines.

CUSHMANN / America 1944–1957
Made by the Johnson-Evinrude outboard motor branch factory at Lincoln, Nebraska, the Cushmann was an early scooter with 4·8 hp and 7·95 hp ohv engines.

CURTISS / America 1903–1912
Glenn Curtiss, the famous pilot and aircraft engine producer, built single and V-twin motorcycles and also supplied his engines to other motorcycle producers, including Marvel. Riding a motorcycle with one of his aircooled V-8 aircraft engines, he broke many records.

CURWY (CURSY) / Germany 1911–1931
Produced mainly 348cc and 498cc sv and ohv machines with own power-units; a few 348cc ohc machines were also built. Curt Szymanski, the designer-manufacturer, changed in 1927 the name Curwy to Cursy, probably because the word 'curwe' means 'prostitute' in German.

CYC-AUTO / England 1934—1956
Wellington Butt's early 'Autocycle' always had the 98cc engine ahead of the cycle pedal bracket, the crankshaft in line with the frame. He used own engine, then Villiers. Cyc Auto was sold to Scott in 1937, who used their own 98cc engine unit, latterly with twin exhaust pipes. Final offering was a real motor cycle with shaft drive, but few, if any, were made or sold.

CYCLON / Germany 1901–1905
Leading producer during the early years of motorcycle manufacture. Used De Dion, Werner and Zedel engines and concentrated eventually on the production of the three-wheeled Cyclonette.

996cc Cyclone (ohc V-twin) 1913

CYCLONE / America 1913–1917
For many years the only commercially built 996cc V-twin with an ohc engine. Designed by Andrew Strand, the Cyclone won many races but became outclassed when big factories including

348cc Curwy (ohv) 1924

Harley-Davidson entered the market with 8-valve 996cc V-twins and entered racing with such machines. Only one other make—Koehler Escoffier in France—built big V-twin ohc machines before 1939.

CYCLOP / *Germany 1922–1925*
Assembled motorcycles with 127cc to 198cc two and four-stroke engines made by Kurier, Bubi, Teco, Namapo and others.

CYKELAID / *England 1919–1926*
Attachment engines of 1·25 hp and 1·50 hp (133cc) for bicycles and also complete lightweight machines with these power units.

CYRUS / *The Netherlands 1931–1971*
Producer of bicycles and mopeds and motorcycles with 49cc to 148cc Villiers, Sachs, and Ilo two-stroke engines.

ČZ / *Czechoslovakia 1932–*
Started production with 73cc and 98cc lightweights and soon became a leading motorcycle factory in the country. Originally belonged to the big Skoda works. ČZ stands for Česká Zbrojovka', ie Czech arms factory. Other pre-

173cc C.Z. (TS) 1935

war models were good-looking 173cc and 248cc unit-design two-strokes with pressed steel frames. The factory also built 348cc two-strokes and even ohv prototypes, which never went into quantity production; a 496cc aircooled vertical twin-cylinder, two-stroke machine had the same fate. After 1945, ČZ became part of the nationalised Czechoslovakian motorcycle industry and also became commercially and technically connected with Jawa. This co-operation increased during the years. Among the first post-war ČZ

248cc C.Z. (dohc single works-racer) 1957

124cc Čezet (TS single) 1982

346cc Čezet (TS twin) 1982

machines were 123cc models, and other versions with tubular frames up to 348cc twins. The big Strakonice works had over the years many superb technicians and designers, including Václav Pavliček, Ignaz Uhl, J. F. Koch, Jaroslav Walter and Jaroslav Pudil; among successful riders in trials and races were Cyril Němec, Čeněk Kohlicek, Eman Marha, Josef Paštika, Milada Bayerová, Ján Bedrna, Bickers, Friedrichs, De Coster, Ján Lucák, František Bartoš, Václav Parus and others. Many among these are moto-cross specialists and while Jawa concentrated more on trials and road races it was up to ČZ to succeed in moto-cross with excellent machines. Since 1949 the Strakonice factory has built superb 123cc, 248cc and 348cc road racing machines with ohc engines, of which most were designed by the late Jaroslav Walter. Redesigned watercooled moto-cross models with 248cc and other engines came into production in 1978 and proved fast and reliable. As part of the nationalised Czechoslovakian motorcycle industry, ČZ (now known also as Čezeta) ceased their own production of motorcycles in 1981, which are now built together with Jawa machines.

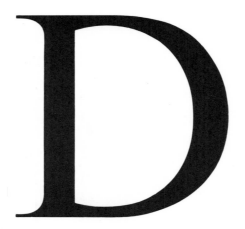

p112

DAK/*Germany 1923–1925*
Association of some German car manufacturers, which also sold 117cc and 147cc deflector-type two-strokes, assembled by Ilo of Pinneberg. When demand for Ilo proprietary engines increased, the factory stopped manufacture of complete machines.

DALESMAN/*England 1969–1974*
Financed mainly by US dollars, Dalesman built good competition machines with 98cc and 123cc Puch as well as 123cc Sachs engines.

DALTON/*England 1920–1922*
Some versions of Dalton motorcycles had disc wheels. The small factory fitted 347cc and 497cc sv Blackburne singles and 688 flat-twin cylinder Coventry-Victor engines into sturdy frames.

DANE/*England 1919–1920*
Limited production using 348cc two and four-stroke Precision engines and 990cc sv V-twin JAP engines.

DANUBIUS/*German 1923–1924*
Made by the big Ratibor machine factory Ganz & Co., the Danubius was a 198cc sv machine of conventional design.

DANUVIA/*Hungary 1955–1963*
Of Czepel design, the Danuvia was a mass-produced 123cc two-stroke machine.

DARDO/*Italy 1924–1929*
Well-made lightweights with flat 132cc and 174cc two-stroke engines.

DARLAN/*Spain 1958–1960*
Limited production of machines with own 94cc two-stroke engines.

DARLING/*Switzerland 1924–1929*
From 1928 produced new 498cc models with sv and ohv Sturmey-Archer single-cylinder engines.

DART/*England 1923–1924*
Built up-to-date 348cc single-cylinder ohc machines with 74mm bore and 81mm stroke. Designer was A. A. Sidney. Few machines were built.

DART/*England 1901–1906*
Designed by Frank Baker—not the Baker of Precision engine manufacture and of Baker motorcycles—the old Dart had 2·5 hp engines made by Minerva and MMC.

DAVENTRY/*Belgium 1951–1955*
Assembled 123cc and 175cc two-strokes with Puch, Sachs, Ilo and other proprietary engines.

DAVISON/*England 1902–1908*
Good early motorcycles with English Simms and Belgian 2 hp and 2·5 hp Minerva engines. .

DAW/*England 1902—1905*
Proprietary engine and carburettor manufacturers, Dalton & Wade also made a small number of motor cycles.

DAW/*Germany 1924–1925*
Unconventional fully enclosed motorcycle. Designed by Ernst Köhler, it had a single-cylinder 405cc two-stroke engine.

DAX/*France 1932–1939*
Excellently designed machines with two-stroke engines from 98cc to 174cc and four-stroke ohv unit-design engines from 123cc to 498cc.

DAY-LEEDS/*England 1912–1914*
Big machine factory which built three wheelers before entering motorcycle manufacture. The only model was a 496cc single with its own ioe engine. WWI stopped manufacture.

DAYTON/*America 1911–1917*
Built by the Huffman Manufacturing Co. at

492cc Dax (ohv) 1932

998cc Della Ferrera (sv V-twin with sidecar) 1924

Elkhart, Indiana, Dayton motorcycles had 7 hp, later 9–10 hp V-twin Spake engines.

DAYTON / *England 1913–1920*
The first product was a 162cc bicycle attachment engine; later Dayton designs had 269cc Villiers two-stroke engines.

DAYTON / *England 1954–1960*
Was among the first producers of modern scooters after WWII. They were nice scooters with 173cc, 198cc and 246cc Villiers engines.

DE-CA / *Italy 1954–1957*
Built interesting 48cc and 98cc ohv singles and also a 123cc vertical ohv twin in limited numbers and for a not very low price. The smallest model had 39mm bore and 40mm stroke. It had 2·4 bhp at 6000 rpm and a 44 mph top speed. The DE-CA range included also a 48cc ohv bicycle engine.

DE-DE / *France 1923–1929*
Limited production of a wide range of models. These included two-strokes from 98cc to 174cc and sv and ohv versions with JAP engines from 248cc to 498cc.

DE DION BOUTON / *France 1926–1930*
There was no real connection between the once famous engine and car factory of the same name and these motorcycles. These had 173cc and 247cc two-stroke, deflector-type engines; a bigger model a 348cc ohv engine.

DEFA / *Germany 1921–1924*
Built not only complete 198cc sv machines, but supplied other builders of motorcycles frames.

DEFY-ALL / *England 1921–1922*
Motorcycles with quite unusual spring frames. The engines fitted were the 269cc Villiers and the 348 sv one-cylinder made by Blackburne.

DEI / *Italy 1932–1966*
When Umberto Dei took over the Ancora motorcycle factory, he produced lightweights with 49cc, 60cc, 73cc and 98cc two-stroke engines, supplied partly by Sachs. Others had Mosquito power units.

DELAPLACE / *France 1951–1953*
Simple machine with 173cc and 247cc Ydral two-stroke engines of good design.

DELIN / *Belgium 1899–1901*
No details are available about this pioneer who, according to some sources, fitted 1·5 hp and 2·5 hp De Dion engines.

246cc Delta Gnom (TS) 1929

248cc Delta Gnom (ohv JAP engine) 1935

DE LUXE / *America 1912–1915*
Made by Excelsior, ie the Schwinn company of Chicago, De Luxe motorcycles had mainly V-twin proprietary engines made by F. W. Spake of Indianapolis.

DE LUXE / *England 1920–1924*
Everyone who bought a De Luxe with the 346cc Barr & Stroud sleeve-valve engine got a free side-car frame. Earlier models had 269cc Villiers engines.

DELLA FERRERA / *Italy 1909–1948*
The Della Ferrera brothers built not very good-looking but interesting machines. Among them were the 498cc V-twin ohc racing machines of 1922, which had the overhead camshafts driven

496cc Della Ferrera (ohv) 1927

by chains. They won many hill-climbs and short-distance races despite the very high saddle position and chains which were not enclosed at all. Production versions included 498cc, 598cc, 746cc and 996cc sv V-twins as well as 498cc ohv and 637cc sv singles. So the models had — even in the 1920s — a rear suspension. The last model built was a unit-design 499cc sv single.

DELOMA / *Germany 1924*
Lightweight built at Magdeburg (now DDR) with Julius Löwy's crude-oil 142cc two-stroke engine.

DELTA / *Germany 1924*
Very unorthodox fully enclosed motorcycle with a dual-seat and rear suspension by semi-elliptic leaf springs. The 499cc single-cylinder two-stroke engine with 75mm bore and 113mm stroke was a three-port deflector-type. Limited production.

DELTA-GNOM / *Austria 1925–1955*
Was a well-known make in Austria. The first machines had their own 246cc two-stroke engines, later versions — with one exception — sv and ohv JAP engines from 346cc to 996cc. The exception was the Hans Pitzek-designed 498cc ohv single, built from 1928 onwards. After 1945 the reorganised factory built only two-stroke

machines with 98cc, 123cc and 173cc. The engines came from Rotax, Puch, Ilo and HMW. Many leading Austrian racing men, including Leopold Killmeyer, Karl Bohmann, Hans Walz, F. J. Meyer, Ladislaus Möslacher and Franz Behrendt rode Delta-Gnom machines in pre-war days.

DEMM / *Italy 1953—1982*

A factory famous in its day for Lightweights of between 50cc and 175cc, both four- and two-stroke, Demm sold engines to other makers from time to time also as proprietary units and made small industrial vehicles. Were involved in racing and record breaking in the 1950s and early 1960s. In later years, concentrated on 50cc motor cycles and mopeds.

174cc Demm (TS) 1955

DENE / *England 1903–1922*

Old motorcycle assembler. Dene machines had 2·5 hp and 3·5 hp Fafnir engines, 2·25 hp to 8 hp Precision engines, 3·75 hp watercooled Green-Precision engines, the 3·75 hp Abingdon and also the 6–8 hp JAP V-twin sv engine. Despite the wide range of models, Dene production was on a limited scale.

DENNELL / *England 1903–1908*

Designed by Herbert Dennell of Leeds, these machines had Minerva, NSU and JAP engines, but among the JAP-engined models was also the

494cc Delta Gnom (ohv) 1929

660cc three-cylinder, which made headlines. The three single-cylinders were aircooled and set in line on a common crankcase. Rear drive was by belt. Dennell also fitted a few four-cylinder in-line Franklin & Isaacsson engines.

DERBI / *Spain 1950—*

Famous for their 50cc models, but also made machines of up to 350cc, all two strokes. Won the 50cc and 125cc world championship, mainly with rider Angel Nieto in 1970/1/2. Today Derbi are Spain's largest and strongest surviving motorcycle makers; they also import Suzuki motor cycles.

DERNY / *France 1949–1957*

Quite unorthodox 123cc and 173cc two-stroke motorcycles in a range which also included 173cc scooters.

660cc Dennell (sv three-cylinder JAP) 1906

DERONZIERE / *France 1903–1914*

Built 282cc singles with their own engines and other models with power units made by Zedel and Peugeot.

DESPATCH-RIDER / *England 1915–1917*

The name more or less states the purpose of these machines. They were powered by 210cc Peco and 269cc Villiers two-stroke engines.

DEVIL / *Italy 1953–1957*

Made at Bergamo, the Devil was a good motorcycle. Production included 48cc and 158cc two-strokes and 123cc and 173cc ohv singles with inclined cylinders on the beautiful Soncini-designed engines. The 173cc version had a five-speed gearbox in unit with the motor, and top speed was 81·2 mph.

DFB / *Germany 1922–1925*

Producer of 159cc two-stroke bicycle engines and of complete machines with the same power units.

DFR / *France 1921–1933*

Ambitious factory. The first models had their own 346cc two-stroke engines, afterwards they also built sv and ohv versions. There was also a

348cc D.F.R. (ohv) 1927

248cc Bradshaw-engined single, probably a sleeved-down oilcooled 346cc engine. The factory raced this machine with a supercharger and with Pierre in the saddle during 1925–1927. There were also MAG-engined 348cc and 498cc ohv singles and soon after 1932 DFR introduced a new model with a pressed steel frame and a 498cc vertical-twin ohv Dresch engine. They were later taken over by Dresch.

DGW / *Germany 1927–1928*
London's 1927 Olympia motorcycle exhibition saw DKW machines with DGW on the petrol tank. The reason was a dispute with another German factory which already used the DKW trade mark.

DIAG / *Germany 1921–1928*
Machine factory, which produced 83cc and 101cc bicycle attachment engines, afterwards also complete 173cc, 246cc and 346cc sv and ohv motorcycles. The frame design had the tubes above the crankcases; the engines virtually hung in the tubular frames. The Diag was never a widely known motorcycle.

DIAMANT / *Germany 1903–1940*
The first Diamant vehicles were three-wheelers and the first motorcycles made had Fafnir power units, afterwards their own single and

498cc Diamant (ohv Kühne) 1929

V-twin engines. From 1907 or 1908 until 1926 there were no motorcycles made, but new models built from 1926 onward were designed by the famous Franz Gnädig and also had Gnädig-designed 346cc Kühne ohv engines, followed by 496cc sv and ohv versions. On special order, JAP engines could be fitted too. During the late 1920s, Diamant and the Elite car factory joined forces and while Elite faded out as a car manufacturer, part of the Diamant factory was taken over by Opel for producing 496cc Opel motorcycles with Duralumin frames, a design by Ernst Neumann-Neander. When this production stopped in the early 1930s, a limited number of new 348cc and 498cc EO (Elite-Opel) machines — with Küchen instead of the original Opel engines — were built before the factory closed forever as a motorcycle and car producer. The frames of the EO were nearly identical to the ones used in the late 1920s and early 1930s by Opel. From 1933 onward, production concentrated on 73cc and 98cc mopeds with Sachs two-stroke engines.

DIAMOND / *England 1910–1938*
Diamond motorcycles were made by the DF&M engineering company in Birmingham, and in the early days showed some remarkable enterprise. In the 1920 250cc class of the Junior TT, they entered an extremely advanced four-valve ohv-engined model, though reports of the time do not say how it performed. Much of Diamond's subsequent production used Villiers two-stroke engines and JAP, Blackburne and Bradshaw oil-cooled proprietary engines. Using JAP engines, Vic Brittain rode in the 250cc, 350cc and 500cc classes in the 1931 TT without any success. Thereafter, Diamond became just another maker of Villiers-engined utility machines, with production ending with the outbreak of war in 1939.

DIETERLE-DESSAU / *Germany 1921–1925*
Known also by the Dreipunkt trade-mark, Dieterle's factory built bicycles and lightweights. The last ones had 'exhaust-injected' 198cc and 248cc sv engines of patented design.

198cc Dieterle-Dessau (sv) 1923

DIFRA / *Germany 1923–1925*
Assembler who fitted mainly 198cc sv Namapo engines into their own frames.

DIHL / *Germany 1923–1924*
Berlin-built 269cc single-cylinder two-stroke machines. Limited production.

4 HP Diamant (sx Forecar) 1905

DILECTA/*France 1920–1939*
Producer of machines with engines from 98cc to 498cc. Engine suppliers were Villiers, Aubier-Dunne, Soyer, Chaise, JAP and others.

DJOUNN/*Germany 1925*
Designed by Alexander von Djounkowski, a former Russian pilot, the Djounn was built in Berlin. Its 499cc single-cylinder engine was full of new and undeveloped innovations which soon caused its commercial demise.

DKF/*Germany 1923–1924*
Assembler of lightweights with 148cc and 198cc sv engines.

DKR/*England 1957–1966*
Manufacturer of Villiers-engined scooters with 148cc, 173cc, 197cc and 247cc single-cylinder and 244cc vertical-twin power units.

DKW/*Germany 1919-1981*
In the 1920s, DKW, founded in 1919 by Danish-born J S Rasmussen, was the world's largest motor cycle factory. It first produced a two-stroke 'clip-on' engine, followed by various small two-strokes, designed by Hugo Ruppe. DKW supplied many other German makes with their two-stroke

122cc D.K.W. (TS 'Golem' scooter) 1921

engines. They raced their Ruppe-designed water-cooled two-strokes, with patent 'Ladepump' inlet charging by a separate piston in the crankcase, in 175cc and later 250cc classes in the 1920s with considerable success. By the decade's end, DKW was producing road machines with single and twin cylinder deflector-piston engines between 150cc, 500cc and even 600cc.

In the 1930s, DKW became part of Auto Union (together with car makers Audi, Horch and Wanderer) and made two-stroke-engined light cars as well as motorcycles. As far as the latter were concerned, two radical decisions were made. One was to exploit the Schnurle 'flat-top piston' patents for road machines, which gave huge advantages in terms of power and reliability. The other decision was to race water-cooled 'split single' two-strokes — still with piston-pump inlet charging — designed by Swiss born Arnold Zoller, and developed through the 1930s by DKW's August Prussing.

These weirdly unorthodox (and very noisy) machines came to dominate the 250cc class and

123cc D.K.W. (TS Model RT-125) 1952

won many Grand Prix events, ridden notably by Walfred Winkler, Ewald Kluge, Siegried Wunsche and many more. Kluge won the 1938 Lightweight TT at record speed. DKW were 1-2-3 in the 1938 250cc European Championship (the first year that a points scoring system was used) with riders Kluge, Petruschke and Gabentz. In 1939 Kluge was 250cc champion and Heiner Fleischman 350cc. The range of road machines covered all classes from 98cc to 500cc — the latter a superb air-cooled twin with electric starting.

Post war, DKW was split. The original factory at Zschopau, in the Russian zone, became IFA, then MZ. DKW itself resumed production at Ingoldstat

346cc D.K.W. (TS 2-Cylinder RT-350) 1955

206cc D.K.W. (TS 206) 1925

174cc D.K.W. (TS watercooled racer) 1926

and later at Dusseldorf, West Germany. Mainstay of early production was an up-dated version of the famous pre-war RT125, this was soon supplemented by 200cc, 250cc and 350cc air-cooled twins. DKW also raced in the 125cc, 250cc and 350cc classes with normal piston-ported two strokes (some had rotary inlet valves) with some success, but not as great as in pre-war days. The 350cc 'three' was especially technically interesting. Designed by Eric Wolf and radically developed by Helmut Görg, it was 'fast but fragile'.

Worrying business trends stopped the racing programme at the end of 1956. In 1957 DKW partly amalgamated with Victoria and Express to form the Zweirad Union, which, in turn, was taken over in 1966 by proprietary engine makers Fichtel and Sachs, who added Hercules to the Union. No longer innovators or leaders in two stroke technology, DKW had become redundant, and the name was gradually subjugated to that of Hercules — though the DKW name was still retained for its earlier prestige in some markets. Apart from some very ordinary mopeds and lightweights, the DKW name was last seen on the Hercules Wankel W2000, which the company made great efforts to

124cc D.K.W. (TS model RT-125) 1972

export to Britain and the USA. The W2000 had a Sachs snow mobile single-rotor air-cooled unit rated as 300cc, for which 32hp at 6500rpm was claimed. It had a 6 speed gearbox and chain drive. The W2000 never achieved acceptance, and it, and the DKW name, disappeared for good in the early 1980s. It was a sad end to a make that in its day had typified ingenuity and forward thinking in motorcycle design.

DLM/*South Korea 1972–*
The Daelim Machinery Co. of Seoul is one of the leading producers of modern 124cc single-cylinder two-stroke machines in the country and produces 5,000 machines monthly. Suzuki has the same production level, while Honda builds 8,000 machines in a month. High taxes and petrol prices are keeping engines to small capacities.

DMF/*The Netherlands 1940–1957*
Owned by former racing driver Joop Verkerke, this assembler used proprietary engines made by Villiers, Ilo and Puch. They were of 123cc, 148cc and 173cc capacity. The last model made by DMF, which stood for Driebergsche Motorrij-wielen Fabriek N.V., was an Ilo-engined 244cc two-stroke twin.

DMG/*Germany 1921–1924*
Limited production of 147cc sv single-cylinder bicycle engines and later of complete motor-cycles with their own 198cc sv power units.

DMW/*England 1945–1971*
DMW made forks, hubs and other components for the trade, plus a range of road bikes, trials bikes and some interesting scooters, including the Villiers 250cc twin-engined Deemster, sold to several police forces. When Villiers stopped making motorcycle engines, DMW took over the stock, jigs and fixtures and still supply Villiers components.
  Under owner Harold Nock, who retired in 1971, DKW were an individualistic company. They made a 250cc Villiers Starmaker-engined road racing model; an interesting prototype had two Star-makers side by side.

DNB/*Japan 1957–1961*
Produced single-cylinder two-stroke machines with 123cc, 197cc and 247cc.

492cc Dollar (ohv) 1931

DNJEPR/*Russia 1967–*
Built as a sidecar machine, the BMW-like Dnjepr, with its 647cc ohv engine and shaft-drive, is the simple home version of the newer Ural-3, which is basically the export model of Dnjepr. Both are built at the Swerdlowsk machine works.

DOBRO-MOTORIST/*Germany 1923–1925*
Made by a branch of Mercur Aircraft of Berlin, this company built 145cc DKW two-stroke and 346cc sv and ohv JAP engines into triangular frames.

DOGLIOLI & CIVARDI/*Italy 1929–1935*
Designed by Cesare Doglioli, these sporting machines had 170cc Norman ohv engines, later versions 173cc, 247cc, 347cc and 498cc JAP and four-valve ohv Python engines. Production was on a limited scale.

148cc Dobro-Motorist (TS D.K.W. engine) 1925

DOLF/*Germany 1922–1925*
Good, but very unorthodox 198cc two-stroke machines with unit-design engines of their own manufacture. The Dolf engines had no less than eight transfer and exhaust ports. In addition, they used a conic inlet rotary sleeve in the crank-case. The 62mm × 66mm bore/stroke engine developed 3 hp.

DOLLAR/*France 1925–1939*
Once a leading French make, Dollar built many different models from 98cc to 748cc. Among them were two-strokes from 98cc to 246cc and 746cc models with four-cylinder unit-design air-cooled ohv engines. There were also Dollar machines with shaft drive and versions with power units made by Chaise.

DOMINISSIMI/*Italy 1924–1928*
Small producer of sporting 172cc and 248cc ohv single-cylinder machines.

746cc Donghai (transverse ohv flat-twin) 1982

DONGHAI/*China 1978–*
The first Chinese make to be exported, the very heavy 745cc vertical twin-cylinder ohv Donghai is, with its 33 bhp at 5000 rpm, built to be driven with a sidecar. With a top speed of not more than

346cc DOT (ohv JAP) 1929

248cc DOT (TS Villiers) 1957

58 mph, it is a sturdy design on basically English lines with some Japanese technical influence. It is a cheap machine without any great performance.

DONISELLI/*Italy 1951–1961*
Once a producer of motorcycles with Ilo and Alpino engines from 63cc to 174cc, Doniselli has concentrated lately on different lightweights with engines of 49cc capacity.

DOPPER/*The Netherlands 1904*
Early ohv design of a 269cc single cylinder machine, which had a long wheelbase and belt drive.

DORION/*France 1932–1936*
Lightweights with 98cc and 123cc Aubier-Dunne two-stroke engines.

DORMAN/*Hungary 1920–1937*
Assembled machines from 172cc to 499 cc with Villiers, MAG and JAP proprietary engines. Limited production.

DOT/*England 1903–1974*
Old established factory, founded by racing motorcyclist Harry Reed, who won the twin-cylinder class in the 1908 TT with a 680cc Peugeot-engined machine. He rode in 1924 in the sidecar TT and finished second on a Bradshaw-engined 348cc machine. DOT's heyday was during the 1920s, when they fitted not only Bradshaw engines, but mainly JAP motors from 246cc to 986cc V-twins. There were also Blackburne-engined 347cc versions and in the late 1920s and early 1930s machines with 173cc and 247cc Villiers two-stroke engines. The Manchester-based company gained further successes in TT races, when Syd Ollerhead was second in the 1924 Junior and Jack Cooke third in the Lightweight of the same year. Two third TT places were won in 1928, with Kenneth Twemlow in the Junior and his brother Eddy in the Lightweight. Kenneth was also second in the 1929 Lightweight. The engines were ohv racing singles, made by JAP. Some experimental racing DOTs had flat cylinders, but these failed to gain success. Motorcycle production stopped in 1932, but a reorganised company re-entered the market after 1948 and built a range of Villiers-engined two-strokes of 123cc to 246cc, of which many were moto-cross and trials machines.

Later, there were also Sachs and Minarelli-engined two-stroke models.

DOTTA/*Italy 1924–1926*
Small assembler who fitted 173cc Piazza two-stroke engines.

DOUE/*France c1903*
Long forgotten make. Fitted 1·5 hp engines into bicycle frames.

DOUGLAS / *England 1907—1956*

Famous for pioneering and for persisting with the flat twin engine, Bristol ironfounders Douglas took over J F Barter's Fairy (Fee) flat-twin motorcycle and developed it, in 350cc form with, from 1910, a two speed gearbox with chain and belt transmission. Douglas were successful in long distance trials and in the TT. Harry Bashall won the 1912 Junior, which led directly to a War Office contract for despatch riders' machines for the British Army — thousands of which were used in WWI. Post war, Les Bailey and Walter Moore designed an ohv model that sold well — the future King George VI owned one! Douglas continued to perform successfully at Brooklands and Freddie Dixon won the 1923 sidecar TT and made fastest lap in the 1924 Senior. Len Parker won the 1925 Sidecar TT. Sales of 350cc, 500cc and 600cc machines continued high through the 1920s. Freddie Dixon and Cyril Pullin designed the EW model with all chain drive, three speeds and 350cc sv engine for 1925. Dixon also designed the 500cc and 600cc RA racing models, later developed into the 'Dirt track' Douglas, and into the super-sporting SW5 and SW6 road bikes.

In 1932, however, the Douglas family sold the company to a finance group and thereafter, the company appeared to lose its way, and was in and out of insolvency for the rest of the decade. However, it managed to produce a neat all-enclosed

350cc Douglas (sv flat twin) 1911

346cc Douglas (ohv transverse flat-twin) 1949

349cc Douglas (sv flat-twin) 1927

346cc Douglas (ohv transverse flat-twin 'Dragonfly') 1957

596cc Douglas (sv flat-twin 'Wessex') 1934

150cc two stroke and side valve flat twins of 250cc — 750cc. In 1935 it was rechristened 'Aero Douglas', but production slowed down to a trickle of 600cc models, while, during WWII, it produced industrial trucks, aircraft parts and auxiliary engines.

The immediate post-war period saw a transverse-engined ohv 350cc with torsion bar suspension, in 1946, this became the T35 model, now with 'Radiadraulic' bottom link front forks. Despite some competition success, however, the T35 and its variants, the Plus 80 and Plus 90, never sold well, while the 350cc Dragonfly, with frame designed by Ernie Earles, did even worse. Production ceased during 1956. What kept the company alive until then was the fact that, since 1951, it had made the Vespa scooter profitably under licence.

D-RAD / *Germany 1921–1933*
Built at a state-owned former arms factory at Berlin-Spandau, the first machine was a 393cc flat twin, designed by Günther. Originally called the Star, it was renamed D-Rad and built until 1926. In the meantime chief designer Christian-

398cc D-Rad (sv flat-twin) 1923

sen created the first true D-Rad, a heavy 496cc single-cylinder sv unit-design machine with a leaf spring fork. The famous Martin Stolle, formerly with BMW and Victoria, joined the Spandau factory in 1927 and developed this design. In 1929 he created an ohv model (R10) with a new fork, coil springs and a separate gearbox, and in 1930 a similar machine, the R11, with an sv engine. The D-Rad motorcycles were always of sturdy design and often ridden with sidecars. Some regarded them as 'farmer's machines', but many big trials and long-distance events were won by these excellent machines, which also competed in races. Stolle was not only

497cc D-Rad (sv Model R-11) 1931

in charge of D-Rad design, but also of the very active competition department. Among leading riders in it were Curt Weichelt, Erich Tennigkeit, Franz Seelos, Max Polster, Hans Przybilski, Franz Ischinger, Paul Bütow, Franz Heck and others. The last models built by D-Rad were 198cc and 246cc two-stroke singles with German Bark engines. Not many were made when NSU at Neckarsulm took over and stopped D-Rad motorcycle production.

DREADNOUGHT / *England 1915–1925*
Made by William Lloyds Cycle Ltd. at Birmingham, where they built Quadrant and LMC motorcycles too. The Dreadnought had an impressive name, but was only an assembled 269cc two-stroke machine with a Villiers engine.

DRESCH / *France 1923–1939*
Built many models over the years. These included 98cc to 246cc two-strokes and sv, ohv and ohc machines with Chaise, Aubier-Dunne,

Stainless, Train, JAP, MAG and other proprietary engines up to 748cc. Among them were models with shaft drive, pressed steel frames and 498cc and 748cc four-cylinder in-line versions. Also a 496cc vertical twin with pressed steel frame and shaft drive was built 1930–1932.

DREVON / *France 1946–1953*
Machines with engines from 98cc to 173cc.

DS / *Sweden 1924–1928*
Made mainly for the Swedish armed forces, the DS had Swiss MAG ioe engines of 746cc.

DSH / *Austria 1924–1932*
The name came from the owners Döller, Seidl and Hauler. The first machines had 172cc and 246cc Villiers engines, later ones also 346cc, 490cc and 746cc sv and ohv JAP and MAG engines. The famous Rupert Karner, many times Austrian Champion, joined DSH in 1927

498cc Dresch (sv two-cylinder, shaft-drive) 1930

746cc DSH (sv V-twin JAP) 1929

as a rider and with commercial interests. His death at the 1928 Hungarian TT when the fork on his 348cc machine broke during the race led to a hiatus for DSH until it was revived in 1929 by Franz Döller. He built new JAP-engined models with 246cc, 497cc and 746cc engines, among them a very sporting 246cc ohv double-port version. Among successful DSH riders were Anton Hunek, Josef Opawsky, Rudolf Runtsch and Friedrich Schwarz.

DS-MALTERRE / France 1920–1958

During the 1920s, production concentrated around a not very modern 496cc single-cylinder sv machine. After the war, DS — it stood for Deblades & Sigran — built Ydral-engined 123cc to 247cc two-stroke and 124cc to 248cc ohv versions with French-made AMC proprietary engines.

248cc DS-Malterre (ohv AMC) 1954

173cc DS-Malterre (ohv AMC) 1955

DSK / Japan 1954–1962

Built many two-strokes from 172cc upwards and also 497cc ohv machines with transverse-mounted flat-twin power units.

DUCATI / Italy 1950—(Cagiva 1985)

Ducati were basically electrical engineers, who, after WW2, were state-aided to produce Aldo Farinelli's 50cc Cucciolo clip-on four-stroke engine for bicycles. At Milan late in 1950, Ducati showed a neat 60cc motorcycle with an enlarged Cucciolo engine, later of 65cc. Later, 98cc and 125cc models were added. In 1954 Ing. Fabio Taglioni was recruited to design sports racing models, first of 100cc then 125cc. These were successful in long-distance races and led to a dohc Grand Prix racer in 1956, which, in turn, led to the 'Desmodromic' 125cc racer of 1957 (Desmodromic valve operation returns the valves to their seats mechanically, without spring's. The 'Desmo' engine was very successful and Ducati riders finished second and third in the 1958 World Championships. Road machines of 175cc and 250cc followed, but racing was curtailed for financial reasons. In the late 1960s 'Desmo' road bikes of 250cc, 350cc and 450cc were offered alongside conventional ohc models and small two strokes. In 1970 Ducati launched their first 90 degree vee twin of 750cc, with conventional ohc valve operation. This marked the start of an intensive development.

In 1972 Paul Smart and Bruno Spaggioni were first and second at Imola, riding 750cc twins. In 1978 Mike Hailwood, after a nine year lay-off, returned to the Isle of Man and on a specially prepared 900cc twin, won the Formula 1 TT at over 108mph! In 1985 Ducati were acquired by the Castiglioni brothers' Cagiva company, who, since 1983, had used Ducati engines. The association has been a fruitful one to the present.

198cc Ducati (ohc) 1958

158cc Ducati (ohc) 1965

904cc Ducati Paso 906 1988.

496cc Ducati (ohc two-cylinder) 1976

DUCATI (MOTOTRANS) / *Spain 1959*

Produced for many years nearly identical models to the Bologna Ducati factory. Mototrans-Ducati of Barcelona is still closely connected with Italian Ducati, which also supplies the licences for the Spanish machines. They are still producing various 340cc ohc singles with touring and sporting specifications and also a 72cc trials two-stroke machine with 6 bhp at 6100 rpm. The latest Spanish-built Ducati (Mototrans) models are improved and developed 246 and 346cc ohc singles, called Forza and Vento.

DUCSON / *Spain late 1950s–early 1960s*

Small producer of 49cc two-stroke machines.

DÜMO / *Germany 1924–1925*

Sporting version of the 198cc Autinag, designed by Frankowski.

DUNELT / *England 1919–1956*

Equipped with double-diameter pistons, the first Dunelt two-strokes had single-cylinder engines with 499cc. A similar version with 248cc was built from the 1920s onwards. From 1929 the factory also fitted 346cc, 498cc and 598cc sv and ohv engines made by Sturmey-Archer, as well as a 246cc version with the Sturmey-Archer face-cam ohc engine. During the following years, the main range consisted of Villiers-engined machines up to 344cc and of sv and ohv models up to 498cc with engines made by Python (Rudge) and JAP. After a reorganization, the Birmingham factory moved in 1931 to Sheffield and discontinued the manufacture of motorcycles in 1935. They re-entered the trade in 1955 with a 49cc moped with its own ohv engine, but had not

246cc Dunelt (TS) 1924

much success. The greatest sporting success gained by Dunelt was winning the 1930 Maudes Trophy in the Isle of Man for the most meritorious performance of the year. Despite severe conditions, a 498cc Dunelt with an ohv engine covered 13,119 miles in 16 days at an average speed of 34·8 mph.

DUNKLEY / *England 1913*

Produced a variety of machines for a very few years with 199, 499, 746 and 988cc Precision engines, 342cc Peco two-strokes and also JAP-engined models from 293cc to 748cc.

DUNKLEY / *England 1957–1959*

Modern mopeds with own 61cc, 64cc and eventually 49cc ohv engines. These were of unit design. 'Whippet' was the trade name of these products.

DUNSTALL / *England 1964—1982*

Paul Dunstall became world famous for custom parts and for his Norton Dunstall Dominator twins, but was also a serious and successful race development engineer. In later years, Dunstall offered various customised bikes with big Japanese high performance engines, special frames etc, but these never had the huge success of his earlier products.

DURAND / *France 1920–1923*

Assembled motorcycles with Zurcher engines. Limited manufacture.

DURANDAL / *France 1925–1932*

Some models had pressed steel frames and most used JAP, Zurcher and Chaise proprietary engines from 246cc to 490cc. There was also a successful works racing machine with a 348cc KTT Velocette ohc engine.

DÜRKOPP / *Germany 1901–1959*

Pioneer of the German motorcycle industry. In 1905, they already produced single and V-twin machines and a four-in-line with aircooled cylinders. Also a leading bicycle and car producer — now a leading manufacturer of needle-

7 hp Dürkopp (sv V-twin) 1903

148cc Dürkopp (TS) 1952

bearings—Dürkopp stopped motorcycle production before WWI, built in the 1930s motorized bicycles and in 1949 resumed motorcycle manufacture with Sachs-engined 98cc and 123cc two-strokes. They also fitted Ilo engines of the same size and built after 1951 their own 147cc,

174cc and 198cc two-stroke engines designed by Goslau. A beautiful scooter, the 198cc Dürkopp Diana, came out in 1953 and was made until the famous factory stopped producing two-wheelers.

DUVAL / *Belgium 1950–1955*
Limited production of small 123cc two-stroke machines with engines supplied mainly by Royal Enfield.

DUX / *England 1904–1906*
Small assembler who used frames made by Rex at Coventry and engines supplied by Minerva, MMC, Sarolea and others. They were singles and V-twins.

DUZMO / *England 1919–1923*
A 496cc single-cylinder ohv machine designed by John Wallace and partly developed by the famous Bert le Vack, who was for a short period with Duzmo.

DWB / *Germany 1924–1926*
After Juhö closed down, Dorko Werke Bamberg took over manufacture of the 195cc sv machines and added in 1925 a 269cc two-stroke model to the range.

DYSON-MOTORETTE / *England 1920–1922*
Scooter-like lightweight with a 1·5 hp engine on the left side and the petrol tank above the rear wheel.

EADIE / *England 1898–1903*
Pioneer make, which first built three-wheelers and then motorcycles with engines made by De Dion, Minerva, MMC and other factories. Eadie was also closely connected with the foundation of the Royal Enfield factory.

EAGLE / *America 1910–1915*
Well-made Spake-engined 4 hp singles and 7 hp and 9 hp V-twins. According to the late Floyd Clymer, the Eagle was one of the best machines ever made in the USA.

EAGLE-TANDEM / *England 1903–1905*
Limited production of De Dion-engined machines, which were fitted with a chairlike seat.

EBE / *Sweden 1919–1930*
After manufacturing 173cc bicycle engines, EBE produced motorcycles with own 172cc ohv and 598cc sv engines.

EBER / *Germany 1924–1928*
Motorcycles of typical English design with 347cc and 497cc sv and ohv Blackburne, then also 348cc and 498cc ohv Kühne and ohc Küchen engines.

EBO / *England 1910–WWI*
Assembler who fitted Precision engines and also single and V-twin JAP engines.

EBS / *Germany 1924–1930*
Berlin-based manufacturer who fitted engines of own manufacture with 198, 246, 348, 398, 496cc and a V-twin with 796cc. After 1928 a Villiers-engined 198cc two-stroke was added. The factory produced also three-wheeled transport vehicles with motorcycle engines.

EBU-STAR / *Japan 1952–1955*
Interesting 248cc twin-cylinder ohv machine with a vertical and a horizontal cylinder.

198cc EBS (sv) 1924

246cc EBS (ohv) 1925

EBW / *Germany 1923–1924*
Assembled 139cc machine with engines made by Bekamo.

ECA / *Germany 1923–1924*
Simple 142cc two-stroke machines made in limited numbers.

ECEKA / *Germany 1924–1925*
Another small make which fitted 145cc and 173cc engines.

ECHO / *Japan late 1950s–early 1960s*
Producer of 123cc and 148cc two-stroke machines and the Pandra scooter.

ECKL / *Germany 1923–1926*
Hugo Eckl first produced bicycle attachment engines, afterwards also a 198cc single with its own ohv engine.

ECONOMIC / *England 1921–1923*
Unusual 165cc twin-cylinder two-stroke machines with friction drive of a design which came from the USA. The first models had the horizontally opposed twin fitted in orthodox fashion – in line. Afterwards it was transverse-mounted in a low duplex frame. Although its price was only £28.10s., it failed to make the grade.

ED / *Germany 1923–1925*
Equipped with low double-loop frames, the 139cc machines had flat single-cylinder Bekamo two-stroke pumping cylinder engines.

EDETA / *Spain 1951–1960*
Two-stroke machines with 147cc and 173cc engines.

EDMONTON / *England 1903–c1910*
Was a small assembler of motorcycles who fitted Minerva and Fafnir engines.

EDMUND / *England 1907—1924*
Made in Chester, the Edmund used Fafnir, MAG, JAP, Blackburne and Barr & Stroud proprietary engines. From about 1911, a 'spring frame' – actually an elaborate sub frame pivoting on leaf springs and isolating the saddle and footrests — was featured, though it is doubtful if it justified its complication.

EENHORN / *Holland 1905–1907*
Based at Rotterdam, Eenhorn (Unicorn) built

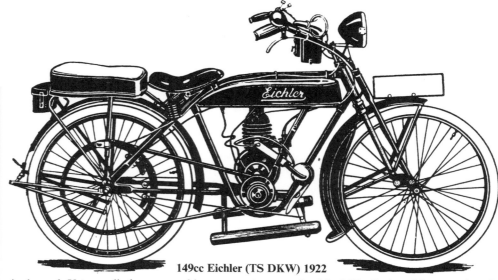
149cc Eichler (TS DKW) 1922

single and V-two-cylinder sv machines on a limited scale. Produced from 3 hp to 5·5 hp.

EGLI / *Switzerland 1968–*
Designed by Fritz W. Egli, the first machines had 996cc Vincent V-twin engines. The latest Egli products include his frames with 1047cc six-cylinder dohc Honda engines, and with 903 to 1100cc four-cylinder dohc Kawasaki motors. There is also a model with a modified turbo-engined Kawasaki version. Kawasaki and Honda also supply big 500 to 600cc single-cylinder ohc engines to Egli.

1047cc Egli (six-cylinder dohc engine) 1982

EGA / *Germany 1922–1926*
Made by the Gaggenau iron works, the EGA machines had own 246cc and 346cc three-port, deflector-type two-stroke engines.

EICHELSDÖRFER / *Germany 1929–1931*
Builder of 198cc machines with ohv engines made by JAP.

EICHLER / *Germany 1920–1925*
Well-known assembler of lightweight motorcycles with 119, 145 and 173cc DKW and 129cc to 149cc Bekamo two-stroke engines. Produced also DKW-designed 123cc Golem and 145cc Lomos scooters, then in Germany called Sessel-räder. Ernst Eichler, founder of the factory, left in the mid-1920s and built machines with pressed-steel frames. After less than a year he

returned to his old Berlin-based factory where he continued producing these red motorcycles.

EISENHAMMER / *Germany 1923–1926*
Two-stroke machines of heavy design with 206cc DKW and 225cc engines of own manufacture.

EISLER / *Czechoslovakia 1920–1926*
Agriculture-machine factory which produced not only 148cc two-stroke bicycle attachment engines, but also complete lightweight motorcycles with these power units.

ELAND / *The Netherlands 1955–1959*
Small assembler, who fitted 123cc to 158cc two-stroke engines, mainly supplied by Sachs, into own frames.

ELECT / *Italy 1920–1923*
Interesting design by Ladetto — later of Ladetto & Blatto fame — Ubertalli and Cavalchini. It was a horizontal twin with 492cc and three valves for each cylinder.

ELFA / *Germany 1926–1932*
Built during the years a variety of models with 73, 98, 123, 198, 298, 346 and 497cc proprietary engines made by DKW, Kühne, Küchen, Windhoff, Sachs, Bark and also JAP. Mofa production continued until 1940.

ELFE / *Germany 1923–1925*
Unorthodox frames with own 196cc three-port deflector-type engines built in small numbers.

ELF-KING / *England 1907–1909*
Equipped with hand-starters like cars, these machines had V-twin Minerva engines.

ELFSON / *England 1923–1925*
Well-designed machines with their own 294cc

three-port two-stroke power units. Another model had 170cc Norman ohv engines.

ELI / *England 1911–1912*
Accessory factory which produced motorcycles with 3·5 hp Precision engines.

ELIE HUIN / *France early 1950s–early 1960s*
The post-war Elie Huin machines had Ydral, AMC and other French proprietary engines from 123cc to 248cc.

ELIG / *Spain 1956–1959*
Small producer who used Hispano Villiers engines from 123cc to 198cc.

ELITE / *Germany 1903–1940*
Founded by Diamant, where motorcycles were built in 1903. Elite started car production in 1914 and the manufacture of a 1 hp engine for bicycles in 1923. Elite and Diamant joined forces in 1927 and produced Diamant motorcycles until 1928–1929, when Opel took over the factory for the manufacture of their own 498cc motorcycles with Duralumin frames. In 1932 these models were succeeded by similar machines called EO (Elite-Opel). These had 348cc and 498cc ohc engines made by Küchen, while the 'real' Opel motorcycles of that period had their own sv and ohv single cylinder power units. Few EOs were actually built.

ELLEHAM / *Denmark 1904–1909*
One of the few Danish producers. The design included an open frame, a larger front wheel and a 2·75 hp Peugeot engine.

ELMDON / *England 1915–1921*
Limited manufacture of 269cc two-strokes with Villiers engines.

ELRING / *Germany 1924–1925*
This was just another name for the 196cc Elfe two-strokes.

ELSINORE / *Japan 1973–1975*
This is not an independent make, but a Honda moto-cross version. It is made with 123cc and 248cc two-stroke high-efficiency engines. The smaller model has 24 bhp at 10,000 rpm, the bigger 33 bhp at 7500 rpm. Most Elsinores are exported to the USA.

ELSTAR / *England 1968–1971*
Produced mainly frames for competition machines, including moto-cross, grass track and speedway. Fitted Jawa, Bultaco and other mainly two-stroke engines. Production stopped when Ellis, the founder, was killed in a road accident.

ELSTER / *Germany 1924–1926*
A comparatively small factory which produced 197cc sv machines with engines of own design and manufacture.

ELSWICK / *England 1903–1920*
Well-known bicycle manufacturer who fitted into 348cc and 498cc single-cylinder motorcycles the proprietary engines made by Precision.

ELVE / *Belgium 1958–early 1960s*
Moped producer who fitted 49cc Sachs engines.

EM / *Austria 1928–1930*
Produced one model only in limited numbers. It was a 497cc single-cylinder ohv machine with the MAG double-port engine.

497cc EM (ohv MAG) 1929

EMA / *Germany 1922–1926*
Designed by Eduard Molitor, these low-built machines had 145cc DKW engines with horizontal cylinder.

206cc EMA (TS DKW) 1925

EMBLEM / *America 1909–1925*
Big 996cc V-twin machines of sound design, which competed with success in sporting events.

EMC / *England 1947–1952*
The first machines had their own 348cc double-piston two-stroke engines. Afterwards the Ehrlich Motor Company fitted 123cc and 248cc Puch engines. A 123cc JAP-engined two-stroke exhibited at Earls Court in 1952 never went into quantity production. Joe Ehrlich built from 1960 to 1964 the 124cc De Havilland rotary disc two-stroke racing machines, which were ridden in races by such famous men as Mike Hailwood, Derek Minter, Phil Read, Rex Avery and Paddy Driver.

EMH / *Germany 1927–1929*
Limited manufacture of 348cc and 498cc machines with open frames and Küchen ohc engines.

EMMAG / *Hungary 1924–1927*
Built unorthodox watercooled 670cc two-stroke twins and also aircooled 495cc two-stroke singles. Production was on a limited scale.

196cc Elster (sv) 1925

340cc EMW (ohv shaft-drive) 1953

EMURO / *Japan 1953–late 1950s*
Produced two-stroke machines with own engines from 98cc to 248cc.

EMW / *East Germany 1945–1956*
Produced in the former Dixi-BMW car and motorcycle factory at Eisenach a 348cc single-cylinder ohv machine with shaft drive and pressed steel frame which was similar to a 1934 BMW model.

EMWE / *Germany 1924–1925*
Using a welded box frame, EMWE fitted a 293cc two-stroke engine of their own design.

ENAG / *Germany 1924–1925*
The Theo Steininger-designed two-stroke machines had 248cc and 348cc capacity, watercooled barrels and aircooled cylinder heads.

ENDRICK / *England 1911–1915*
Built different machines with Fafnir, Peugeot and JAP engines, until the Olton (Birmingham) factory concentrated on models with 346cc Peco two-stroke and 496cc Precision sv engines.

ENDURANCE / *England 1909–1924*
Among the C. B. Harrison-designed models were those with 269cc Villiers engines and versions with their own 259cc and 297cc two-stroke three-port motors.

ENERGETTE / *England 1907–1911*
Designed by the famous J. L. Norton — founder of the Norton factory — the Energette had a British-built Moto-Rêve engine of 274cc. It was a V-twin with 50mm bore and 70mm stroke.

ENFIELD / *India 1970—*
Motor cycles from a time-warp! Royal Enfield of Redditch sold their old tooling to Enfield India, who first made small two strokes, then the 346cc ohv Bullet, and now the 493cc ohv model as well. Sensibly modernised and developed, these handsome and nicely made 'Classics' are exported to Britain and Europe.

ENGEE / *Germany 1925*
Single-cylinder ohv machines with Kühne proprietary power units. Apparently only a 348cc model was marketed.

EO / *Germany 1930–1931*
Mentioned already under Elite, the EO had an Opel-like frame made from Duralumin and 348cc and 498cc ohc Küchen engines. Designer of the frame was Ernst Neumann-Neander.

EOLE / *Belgium c1900*
Built in the pioneer period, the Eole had Kelecom and Fafnir engines.

EPA / *Germany 1924–1925*
Small assembler, who fitted 293cc JAP sv engines into own frames.

ERCOLI-CAVALLONE / *Italy 1922–1923*
One of the few makes in the world which produced 496cc V-twin machines with two-stroke engines. Others were the British Stanger and WAG. None had much success and soon all disappeared from the market.

ERIE / *America 1905–1911*
The Hammondsport factory fitted Minerva, Spake and Curtiss engines and was commercially connected with the Glenn Curtiss factory.

ERIOL / *France 1932–1939*
Lightweight motorcycles with 98cc two-stroke engines.

ERKA / *Germany 1924–1925*
Simple 269cc two-stroke machines made by a small factory.

ERKÖ / *Germany 1922–1924*
Another small producer of lightweights with 145cc DKW motors.

ERMAG / *Germany 1923–1930*
Good machines designed by ex-Ziro designer Albert Roder. The first 246cc Ermag had a

497cc EO (ohc Küchen Prototype) 1930

498cc Ermag (sv) 1927

246cc Ermag (ohv) 1927

Dunelt-like double diameter piston and a rotary inlet valve for the single-cylinder two-stroke engine. From 1925 Ermag produced a fast 246cc ohv machine and sv singles with 497cc and 547cc capacity. Successful Ermag riders: Hans Hieronymus, Karl Perl, Paul Bittorf. Roder was with Victoria in the 1930s and before the war joined the NSU works at Neckarsulm.

ERNST EICHLER / *Germany 1924–1925*
Originally the founder of the Berlin-based Eichler motorcycle factory, Ernst Eichler left the works after differences and set up a new factory. There he created some interesting 142cc two-stroke and 172cc two and four-stroke sv machines with frames made from pressed steel. After a comparatively short period he returned.

ERNST-MAG / *Germany 1926–1930*
The first machines had 348cc and 498cc ohc engines made by Küchen, but from 1928 onwards the Silesian factory relied exclusively on

Swiss MAG engines of 348, 498, 598, 746 and 996cc capacity. Among them were fast 348cc ohv double-port singles and 498cc and 598cc ohv V-twins. Factory riders even had some 498cc ohc V-twins. These included Landolph Rhode, Edgar Kittner and Orlindo Geissler.

ERR-ZETT / *Austria 1938*
Lightweights with 98cc Sachs and Ilo engines.

As result of political circumstances at that period in Austria, only few of these machines were actually built.

ESCHAG / *Germany 1923–1925*
Simple 298cc two-stroke machines with belt drive to the rear wheel.

ESCH-REKORD / *Germany 1927–1930*
Designed and built by racing motorcyclist Adolf Esch, these racing machines used 248cc, 348cc and 498cc engines made by Blackburne, MAG and JAP. Among the riders were Joseph Wenzel and Wilhelm Etzbach. The design resembled that of leading English machines.

ESCOL / *Belgium 1925–1938*
Built on English lines in limited numbers, Escol used Villiers engines from 147cc to 247cc. Larger models had 248cc to 596cc JAP and Python engines. The last Escol had its own 348cc two-stroke engine.

ESO / *Czechoslovakia 1949–1962*
Now part of the Jawa factory (and sold with the Jawa trade mark), Eso was founded by ex-racing rider Jaroslav Simandl for the purpose of producing 498cc speedway ohv single-cylinder engines. Afterwards they built at the Divišov factory not only complete speedway machines but also models with modified 348cc and 498cc engines for road races and moto-cross events. Now they produce track engines and ice-racing versions. The latest Jawa (née Eso) speedway engines and machines have four-valve cylinder heads and are very successful.

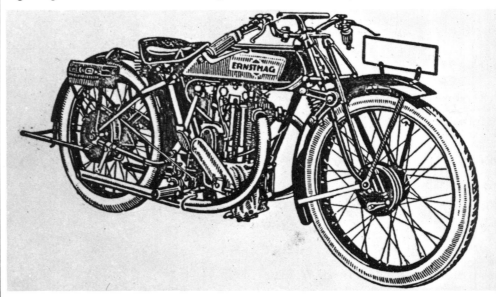

347cc Ernst-MAG (ohv MAG) 1927

198cc Europa (TS Schliha) 1933

ETA / *England 1921*
Interesting 870cc three-cylinder machine with a radial engine, unit-design and shaft drive. The Eta never went into quantity production.

ETOILE / *France 1933–1939*
Aubier-Dunne-engined two-strokes from 98cc to 198cc.

EUROPA / *Germany 1931–1933*
Officially made at Munich with 98cc and 146cc Villiers engines as well as with Berlin-built 147cc and 198cc Schliha two-strokes.

EVANS / *America 1919–1924*
One of the finest American lightweights ever built, the Evans had a 119cc two-stroke engine and also gained popularity in Germany. The Berlin-based Stock factory, then part of the Kuhn industrial empire, eventually took the Evans licence and built these machines in improved form as the first models made by Stock.

EVANS-PONDORF / *Germany 1924–1925*
Built also the 119cc Evans, but ran into licence problems with Stock and tried to enter the market with a beautiful 496cc single of advanced design, which included foot gear change. Unfortunately lack of money prevented quantity production of this Pondorf design.

119cc Evans (TS) 1922

EVART-HALL / *England 1903–1905*
The first machines had single-cylinder engines fitted into strengthened bicycle frames and mounted near-horizontally above the pedalling gear. The 2·5 hp engines had sight-feed lubrication, spray or surface carburetters and back-pedalling hub brakes. From 1904 onwards, Evart-Hall produced also the aircooled in-line four-cylinder 385cc machine designed by Binks.

EVEREST / *Germany 1925–1926*
Offered by a Berlin-based company, the Everest was actually built by the G. A. Rempp factory at Münster. It was a heavy 496cc single with its own ohv engine.

EVO / *Germany 1923–1925*
Designed by well-known motorcycle journalist Eduard Voigt, 146cc Evo machines had Ilo as well as their own two-stroke engines.

EVYCSA / *Spain c1956*
Well-designed 173cc machines with four-speed gearboxes made in limited numbers.

EWABRA / *Germany 1921–1924*
Heavy 550cc single-cylinder sv machines, designed and built by Ewald Brackelsberg, a cousin of the late Bugatti driver Karl Brackelsberg.

EXCELSIOR / *England 1896—1964*

Baylis-Thomas of Coventry used De Dion, MMC and Minerva engines as early as 1900 and Harry Martin broke records at Canning Town cycle track on an Excelsior in 1903. A pause followed until 1910, when motor cycle production resumed under W H Carson, an advocate of 'big singles'. Pre

war, an 850cc S.V. single was offered. In 1920 there was a tie up with the Walker family of Tyseley, Birmingham, and Eric Walker took over the company's direction. In the 1920s, Villiers, JAP and Blackburne engines were used, and Excelsior-JAPs gained a reputation in racing. In 1933 a special Blackburne engine with four radial valves and twin carburettors was used, Syd Gleave winning the Lightweight TT with it on its first appearance. Its subsequent record was disappointing.

In 1934 the Excelsior Manxman was produced,

with a single ohc engine of 250cc and 350cc (and later 500cc); it was also sold in genuine racing form. For 1936, Excelsior made the 'Manxman' engines in their own factory, and, in 1937 and 1938, produced ohc four valve racer engines (under Rudge patents) in 250cc and 350cc for works riders Tyrell Smith, Ginger Wood and occasionally Charlie Manders. Development was in the hands of Australian Alan Bruce. The four valve engines were never sold to the public and for 1938 the factory reverted to two valves. Excelsior never won a TT with the Manxman (though they won several Grand Prix), but were second in 1937 and 1938.

248cc Excelsior (ohc 'Manxman') 1936 GB

Dennis Parkinson won the Manx Grand Prix in 1936, 1937 and 1938, on the last occasion with a rear sprung machine.

Excelsior built the war time 'Welbike' with 98cc Villiers engine for airborne dropping for the army. Post war, this — with a 98cc Excelsior engine — became the Brockhouse Corgi scooter. Excelsior now made their own 98cc, 125cc and twin 250cc engines — all two strokes, and their Talisman twins, 250cc then 330cc became highly popular. Excelsior lightweights, with their own engines and later with Villiers units, sold well at home and in export, but with the death of the energetic Eric Walker, the

490cc Excelsior (ohv JAP) 1930 GB

company lost its driving force. Over a period of time production and sales fell away, until in the end only the 'Universal' model was being offered as a 'do it yourself' kit. The Walker brothers, Eric Walker's sons, eventually sold the factory to accessory makers and seat belt pioneers Britax.

EXCELSIOR / Germany 1923–1924

This company was evidently not considered a problem for the older German Excelsior factory at Brandenburg, for they apparently never fought the use of the Excelsior trade mark. The short-lived Munich firm built only a simple 245cc two-stroke machine.

EXCELSIOR / Germany 1901–1939

This was originally a bicycle factory at Brandenburg, now in East Germany. After using Minerva, Zedel and Fafnir engines, during the 1920s the factory used English 198cc, 298cc and 346cc sv and ohv JAP engines too. Their motorcycles, of typical English design, were not unsimilar to English Excelsiors, although there was no direct connection between Excelsior-Birmingham and

192cc Excelsior (TS Bark) 1936 D

Excelsior-Brandenburg. Never as famous as the English make, the German factory fitted in the 1930s 198cc two-stroke and 196cc to 496cc sv engines made by Bark of Dresden, and while Walker built successful racing machines, Conrad & Patz — owners of the German factory — never showed any interest in sporting events.

EXCELSIOR / America 1908–1931

This was the biggest factory producing Excelsior motorcycles. It was the Excelsior Supply & Mfg. Co at Chicago, part of the still-existing Schwinn bicycle empire. The range consisted of 269cc

269cc Excelsior (TS) 1914 USA

992cc Excelsior (ioe V-twin) 1922 USA

two-strokes built along the lines of the English Triumph Baby and of 499cc singles and 746cc to 996cc V-twins with their own ioe engines. Only a few 499cc and 996cc works racing models had ohc power units. There was a problem when the Chicago-based factory sold machines to England. These had the name American-X and in the mid-1920s all V-twins built by Schwinn were renamed Super-X. In addition, the factory produced since 1919 the famous Bill Henderson-designed four-in-line machines, of which the last version had 1301cc with ioe valves, separate cylinder barrels and a common cylinder head. Super-X and Henderson had next to Indian and Harley-Davidson the largest motorcycle production in the USA when Ignaz Schwinn decided in 1931 to stop manufacture of motorcycles.

EXPRESS / Germany 1903–late 1950s

Produced Fafnir-engined motorcycles in the early years of motorcycling. Resumed manufacture of mofas in the 1930s with 74cc and 98cc two-stroke engines and re-entered the market in 1949 with two-stroke motorcycles up to 248cc. An old bicycle factory, Express also supplied mofas and mopeds again. These now had 47cc engines. Experiments in the mid-1950s with the Küchen-designed 248cc twin-cylinder ohe engine proved not very successful. In 1957 Express became part of the then newly-founded Zweirad-Union at Nuremberg, together with Victoria and DKW, but the name Express was soon dropped.

247cc Express (TS ILO 'Radex') 1952

EYSINK/*The Netherlands 1899–1956*
Leading Dutch motorcycle factory. Fitted first Minerva, Fafnir and other engines into own frames, built in 1905 vertical twins with Kindermann-designed Bercley engines and also entered car production. The most famous pre-1914 models were the 365cc and 425cc singles, used also by the Dutch forces during the war. There were also 366cc and 409cc singles and 774cc V-twins with own engines. During the early 1920s, a flat twin came into being. It had 702cc and its engine was unsimilar to the British Raleigh of that period. The first Villiers-engined two-strokes were built in 1926. Eysink built 147cc, 172cc and 198cc versions. The Dutch factory was also closely connected with foreign factories including New Hudson and Sunbeam in England and Dollar in France, which supplied certain parts to the Dutch. They also fitted the English Rudge-built 348cc and 498cc four-valve Python ohv engines and some JAP engines, including racing versions. In the mid-1930s bread-and-butter versions with Sachs and Ilo two-stroke engines up to 198cc came into production at the Amersfoort factory, then headed by Dick Eysink. After 1945 most Eysink machines had Villiers engines. During the late 1940s and early 1950s, very fast 172cc machines were developed.

123cc Eysink (TS Villiers) 1939

F

FABULA/*Germany 1922–1924*
Designed by ex-Dürkopp designer Nikolaus Henzel, the Fabula was of very advanced design. It had its own 246cc unit-design two-stroke

246cc Fabula (TS shaft-drive) 1923

deflector-type engine and shaft drive to the rear wheel. Many parts of it were made for Fabula by the superbly equipped Dürkopp factory at Bielefeld.

492cc Fadag (ohv) 1926

FADAG/*Germany 1921–1925*
Made by a car factory, Fadag's first product in the sphere of two-wheelers was a 118cc bicycle attachment engine. Motorcycles, built from 1923 onward, had 'own' 497cc single cylinder sv and ohv engines which—according to unconfirmed sources—were supplied by Sarolea of Belgium to the Düsseldorf-based factory.

FAFNIR/*Germany 1900–1914*
Pioneer producer of proprietary engines and from 1903 onward of complete motorcycles, Fafnir supplied in the early years most German-made motorcycle power units. The Aachen-based factory had the Werner brothers licence for the manufacture of proprietary engines and produced many versions up to 8 hp V-twins.

FAGAN/*Ireland 1935–1937*
Only one model, a Villiers-engined 123cc single, was made by the Irish factory.

FAGARD/*Germany 1923–1925*
Limited production of 145cc two-stroke machines with DKW engines, also known as FG.

FAGGI / *Italy 1950–1953*
Lightweight machines with Villiers engines from 123cc to 147cc. Good design, small production.

FAINI / *Italy 1923–1927*
Manufacturer of 108cc bicycle engines and of 198cc motorcycles with own sv engines.

FAIRFIELD / *England 1914–1915*
Only one model, a 269cc two-stroke, was built by this Warrington factory. WWI prevented a large output.

FAKA / *Germany 1952–1957*
A scooter with 8 inch and later 10 inch wheels and Ilo engines of 147cc, 174cc and 197cc capacity.

FALCO / *Italy 1950–1953*
Built at Vercelli, the Falco was powered by German 98cc and 147cc Sachs engines.

FALKE / *Germany 1923–1925*
Assembled machines with 142cc Grade and 145cc DKW three-port, deflector-type two-stroke engines.

FALTER / *Germany 1952–*
Moped and mofa producer, whose products were also known as Stoewer Greif. The still-existing Bielefeld-based factory used mainly 49cc engines.

FAM / *Italy 1951–1969*
Founded by Giovanni Benelli — one of the five brothers of Benelli motorcycle fame of Pesaro — the FAM produced 115cc singles and 195cc flat-twins which had the B trade mark. The egg-shaped engines were of modern design.

FAMA / *Germany 1923–1925*
Limited manufacture of 190cc ohv and 420cc sv single-cylinder machines with own engines.

FAMO / *Germany 1923–1926*
Triangular frames and 127cc two-stroke three-port engines formed the basis of all Famo models.

127cc Famo (TS) 1925

49cc TS Fantic GT Super, 1976

123cc TS Fantic Caballero 125 RC, 1976

79cc Fantic (TS cross comp. model) 1982

FANTIC / *Italy 1968–*
Sporting 49cc and 124cc two-strokes built with an eye on the American market. Produces many models, including choppers, trials and moto-cross versions. Some belong to the Caballero range with 124cc 21 bhp at 9500 rpm engines and six-speed gearboxes, while moto-cross versions have 26 bhp at 10,000 rpm. Famous for the trial models of 79, 124, 157 and 212cc two-strokes.

FAR / *Austria 1924–1927*
Assembled machines with 346cc and 490cc single-cylinder sv and ohv JAP engines. The name stood for Franz and Anton Rumpler.

FARNELL / *England c1901*
Long forgotten make which had 2·75 hp Minerva engines fitted into bicycle frames.

FAVOR / *France 1919–1959*
Was a well-known make in France. Built two-strokes from 98cc to 248cc and JAP-engined sv and ohv models with 346cc single-cylinder power units. After the war the Favor range included Aubier-Dunne-engined two-strokes and AMC-engined ohv singles up to 248cc.

FAVORIT / *Germany 1933–1938*
The first machines had 996cc V-twin JAP engines, afterwards the small manufacturer concentrated on 98cc and 123cc lightweights with Sachs engines. Favorit's main product was sidecars.

FB / *Germany 1923–1925*
The first machines were 269cc two-strokes, afterwards JAP and Blackburne-engined 348cc and 498cc sv and ohv models came into being. Designed by Friedrich Benz, these machines were also known with the Meteor transfer on the petrol tank.

FB / *England 1913–1922*
Fowler and Bingham built proprietary two-stroke engines of 206cc, 269cc and 411cc and also complete motorcycles.

F.B. MONDIAL / *Italy 1948–1979*
Fratelli Boselli — the Boselli brothers — built industrial three-wheelers until 1944. Post war, Count Giuseppe Bosselli decided to advertise by racing in the new 125cc class and the 125cc dohc Mondial, designed by Alfonso Drusiani, swept all before it in 1948 and 1949. In 1949 Nello Pagani was world

champion, in 1950, Bruno Ruffo and in 1951 Carlo Ubbiali. Cromie McCandless won the first 125cc TT for Mondial in 1951. 1950 saw the debut of Mondial's 125cc push-rod ohv road machines. Later production ranged from 50cc to 250cc two-strokes and four strokes. Mondial were always interested in racing and in 1957 Tarquinio Provini won the 125cc and Cecil Sandford the 250cc world titles. After 1960 Mondial raced two strokes designed by Francesco Villa, though not very successfully. Thereafter, Mondial's fortunes declined, they became just another Italian company and late models even had Sachs engines.

FBM / *Italy 1950–1955*
Interesting design with partly pressed steel frames and the flat single-cylinder engines mounted directly on the swinging arm of the rear suspension. The range included 48cc and 74cc two-strokes and ohv engines with 158cc and 198cc capacity.

269cc Federal (TS Villiers) 1921

FECHTEL / *Germany 1924–1926*
Small assembler who fitted Hansa-built 198cc ohv engines into their own frames.

FEDERATION / *England 1919–1937*
The Co-op machine, built at Birmingham, was also known with the Federal trade mark. Most models had the 269cc Villiers engine, later ones 147cc Villiers and 246cc ohv JAP engines. The price for the smaller model in 1936 was £25, for the bigger £44.

FEE / *England 1905–1908*
The Barter-designed sv flat twins had 198cc, 346cc and 676cc engines. Also known as the Fairy, the Fee was really the forerunner of the Douglas machines.

FEILBACH LIMITED / *America 1912–1915*
Like the Harley-Davidson, the Feilbach Limited was built at Milwaukee, Wisconsin, but unfortunately for a short period only. The range consisted of 548cc singles and 990cc to 1130cc V-twins with their own ioe engines. Most models could be obtained with either chain or shaft drive.

FEMINIA / *France 1933–1936*
Assembled lightweights with 98cc and 123cc Aubier-Dunne and Stainless two-stroke engines.

FERBEDO / *Germany 1954*
Very simple but unsuccessful mini-scooter with 49cc Zündapp engines.

FERRARI / *Italy 1951–1954*
A big name, but a small factory. There was no connection with Enzo Ferrari and his cars. Still, Ferrari motorcycles were of sound design and the range included two-stroke and ohv machines from 123cc to 248cc. The last model was a beautiful 173cc vertical-twin ohc machine.

FERRARIS / *Italy 1903*
Short-lived make which had 2 hp Peugeot engines in bicycle frames.

FERT / *Italy 1926–1929*
Calamidas Fert machines had no connection with the then well-known Italian plug of the same name. The motorcycles used 173cc ohv engines of Fert's own design and manufacture. Ridden by Passera and Aldi in races, they were not successful.

FEW-PARAMOUNT / *England 1920–1927*
Waller's long wheelbase design with two bucket seats and a fully enclosed engine was not the dream of many customers. Offered with 498cc JAP and Blackburne as well as with 996cc V-twin JAP engines, only few of these unorthodox machines were actually built.

490cc FEW-Paramount (sv JAP) 1927

FEX / *Germany 1923–1924*
Fitted DKW and Bekamo engines, after his own 170cc two-stroke proved to be a technical failure.

FG / *Germany 1923–1925*
Identical with Fagard.

FHG / *Germany 1927–1929*
Offered by the German AJS importer Pleus & Co., the FHG was probably a French Grimpeur 173cc two-stroke built to the Pleus specification.

FIAM / *Italy 1923–1925*
A 110cc bicycle attachment engine designed by Lelio Antonioli and built in limited numbers.

FIAMC / *Germany 1951–1953*
Producer of 123cc two-stroke motorcycles and of scooters with identical engines.

1196cc Feilbach (ioe V-twin) 1914

FIDUCIA/*Switzerland 1902–1905*
Made by the Weber foundry at Zürich-Uster, these machines had own 450cc single-cylinder engines.

FIFI/*Germany 1923–1924*
Another name for the 145cc and 173cc Eichler motorcycles.

FIGINI/*Italy 1898–1910*
Luigi Figini together with Lazzati were pioneers in the motorcycle field. They produced their first machine in 1899 and entered commercial manufacture of motorcycles in 1902.

FINZI/*Italy 1923–1925*
Built actually at the Maxima factory, the Finzi was a machine of advanced design with the 598cc ohv V-twin unit-design engine transverse-mounted. It had a saddle sprung by leaf springs and a fully enclosed rear chain. Despite the modern conception, the Finzi was not a commercial success.

FIORELLI/*Italy 1951–1968*
Assembled machines with 123cc and 173cc Ilo engines and concentrated afterwards on the production of components for other factories and on bicycles and mopeds.

FIT/*Italy 1950–1954*
Another assembler, who fitted Ilo engines of 123cc and 147cc into own frames.

FIX/*Germany 1922–1926*
A branch of the Hansa-Lloyd car factory, Fix produced two-strokes with own 3 hp engines.

FKS/*Germany 1921–1926*
Produced a range of machines with 149cc two-stroke engines. These were mounted originally above the front wheel, afterwards above the pedalling gear. Another model was a 298cc flat-twin two-stroke, not unsimilar to the KC.

FLANDERS/*America 1911–1914*
Made by the Michigan car factory of the same name, the Flanders was a 499cc sv single with the exhaust valve on the rear side of the cylinder.

496cc Finzi (ohv transverse V-twin) 1924

298cc FKS (TS flat-twin) 1923

497cc Flanders (sv) 1913

135

FLANDRIA / *Belgium late 1950s–*
Well-known manufacturer of bicycles, mofas, mopeds and lightweight machines with 49cc two-stroke engines. Showed in 1976 a very sporting motorcycle with a six-speed gearbox and 17 inch alloy wheels. All engines are made by the A. Claeys-Flandria N.V. at Zedelgem.

FLINK / *Germany 1920–1922*
Built by a company which is now part of BMW at Munich, the Flink was a 148cc two-stroke machine with a Kurier deflector-type proprietary engine. Not a very successful design.

FLM / *England 1951–1953*
Designed by former P&M Panther designer Frank Leach, the little lightweight had 123cc

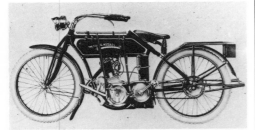

490cc Flying Merkel (sv single) 1917

119cc Flottweg (TS) 1922

Villiers and JAP two-stroke engines and also 198cc Villiers power units.

FLOTTWEG / *Germany 1921–1937*
The first products were good 119cc bicycle attachment engines over the front wheel. They were followed by 183cc and 246cc ohv machines with their own engines. JAP-built 198cc and 346cc ohv engines powered Flatwegg machines from 1928 to 1931. After an interruption, new models again with their own 198cc ohv engines came into being but did not make headlines. The factory—not far from BMW at Munich—was eventually sold to that maker.

FLUX / *Germany 1923–1924*
Assembled motorcycles in limited numbers with 198cc two-stroke engines.

FLYING MERKEL / *America 1909–1915*
The yellow Merkels were machines of modern and advanced design. The Middletown factory built 545cc singles and 980cc ioe V-twins and in 1913 built models which had not only two-speed gearboxes, but spring frames and some electric starters.

FM / *Italy 1925–1927*
Very unorthodox frame, designed by the Molteni brothers. (Fratelli Molteni means Molteni Brothers in Italian.) The frame was made from cast alu-alloy and allowed a low saddle position; it was also nice looking. Engines fitted were the 346cc MAG single and afterwards the 346cc ohv Bradshaw with oilcooling.

FMT / *Italy 1922–1930*
Small 124cc two-strokes built in limited numbers by Fratelli Mattarollo of Torino.

FN / *Belgium 1901–1957*
Pioneer in the motorcycle field and for many years the leading make in Belgium. Became famous for using shaft drive from 1903 to 1923, for great successes in races and long distance events and after 1945 in moto-cross. Great

designers, including Paul Kelecom, Van Hout, Dougal Marchant, George-William Patchett and others have been connected with this big factory of arms, motorcycles and cars. There were also famous racing men like Kicken, Flintermann, Lovinfosse, Lempereur, Sbaiz, De Grady, Milhoux, Charlier, Demuiter, Noir, Van Gent, Renier, S. 'Ginger' Wood, Handley Mellors, Abarth and others, who—like Mingels, Leloup and R. Beaten in moto-cross—won many races. The first FN machines had 225cc and 286cc

283cc FN (sv shaft-drive) 1921

748cc FN (sv four-cylinder shaft-drive) 1922

single-cylinder and 496cc and 748cc four-cylinder in-line engines. All models from 1924 onwards had chain-drive to the rear-wheel, as shaft drive production was then too expensive. Afterwards mainly 348cc and 498cc sv and ohv models were built. All had unit-design engines. There were also 596cc ohv versions, and in 1937 a BMW-like 992cc four-cylinder machine with a tranverse-mounted, aircooled sv engine was made for the Army. Already in 1931 there was a 198cc Villiers-

980cc Flying Merkel (sv twin) 1913

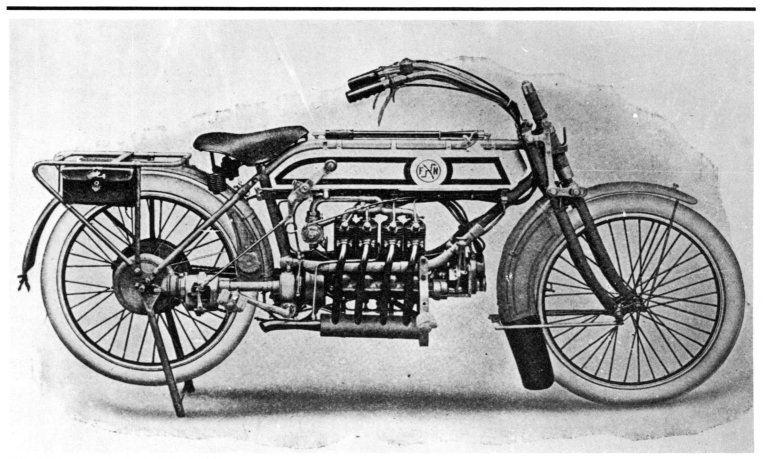

493cc FN (sv four-cylinder shaft-drive) 1908

498cc FN (ohv 'Super-Sport') 1936

engined two-stroke in the FN range and when Marchant joined the Belgian factory in 1930, he created very fast 348cc and 498cc racing ohc singles. Van Hout developed these during the following years and designed in 1937 a supercharged 498cc vertical twin-cylinder ohc racing machine, which was ridden in 1938 by 'Ginger' Wood. The war prevented more successes by this fast machine. After the war, FN built a range of sv and ohv unit-design models with 249cc, 344cc, 444cc and 498cc and also two-strokes from 49cc to 248cc, mainly with their own Ilo engines. With mainly Belgian riders, they competed successfully with 498cc machines in moto-cross events, but withdrew in the mid-1950s. FN car production stopped before WWII.

446cc FN (ohv) 1954

FOCESI / *Italy 1952–1956*
Well-designed 49cc two-stroke machines with the flat unit-design engine mounted directly on the swinging arm of the rear wheel. The machines became known under the Gloria trade mark.

FOCHJ / *Italy 1954–1957*
Assembler who used German NSU two and four-stroke engines from 49cc to 246cc. They included the famous Max single-cam engine.

FOLLIS / *France 1903–1960*
Fitted in pre-1939 days different proprietary engines made by JAP, Python and Blackburne; after 1945 machines from 124cc to 248cc with Ydral two-stroke and AMC ohv engines. The factory was at Lyon.

FONGRI / *Italy 1919–1925*
Designed by Eugenio Grignani, Fongri — the name came from Fontana and Fratelli Grignani — concentrated on machines with sv opposing twins having capacities of 579cc, 575cc and 499cc.

FORCE / *Austria 1925–1926*
Small producer of 346cc single-cylinder, two-stroke machines with their own three-port, deflector-type engines.

349cc Force (TS) 1925

FORELLE / *Germany 1955–1958*
Bicycle factory, which built 49cc mopeds with Sachs and Ilo engines.

FORSTER / *Switzerland 1921–1932*
Producer of two-stroke machines with 140cc, 198cc and 246cc. Designer was Karl Kirschbaum.

FORTONIA / *Germany 1924–1925*
Motorcycles with 2·5 hp and 3·8 hp single-cylinder engines.

FORTUNA / *Germany 1921–1928*
Two-strokes with 247cc and 297cc three-port engines and big outside flywheels.

FORWARD / *England 1909–1915*
Produced by a leading bicycle, accessory and parts manufacturer, the Forward was really a comparatively backward motorcycle design with a strengthened bicycle frame and its own V-twin engines of 339cc and 479cc.

FP / *Hungary 1924–1925*
Single-cylinder machines with own 346cc sv engines.

FRANCE / *France 1931–1935*
Two-stroke machines with own engines from 98cc to 245cc. The frames were of simple design.

FRANCIS-BARNETT / *England 1919–1964*
The first models had 293cc and 346cc sv JAP engines. From 1924 onwards, the Coventry-based factory concentrated on screwed triangular

frames, in which Villiers engines from 147cc to 344cc and JAP sv engines of 174cc and 346cc

Francis-Barnett

were fitted. Among them also — from 1927 onwards — the vertical-twin two-stroke of 344cc, made by Villiers. During the 1930s they built Villiers-engined machines from 148cc to 248cc with the exception of the Stag, which had a Blackburne-built 248cc ohv engine with entirely enclosed valve mechanism and crossed push-rods. Once more Villiers-engined two-strokes formed the backbone of the Francis-Barnett programme after the war; they were 98cc to 248cc. In the late 1950s AMC (Associated Motor Cycles Ltd.) took over the Coventry factory and built Piatti-designed 248cc two-stroke engines. It was not a successful venture and soon they

346cc Francis-Barnett (sv JAP) 1927

246cc Francis-Barnett (TS Villiers 'Cruiser') 1936

248cc Francis-Barnett (TS Model M/C 82) 1960

reverted to Villiers power units. They also moved FB production to the James Works at Birmingham, another factory which belonged to AMC Ltd. Afterwards both makes ceased to exist.

FRANCHI / *Italy 1950–late 1950s*
Assembler, who fitted Sachs two-stroke engines of 98, 123, 147 and 174cc and also called his machines Franchi-Sachs.

FRANKONIA / *Germany 1923–1925*
Another assembled machine. Used 145cc DKW engines with horizontal cylinders.

FRANZANI / *Germany 1923–1932*
Small factory. First used their own 283cc two-stroke engines, afterwards 198cc to 490cc JAP engines and the German 497cc Küchen ohc proprietary power unit.

FRECO / *Germany 1923–1925*
Fitted 145cc and 173cc DKW two-strokes, 197cc Runge sv engines and for racing purposes 173cc and 247cc ohv Blackburne engines. Production was on a limited scale.

FREITAL / *Germany 1925–1926*
For commercial reasons, the DKW factory at Zschopau used this name for a short period on 173cc machines.

FREJUS / *Italy 1960–1968*
Turin-built machines, including mofas, mopeds etc, from 48cc to 198cc.

FRERA / *Italy 1906–1956*
For many years a leading make. Built 320cc and 570cc singles and 795cc V-twins, afterwards also a big 1140cc sv V-twin. During the 1920s, Frera machines had a very Sunbeam-like black and gold appearance and were designed on English

123cc Frera (TS) 1958

lines. A 269cc two-stroke was made for a short period, but 346cc and 496cc sv and ohv singles formed the main range in the period between the wars. Leading riders: Felice Macchi, Virginio Fieschi, Mario Acerboni, Edoardo Self, Mario Ventura, F. J. Meyer. Reorganisation after 1945 resulted in 73cc and 124cc two-strokes and a 147cc ohv machine. The founder, Corrado Frera, died before the last war.

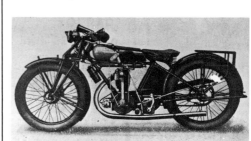

346cc Freyler (ohc sleeve-valve engine) 1929

FREYLER / *Austria 1928–1929*
This was a 'valveless' ohc machine of 348cc capacity. It used a rotary valve—driven by a vertical shaft—in the cylinder head. The interesting design by Adalbert Freyler was not fully developed when the Vienna-based factory closed.

FREYER & MILLER/ *America c1902*
Had the engine behind the saddle and the petrol
tank was mounted above the rear wheel. The
Freyer & Miller was one of the first machines
using a rotation magneto.

FRIMA/*Germany 1923–1924*
Made by Friedrich Marquardt of Friedburg, the
Frima had an own 2·5 hp two-stroke engine.

FRIMO/*Germany 1923–1925*
Made by the Vis AG., producer of Vis-Simplex
and Vis-Duplex machines, the Frimo was a conventional 246cc two-stroke machine with a three
port engine.

FRISCHAUF/*Germany 1928–1933*
Assembled 198cc sv singles with JAP and Black-
burne engines and 497cc ohc machines with the
Küchen proprietary engine.

FRISONI/*Italy 1951–1957*
Produced 123cc Villiers-engined two-strokes
and 160cc scooters in limited numbers.

FUBO/*Germany 1923–1925*
Two-strokes of 170cc and 269cc with their own
engines, but also supplied 247cc and 347cc
models with sv and ohv Blackburne engines.

FUCHS/*Italy 1953–1957*
Produced bicycle engines and 124cc to 159cc
motorcycles with two-stroke and ohv engines.

FUJI/*Japan early 1950s–early 1960s*
Producer of the Gasuden scooter and of two-
stroke machines from 49cc to 249cc. This
factory was not the same as the Fuji Heavy
Industries Ltd.

FULGOR/*Italy 1922–1926*
Lightweight two-strokes of 143cc, made by a
small factory at Milan.

198cc Frischauf (TS Villiers) 1932

FURCH/*Germany 1924–1925*
Yet another small Berlin-built motorcycle which
had an own 2·5 hp sv motor. The production was
on a limited scale.

FUSI/*Italy 1932–1957*
For many years Italian FN importer, Fusi
bought the CF motorcycle factory in 1937 and
produced first a 248cc ohc machine. They fitted
174cc, 246cc and 490cc JAP engines into own
frames, which had also many FN parts; according to some sources, FN even built the frames for
Fusi machines. The JAP engines were made in
Italy under licence. After 1945, Fusi built an
improved 248cc machine with the old but
developed CF ohc engine.

173cc FVL (ohv Moser) 1929

FVL/*Italy 1926–1935*
Designed by former racing motorcyclist Francesco Vincenzo Lanfranchi, the first FVL lightweight machines had 124cc and 174cc ohv Moser
engines. Bonamore and Forlani, designers of the
now defunct Fert factory, joined the Lanfranchi
works in 1929 and created beautiful ohv machines with 174cc and in 1932 a 248cc. Another
version had a 174cc ohc power unit.

496cc Fusi (ohv) 1939

G

GA/*Italy 1925–1927*
Assembler of sporting V-twin machines, Franco Azzara fitted 678cc ohv engines made by Blackburne in England.

GABBIANO / *Italy 1954—1956*
One model, a 125cc two stroke single.

GABY / *England 1914–1915*
Well-made 269cc machines with Metro three-port, deflector-type engines.

GADABOUT / *England 1948–1951*
Made by the Swallow sidecar factory, the Villiers-engined Gadabout was a 123cc scooter, which for various reasons could not beat the leading foreign scooters in England.

GAGGENAU/*Germany 1925–1927*
Sturdy two-stroke singles with own 346cc and 396cc unit-design engines of own manufacture.

GAIA/*Italy 1922–1932*
The Turin-based factory always built machines of sound design. The first products were bicycles fitted with Rubinelli engines; the next were motorcycles with the then popular Swiss 123cc

346cc Galloni (sv Sport) 1924

496cc Galbusera (TS V-8 cylinder Prototype) 38

and 173cc ohv Moser engines. After 1927, most models had Ladetto & Blatto 173cc ohv units.

GALBAI/*1921–1925*
Producer of 276cc, 301cc and 348cc two-stroke machines with own engines. Other models had 492cc V-twin MAG and oilcooled 346cc single-cylinder Bradshaw ohv engines.

GALBUSERA/*Italy 1934–1955*
Sensationally exhibited an in-line mounted supercharged 498cc two-stroke V-8 cylinder prototype at the 1938 Milan show. There was also a V-4 version of 248cc, built on identical lines. Plinio Galbusera's bread-and-butter models had 173, 246, 348 and 498cc Rudge-built (Python) four-valve ohv engines, the smallest version supplied by Miller, which had exclusive rights for this engine. Technical head of Galbusera was Egyptian-born Adolf Marama, who rode Rudge-engined machines in all kinds of races. He was

also responsible for the design of the speedway frames made by this Brescia factory, which after 1945 concentrated on lightweight machines with Sachs engines from 98cc to 173cc. The sensational two-strokes of the immediate pre-war period never went into production.

GALLONI/*Italy 1920–1931*
Was a leading make and also successful in many races with Alfredo Panella, Nino Bianchi and Augusto Rava. The early models had 494cc and 746cc V-twin sv engines; later ones 249cc, 349cc and 499cc sv and ohv single-cylinder engines of their own design and manufacture. From 1927 the red Galloni was overshadowed by the Bianchi, Frera and Moto-Guzzi. The last Galloni was a 173cc ohv machine with a Blackburne engine.

GAMAGE/*England c1905–1924*
The motorcycles sold by the Gamage stores were made mainly in England by factories which in-

Advertisement from Gamage's 1913 catalogue

cluded Wolfruna, Omega, Radco and others. The models included 269cc two-strokes and 293cc, 347cc and 497cc single-cylinder sv machines.

290cc Gamage (sv) 1903

GANNA / *Italy 1923–late 1960s*
Varese-built, the Ganna was a good machine with many different engines fitted during the years. Among the first were 347cc sv and ohv Blackburnes, afterwards 173, 248, 348 and 498cc JAP engines, partly built under licence in Italy.

There was in 1936 an interesting 499cc four-valve ohc model with a Ganna-designed and built engine. After the war and a reorganisation of the company, most Gannas had two-stroke engines made by Puch, Sachs and Minarelli. They were from 48cc to 248cc. In addition, a 174cc ohv model was in the range too. Although Ganna never belonged to the leading makes in races, all models had a very sporting appearance and a superb finish.

GAR / *Germany 1924–1926*
The Rempp-designed 499cc ohv machines had their own single-cylinder engines and were built in limited numbers only.

GARABELLO / *Italy 1906–1929*
Francesco Garabello was one of the pioneers of the Italian motorcycle industry. He produced 240cc and 480cc singles and from 1922 onward a big, watercooled 984cc four-cylinder in-line model with shaft drive. Although a clever techni-

996cc Garabello (sv watercooled four-cylinder) 1926

cian, he never achieved financial success. When Luigi Comini took over the Alba factory, he transferred it to Turin. Garabello's last (and unorthodox) design was a 173cc single with watercooling and a rotary valve in the head. The drive to this valve as well as the rear wheel drive was by shaft. The radiator was mounted directly in front of the petrol tank, the carburettor in front of the vertically mounted cylinder. The design was unsuccessful.

GARANZINI / *Italy 1921–1931*
Made by a racing motorcyclist Oreste Garanzini —who imported the English Verus machines which were renamed Veros in Italy — the design was on typical English lines. Also from England came the 346cc sv JAP engines and on later models 147cc to 248cc Villiers and 248cc to 490cc sv and ohv power units made by JAP and Blackburne. Garanzini rode his machines in many races during the mid-1920s.

346cc Garelli (TS double-piston single racer) 1926

346cc Garanzini (sv JAP) 1926

GARELLI / *Italy 1918—*
Alberto Garelli developed his 'split single' two-stroke between 1912 and 1918 and offered a 350cc version for sale in 1919. Successful in racing and record breaking, it sold freely until 1935, when the factory switched to aero engines. Post-war production resumed with the Mosquito cycle attachment, made between 1947 and 1956. Between 1958 and 1961, Garelli merged with Agrati and thereafter

346cc Garelli (TS double-piston single) 1935

346cc Garelli (TS double-piston single racer) 1924

specialised in mopeds and 50cc and 80cc lightweights. In the 1980s, it entered the 125cc class both for the road and racing and won the 125cc championship in 1982 and 1983, with rider Angel Nieto. Thereafter, Garelli sold 125cc roadsters and trail bikes. In 1986 Luca Caladora won the 125cc world title, but sales were sliding, and production was cut back to concentrate on mopeds and bicycles. Garelli withdrew from racing and entered the 1990s very much on the defensive in the face of recession.

GARIN / *France 1950–1953*
Small producer of 49cc mopeds and 98cc two-stroke motorcycles.

GARLASCHELLI / *Italy 1922–1927*
Produced 65cc and 123cc two-strokes, from 1925 onwards also 173cc machines with two-stroke ohv engines.

GATTI / *Italy 1904–1906*
Pioneer who fitted 1·75 hp De Dion engines into strengthened bicycle frames.

GAZDA / *Austria 1926–1927*
Created by the inventor of the Gazda leaf-spring handlebars Anton Gazda, the 246cc two-stroke machines — built in small numbers only — were of unorthodox design. They had a pumping cylinder and three ports.

GAZELLE / *The Netherlands 1903*
Famous bicycle factory which fitted Sarolea engines into the first motorcycles made at the

Dieren works. Resumed production of motorised two-wheelers in 1932 with Ilo-engined 60cc and 75cc machines. Motorcycles with Ilo and Villiers engines followed in the mid-1930s. They had 98cc, 123cc and 148cc. The range was similar after the war, until the Dutch factory concentrated on various models with 49cc engines, many of which had Minarelli engines.

246cc Gazda (TS Prototype) 1926

GAZZI / *Italy 1929–1932*
A small factory which produced well-made 173cc ohv machines of modern design.

GB / *England 1905–1907*
Motorcycles with different Minerva engines from 3·5 hp to 5 hp and a very long wheelbase.

GCS / *Australia 1914–1917*
Designed and built by George Charles Stilwell at Melbourne, GCS motorcycles were mainly V-twins with various sv engines made by JAP in England. Among them 490 and 746cc models.

GD / *Italy 1923–1938*
Very fast 122cc two-strokes with a great racing history, ridden by such famous riders as Alfonso Drusiani, Frederico Castellani, Guglielmo Sandri, and Amilcare Rosetti. The GD stood for Ghirardi and Dall'-Oglio. From 1928, the factory built besides these flat singles also 248cc vertical twin two-strokes, 173cc ohc singles and 98cc two-stroke machines.

GÉCO-HERSTAL / *France 1924–1928*
Gérkinet's factory was closely connected with the Belgian Gillet works at Herstal, and also built part of the Gillet model range. In addition, they had their own 173cc to 346cc sv models.

GEER / *America 1905–1909*
Early producer of single and V-twin machines. Fitted their own engines into strengthened bicycle frames.

148cc Geier (TS Sachs) 1954

GEHA / *Germany 1920–1924*
Lightweight machines with their own 1·5 hp two-stroke engines.

148cc Geha (TS) 1922

GEIER / *Germany 1934–early 1960s*
Built mofas and motorcycles with 73cc, 98cc and after 1945 also 123cc, 147cc and 173cc Ilo and Sachs two-stroke engines.

GEKA / *Germany 1924–1925*
Fitted 173cc DKW engines into lightweights. Limited production.

GE-MA-HI / *Germany 1924–1927*
Built a wide range of machines with tubular and also with wide-tube petrol tank frames. The last ones were partly made from welded steel, not unlike the big Mars. Among the engines fitted were the 131cc Esbe, 149cc Bekamo, 149cc Grade and also the 147cc and 173cc DKW.

GEMINI / *Taiwan 1970–*
Partly Suzuki-licence machines, including many having the 'off-the-road' look. Among them 49cc

versions with 8 inch wheels and more orthodox 78cc, 123cc and 173cc models, of which many are exported to the USA.

GEMS / *Italy 1921–1923*
Light machines with 269cc two-stroke engines.

GENIAL-LUCIFER / *France 1928–1956*
Assembler of two-stroke machines with 98cc to 246cc Aubier Dunne, Train and Sabb engines.

GENTIL / *France 1903–1904*
With the horizontal single-cylinder engine in front of the pedalling gear, the Gentil had the look of a modern moped. Produced also V-twin machines and 98cc mopeds.

GEORGES RICHARD / *France c1899*
Assembled motorcycles with Minerva, Buchet, Zedel, Peugeot and other engines and later became part of the Unic car factory.

GEPPERT / *Germany 1925–1926*
Small factory which assembled two-stroke machines with 147cc Grade and DKW engines.

GERALD / *France 1927–1932*
Designed by Charles Gerald, these machines had 98cc and 173cc Aubier-Dunne two-stroke engines. Other models were powered by 248cc ohv JAP and 348cc and 498cc ohc Chaise power units.

GERARD / *England 1913–1915*
Of simple design, the 269cc Gerard had a Villiers engine and was built at Birmingham.

GERBI / *Italy 1952–1953*
Sachs-engined 98cc, 123cc and 173cc machines.

GERMAAN / *The Netherlands 1935–1966*
Another Dutch bicycle factory, which assembled good lightweight machines with 98cc Sachs and Ilo, as well as 123cc Ilo and 147cc Villiers engines. After the war, Germaan also used Hungarian 123cc Czepel engines and Ilo engines which included the 244cc vertical twin two-stroke. Germaan is now part of the Batavus group.

GERMANIA / *Germany 1901–1908*
These were actually Czechoslovakian Laurin & Klement motorcycles, built by the once famous Seidel & Naumann typewriter factory at Dresden under licence. The range of models included 3·5

615cc Germania (sv V-twin) 1904

hp and 4·5 hp V-twins. Laurin & Klement was the forerunner of the present Skoda car factory.

GEROSA/*Italy 1953–*
One of the younger makes, which produces at Brescia a variety of 49cc models and also 123cc two-strokes of sound design. Earlier, there were also 124cc and 174cc ohv machines in the range.

GERVO/*Germany 1924–1925*
Limited production of 198cc sv and 173cc DKW-engined two-stroke machines.

GH/*Czechoslovakia 1924–1925*
Gustav Heinz designed 172cc machines with Villiers power units. Heinz also produced Sirocco and Velamos motorcycles. Now nationalised, Velamos is one of the leading bicycle factories in the country.

GIACOMASSO/*Italy 1926–1935*
Superbly designed machines with 174cc Moser ohv engines, but from 1927 onward Felice Giacomasso designed his own power units with ohv and even ohc. New 489cc and 595cc ohv vertical twins appeared in 1933.

GIGANT/*Austria 1936–1938*
Designed by the former Delta-Gnom technician Johann Teichert, the light-green Gigant machines had 498cc and 598cc ohv and 746cc V-twin sv engines. All were of JAP manufacture. Also produced successful racing machines with 498cc ohv JAP and Husqvarna single-cylinder engines, which were ridden by the Austrian champion Martin Schneeweiss, Josef Lukeš and others.

490cc Gigant (ohv JAP) 1936

GIGUET/*France 1903*
Equipped with strong frames, Giguet motorcycles had De Dion and Minerva engines.

GILERA / *Italy 1909—*

Giuseppe Gilera started his business in 1909 in Milan, but full-scale production only began when he moved to Arcore in 1920. Early models were sturdy sidevalves of 350cc, 500cc and 600cc. These sold well and competed in the ISDT, winning for Italy in 1930 and 1931. They also did well in races such as the Milan-Taranto. In 1935 Gilera bought the rights to the water-cooled, super-charged Rondine, which, under the direction of Gilera and Piero Taruffi, became the famous Gilera 'four'. With all-enclosing streamlining, Taruffi broke the world's fastest record at 170.15mph. The Gilera, ridden by Dorino Serafini won the 1939 European championship.

Post war, road bike manufacture began with the 500cc ohv Saturno, which was also developed as a 'production' racer to considerable effect. In 1947, Piero Remor (designer of the Rondine) designed a normally aspirated 500cc four for Gilera, which was to be extensively developed by Francesco Passoni. This machine took the 500cc world title in 1950 and 1952, ridden by Umberto Masetti and in 1953, 1954 and 1955 by Geoff Duke.

Duke also won the Senior TT in 1955, while Bob McIntyre did the 'double' — Junior and Senior TTs and the first-ever 100mph lap in the Isle of Man in 1957. After this, Gilera withdrew from racing, only to be tempted back later in 1963, against their better judgement. Meanwhile, for the road, there were mainly rather depressingly uninspired ohv lightweights of 125cc, 175cc and a 300cc twin. The beautiful Saturno went out of production in 1959. Racing had all but bankrupted Gilera, while founder Giusepe Gilera had been deeply affected by the death of his energetic son Ferruccio in 1955 from a heart attack. In 1969, aged 80, Gilera sold his faltering company to Piaggio, maker of the Vespa scooter. Piaggio brought new energy to the production of lightweights from 50cc to 200cc, both two-strokes and four-strokes. Involvement in

498cc Gilera (dohc 4-cylinder racer) 1939

496cc Gilera (sv) 1921

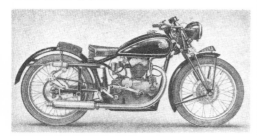
250cc Gilera ohv 'Nettuno' (Neptune) sports, 1946

498cc Gilera (dohc aircooled 4-cylinder racer) 1952

496cc Gilera (ohv 'Saturno') 1939

498cc Gilera (dohc aircooled 4-cylinder racer) 1953

49cc Gilera (TS Trial) 1982

trials and moto-cross followed with no overwhelming success. However, the development work involved paid off in very sporting 125cc models for the road in the 1980s, which enjoyed a considerable domestic sale. Like most Italian companies, Gilera made 50cc mopeds, and still does, but they are not in the early 1990s, entirely dependent upon these. In fact, a 1980s — even 1990s — version of the Saturno was developed with dohc specifically for the Japanese market, though it sells well elsewhere in Europe, too. Though Gilera have found the going hard at times, they enter the 1990s in better shape than some Italian manufacturers, and appear to have a future before them.

GILLET-HERSTAL / *Belgium 1919–early 1960s*
Together with FN and Sarolea, among the leading Belgian makes. Became famous with the rotary-valve 346cc two-stroke, which Robert Sexé rode around the world. This was in the mid-1920s. Other models included 348cc and 498cc unit-design sv and ohv machines and a 996cc V-twin with the ioe engine, made by MAG in Switzerland. The factory also showed great interest in racing and had such riders as Kicken, Debay, Bentley, Milhoux, Jackl, Deimel, Uvira and others. Chief designer Van Oirbeck created in 1929 works machines with single-cylinder ohc engines and René Milhoux broke many records with them. Two-strokes from 98cc to 248cc were built after the war and there were also vertical-twins up to 720cc.

GIMA / *France 1947–1956*
The machines were beautiful lightweights with Ydral, AMC and other 123cc to 248cc engines.

GIMSON / *Spain 1956–1964*
Bicycle factory which built 49cc and 65cc mopeds.

GIRARDENGO / *Italy 1951–1954*
Another Italian assembler who produced 123cc, 147cc and 173cc two-stroke engines.

GITAN / *Italy 1951*
Old established producer of 49cc two-strokes, including moto-cross versions. In the early years

of the company, motorcycles with up to 198cc two and four-stroke Minarelli engines were also built.

GITANE / *France 1953–early 1960s*
Well-known bicycle manufacturer, whose motorcycles had 49cc to 173cc and engines made by Ydral, VAP and Mistral.

GIULIETTA / *Italy 1957–1980*
Under this name and also that of Peripoli and, in England, AJW, Giulietta sold a wide range of mopeds and 50cc motor cycles using Sachs, Morini and Minarelli two-stroke engines. Popular and stylish in their day, but of no particular merit.

p147

GIVAUDAN / *England 1908–1914*
An 'assembler' company that used various engines, including Precision and Blumfeld. A few used the Villiers four-stroke.

GKD / *Italy 1978–*
New manufacturer which concentrates on 99, 123 and 242cc trial and moto-cross two-stroke singles, of which the 242cc cross has 37·7 bhp at 8700 rpm.

GL / *France 1919–1921*
Mainly built from English components, this French design by Georges Lévy, had a 990cc V-twin JAP sv engine, Sturmey-Archer gearbox and Binks carburettor.

GLENDALE / *England 1920–1921*
Simple assembled machines with 269cc Villiers and 346cc Blackburne engines.

GLOBE / *England 1901–1911*
Produced different models with Minerva, MMC and Sarolea engines.

346cc Gillet-Herstal (TS Tour du Monde) 1929

GLORIA/*England 1924–1925*
With frames built by Campion in Nottingham, the Gloria also had strong ties with France. In both countries it was sold with the 173cc Train two-stroke engine.

GLORIA/*England 1931–1933*
Made by Triumph at Coventry, this Gloria had a 98cc Villiers two-stroke engine.

GLORIA/*Italy 1948–1955*
Designed by Alfredo Focesi, the little Gloria had the 48cc two-stroke engine mounted directly on the swinging arm of the rear wheel.

GLORIA-REKORD/*Germany 1924–1925*
One of the many German companies which entered the market in the mid-twenties with an unsuccessful 3 hp single-cylinder two-stroke.

GN/*Italy 1920–1925*
Assembled mainly from English components, Giuseppe Navone's motorcycles had 346cc two-stroke single-cylinder engines. Navone was also closely connected with the Italian branch of the French Train engine works.

GNÄDIG/*Germany 1925–1926*
When KG at Suhl was sold to Allright, Franz Gnädig—one of the designers—left for Berlin and built there his own 348cc ohv machines. Afterwards he took the design to Kühne at Dresden and this was the first engine built by this proprietary engine factory.

GNOM/*Germany 1921–1923*
Bicycle attachment engine of 63cc, built by the Columbus engine factory, which was eventually taken over by Horex of Bad Homburg.

GNOME & RHONE/*France 1919–1959*
Famous for their aircraft engines in the First World War; Gnome & Rhône built first the English Bradshaw-designed 398cc, afterwards also a 498cc ABC with the flat-twin ohv engine transverse-mounted under licence. Cpt. Bartlett headed the manufacture at the big Paris factory. Together with Naas he also won many races. From 1923 onwards, single-cylinder machines of own designs came into being. They consisted of 306cc sv, 344cc ohv and 498cc sv and ohv versions and again Naas, together with Georges Bernard, gained many successes. During the late 1920s, BMW-like sv and ohv flat twins, transverse-mounted in pressed steel frames, came into

492cc Gnome-Rhône (ohv Super-Sport) 1927

The French Gnome-Rhône production programme in 1938

production. They had 495cc and 745cc capacity. After 1945, Gnome & Rhône concentrated on small two-stroke machines, of which most had 124cc and 174cc.

GODDEN/*England 1978–*
Concentrates on the manufacture of track racing machines with own ohv and sohc engines, including a 498cc sohc four-valve model with 64 bhp.

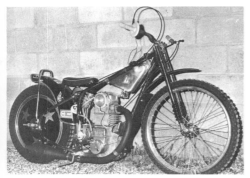

499cc Godden (sohc Speedway model) 1982

GOEBEL/*Germany 1951–1972*
Still a producer of mofas and mopeds, Goebel uses 49cc Sachs engines for his product.

GOETZ/*Germany 1925–1935*
Built in 10 years a total of 79 machines, most individually at the request of customers. They had 246cc Villiers, 346cc, 498cc and 676cc JAP, 498cc Küchen and even 796cc vertical twin Columbus (ohc) engines.

GOLEM/*Germany 1921–1923*
Called Sesselrad (chair-wheel), the DKW-built Golem was a scooter-like vehicle with a 122cc two-stroke engine which had a horizontal cylinder. The improved successor was the 144cc Lomos. When DKW dropped the production, Eichler at Berlin bought the production equipment and all rights for both designs.

GOGGO/*Germany 1951–1954*
Now part of BMW, the Glas factory at Dingolfing built a range of nice scooters with 123cc, 147cc and 173cc Ilo engines. Afterwards they created the 248cc Goggomobil and scooter sales went down.

124cc Gori (TS Sachs Racing) 1974

GOLD-RAD/*Germany 1952–*
Producer of mofas, mopeds etc. with 49cc Sachs and Ilo engines; now mainly importer of Italian Motograziela products, which also have 49cc power units.

GOLO/*Austria 1923–1925*
Limited manufacture of machines with 346cc and 490cc JAP and 347cc Bradshaw engines.

GONTHIER/*Belgium 1907–1910*
Early 748cc design with an aircooled four-cylinder in-line engine of own manufacture, double-loop frame and chain drive.

490cc Goetz (ohv JAP) 1933

GORI / *Italy 1969—early 1980s*
Gori produced sporting off-road and road-racing machines with highly-tuned Sachs 125cc engines. These enjoyed considerable succes in Italy in the 1970s, with the result that the company was taken over by their ambitious rivals, SWM, in 1979. SWM renamed the Gori 'Go-Motor' and continued production, but this ended shortly before SWM themselves collapsed.

GÖRICKE / *Germany 1903–*
Once well-known for racing bicycles, Göricke was one of the pioneer motorcycle producers in Germany. Built in the early days single and V-twin machines and during the 1920s assembled models with 172cc to 247cc Villiers as well as 346cc and 496cc MAG engines. Touring versions had ioe and sporting machines ohv engines. There were also Blackburne-engined Göricke machines, but the motorcycle production was never very big. Designer was Alfred Ostertag. Still building mofas etc., Göricke also produced until the mid-1950s Sachs and Ilo-engined two-strokes from 98cc to 198cc.

GORRION / *Spain 1952–1955*
Sachs-engined mopeds and motorcycles. The range also included 124cc and 174cc machines.

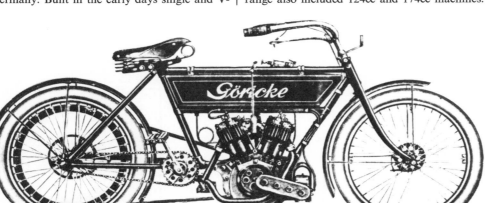

4½ hp Göricke (sv V-twin) 1905

4½ hp Göricke (sv V-twin Forecar) 1905

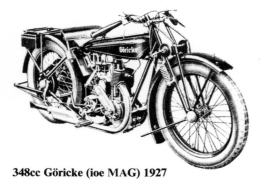

348cc Göricke (ioe MAG) 1927

49cc Göricke (TS Sachs) 1956

GOUGH / *England 1920–1923*
Assembled machines with 293cc sv JAP and 548cc sv Blackburne engines.

GOUVERNEUR / *Germany 1903–1907*
Long forgotten make which used 3·5 hp GN engines.

GR / *Italy 1925–1926*
After Count Mario Revelli won the 500cc class of the Grand Prix des Nations at Monza in 1925 on an Antonio Boudo-designed 490cc JAP-engined ohv single-cylinder machine, his brother Count Gino Revelli built these machines with the GR trade mark in limited numbers.

GRADE / *Germany 1903–1925*
Designed by Hans Grade, a leading aircraft pioneer, all the products (airplanes, cars and motorcycles) had two-stroke engines. He also supplied engines to other producers. His 118cc and 132cc motorcycles were very successful and were really a creation of his designer-in-chief, Hans Plog. Leading Grade riders: Hans Przybilski and the Hartmann brothers.

132cc Grade (TS) 1924

GRANDEX-PRECISION (GRANDEX) /
England 1917
As the factory first fitted Precision engines from 2·5 hp to 6 hp, the early machines used the Grandex-Precision trade mark. The Precision was dropped when the factory also fitted 225, 293, 490, 597 and 746cc JAP engines. Most of them were sv models.

GRAPHIC / *England 1903–1906*
Small producer who fitted De Dion, Minerva and MMC engines.

GRASETTI / *Italy 1952–1965*
Produced 123cc and 148cc machines with their own two-stroke power units.

GRATIEUX / *France 1919–1921*
Aircraft engine producer who tried building motorcycles with two-stroke radial engines.

247cc Greeves (TS Villiers) 1963

GRAVES / *England 1914–1915*
This was a supermarket of that period which sold Speed King motorcycles with 293cc JAP sv engines and a simple specification. Producer was Omega at Wolverhampton on behalf of Graves.

GREEN / *England 1919–1923*
In pre-WWI days closely connected with Green-Precision and Regal-Green. Charles Green was mainly an engine producer and a strong supporter of watercooled power units. He produced mainly 3·33 hp and 4 hp singles. After the war he tried again to join the ranks of motorcycle manufacturers, but was not very successful. In his last years he offered to rebuild aircooled Precision engines to watercooled versions.

GREEVES / *England 1952—1978*
Unorthodox and sturdy machines with partly cast aluminium frames and own leading link front forks, designed by Bert Greeves. Most used Villiers engine-gear units, but Greeves developed special cylinders and, later, complete engines. Brian Stonebridge pioneered Greeves' moto-cross career, but sales took off when Dave Bickers won the 1960 European Championship. The bikes, such as the 360cc and 380cc moto-cross models, were almost unbeatable in British scrambles and trials. Greeves also made a road racer, the 250cc

248cc Greeves (TS Villiers racer) 1963

Silverstone, which, ridden by Tom Phillips, won the ACU star in 1963, the 250cc Manx Grand Prix in 1964 (Gordon Keith) and in 1965 (Dennis Craine). There were road bikes, too — the 2T Villiers engined 'Essex Twin' being very well thought of. When Bert Greeves retired in 1973, the factory lost its lucrative American connection and declined.

GREYHOUND / *England 1905–1907*
Small assembler, who fitted proprietary engines made by Minerva, MMC and Fafnir.

GREYHOUND / *America 1907–1914*
Once a well-known make. The 4·5 hp single-cylinder was developed and built at the Thor factory.

197cc Greeves (TS Villiers) 1963

GRG / *Italy 1926–1927*
Technically interesting design with two coupled 174cc Della Ferrera single-cylinder ohv engines and rear suspension.

GRI / *England 1921—1922*
G R Inshaw's 350cc and 500cc engines used a combination of poppet valves and a rotary valve. As with so many rotary valves, this was not really satisfactory in practice.

GRIFFON / *France 1902–late 1920s*
Old established and once very successful make at races. Built singles and V-twins, but the last model was a nice 348cc single with sv and ohv engines. In the 1920's Peugeot took over Griffon.

343cc Grigg (TS Villiers) 1923

GRIGG / *England 1920–1925*
A 1·75 hp scooter was the first Grigg product. It was followed by a 161cc two-stroke and a 181cc ohv machine with their own engines. Other models had Villiers and Blackburne single and V-twin engines up to 680cc. The biggest model had the rare 990cc V-twin sv B&H engine.

GRINDLAY-PEERLESS / *England 1923–1934*
Originally a factory for sidecars, the first motorcycle models had 490cc JAP single-cylinder and 996cc Barr & Stroud sleeve-valve V-twin engines. Machines with 346cc and 496cc single-cylinder Barr & Stroud motors followed. Many models had sv and ohv JAP engines from 248cc to 996cc and Brough-Superior-like petrol tanks and there was a 490cc JAP-engined version with a Castle-type fork. Small models from 147cc to 247cc were powered by Villiers two-stroke engines and there were also Grindlay-Peerless

346cc Grindlay-Peerless (sleeve-valve Barr & Stroud) 1924

49cc Gritzner (TS Sachs) 1962

machines with Rudge-built Python four-valve ohv engines from 248cc to 498cc. Bill Lacey, famous tuner and rider, broke many records on JAP engined machines while Karl Abarth of Austria and Jan Mocchari of Czechoslovakia gained many successes in road-races and hill-climbs with various grand prix machines. The Grindlay-Peerless factory was only a few hundred yards from the former Rudge works.

GRINGO / *America 1973–*
Newer make which concentrates on 248cc and 358cc single-cylinder two-stroke machines for moto-cross and flat tracks. The frames are made from chrome light alloy.

GRITZNER / *Germany 1903–1962*
A famous sewing-machine factory, which during the early years built Fafnir-engined singles and

V-twins. After WWII, motorcycle manufacture was resumed and Sachs engines of 98cc, 147cc, and 174cc fitted. The last Gritzner was a 49cc motorcycle of very sporting appearance and originally known as the Mars-built Monza. Gritzner-Kaiser AG is the factory name and the Kaiser part built three-wheelers in 1901.

GRIZZLY / *Czechoslovakia 1925–1932*
Designed by Josef Matyaš, the Grizzly was a modern 246cc two-stroke machine with deflector-type three-port engine. The range included after 1929 348cc MAG-engined ioe and ohv models. Works rider Zdenek Hermann had a 348cc ohc MAG engine in his machine. Other riders: Trnka, Adamek, Korbel.

246cc Grizzly (TS) 1929

GROSE-SPUR / *England 1934–1939*
Lightweight machines with 123cc Villiers engines built by Carlton for the London-based dealer Grose.

GROTE / *Germany 1924–1925*
Very unorthodox 305cc two-stroke singles, which — by adding one or two more engines! — could be brought to 614cc or 921cc.

490cc Grindlay-Peerless (ohv JAP) 1929

148cc Guazzoni (TS) 1966

GRÜCO/*Germany 1924–1925*
Assembler who fitted 346cc Kühne ohv engines into simpler frames.

GRUHN/*Germany 1909–1932*
Old established Berlin-based manufacturer of sv machines and proprietary engines with 148cc, 196cc and 246cc. A new 198cc single-cylinder ohv machine came into production in 1928. It had shaft drive to the rear wheel and was of up-to-date design. The last Gruhn was a 123cc two-stroke. Richard Gruhn's machines never had any kind of sporting image.

198cc Gruhn (sv) 1922

GRUHN/*Germany 1920–1926*
Another Berlin-based Gruhn, owned by Hugo Gruhn. He was Richard Gruhn's brother and concentrated mainly on the production of frames for others. His own machines housed the 198cc Alba single-cylinder sv engine.

GRUTZENA/*Germany 1925–1926*
Sturdy but not very modern 348cc singles with Kühne ohv engines. Production was on a limited scale.

GS/*Germany 1920–1924*
Lightweight machines with 129cc two-stroke engines. These could be bought also as bicycle attachments. This was the Gustav Schulze GS.

GS/*Germany 1923–1925*
This, the Georg Schroff — Berlin built — GS was a 145cc machine with Gruhn sv engines as well as many other Gruhn parts.

GSD/*England 1921–1923*
R. E. D. Grant's interesting design had a transverse-mounted 496cc flat-twin engine, four speeds and shaft drive to the rear wheel. A second model housed the 342cc White & Poppe single-cylinder two-stroke and also had shaft drive.

GUARALDI/*Italy 1905–1916*
The first machines had German Fafnir, later ones Belgian Sarolea engines with capacities up to 550cc.

348cc Grutzena (ohv Kühne) 1925

GUAZZONI/*Italy 1949–1977*
After Aldo Guazzoni left Moto Morini, he created many interesting two-strokes and ohv models up to 248cc. Among them were some very fast 49cc versions. Lately Guazzoni has concentrated on 49cc mini-machines and 123cc models — two-strokes — for trials and moto-cross.

GUIA/*Italy 1950–1954*
Small assembler of 98cc, 123cc and 147cc two-stroke machines.

GUIGNARD/*France 1933–1938*
Jéan Guignard produced mainly 98cc and 123cc two-stroke machines.

GUILLER/*France 1950–late 1950s*
One of the leading French factories after WWII. Built two and four-stroke ohv machines from 49cc to 248cc with engines supplied by Ydral, AMC, VAP, Aubier-Dunne and others.

GUIZZARDI/*Italy 1926–1932*
Produced 124cc and 174cc ohv and also 174cc ohc singles with their own power units. They were modern machines of sound design.

GUIZZO/*Italy 1955–1962*
Built 48cc mopeds and a well-designed 149cc scooter in a period when others had dropped scooter manufacture.

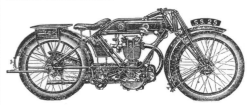

490cc Güldner (ohv) 1925

GÜLDNER/*Germany 1925*
A short-lived but superb Norton-like 490cc ohv single-cylinder machine, built by a well-known agriculture machine factory. Dr. Güldner's design was so Norton-like that it was possible to use Norton spare parts after Güldner dropped motorcycle production. Top rider was Josef Klein, who later rode for DKW and Horex.

GUSTLOFF/*Germany 1934–1940*
Mopeds with 98cc Sachs engines, designed by Martin Stolle of D-Rad fame.

G&W/*England 1902–1906*
Long forgotten assembler who used Minerva, Peugeot and Fafnir proprietary engines.

H

HACK / *England 1920–1923*
Mini-scooter with 103cc and 110cc Simplex two-stroke engines built in limited numbers.

HADEN / *England 1920–1924*
Built a single model only. It had a 347cc Precision two-stroke engine.

HAGEL / *Germany 1925*
Two-stroke machines with their own 247cc three-port engines.

HÄGGLUND / *Sweden 1973–1978*
Developed for the Swedish Army, this machine had a single-cylinder 345cc Rotax two-stroke engine with 76mm bore and stroke. It developed 24 bhp at 5300 rpm. The monocoque frame included the petrol tank; drive was by shaft, and the wheels were made from pressed steel. The weight was 135 kg. Late in 1976, Husqvarna got the army order and the fate of the Hägglund was in the balance.

HAI / *Austria 1938*
Cast aluminium frame including the petrol tank. Own 110cc two stroke engine. Hitler's production plans for the industry brought production of the Hai to an end.

HAJA / *Germany 1924–1925*
Simple 198cc sv machines with Hansa-built single-cylinder engines.

HAKO / *Germany 1924–1925*
Copies of HRD machines. Even the 348cc and 490cc ohv JAP engines used were identical.

HALUMO / *Germany 1923–1926*
Produced 147cc two-strokes, afterwards 146cc

248cc Hansa (ohv) 1926

and 198cc ohv machines with their own engines.

HAM / *The Netherlands 1902–1906*
Single-cylinder machines with 2 hp (at 2000 rpm) Altena engines.

HAMILTON / *England 1901–1907*
Built 2·25, 3·25 and 4 hp singles as well as 4·5 hp V-twins and sold power units to other producers.

HAMPTON / *England 1912–1914*
Well-made 492cc sv machines with single-cylinder power units made by T. D. Cross.

HANFLAND / *Germany 1920–1925*
Built Hanfland and Kurier motorcycles with own 147cc two-stroke engines. Curt Hanfland also supplied these engines to Flink, a branch of the famous BMW factory.

HANSA / *Germany 1922–1926*
Once a well-known factory at Bielefeld, Hansa produced two and four-stroke singles from 148cc to 246cc. The last models had 198cc and 246cc ohv engines with horizontally-mounted valves and low triangular duplex frames.

HANSAN / *England 1920–1922*
Assembler who fitted 269cc Arden two-stroke and 346cc Blackburne sv engines.

148cc Hanfland (TS Model Sport) 1922

HAPAMEE / *Germany 1925–1926*
Meinke-designed 198cc and 246cc two-strokes with own deflector-type motors.

HARDING-JAP / *France 1912–1914*
Built from English components, the Harding motorcycle had a 496cc V-twin JAP engine. H. J. Harding was an Englishman living in St. Cyr.

HAREWOOD / *England 1920*
Assembled machines with 269cc Villiers two-stroke and 346cc Precision sv engines.

HARLETTE / *France & Belgium 1925—1928*
Puch split single two-stroke made under licence and sold as Harlettes in France, Belgium and Italy. However Gerkinet in France also made a 175cc model with an ohv Gillet Herstal engine. Painted to look like a miniature Harley Davidson (though no connection) and sold in France and Belgium.

HARLEY DAVIDSON / *USA 1903—*
Harley Davidson is not only the USA's sole surviving native motorcycle manufacturer — the company can also claim a further unique distinction. Having made and sold motorcycles under its own

HARLEY-DAVIDSON

name since 1905, it is undeniably the oldest surviivng motorcycle concern in the world.

Harley Davidson has come a long way from that far-off year, when pattern maker Arthur Davidson and draughtsman William Harley came together to build their first motorcycles, with Davidson's brother, Walter, helping. When, in 1907, working from a small backyard shed, production reached 50, they decided to give up their regular jobs, and joined by another Davidson, brother William, they

incorporated the company and moved into a larger factory. Progress from here was quite remarkable; by the time the USA entered WWI in 1917, Harley Davidson were making 17,000 motorcycles a year.

The 1907 model had a 475cc engine with an inlet valve opened by atmospheric pressure over the side exhaust valve, the engine being inclined forward in a sturdy loop frame, with characteristic bottom link front forks. The single speed transmission was by flat belt, tensioned by a jockey pully. Surprisingly, almost alone in the USA, Harley persisted with belt drive until as late as 1913.

61 Twin . . . from 1915 brochure

The company's first 800cc 45° V twin came in 1909. It had mechanically operated overhead inlet valves, a Schebler carburettor and a Bosch magneto. Engine capacity rose to 980cc in 1912. There was a clutch in 1911, a two-speed gear and chain drive for 1914 and a three-speed gear and kickstart a year later. In the war, Harley produced over 20,000 twins, most with sidecars for the US forces, of which about 7,000 went to France.

Post war, a novel offering was a 600cc fore-and-aft flat twin, but it lasted for only four seasons, main production consisting of 1000cc and 1200 V twins. Cheap car prices forced a degree of conservatism

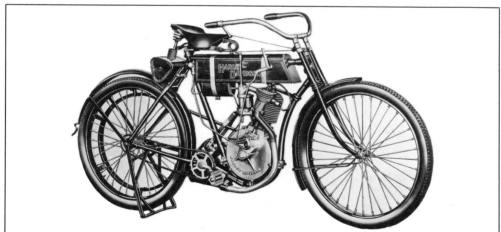
3 hp Harley-Davidson (sv) 1903

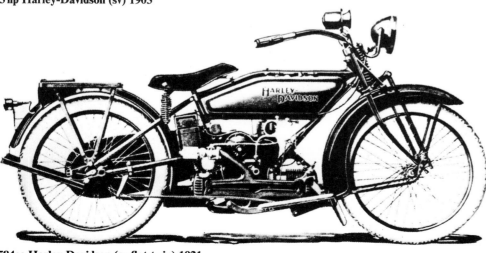
584cc Harley Davidson (sv flat-twin) 1921

346cc Harley-Davidson (ohv 'Peashooter' racer) 1930

on the company, which cut down on model changes, but, in 1928, a significant development took place, with the introduction of the 750cc 'Forty five' with a straightforward side-valve layout. This D series twin was uprated until 1951, while its engine lasted for even longer, being used in the three-wheeled utility 'Servicar' from 1932 until 1975! There were also side valve and ohv 350cc singles, perhaps owing something to the British AJS and intended more for export than for dom-

998cc Harley-Davidson (ohv V-twin) 1936

901cc Harley-Davidson (ohv V-twin 'Sportster CH') 1965

347cc Harley-Davidson (ohv) 1974

estic sale. Harley's first ohv twin was the 1000cc 'Knucklehead' of 1936, supplemented in 1941 by a similar 1200cc version.

Post WWII, Harley branched into lightweights with the 125cc Hummer an even franker copy of the DKW RT125 than BSA's Bantam. This was uprated to 165cc before being dropped after 1952. Harley also briefly made a 165cc two stroke scooter. Serious production, however, centred on the big twins, particularly on the 1948 'Panhead' ohv with light alloy heads and hydraulic tappets. This came in 1000cc and 1200cc capacities. In 1949, hydraulically-damped telescopic front forks

883cc Harley-Davidson (ohv V-twin 'Sportster CH') 1958

1215cc Harley-Davidson (ohv V-twin 'Duo Glide') 1963

were added and it was rechristened the Hydra-Glide. In 1958, with rear suspension, it became the Duo-Glide and, in 1965, with 12 volt electric starting, the Electra-Glide; it was then redesigned with 1200cc and 1340cc engines as the F series. In 1952 the unit constructed s.v. K series was introduced, followed by the X series ohv in 1957, which is still in production. The original XL Sportster had a totally new 833cc engine and, for the first time, a unit construction gearbox. Continually developed since then, with a 1000cc option being introduced in 1972, there have been a bewildering number of permutations of this basic model.

Before WWI Harley were content to let their customers' race results speak for themselves, but in 1916 they built special eight-valve ohv models, which were raced into the early 1920s by Harley's

own team. Thereafter, racing models were sold, including the 350cc ohv 'Peashooter'. Originally intended for professional US dirt track and speedway racing, the 'Peashooter' had a significant influence on dirt track racing, first in Australia and then in Britain.

In the 1930s Class C amateur racing called for stock machines of 750cc, relieving Harley and their rivals from the task of fielding factory teams. But, inevitably, special machines were made and supplied to favoured dealers and riders — especially when Class C began to centre on the 200-mile race at Daytona beach. In the late 1930s honours in Class C were about equal between Indian and Harley, but in 1941 both concerns were shocked when the Daytona 200 was won by Canadian Billy Matthews on a 500cc ohc Norton. Another Norton

1338cc Harley-Davidson (ohv Low Rider)

1338cc Harley-Davidson (V-ohv twin FLTC) 1982

came second in 1948, while Nortons won the race outright from 1949 and through to 1952. In 1953, however, Harley struck back with the remarkable KR 750cc side-valve, which became legendary before being replaced by the ohv XR750 in 1970.

Between 1960 and 1978 Harley Davidson at first partly- and then fully-owned the Italian Aermacchi company, a link that provided them with a ready-made range of smaller machines for the domestic market. It also provided racing models, at first ohv four-strokes and, later, two-strokes. In 1974, 1975 and 1976 Walter Villa was 250cc road racing champion and in 1977 350cc champion on Harley Davidson two-stroke twins. Aermacchi was sold to a new company, Cagiva, when US exhaust emission legislation made the continued sale of two-strokes impractical.

In 1968 Harley Davidson was bought by the large US conglomerate AMF American Machine and Foundry. Though the Davidson family were nominally involved, first Walter, then William S — chairman in 1971 — and John A Davidson left the board. The AMF period has been painted as a disaster for Harley, but, in fact, sales trebled, while they also lobbied against the unfair pricing of Japanese imports forcefully — eventually the US government imposed tariffs on imported motorcyles of 700cc and over. By 1980, however, AMF were disenchanted with the business, since it appeared difficult to make profits commensurate with the capital they had invested, so they responded favourably to offers of a buy-back by former and current members of the senior management, including William S Davidson — but not brother John. The buy-back took place amicably for $75,000,000 in June 1981. Strong, imaginative aggressive management since then now sees Harley Davidson in a strong position as it approaches its 90th anniversary; to all appearances, the company is well placed to celebrate 100 years of making America's best-known, best-loved motorcycle.

1340cc Harley Davidson FXSTS Solfail Springer (1990).

1208cc Harley Davidson FLH (ohv V-twin) 1977

157

HARPER / *England 1954–1955*
Scooter with 198cc Villiers two-stroke engine. The production was on a limited scale.

HARRAS / *Germany 1922–1925*
Fitted Ruppe's Bekamo two-stroke engines — built under licence — into own frames. They had 139cc and 145cc and a pumping cylinder, housed at the bottom of the crankcase.

HARSO / *Germany 1925–1926*
Small machines built by a small company, which fitted 174 and 206cc DKW two-stroke proprietary engines into open frames.

HASCHO / *Germany 1923–1926*
Fitted first 143cc and 173cc DKW engines, superseded by English Villiers two-strokes.

HASCHÜT / *Germany 1929–1931*
Limited production of machines with 172cc Villiers deflector-type engines.

HASTY / *France 1930–1934*
Lightweights with 98cc Aubier-Dunne two-stroke power units.

HAUSER / *Germany 1981–*
Took over the manufacture of the well-known Kramer trial, enduro and moto-cross machines. The range includes 124, 248 and 406cc versions with membrane and rotary-valve two-stroke engines.

HAVERFORD / *America 1909–1914*
Small American factory. Built 4 hp single-cylinder machines with automatic inlet valves.

346cc Haweka (sv) 1926

HAWEKA / *Germany 1923–1926*
Very English-looking motorcycles with 348cc, 490cc and 678cc sv and ohv JAP engines. Another model had the 497cc ioe MAG single-cylinder engine. Leading riders: Bremer and Schulz.

HAWKER / *England 1920–1923*
When ABC were liquidated, Tom Sopwith and Harry Hawker — Sopwith's test pilot — used the factory to make a small 300cc two-stroke motorcycle. Subsequently, Hawkers used 350cc and 550cc side-valve Blackburne engines. Hawker died in a flying accident in 1921 and production of Hawkers ended as Sopwith re-entered aircraft manufacture.

HAXEL-JAP / *England 1911–1913*
Assembler who fitted the 293cc JAP sv engine into a limited number of frames.

HAZEL / *England 1906–1911*
This was another assembler which fitted first V-twin Peugeot and from 1909 also 393cc JAP engines.

HAZLEWOOD / *England 1905–1923*
Once a big motorcycle factory, but never a well-known one at home. The Hazlewood production included V-twin sv machines of 499cc to 998cc and JAP-engined models from 245cc to 548cc and V-twins to 996cc in strong duplex frames.

199cc Hecker (ohv JAP) 1931

247cc Hecker (TS Ilo) 1954

These were exported to the British Colonies: few reached the home market. A make which built exclusively road-going models.

HB / *England 1919–1924*
Simple well-made machines with 346cc and 498cc sv and ohv Blackburne engines.

HEC / *England 1922–1923*
The Hewin-built machine had 247cc Villiers two-stroke engines.

HEC / *England 1938–1940*
First seen at the 1938 Motor Cycle Show, the HEC was distinguished from most autocycles through its use of an 80cc engine made by the famous Levis factory at Stechford, Birmingham. When Levis were sold, supply of engines ceased and so did HEC production.

HECKER / *Germany 1921–1956*
Was a leading factory. Built 245cc two-stroke machines with their own engines, afterwards 346cc ohv models, with power units not un-

158

493cc Helios (sv flat-twin BMW-engine) 1922

similar to the AJS of that period. They were followed by JAP-engined machines from 198cc to 548cc and a 746cc V-twin with the ioe MAG engine. The range also included from 1931 onward Sachs-engined 73cc and 98cc two-strokes, some with frames made from square tubes. After 1945 Hecker machines housed Sachs and Ilo engines from 98cc to 248cc.

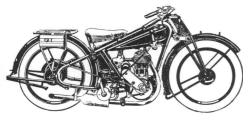

490cc Hecker (sv JAP) 1928

HEIDEMANN / *Germany 1949–1952*
Well-known bicycle factory which built lightweights with 98cc and 123cc Sachs engines.

HEILO / *Germany 1924–1925*
Well-designed 348cc deflector-type, three-port, two-stroke single with own engine. Experimented also with super-charged two-strokes.

HEINKEL / *Germany 1952–1962*
Built 49cc mopeds and scooters with own 149cc

ohv engines in a former aircraft factory. The range was extended by 123cc two-stroke and 174cc ohv scooters, which gained commercial success.

HELI / *Germany 1923–1925*
Watercooled 246cc two-stroke, unit-design engine in tubular duplex frame, with belt drive and leaf-spring fork.

HELIOS / *Germany 1921–1922*
Although not designed by BMW, the machine was actually BMW built. Its engine was a 493cc BMW-made M2B15 proprietary sv flat-twin. The Helios had many faults and so BMW decided to produce completely new motorcycles with transverse-mounted flat-twin engines.

147cc Hella (TS) 1922

HELLA / *Germany 1921–1924*
Built at Munich, the Hella was a two-stroke with a flat cylinder. The range consisted of 147cc and 183cc models.

HELLER / *Germany 1923–1926*
Used, like the Helios, the 493cc flat-twin BMW M2B15 engine; from 1924 onwards also the similarly-built 746cc MJ (Mehne) sv flat-twin power unit.

HELO / *Germany 1923–1925*
Fitted with 149cc Bekamo-type two-stroke, which had an additional piston in the crankcase. Production was on a small scale.

HELVETIA / *Switzerland 1927–1930*
Built by the Universal company, the little Helvetia had a 190cc PA two-stroke engine.

HELYETT / *France 1926–1955*
Produced motorcycles with 98cc to 996cc V-twins. Among them were transverse-mounted JAP-engined 746cc V-twins with shaft drive, which had the gearbox in unit with the engine. Also built some fast 996cc racing machines with 45 bhp and 55 bhp ohv JAP engines. After 1945 only two-strokes from 48cc to 123cc were made.

HENDERSON / *America 1911–1931*

A famous four-cylinder design by William 'Bill' Henderson, whose father built Henderson cars. The motorcycles had aircooled in-line unit-design engines with 1068cc and 1301cc; for a short period also 1168cc. The designer sold his creation to the Chicago-based Schwinn factory in 1917 and created afterwards the not un-similar ACE. He was killed in 1922 in a road accident. Henderson motorcycles had three-speed gearboxes with a reverse gear.

Another famous American designer, Arthur Lemon, continued after Henderson's death in developing the big four-cylinder until 1931, when Ignaz Schwinn decided to withdraw from the manufacture of motorcycles. According to experts who knew most American fours, which included the Militaire, the Champion, the Cleveland, the ACE and Indian-ACE and others, the big Henderson was the finest of them all. Red Wolverton, who rode Hendersons in the mid-1920s' won many races on them.

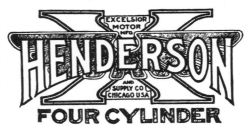

1301cc Henderson De Luxe 1925

HENKEL / *Germany 1927–1932*

Was the last in the line who built the once-famous 503cc and 497cc Krieger Gnädig (KG) motor-cycles. This unit-design single with shaft drive was originally designed by the Kreiger brothers and Franz Gnädig. They handed production over to the Cito works, which eventually became part of the Allright factory. When Allright decided in 1927 to drop motorcycle production in favour of the manufacture of forks, hubs etc., it was Paul Henkel who built these machines. Rudi Albert had them redesign-ed and developed in the mid-1920s, but by 1932 they were outmoded. Henkel made after 1929 a 198cc sv single with a Blackburne engine.

HENLEY / *England 1920–1929*

Assembled machines with modern tubular frames. The first models had 269cc Villiers two-stroke and 497cc Blackburne sv engines. Other models with 248cc, 293cc and 346cc sv and ohv JAP and Blackburne engines followed. After a reorganisation in 1927, the name became New Henley. Afterwards the make was bought by Arthur Greenwood and Jack Crump, and was transferred to Oldham from Birmingham. Among new models were 678cc and 748cc sv V-twins. Henley would fit MAG engines if required, mainly the 497cc double-port ohv model.

HERBI / *Germany 1928–1932*

Two models of sound design formed the Herbi production. One was a 198cc sv machine with Blackburne engine, the other a 498cc model with the ohc three-valve Küchen motor.

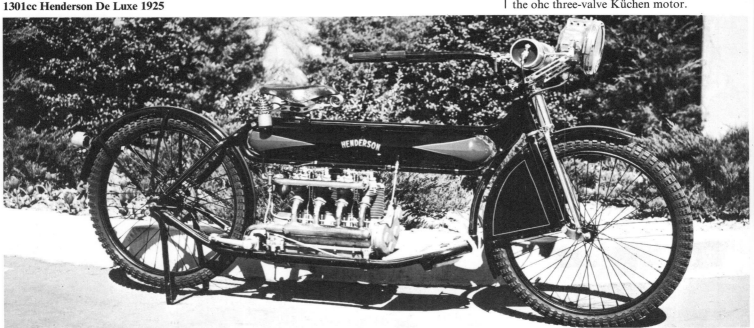

7 hp Henderson (sv 4-cylinder) 1913

HERCULES / *Germany 1904—*

Today Hercules, owned by engine makers Sachs, survives only as a producer of mopeds. Hercules, from its start, used proprietary engines from many sources; and in the 1930s; it achieved some good racing results with JAP-powered models. The company also made lightweights, down to as small as 75cc. Wartime bombing of Nuremburg put the Hercules factory out of action until 1950, when 98cc Sachs-engined and 125cc Ilo-engined models

were both shown for the first time. Both sold well and were joined a year later by other lightweight models. By the mid-1950s, Hercules was exporting throughout Europe with models from 100cc to 250cc, the top of the range using a 250cc Ilo twin-cylinder engine. The company survived the problematical late 1950s that saw so many German motorcycle concerns founder, becoming part of the Zweirad Union in 1966. Three years later, this was taken over by Fichtel and Sachs, who kept the

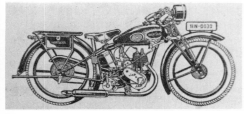

198cc Hercules (sv JAP) 1930

197cc Hercules (ohv Moser) 1931

famous name alive. The W2000 Wankel-engined model (promoted outside Germany as a DKW) followed in 1970. More profitable was a 125cc Sachs-engined model sold in large numbers to the German army. As part of their efforts to keep Hercules afloat, Sachs, for a while, sold a reasonably large range between 125cc and 350cc as Enduro models in the USA. However, economic circumstances were not to be denied and in 1980 the range was cut down to machines of 80cc, using a water-cooled Sachs two-stroke. This remains the current situation.

198cc Hercules (TS ILO) 1951

49cc Hercules (TS Sachs K50RX) 1971

294cc Hercules (Wankel-engine) 1975

49cc Hercules (TS Sachs K50RL) 1977

992cc Hesketh (ohc eight-valve V-twin) 1982

HERCULES / *England 1902*
Assembler who used engines made by MMC, Minerva and White & Poppe.

HERDTLE-BRUNEAU / *France 1902–1914*
Produced a range of unorthodox motorcycles including a watercooled 264cc (48mm bore × 73mm stroke) vertical twin. Other models had V-twin Bichrone two-stroke engines. Herdtle-Bruneau was also among the first motorcycle manufacturers using ohv engines.

HERKO / *Germany 1922–1925*
Built lightweight machines with 122cc and 158cc two-stroke engines and also 198cc sv engines. Engines as well as frames were also supplied to other makes.

HERKRA / *Germany 1922–1923*
Another small manufacturer of motorcycles with their own 141cc two-stroke engines.

HERMA / *Germany 1921–1924*
Bicycle attachment engines which could be fitted on either front wheel or the rear. They were of Herma design and had 148cc.

HERMES / *Germany 1922–1925*
Designed by Berwald, the Cockerell-like machines with a flat single-cylinder two-stroke engine had 124cc.

HERMES / *Germany 1924–1925*
JAP-engined 348cc, 490cc and 678cc motorcycles with sv engines and open frames. Production was on a limited scale.

HEROS / *Germany 1921–1929*
Built in the Saxonian part of the country, Heros machines had own 155cc, 185cc and 247cc engines with outside flywheels and used also two and three-speed gearboxes of own manufacture. The engines were two-strokes as well as four-strokes. The last ones had sv, in some cases also overhead-inlet and side-exhaust valves.

HEROS / *Germany 1923–1924*
Another Heros, made by a Berlin-based factory, which used 142cc DKW two-stroke engines.

HERTHA / *Germany 1924–1925*
Lightweights, made on the line of the Eichler. Also the Hertha had a 142cc DKW engine.

HESKETH / *England 1981–*
An impressive looking, but highly flawed, attempt to market a British 'Super Bike' with 1000cc ohc 90° V twin engine based on a Weslake design. The Hesketh had many other advanced features, but extremely serious gearbox problems delayed its launch and only about 150 were delivered before financial problems hit the company, with the loss of substantial sums of money. Nevertheless, Hesketh remain in very limited production to order.

HESS / *Germany 1925*
Made by a Darmstadt machine factory, the Hess was a 799cc aircooled four-cylinder in-line motorcycle; the only such design ever made in Germany. Production was on a limited scale only.

HESSRAD / *Germany 1923–1925*
Single cylinder sv-machines with own 297cc and 347cc engines, built on a limited scale.

HEXE / *Germany 1923–1925*
Producer of bicycle attachment engines and of 142cc and 269cc two-stroke motorcycles. The last model was a 346cc sv single with belt drive.

HIEKEL / *Germany 1925–1932*
Only a single model was ever made by Hiekel. It was a sturdily built 348cc single-cylinder three-port two-stroke with a strong triangular frame, which provided a low saddle position.

HILAMAN / *America 1906–late 1910s*
Produced ioe single-cylinder and in 1912 also V-twin models with strong frames. Good machines.

HILDEBRAND & WOLFMÜLLER / *Germany 1894–1897*
This was the first motorcycle built in the world on commercial lines. It was also the first two-wheeled machine called a *Motorrad* (motorcycle). Heinrich Hildebrand and Alois Wolfmüller created it together with Hans Geisenhof, a clever mechanic. The Munich-based factory soon had five branch factories also at Munich, but luck was not with them. After less than four years, the production of the Hildebrand & Wolfmüller had to be stopped forever. While this factory stopped development and became uncompetitive, other factories — especially Werner in France — went on developing motorcycles. The number of machines made by Hildebrand & Wolfmüller is not known exactly. Some sources claim there were 2000 made; others say there were no more than 800 produced.

The Hildebrand & Wolfmüller had a low frame made from steel tubes and a flat four-stroke twin-cylinder engine, which developed 2·5 hp at 240 rpm. With a 90mm bore and 117mm stroke, it had a capacity of 1488cc. The connecting rods of both cylinders were connected directly with the rear wheel, which acted also as flywheel. Rubber bands assisted the rods in returning while the rear mudguard housed the radiator for watercooling the engine. Total loss lubrication,

1488cc Hildebrand & Wolfmüller (Twin-cylinder 2.5 hp at 240 rpm) 1894

glow combustion and a surface carburettor were other features of this design.

Mr. Moritz Schulte bought such a machine in 1895 and took it to England, where it created great interest. A few years afterwards, Schulte became a director of Triumph at Coventry, but by then the original Hildebrand & Wolfmüller design was a thing of the past. Heinrich Hildebrand designed more engines in later years, but never regained the fame which he had with his original motorcycle.

HINDE / The Netherlands c1900–1938
Pioneer who used 2 hp De Dion engines in his first motorcycles. After an interruption of many years, the reorganised factory built in the second part of the 1930s 98cc and 118cc two-stroke machines with Ilo engines.

HIRANO / Japan 1952–1961
Mini-scooter producer, who used 49cc and 78cc two-stroke engines. The motorcycle production included models with 123cc and 173cc two-stroke engines.

HIRONDELLE / France 1921–1926
Former arms factory which built motorcycles with 198cc sv and also other engines.

HIRSCH / Germany 1923–1924
Two-stroke machines with own 128cc and DKW 142cc engines. Small production. This was one of the many Berlin-based companies which built two-stroke motorcycles during the 1920s.

HIRTH / Germany 1923–1926
Racing two-strokes with watercooled double-piston engines, designed for experimental purposes by the famous WWI pilot and racing car driver Helmut Hirth. The experiments concerned the material 'Electron', used on these comparatively very powerful 144cc singles and 244cc vertical twins. Ridden by Hirth's famous brother Wolf Hirth, by Erwin Gehrung, Karl Fischer and others, these machines won many races. After they ceased racing, the Stuttgart Bosch factory used them for plug-testing purposes.

HJ / England 1920–1921
Assembled machines which housed 269cc Liberty and Villiers engines.

HJH / Wales 1954–1956
Built in Neath in Wales, the Hulsman motorcycles were of orthodox design and housed 147cc, 197cc and 247cc Villiers two-stroke engines.

HKR / Germany 1925–1926
After a reorganisation at Hako, these HRD-like machines became known as HKR, which stood for Hans Korn, Rothenburg. The range of these sporting machines included 348cc and 498cc models with sv and ohv engines made by JAP in London.

HMK / Austria 1937–1938
Built in limited numbers, also the HMK was a JAP-engined motorcycle built on typical English lines. Production included sv, but mainly ohv models from 248cc to 594cc with single-cylinder engines.

490cc HMK (ohv JAP) 1938

HMW / Germany 1923–1928
Heavy single-cylinder 3 hp machines with their own sv engines.

HMW / Austria 1949–1964
The first product was the 49cc Fuchs bicycle engine. Afterwards a wide range of nice 49cc two-stroke mopeds and lightweight machines were built. The factory also supplied engines to other manufacturers.

HOBART / England 1901–1923
A big, Coventry-based factory which also supplied engines, frames and other parts to motorcycle assemblers. Built own machines with single-cylinder and V-twin engines, but used also own two-strokes as well as proprietary engines made by Morris, JAP, Villiers and Blackburne. 170cc Hobart two-strokes were popular. The last model built was a 246cc two-stroke with internal flywheel. McKenzie motorcycles also came from the Hobart works.

2¾ hp Hobart (sv) 1904

HOCHLAND / Germany 1926–1927
Limited in production numbers, the Hochland, designed by Emslander, was a well-made 496cc flat-twin ohv machine.

HOCKLEY / England 1914–1916
As a result of WWI only a limited number of Hockley machines with 269cc two-stroke Liberty and Villiers engines came into being.

HOCO / Germany 1924–1928
Interesting design with a wooden frame and on some models a fully enclosed engine. Nabob

498cc Hochland (ohv flat-twin) 1926

supplied 146cc and 246cc two-stroke engines; JAP sv engines of 293cc and 346cc capacity were also fitted.

HODAKA/*Japan 1964–1977*

When Yamaguchi, once a well-known motor-cycle factory, closed down, the American Henry Koepke resumed work in this Negoya-based Japanese factory and called his new machines Hodaka. Main production went to the USA, although he also tried to gain part of European markets. Main production concentrates around moto-cross and enduro machines with 98cc, 123cc and 246cc two-stroke engines of modern design. The American base of Hodaka is the Pacific Basin Trading Co. at Athena, Oregon.

HOENSON/*The Netherlands 1953–1955*

Bicycle factory, which built good-looking motor-cycles with 147cc Sachs and 198cc Ilo single-cylinder two-stroke engines. The last model had the 244cc Ilo twin two-stroke motor.

HOFFMANN/*Germany 1949–1954*

Produced the Italian Vespa scooter under licence for Germany, and in addition two-stroke motorcycles with Sachs and Ilo engines from 98cc to 247cc. Richard Küchen, one of the leading German motorcycles designers, created in the early 1950s beautiful BMW-like 246cc and 298cc machines with transverse-mounted horizontally-opposed twin-cylinder ohv unit design engines and shaft drive to the rear wheel. Called Gouverneur, these Hoffmann machines were of clean and up-to-date design with telescopic forks and plunger-type rear suspension. They were quite expensive in production and the motorcycle market was not good in those days.

HOLDEN/*England 1898–1903*

Designed by Colonel H. Capel Holden, this machine had a watercooled 3 hp four-cylinder engine with direct drive to the small rear wheel. Some of these interesting machines are still in existence. Colonel Holden afterwards went to Australia.

HOLLEY/*America 1902–late 1910s*

One of the first companies in the USA building motorcycles on a commercial basis. The machines had a rearward facing single-cylinder engine of about 2 hp which was mounted in a strengthened bicycle frame.

HOLROYD/*England 1922*

Racing motorcyclist Jack Holroyd built a number of sporting machines with 246cc and 346cc ohv JAP engines, without much success.

123cc Hodaka (TS) 1974

246cc Hoffman (ohv flat-twin transverse mounted) 1953

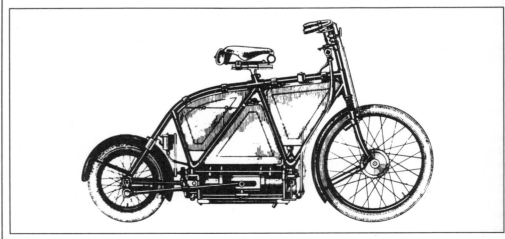

3 hp Holden (First four-cylinder built) 1897

HONDA / *Japan 1948—*

The 40-year-old Soichiro Honda already had one successful career behind him, having sold his piston ring manufacturing business just after WWII, which left him at a loose end in 1946. More as a hobby than anything else, he began converting surplus army two-stroke engines to power bicycles and the ready sale of these led him to design a motorcycle of his own. In 1948 the Honda Motor Co Ltd was incorporated; by 1950, production of the 98cc model D two-stroke was over 3,500. Honda's Model E was his first four-stroke. It had a pressed steel frame, telescopic front forks, and a 5.5hp, 150cc ohv engine. In 1953 Honda produced

98cc TS Honda D-Type single 1947

146cc Honda (ohv single 3E-Type) 1953

98cc Honda (TS) 1951

32,000 of this model — very profitably. At the urging of financial partner Takeo Fujisawa (who steered the infant Honda Co through some difficult times), that profit was almost entirely ploughed back into the developing business.

In 1954 Honda and Fujisawa, who had decided that the company had to export or die, visited Europe. Grasping the advertising possibilities of racing they attended the 1954 TT in the Isle of Man and were overwhelmed by what they saw. In particular Honda was deeply impressed by the 125cc and 250cc NSU team, who won both their races (they were double world champions that year) and who displayed remarkable organisation and efficiency. 'I decided there and then that when Honda went racing that was how we too would do it, and that those were the sort of results that we, too, would obtain,' he later commented.

Starting in 1959 when Honda 125cc twins won the team prize in the TT, Honda were indeed obtaining 'those sort of results' by 1961; between then and 1967, the company won every class in the TT — 18 victories in all — and had 16 world championships to its credit. Honda riders in those years included Tom Phillis, Tommy Robb, Mike Hailwood, Luigi Taveri, Ralph Bryans, and Jim Redman.

Other makers had won racing fame without parallel successful sales of road machines, but Honda combined the two. Its early 1960s road bikes were as strikingly different as their twin-, four- and five- and six-cylinder racers. The 125cc twin Benly and 250cc twin Dream had sturdy ohc engines that ran at very high rpm and produced remarkable power with very quiet exhausts. Pressed steel frames were used, while some models had electric starting.

Honda used clever advertising, and insisted on

246cc Honda (ohc 'Dream') 1960

161cc Honda (ohc Model CB 160) 1965

408cc Honda (ohc four-cylinder) 1977

748cc Honda VFR750R (RC30) 1988.

the competence of their sales outlets — a major reason for their success. Their 50cc Cub — and later 70cc and 90cc variants of this little 'step through' — achieved a market breakthrough rarely achieved before or since. Within a year of the Cub's introduction in 1959, nearly 170,000 had been sold. By the mid-1960s, Honda production of all models was 130,000 per month!

The first hint of a challenge to British big bikes was the CB450 vertical twin of 1965, but neither it nor the later, larger CB500 were really successful, and British manufacturers gave a premature sigh of relief. But in 1969 the stunning CB750 four appeared, a magnificently-styled machine with its transverse four-cylinder ohc engine, with four carburettors, a disc front brake and, of course, electric starting. The CB750 moved motor cycling into a new dimension. It was made in thousands, where British bikes were made only in hundreds, and it cut the heart out of the ailing British industry. Honda never looked back, even though Soichiro Honda and Takeo Fujisawa both retired at the end of 1973.

The next two decades saw a constant flow of innovation, always backed up by a range of down-to-earth reliable models for basic transportation. 1971 saw the delightful CB500 four and 1975 the

CB400. The same year, the then incredible 1000cc flat 4 watercooled, shaft-drive Gold Wing appeared (shades of George Brough!) to grow up over the years to the Aspencade and eventually the flat six cylinder GL1500. This variant, at a price of £10,000, was not a best seller in Britain, but it still found a market in the USA.

More realistic was the transverse water-cooled V twin CX500 of 1978, which grew into the CX650. The six cylinder 1000cc CBX of the same years was yet another demonstration of Honda versatility, with its double ohc engine set transversely. Like the Gold Wing, it was made at Maryville, Ohio, in a new US factory. By that time Honda had set up plants in Belgium, Taiwan, Thailand, Mexico and Brazil. They now have one in Italy as well, plus an engine plant in Pakistan.

After 10 years' abeyance, Honda made a disastrous return to racing in 1979 with the infamous oval-piston V4 NR500. One of Honda's few outright failures, this was eventually replaced by a two-stroke for Grand Prix racing, since when Honda have been content to stay with the crowd. However, the NR500 inspired a new generation of V4 engines — with conventional pistons — that is still in production in the 1990s, and highly successful in production and production-based racing.

1085cc Honda (Gold Wing flat-four) 1982

748cc Honda (four-cylinder dohc) 1982

493cc Honda (watercooled transverse ohv V-twin) 1982

HOOCK/*Germany 1926–1928*
Hoock & Co. of Cologne were importers of English Villiers engines and built the 342cc single-cylinder three-port version into their own frames. Not many were actually made.

HOREX/*Germany 1923–*
Built at Bad Homburg, the Horex was for many years a leading make in Germany. Fritz Kleemann, a well-known racing motorist, founded the factory together with his father, whose factory produced glassware under the Rex trade mark. From this name and from the first two letters of Homburg emerged the Horex trade mark. Closely connected with it was the Columbus proprietary engine factory; nearly all Horex motorcycles used these power units, although around 1930 some engines were made under Sturmey-Archer licence. In addition, Columbus engines were used by other motorcycle factories including Victoria, AWD, Tornax etc. The first design was the Gnom, a 63cc bicycle attachment, which was fitted in front of the pedalling gear. The first Horex was a good-looking 246cc ohv single, which — ridden by Fritz Kleemann Junior and Phillip Karrer — won many sporting events. Bigger 498cc and 598cc sv and ohv singles and also 198cc, 298cc and 346cc ohv models followed. Hermann Reeb, then chief designer at Bad Homburg, created in 1932 sensational 598cc and 796cc vertical twins with chain drive to the ohc. This was a technically very advanced design. Some of the bigger versions had their capacity increased to 980cc and competed successfully in the 1000cc

792cc Horex (ohc twin Columbus) 1934

sidecar racing class. Karl Braun used a supercharger on such an engine and won many races. Other models, especially 248cc and 498cc versions, ridden by Josef Klein, Franz Islinger and others were successful too and when Tom Bullus rode a 498cc Horex in the 1929 Grand Prix at the Nürburgring, he was leading the race until he had to retire. In the mid-1930s Horex also built 498cc four-valve ohv singles. After 1945, Horex was the first German motorcycle factory to get permission to build a motorcycle with more than 250cc. Some claimed it was because the Kleemanns had close connections with the Americans. At any rate the 349cc Horex Regina, an ohv single, was an excellent machine. There were also 248cc and 398cc versions of it, but none could outsell the 349cc version. It was, after many

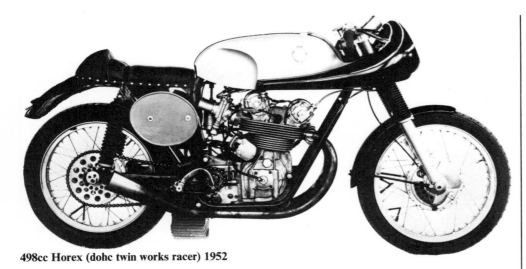

498cc Horex (dohc twin works racer) 1952

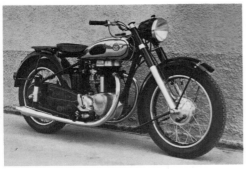

346cc Horex (ohv 'Regina' Columbus) 1950

years, replaced by 248cc and 348cc Resident singles and 398cc, 448cc and 498cc Imperator vertical twins. All these new models had modern ohv engines. In addition, Horex also produced 348cc and 498cc twin-cylinder double ohc machines for the works team, which included such famous riders as Kurt Mansfeld, Hugo Schmitz, Friedl Schön, Werner Gerber and Bill Petch. The last Horex racing machines were Apfelbeck-designed 348cc vertical dohc twins, ridden by Hans Bartl and Fritz Kläger. Kläger rode together with H. P. Müller, designer Roland Schnell, Georg Braun, Hermann Gablenz, Erwin Aldinger and Robert Zeller. Schnell also designed dohc 248, 348 and 498cc singles which he built in conjunction with Horex. After the name Horex was sold during the late 1970s, new 49 and 79cc two-strokes with German Sachs engines came into being. There is also the Horex Motorrad GmbH where the well-known designer Friedl Munch still builds—on order with six months' delivery—the luxurious 1326cc 'four in line' Horex 1400 TI with 100 bhp. The price of this hand-built motorcycle in 1982 was approximately £22,000. 48cc and 78cc Sachs-engined.

Horex two-strokes are built by Zweirad-Röth, 6 Schulstrasse, 6149 Hammelbach (Germany).

HORSY / *France 1952–1953*
Scooter with a 83cc two-stroke engine, made by a small factory.

HOSK / *Japan 1953–early 1960s*
Produced 123cc two-strokes, 248cc and 348cc ohv singles as well as 498cc vertical twins, which were not unlike the German Horex motorcycles.

HOSKISON / *England 1919–1922*
Assembler whose range consisted of three basic models: 269cc Villiers, 292cc Union and 497cc sv Blackburne-engined. Small output and orthodox open frames. Like the Villiers, the Union was also a three-port two-stroke.

HOWARD / *England 1905–1907*
Interesting 2·5 hp single, because the designer used fuel injection instead of a carburettor.

H&R (R&H) / *England 1922–1925*
A simple 147cc Villiers-engined two-stroke, hailing from Coventry. The H&R stood for Hailstone and Ravenhall, which occasionally became Ravenhall and Hailstone.

H&R / *Germany 1921–1925*
This H&R stood for Hartmann and Richter, the original name for Heros motorcycles which had their own 155cc, 185cc and 249cc sv engines.

HRD / *England 1924–1950*
Founded by famous racing motorcyclist Howard R. Davis, the company built Massey-designed machines of advanced design. They had 348 and 490cc sv and mainly ohv JAP engines, a low saddle position and a very sporting appearance. H. R. Davis himself won the 1925 Senior TT and Freddy Dixon the 1927 Junior TT on these

490cc HRD (ohv JAP Racer) 1925

498cc HRD (hc Vincent-engine Racer) 1934

998cc HRD (hc V-twin Vincent-engine) 1946

machines. In 1928 Bill Humphries of OK-Supreme fame bought HRD but soon sold it again to Phil Vincent, who continued production at Stevenage. In addition to JAP engines, he also used in the following years Villiers, Blackburne and four-valve ohv Python engines from 248cc to 498cc and fitted on all frames his unusual rear suspension. From 1934 onwards, his own high-camshaft 496cc ohv singles and from 1937 his 996cc high-camshaft V-twins came into modern frames. (See also Vincent-HRD.) The original HRD design was copied by many other producers, including Hako.

HRD/*Italy 1980–*
Sporting machines with 49 and 79cc two-strokes.

HT/*England 1920–1922*
Scooter-like design with two seats and with leaf rear suspension. Used first 292cc Union two-stroke, afterwards 346cc Barr & Stroud sleeve-valve engines. The engines were fully enclosed. The production was on a limited scale.

HUC/*Germany 1924–1925*
Designed by Max Hecker of Berlin, the HUC was fitted with 145cc and 172cc DKW two-stroke proprietary engines.

HUCKE-RINNE/*Germany 1924–1926*
Racing motorcyclist Max Hucke was building frames for 124cc, 174cc and 247cc Rinne engines, which had evaporation cooling. They were fast two-strokes and—ridden by Hucke, Rannacher, Lücke, Michael, Köhler etc.—won many races.

HÜFFER/*Germany 1923–1925*
Assembler of lightweights, who fitted 150cc to 198cc engines made by DKW, Rapid, Baumi etc.

HULBERT-BRAMLEY/*England 1903–1906*
Successor to the Booth Motor Company. Produced three-wheelers, lightweights and the Binks-designed 385cc four-cylinder in-line machine.

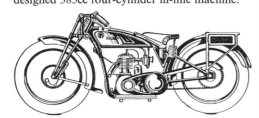

293cc Hulla (sv JAP) 1931

HULLA/*Germany 1925–1932*
Fitted mainly DKW two-stroke engines of 173cc, 198cc, 206cc and 298cc into own frames. There was another model which housed the 293cc JAP sv engine. Hulla sales were concentrated in the northern parts of Germany.

HULSMANN/*The Netherlands 1939–1955*
Bicycle factory which fitted for a long period 123cc Villiers engines. During the 1950s, Villiers-engined 198cc and 225cc machines were added.

498cc Humber (sv flat-twin) 1924

346cc Humber (ohc single) 1929

HUMBER/*England 1900–1930*
Famous manufacturer of De Dion-engined three-wheelers and of cars, whose first motorcycles were built under Phelon & Moore licence with a forward inclined single-cylinder engine. Models of own design had 496cc, 596cc and 746cc sv flat twin engines, of which the 596cc version was built until 1923. Afterwards Humber concentrated on 347cc singles with sv, ohv and ohc. A Humber ridden by P. J. Evans won the 1911 Junior TT.

HUMMEL/*Germany 1951–1954*
Became known as producer of the Sitta scooter, which had 120cc, 123cc and 149cc Ilo engines. Motorcycles also had 49cc to 248cc Ilo two-stroke engines.

HURIKAN/*Czechoslovakia 1947–1949*
Designed by Jaroslav Vlk, the Hurikan was a luxurious 247cc ohc sports machine of advanced design. Only a few were made.

HURRICANE/*Japan late 1950s–1961*
Producer of the 90cc and 123cc Rabbit scooters and of motorcycles with two-stroke engines up to 248cc. The biggest model was a 348cc ohv single.

HURTU/*France 1903–late 1950s*
Once a well-known car factory which built lightweight motorcycles and after WWII also 49cc attachment engines for bicycles.

HUSAR/*Germany 1923–1925*
A rear suspension by means of leaf-springs was common to all Husar machines. Engines fitted were side-valve singles of 296cc capacity.

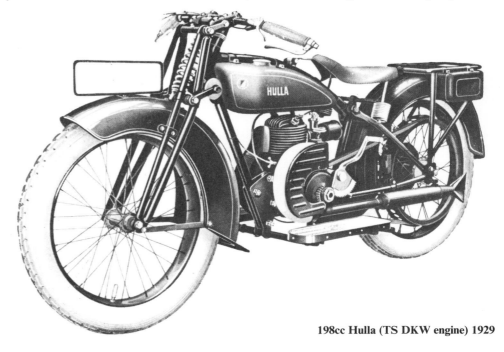

198cc Hulla (TS DKW engine) 1929

HUSQVARNA / Sweden 1903—

As an industrial conglomerate, Husqvarna was not dependent upon the vagaries of the motorcycle trade for its prosperity, so production was spasmodic, rather than continuous, between 1903, when a proprietary engine was first fitted to a Husqvarna bicycle, and 1986 when the American dealer network was sold to the Italian Cagiva company. In the 1920s most models used JAP engines, though a 735 cc ohv V twin, specifically for sidecar use was designed for 1926, and 500cc versions were made for the ISDT in 1929. These engines were used very successfully for ice — and later for road racing, though several excursions to the TT in the 1930s brought indifferent results. Husqvarna's best year was 1934, when Ernie Nott was third on a 350cc version in the Junior race and Stanley Woods made fastest lap in the Senior before running out of fuel.

The factory then largely switched to making ultra-lightweight two-strokes, and continued along much the same lines after WWII, with 120cc and 150cc models. In the early 1950s, however, Husqvarna began to take trials and moto-cross seriously, offering special 175cc and 200cc machines that became extremely popular. By 1959, engine capacity was up to 250cc, and rider Rolf Tiblin contested and won the European 250cc Moto-Cross championship.

Another remarkable achievement followed in 1960, when Husqvarna built a 500cc machine from scratch and won the 500cc championship. However, sales had plunged — for all their competition successes, Husqvarna sold only 420 motor cycles in 1961 — and manufacture of road-going motorcycles accordingly ·halted. Only 250cc competition and off-road models were now made, and a determined effort to sell them in the USA gradually succeeded. In 1962 Torsten Hallman won the World Moto Cross Championship and Rolf Tiblin the 500cc, though no 500cc machines were on offer to customers.

With some half-hearted excursions into road racing, Husqvarna thereafter concentrated on the off-road and competition market. A development in the 1970s was a 'clutchless' trial bike, followed by a genuinely fully automatic four-speed gearbox. Capacities grew to 360cc and 390cc, then to 430cc. However, with the onset of anti-pollution laws in the USA putting an end to the future of two-strokes, Husqvarna may well have seen Cagiva's bid for their USA dealer network as an ideal chance to put the effort devoted to making motorcycles to better use, switching to the manufacture of sewing machines, refrigerators and lawn mowers.

HUY / Germany 1923—1926

The first model made by this firm used the 198cc side-valve single engine built by Alba at Stettin. It won some popularity, although it had a very high riding position and somewhat uncomfortable front springing. Later, an additional model featured a

498cc Husqvarna (ohv V-twin Racer) 1934

354cc Husqvarna Automatic, single-cylinder, two stroke. 1976

350cc 100 MAG engine, although in all probability this was made only in limited numbers.

124cc Husqvarna MC 125 CR-76. 1976

IBIS / *Italy 1925–1928*
Piazza-engined 173cc sports machines with ohv and an open frame built on English lines.

IDEAL / *Germany 1924–1925*
Two-strokes with 173cc deflector-type three-port engines of own manufacture.

IDEAL-JAWA / *India 1961–*
Closely connected with Jawa of Czechoslovakia, the Mysore factory started with the production of 248cc Jawa two-stroke singles, which were known also as 'Jawa-Jezdi'. Other models based on original Jawa designs followed.

IDRA / *Italy 1923–1926*
Designed by O. Idra, this 123cc ohv engine could be fitted into bicycles and was obtainable also as a complete lightweight with a strengthened bicycle frame.

IDROFLEX / *Italy 1949–1954*
Unusual 105cc two-stroke engine fitted to the swinging arm of the rear wheel.

IFA / *East Germany 1945–1960*
Successor to the pre-war DKW motorcycles and made at the former DKW factory at Zschopau, the name IFA disappeared when it became superseded by the name MZ, which stands for Motorradwerke Zschopau. A nationalised factory, the

342cc Ifa (TS transverse flat-twin) 1955

production concentrated around two-stroke singles from 98cc to 298cc, built in large numbers. Most interesting was a twin-cylinder two-stroke of 346cc, which had the flat twin mounted transverse. It had also shaft drive to the rear wheel. The unique engine had 58mm bore, 65mm stroke and 15 bhp at 5000 rpm. Not a big output, but everyone was at that period glad to get a motorcycle at all. In addition, the 346cc IFA was comparatively cheap. When IFA disappeared and MZ took over, the only difference on the single-cylinder two-strokes up to 298cc was the different badge on the petrol tank. IFA also built aircooled 123cc and 248cc racing two-strokes. Among riders were such famous names as Petruschke, Brehm, Krumpholz, Fügner, Degner, etc. Racing manager was Walter Kaaden, also responsible for part of the development.

147cc Ilo (TS) 1923

ILO / *Germany 1923–1925*
Famous manufacturer of two-stroke proprietary engines, who also built complete 117cc, 132cc, 147cc and 170cc motorcycles until the demand for engines forced the Pinneberg factory to give up manufacture of frames and other parts.

IMHOLZ / *Switzerland 1924–1927*
Built 123cc two-strokes, afterwards also 173cc versions with their own two-strokes and 173cc Moser ohv engines. Limited production.

IMME / *Germany 1948–1951*
Unorthodox 98cc two-stroke with a pressed steel frame. The Imme had the power-egg swung

together with the rear wheel, which was connected via the exhaust pipe—which acted as one side of the frame—to the centre of the machine. Similarly unorthodox was the one-sided front fork. Before Imme closed down forever Norbert Riedl, the creator of this design, produced a similar 148cc twin-cylinder model, which was made in small numbers only.

98cc Imme (TS) 1949

IMN / *Italy 1950–1958*
Concentrated first on 49cc to 248cc two-strokes, also built ohv machines and failed. They then created a sensational 198cc flat-twin ohv of unit design with shaft drive. This design was not fully developed when it was put on the market, and that was the end of the IMN Rocket.

IMPERIA / *Germany 1923–1925*
Assembler who fitted 346cc and 496cc JAP engines into open frames. No connection with the other German Imperia.

IMPERIA / *Germany 1924–1935*
Becker's Imperia factory at Cologne was building 247cc and 347cc ohv Blackburne-engined machines and also versions with the 490cc single-cylinder ohv JAP, but most had Swiss MAG power units of 346cc, 496cc, 596cc, 746cc and 996cc. With the exception of the smallest, all were V-twins with ioe and ohv. Becker went broke in 1926 and the Schrödter family of Bad Godesberg bought Imperia. New models with

498cc single-cylinder double-port MAG ohv engines and 678cc V-twin ohv JAP engines came into being. During the 1930s there were also other models with MAG and Bark engines, but mainly 248cc, 348cc and 498cc four-valve ohv singles with Rudge-built Python proprietary power units. Racing versions ridden by Ernst Loof, A. F. Dom, Wilhelm Schminke, Sebastian Roth, Gerd in der Elst, Otto Kohfink etc. won many races and championships. Dom, born in the Dutch East Indies and formerly with Motosacoche and Standard, was a famous designer-rider. The same was the case with Ernst Loof, the top Imperia rider. In the mid-1930s import of foreign engines into Germany became nearly impossible. As a result, Imperia boss Rolf Schrödter designed a range of new and very unconventional two-strokes. The first was a 348cc double-piston single with the pistons running in opposite directions and the single plug in the centre. There were really two crankcases, one on each side of the cylinder. They were connected by a chain and on top was a supercharger. This aircooled engine was not fully developed when Imperia ran out of money;

the reason for this was too many unconventional designs to produce with limited means. These included a 498cc transverse-mounted flat-twin two-stroke with Trilok gearbox and shaft drive as well as 746cc sports and racing cars.

IMPERIAL / *England 1901–c1910*
Fitted with 3·5 hp Coronet engines, these machines had a kind of disc brake.

IMPERIAL / *America 1903–c1910*
This was a 444cc single-cylinder machine, of which nothing else is known.

497cc Imperia (ohv MAG) 1928

678cc Imperia (ohv JAP V-twin) 1929

346cc Imperia (ohv Bark engine) 1934

INDIAN / *1901—early 1950s*
Though not the USA's first motorcycle concern, Indian was an early pioneer and, for many years, indisputably the country's leading make. Its story started when a successful bicycle manufacturer George M Hendee commissioned an engine design

from toolmaker Oscar Hedstrom, who was familiar with the De Dion. Hedstrom's engine, with automatic overhead inlet valve and a spray carburettor, was fitted into a cycle frame forming part of the seat pillar, and driving the rear wheel by chain. Three machines were extensively tested in 1901 and proved notably easy to start and control, due to the excellence of Hedstrom's carburettor. The next year, 143 Indians were sold and, from then on, progress was swift. The first 600cc V twin appeared in 1907, it rapidly gained a spring front fork, twist grip throttle control and an engine shaft shock absorber.

Indians won races and broke records. Their British agent, Billy Wells, entered George Lee Evans in the 1909 TT and Evans led for half the race to finish second. Always with an eye on export sales, Hendee entered four riders for the 1911 Senior TT on the Mountain circuit. In a thrilling race, Indian riders, helped by the new two-speed gearboxes, finished 1-2-3 and Indian's name was made in Europe. In 1912, over 20,000 machines were sold.

By 1914, Indian were offering a 7hp (1000cc) twin with spring frame electric lights and even electric starting. Unfortunately, with this latter advance, Indian had over-reached themselves, since the innovation was a disaster. Even more unfortunately, the electric starting controversy had already led Oscar Hedstrom to leave the company, and indirectly to Hendee himself leaving in 1916. Hedstrom's replacements were Charles Gustafson and C B Franklin. Gustafson abandoned Hedstrom's inlet-over-exhaust-valve layout in favour of side-by-side valves with the 1000cc Powerplus of 1915. Franklin was to design the 600cc sidevalve Scout for 1919. During WWI, Indian supplied 40,000 motor cycles to the US government.

346cc Indian (sv 'Prince') 1926

In the 1920s Indian consolidated its image with the Scout, the uprated Powerplus, the Chief, and the 1200cc Big Chief. There were also various smaller single-cylinder models, rather on European lines. Racing and record breaking were still important, as was the popular sport of hillclimbing.

Exports to Britain were devastated by tariffs imposed in 1924, indeed, in the later 1920s, Indian profits were eroded overall by ever-cheaper motor cars that cost little more tha a high-quality motor cycle. Nevertheless, Indian were able to acquire the moribund Ace company, makers of a famous four cylinder motorcycle in 1927, together with the services of designer Arthur Lemon. Sold at first as the Indian Ace, later as the Indian four, the machine remained in production until 1942. Another new design in 1927 was the first 750cc Franklyn-designed Indian twin, which was to feature more importantly in Class C racing in the 1930s.

In 1930, Indian were taken over by E P Du Pont at a particularly difficult time. Production plunged, in 1933, for example, it was down to a miserable 1660 machines. Indeed, though Indian strove manfully to do so, the concern never really recovered from these grim depression years. Charles Franklyn died in 1932 and was replaced by Briggs

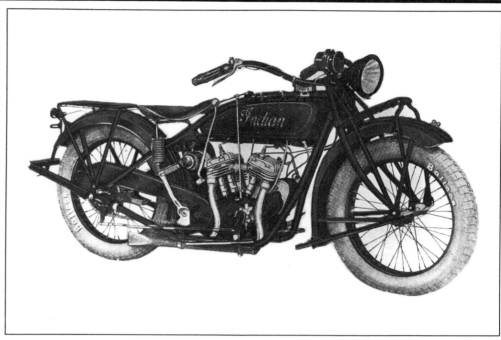

596cc Indian (sv V-twin 'Scout') 1926

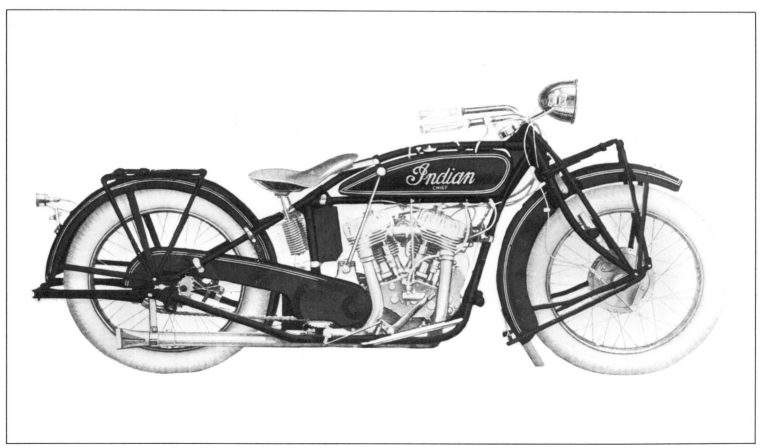

998cc Indian (Chief sv V-twin) 1928

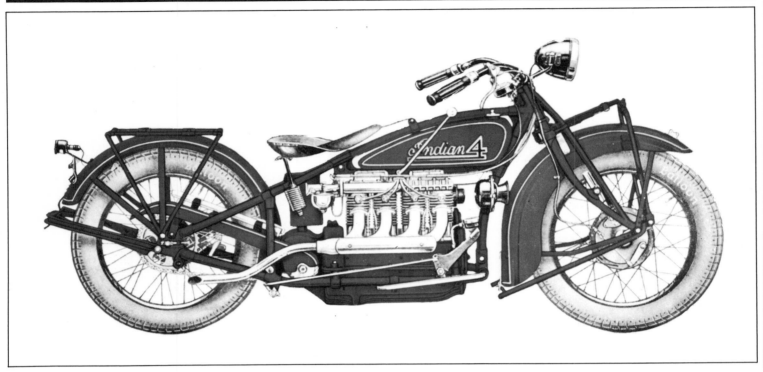

1200cc Indian-4 1931

Weaver. One of his early designs was the 750cc Sport Scout, which sold very well and became Indian's mainstay in Class C racing. Even so, Indian were, in the 1930s, running a poor second in sales to Harley Davidson. Post war, Paul Du Pont sold Indian to industrialist Ralph B Rogers, owner of Torque Engineering. While continuing to make the 1200cc Chief, Rogers instituted the Torque series of European-style singles and twins, designed by Briggs Weaver, that came on the market in 1947.

Unfortunately the Torque models were mechanically so unreliable that they earned themeselves an unenviable reputation. Money was injected into the company by British entrepreneur John Brockhouse, whose Brockhouse Engineering also provided a 250cc side-valve model, the Indian Brave. When Rogers resigned from Indian in 1949, Brockhouse assumed control, but continuing losses meant that in 1953 production in the USA was terminated, the separate Indian Sales Corporation being subsequently sold. Some European motorcycles were imported as Indians, and numerous attempts were made to revive a 'real' Indian, but in vain.

INDUS / Germany 1924–1927
Fitted with 346cc ohv Kühne engines, 346cc and 490cc ohv JAP engines and the 497cc ohc three-valve Küchen single-cylinder engine, Indus machines were built in limited numbers only. They had front and rear leaf-spring suspension.

746cc Indian (sv V-twin 'Police Scout') 1931

218cc Indian (ohv) 1949

246cc Indian (sv Brockhouse-made 'Brave') 1955

INTRAMOTOR / *Italy 1971–*
Produces a variety of 49cc models with Minarelli two-stroke engines and also 122cc trials and moto-cross machines.

INVICTA / *England 1902–1906*
Assembled machines with Minerva and Kelecom engines.

INVICTA / *England 1913–1923*
Built at the Francis-Barnett factory at Coventry, the Arthur Barnett-designed machines had 269cc Villiers two-stroke engines, other models 499cc sv Abingdon and 346cc and 678cc sv JAP engines.

293cc Invicta (sv JAP) 1921

INVICTA / *Italy 1951–1954*
Two-strokes with engines from 74cc to 123cc of typical Italian design.

IRESA / *Spain 1956–1959*
Small assembler who fitted Spanish-built Villiers engines up to 198cc into own frames.

IRIS / *England 1902–1906*
Quite unorthodox machines with 5 hp V-twin watercooled engines. There was also a hand starter and a friction clutch.

IRIS / *Italy 1952–1953*
Two-stroke machines with German 123cc Ilo engines. Limited production.

IRUNA / *Spain 1953–late 1950s*
Produced 123cc scooters with their own two-stroke engines.

ISH – *Russia 1928–*
The oldest Russian factory at Izevsk. Early models had 1200cc V-twin sv and 746cc ohv engines. They were followed by 198cc two-strokes and a Neander-like 498cc ohc machine. From 1938 onwards, the 348cc single-cylinder two-stroke Ish came into being and was built in large numbers. Early models had 18 bhp, later ones 25 bhp. Successor to this model is the 347cc Jupiter-3 with a twin-cylinder, two-stroke engine, designed on German lines. This engine has

25 bhp at 4600 rpm. Another version is the single-cylinder Jupiter Planeta Sport, whose 348cc two-stroke engine has 76mm bore, 75mm stroke and 32 bhp at 6500 rpm. Top speed is 87·5 mph.

ISLO / *Mexico 1960–*
With two-stroke engines built under Sachs licence from 48cc to 248cc. Supplies also the Cooper-Islo machines for America.

ISO / *Italy 1949–1964*
Once a famous producer of luxury cars and also of scooters and motorcycles with their own double-piston two-stroke engines of up to 248cc. Fitted also 123cc and 173cc ohv engines, but a BMW-like 499cc machine with transverse-mounted ohv flat twin never went into quantity production.

ITALA / *Italy 1933–1939*
Giuseppe Navone's motorcycles were of sound design, but built in limited quantities. As he was importer of French Train proprietary engines, his first models used the 98cc Train two-stroke. Afterwards he used 173cc, 246cc and 346cc Chaise, as well as English 248cc, 348cc and 498cc Python four-valve ohv engines. The Super-Itala had an aircooled 498cc Chaise four-cylinder engine.

ITALEMMEZETA / *Italy 1958–1966*
Designed by Leopoldo Tartarini, this machine was really an MZ built on Italian lines with MZ two-stroke engines from 98cc to 248cc.

ITAL JET / *Italy 1966–*
Evolved out of Leo Tartarini's Italemzetta made from 1958 as a re-styled MZ for Italy. A wide variety of models were produced, from 50cc up to a Triumph 650cc-engined road bike, though the concentration was on miniature motor cycles for children and similar novelties. Attempts to move into more serious manufacture in the 1980s led to financial problems that Tartarini was lucky to overcome. He had to forego his motor cycle ambitions, however, and now the company largely make 'fun' bikes, three wheelers, beach machines etc.

ITAR / *Czechoslovakia 1921–1929*
Produced the Zubaty-designed 750cc SV flat twin

746cc Itar (sv flat-twin) 1929

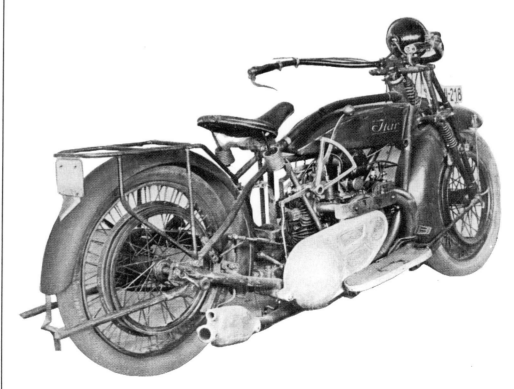

746cc Itar (sv flat-twin) 1922

used by the Czechoslovakian army and also a civilian version. A 350cc single never came into quantity production. For 1928, they switched to 350cc and 500cc SV JAP engines.

ITOM / *Italy 1948—1968*
Makers of superb 50cc mopeds and lightweight motorcycles. The latter were the backbone of 50cc racing in Britain from 1958 to 1962, but the concern did not keep up with progress.

IVEL / *England 1902—c1905*
Used De Dion and MMC engines in strengthened bicycle frames.

IVER-JOHNSON / *America 1907–1915*
Superbly designed singles and V-twins with capacities up to 1090cc. Some models had rear suspension.

IVO LOLA RIBAR / *Yugoslavia 1956–*
Produced Italian 123cc Vespa scooters under licence.

IVY / *England 1908–1932*
Newman's first machines had Precision, water-cooled Green-Precision and JAP proprietary

1090cc Iver-Johnson (sv V-twin) 1914

engines. Own two-stroke engines had 225cc and 296cc; after 1919 there were also 246cc and 346cc versions with outside flywheels. After an interruption of some years, Ivy returned to motorcycle production with 248cc two-strokes and 293cc JAP-engined sv singles.

IXION / *England 1901–1903*
Bicycle producer who fitted De Dion, MMC and — according to unconfirmed sources — also French 1·5 hp Bichrone two-stroke engines.

IXION / *England c1900s–1923*
The green machines had a variety of engines. Among them were the 670cc Abingdon V-twin, the 499cc and 597cc Precision sv singles and 349cc Precision and 293cc Peco two-strokes. When Ixion closed New Hudson bought the trade mark.

J

JAC/*Czechoslovakia 1929–1932*
Interesting 498cc single-cylinder sleeve-valve unit-design machine with shaft drive and a welded frame of triangular design, made from pressed steel. Designed by J. A. Cvach, the machine had a leaf-spring fork, a low saddle position and the triangular fuel tank between saddle and gearbox.

JACKSON-ROTRAX / *England 1949–1966*
Speedway machines with 499cc JAP single-cylinder ohv Speedway engines, designed and built by former rider Alec Jackson.

JACK SPORT / *France 1927–1931*
Assembler of motorcycles with 348cc and 498cc sv and ohv engines.

JAK / *Germany 1922–1925*
Lightweight machines, fitted with 119cc, 142cc

498cc JAC (Sleeve valve, shaft drive) 1930

and 173cc DKW and 129cc Bekamo engines, which had a charge-pump in the crankcase.

JALE / *Germany 1923–1925*
Produced air and watercooled 170cc two-strokes with deflector-type, three-port engines in limited numbers.

JAMATHI / *The Netherlands 1973–*
Limited manufacture of sporting 49cc two-strokes.

JAMES / *England 1902—1964*
Originally cycle makers, whose first motorcycle used a Minerva engine in a standard cycle frame. This was the work of Frank Kimberley, who was to be with James for the next 53 years, most of them as managing director. In 1908, the concern moved to a new factory at Greet, near Birmingham, where they remained until 1964, and expanded their production accordingly. The Safety James, a PL Renouf design with James' own 500cc engine, sold badly, but they soon were offering a lightweight two stroke, a 500cc V twin and a 600cc single. Post WWI, a fire at Greet meant that full production did not start until 1922, but for the rest of the 1920s, James were prominent on the trials scene, with the 500cc V twin as their prestige model. An ohv model was made in 1930, by which time James also had a range of Villiers two-strokes, based on Frank Baker's designs, which they had acquired. During the early 1930s, the fortunes of the four-strokes declined; by 1935 only two-strokes were being made, including, from 1939, an Autocycle. During WWII James supplied the Military Lightweight, with Villiers 125cc 9D engine, to the British Army, phasing it in as a civilian model, the ML, after 1945.

In 1951, Kimberley sold James to AMC of Woolwich. In the early 1960s, James used the disastrous AMC Piatti-designed two-stroke engine, as did AMC's other lightweight maker Francis Barnett, which had been moved from Coventry to Greet. An unsuccessful James scooter was another nail in the coffin. AMC fortunes declined and, in 1966, the group — AJS, Matchless, Norton, James and Francis Barnett — was sold to Manganese Bronze Holdings. Norton alone was to be revived.

2¾ hp James (sv) 1911

346cc James (sv) 1923

498cc James (ohv V-twin) 1929

248cc James (TS 'Cotswold M/C')

198cc James (TS 'Captain') 1957

JAP / *England 1904–1908*
Famous as manufacturer of proprietary engines from 123cc to 1098cc, JAP also built complete motorcycles until 1908, when J. A. Prestwich of Tottenham (London) decided to concentrate on building power units only. After 1945 the engine factory was taken over by Villiers.

JAVON / *Germany 1929–1932*
Small assembler of JAP-engined motorcycles with 198cc and 498cc single-cylinder sv engines.

JAWA / Czechoslovakia 1929–

In 1929 the manufacturer of arms František Janeček of Prague decided on the production of motorcycles. He got the licence of the German Wanderer design, bought eventually the production equipment for this model and thus entered the motorcycle market with a 498cc single-cylinder unit-design ohv machine with shaft drive and a pressed steel frame. The leaf-sprung fork was also made from pressed steel. The whole design was expensive to produce and not fully developed when it was bought. There were many teething troubles with the lubrication system, the valve gear and the frame. The name Jawa was a combination of the first two letters of the names Janeček and Wanderer. This model despite its faults was quite successful in big trials, including the Sixdays, with riders who included Jaroslav Kaiser, Antonin Vitvar, Franta Brand, Richard Dusil, Zdenek Houška, Robert Uvira and others.

George-William Patchett, the famous English designer, joined the Jawa factory in 1930 and soon created new racing machines with 498cc unit-design ohv engines and chain drive to the rear wheel. In later years they got separate gear-boxes and were followed by 348cc, eventually 248cc and 173cc models, used exclusively by works riders such as Franta Juhan, Fritz Bardas,

246cc Jawa (TS A.-U. Patent engine) 1936

Leopold Killmayer, Václav Stanislav, Lada Ne-rad, Josef Paštika, Jiři Bayer, Hermann Gunzenhauser and others. Patchett himself was also a good rider, besides being designer-in-chief. The big 498cc production (ex-Wanderer) model was not a commercial success, but when Jawa in 1932 introduced a very nice-looking 173cc two-stroke with Villiers deflector-type engine and a tri-angular frame also made from pressed steel, it was immediately a bestseller. These red-yellow machines became very popular; they were comparatively cheap as well as good-looking. Many riders who afterwards became famous started their careers on tuned versions of this little machine. Jawa afterwards built the Villiers engines under licence, while a 246cc two-stroke version of 1934 introduced the Schnürle patent flat-top two-stroke engine as then used by DKW in Germany, also under licence.

Patchett-designed 346cc sv and afterwards ohv models completed the Jawa range in the mid-1930s. The last pre-war version was the Robot, designed by the famous Czech designer Josef Jozif. This was a 98cc two-stroke model. When the war broke out, Patchett returned to England and concentrated on the design of arms for Enfields and other firms, a job which brought him fame and financial rewards. Jawa at the Prague-Nusle and Tynec factories repaired motorcycles during the war for the German occupants, but Czech designers and other technicians secretly developed new machines for the immediate post-war period under the noses of the Germans. Among them was a highly sophisticated 248cc two-stroke single with unit design, automatic clutch, telescopic fork and plunger-type rear suspension. In 1947 Jawa took over the Ogar factory and added a new 346cc two-stroke

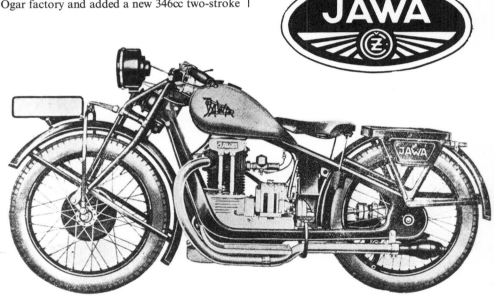

497cc Jawa (ohv shaft-drive) 1929

twin in a frame identical to the 248cc machine to the range. Václav Sklenář, another Czech designer, created in the same period new 348cc and 498cc supercharged and unsupercharged vertical-twin double ohc racing machines for the works riders. These included again Antonin Vitvar, Richard Dusil, Jan Novotny, Karel Rykr, Ladia Stainer and others. During the 1950s and 1960s, new racing twins came into being. Designers have been Josef Jozif, Jan Křivka and others. These new double-ohc models had 248cc, 348cc and 498cc and in the mid-1950s there was a 498cc production model

98cc Jawa (TS 'Robot') 1938

174cc Jawa (TS) 1966

343cc Jawa (TS two-cylinder) 1982

498cc Jawa (dohc twin-cylinder works racer) 1955

with a single ohc vertical twin engine. With František Stastny and Gustav Havel in the saddle, the 348cc racing twins won many road races in the late 1950s and early 1960s. Afterwards Jawa—since 1945 a nationalised factory —built two-stroke machines—including 248cc and 348cc racing versions—only. They also produced very successful trials and moto-cross versions and, after taking over the Eso factory, very successful 498cc ohv singles for speedway, ice racing and so forth. Many of these machines are exported to nearly every country in the world but especially to Russia, Poland, East Germany, etc. Even Barry Briggs and Ivan Mauger ride Jawa speedway machines. Jawa riders won many trials and they form—since 1931—the Trophy Team at the Sixdays. The present Jawa range (with the exception of the speedway models) consists of two-strokes from 49cc to 362cc; the machines are of sound design and developed from the early 248cc model of 1946. The smallest model currently in production is a 49cc machine with a flat single-cylinder 4 bhp (at 6500 rpm) engine, the largest road-going version the 343cc vertical-twin with 26 bhp at 5250 rpm. Among trials Jawas, the 174cc has 22·5 bhp at 7000, the 246cc 28·5 bhp at 7000, the 344cc 35 bhp at 6400 and the 362cc 36 bhp at 6500 rpm. These machines are excellent in performance, reliability Jawa for 1969. In his hands, the V4 showed promise, but, tragically he was killed in practice for the Sachsenring; his team-mate Bocek, died at Brno only a week later.

Jawa took over ESO in 1962 and thereafter produced Jawa-ESO speedway machines in large

numbers, exporting them over the world. Production of somewhat stagnant designs for the road continue to the present, with two-strokes ranging from 50cc to 370cc.

In 1981 Jawa took over CZ, with whom they had long been associated on a co-operative basis. As part of the Eastern European block, Jawa CZ often suffered from the apparent advantage of a captive market and design stagnated. Currently, they are thought to be the subject of interest from the Italian Cagiva company.

JD–*England 1920–1926*
Made by Bowden, the JD was a 116cc bicycle attachment engine. It was also supplied with a strengthened bicycle frame.

116cc JD (TS) 1923

JE-BE / *America late 1950s to late 1960s*
For the US market, built in Germany 98cc and

123cc two-stroke machines with engines made by Fichtel & Sachs. The name stood for Joe Berliner, the importer.

JEAN THOMANN / *France 1920–1930*
Was part of the Alcyon Group and produced two-strokes from 98cc to 248cc. There was also a 499cc ohv single with a big outside flywheel.

JEECY-VEA / *Belgium 1923–1927*
Concentrated on producing motorcycles with opposing flat-twin engines. These power units were 498cc ohv and 688cc sv Coventry-Victor as well as 746cc sv Watelet engines. The late King Albert of Belgium rode such a machine in the mid-1920s.

998cc Jefferson (ohv V-twin) 1914

JEFFERSON / *America 1911–1914*
The superb Jefferson was a development of the Perry E. Mack-designed PEM machines. It had its own ohv engines of 499cc (singles) and 998cc (V-twins), a swinging arm fork and rear suspension.

JEHU / *England 1901–c1910*
Was in the pioneering years a well-known factory. The engines fitted were Minerva, MMC and also of the company's own design and manufacture. They had 2·25 hp, 2·5 hp and 3 hp.

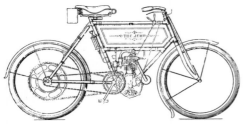

2 hp Jehu (sv) 1903

JELINEK / *Czechoslovakia 1904–1907*
Produced motorcycles with engines made by Minerva, Orion and Fafnir. These had from 2·5 hp to 5 hp.

JES / *England 1910–1924*
In pre-1914 days was already building 116cc and 189cc ohv machines. In the 1920s, models with 169cc and 247cc two-strokes came into production. There were also 246cc and 498cc sv and ohv singles with Blackburne engines when JES was taken over by Connaught.

JESMOND / *England 1899–1907*
One of the pioneers in the motorcycle trade. Fitted De Dion, MMC and Sarolea engines into the strengthened bicycle frames.

JFK / *Czechoslovakia 1923–1926*
Designed by J. F. Koch, this 348cc ohc single was of modern design. Koch was also the creator of BD, Praga, Koch and some CZ designs.

JH / *England 1913–1915*
Assembled machines with various JAP and 269cc Villiers engines. There was also a model with the 6 hp V-twin MAG engine.

JHC / *Germany 1922–1924*
Simple 183cc machines with their own three-port, two-stroke engines.

JNU / *England 1920–1922*
The only model made had a 312cc two-stroke Dalm engine. The production was limited.

JNZ / *New Zealand 1960–*
The JNZ stands for Jawa New Zealand; the machine is built under Jawa licence.

JOERNS / *America 1910–1915*
Once a well-known motorcycle factory. Built singles and V-twins and fitted two-speed gearboxes. Produced also the 996cc Cyclone, probably the first V-twin ohc machine built in large numbers.

JONGHI / *France 1931–1956*
Concentrated first on 348cc sv singles, designed by the Italian Giuseppe Remondini, who came to Jonghi from Negas & Ray. His first 348cc ohc machines were made in 1933 and were successful in races. Afterwards he built also 248cc and 173cc ohc versions. Famous Jonghi riders were Jeanin, Perrin, Renier (Sen.) and the great Georges Monneret. The factory also built small two-strokes with Aubier-Dunne engines. In the mid-1930s, Jonghi amalgamated with Prester. Most models built after 1945 had two-stroke engines from 98cc to 248cc. Jonghi machines also broke many long-distance records at the Montlhéry race track.

123cc Jonghi (ohv) 1952

JOOS / *Germany 1900–1907*
Machine factory which built engines, later also motorcycles, with horizontal twin-cylinder engines. Later models were orthodox singles and V-twins with Fafnir engines.

JOUCLARD / *France 1903–1907*
Was a machine equipped with 1·5 hp and 2·25 hp single-cylinder engines.

JOYBIKE / *England 1959–1960*
This was a cross between a lightweight and a scooter. It was powered by 70cc JAP and 49cc Trojan two-stroke engines.

JSL / *Germany 1923–1925*
Lightweights with own 132cc and 180cc as well as 206cc DKW two-stroke three-port deflector-type engines.

JUCKES / *England 1910–1926*
Very underrated machines, made by a well-known engineering company at Wolverhampton. Produced well-made two-strokes of 269cc, 274cc and 399cc and a 348cc ohv single. All had their

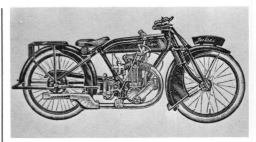

346cc Juckes (ohv) 1925

own engines and gearboxes; the last version of the four-stroke also had an additional tube on both sides, leading from the bottom of the steering head directly to the hub of the rear wheel.

JUERGENSEN / *Denmark 1904–WWI*
One of the first Danish motorcycle factories. Built English Humber machines under licence, which is interesting because these early Humber machines, with the cylinder inclined to the front and forming part of the front down-tube, were themselves made under Phelon & Moore licence.

JUERY / *France 1931–1939*
Paris-built 346cc and 498cc sv and ohv singles with Chaise as well as own engines.

198cc Juhö (sv) 1923

JUHÖ / *Germany 1922–1924*
The name came from the manufacturer Julius Höflich. Designed by Leo Falk with own 148cc sv and 195cc two-stroke engines.

JULES / *Czechoslovakia 1929–1934*
These were 120cc two-stroke bicycle engines and were sold also complete with the Leopold Skřivanek-designed Praga bicycles. They had a single leaf spring below the saddle as suspension for the rear wheel. There was no connection between Praga motorcycles and the Jules.

JUNAK / *Poland 1956–1964*
Made at the former German town of Stettin, the Junak was the only four-stroke machine made after 1945 in Poland. Of sound design, it had its own 247cc and 347cc ohv single-cylinder engine.

JUNCKER/*The Netherlands 1932–1935*
Basically a bicycle factory, the Dutch firm built a range of two-strokes from 98cc to 198cc with Ilo and Villiers proprietary engines. They used triangular frames on some models, which were so similar to German Europa motorcycle frames that the impression was created that Juncker built them for the Munich company, although there was in fact no connection. After the war Juncker merged with Gazelle, another famous Dutch bicycle factory.

JUNCKER/*France 1935–1937*
Stainless and Aubier-Dunne two-stroke engines propelled these French-built 98cc, 123cc and 147cc lightweight machines.

JUNIOR/*Italy 1924–1935*
This Italian machine was made by Edoardo Mascagni, son of the opera composer Pietro Mascagni. Equipped with triangular duplex frames, the Junior housed its own 174cc and 346cc two-stroke engines, later models also 173cc to 499cc sv and ohv JAP and 248cc and 348cc ohv Blackburne engines. The end came when Edoardo Mascagni lost his life with Italian forces in Abyssynia.

JUNO/*England 1911–1923*
Small assembler. When demand rose, it was the Birmingham-based Sun motorcycle factory which supplied the London-based Juno works with frames. Among the engines used were the 269cc Villiers, 597cc Precision and 770cc V-twin JAP. There was also a 147cc Villiers-engined model. If required Juno were also prepared to supply motorcycles equipped with other proprietary engines.

JUPITER/*Russia 1973–*
Built in the same factory as the Ish the modern Jupiter, created in 1981, has a 346cc two-stroke two-cylinder engine with 28 bhp, while a racing version of this machine develops 35 bhp and reaches 112 mph. There is also the older 346cc two-stroke single, which develops 32 bhp and which looks like a combination of older DKW and new Jawa and MZ models.

JUPP/*England 1921–1924*
The Baker-designed Jupp was a cross between a scooter and a motorcycle. It had an open frame, rear suspension and a 269cc Liberty two-stroke engine.

246cc Jurisch (TS four-cylinder w/c racer Prototype) 1926

JURISCH/*Germany 1926–1930*
The designer/producer of this very unorthodox two-stroke was Carl Jurisch, a well-known technician and racing motorist. His own 248cc double-piston twin-cylinder racing machine was watercooled and supercharged. Jurisch was a two-stroke specialist, who rode many such machines including Bekamo, Puch and DKW.

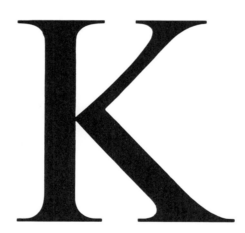

K

KADI/*Germany 1924–1930*
Small producer of good 198cc sv machines and of 498cc versions with the three-valve ohc Küchen proprietary single-cylinder engine.

KANTO/*Japan 1957–1960*
Was one of the many Japanese factories which produced two-strokes, in this case a 124cc model only.

KAPTEIN/*The Netherlands 1938–1951*
Was closely connected with the French Motobecane factory and fitted 123cc sv and 173cc ohv Motobecane engines into his machines, which had many other parts from that source.

KARÜ/*Germany 1922–1924*
Designed by Dr. Karl Rühmer, who was also behind SMW motorcycles, these machines had opposing flat-twin engines. One was the 398cc

398cc Karü (sv flat-twin Bosch-Douglas) 1923

Bosch-Douglas, built by SMW under licence, the other the 492cc BMW flat-twin.

KATAKURA/*Japan late 1950s to late 1960s*
Built a variety of two-strokes, including mofas, mopeds etc., from 48cc to 248cc.

KATHO/*Germany 1923–1925*
Assembler of 198cc sv machines with engines supplied by Alba.

KAUBA/*Austria 1953–1955*
Scooters with 98cc and 124cc Rotax-Sachs engines, built in limited numbers.

KAWASAKI / *Japan 19632—*

Kawasaki were late starters among Japanese motorcycle manufacturers. Although the Kawasaki aircraft company had been making small two-stroke and four-stroke engines, since the early 1950s, this was a minor activity until 1961, when Kawasaki Auto Sales was not formed specifically to make motorcycles. Their first move was to take over manufacture of the Meguro, a 500cc BSA A7 lookalike. The all-Kawasaki B8 125cc two-stroke followed in 1962, and soon there was a range from 50cc to 250cc, including the disc valve induction 250cc twin 'Samurai', which sold well in the USA. Following internal reorganization in 1969, the first of Kawasaki's three-cylinder air-cooled two strokes, the 500cc H1, was produced. Its abysmal handling and terrible thirst for petrol did not stop it becoming a cult motor cycle in the USA due to its straight line performance, so the three-cylinder style was carried into 250cc, 350cc and 750cc versions. The 500cc H1R and H2R racer versions

were extremely successful on the track, both as raced by the factory and as sold to private owners.

With the advent of new, strict, air pollution laws in the USA, Kawasaki planned a new range of four-strokes, the outcome being the 900cc double ohc Z1 of 1972, with its transverse in line air-cooled four-cylinder engine. The Z1 won itself a tremendous reputation, establishing Kawasaki as contenders on the US motorcycle scene. The company still raced the three-cylinder two-strokes, however, and built successful single-cylinder motocross machines.

The Z1's success led to similar 650cc and 1000cc models while 250cc and 350cc twins also appeared. However, the ultimate second generation Kawasaki was the remarkable 1300cc six-cylinder water-cooled dohc Z 1300, the flagship of the company's fleet in the early 1980s.

Kawasaki had always raced what were basically standard road machines, but sprang a surprise in 1975 with an in-line 250cc two-stroke — in effect,

two 125cc singles one behind the other. This was not a new idea, (in fact, copied from MZ) and the famous Rotax engine is also built on the same principle. The advantage of the layout is that the design of the transfer passages is unrestricted by the need to place the cylinders as close to one another as possible, as on a conventional twin. However, the in-line twin was a disappointment at first, since it suffered from severe vibration. Eventually, this was cured, and Mick Grant rode it in 1977 to good effect. In 1978, it was joined by a 350cc version, and South African Kork Ballington, with a series of excellent rides, won both the 250cc and 350cc world championships.

Through the 1980s Kawasaki maintained a full range of motorcycles, and preserved a forward-looking technical outlook. In common with all the Japanese motorcycle concerns, they suffered to some extent from the worldwide decline of the commuter market and consequently the reduced sales of smaller machines. This led to undue

85cc Kawasaki (TS) 1965

123cc Kawasaki (TS racer) 1966

652cc Kawasaki (dohc four-cylinder 'Z 650') 1977

498cc Kawasaki (TS three-cylinder 'KH 500') 1977

748cc Kawasaki Mach IV Model H2 1972

1286cc Kawasaki (watercooled six-cylinder dohc) 1979

647cc Kawasaki (dohc four-cylinder) 1979

248cc Kawasaki (ohc twin) 1980

emphasis on horsepower, though improved suspension, brakes and 'body work' — total enclosure — and almost universal use of liquid cooling were benefits that came out of this. However, interestingly, Kawasaki's unusual current 1990s offering is the 'Retro-styled' 550c and 750cc Zephyr models, which are 'simple' air-cooled transverse four-cylinder motorcycles bereft of any modern styling and encumbrances in a fashion reminiscent of the 1970s rather than the 1990s. Kawasaki always have been different from the run of the mill!

KC/*Germany 1921–1924*
Designed by the motoring pioneer Fritz Kirchheim, the first KC product was a 105cc rotary-valve two-stroke bicycle engine with 1·2 hp at

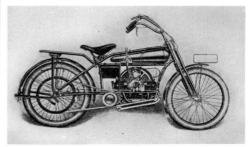

257cc KC (TS flat-twin) 1923

2100 rpm. Another product by KC—which stood for Kirchheim & Co.—was an opposing flat-twin motorcycle with 257cc. This was also a two-stroke. Most parts including even the carburettor were made by KC.

KELLER / *Switzerland 1930–1932*
Equipped with a triangular duplex frame of strong design, the 347cc Keller had its own sv single-cylinder unit-design engine of very clean lines. It could be taken very easily out of the frame and dismantled using very few tools. Still, the Keller was not very successful.

KEMPTON / *England 1921–1922*
Lightweight machines and scooters with 124cc ohv engines supplied by ABC.

KENI / *Germany 1921–1923*
Yet another Berlin-based producer of two-stroke machines. The Kempff-designed machines had 145cc and 158cc deflector-type, three-port engines.

145cc Keni (TS) 1923

KENZLER-WAVERLEY / *America 1910–1914*
Closely connected with Jefferson, Kenzler-Waverley also produced singles and V-twins with their own ohv engines.

KENILWORTH / *England 1919–1924*
Produced orthodox motorcycles with 293cc single-cylinder sv JAP engines. Another product was a scooter, supplied with various engines including the 143cc ohv Norman, 269cc Villiers and 293cc JAP. They had front and rear suspension and a hand starter. Despite the advanced design, sales figures did not show any scooter boom.

KERRY / *England 1902–early 1960s*
Various sources claim that the first Kerry machines—equipped with Kelecom and FN engines—were made in Belgium for the London-based East London Rubber Co., who sold these machines in England. From 1910 onward Kerrys were made at the Abingdon factory with 499cc

347cc Keller (sv) 1932

sv single-cylinder and 670cc V-twin sv engines. Production finished when WWI broke out, but entirely different Kerry machines—49cc mopeds—appeared in the late 1950s.

KESTREL / *England 1903*
Assembled machines with 211cc Minerva and MMC engines.

KG / *Germany 1919–1932*
Very advanced single-cylinder design by the Krieger brothers and Franz Gnädig. The first models had 503cc ioe, later ones 499cc ohv unit-design engines with shaft drive to the rear wheel. Early models had leaf-spring forks; from 1922 onwards, girder forks were used. At that date, the KG was being built by the Cito works of Suhl in Thuringia, which in 1923 became part of the Allright factory at Cologne. When they stopped building motorcycles, Paul Henkel—formerly with Cito—bought in 1927 the whole design including the production equipment and moved it to his works at Mäbendorf near Suhl. So the original KG became the Cito-KG, the Allright-KG and eventually the Henkel-KG, but was after 1927 only a shadow of the big make of the early 1920s. Rudi Albert had it redesigned in 1924 and fitted with a horizontal shaft, but it could not compete with the latest BMW and other designs. Until the mid-1920s these machines

498cc KG (ohv shaft-drive) 1924

gained many successes in sporting events. Leading riders were Max and Oskar Krieger, Hemming, Kniebecke, Faust, Ehrlenbruch, Greifzu, Roggebuck and others. When Allright took over, the Krieger brothers and Gnädig left the factory. The Kriegers afterwards built 'Original Krieger' motorcycles with Blackburne engines, and Gnädig created new 348cc ohv singles, bearing his name and eventually built by the Diamant works.

KIEFT / *England 1955–1957*
Produced small sports and racing cars and sold Hercules (Nuremberg-built) 147cc and 198cc scooters and 197cc two-stroke Sachs-engined motorcycles in England under the Kieft trade mark.

KILEAR / *Czechoslovakia 1924–1926*
Brno-based machine factory which built 247cc two-stroke machines with three-port, deflector-type engines.

KING / *England 1901–1907*
Pioneer who built three-wheelers and afterwards motorcycles. Both had De Dion Bouton engines, the motorcycles also Minerva, MMC, DAW, Antoine, Sarolea and other power units.

KING-JAP / *Germany 1928–1931*
Although built in Germany, most parts—including the 198cc, 346cc, 490cc and 545cc sv and ohv JAP engines—came from England.

KINGSBURY / *England 1919–1923*
Aircraft engine factory, which produced after WWI small cars, scooters not unlike the Autoped and Krupp and also 261cc motorcycles with their own engines.

KINGSWAY / *England 1921–1923*
Motorcycles of simple design with 293cc sv JAP engines.

K&K / *Germany 1924–1925*
Two-stroke machines with own 170cc and 289cc three-port engines.

KLOTZ / *Germany 1923–1926*
Excellent 246cc two-stroke three-port deflector-type engines of their own manufacture in modern frames (for that period) of good design. Ridden by Gebhardt and others, Klotz machines gained many successes in trials and races. Connected with Klotz was Wilhelm Gutbrod, who after the demise of the Klotz make founded the Standard motorcycle factory.

246cc Klotz (TS) 1925

KM / *Germany 1924–1926*
Produced 142 and 159cc two-stroke machines with own three-port engines in limited numbers.

KMB / *Germany 1923–1926*
Built single-cylinder machines with 4·2 hp two-valve and 6 hp four-valve engines of own design and manufacture.

4.2 hp KMB (sv) 1923

KMS / *Germany 1922–1924*
Interesting 196cc ohv singles with the valves in a sloping position. These engines were of own design and manufacture. A smaller model had the 142cc Grade two-stroke power unit.

KÖBO / *Germany 1923–1926*
Köhler & Bovenkamp at Barmen-Hatzfeld was a well-known factory for chains. Motorcycles made by this company had own 276cc two-stroke engines and never gained the reputation of the chains made by Köbo.

KOCH / *Czechoslovakia 1934–1935*
When the Praga factory decided to give up manufacture of motorcycles, chief designer J. F. Koch founded his own factory. There he built very advanced 348cc unit-design ohc singles with four-speed gear-boxes. Production was on a limited scale.

KOEHLER-ESCOFFIER / *France 1912–1957*
Designed by Roger Guignet, Koehler-Escoffier machines became famous during the 1920s with

347cc Koehler-Escoffier (ohv) 1929

497cc Koehler-Escoffier (ohc) 1929

a 996cc V-twin which had — as the only machine of this capacity and configuration in the world — an ohc engine of their own design and manufacture. There was also a 498cc ohc single with a sloping cylinder. Other versions had 347cc and

497cc MAG and Chaise single-cylinder ohv engines. There was a great similarity with Monet-Goyon motorcycles, after the MG factory at Macon took over the Guignet works in 1929. After 1945 Monet Goyon and Koehler-Escoffier motorcycles were near-identical. Most models had 98cc to 248cc Villiers two-stroke engines with J. A. Gregoire rear suspension. Among successful Koehler-Escoffier riders were the famous George Monneret and Jean Eddoura.

KOFA / *Germany 1923–1925*
Assembled machines with 283cc two-stroke engines.

KOHOUT / *Czechoslovakia 1904–1906*
Minerva and Fafnir-engined 2·5 hp and 2·75 hp single-cylinder machines.

KOLIBRI / *Germany 1923–1930*
A good 110cc two-stroke attachment engine supplied for existing bicycles and also with the firm's own bicycle.

KOMÁR / *Poland late 1950s to late 1960s*
Nationalised producer of various 48cc two-stroke mopeds.

KOMET / *Germany 1902–1905*
Originally a bicycle factory, Komet was among the first producers of two-stroke motorcycles in Germany. These engines were made under French Ixion licence and had from 1 hp to 4 hp.

KONDOR / *Germany 1924–1925*
A two-model range which consisted of a 3 hp version with an Ideal sv engine and a 3·5 hp

3 hp Komet (TS) 1905

185

model, which had a Simplex single-cylinder two-stroke power unit.

KOSMOS / *Italy 1978–*
Enduro and moto-cross machines with 123, 246, 310, 348 and 480 single-cylinder Sachs engines, including a 246cc version with 45 bhp, built at Liscate near Milano.

KOSTER (KS) / *Germany 1923–1925*
Unorthodox lightweight with a frame made partly from pressed steel, partly from tubes. It was supplied with 123cc Bekamo or with 144cc Cockerell engines. The wheels were disc wheels, the drives (chain and belt) fully enclosed while the petrol tank formed the top part of the frame.

KOVROVETZ / *early 1960s*
Was for a few years the leading 123cc and 174cc two-stroke single in Russia. Eventually superseded by the Voskhod.

KR / *Germany 1924–1925*
Successor to the Karü, the KR had also the old 492cc sv flat-twin BMW proprietary engines; another model was the big 998cc V-twin MAG with ioe valves and a duplex cradle frame.

KR / *Germany 1930–1933*
Although both KR machines were made at Munich, they had nothing in common. This one was an assembled machine with 198cc sv and ohv as well as 298cc sv engines made by JAP.

KRAMER / *Germany 1977—1985*
Manufacturers of trials, moto-cross and enduro models, with Rotax two-stroke engines of between 125cc and 280cc, which competed in the ISDT and later the ISD Enduro with distinction. Even so, falling sales meant an end to production in the mid-1980s.

KRAMER / *Italy 1979–*
Linked to, but independent of, the German Kramer factory and makers of similar Rotax-engined machines.

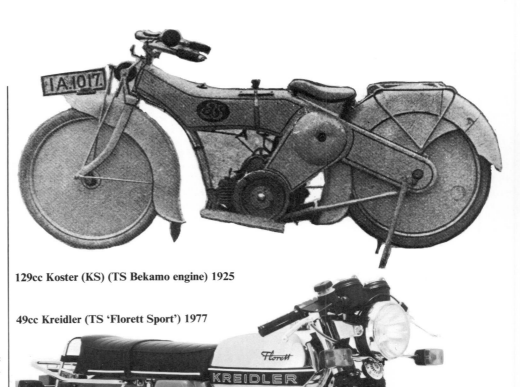

129cc Koster (KS) (TS Bekamo engine) 1925

49cc Kreidler (TS 'Florett Sport') 1977

KRAMMER / *Austria 1926–1929*
Vienna-based Rudolf Krammer's first machines had 172cc Villiers two-stroke engines. His 496cc ohv models had the rare single-cylinder Anzani or the MAG engine; the 996cc V-twin versions housed 8-valve Anzani ohv engines. The production was on a limited scale.

KRASNY-OKTOBR / *Russia 1930–1934*
These were the first motorcycles made in large numbers in Russia. They were not unlike the German DKW machines of that period and had 296cc two-stroke engines.

KREIDLER / *Germany 1951–*
Concentrated on the production of 50cc machines, including mofas, mopeds etc. As a result of steady development, the motorcycles — equipped with flat two-stroke engines of 40mm bore, 39·7mm stroke and 6·25 hp at 8500 rpm — are among the leaders in this class. The Kreidler frames are made from pressed steel, the wheels on some

497cc Krammer (ohv Anzani engine) 1928

49cc Kreidler (TS 'Florett Touring') 1974

49cc Kreidler (TS 'Super TS') 1966

models from light alloy. Top speed of the Florett is around 53 mph. Designed by chief engineer Hilber, Kreidler machines include some very fast 49cc racing machines which have broken world records. Among leading riders were Anscheidt, Kunz (father and son), Rittenberger, Lazzarini, Dörflinger and other successful men. In 1981 commercial difficulties led to a reorganisation and new ownership of Kreidler, but to no avail. In 1982 the factory closed.

KRIEGER (ORIGINAL KRIEGER)/Germany 1925–1926

After the Krieger brothers left the KG factory (taken over by Allright), they founded at Suhl in Thuringia another motorcycle factory, this time with the Original Krieger trade mark. With frames very similar to the KG, this new machine had a 347cc sv Blackburne engine, but failed to gain much popularity. Interesting is the fact that the Kriegers also offered their old 499cc ohv single with its shaft drive until 1926, although the machine was made by then at the Allright-owned Cito factory at Suhl. They also produced frames for other companies and a Hamburg company supplied KG frames with various JAP engines.

KROBOTH/Germany 1951–1954

Produced scooters of sound design with 98cc, 147cc and 173cc Sachs two-stroke engines. Was already during the 1920s connected with motorcycles, when he not only raced on Roconova and Gillet-Herstal machines, but when the K&R (Kroboth & Richter) motorcycle was made. In the 1930s he was also behind the design of Favorit and Kroboth light cars.

KRS/Germany 1921–1926

Assembler, who fitted 148cc and 198cc ohv Paqué proprietary engines and also the 293cc Bosch-Douglas flat twin, made under licence by SMW.

KRUPP/Germany 1919–1921

The autoped-like scooters—called at that time Motorläufer in Germany—had 185cc and 198cc engines fitted outside the small front wheel. Producing scooters was not a good proposition then and even the financially strong Krupp group was not in the trade for long.

KSB/Germany 1924–1929

Small, but very active make. Fitted a variety of engines into own frames. These included the 142cc and 173cc DKW, 348cc ohv Kühne, 248cc Blackburne and eventually the 248cc and 490cc sv and ohv JAP single-cylinder.

KTM / Austria 1953—

A make that seemed to spring from nowhere, and, for no particular reason at first, became extremely popular very quickly. Excellent styling was probably the reason, which helped KTM build up a following among younger riders of 50cc machines.

49cc KTM (TS Sachs 'Comet GP 50RS) 1977

390cc KTM (GS 390 TS) 1982

Their bikes used 125cc and 150cc Rotax and also Puch and Sachs engines. In the 1960s KTM began serious efforts in trials and moto cross, progressing, in the 1970s, to making their own two-stroke engine/gearbox units, though a number of Rotax engines, made under licence in Austria, still featured. In the 1980s KTM became ever more deeply involved in world moto cross competition with typical single-cylinder water-cooled two-stroke machines. Success on the tracks, however, did not bring the rewards that might have been

49cc KTM (TS Sachs 'Comet') 1971

246cc KTM (TS Own eng. '250 GS') 1977

expected — or hoped for. By the end of 1991, KTM's financial situation was such that the company was expected to collapse. A management buy-out rescued the situation, but the new company currently faces an uncertain future.

KUMFURT / *England 1914–1916*
With frames made under Waigh patents, these machines housed 269cc Villiers and 496cc Precision V-twin engines.

KURIER / *Germany 1921–1924*
Designed by Curt Hanfland, these 147cc two-stroke engines had square-finned barrels. Hanfland supplied such engines also to other manufacturers, including the Bavarian Flink.

KURRAS / *Germany 1925–1927*
The Kurras sport machines had triangular frames with watercooled 173cc Bekamo two-stroke engines, which had an additional pumping piston at the bottom of the crankcase. Not many were actually made.

KV / *Germany 1924–1927*
Simple ohv machines with own 197cc and 246cc single-cylinder engines.

KYNOCH / *England 1912–1913*
Now an unknown make, but Kynoch was once a famous arms factory at Birmingham. Produced mainly 488cc single-cylinder and 770cc V-twin sv machines with own engines of first class design and quality. Kynoch's Perry Barr factory housed afterwards the Amal carburettor works.

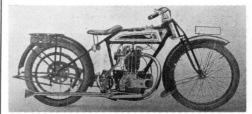

346cc KZ (ohv Kühne engine) 1925

KZ / *Germany 1924–1925*
Assembler, who fitted besides 198cc sv Alba engines, also 348cc ohv engines, made by Kühne at Dresden. They were designed by Franz Gnädig, formerly of KG (Krieger-Gnädig) fame.

L

L-300/*Russia 1932–*
Produced DKW-like 294cc and 346cc two-strokes and—in 1940—also a 348cc single-cylinder machine. The two-strokes were built in large numbers for the Russian forces.

LABOR/*France 1908–1960*
One of the many motorcycle factories belonging to the Alcyon group of companies. Labor produced 98cc to 248cc two-strokes and mainly ohv models from 174cc to 498cc.

LADETTO (LADETTO & BLATTO)/*Italy 1923–1932*
Like other Italian factories, Ladetto's first machines were 123cc and 173cc two-strokes. After Emilio and Giovanni Ladetto were joined by Angelo Blatto they built potent 173cc sv and ohv models and a 247cc sv machine with own engines. Alfredo Panella won his class in the 1928 Grand Prix of Europe at the Meyrin Circuit in Switzerland, where the 173cc Ladetto & Blatto was extremely fast. Blatto left the Turin-based factory in 1930.

LADIES PACER/*England 1914*
Built in Guernsey, this open-framed machine housed a 110cc two-stroke engine, made by JES at Gloucester.

LADY/*Belgium 1925–1938*
Designed by Lambert van Ouwerkerk, these well-made machines had 172cc to 498cc proprietary engines made by Villiers, MAG, Blackburne, JAP and Python (Rudge) and—on some models—already in 1932 a good rear suspension.

LAFOUR & NOUGIER/*France 1927–1936*
A variety of engines made by Aubier-Dunne, Chaise, Stainless, Train, Villiers and JAP powered these machines, from 98cc to 498cc capacity.

LAG/*Austria 1921–1929*
The first products were 118cc and 148cc two-stroke bicycle engines. Afterwards a few JAP engines with 346cc and 490cc were fitted into LAG frames. A 246cc two-stroke came into production in 1925, but from 1927 until the demise of motorcycle manufacture, only a single model with a 346cc two-stroke engine was made by the Liesing (near Vienna) factory. They fitted these engines also to Draisines. A 348cc model with an ohc engine, designed by LAG designer Ludwig Stein, never came into quantity production. The two-strokes had 70mm bore, 90mm stroke, Tiger forks, Sturmey-Archer 3-speed gearboxes and —in the last models—modern saddle tanks.

497cc Lady (sv Blackburne engine) 1930

LA GALBAI/*Italy 1921–1925*
Equipped with own 276cc, 301 and 347cc single-cylinder and 492cc V-twin two-stroke engines of own design and manufacture, these machines were not well-known internationally.

LAGONDA/*England 1902–1905*
The Lagonda factory owner was an American, Wilbur Gunn, who came to England to build motor vehicles. His first products were three wheelers, followed by cars and motorcycles. Most had De Dion, MMC or Minerva engines.

L'ALBA/*Italy 1924–1926*
Slightly modified German 198cc Alba sv machines, assembled at Milan by Valeri.

LA LORRAINE/*France 1922–1925*
Lightweight machines with own two-stroke engines from 98cc to 248cc.

LAMAUDIÈRE/*France 1901–1907*
Used big engines and there was even a single-cylinder engine with a capacity of 942cc.

LAMBRETTA/*Italy (Spain) 1946–*
The Innocenti-built Lambretta was one of the first and most successful scooters on the international market. It had engines from 123cc to 198cc and there were also 49cc mopeds and for a short period also 123cc motorcycles. A special racing machine bearing the name Lambretta and designed by the famous Salmaggi was a 248cc transverse-mounted double ohc V-twin. Pagani rode it in a few races during the early 1950s.

LA MONDIALE/*Belgium 1924–1933*
These machines had nothing in common with the Italian-built Mondial. Blavier's La Mondiale, built at Brussels, was one of the first machines using a pressed steel frame and fork. The two-stroke engines had 308cc (75mm × 68mm bore/stroke) and 349cc (75mm × 79mm bore/stroke); bigger versions used 346cc and 498cc Chaise ohc engines. There was also a 347cc Villiers-engined model and there were JAP-engined 346cc (70mm × 90mm bore/stroke) and 490cc (85·7mm × 85mm bore/stroke) sv and ohv singles. Thanks to triangular frames, La

496cc La Mondiale (ohc Chaise engine) 1928

Mondiale machines had a very low saddle position. Among the works riders were Fondu and Schuoppe, who rode 248cc ohv racing machines with JAP engines.

LAMPO / *Italy 1925–1927*
Well-designed lightweight machines with 123cc, 173cc, 198cc and 247cc two-stroke and 173cc ohv engines. The last came from Piazza.

LANCER / *England c1904*
Minerva, MMC and their own engines powered these 2 hp, 2·75 hp and 3·5 hp machines.

LANCER / *Japan 1957–early 1960s*
Produced two-stroke machines up to 248cc and built eventually a Lilac-like 248cc V-twin, which was transverse-mounted in the frame and had shaft drive to the rear wheel.

LANCO / *Austria 1922–1926*
The best-known model built by Lanco was the Josef Wild-designed 496cc machine with its own ohv single-cylinder engine. There was also an sv

496cc Lanco (ohv) 1924

version and earlier models had 492cc, 746cc and 986cc ioe MAG engines.

LANDI / *Italy 1923–1926*
Built 122cc and 172cc machines with own two-stroke three-port deflector-type engines.

LA PANTHERRE / *France 1928–1932*
Chiefly assembled orthodox machines with 346cc and 490cc sv and ohv JAP engines.

LAPIZE / *France 1930–1937*
Another small but active factory. Fitted different engines, including Aubier-Dunne, LMP, JAP and others into machines from 98cc to 498cc.

LATSCHA / *France 1948–1953*
Assembler, who fitted 98cc and 123cc Aubier-Dunne two-stroke engines into own frames.

LAURIN & KLEMENT / *Austria (Czechoslovakia) 1899–1908*
One of the leading motorcycle factories in the early years, Laurin & Klement produced singles, V-twins and even four-cylinder in-line machines. Some models were watercooled. The first models had the engine above the front wheel; thereafter a wide variety of engine placements were designed. Famous were the single-cylinder models BZ with 2·5 hp, L with 2·75–3 hp and BZP with 2·5 hp. The model CC was a V-twin with 3 hp and front suspension, the CCD a stronger version

4 hp Laurin & Klement (sv Type 'CCD' V-twin) 1904

3 hp Laurin & Klement (sv Type 'B') 1903

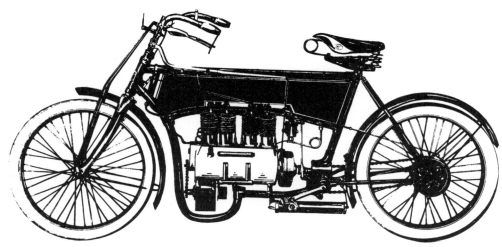

5 hp Laurin & Klement (sv Type 'CCCC II') 1905

75cc Laverda (ohv) 1951

98cc Laverda (ohv) 1956

with 3·5 to 4 hp and the CCRW was a water-cooled 4·5 to 5 hp machine. The first four-in-line was built in 1905. Motorcycle production stopped when Laurin & Klement concentrated in 1908 on car production. The L&K motorcycles — then an Austrian make — were built in Germany with the Germania trade mark under licence. In the mid-1920s, Laurin & Klement was bought by the Skoda works. While producing motorcycles, the factory won many big races with riders who included Vondřich, Podsedniček, Toman, Count Kolowrat, Merfeit etc.

L'AVENIR / *Belgium 1959–*
Producer of 49cc mofas, mopeds etc. with HMW and Sachs engines.

LAVERDA / *Italy 1949–*
Francesco Laverda made his first 75cc ohv motor cycle entirely on his own solely for his own personal use. Local enthusiasm pushed him into making replicas for sale, and by 1951, 500 had been produced. Entries in the Milan-Taranto road race culminated in 1953 in Laverdas taking the first 14 places in their class! Next came a 100cc model and 50cc and 60cc scooters.

Laverda embarked on a totally new direction in 1961 with a 200cc ohc twin, but the company's for-

124cc Laverda (ohv 'Trail') 1969

744cc Laverda (ohc twin Model 750 S) 1969

tunes were really transformed by a brand-new 650cc ohc twin, designed by Francesco Laverda's son, Massimo, and launched in 1967. Quickly uprated to 750cc, the twin sold well, but Laverda had ambitions for a 900cc three-cylinder, which appeared in 1973 — and nearly foundered due to electrical problems. These were eventually resolved, and by 1975 the 3C was well established. The Jota sports model of 1976 consolidated Laverda's position. In 1978 a prototype V-6 was built and raced at the Bol d'Or, only to retire with drive shaft problems. Smaller two-stroke and four-stroke machines were made, but enjoyed limited popularity, leading to financial problems for the company in the 1980s. So did a venture into off-road four-wheelers and diesel engines.

In 1985 the company was forced to retrench and concentrate on the three-cylinder 1000cc SFC. Even so, production ground to a halt over 1988 and 1989, and a rescue operation was required. The result was the formation of Nuovo Moto Laverda, without the Laverda family. Various new designs were proposed, with a revival of the extraordinary in-line V6 among the possibilities. But, in common with so many other once-successful European motorcycle concerns, Laverda entered the 1990s in a state of uncertainty.

LAZZATI / *Italy 1899–1904*
The Milan factory was among the first in Italy producing motorcycles. The De Dion engines were mounted into strengthened bicycle frames.

L&C / *London c1904*
Small assembler, who fitted De Dion, Minerva and Antoine engines.

LDR / *Germany 1922–1925*
Designed by Josef Herz, the 548cc sv single was a primitive design, although it had a low saddle position. The engine had an outside flywheel and neither chain was sufficiently enclosed. Early machines had belt drive to the rear wheel.

LEA FRANCIS / *England 1911–1926*
George Bernard Shaw was one of the Lea Francis customers. He rode a MAG-engined 592cc ioe V-twin. Other models had 496cc versions of the same make of engine. Until 1920, the Coventry-based car and motorcycle factory also fitted

592cc Lea-Francis (ioe V-twin MAG) 1923

981cc Laverda (three-cylinder dohc RGS 1000) 1982

V-twin sv JAP engines — including 746cc power units — into their own frames.

LEBELT / *Germany 1924–1925*
Small producer of machines with own 3·8 hp two-stroke and 4·6 hp sv engines.

LECCE / *Italy 1930–1932*
Built 173cc ohv machines with modified Swiss-made Moser engines. Otello Albanese, the Lecce boss, modified the cylinder-heads to V-valves.

LE FRANCAISE-DIAMANT / *France 1912–1959*
Another Alcyon-owned motorcycle producer, who built machines from 98cc to 498cc. After the war, only two-strokes up to 248cc were made.

LEGNANO / *Italy 1954–*
Concentrated on mopeds, mofas and other lightweights with 49cc engines, made mainly by Sachs and Minarelli.

LE GRIMPEUR / *France c1900–1932*
Produced a variety of machines from 98cc two-strokes to big V-twins with engines made by MAG, JAP, Aubier-Dunne, Stainless, Chaise etc. Another French factory, Dresch bought Le Grimpeur in the late 1920s.

LEIFA / *Germany 1924–1925*
Lightweights with 148cc sv engines, built by a former shipyard.

981cc Laverda (three-cylinder dohc Jota) 1982

497cc Laverda two-cylinder 1977

980cc Laverda (ohc) 1972

LELIOR/*France 1922–1924*
Built an Evans-like 246cc two-stroke machine and also a 174cc two-stroke flat-twin.

LEM / *Italy 1974—1983*
Produced a range of lightweights and children's motorcycles, using 50cc Morini and Minarelli engines.

LEONARD / *England 1903–1906*
Small assembler of motorcycles with Minerva, MMC and Fafnir engines.

LEONARDO FRERA/*Italy 1930–1934*
When Frera founder Corrado Frera retired in 1929 and Emilio Fossio took over the famous factory, young Leonard Frera became technical director. Two years later he left and founded his own motorcycle works at Tradate. He built there 173cc to 346cc sv and ohv machines with JAP single-cylinder engines.

LEOPARD/*Germany 1921–1926*
Produced 248cc and 346cc two-strokes with their own engines, afterwards also 248cc and 348cc ohv models.

LEPROTTO/*Italy 1951–1954*
Well-made two and four-stroke (ohv) models of 123cc, 158cc and 198cc capacity.

LETHBRIDGE/*England 1922–1923*
Small assembler of machines with 247cc and 269cc Villiers two-stroke three-port engines.

LETO/*Germany 1926–1928*
Interesting design with a frame made of pressed steel, which was welded together and included the petrol tank. Lehmann, the designer, fitted 173cc and 198cc Rinne two-stroke engines into his unusual frames.

LE VACK/*England 1923*
Famous designer-rider Herbert Le Vack — who was also with JAP, Duzmo, New Hudson, Indian, Motosacoche — built for a short period his own 346cc ohv single-cylinder machines, using JAP engines.

LEVIS/*England 1911—1939*
Levis made the first practical lightweight two-stroke motorcycle and led the world in two-stroke development into the 1920s. For many years, they

246cc Levis (TS Model 'K') 1926

were one of England's leading manufacturers of two-stroke machines. Racing successes included winning the 250cc class of the 1920 Junior TT and the first Lightweight TT, the French and Belgian Grand Prix — all in 1922. Top Levis riders including Geoff Davidson, R.O. Clark and Phil Pike, among others. Lightweights of first 211cc and then 250cc were very popular in the early 1920s, and sold all over the world. For 1927 Levis designer and development engineer Bob Newey,

246cc Levis (TS Model 'O') 1927

346cc Levis (ohv mod. A) 1928

the brother-in-law of the Butterfield brothers, who owned the company, devised a simple 350cc ohv four-stroke engine that was originally offered in the same frame as the current model O 250cc two-stroke. Though two-strokes continued to be produced, the ohv machines gained in popularity and were made in 250cc, 350cc, 500cc and latterly 600cc versions.

Though never a high volume producer, Levis were highly regarded. However, in 1939, the But-

Percy Hunt, the great Norton rider, rode a 348cc Levis in the 1928 Amateur T.T.

496cc Levis (ohv mod. D-Special) 1938

193

terfield brothers sold the factory to an air compressor manufacturer, the marque coming to an end as a result.

LEWIS/*Australia 1911–1913*
Small factory at Adelaide which used English 546cc single-cylinder watercooled precision engines in own simple and open frames.

LFG/*Germany 1921–1925*
The first product of this former airship producer was a separate small wheel with a 163·5cc sv engine, which could be attached to any bicycle. More unorthodox was a 305cc single-cylinder two-stroke motorcycle, which had an airship-like body.

LGC/*England 1926–1932*
Made at Birmingham by the Leonard Gundle Motor Co., a manufacturer of delivery three-wheelers, the machine had a very sporting appearance, but was never built in large quantities. Engines fitted were the 247cc Villiers, 293cc sv JAP and both 346cc sv and ohv JAP single-cylinder versions.

LIAUDOIS/*France 1923–1927*
Assembled machines with Train two-stroke engines from 98cc to 173cc.

LIBERATOR/*France 1902–late 1920s*
Old producer who fitted mainly Antoine, Sarolea and JAP proprietary engines.

LIBERIA/*France 1920–1965*
Bicycle factory which produced motorcycles with mainly Aubier-Dunne two-stroke engines from 98cc to 248cc.

LILAC/*Japan 1952–1961*
Was a leading make and built many expensive and luxurious models. Among them were shaft-driven 246cc flat and transverse-mounted ohv V-twins, 173cc ohv singles with shaft drive, etc. Lilac produced also 49cc mopeds, mofas, etc.

246cc Lilac (ohv transverse V-twin) 1960

LILIPUT/*Germany 1923–1926*
Assembled in a modest way motorcycles with proprietary engines made by Namapo, DKW, Baumi, Gruhn and others.

LILLIPUT/*Italy 1899–c1906*
Produced machines with 269, 293 and 499cc engines. Made by Minerva, Villiers and TDC.

LILY/*England 1906–1914*
Another assembler of motorcycles with 269cc, 293cc and 499cc engines, made by Minerva, Villiers and TDC (Cross).

LINCOLN-ELK/*England 1902–1924*
Was a well-known make. Designed by James Kirby, pre-WWI models had his own 402cc and 499cc single-cylinder sv engines. After the war, production concentrated around 349cc and 596cc sv singles and 770cc sv V-twins.

LINER–*Japan 1961*
Like Lilac, Liner also built quite expensive motorcycles. Among them were 148cc ohv singles and a 246cc vertical twin, which had—like the Sunbeam S7 and 8 models — one cylinder behind the other. It had an ohc unit-design engine and also shaft-drive to the rear wheel.

LINSER/*Austria (Czechoslovakia) 1904–1910*
Linser motorcycles were also known under the Zeus trade mark. The range consisted of 492cc singles and 618cc V-twins with their own sv power units.

LINSNER/*Germany 1922–1924*
Assembled flat-twin machines with 293cc Bosch-Douglas and 492cc BMW sv proprietary engines.

LINTO/*Italy 1965–1968*
Designed by the famous Lino Tonti, these 498cc

5 hp Linser (sv V-twin) 1905

3½ hp Linser (sv) 1905

490cc Lloyd (ohv JAP) 1925

vertical twins were double-ohc road racing machines, built in very limited numbers. The riders included Alberto Pagani, Jack Findlay, John Dodds and Marszowsky.

LINX / *Italy 1929–1941*
Made by a small factory, Linx motorcycles were of modern design. The engines were 173cc to 598cc sv and ohv singles, made by Blackburne, Piazza, and JAP, and the four-valve Rudge-built Python.

LION-RAPIDE / *Belgium 1936–1953*
Assembled machines with 98cc to 247cc Villiers and Ilo two-stroke engines and there were also models with the 347cc FN engine.

LITO / *Sweden 1959–1965*
Produced 498cc ohv motocross machines with modified single-cylinder BSA and Husqvarna engines. An engine, designed by Folke Manner-stedt, had 87mm bore, 83·5mm stroke, 496cc and a semi-desmodromic valve gear for the ohv. The clutch and the declutching mechanism was built into the graduated flywheel.

LITTLE GIANT / *England 1913–1915*
Assembled machines with 225cc two-stroke and 199cc sv single-cylinder Precision engines.

LLOYD / *England 1903–1923*
Heavy machines, built mainly for use in the former British Colonies. The range included 499cc and 497cc singles and 842cc V-twins, all with their own sv engines.

LLOYD / *Germany 1922–1926*
Produced a single model, a 144cc two-stroke version, only.

LLOYD / *Germany 1923–1926*
The first product was an Ottmar Cramer-designed 137cc bicycle engine. Bigger machines included 293cc, 346cc and 490cc JAP-engined sv and ohv models of typical English design and with many parts made in England.

LLOYD / *The Netherlands 1930–1931*
Was closely connected with the German DKW and Hulla factories, which supplied the 198cc two-stroke engine and (Hulla) most of the parts for the frames. The frame was made from pressed steel.

LMP / *France 1921–1931*
Was really an engine factory which built also JAP engines under licence in France. The range of LMP motorcycles included 173cc and 248cc two-strokes and sv and ohv single-cylinder models from 247cc to 497cc. Marc and CP Roleo fitted LMP engines.

LMS / *Germany 1923*
Another builder of airships, which tried to produce unorthodox motorcycles with airship-like bodies. In fact only a very few machines were built and all of these had 142cc DKW engines before production ceased.

LOCOMOTIEF *The Netherlands 1957–early 1960s*
Mopeds with 49cc Pluvier and Sachs engines. Successful but little known.

LOHNER / *Austria 1950–1958*
Produced first class car bodies etc. and also Porsche-designed electro-motor vehicles. The scooters had 98cc and 123cc Rotax-Sachs and 198cc Ilo engines.

98cc Lohner (TS Ilo engine) 1955

LOMOS/*Germany 1922–1924*
Early scooter with a pressed steel frame, made by DKW and afterwards by Eichler of Berlin. A 142cc DKW two-stroke engine was used.

LONDON/*England c1903*
Forgotten producer, whose machines housed De Dion, Minerva and MMC engines.

LORD/*Germany 1929–1931*
Despite the English name, a German machine with a 198cc JAP sv engine.

LORENZ/*Germany 1921–1922*
Another early scooter with a 211cc two-stroke engine which soon disappeared from the market.

LORENZ/*Germany 1921–1925*
Known also as the Rapid bicycle attachment engine, the interesting Lorenz was a 126cc two-stroke flat-twin with the cylinders set opposite. It was supplied also as a complete machine with a strengthened bicycle frame.

LORIOT/*France 1927–1930*
Bredier & Charon, a French gearbox factory, supplied units which could be attached to existing JAP proprietary engines for the use of shaft drive to the rear wheel.

LOT/*Poland 1937*
Unit-design machine with a 346cc single-cylinder two-stroke engine and shaft drive, built in limited numbers.

LOUIS CLEMENT/*France 1920–1932*
Limited production of 598cc and 996cc V-twins with own ohc engines. From 1928 onwards, manufacture concentrated around 98cc two-stroke machines.

LOUIS JANIOR/*France 1921–1924*
Heavy machines with 499cc flat-twin sv engines.

LUBE/*Spain 1949–1965*
For many years closely connected with NSU of Germany, Louis Bojarano, the head of this Spanish factory, built NSU-engined two and four-strokes from 49cc to 246cc into his own frames. Only after NSU gave up motorcycle production did Lube build their own two-strokes.

LUCAS/*Germany 1923–1924*
The first models had the 129cc Bekamo two-

126cc Lorenz (TS flat-twin bicycle engine) 1923

stroke engine with pumping cylinder; later ones their own 148cc ohv engines.

LUCER/*France 1953–1956*
Most models had 173cc AMC ohv engines, others the Aubier-Dunne two-strokes from 98cc to 173cc.

LUCIFER/*France 1928–1956*
Used a variety of the proprietary engines. These included the 98cc to 246cc two-stroke Train, 248cc to 496cc ohv MAG and Chaise and also the 498cc unit-design ohc Chaise.

LUDOLPH/*Germany 1924–1926*
Fitted own two-strokes of 247cc and 299cc into simple frames.

LUGTON/*England 1912–1914*
Limited production of 498cc machines with Precision and JAP engines.

LUPUS/*Germany 1923–1926*
The Stuttgart-based factory concentrated production on a single model with its own 148cc two-stroke engine.

LUTÈCE/*France 1921–1926*
Heavy and luxurious 997cc and 1016cc vertical twins with strong duplex frames, built much on American lines. They had shaft drive to the rear wheel. The last model was a 98cc two-stroke with belt drive.

LUTRAU/*Germany 1924–1933*
A producer of car accessories, whose two-stroke singles had 198cc, 246cc and 346cc engines of own design and manufacture. There was also a 497cc sv single-cylinder model. Designer: Ludwig Traunspurger.

348cc Latrau 1928

LUTZ/*Germany 1949–1954*
Produced 48cc and 49cc two-strokes, mainly scooters and mopeds. The last Lutz scooter had a 173cc two-stroke engine.

LUWE/*Germany 1924–1928*
Designed by Ludwig Weber, the first models had 148cc and 198cc Paqué ohv engines. There was also a version with the 198cc ohc engine made by Paqué. Other models used the 348cc ohv Kühne engine and 348cc to 746cc singles and V-twins made by JAP, MAG and Blackburne.

LWD/*Germany 1923–1926*
A small factory, which produced 197cc and 247cc sv engines and fitted them into simple tubular frames.

M

MABECO/*Germany 1923–1927*
This design was a perfect copy of the American Indian Scout. Built by Max Bernhardt & Co. at Berlin, the engines were really made by Siemens & Halske. They were 596cc and 749cc sv V-twins and in 1925 a 749cc ohv version which in racing trim had four exhaust pipes, was added. Originally green in colour, Mabecos became eventually red like the Indians of that period. This led to difficulties, as the Springfield company went to court. Mabeco was liquidated, but after a change of name from Max Bernhardt & Co. to Mabeco-Werke GmbH, they re-entered motorcycle production, still with the big Siemens & Halske Group as the main shareholder. A few 996cc ohv racing-machines and 346cc double-piston single-cylinder two-strokes built under Garelli licence were made too. Mabeco gained many racing successes with such riders as Hermann Rossner, Erich Tennigkeit and others.

749cc Mabeco (sv V-twin Model 'Luxus') 1927

749cc Mabeco (ohv V-twin Model 'Sport') 1927

MABON/*England c1905*
Strengthened bicycle frames with MMC, Fafnir and own engines. Limited production.

MABRET/*Germany 1927–1928*
Small assembler, whose machines had 346cc sv and ohv Kühne engines; a few also the 496cc Kühne sv single.

MACKLUM/*England 1920–1922*
Scooter-like machines with 292cc Union two-stroke engines. Production was on a limited scale.

MACO/*Germany 1921–1926*
Produced a variety of DKW-engined two-strokes and also 198cc sv machines with own engines.

MACQUET/*France 1951–1954*
Two-strokes with 123cc and 174cc, built into modern frames.

MADC/*Switzerland 1901–1905*
This was the original name for the 215cc Motosacoche bicycle-attachment engines, built by the Dufaux brothers.

MAER/*Italy 1978–*
One of the many new German producers of 123cc and 246cc moto-cross and trial (enduro) two-strokes.

MAFA/*Germany 1923–1927*
Bicycle factory which used 119cc to 246cc DKW two-stroke engines as well as the 348cc ohv and 496cc sv single-cylinder Kühne power units.

MAFALDA/*Italy 1923–1928*
Sporting two-stroke machines with own 123cc and 173cc three-port, deflector-type engines.

MAFFEIS/*Italy 1903–1935*
Like the Maserati brothers in the racing car field, the Maffeis brothers built and raced their own product. The first Maffeis machines had Belgian 2·25 hp Sarolea engines. Maffeis chief Bernardo Maffeis later designed 348cc single-cylinder and also V-twin models, but concentrated during the 1920s on producing machines with 248cc, 348cc and 496cc sv and ohv Blackburne engines.

MAGATY / *France 1931–1937*
Small assembler of 98cc two-stroke machines with Train and Stainless engines.

MAGDA / *France 1933–1936*
Small production of 98cc and 123cc two-stroke machines.

MAGNAT-DEBON / *France 1906–late 1950s*
Was among the leading French makes. Built different V-twins partly with Moto-Rêve engines in pre-1914 days. After WWI new two-strokes and single-cylinder sv and ohv models to 498cc capacity were built. Became part of Terrot in Dijon during the 1930s and had more or less identical models to the Terrot, among them, after 1945, mopeds, scooters and ohv singles up to 499cc with their own single-cylinder power units. Top rider in pre-war days was Paul Boetsch, who joined Terrot together with others when Magnat-Debon was taken over.

MAGNAT-MOSER / *France 1906–1914*
A Magnat-Debon branch factory—also at Grenoble—which fitted Swiss Moser engines up to 746cc.

MAGNEET / *The Netherlands 1950s to early 1960s*
Moped and mofa producer. Used mainly 48cc Sachs two-stroke engines.

MAGNET / *Germany 1901–1924*
Leading motorcycle producer in pre-1914 days, who also built own ioe and sv engines. Most famous was the 4·5 hp V-twin model.

4½ hp Magnet (sv V-twin) 1906

MAGNI / *Italy 1928–1930*
The most interesting model which appeared under this name was a 348cc ohc twin-cylinder machine with the two cylinders facing forward. Another model had a vertical 498cc single-cylinder. Both models were put into limited production by the designer Luigi Magni.

MAICO / *Germany 1935—1987*
The first pre-WWII Maicos used 120cc and 145cc Ilo two stroke engines, but when motorcycle production resumed after the war in 1948, Maico's own 125cc two-stroke took their place. In 1951, the company launched the sensational enclosed Maico Mobil, with a 175cc fan-cooled engine; this was not a scooter, but had many of a scooter's good points. With more conventional 175cc machinery, Maico took part in the ISDT and similar events successfully, also becoming increasingly involved in moto-cross. For 1954, there was the 350cc or 400cc two-stroke twin Taifun, with beautifully detailed pressed frame-cum-bodyworks, and, for 1955, the new Maicoletta scooter.

Through the years Maico's involvement with off-road sport increased, and many machines were sold in the USA. There was also some involvement with road racing in the 125cc class and the Maico 125cc R5 model was popular and successful with private owners. The German Army used 250cc Maicos, based on the company's moto-cross experience, in the 1970s. In the 1980s, however, financial problems dictated a policy of making only off-road models, or lightweights with off-road styling, with water cooling, monoshock suspension etc.

In 1987, Maico collapsed, most of its employees being dismissed. However, a buyer was at hand, the concern moving to Bavaria as a result Restarting production again took time, and it is not yet possible to predict what the future holds for Maico motorcycles, though sales in export markets appear to be being maintained.

174cc Maico (TS Model 175 SS) 1960

123cc Maico (TS Model 'MD 125' Racer) 1969

386cc Maico (TS Model 'MC 400 Moto-Cross') 1977

490cc Maico (TS moto-cross) 1982

MAGNI / *Italy 1977*
Once MV's race chief, Arturo Magni made special accessories, then used Honda CB900, BMW and Moto Guzzi 1000cc V twin engines in special frames. Limited production to special order.

MAINO / *Italy 1902–1956*
A small factory which built motorcycles in limited numbers and with interruption. In early years they fitted Swiss 2·25 hp Souverain engines; after a long period of abstaining from building motorcycles, Giovanni Maino produced after 1945 lightweights with 38cc Mosquito and Sachs and NSU engines from 98cc to 147cc.

MAJESTIC / *England 1933*
An attempt by Ernie Humphries of OK Supreme to move up-market in the early 1930s. The very nicely styled and made 250cc, 350cc and 500cc Majestic had engines made by the Stevens brothers under the name AJAX, after they had been forced to sell their AJS company to the London Matchless firm.

MAJESTIC / *Belgium 1928–1931*
Made from English components, this machine was fitted with 346cc and 490cc single-cylinder sv and ohv JAP engines, Burman gearboxes, Amal carburettors and other proprietary parts.

MAJESTIC / *France 1927–1934*
Another assembled machine, using Train, Chaise and JAP engines up to 498cc. A sensational 498cc four-in-line model with an aircooled Train engine and a car-like bonnet over the power unit, with duplex steering, a car-like frame and rear suspension, never went into quantity production.

MAJOR / *Italy 1947–1948*
Yet another motorcycle with a fully enclosed engine and with shaft-drive to the rear wheel. Designed by Salvatore Majorca, this machine had a 347cc engine of his own design.

MALAGUTI / *Italy 1958–*
Makers of small motorcycles and high tech children's motor cycles. Originally used Mosquito, then Sachs and now Franco Morini engines, all of 50cc, on which the company now concentrate. Malaguti are one of the leaders in their field, strong in export and still expanding.

MALANCA / *Italy 1957–*
Produces like Malaguti a wide range of 49cc mopeds etc. and also 124cc and 149cc two-

346cc Mammut (sv JAP) 1925

stroke machines with twin-cylinder engines. Malanca's 123cc watercooled two-stroke racer built in the mid-1970s was a very successful vertical twin.

MAMMUT / *Germany 1925–1933*
The first models had 198cc Baumi, afterwards 197cc and 246cc own two-stroke engines. From 1928 onwards, Mammut used 198cc Villiers and 198cc to 497cc Blackburne engines. Mammut also built Coventry-Eagle frames under licence. They were made from pressed and rivetted steel.

198cc Mammut (sv JAP) 1931

MAMMUT / *Germany 1953–1956*
Had nothing in common with the other Mammut. Production concentrated on 49cc mopeds and lightweights of 123cc, 147cc, 173cc and 198cc two-stroke machines with Sachs and Ilo

proprietary engines. Identical to these Bielefeld-built machines were also Meister and Phäno-men motorcycles, also Doppler products.

MAMOF / *Germany 1922–1924*
Assembled machines with 145cc DKW and Grade two-stroke engines. Also small production of machines with own 155cc sv motors.

MANET / *Czechoslovakia 1948–1967*
This factory in Slovakia is part of the national-ised Czechoslovakian motorcycle industry. The only motorcycle built under this name was an 89cc double-piston two-stroke single, designed by Vincenz Sklenář; afterwards the factory produced scooters with 123cc engines and is still working closely together with Jawa and CZ.

MANON / *France 1903–c1906*
Strengthened bicycle frames with their own 1·5 hp engines.

MANTOVANI / *Italy 1902–1910*
Produced 1·5 hp, 2·75 hp and 4 hp machines, of which some had watercooled engines of own manufacture.

124cc Malanca (TS Model 'Sport') 1976

MANURHIN / *France 1955–1962*
After DKW (Auto Union) stopped manufacture of the Hobby scooter in 1955, Manurhin took over production and supplied it with a 75cc two-stroke engine.

MANUFRANCE / *France 1951–1955*
Lightweight machines and scooters with 124cc and 174cc engines.

MARANELLO-MOTO / *Italy 1977–*
Sachs, Simonini and other two-stroke engines of 49, 123 and 247cc are used by this small company for powering a variety of trial, moto-cross and other competition machinery.

MARATHON / *America 1910*
A two-stroke twin with shaft drive. It has been impossible to find out if this design was marketed.

MARC / *France 1926–1951*
Well-known make which built machines of typical English design. The range included models with 247cc Staub-JAP and 347cc and 490cc sv and ohv engines made by JAP and LMP.

MARCK / *Belgium 1904–1908*
Produced single-cylinder machines with own 499cc ioe engines.

MARIANI / *Italy 1930–1934*
Interesting 496cc single-cylinder sv machines, supplied with two valves for the use of petrol and with three valves for running on naphta. They never became a world-sensation.

MARINI / *Italy 1924–1928*
Not to be confounded with Morini, Emilio Marini's machines — built in limited numbers — had 124cc two-stroke engines.

MARLOE / *England 1920–1922*
Small assembler, who fitted 346cc Precision and 348cc and 498cc sv Blackburne engines into open frames.

MARLOW / *England 1920–1922*
There have been discussions in the motorcycle press about whether this make was identical with the Marloe, which was made at Birmingham. There was really no connection with the Warwick-built Marlow, where the main production concentrated on 269cc Villiers-engined ma-

MARS (MA) / *Germany 1903–1957*
Swiss Zedel and German Fafnir engines powered Mars motorcycles built in Nuremberg before WWI. Fame came in 1920 when Franzenberg designed the famous white Mars with a box frame made from welded and rivetted pressed steel. The engine was exclusively made by the Maybach car and aircraft engine factory for Mars. It was a 956cc sv flat twin with opposing cylinders. The first models had a two-speed gearbox with two chains to the rear wheel; from 1927 onwards, a three-speed gearbox was used. There was a hand starter below the low saddle; the gear change was inside the petrol tank and so was the tool kit. Early models had a swinging arm on the front, later ones a Druid-like Tiger fork. Half of the rear wheel was enclosed and leg shields were standard. For a couple of years, this Mars — which was delivered in white, afterwards also in green, violet and dark red — was a good seller. During the inflation in Germany the factory ran into difficulties, and production stopped between late 1924 and 1926, when Johann and Karl Müller,

two leading technicians of the Mars works, started up again with improved models. As they could not use the Mars trade mark, the machines were known for a while as 'MA'. In 1929 they added new models with MAG, later also with Sturmey-Archer, JAP and Villiers engines from 198cc to 596cc. During the 1930s, manufacture concentrated on bicycles and mopeds with 75cc and 98cc Sachs engines. There was a 60cc two-stroke lightweight with 57mm bore × 68mm stroke. Typical for all Mars and MA products was the excellent workmanship and finish. This was still true after 1945, when Rudi Albert — formerly designer with Allright and Phänomen — created the unorthodox Mars Stella, with a low frame, small-diameter wheels and rubber suspension for the fork and the saddle. Sachs supplied the 147cc, 174cc and 198cc two-stroke engines. Albert also designed the last Mars model, the sporty Monza with a Sachs 49cc engine. When the factory closed down, Gritzner took over manufacture of this lightweight. Chief designer Albert left and joined the Fichtel & Sachs proprietary engine factory.

956cc Mars (sv flat-twin Maybach engine) 1923 (D)

497cc Mars (ioe MAG) 1929 (D)

147cc Mars (TS Sachs Model 'Stella') 1952 (D)

chines. Models with 346cc and 490cc JAP engines were built to order.

MARMONNIER / *France 1947–1951*
Produced mainly 124cc and 174cc machines with Aubier-Dunne engines.

MARS / *England 1905–1908*
Small factory which—like the German Mars—also fitted Fafnir engines into strengthened bicycle frames. It is not known if there was a connection with the German factory. The London-based firm also used the 211cc Minerva engine, which was not used by Mars in Germany.

MARS / *England 1923–1926*
A variety of engines powered these well-made machines, built in Coventry. Among them were the 247cc Villiers two-stroke, 293cc and 346cc JAP sv models, the 348cc sleeve-valve Barr & Stroud and the 348cc oilcooled Bradshaw. Production was on a small scale, but workmanship was excellent. Mars already used modern saddle tanks in late 1923.

MARSH / *America 1901–late 1910s*
Pioneer of the American motorcycle industry. Produced singles and V-twins with their own engines. After they bought the Metz motorcycle factory, Marsh's machines became known as MM, which stood for Marsh-Metz.

MARSEEL / *England 1920–1921*
Designed by racing-driver D. M. K. Marendaz, the Marseel was a 232cc scooter which failed to make the grade.

MARTIN / *England 1911–1922*
Assembled standard-looking machines with 198cc Precision and 293cc, 347cc and 490cc sv JAP engines. There was also a V-twin with the 64·5mm × 76mm bore/stroke 498cc JAP engine.

MARTIN / *Japan 1956–1961*
Assembled two-stroke singles with 124cc, 198cc and 246cc engines.

MARTINA / *Italy 1924–1927*
Small producer of 173cc two-stroke machines.

MARTIN-JAP / *England 1929–1957*
Specialist in the manufacture of JAP-engined 348cc and 498cc speedway machines. Was known all over the world and supplied such machines to many famous riders.

MARTINSHAW / *England 1923–1924*
Fitted the 346cc Bradshaw 'oilboiler' (oilcooled) engine into their own frames. Production of this ohv single was limited.

MARTINSYDE / *England 1919–1925*
A former aircraft factory which built 346cc singles and 498cc to 676cc V-twins with their own eoi (exhaust over inlet) engines. Of good design and quality, the biggest version had 70mm bore and 88mm stroke, drip lubrication, an AJS three-speed gearbox and Amac carburettor. When this factory closed down, BAT in London bought the remains and the name.

346cc Martinsyde (ioe) 1923

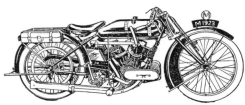

676cc Martinsyde (ioe V-twin) 1923

MARUSHO / *Japan 1966–c1970*
Was a very BMW-like 498cc transverse-mounted ohv flat-twin with unit-design engine, four-speed gearbox and shaft drive to the rear wheel. The Marusho was built in the former Lilac factory and destined mainly for the USA market.

MARVEL / *America 1910–1913*
Closely connected with Glenn Curtiss, Marvel used Curtiss single-cylinder and V-twin engines.

MARVEL-JAP / *England 1909–1912*
Fitted JAP proprietary engines into standard frames, especially the 4·5 hp V-twins. Limited production.

MAS / *Italy 1920–1956*
Founded by Alberico Seilig, one of Italy's leading designers of motorcycles, the first machines were strengthened bicycles with their own 123cc ohv engines. The first motorcycles made by MAS had 148cc and 173cc ohv engines with big outside flywheels and pedalling gears. 173cc sv and 244cc ohv singles followed. During the 1930s the range included 248cc and 348cc sv machines and a 568cc sv single. There were also 348cc and 498cc ohv models, which—like the sv versions—had inclined cylinders. Although main production concentrated for a long time on 173cc ohv models in different shapes, Seilig had already designed in 1929 a modern 492cc vertical-twin with an sv engine, and later, very good rear suspensions for nearly the whole range. He left the MAS factory in 1938 and founded the Altea. After the war he was in Argentina for many years, but eventually returned to Italy, where he died. MAS during the war supplied 498cc ohv singles to the Italian forces and also produced the 173cc Lupatta two-stroke, followed by a 340cc sv and a new version of the 598cc ohv model. The 122cc Stella Alpina, with cooling by forced air, was interesting but not a success. That was soon after the war, and in 1950 a new 492cc vertical-twin with a single

498cc Marusho (ohv transverse flat-twin Model 'Magnum') 1965

496cc MAS (ohv) 1938 (I)

ohc engine also failed to make the grade. Better was the 173cc Zenith of 1951, a very modern ohv single with telescopic fork and swinging-arm rear suspension. Another model had a 173cc ohc engine and was exhibited in 1954 at the Milan show. Other models included a range of 124cc two-strokes and a Sachs-engined 49cc mini-scooter.

MAS / *Germany 1923–1924*
Built 183cc two-strokes in small numbers.

MASCOTTE / *France 1923–1924*
Lightweight machines with own 174cc sv engines.

MASERATI / *Italy 1953–1961*
Famous factory which entered motorcycle production with modern 123cc two-strokes and 158cc ohv models. There were also 248cc ohv and 173cc ohc singles, a 158cc two-stroke and eventually a 248cc vertical-twin with an ohc engine, built in small numbers only. Although of excellent design and finish, Maserati motorcycles never became as famous as the cars.

248cc Maserati (ohv) 1955

MASON & BROWN / *England 1904–c1908*
Assembled machines with De Dion, Antoine and mainly the 2 hp Minerva engine.

MASSEY (MASSEY-ARRAN) / *England 1920–1931*
Designed by E. J. Massey, these machines had a hectic life, as the company moved nearly every year. They built good, light motorcycles with 172cc to 490cc engines made by Villiers, Jap, Blackburne and Bradshaw. Massey also designed the first HRD motorcycles.

MAT / *Czechoslovakia 1929–1930*
Not unlike the Ariel Square Four, the 498cc Votroubek-designed MAT had a square four-cylinder engine, but Votroubek used an sv design with shaft drive to the rear wheel. The factory, owned by Bugatti racing driver Miloš Bondy, built only few of these machines.

MATADOR / *Germany 1925–1926*
Limited production of lightweights with their own 269cc two-stroke engines.

MATADOR / *England 1922–1927*
Concentrated on 348cc machines with Blackburne sv and ohv engines and with the oilcooled Bradshaw ohv engine. Bert Houlding, the designer, also built Toreador motorcycles. Successful riders: B. Houlding, A. Tinkler.

159cc Maserati (ohv) 1953

MATCHLESS / *England 1901-1969 (revived 1987)*
Harry Collier senior and his sons Harry and Charlie Collier were famous pioneers, who started the Matchless company in London in 1901 using De Dion and MMC engines from a very early date. They were early customers, too, for JAP engines, which they raced successfully. Competing in the scandalous International Cup Race in Austria in 1906 so disgusted them that they urged the Auto Cycle Club to stage a 'fair' race in the Isle of Man. As a result the TT was born. The Collier brothers won, or were second, in six TT races between 1907 and 1911 and set many records at Brooklands and elsewhere.

By this time, Matchless was mainly using JAP and MAG engines, but they began to make their own after WWI. In the 1920s, Harry and Charlie Collier were joined by Bert Collier, their younger brother, though their father died in 1926. Two years later, 1928 Matchless became a public company. The designs of the period were unexciting by and large, and not enhanced by the strange shade of khaki green chosen for most models. Matchless briefly flirted with Brough Superior-type petrol tanks, before settling on somewhat slab-sided saddle tanks, enamelled white with black lining.

Two designs of more interest were the Silver Arrow of 1929 and Silver Hawk of 1930. Both had very narrow-angle V engines — a side-valve twin of 400cc for the Arrow and, for the Hawk, a 600cc four with overhead camshaft. Despite their advanced specifications, including spring frmaes, neither was a sales success.

Even so, Matchless was a well run and profitable company, as became evident in 1931, when AJS at Wolverhampton hit financial trouble. Matchless outbid BSA to acquire the company. At first, Matchless made the AJS as a separate range, but, as parts were used up, the two makes were rationalised and, by the end of the 1930s, were virtually identical, the exception being the 350cc and 500cc ohc race models. These were sold only as AJS.

Associated Motor Cycles — AMC, is frequently termed the Matchless/AJS set-up — also built and raced a most impressive supercharged ohc V4 500cc AJS, originally seen at the 1935 Show as a sports model! After a disappointing 1936 season, it

986cc Matchless (sv flat-twin) 1916

976cc Matchless (sv V-twin JAP) 1923

347cc Matchless (sv Model 'Comfort') 1925

398cc Matchless (sv V-twin 'Silver Arrow') 1930

346cc Matchless (ohv) 1947

646cc Matchless (ohv twin Model G12 CSR) 1961

496cc Matchless G6 (ohc single) 1960

347cc Matchless G3 (ohv single) 1960

496cc Matchless G50 (ohc single) 1960

497cc Matchless (ohv Model G80CS Trails) 1961

498cc Matchless G9 (vertical twin) 1960

pany's new sales manager. There were also a 500cc vertical twin, followed by 550cc, 600cc and 650cc variants, all of which shared a central main bearing.

In the 1950s, Matchless acquired the Norton, Francis Barnett and James companies and the Matchless name appeared for the first time in many years on a racing model. This was the G45, a 500cc twin, which was followed by the 500cc G50, in effect a stretched 7R.

With the passing of the Collier brothers, however, the quality of AMC's management declined sharply and rapidly and the decision to manufacture an AMC two-stroke engine for the use in the James and Francis Barnett range proved disastrous.

The design of 'Lightweight' 250cc and 350cc models, and a frantic mix of AMC and Norton parts to create special bikes for the US market did little to arrest the company's slide. As early as 1961, there had been a shareholders' revolt, but, as so frequently happens, this led to nothing. Jock West resigned in disgust. Matchless management quarrelled with their American distributor, the able and energetic Joe Berliner, and became involved with the moribund Indian Sales Corporation, which by that time had nothing to do with manufacturing. By 1969 AMC — Matchless — were effectively bankrupt and were sold to Dennis Poore's Manganese Bronze Holdings group. Norton was revived and AJS put on hold. Matchless simply disappeared.

However, in 1987, the name was revived. Les Harris, 'spares king' and maker (under licence) of the post-Triumph 'Bonneville' bought the Matchless name from Manganese Bronze and launched a new machine with an ohc 494cc Austrian Rotax engine. The frame was British-built, but it was largely equipped with Italian hubs, brakes, front forks and rear suspension. Called the G80, the new model, unfortunately did not even look British, and its angular petrol tank was a styling disaster that so eaily could have been avoided.

Despite some enthusiastic write-ups, the 'new' G80 failed to sell in the home market in sufficient quantities and it was announced that production would end. However, to date, sales abroad have ensured its continuation.

disappeared, only to return in 1938, now water-cooled with a spring frame. Ferociously fast, it was almost unrideable, and won no races before the war. However, ridden by Jock West, it did win the 1946 Albi Grand Prix, before the FICM banned supercharging. Following WWII, AMC launched the 500cc twin 'Porcupine' and the 350cc single-cylinder 7R, both with AJS on the tank.

During the war, Matchless supplied many thousands of G3 and then G3L (Lightweight) 350cc machines to the armed forces. Fitted with AMC's version of a BMW hydraulically damped telescopic ('Teledraulic') front form, the G3L was the favourite of many wartime desptach riders. Post war, similar 350cc and 500cc singles soon were also fitted with oil-damped swinging arm rear suspension at the insistence of Jock West, the com-

MATRA/ *Hungary 1938–1947*
Designed by former racing motorcyclist Laszlo Urbach, these machines had 98cc and 198cc Sachs and Ardie two-stroke engines.

MAURER/ *Germany 1922–1926*
Produced 1·5 hp bicycle attachments with rotary disc-valve two-stroke engines. Maurer motorcycles had watercooled vertical 247cc and horizontal watercooled 494cc twin-cylinder two-stroke motors. With its opposing cylinders in line with the duplex frame, this model was probably the only watercooled two-stroke flat-twin built as a production model. Production was not large-scale. Interesting was the big outside flywheel and the position of the forward-facing carburettor, which was connected with the rearward-facing cylinder via a long inlet pipe and had a shorter pipe to the forward-facing cylinder. It is unlikely that this unusual system worked satisfactorily. Unusual also was the position of the radiator. The single-cylinder Maurer had it below the saddle, where four-strokes usually have the oil tank. The flat-twin had the radiator directly below the full length of the petrol tank.

MAUSER/ *Germany 1924–1927 (1932)*
Extremely unorthodox two-wheeler with a car-like body and with outrigger wheels on both sides. The chassis comprised two pressed steel channel members, while steering was by a huge D-shaped handlebar. The watercooled single-cylinder 510cc sv engine had 10 bhp at 3400 rpm. It was mounted in front of the rear wheel and had the cylinder mounted horizontally. Chains drove the gearbox and rear wheel. At 638 lb it was a heavy vehicle and business for the producer, the Mauser arms factory, was not brisk. The Mauser did not look very safe. When Mauser in 1927 abandoned manufacture of this 'Einspurauto' (single-track car), another company at Oberndorf/Neckar — Gustav Winkler —continued production until 1932. During the second half of the 1920s, the French firm Monotrace built the Mauser under licence.

496cc Maxima (sv flat-twin) 1922

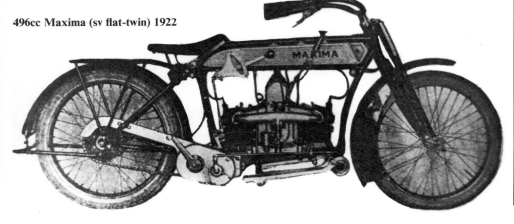

MAV/ *Italy 1977–*
Another Italian assembler of moto-cross and trial machines with 49, 123 and 244cc two-stroke singles, made by Minarelli, Hiro and Sachs.

MAVISA/ *Spain 1957–c1960*
Luxurious lightweight with a horizontal 248cc two-stroke, twin-cylinder engine of unit design and with shaft drive to the rear wheel.

490cc Mawi (sv JAP) 1930

MAWI/ *Germany 1923–1930*
Assembled machines with 142cc and 173cc DKW two-stroke and 198cc to 546cc sv and ohv single-cylinder four-stroke JAP engines.

MAX/ *Germany 1924–1925*
Produced 180cc two-stroke and 446cc sv machines with their own power units.

MAX/ *France 1927–1930*
French and English proprietary engines from 98cc to 496cc were fitted into motorcycles made by this small company.

MAXIM/ *England 1919–1921*
One of the many assemblers. Fitted 318cc Dalm single-cylinder two-stroke engines.

MAXIMA/ *Italy 1920–1925*
Well-designed 690cc and 747cc horizontal twins with opposing cylinders. The sv engines were of their own design and manufacture.

MAY BROS/ *England 1903–1906*
Motorcycles with Minerva, MMC, Sarolea and other engines made to order.

MAZUÉ/ *France 1911–1914*
This company built at Lyon 346 and 496cc single-cylinder machines with ohv engines of their own manufacture.

MAZZUCHELLI/ *Italy 1925–1928*
A long name, a small factory and a German 198cc Alba single-cylinder sv engine in a simple frame.

MB/ *Czechoslovakia 1927–1928*
Built, like the Mat, in the Avia factory of racing car driver Miloš Bondy, the Šlechta-designed 498cc single-cylinder MB machine was quite unusual, because it had a rotary valve in the cylinder head, which steered the incoming and outgoing fuel mixtures and gases respectively. The design was never fully developed and became superseded by the Mat.

MB/ *America 1916–1920*
Modern machines with 746cc parallel-twin engines and shaft drive to the rear wheel. The The design was never fully developed.

MBM/ *Italy 1974–*
Concentrates on 49cc mopeds and similar small transport.

MBR/ *Italy 1924–1926*
This firm was a small producer of 124cc two-stroke machines.

MC/ *Czechoslovakia 1924–1927*
Concentrated on the manufacture of a 996cc V-twin sv machine for use with a sidecar. The design by Vladimir Guth was based on English lines.

MCB/ *Sweden 1902–*
Famous factory which now includes former motorcycle producers as Hermes, Monark (Esse), Nordstjernan, NV-Bohlin, Apollo and others. The main range of models includes two-strokes from 48cc to 123cc with mainly Sachs and Franco-Morini engines.

MCC/ *England 1903–c1910*
Fitted De Dion, Minerva and other engines. Produced also their own engines using Minerva patents.

McEVOY / *England 1926–1929*
Michael McEvoy, the founder of this Derby-based factory, was earlier with Rolls-Royce; Cecil Allerhead Birkin, who financed the enterprise, was a brother of famous racing-car driver Tim Birkin; and George Patchett, the leading technician, came from George Brough's Brough-Superior works at Nottingham. McEvoy soon offered machines from the Villiers-engined 172cc two-stroke and 248cc, 348cc and 498cc sv and ohv singles with Blackburne and JAP engines, to 998cc JAP and Anzani-engined sv and ohv V-twins, including 8-valve versions and racing engines. George Patchett—who eventually became FN and Jawa designer—also rode in 1926–1927 a supercharged 996cc McEvoy with the big JAP racing engine. McEvoy and Cecil Birkin also competed in sporting events and when Birkin was killed in a TT practice accident in 1927, the factory got into difficulties. Before McEvoy closed down, he built prototypes of a 346cc three-valve ohc single and of an aircooled 498cc four-in-line, which was also an ohc design. He was an expert on supercharging, represented afterwards German Zoller superchargers in England and also built some supercharged cars.

McKECHNIE / *England 1922*
Luxurious twin-cylinder with a 688cc Coventry-Victor flat-twin engine. The McKechnie had rear suspension and a very strong duplex frame. The production was on a limited scale.

McKENZIE / *England 1921–1925*
Lightweight machine with 169cc two-stroke engine, which was also supplied in open frames for ladies. McKenzie machines were made for this London-based company by the Hobart works at Coventry.

MDS / *Italy 1955–1960*
Produced modern lightweights with own unit-design, single-cylinder ohv engines of 65cc, 70cc, 75cc and 80cc. There was also a miniscooter with a 65cc engine. Some versions of the motorcycle had separate gearboxes.

MEAD / *England 1911–1916*
According to some sources, Premier in Coventry was the actual producer of the machines for the Liverpool-based Mead Cycle Co. The range included Precision-engined 198cc, 492cc and 592cc models, 293cc JAP-engined singles and 746cc and 980cc versions with V-twin Premier engines.

MEAD / *England 1922–1924*
Assembler, who used 1·75, 2·75 and 3·75 hp Precision, Wall and Villiers engines.

MEGOLA / *Germany 1921–1925*
This was probably the most unorthodox motorcycle ever made on a commercial basis. Designed by Fritz Cockerell, the 640cc Megola had an aircooled 5-cylinder radial engine with the side-valves built directly into the front wheel. It had no clutch or gearbox, but a lot of power at the low end. Starting was by pushing or by 'kicking with the heel into the spokes of the front wheel' while the machine was on the stand. The petrol tank was in the normal position, but petrol first had to be pumped into a smaller tank, mounted on the right side of the leaf-sprung fork. Below it, outside the front axle, was the carburettor, on the opposite side the magneto. Some models also had rear suspension by means of half-elliptic springs. Changing ratios was by using bigger front wheels. Racing models had top speeds of around 85 mph, production versions of 68 to 70 mph. Thanks to the low centre of gravity, Megolas had first class road-holding quality. They won many races and trials with a works team which consisted of Toni Bauhofer,

Sepp Stelzer and Albin Tommasi. The name Megola came from the first two letters of the three men who founded this Munich-based factory: Meixner, Cockerell and Landgraf. Interesting, because Cockerell in this case wrote his name with G instead of the usual C as with his second motorcycle enterprise, the Cockerell lightweight motorcycles. He was quite clever, although it would now not be possible to use a gear and clutchless motorcycle in modern traffic conditions. The design of the spokes of the front wheel enabled the dismantling of the cylinders without taking a spoke out of the wheel. There was also a specially designed tube in the tyres. It could be changed without dismantling the wheel, ie it was an open tube, which could be 'pushed' together. The five small cylinders had 52mm bore and 60mm stroke; the frame consisted of a welded and rivetted box. Touring models had mostly bucket-seats; sports versions had saddles. Today, the Megola—of which nearly 2000 were made—is one of the most valued collector's items.

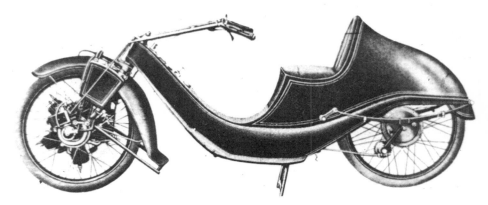
540cc Megola (sv 5-cylinder radial engine) 1921

540cc Megola (sv 5-cylinder radial engine model 'Sport') 1923

MEGURO / *Japan 1937–1964*
Once a leading Japanese factory, which eventually was taken over by Kawasaki. Produced mainly singles with capacities from 124cc to 498cc and also a 498cc vertical-twin ohv model. All were designed on typical English lines.

MEIHATSU / *Japan 1953–1961*
Was also part of the Kawasaki group and concentrated on two-strokes up to 248cc capacity. There were also twin-cylinder models.

MEISTER / *Germany 1949–early 1960s*
The Alfred Ostertag-designed machines were of standard design and good finish. Production included 49cc Zündapp-engined mopeds and motorcycles with 98cc, 123cc, 147cc, 173cc and 198cc Sachs as well as Ilo two-stroke power units.

MELDI / *Italy 1927–1937*
Concentrated on the production of racing machines with 248cc, 348cc and 498cc ohv JAP and Python (Rudge product) engines.

MEMINI / *Italy 1946–1947*
Concentrated on a limited manufacture of 173cc two-strokes with own engines.

MENON / *Italy 1930–1932*
Touring machines with inclined 174cc and 198cc single-cylinder sv engines.

MENOS / *Germany 1922–1923*
This was nothing else but a slightly redesigned and renamed Aristos. Identical was the water-cooled 614cc flat-twin sv engine, the rivetted and welded box frame made from pressed steel and the position of the radiators on both sides

498cc Meguro (ohv twin-cylinder) 1959

of the rear wheel. Only differences were a new fork design and a Zebra-like enamelling of the whole machine.

MERAY / *Hungary 1921–1944*
Was once the leading Hungarian make over the years produced machines from 172cc to 996cc with Villiers, Moto-Rêve, Puch, Blackburne

and JAP engines. After 1936 also had their own 346cc and 496cc single-cylinder engines. Ferencz Meray, Laszlo Erdély, Bertalan Szoter, Josef Weber etc. won many races on these machines.

346cc Méray (ohv JAP) 1929

614cc Menos (sv flat-twin watercooled) 1923

MERCIER / *France 1950–1962*
Built 49cc machines, mainly mofas, with Lafalette engines. Also miniscooters and afterwards motorcycles with from 98cc to 173cc Villiers and Ydral engines.

MERCO / *Germany 1922–1924*
Very simple design of 148cc two-stroke machines with deflector-type three-port engines of their own manufacture.

MERCURY / *England 1956–1958*
Offered a wide range of 49cc and 98cc motorcycles and miniscooters, but actual production was limited. Among the models were the Dolphin, Hermes and Whippet scooters.

MERKEL/*America 1902–1922*
For many years a leading make, Merkel built well-designed singles and V-twins up to 986cc. Some models already had rear suspension before WWI. The end came when Indian bought the Milwaukee factory.

MERLI/*Italy 1929–1931*
Small production of 173cc two-stroke machines with French Train engines.

MERLIN/*Spain 1982–*
A new competition machine designed by Ignacio Bulto, formerly of Bultaco fame. Merlins are using Italian 248cc Cagiva two-stroke engines.

MERLONGHI/*Italy 1927–1930*
Another small producer of small 132cc two-stroke two-speed machines.

MESSNER/*Austria 1928–1933*
Racing motorcyclist who produced 248cc racing machines with ohv JAP and his own ohc engines.

METEOR/*Czechoslovakia 1909–1926*
The first products were 211cc bicycle attachment engines. The motorcycles had 147cc and 169cc two-stroke deflector-type three-port engines.

METEOR/*Germany 1925–1926*
Simple machines with 185cc sv engines. Limited production.

METEOR/*Germany 1924–1926*
Lightweights with 172cc two-stroke engines which came probably from Thumann in France.

METEORA/*Italy 1955–1966*
Produced 49cc NSU-engined and 123cc FBM-engined two-strokes and also a 148cc ohv model. Later models had 49cc Franco-Morini engines and included moto-cross versions.

METISSE/*England 1962–mid 1980s*
Famous moto-cross riders Don and Derek Rickman built their own machines using Triumph engines, which became very popular and successful. They diversified into road racing and pioneered disc brakes. They also made road machinery with both British and Japanese engines, and even sold such machines to the police. They abandoned motor cycles in the 1980s.

METRO/*England 1912–1919*

652cc M.F. (ohv flat-twin model 650 R) 1982

Well-made machines with own 269cc two-stroke engines. *See also* next entry.

METRO-TYLER/*England 1919–1923*
The Metro became the Metro-Tyler when the London-based Tyler Apparatus Co., Ltd. bought the remains of the Birmingham-based Metro Manufacturing and Engineering Co. The price in 1921 for the 269cc two-speed model was £80, for the three-speed version £85.

MEYBEIN/*Germany 1922–1926*
Fitted 119cc and 142cc DKW two-stroke engines into their own very low and very simple frames. Some versions had a horizontal cylinder.

MEYBRA/*Germany 1923–1925*
Another simple machine with its own 168cc two-stroke engine.

MEZO/*Austria 1923–1926*
Designed by Medinger, who was a racing motorcyclist and also importer of English engines into Austria, the Mezo range included 172cc and 247cc two-strokes with Villiers engines and 293cc, 346cc and 490cc sv and ohv singles with JAP engines. Actual production was on a limited scale, partly because of Medinger's injuries, sustained in 1924 in the Austrian Tourist Trophy race.

MF/*France 1981—1982*
The MF used a modified Citroen 'Visa' flat twin car engine of 650cc in a nicely styled chassis of what was at the time modern design with cast-alloy wheels and so on. Very few were made, however, and a potential superbike soon disappeared.

MF/*Germany 1922–1925*
The Nuremberg-built, Max Fischer-designed machine first had 492cc flat-twin sv engines made by BMW, afterwards 347cc and 497cc sv engines made by Blackburne in England.

MFB/*Germany 1923–1924*
The frames were made of wood. Engines fitted were the German 198cc Nabob and the English 293cc sv JAP. When this Hamburg factory went bust, Hoco in Minden took over.

MFB/*Germany 1925–1926*
Small assembler of 206cc two-stroke machines with DKW engines.

MFB/*Italy 1957–1964*
Bologna-built 48cc, 74cc and 124cc two-strokes and 174cc ohv singles.

MFZ/*Germany 1921–1928*
Produced always 'farmer's' motorcycles and

346cc MFZ (ohv) 1927

never any kind of 'hot' design. Nearly all models had their own ohv engines with 198cc, 247cc and 347cc capacity. The biggest version had in 1926 chain-drive and three instead of two speeds.

MGC / *France 1927–1929*
Interesting design with a light-alloy frame which included the petrol tank. Most engines fitted were JAP or Chaise of 248cc, 348cc and 498cc with ohv heads.

MGF / *Italy 1921–1925*
Designed by a well-known racing motorcyclist, the MGF — Motocicli Garanzini Francesco — machines had Blackburne ohv engines from 248cc to 498cc and also their own 142cc two-stroke engines.

MGF / *Germany 1923–1931*
Produced quite a large number of 122cc, 140cc, 173cc and 198cc two-stroke three-port and also Bekamo-licence pumping-cylinder two-stroke machines. Also made engines for other assemblers of lightweights.

MG-TAURUS / *Italy 1933–late 1950s*
Vittorio Guerzoni's first machines had 173cc two-stroke Train engines. Afterwards he built own 248cc ohv and 496cc ohv and eventually ohc models. There were also Sachs-engined mofas and after 1945 two-strokes and ohv models from 75cc to 198cc.

MIAMI / *America 1905–1923*
Was closely connected for some time with the manufacture of the Flying Merkel and produced also their own 298cc sv singles with pedalling gears and a rearward facing cylinder.

246cc Miami (sv) 1916

MICHAELSON / *America 1910–1915*
A well-made machine with 492cc single-cylinder and 992cc V-twin engines. They had oh inlet and side exhaust valves, duplex frames, leaf-sprung forks and chain drive to the rear wheel, when most other factories used belt drive.

13 hp Michaelson (ioe V-twin) 1913

MIDGET BICAR / *England 1908–1912, USA / 1908–1909*
Made by J F Brown of Reading, England, the Midget Bicar featured a pressed and rivetted sheet steel frame, and a variable pulley gear. Late models had 500cc and 600cc Precision engines. The design was licensed to the American Walton Motor Coy, who used their own V twin engines to power it.

MIELE / *Germany 1953–1962*
Big and still famous factory which before WWII built bicycles with 73cc and 98cc Sachs two-stroke engines. After the war, the same make of proprietary engine powered machines from

48cc to 147cc. Miele products were known for their high quality.

MIGNON / *Italy 1923–1932*
After producing 123cc bicycle attachment engines, Vittorio Guerzoni designed the modern Mignon with a vertical 246cc twin-cylinder sv engine and a crank case made of Electron. That was in 1925 and in 1932 his next design appeared.

246cc Mignon (TS twin) 1926

This was a 498cc single with ohv and chain-driven ohc. Other models were 173cc versions with ioe and also ohv.

MILANI / *Italy 1970–*
Produces a wide range of Minarelli-engined 49cc models and also 124cc models for trials and moto-cross. Most of the production goes to the USA.

98cc Miele (TS) 1952

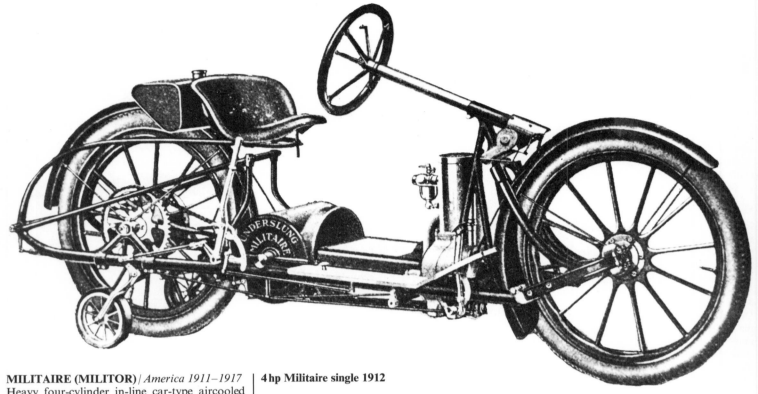

4 hp Militaire single 1912

MILITAIRE (MILITOR)/*America 1911–1917*

Heavy four-cylinder in-line car-type aircooled 1306cc ohv unit-design engine fitted into unusual frames with shaft drive. The frames consisted of a one piece stamping while the front suspension embodied coil springs in the front fork tubes. There was also a rear suspension which included quarter-elliptic cantilever springs mounted on a patented axle suspension. The gearbox had three speeds and a reverse gear; lubrication was full force feed by gear pump. The whole design was unorthodox and very expensive in production. In the seven years of limited production, these machines were made by not less than eight companies in Cleveland, Buffalo, New Jersey, Springfield and Bridgeport. The total output was probably less than 100 units. A single-cylinder version, built in the early years, never reached even this figure. This single had 480cc, a steering wheel instead of handlebars, a bucket seat instead of a saddle and, like the four, wheels with wooden spokes.

1306cc Militaire (ioe four-in-line) 1915

MILLER-BALSAMO/*Italy 1921–1959*

Was a leading make in Italy, first with 123cc two-strokes, afterwards with very fast 174cc ohv machines, which had Swiss Moser and afterwards also Miller-built English Rudge (Python) four-valve single-cylinder engines. In addition, there were also Miller models with 248cc, 348cc and 498cc four-valve Pythons. Carlo Fumagalli, Aldo Pigorini, Silvio Vailati, Gino Zanchetta and others won many races and on 174cc Python-engined racing machines broke

173cc Miller (ohv Moser engine) 1926

world records. The range of models included after 1934 98cc Sachs-engined two-strokes and a 246cc ohv model with its own single-cylinder engine. A completely enclosed version, built just before the war, had a 198cc two-stroke engine. After 1945, production concentrated around two-strokes from 123cc to 246cc and the 246cc ohv model, but Ernest Balsamo's machines never regained the popularity they had in the late 1920s and early 1930s. The big 499cc ohv singles, built after the war, were basically pre-war models slightly modernised. They were soon dropped, while a new 169cc ohc single made its appearance in the 1950s. The last model was a 49cc two-stroke.

MILLIONMOBILE / *England c1902*
Motorised bicycle with a 1·5 hp engine.

MIMOA / *Germany 1924*
Used a 142cc Albertus two-stroke engine, designed by Julius Löwy. This power unit could be run also on crude oil, but lacked power and reliability.

MINERVA / *Belgium 1901–1914*
A famous name in the motoring world, Minerva not only built complete motorcycles with their own engines from 2 hp to 8 hp, but supplied these engines to other producers, as well as licences for manufacture in other countries.

MINETTI / *Italy 1924–1927*
One of the many small Italian producers of 124cc two-strokes with three-port engines.

MINEUR / *Belgium 1924–1928*
Liège was once the centre of the motorcycle industry in Belgium. Paul Mineur produced there his 348cc and 496cc sv and ohv singles with a variety of proprietary engines. These included JAP, Bradshaw, MAG and Liége-built Sarolea motors.

MINISCOOT / *France 1960–1962*
This was a folding miniscooter with a 74cc two-stroke engine.

MINNEAPOLIS / *America c1900–1915*
Well-designed singles and V-twins with two-speed gearboxes in unit. The Minneapolis-based factory used telescopic forks and produced also three-wheelers.

MINSK / *Russia 1954–early 1960s*
Produced inside the Russian motorcycle industry two-strokes up to 246cc vertical-twins, but was also closely connected with other Russian works via the CKEB, the common design centre.

MIRANDA / *Germany 1951–1954*
Originally known as Schweppe scooter, the design was renamed Miranda when the Dortmund-based Pirol works took over its manufacture. It was offered with 173cc Sachs and 198cc Küchen two-stroke engines.

MISTRAL / *France 1902–early 1960s*
Produced lightweights with 1·75 hp engines and after WWII modern lightweights from 49cc to 247cc until they specialised in various 49cc models and also supplied the power units to other mofa and moped manufacturers.

MITCHELL / *America 1901–c1906*
Was a famous car factory which also built 345cc single-cylinder motorcycles with rearward-facing cylinders.

MIVAL / *Italy 1950–1966*
Produced 123cc two-strokes and in 1954 took over the licence for the German Messerschmitt cabin-scooter. They fitted a 172cc two-stroke engine into this three-wheeled vehicle and used a four-speed gearbox with it. New motorcycles included 123cc, 174cc and 199cc ohv versions. There was also a racy-looking 174cc single-cylinder double-ohc machine and a similar moto-cross version with a single-ohc engine. The production included 49cc bicycle attachment engines and also 248cc ohc moto-cross models, of which some had five and even six-speed gearboxes. Mival also built trials versions.

MIYATA / *Japan 1909–1964*
Old factory which produced Asahi motorcycles after WWII. Among the models were 249cc sv and ohv singles, 344cc ohv singles and 496cc vertical twins with ohv engines. Other models included 123cc two-strokes. Based on English lines, Asahi's were never imported into Europe.

MJ / *Germany 1925*
Produced experimental 249cc two-stroke machines which never went into quantity production. Concentrated on the manufacture of air and watercooled flat twin engines with opposing cylinders of 596cc and 746cc, supplied to motorcycle producers such as Heller. Mehne, another machine factory, took over MJ when they ran into financial difficulties.

MJS / *Germany 1924–1925*
Motorcycles of simple design with their own 245cc three-port deflector-type two-stroke engines.

MM / *America 1906–WWI*
The MM had, like other early American motorcycles, single-cylinder rearward facing sv engines, supplied by Thomas. Afterwards they used single-cylinder and V-twin power units made by Marsh, Royal, Holley and Pope.

MM / *Italy 1924–1964*
This MM was founded by Angelo Mattei, Mario Mazzetti, Alfonso Morini (who became founder of the Morini works) and Giuseppe Massi. Afterwards Massi and Mattei left and Antonio Salvia joined the MM factory, where they built superb 123cc and later 173cc two-strokes with a forward-facing horizontal cylinder. In 1927 Alfonso Morini and Amedeo Tigli, riding 123cc two-strokes which had the gearbox in unit with the engine, broke world records and reached speeds of over 66 mph. A 173cc ohv machine and 348cc sv and ohv singles as well as 248cc ohv and 496cc sv models followed. New racing singles with 173cc and 348cc chain-driven ohc engines came into production in 1932 and 1936 respectively. Both proved to be very successful. Luigi Bonazzi broke the world record for the flying kilometre with the 348cc version and reached 116·6 mph, while Guglielmo Sandri won many races with this machine. He also ran it under the CM trade mark. Michaele Mangione became Champion of Italy in 1938 on an im-

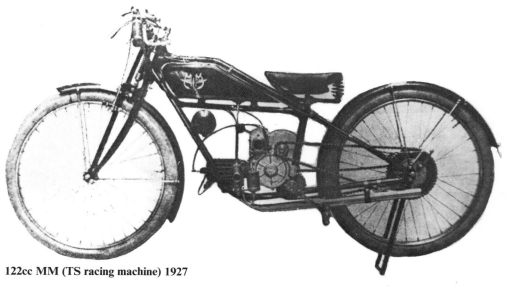
122cc MM (TS racing machine) 1927

246cc MM (ohv) 1936

248cc MM (ohv 'Super-Sports') 1956

proved version of this 348cc single with the chain-drive single ohc engine; Salvia was responsible for the design. All MM machines were superbly made and had an excellent finish; this was the case with a new 248cc ohc single built in 1947, and with 346cc and 492cc sv singles made in the same period. MM afterwards dropped the big model and concentrated on 247cc and 347cc ohc singles. Unfortunately they never built racing machines after the war, but only 247cc moto-cross versions. The last MM design was a 173cc ohc single, although they also built 123cc two-strokes of excellent design. A 247cc production racer was the 1956-built Sport SS, with a single ohc unit-design engine.

M&M / *England 1914*
Assembled machine with open frame and 269cc Villiers two-stroke engine.

MMM / *Germany 1925–1927*
Small producer of 148cc two-stroke machines.

MOCHET / *France 1950–1955*
Lightweights with 149cc Ydral two-stroke engines.

MOFA / *Germany 1920–1925*
Produced 70cc and 148cc bicycle attachment engines and also complete lightweight machines.

MOHAWK / *England 1903–1925*
The first models had 2·5 hp and 3 hp engines. After an interruption of some years, the bicycle factory re-entered the motorcycle market in the 1920s. The wide range of assembled machines included models with 269cc Villiers, 293cc JAP and 492cc Abingdon engines. Other models used a 154cc two-stroke flat-twin Economic power unit and a 346cc sv JAP engine.

MOLARONI / *Italy 1921–1927*
Made by the Molaroni brothers at Pesaro, early models were 296cc two-stroke singles of their

own design and manufacture. Others housed a 596cc flat twin two-stroke with opposing cylinders and automatic lubrication. Designed by Alfredo Sgrignani, a new range of models included the improved 296cc model with 70mm bore and 78mm stroke, a 344cc version with 75mm bore and 78mm stroke and a 348cc ohv single with 74mm bore and 81mm stroke which had a Blackburne engine.

MOLTENI / *Italy 1925–1927*
Very ambitious design of a frame and fork, chain cases etc. made from aluminium alloy. The good-looking Molteni, fitted with 348cc oilcooled Bradshaw and with 492cc MAG single-cylinder engines, was not a commercial success.

MONACO-BAUDO / *Italy 1926–1928*
After Augusto Monaco produced an experimental 246cc vertical twin engine at the Della Ferrera factory, he built a 496cc single-cylinder sv model with a unit-design engine and a big outside flywheel. Co-designer was Antonio Baudo, whose earlier V-twin engines had 474cc, 686cc and 996cc capacity. Other models housed 346cc and 490cc single-cylinder JAP and Blackburne sv and ohv engines.

MONARCH / *America 1912–1915*
Another USA factory which produced 496cc singles and 990cc V-twins with their own ioe engines and spring frames.

10 hp Monarch (ioe V-twin) 1913

MONARCH / *England 1919–1921*
Actually made by Excelsior of Birmingham, the Monarch was a cheaper version. It had 296cc Villiers and 293cc JAP sv engines.

MONARCH / *Japan 1955–1962*
Produced Norton-like 346cc and 496cc ohv single-cylinder machines.

MONARK / Sweden 1920—late 1970s

Monark began by making a 175cc two-stroke mot-orised bicycle under the name of Essc, but changed this when they started making four-strokes, from 250cc to 600cc. In the 1930s, they began to use Ilo two-strokes, and, during the war, 500cc Husqvarna four-strokes. Post war, production was of lightweights, again with proprietary engines. BSA originally made the 'Bantam' engine for Monark, with others coming from Ilo, CZ and Adler. In the late 1950s and early 1960s, Monark built 500cc ohv moto-cross machines and rider Sten Lundin, supported by Ove Lundell, won the world championship in 1959 and 1961. However, production increasingly centred on 50cc off-road machines with Sachs and Franco Morini engines, headed by the 175cc Enduro model. Monark, like several other Swedish motor cycle manufacturers, were owned by the MCB group, who, in the late 1970s, decided to concentrate on enterprises other than motorcycle racing.

244cc Monark (TS Ilo twin) 1952

498cc Monark (ohv moto-cross works-machine) 1959

MONET GOYON / France 1917–1957

Was for many years a leading make successful in races. The first product was a wheel with a small engine, which could be attached to any bicycle. It had 114cc and ioe valves. Motorcycles made by the Macon works used for many years 147cc, 172cc, 247cc and 342cc Villiers two-stroke and 347cc and 497cc ioe and ohv single-cylinder MAG power units. With Sourdot, Hommaire, Goussorgues and Debaisieux many races were won, partly with Brooklands-Villiers 172cc two-stroke engines, partly with ohv and ohc MAG 347cc and 497cc singles. The ohc versions were works engines; Monet Goyon as one of the biggest MAG engine customers was the only French factory to get them from the Swiss engine works. The only engine built by Monet Goyon around the early 1930s was a 344cc sv single of unit design and with a slightly inclined cylinder. After the war, new 98cc, 124cc, 198cc and 232cc two-strokes and 345cc sv and ohv singles came into production. There was also — from 1953 onwards — the Starlet, a nice 98cc two-stroke scooter. Many of these machines had J. A. Grégoire rear suspension. The same was the case with similar Koehler Escoffier models, which were also built by Monet Goyon. Both makes used Villiers engines made under licence. They were fitted also to the Lemardelé-designed fully enclosed motorcycles and scooters.

498cc Monet-Goyon (ohv MAG) 1931

342cc Monet-Goyon (TS Villiers) 1930

346cc Monet-Goyon (sv) 1931

MONFORT / Spain late 1950s

Assembled machines with 124cc and 198cc two-stroke engines in limited numbers.

MONOPOLE / England 1911–1924

One of the best assembled machines. Fitted 247cc and 269cc Villiers engines, 293cc and 680cc sv JAP motors and also the 499cc Abingdon single-cylinder sv engine.

MONOTRACE / France 1926–1928

Licence-built German Mauser one-track car. Had a watercooled 520cc engine, a car-like open body and on each side an outrigger wheel.

MONTEROSA / Italy 1954–1958

Producer of 49cc mopeds. Small factory and limited output.

MONTESA / *Spain 1945—*

Pedro Permanyar and Xavier Bulto built up Spain's first post-war motorcycle factory with 100cc and 125cc two-stroke machines of Bulto's design. They did well in racing, and in 1956 Marcello Cama finished second in the 125cc TT. Bulto left the company in 1958, to be replaced by Leo Mila, who designed the 175cc two-stroke Impala. Its excellent sales led to another model, the 250cc Sport. Both models did well in long distance races, such as the Barcelona 24 hours.

From the early 1960s, too, sales were good in the USA, especially of 'trial' bikes for off-road riding, while, in Europe, Montesas had a real place in the world of one-day trials. By the late 1970s, they offered a full range of two-strokes from 50cc to 350cc. With the general decline of the Spanish industry, however, Montesa were taken over by Honda. They now make Honda-engined mopeds, but, curiously, production of the 'traditional' two-stroke trials and trail bikes still continues.

349cc Montesa (TS Enduro 360H7) 1982

247cc Montesa (TS 'Cota') 1974

247cc Montesa (TS 'Cappra') 1974

MONTGOMERY / *England 1902–1939*

Before WWI William Montgomery built motorcycles with proprietary engines at Bury St. Edmunds. Afterwards he moved to Coventry, where his products included not only a model with a 688cc flat twin sv engine but also sidecars. After the war his son Jack Montgomery resumed motorcycle production and built a wide range of machines from 147cc Villiers-engined two-strokes to 996cc V-twins with ohv Anzani and JAP engines. There were also models with 348cc Bradshaw engines, but from the mid-1930s onwards, only 246cc, 346cc and 496cc ohv JAP engines were fitted. The sporting Greyhound models with JAP special engines were famous; successful also were some JAP-engined

490cc Montgomery (ohv JAP engine) 1939

996cc Montgomery (ohv Anzani V-twin) 1923

racing models. Riders included Sid Jackson, Erich Hiller, Otto Kohfink and Mita Vychodil. Montgomery built the first Brough-Superior frames in 1920/1922 and afterwards produced the P&P motorcycle frames. In 1925 a fire destroyed the Montgomery works; P&P also had to interrupt production.

MONTLHERY / *Austria 1926–1928*
Limited production of 346cc sv and ohv machines with JAP engines.

MONVISO / *Italy 1951–1956*
Sachs-engined 98cc, 123cc, 147cc and 173cc two-strokes of typical Italian design.

MOONBEAM / *England 1920–1921*
Utility machines with 296cc Villiers two-stroke

MORIDELLI (MBA) / *Italy 1969–1982*
Racing enthusiast Giancario Morbidelli sponsored 50cc and then 125cc racing two-strokes, designed by Franco Rhingini. This was followed by a water-cooled 125cc twin with disc valve induction, which ridden by Gilberto Parlotti, was sensationally successful in 1970 and 1971. Following Parlotti's death in the 1972 TT, Morbidelli partially withdrew from racing for the next two years; however, with riders Pileri and Bianchi, they later dominated the 125cc class, winning the world title for three years in a row from 1975. The same year, they produced a 250cc twin in a Bimota frame, with which Mario Lega won the 250cc world championship in 1977.

In 1978, Morbidelli 125cc and 250cc racers, built at the nearby Benelli Armi factory, were offered for sale for the first time and quickly became enormously successful in the hands of private owners. Designer Jorg Moller, the brains behind the earlier Van Veean Kreidlers, was associated with these later machines. Giancarlo Morbidelli himself withdrew after overspending on unsuccessful 350cc and 500cc four-cylinder machinery, but by now the marque was well established as MBA (Morbidelli Benelli Armi).

MORETTI / *Italy 1934–1952*
Known as producer of small sports cars, Giovanni Moretti began producing machines with Ladetto, DKW and JAP engines, mainly lightweights up to 248cc. After 1945 the range included 123cc and 248cc ohc machines and also a 246cc vertical twin with shaft-drive.

MORINI / *Italy 1946—1987*
Alfonso Morini, Mario Mazzetti's one-time partner in the pre-war MM company, began

174cc Morini (dohc 'Rebello' racer) 1957

motorcycle manufacture on his own account with yet another copy of the RT125 DKW. Production racers soon followed, with works two-strokes being raced by Nello Pagani. To try to match the all-conquering Mondials, Morini turned to four-strokes in 1950. A 175cc ohv road model appeared in 1952 and in 1955, the ohc 175cc Rebelo was introduced, much used in production racing. The 1958 dohc 250cc was so successful that the great Tarquinio Provini joined the works team for the 1960 season. Over the next four seasons, Provini was to challenge the world, almost, but not quite, winning the 1963 world title.

In 1973 Morini broke away from run-of-the-mill production of 125cc and 150cc models with the very unusual 350cc '3½' V twin. This introduced a concept that has lasted for 20 years, continuously developed and uprated by designer Franco Lambertini. Aircooled, and using flat cylinder heads with combustion chambers in the pistons (Heron configuration), the V twin engine has since been made in 250cc and 500cc configurations, while 125cc and 250cc singles were also part of the range.

In the mid-1980s, Morini followed the common trend and styled many of their machines in off-road guise. Worries about future development costs were in the air, as it was evident that a new generation of water-cooled engines would soon be necessary. However, in 1987, Morini, together with several other companies, was absorbed by the growing Cagiva company.

MORRIS / *England 1902–1905*
Founder of this factory was William Morris, who later became Lord Nuffield of what is now the Leyland car group. His motorcycles had 2·75hp single-cylinder engines made by De Dion and MMC.

MORRIS / *England 1913–1922*
Had no connection to the above factory. Produced a single model, a 247cc two-stroke with its own three-port, deflector-type engine.

MORRIS-WARNE / *England 1922*
A 248cc two-stroke single, which was offered with a vertical as well as with a horizontal cylinder. They were built in limited numbers.

MORS (SPEED) / *France 1951–1956*
Cars bearing this name were among the finest products in the pioneer period. In the 1950s a branch of the original Mors factory produced scooters with 60cc, 115cc and 124cc two-stroke engines.

MORSE-BEAUREGARD / *America 1912–1917*
Very advanced 492cc vertical-twin unit-design machines, which had the cylinders mounted in line with the frame. Drive to the rear wheel was by shaft.

MORTON-ADAM / *England 1923–1924*
Produced 292cc three-port, deflector-type two-strokes in small numbers and also Harry Sidney-designed 248cc and 348cc ohc models with chain-driven camshafts.

MOSER / *Switzerland 1905–1935*
Was — like Motosacoche — not only producing complete motorcycles from 123cc to 598cc, but also a leading supplier of proprietary engines to factories like Miller-Balsamo, FVL, Lecco, Dollar and others. Most were ohv singles and the 123cc and 173cc versions gained great popularity, especially in Italy. Both models also won many big races and during the 1920s in a Grand Prix in Switzerland, Lehman and Brehm riding 123cc ohv Moser machines gained first and second place with the great Italian rider Omobono Tenni on a GD in third position. Another quite popular Moser model was the 198cc ohv version fitted also by Hercules of Germany in the early 1930s. These engines had 60mm bore and 70mm stroke, the 173cc version 60mm bore and 61mm stroke. The biggest Moser engine, the 598cc single, had 85mm bore and 106mm stroke, double-port and a JAP-like appearance.

123cc Moser (ohv) 1927

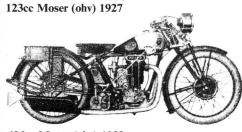
496cc Moser (ohv) 1932

MOSER/ *Austria 1953–*
This make, which produced 98cc and 123cc two-stroke machines with Rotax engines has been defunct for many years. Actually it was the make from which the present KTM motorcycles were developed.

MOSKVA/ *Russia 1940–early 1960s*
Produced during the war, heavy V-twins, called M-72, for the Russian forces. Peace-time production consisted of 123cc and 173cc DKW-like two-strokes, which are now superseded by the 174cc Voskhod. Other models connected with this factory were the shaft-driven M-31 with a 346cc ohv engine and the BMW-like M-61, a 592cc ohv flat-twin, transverse-mounted, which eventually became the 649cc Dneipr M-10, with 34 bhp at 5200 rpm.

MOTAG/ *Germany 1923–1924*
Advanced design by Josef Schneeweiss. The Motag had a cast alloy-frame made from Electron and was offered with three variants of vertical twin-cylinder ohv engines and also — as required — with air or watercooling. The engines had 514cc, 642cc and 804cc. The production must have been very small, as only very few of these machines actually reached the market.

346cc Motobécane (ohv) 1939

MOTOBECANE / *France 1923—*
For many years, Motobécane was France's largest motorcycle manufacturer; not the least of the company's claims to fame is to have made the Mobylette moped from 1949 onwards. Motobécane took over engine builders Polymechanique in 1928 and Motoconfort in 1930 and applied the Motoconfort name to some models — notably a

as 1963. Post war, too, there was a neat and technically interesting 350cc vertical twin but, as ever, the real profits were in moped manufacture. Again, in 1972, Motobecane produced a range of modern Japanese-styled two-strokes, but these were too expensive, and the Mobylette range continued to be the company's salvation. Alessandro de Tomaso briefly owned Motobecane in the late 1970s, but sold out to Yamaha in the early 1980s. Manufacture of 50cc machinery continues under the name of Motobécane at present.

652cc Motag (ohv watercooled twin-cylinder) 1923

MOTA-WIESEL/ *Germany 1948–1952*
The original name was Motra-Wiesel. It was a cross between moped and scooter with small wheels and 74cc and 98cc two-stroke engines.

MOTEURCYCLE/ *France 1921–1924*
Unusual 206cc two-stroke machine with friction drive to the rear wheel.

superb 500cc in-line four-cylinder side valve (later 750cc ohc), with unit gearbox and shaft drive, sold in the early 1930s as both Motobécane and Motoconfort. Such flights of fancy were rare, though Motobécane prided themselves on some nice British-styled ohv singles. Best seller in the 1930s, apart from the inevitable Velometeur type of machine, was the 100cc ohv model Z (later in 125cc and 175cc versions) that lasted until as late

348cc Motobécane (ohv twin) 1952

MOTOBI/ *Italy 1951–1976*
Designed by Giovanni Benelli, who had left his brothers in the Pesaro factory but later returned — now with the Motobi — to the old Benelli home, the first Motobi machines had 98cc, 114cc and 123cc flat single-cylinder egg-shaped two-stroke engines and also 198cc twin-cylinder versions. Afterwards he also built ohv models of similar design with capacities up to 248cc. That was in 1956, when the B on the petrol tanks was superseded by the Motobi transfer. Bestsellers were the 173cc Catria single with ohv, and 198cc and 248cc Spring Lasting two-stroke twins. A

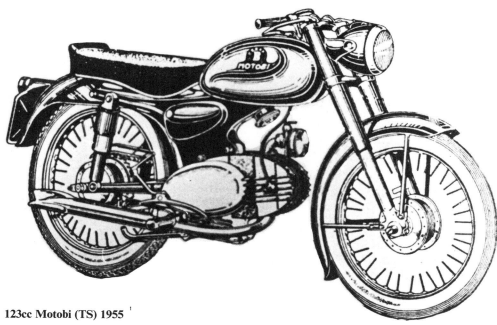

123cc Motobi (TS) 1955

scooter with a 74cc two-stroke engine failed to succeed. After the return of Motobi to Benelli, some models stayed in production and there were others sold with both names, according to the demand. There were still 123cc and 245cc ohv singles with Benelli transfers on the petrol tank in 1976 catalogues. The only model in the increasingly rare Motobi range was the 231cc ohc four-cylinder ohc version, built on order with a 26bhp engine. The last model offered was the 250cc Cafe Racer twin — really a Benelli — after which the Motobi name disappeared.

MOTOBIC / *Spain 1949/1965*
Began with 50cc mopeds, then made a motorcycle with 125cc Hispano Villiers engine.

MOTOBIMM / *Italy 1969–1971*
Was a small factory which built 49cc moto-cross and trials machines with FB-Minarelli two-stroke engines.

MOTOBLOC / *France 1948–late 1950s*
Made at Vichy, the Motobloc products included 44cc mopeds, 65cc Sulky scooters and motorcycles from 124cc to 248cc with Villiers and Aubier-Dunn two-strokes and French AMC 123cc and 248cc ohv engines.

MOTO-BORGO / *Italy 1906–1926*
Designed by Carlo and Alberto Borgo — and also successfully raced by them — the early single-cylinder models had 493cc, 693cc and even 827cc. During WWI V-twins with 990cc and afterwards 746cc came into being. Most of these machines had overhead-inlet and side-

exhaust valves and there was at that period a co-operation with the English Rudge-Whitworth works at Coventry too; therefore a certain similarity between Borgo and Rudge machines. New 477cc V-twins with unit-design ohv engines came into production in 1921. Improved versions for sporting purposes had four-valve heads. The last Moto-Borgo, built from 1925 onwards, was of clean design and had a two-speed gearbox built into the engine unit; it was one of the few 492cc ohv V-twins ever made on a commercial basis. The Borgos gave up motorcycle production soon afterwards and subsequently concentrated their efforts on the manufacture of pistons.

Moto-Borgo

496cc Moto-Borgo (ohv V-twin) 1926

MOTOCLETTE / *Switzerland 1904–1915*
Small producer who fitted Zedel and afterwards Moser single-cylinder proprietary engines.

MOTO GELIS / *Argentina 1963–*
Two-stroke machines up to 246cc with engines and other parts imported from Italy.

Engineer Carlo Guzzi and wealthy enthusiast Giorgio Parodi created the first horizontally-engined Moto Guzzi at Mandello del Lario in 1921 and continued to work together amicably for 30 odd more years. The Moto Guzzi theme of a horizontal engine with outside flywheel and unit

MOTO GUZZI

gearbox in a low-built frame similarly lasted until the late 1960s with one or two variations.

The first Guzzis were 500cc; as early as 1923, now with overhead camshaft valve operation, they were already famous in racing. In 1926 Carlo Guzzi designed a similar 250cc machine; in that year's TT, Pietro Gherzi made fastest lap in the Lightweight TT and finished second — only to be disqualified over a technicality. Their natural disappointment did not stop Guzzi returning to the Isle of Man, a course of action that culminated in

499cc Moto Guzzi (ioe) 1921

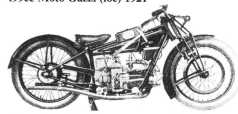

499cc Moto Guzzi (ohc racing machine) 1926

498cc Moto Guzzi (ohc V-twin racer) 1935

Stanley Wood's magnificent double win in Light-weight and Senior races in 1935. The Senior win was on the wide angle even-firing 'Bicylindrica' 120° V twin, a 1933 Carlo Guzzi design, while both wins were the first ever by machines with spring frames, of a type designed by Carlo Guzzi in 1928. The victories were the first of a total of nine TT triumphs before Moto Guzzi withdrew from racing after 1957.

Successful production of motor cycles and light trucks continued in the 1930s and a prestige model, the 500cc transverse three-cylinder, was an interesting, if little known offering, in 1932 and 1933. The horizontal single-cylinder models were much more popular and, in the 1930s Guzzi were one of the few to successfully supercharge a single. It was with such a supercharged model that Stanley Woods made fastest lap in the 1939 Lightweight TT.

499cc Moto Guzzi (dohc 3-cylinder works supercharger racer) 1940

98cc Moto Guzzi (TS Model 'Zigolo') 1958

246cc Moto Guzzi (ohc Model 'Albatros') 1947

499cc Moto Guzzi (dohc watercooled 4-cylinder works racer) 1953

498cc Moto Guzzi (dohc 8-cylinder watercooled works racer) 1955

Post war, the 500cc Bicylindrica was redesigned by Ing. Antonio Miccuchi, who also designed from scratch a superb 250cc twin that was foolishly discarded when Miccuchi took over the design of the road models. He had already laid the foundations of Moto Guzzi's post-war prosperity with the 1946 design of the 65cc two-stroke Moto Leggera that sold in tens of thousands. Other post-war designs included the Galletto — a cross between a motor-cycle and a scooter, and the Zigolo, an all-enclosed 100cc (later 110cc) two-stroke with a rotary inlet valve. Another post-war design — Carlo Guzzi's own — was the 175cc (later 235cc) Lodola of 1956, with a sloping, rather than horizontal, cylinder. The Lodola was very successful in the ISDT and similar events, as well as selling well in standard form. The traditional horizontal singles continued as the 250cc Airone and the 500cc Astora and Falcone.

Post-war racing took off in 1949 with, for the first time, an integrated factory racing department with Ing. Giulio Carcano in charge and British rider Fergus Anderson as development rider and team leader. After a promising start with 250cc singles and yet another redesign of the 500cc twin, with

948cc Moto Guzzi (ohv V-twin California II) 1982

Bruno Ruffo winning the 250cc world championship Moto Guzzi had a poor year in 1950 and withdrew to recoup. In 1951 Moto Guzzi rider Tommy Wood won the Lightweight TT and Bruno Ruffo again won the 250cc Championship. In 1952 Guzzi were 1-2-3 in the Lightweight TT and Enrico Lorenzetti was world champion.

This, however, was Moto Guzzi's last year of 250cc supremacy, for in 1953 and 1954 they were overwhelmed by the German NSU twins. Now Carcano developed single-cylinder 350cc machines that had a remarkable run of success over the next four seasons, with two Junior TT wins and four consecutive world titles. Not so good was the record of an in-line 500cc water-cooled four-cylinder racer with shaft drive, one that had been commissioned elsewhere by Giorgio Parodi. Though bristling with novelties, it was not an easy machine to ride, and was abandoned after a couple of half-hearted seasons, perhaps prematurely.

Its immediate replacement was another single-cylinder model, but this was a relatively unsuccessful stop gap. For 1955, Carcano designed one of the most extraordinary racing motor cycles of all time, the 500cc V eight. Of incredible complexity, its technical brilliance seems to have blinded many commentators to the fact that, even with two full seasons of development behind it, it was really a failure. It was also hideously expensive, and no doubt contributed considerably to the financial troubles that forced Moto Guzzi to withdraw from racing at the end of 1957 and disband the racing department.

For a time, Moto Guzzi were in grave danger of collapse, and indeed were briefly in receivership. The situation was narrowly retrieved by the intro-duction of the 700cc V7, a transverse V twin on which almost all of Moto Guzzi's future was to depend. Using an engine designed by Micuchi, Carcano had built a prototype, which was developed by his successor Lino Tonti into the shaft-drive model that has since served Moto Guzzi so well. In 1971 the first model appeared, and, successively modified, it is still in production in a variety of styles and capacities.

Since 1971 Moto Guzzi has been owned by Allesandro de Tomaso, who also owns Benelli. A few models were made in common, but were not really successful. Moto Guzzi in the 1990s is still developing and still deeply committed to the big transverse engined shaft-drive V twins.

948cc Moto Guzzi (ohv V-twin V-1000) 1982

346cc Moto Guzzi (ohv V-twin Imola) 1982

MOTOM / *Italy 1947–early 1960s*
Produced a variety of lightweight-machines with pressed steel frames. Most engines used were ohv units; the first a 48cc bicycle engine with pedalling gear. The next design was the 147cc Delfino, which eventually got a 163cc ohv engine. In this form it had 8 bhp at 6000 rpm. Very popular was a 98cc ohv model with a horizontal fully-enclosed engine. There were also versions with 92cc and 98cc, models with tubular frames and also — in 1964 — a 48cc version with a Peugeot two-stroke engine. There were many versions with automatic gearboxes, moto-cross models and machines with partly foreign engines, including the 49cc Zündapp two-stroke, which had a four-speed gearbox.

48cc Motom (ohv) 1958

MOTO MONTE / *France 1932–WWII*
Small manufacturer of 98cc two-stroke machines.

MOTOPEDALE / *France 1933–1939*
Two-strokes with 98cc and 123cc Aubier-Dunne engines. Other models included 248cc, 348cc and 498cc JAP and Python single cylinder engines. Limited production.

MOTOPIANA / *Italy 1923–1931*
Assembled for years 147cc to 247cc Villiers-engines and also 246cc to 490cc JAP sv and ohv motors into their own very sporty frames. Late in 1927, Gualtiero Piana produced his first 248cc sv engine, afterwards also an ohv version.

MOTO RÊVE / *Switzerland (England) 1904–1925*
Once a leading motorcycle and proprietary engine manufacturer. Built 298cc, 403cc and 497cc V-twins and already in 1909 a vertical twin. They had a branch factory in England which produced Alp motorcycles. Their last model, in 1925, had a modern 346cc ohv engine.

MOTORMEYER / *The Netherlands 1949–1951*
Built a limited number of 346cc two-stroke, double-piston, single-cylinder machines.

MOTOSACOCHE (MAG) / *Switzerland 1899–1957*
Founders Armand and Henry Dufaux gained fame with 241cc and 290cc bicycle attachments. Afterwards they built a seven-cylinder radial engine, but production models had 247cc to 996cc ioe and partly ohv single-cylinder and V-twin engines. From 1930 onward new sv versions superseded the ioe engines. In addition to motorcycles, the Swiss factory also supplied proprietary power units to motorcycle factories in many countries. There were also branch factories in Lyon and Milan; other firms including Royal-Enfield in England and Triumph in Germany built Motosacoche engines under licence. Among factories which fitted these superb engines in England were Brough-Superior, Matchless, Ariel, Rex Acme, New Henley, Lea Francis, Morgan and New Hudson. Motosacoche proprietary engines were also known as MAG. Other factories included the German Standard, OD, Triumph (Orial), Imperia, Spiegler, MA, Bayern, Neander, Luwe, Hecker, Bücker; the Austrian DSH, Werner-MAG, EM; the French Monet Goyon; the Hungarian Meray, the Swiss Condor and Allegro. Very prominent were the 347cc and 498cc ohv singles, also 497cc and 597cc ioe and ohv V-twins.

Dougal Marchant and Bert Le Vack were among leading Motosacoche designers and it was Marchant who produced between 1927 and 1929 extremely fast 248cc, 348cc and 498cc ohc single-cylinder works racing engines. Only a few good MAG engine customers, including Standard, Triumph, Monet-Goyon etc., got such engines for their works riders. Wal Handley won in 1928 the 350cc and 500cc class in the Grand Prix of Europe on them. For their own works riders, Motosacoche also had in the years up to 1927 a few 498cc and 748cc V-twins with ohc engines, but these were suitable only for the many hillclimbs of that period. Among leading Motosacoche works riders were Francesco Franconi, Luigi and Bruno Martinelli, Paul Oilter, Artur Bizzozero, Ernst Haenny, Jean Gex, Augsburger, Rossi and among foreign works riders besides Handley, Luigi Arcangeli, Carlo Barsanti, Charly Dodson, Artur Simcock, Ignaco Faura, Hans Soenius and Anton Uroič. There were also other riders such as Otto Ley, Toni Fleischmann (both Triumph); Artur Dom, Karl Gall, Paul Rüttchen, Rudi Ecker and Hermann

498cc Motosacoche (ioe V-twin) 1924

598cc Motosacoche (ohv V-twin) 1926

Lang (all Standard); Jean Goussorgues and Pierre Debasieux (all Monet Goyon) etc. who won races on MAG-engined machines.

Privateers got from 1931 onward a 498cc ohv racer, the D50, with a special engine which had both push-rods in a centre-tube and looked like an ohc design. These engines were catalogued not only in Motosacoche's own motorcycles, but also at Standard, OD, Triumph and other factories. Among riders of such 'private' racers were Count von Alvensleben, Fritz Köhler, Franz Hecker and others. Production engines of the 1930s included besides 347cc and 497cc sv singles and 497cc ohv singles also a superb 846cc sv V-twin touring model, the last Le Vack design before he was killed when testing a model. A few new 498cc ohc singles were built in the mid-1930s for the works team, but no new designs appeared from that time until after the war, when Dougal Marchant created a very unorthodox 235cc single-cylinder sv model, which never went into quantity production. The only post-war versions built were a 248cc ohv single with unit-design engine and shaft-drive and a 246cc vertical twin with the Richard Küchen-designed Opti ohc motor.

496cc Motosacoche (sv) 1933

496cc Motosacoche (ohv) 1929

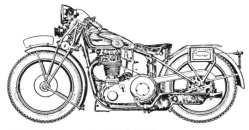

498cc Motosacoche (ohv) 1931

746cc Motosacoche (ioe V-twin) 1931

498cc Motosacoche (sv) 1931

246cc Motosacoche (ohc twin-cylinder Opti) 1955

MOTOTRANS / *Spain 1957—1982*
Under the Franco regime, the import of foreign motor cycles into Spain was prohibited, so Moto-trans manufactured Italian Ducati designs. In time, the company branched out with its own machines, mainly off-road and trial bikes with proprietary two-stroke engines of 50cc. Mototrans was taken over and closed by Semsa Yamaha in 1982.

MOUNTAINEER / *England 1902–1926*
Early machines had Minerva, Fafnir and MMC engines. After the war, only one model, a 269cc two-stroke with a three-port engine, was built in small numbers. It had an Albion two-speed gearbox and belt drive.

MOVESA / *Spain 1952–early 1960s*
Closely connected with Peugeot of France, the Movesa had a 173cc Peugeot two-stroke engine.

MOVEO / *England c1907*
Assembled machines with 3·5 hp single-cylinder and 5 hp V-twin JAP engines.

MÖWE / *Germany 1903–1908*
Produced by the same factory which in later years built Walter motorcycles, the Möwe was equipped with 3·25 hp and 3·50 hp single-cylinder and 5 hp V-twin Fafnir engines.

MOY / *Poland 1937–1940*
Small factory which produced lightweights with own 172cc two-stroke engines.

M&P / *France late 1920s to late 1930s*
Producer of lightweight-machines with 98cc and 123cc Aubier-Dunne engines.

MP / *Italy 1934–1935*
Built by Mario Penazio at Turin, the MP had a modern pressed steel frame and English Sturmey-Archer proprietary engines, ie ohv singles with 347cc and 497cc.

MPH / *England 1920–1924*
Like the Mountaineer a very simple machine. The 269cc Wall two-stroke engine was fitted. The gearbox was a two-speed Roc.

MR / *France 1924–1926*
Equipped with various Train engines, the Italian MR was made by the Officine Mecchaniche Romeo Raimondi at Turin. Most versions had 174cc two-stroke engines; earlier ones 98cc.

MR / *France 1926*
This MR also concentrated on lightweights. 98cc and 123cc Aubier-Dunne, Ydral and Sachs engines played a major part. Special versions made by the factory competed successfully at long-distance events.

MT / *Italy 1949–1953*
Teresio Muratore designed modern 248cc vertical ohc twins, but was unable to produce larger numbers of these interesting touring and sports machines.

MT / *Austria 1925–1937*
The Austrian MT was designed by Count Matthias Thun on typical English lines with mainly English parts. Among them were 147cc to 344cc Villiers engines as well as 346cc, 490cc and 746cc JAP sv and ohv engines. The last ones were V-twins. Special models, mainly racing machines, had also 248cc ohv Blackburne and 497cc ohv MAG motors. Thun, who also imported Villiers engines into Austria, used the 344cc Villiers vertical-twin and the watercooled 247cc single-cylinder engine. Among leading MT riders were Count Phillip Boos-Waldeck, Josef Opawsky, Friedrich Schwarz, Robert Wolf, F. J. Meyer and Lorenz Hubbauer, to name just a few of the notables.

MÜCO / *Germany 1921–1924*
Bicycle attachment engines of 118cc, which had to be fitted outside of the rear wheels.

MUFI (IMPERATOR) / *Germany 1925–1926*
Built one model only. This was a simple 348cc two-stroke machine with a three-port, deflector-type engine.

MULLER / *Italy 1950—late 1970s*
Made by a German expatriate, these machines used both two and four-stroke NSU engines. With NSU's withdrawal from manufacturing, Müller switched to Sachs, Franco Morini and latterly Hiro engines for their trail models.

MÜLLER / *Austria 1924–1926*
Another two-stroke and yet another simple design, the Austrian Müller was a 183cc machine with a strengthened bicycle frame and a unit-design engine, which had a two-speed gearbox and a big outside flywheel.

MUNCH / *Germany 1966—*
For many years, Friedl Münch worked in the racing department at Horex. After Horex closed in 1959, he was involved in a number of racing projects, plus

a collaboration with American Floyd Clymer in an abortive effort to revive manufacture of the Indian motorcycle. Another involvement was with Helmut Fath and the four-cylinder URS engine. However, he is best-known for his design and construction of the 'Mammoth' four cylinder motorcycle, using a modified NSU Prinz car engine, a

1197cc Münch 4 (ohc four-cylinder NSU engine) 1971

1000cc air-cooled ohc four cylinder that gave 55hp at 5800rpm, the engine being set transversely and driving a special four-speed gearbox by chain. Subsequent 1300cc engines gave considerably more power.

The Mammoth was no one-off special, but a series-produced machine, though, being hand made and very expensive, it was not produced in large numbers. Over the years several different backers came and went, but despite financial ups and downs the enterprise continued. Though at the time of writing it is not entirely clear whether Münch is currently building Mammoths to order (he is now well into his 60s) the project has never been publicly abandoned. Even today there may still be a tiny market for a 'superbike' that is of 'traditional' design rather than aping all the lookalike Japanese models.

MUSTANG / *America 1946–1964*
Destined mainly for town-riding, the primitively built Mustang had a 314cc sv single-cylinder engine.

498cc MV Agusta (dohc four-cylinder works racing machine) 1952

MV AGUSTA / *Italy 1945—1978*
Moto Verghera-Agusta holds the considerable distinction of having won more world titles in road racing than almost all other makes put together. Between 1952 and 1974, the company captured no fewer than 37 titles in every class from 125cc to 500cc — all this from a company whose main business was not motor cycles at all, but the design and manufacture of helicopters.

The first MV dates from 1945. Conceived by aircraft manufacturer Count Domenico Agusta to take advantage of the post-war shortage of transport, it was a 100cc two-stroke with two-speed gear. A 125cc, four-speed racing version, with three gears and telescopic forks, appeared in 1948.

The two-stroke MV was no match for the dohc FB Mondial, however, so Count Agusta poached Arturo Magini and Ing. Pietro Remor from Gilera and set them to work. Remor designed a 125cc dohc single and a 500cc four and Magni had them running within six months, the new machines first appearing at the 1950 Belgian Grand Prix. It was not until 1952, however, that they really started to make a mark, with Cecil Sandford winning the 125cc TT and Les Graham's excellent second in the Senior on the four. Sandford went on to win that year's 125cc championship, but the MV four continued to be overshadowed by the Gilera until Gilera withdrew from racing at the end of 1957. Thereafter, with the removal of direct competition from the racing scene, winning the Senior world title became almost taken for granted.

In contrast to the long record of track success, MV's road-going machinery was almost all thoroughly uninspired. It lacked any hint of the style of the racing bikes, and the factory seemed for a long time to be more interested in scooters than in designing and making road-going motorcycles. Attempts to export to England even when the MV name was at the height of its fame were almost entirely fruitless, while so few of the later four-cylinder road bikes were produced that they might as well have been made to special order.

Racing success continued, however. In 1953, a 350cc four appeared alongside the 500cc model, but that same year Les Graham was tragically killed in the Senior TT, so little development work was done on it. It was not until 1956 that the fours really lived up to their promise, with John Surtees riding for MV. Remor had left MV by then, development thereafter being in the hands of Arturo Magni. Over the years, the MV fours (and three-cylinder models) were to be ridden by some of the world's finest — including Mike Hailwood, Giacomo Agostini and Phil Read. On 125cc and 250cc, there were such legends as Carlo Ubbialli, Tarquinio Provini and Luigi Taveri. When the Japanese began their thrust forward in the 125cc and 250cc classes, MV withdrew to concentrate on the larger ones, Ubbiali's 125cc and 250cc titles in 1960 were the last for MV.

When Count Agusta died in 1971, it was universally expected that MV's racing involvement would

147cc MV Águsta (TS) 1957

743cc MV Agusta (dohc four-cylinder Model 750 S) 1975

349cc MV Agusta (ohv two-cylinder Model 350 GT EL) 1975

743cc MV Agusta (dohc four-cylinder Model 750 GT) 1975

cease, especially as the Japanese were now threatening to compete in the larger classes, while, lack of racing success by three and four cylinder racing models added to the pessimism that started to pervade the works. However, Corrido Agusta took up the challenge, and Arturo Magni and designer Ruggero Mazza kept MV ahead, but only for a few short years. The . helicopter business had grown in importance, and, with major government contracts in hand in the late 1970s, not only racing, but the manufacture of ordinary motorcycles, ceased.

MVB / *Italy 1954–1956*
Produced 49cc mopeds and motorcycles with 123cc and 147cc two-strokes in limited numbers.

MW / *Germany 1923–1926*
The MW, designed by Paul Paffrath, was an unorthodox design with a frame part of which was cast from light alloy and part made from pressed steel, welded and rivetted. The first version had a 249cc ohv single-cylinder engine

and three-speed gearbox; the second model a 144cc two-stroke vertical-twin of own design and manufacture. Both machines had rear suspension. After WWII, Paffrath — whose original home was in East Germany — lived in West Germany and produced from 1949 to 1953 a bicycle attachment engine, called Eilenriede.

MYMSA / *Spain 1953–1962*
Produced a wide range of small two-strokes of 75cc, 99cc, 123cc and 175cc in limited numbers.

MZ / (East) Germany 1953—

MZ (Motorad Zschopau) was the successor of IFA, itself, between 1946 and 1953, the successor to pre-war DKW, working from the old DKW factory at Zschopau. Taking the pre-war DKW RT125 as a basis, Walter Kaaden developed 125cc single and 250cc twin racers, with disc valve induction, which, by the late 1950s, first matched and then exceeded the specific power outputs of the best four-strokes of the day. A major blow at the end of 1961 was the defection of top rider Ernst Deger to Suzuki, to whom he revealed most of MZ's technology and, though MZ continued to race, they now put more emphasis on models for the ISDT and similar events.

Road machines of 125cc and 250cc based on this experience were offered for sale and exported to a number of countries at very competitive prices. However, when faced with the ramshackle East German economy, even Walter Kaaden's dedication and hard work on the development side was not enough to keep MZ ahead. Though their domestic customers had no choice, other European customers did, and MZ gradually lost sales to the Japanese industry. Long before the re-unification of Germany, MZ were in financial difficulties, and, when state aid was withdrawn, the company came near to collapse.

At the end of 1991 the company shed many jobs and announced plans for drastic reorganization — a tale that had been, and continues to be told by motorcycle makers, not only in East Germany! Like so many others, MZ face an uncertain future in the last decade of the 20th century.

248cc MZ (TS aircooled twin-cylinder works-racer) 1959

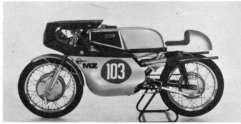

248cc MZ (TS watercooled twin-cylinder works racer) 1972

243cc MZ (TS model ETZ 250) 1982

123cc MZ (TS Model 125/G) 1966

248cc MZ (TS Model 250/1 G) 1967

N

NAMAPO / *Germany 1921–1924*
Designed by Bernhard Nagl, the Namapo was built in the northern part of Germany — at Stettin which belongs now to Poland — and was nearly unknown in the south. It was made with own 147cc and 197cc sv single-cylinder engines. The smaller version was sold also as a bicycle attachment engine.

NARCISSE / *France 1950–1953*
Assembler of two-stroke machines with 48cc and 98cc Aubier-Dunne and partly also Sachs engines.

NARCLA / *Spain 1955–1967*
Small assembler who concentrated on 123cc two-strokes.

NASSETTI / *Italy 1951–1957*
Manufacturer of accessories, whose lightweight motorcycles — which included the 49cc Pellegrino with a horizontal cylinder and friction drive — had two-stroke engines and modern frames with telescopic forks. Ettore Nassetti, the designer-manufacturer, used tubular and pressed steel frames for his motorcycles.

NASSOVIA / *Germany 1925*
Small producer, whose motorcycles had the rare 2·75 hp Anzani engine.

NAZZARO / *Italy 1926–1928*
Made by Eugenio Nazzaro of Turin, brother of the famous racing-car driver Felice Nazzaro (Fiat), the machine had a 173cc ohv engine and was built in limited numbers only.

NEALL / *England 1910–1914*
Fitted with 2·5 hp and 3 hp Precision proprietary engines, the Neall was an assembled machine.

NEANDER / *Germany 1924–1929*
Designed by the famous Ernst Neumann-Neander, who was known for his unorthodox creations, the Neander had a frame made from Duralumin covered with cadmium, so that enamelling of the frame was not necessary. The frame included the petrol tank. A fork with small leaf springs and a bucket seat were other features of the Neander, which was also built under licence by the famous Opel car factory. While Opel fitted own 498cc engines, all Neander machines had proprietary power units from 122cc to 996cc. These were Villiers two-strokes, Küchen single-cylinder ohc engines of 347cc and 497cc, MAG engines with ioe valves of 497cc, 746cc and 996cc, JAP sv and ohv engines from 490cc to 996cc and if required other power units could also be fitted. Racing successes were gained by 172cc models with Villiers Brooklands engines ridden by Gohr and Goretzki.

172cc Neander (TS Villiers) 1925

996cc Neander (ioe MAG V-twin) 1929

NECCHI / *Italy 1951–1953*
Assembled motorcycles with 98cc and 123cc Villiers two-stroke engines.

NECO / *Czechoslovakia 1923–1927*
Limited production of 346cc and 490cc sv and ohv machines with JAP engines.

NEGAS & RAY / *Italy 1925–1928*
Milan motorcycle importers which ventured into motorcycle production with 348cc unit-design sv singles which had big outside flywheels. Giuseppe Remondini, the designer, also built an ohv version in 1927 and in the 1930s joined the French Jonghi factory.

NEGRINI / *Italy 1954–*
Concentrates on the quantity production of 48cc and 49cc two-stroke machines, some with three and even four speeds. Also moto-cross versions are in the Negrini range. Earlier models had 110cc and 123cc two-stroke engines.

NEMALETTE / *Germany 1924–1925*
Unorthodox design with two rear wheels, a car-like body and a 173cc DKW two-stroke engine. It is not known if this machine was produced in any large quantities.

NERA / *Germany 1949–1950*
Designed by W. Neuscheler, the Nera was among the first post-war scooters in the country. Engines used were the 120cc Ilo and the 149cc Sachs.

NERACAR / *America (England) 1921–1926*
Designed by J. Neracher, the American-built machine had a low, channel-steel car-like frame. The engine used was a 283cc two-stroke with friction drive to the rear wheel. Built under

licence in England, developed versions of this unorthodox machine had 347cc Blackburne sv and ohv engines. Some models built in 1925 and 1926 also had bucket seats and deeply valanced mudguards. The Neracar was a comfortable machine with excellent road-holding. The machines built in England had chain drive and also an improved fork design.

348cc Neracar (sv Blackburne 'De Luxe') 1924

348cc Neracar (sv Blackburne) 1924

285cc Neracar (TS Simplex engine) 1923

NERVOR / *France 1947–1958*
Closely connected with Radior, Nervor produced well-finished machines with engines from 48cc to 248cc. Among them were their own power units, but also proprietary engines made by NSU and the French AMC. Nervor's top model was a 248cc vertical two-stroke twin with aircooling.

NESTOR / *England 1913–1914*
Produced in limited numbers Villiers-engined 269cc two-strokes and Precision-engined 296cc and 347cc sv machines.

NESTORIA / *Germany 1923–1931*
Produced 289cc and 346cc two-strokes with their own engines; took over the Astoria factory in 1925 and built afterwards Küchen-engined 348cc and 498cc three-valve, single-cylinder ohc machines. Other versions had 496cc and 596cc MAG engines with ioe valves and eventually 198cc ohv Sturmey-Archer and 497cc sv Sturmey-Archer single-cylinder engines.

346cc Nestoria (TS) 1925

496cc Nestoria (sv Sturmey-Archer engine) 1930

NETTUNIA / *Italy 1950–1953*
Equipped with Busi-designed 123cc and 158cc two-stroke engines, all Nettunia machines were equipped with four-speed gearboxes and were of sound design.

NEVA / *France 1926–1927*
Made by a small factory, these machines had 347cc ohv Anzani single-cylinder engines.

NEVE-ILO / *Germany 1924–1926*
Was among the first factories which fitted the then new 132cc and 170cc Ilo two-stroke proprietary engines into their own frames. Ilo became eventually one of the leading producers of two-stroke proprietary engines in the world.

NEW COMET / *England 1905–1932*
Built motorcycles with interruptions. Haden, the designer-manufacturer, used Villiers, Peco, JAP and Precision engines for his frames and there was also a Climax-engined 293cc two-stroke version. An interruption was from 1924 to 1931, when the last New Comet machines were built. They were equipped with 198cc Villiers engines.

NEW COULSON / *England 1922–1924*
Originally the Coulson-B, the New Coulson had long leaf springs on either side of the rear wheel and a double leaf-sprung front fork. Otherwise it was a normal motorcycle with 269cc two-stroke and 346cc and 498cc sv and ohv engines made by Bradshaw and by Blackburne. Eric Longden won many races on Blackburne-engined machines. Some racing models had also JAP engines, including a V-twin ohv version of 496cc.

NEW ERA / *America c1908–1913*
Open-framed unorthodox design with a 546cc sv engine below the bucket seat and the petrol tank above the rear wheel.

NEW ERA / *England 1920–1922*
Used mainly the 311cc Dalm two-stroke engine, but also other power units made by Precision and JAP.

NEW GERRARD / *England 1922–1940*
To be exact, this machine was really a Scottish product, made by famous racing motorcyclist Jock Porter. For a period when demand was bigger than production at Edinburgh, Campion in Nottingham produced frames on behalf of the Scottish factory. For years Porter fitted Blackburne engines from 173cc to 498cc into good and comparatively light frames, but concentrated from the late 1920s onward on 348cc models with ohv engines. When Blackburne stopped supplying such engines, Porter switched to JAP. He won TT and Grand Prix races on his machines. Other successful riders were the Austrians Georg Gartner, Karl Gall, Willi Melichar and Franz Putzker. Scottish patriots could get Scottish proprietary engines fitted; around 1922–1923 346cc sleeve-valve Barr & Stroud engines were available.

348cc New Gerrard (ohv JAP) 1928

NEW HENLEY / *England 1920–1929*
This make already mentioned under Henley, as there was not much difference between the Henley and the New Henley. The Clarke brothers, original owners of the Birmingham-based factory, had to sell it when their own father, who put up the money, withdrew his support.

348cc New Henley (ohv JAP) 1929

NEW HUDSON / *England 1909–1957*
Was a well-known motorcycle factory, which had with Fred Hutton and Bert Le Vack two leading designers and riders. Other famous racing men with this make were Jimmy Guthrie and Tom Bullus. Most models built were sv and ohv singles with own 346cc, 496cc and 598cc engines, although a 211cc two-stroke was also made around WWI. This nice little machine had 62mm × 70mm bore/stroke, a two-speed gearbox, and according to the model, belt or chain drive. Le Vack broke many records at Brooklands in the late 1920s; soon afterwards further development led to models with sheetmetal panels over engines and gearboxes. Vic Mole, a motorcycle sales expert, was the man behind this idea, which was not too successful. Motor-

346cc New Hudson (ohv) 1927

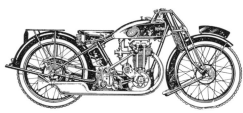

496cc New Hudson (ohv) 1929

496cc New Hudson (ohv) 1930

cycle production was stopped in 1933 and the name revived by BSA after 1945, when they produced mopeds with 98cc Villiers engines, in contrast to the big V-twins also made by New Hudson in pre-WWI days. There were also MAG-engined three-wheelers built between the wars; via Bert Le Vack, the English factory had good connections with the Swiss make.

NEW IMPERIAL / *England 1910–1939*
Norman T Downs, who presided over New Imperial from 1899 to his death in 1936, made his first JAP-engined motorcycle in 1910. After WWI, they concentrated on JAP-engined lightweights, scoring their first TT win in the 1921 Lightweight race and their last (of six) in 1936 — the last time a British bike won the race. From 1926, New Imperial made their own engine, designed by the 20-year-old Matt Wright, who remained development engineer and in charge of racing until 1937. Very well made and sporting, the marque sold well in the 1920s. In the 1930s 150cc, 250cc, 350cc and 500cc unit construction models, were developed, offered later with optional spring frames. In 1934 Wright built a 500cc V twin that Ginger Wood rode at Brooklands to put 102.27 miles into an hour — the first 'hour' at over 100mph by a 500cc 'multi'. A supercharged version was also built. Unlike the 250cc racers, the V twin was a notoriously difficult machine to race — so much so that Stanley Woods, declined to ride it after one trial!

New Imperial were very successful until Norman Downs' death late in 1936. Bob Foster's TT win that year brought business with which the factory could not cope, and they resorted to sub-contracting with disastrous results. The resulting claims for rectification work bankrupted the concern, which was sold to Triumph's Jack Sangster in 1939 and moved to Coventry. It was Sangster's intention to revive New Imperial after the war, but German bombing destroyed the factory.

246cc New Imperial (ohv) 1926

246cc New Imperial (ohv JAP engine) 1927

248cc New Imperial (ohv Grand Prix) 1938

496cc New Imperial (ohv) 1936

246cc New Imperial (ohv) 1938

NEW KNIGHT/*England 1923–1931*
Small assembler of motorcycles with 147cc to 344cc Villiers two-stroke and 293cc JAP sv engines.

NEW MAP/*France 1920–late 1950s*
Built during the years a wide range of assembled machines with engines from 98cc to 998cc and engines made by Zurcher, JAP, Chaise, Blackburne, MAG, Ydral, AMC, Aubier Dunne, Sachs and Opti. New Map built also Mistral-engined 48cc mopeds and even small minicars with 123cc two-stroke engines. That was in the early 1950s, when motorcycle production concentrated around Ydral and AMC-engined models from 98cc to 248cc with two-stroke and ohv power units. Scooters and fully enclosed motorcycles were other products of this very versatile French factory.

NEW MOTORCYCLE/*France 1925–1930*
The Georges Roy-designed New Motorcycle had 246cc two-stroke and also 346cc ohv and ohc engines made by Chaise and MAG. Other power units made by these factories were also fitted.

NEWMOUNT/*England 1929–1933*
These machines—put together at Coventry—were really German Zündapp products with tubular frames. Engines fitted were 198cc, 248cc and 298cc Zündapp three-port deflector-type two-strokes and 348cc and 498cc Python four-valve ohv single-cylinders.

NEW PARAGON/*England 1919–1923*
Produced a range of single-cylinder two-stroke

machines with 235cc, 347cc and 478cc engines of own manufacture and with half-elliptic leaf-springs.

NEW RAPID/*The Netherlands 1933–1936*
Made by the Amsterdam factory of P. J. Meyer, New Rapid supplied Villiers-engined two-strokes of 98cc, 148cc, 196cc, 248cc and 346cc and four-strokes with ohv engines. These included 248cc, 348cc and 498cc four-valve Python engines and also 346cc and 498cc two-valve JAP ohv versions.

NEW RYDER/*England 1913–1922*
Assembled machines with single-cylinder and V-twin Precision engines in early years, but concentrated after 1918 on Villiers-engined 269cc models.

NEW SCALE/*England 1909–1925*
Harry Scale first built his Scale motorcycles in very small numbers, but when he reorganised his production in 1919, he called them New Scale. They were assembled machines with 348cc Precision two-stroke and 499cc Blackburne sv engines. They had two-speed gears and chain-cum-belt drive. Later the range of models increased by 346cc versions with Bradshaw ohv engines and mainly with sv and ohv Blackburne engines of similar size. An interesting model which was built by order had the 347cc ohc Dart engine, designed by Sidney. When New Scale came into difficulties, the factory was taken over by Dot.

NEWTON/*England 1921–1922*
Villiers-engined 269cc two-strokes of cheap design.

NICHOLAS/*England pre-WWI*
This small and now completely forgotten producer of motorcycles produced machines equipped with 1·5 hp engines which were probably made by MMC.

NICKSON/*England 1920–1924*
Assembled a variety of models with proprietary engines. These included the 247cc and 269cc Villiers two-strokes, the oilcooled 348cc ohv Bradshaw and Blackburne's 346cc, 499cc to 546cc sv singles.

NIESNER/*Austria 1905–1911*
Designed by Josef Niesner, the Vienna-built 3 hp, 3·5 hp and 5 hp Minerva- and Fafnir-engined motorcycles were among the first made in the old Austro-Hungarian Empire. They were of sound and strong design. Niesner was after-

wards Austrian importer for Norton, Royal Enfield and other makes.

NIMBUS/*Denmark 1920–1957*
Denmark's largest motorcycle factory ever, Fisker & Nielsen Ltd. at Copenhagen, concentrated all those years on only one model. This was a 746cc aircooled four-in-line with ioe and later ohv unit-design engines. With frames made from pressed steel, early models already had a rear suspension by means of open coil springs and a tank consisting of a wide-diameter tube. The trailing arm front suspension was superseded by a telefork and a triangular tank superseded the earlier one. Common to all Nimbus models was shaft drive and a very limited export.

746cc Nimbus (ioe four-cylinder spring-frame) 1924

746cc Nimbus (ohc four-cylinder) 1935

NINON/*France 1931–1935*
Small producer of 499cc JAP-engined ohv.

NIS/*Germany 1925–1926*
Another small factory which fitted 269cc two-stroke and mainly 293cc JAP sv engines into orthodox frames of own manufacture.

NISSAN/*Japan 1951–1956*
A range of 60cc machines with own ohv single-cylinder engines, made by a famous car firm.

NKF/*Germany 1924–1925*
Lightweight motorcycles with 132cc Bekamo-licence engines, which used a pumping piston in the crankcase.

NLG/*England 1905–1912*
This maker achieved fame when a NLG racing

machine with a large, 2913cc ohv V-twin JAP engine ridden by Cook reached 90 mph in 1909. Production versions housed 499cc single and 770cc V-twin JAP engines.

NMC / *Japan early 1950s–early 1960s*
Small 123cc and 173cc two-stroke machines, built by a small factory.

NOBLE / *England 1901–c1906*
The Noble was one of the first makes using the new central Werner position of engine location. The 2·25 to 4·5 bhp engines came from De Dion, Minerva, MMC, Coronet and also from their own production.

NORBRECK / *England 1921–1924*
D. H. Valentine's Norbreck machines housed 269cc Villiers and Arden (70mm bore × 70mm stroke) two-stroke engines. Models with 346cc and 496cc sv Blackburne engines were built on request.

NORDSTERN / *Germany 1922–1924*
Produced 2·5 hp two-strokes with own deflector-type engines. SFW took over this design when the original producer went bankrupt.

NORICUM / *Austria (Czechoslovakia) 1903–1906*
Built actually by Cless & Plessing at Graz in Austria, then the Austro-Hungarian Empire, the 2·75 hp and 3·5 hp singles and 5 hp V-twins supplied to the Czechoslovakian part of the Empire were renamed Noricum.

NORMAN / *England 1937–1961*
Entered the market with 98cc Autocycles, took over the design and production equipment for the 98cc Rudge Autocycle and also built motorcycles with 98cc to 247cc Villiers two-stroke engines. In some countries they were renamed Rambler. In the late 1950s they bought the remains of the German Achilles factory. In the early 1960s the Norman brothers sold out to the big Raleigh group of companies, and manufacture of Norman motorcycles came to an end.

246cc Norman (TS Villiers 'Trials') 1962

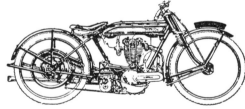

NORTON / *England 1902—*
James Lansdowne Norton made his first Norton motor cycle in 1902, using a French Clement engine in his own frame. This was soon supplemented by a Peugeot-engined v twin model, on one of which Rem Fowler won the twin-cylinder race in the first TT of 1907. In the same year, Norton designed the first engine of his own manufacture. He himself competed in the TT in 1909, 1910 and 1911, on the last occasion using the first of his 'Long stroke' engines of 79mm x 100mm, 490cc, dimensions that were to become a Norton tradition.

Illness meant that in 1911 Norton lost control of his own company, which passed to the Vandervell family, though Norton remained as joint managing director with R T Shelley. Though Norton did not win a TT again until 1924 (one was second in the 1920 Senior), the exploits at Brooklands of record breaker 'Wizard' O'Donovan meant a ready sale for 490cc side valve Brooklands Road Special models in the days just before and just after World War I. Post war, Norton took on an even more sporting image, and in 1922 raced an ohv model. 1924 saw Alex Bennett win the Senior TT and George Tucker the sidecar race, whilst O'Don-

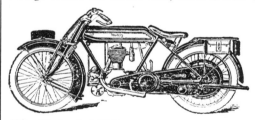

490cc Norton (sv) 1921

ovan, Rex Judd and, later, Bert Denly continued to break records at Brooklands.

Through these years, Norton offered 500cc side valve (16H) 633cc side valve (Big four) and 500cc ohv (model 18) variants. Though James Norton himself, a victim of heart trouble, died in April 1925, the greatest days of his company were still to come. Norton won the Maudes trophy for various achievements five times during the 1920s. They also won the 1926 and 1927 Senior TTs, the latter with the first ohc Norton, which became the CSI model. This engine however, was, relatively unsuccessful, and was redesigned in both 500cc and 350cc form by Arthur Carroll for 1931. Standing over Carroll's shoulder was Irishman Joe Craig, a Norton rider of the 1920s who, between 1926 and 1955, masterminded Norton's racing success. During the 1930s the ohc Nortons won no less than 14 TTs. At the top of the range, the CSI and 350cc CSJ were superceded by 'International' models, which 'prepared to Manx specification' were offered for sale as genuine racing machines.

In the years between the two world wars, there is no doubt that the Norton racing success of such star riders as Alex Bennet, Stanley Woods, Tim Hunt, Harold Daniel, Fréddie Frith and many more, effectively sold the more mundane road machinery. Successes after 1945 continued the process, as newer stars like Artie Bell and, above all, Geoff Duke continued to win, aided and abetted by the extraordinarily successful Featherbed frame of 1950 and engine development by Joe Craig and Leo Kuzmicki. However, the single-

490cc Norton (ohv) 1924

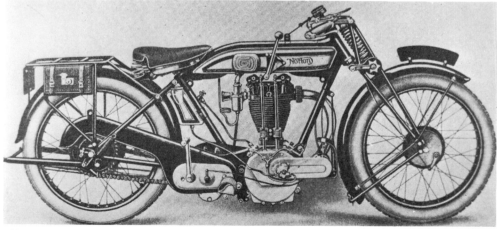

490cc Norton (ohv) 1926

cylinder Norton could not stave off the challenge of the Gilera 4 for ever. Even so, after Gilera withdrew from racing, Norton scored one last TT 'double', with Mike Hailwood winning the 1961 Senior race and Phil Read the Junior, and Nortons continued to win the Manx Grand Prix for some years to come.

Norton's 500cc vertical twin, the Dominator, was designed by Bert Hopwood in 1947, but not marketed until after he had left the company, in 1949. During the 1950s Norton design by and large stagnated, though the Featherbed frame became common to all models even including the venerable 16H side-valve which finally expired in 1954. Hopwood returned to Norton to design the 250cc Jubilee twin of 1958 and the 350cc Navigator in 1960. By that time Norton was owned by AMC (Matchless and AJS) having been sold in anticipation of death duties by the Vandervell family in 1952. The company eventually moved from Birmingham to the AMC factory in Plumstead in 1962. In 1966, AMC collapsed and was sold to Dennis Poore's Manganese Bronze Hold-

ings who perforce concentrated their efforts on the Atlas engine, as the 750cc version was known, the original Dominator twin having been increased in capacity over the years from 500cc to 600cc, 650cc and finally 750cc.

A totally new frame was conceived that isolated engine vibration from the main frame — the 'Isolastic' system — and the Norton Commando was revealed at the 1967 Motorcycle Show. The Commando launched a remarkable revival of Norton's fortunes, and in uprated form, stayed in production for ten years. Its engine also formed the basis of Norton's successful re-entry into racing in the production class, and also in the newly instituted Formula 750cc class. Rider-designer Peter Williams was responsible for much of the riding and almost all of the design work involved. After an encouraging second place in the 1970 production TT with a Commando, Dennis Poore gave the go ahead for a F750 TT and an enthusiastic Poore obtained sponsorship for a full racing team from Imperial Tobacco, who financed the F750 John Player Nortons in 1972, 1973 and 1974. In a pro-

gramme that had its ups and downs over the three seasons, the highest spot was the win in the 1973 F750 TT at over 105mph by Williams with team-mate Mick Grant second. The machines in question employed superb streamlining and stainless steel monocoque frames designed by Williams.

However, 1974 was not so fortunate, with Williams suffering an accident half way through the season. Sponsorship ended — just as a brilliant new engine, the 'Challenge', designed by Keith Duckworth of Cosworth Engineering, became available. Planned not only as a 100bhp racing engine, but as the basis of a whole new generation of Norton road bikes, it incorporated four-valve cylinder heads, water cooling, balancer shafts and a superb unit five-speed gearbox. Alas, it was to come to nothing — a Challenge racer was ridden just once by Dave Croxford at the end of 1975 when it was eliminated by a first lap crash. Nor was the road bike ever built. Denis Poore's Norton-Villiers company had, in 1973, been asked to take over the ailing Triumph-BSA company, and NVT — Norton-Villiers-Triumph — had been formed. But almost immediately, the new company was in trouble with its work force at the Triumph factory at Meriden, which Poore estimated last cost NVT £20,000 a week in disputes and disrupted production, not only at Meriden but as BSA as well. In 1976 the position became impossible and, though government aid was promised, it was not forthcoming in the event. In effect, production ceased, though quite a few Commandos and Interpol police bikes were assembled in 1977 and early 1978.

However, it was not the end. Poore retained the Norton name, and set up a new division at Andover. Part of this was given the name Norton Motors (1978) Ltd and its brief was to continue the pursuit of a motorcycle powered by a Wankel rotary engine design that Poore had inherited from BSA in 1973. Quite a bit of work had already been done on the running gear, and in 1979 25 machines were made with air-cooled rotary engines for evaluation and testing. In 1981-82, an improved

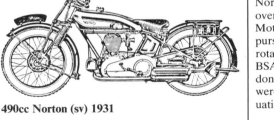
490cc Norton (ohc Model CS 1) 1927   490cc Norton (ohc Model CS 1) 1930

490cc Norton (ohv Model 18) 1927   490cc Norton (sv) 1931

490cc Norton (ohv 'Trials') 1935

490cc Norton (ohc 'International') 1933

496cc Norton (ohc 'International') 1935

machine was developed, famous ex Norton and Triumph development engineeer Doug Hele joined the company and in 1983 about 170 'Interpol II' rotary-engined machines were sold to police, armed forces and the RAC. Overheating and other problems dictated a water-cooled engine and development began again.

In 1987, the company was sold as part of a package to financier Phillippe le Roux and renamed Norton plc. Fascinated by the Norton name, and impressed by the work in hand, Le Roux demanded a production model. As a token for the future, 100 air cooled 'Classic' models were made and sold. At the same time, the engine was being developed for light aircraft and a racing project had been set up which was to produce some encou-

raging results.

The water-cooled engine appeared in the Commander, at first a police model, but, from June 1988, on sale to the public. This in turn led to the Formula One of 1989/90. Unfortunately the energetic le Roux left the board of Norton in 1991 over difficulties with American and German subsidiaries, and his departure coincided with a downturn in trade. Like so many more, the rotary-engined Norton's future is uncertain.

Norton (liquid-cooled rotary) Commander, 1988.

828cc Norton (ohv twin 'Commando Roadster') 1974

498cc Norton (ohc 'Manx') 1947

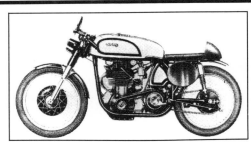

498cc Norton (dohc 'Manx') 1962

Norton (rotary engined) F1, 1990.

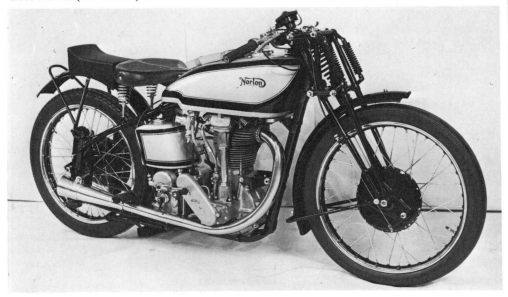

348cc Norton (ohc 'Manx') 1938

828cc Norton (ohv twin 'Commando Interpol') 1974

NORVED / *Germany 1924–1925*
Limited assembly of 348cc and 498cc machines with ohv and sv Kühne proprietary engines. Blackburne single-cylinder engines could be fitted on order.

NOVA / *Hungary 1925–1928*
Produced sporting machines with engines from 248cc to 498cc. The single-cylinder engines came from the JAP and Blackburne factories. Also most other parts such as Amal carburettors, Best & Lloyd oil pumps, Sturmey-Archer gearboxes, Druid forks etc. came from England. Among successful Nova riders in races were both Stefan and Nikolaus von Horthy, the sons of Hungary's Reichsverweser (head of state), Stephan Kiss and Karoly von Hild.

NOVY / *Belgium early 1930s to early 1960s*
Produced two-strokes from 48cc to 244cc with mainly Ilo engines. Among the models also was a vertical twin.

NSH / *Germany 1923–1928*
Not to be confused with NSU, the NSH was an assembled machine with 173, 346cc Villiers and 490cc JAP engines. The Villiers-engined versions included the vertical 344cc twin of 1927–1928.

344cc NSH (TS Villiers twin) 1927

NSU / *Germany 1901—1965*

A pioneer firm, who began by fitting Swiss Zedel engines to ordinary bicycles before making their own engines from 1903. NSU developed a simple free-engine clutch and a two-speed epicyclic gear that fitted into the engine pulley of the belt drive. They were strong exporters, even penetrating the US market at an early date, but, though they competed in the TT before World War I, they met with no great success. In the 1920s, NSU pioneered mass production; in the 1930s, they concentrated on smaller machines, though there were larger prestige models. Walter Moore, from Norton, was the designer at that time. He is best remembered by his Norton lookalike ohc racer, though he actually developed a wide range of models, including the 98cc Quick two-stroke, in production from 1936 to 1953. The English rider Tommy Bullus joined NSU at about the same time and won many racing successes for them in the early 1930s.

Both men returned to England in 1939. Post war, designer Albert Roder introduced pressed steel frames and patent leading link forks. In 1949 NSU signed an agreement to make and sell the

1¾ hp NSU (sv Zedel-engine) 1903

4 hp NSU (sv watercooled engine) 1905

6 hp NSU (ohv V-twin racing machine) 1909

326cc NSU (sv spring-frame) 1914

497cc NSU (sv) 1927

Lambretta scooter in Germany, which became a steady and lucrative source of income.

For 1953, they announced a new ohc 250cc four-stroke, with some striking features that included drive to the camshaft by eccentrics and straps (the system used by the Dart motorcycle 30 years earlier, and also by W O Bentley for some of his car engines). The Max, Special Max and Super Max were in production until 1963, and set new standards of excellence in the 250cc class. So did NSU's racing motorcycles of 1953 and 1954, the 125cc single-cylinder Rennfox and 250cc Rennmax twin. Derived from an earlier and relatively unsuccessful 500cc four, these machines won the 125cc and 250cc titles in 1953 and 1954 and, ridden by Werner Haas, Rupert Hollaus, H P Muller and Irishman Reg Armstrong, dominated their classes.

NSU were also in the forefront of record breaking. In 1951 Willi Herz had broken the world speed record on a streamlined 500cc supercharged twin that dated back to before the war, at a top speed of over 180mph. In April 1954 Gustav Baum broke world records in the 50cc and 100cc classes on (or rather in) a streamlined, cigar-shaped, feet first projectile that became known as the 'Flying Hammock'. Later he was to achieve over 134mph, using a 125cc engine.

NSU also sold a 'production racer', the 250cc Sportmax that earned an enviable reputation in

private hands between 1954 and about 1962. Though engine and frame closely resembled those of the 250cc road-going Max, they were in fact very special, and commanded a high price. Riders such as John Surtees, Mike Hailwood, Dan Shorey and many more were customers. H P Muller actually won the 1955 Riders' Championship in the 250cc road racing class using a Sportmax.

However, NSU had no hesitation in abandoning racing at the end of 1954. They had proved their point and that was enough. They were anticipating the expiry of their Lambretta licence, and needed to develop their own scooter model, the NSU Prima. Announced in January 1956 it was another success. So, too, was the 50cc NSU Quickly, the original 'moped' first sold in 1953 and of which NSU made well over a million. Later 50cc models were the sporting miniature motor cycles, the

498cc NSU (dohc twin-cylinder supercharged works-racer) 1950

Quickly Cavallino and Quick 50.

By the late 1950s, however, NSU were finding the going harder than it should have been. As with most of the German industry, motorcycle sales were suffering, as growing affluence made light cars available to a wider public. NSU themselves, in fact, had begun to make four wheelers, after a long lapse, with the Prinz air cooled car, and felt reasonably confident of being able to successfully 'change horses'. In fact they might well have done so, but for their unfortunate obsession with the Wankel rotary engine. Motorcycle production was deliberately run down, as the company devoted more and more time and money to the Wankel. By 1969 the company had gone, ruined by warranty claims on the disastrous NSU RO80 car. They were taken over by VW-Audi and the name was abandoned.

174cc NSU (ohc model 'Maxi') 1957

592cc NSU (sv) 1935

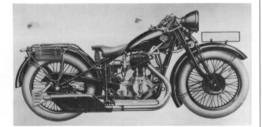
494cc NSU (ohv Model 'Sport') 1935

124cc NSU (TS 'Fox') 1951

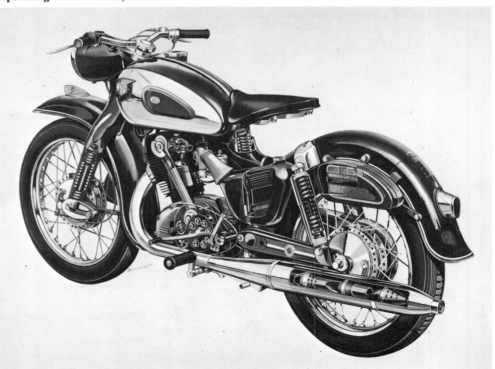
248cc NSU (ohc model 'Supermax') 1957

NUT / *England 1912–1933*

Although founded only in 1912, NUT was already in 1913 a TT winner, when Hugh Mason won on a V-twin the Junior TT in the Isle of Man. The name was always closely connected with V-twins, with machines of 498, 678, 698 and 746cc capacity. Engines came from JAP as well as from their own production. There were

698cc NUT (sv V-twin) 1923

498cc NUT (ohv V-twin four-port) 1927

four-port 498cc and 698cc ohv models, and there were also 172cc Villiers-engined two-strokes and 248cc and 348cc ohv singles with JAP power units.

NUX / *Germany 1924–1925*

Small producer of 170cc machines with own three-port deflector-type two-stroke engines.

NV / *Sweden 1926–*

Now part of the big MCB-Monark group of companies, NV became known for fast 246cc ohv single-cylinder unit-design engines in excellent frames. There were afterwards two-strokes up to 123cc in production which had proprietary engines made by DKW, Royal Enfield, Sachs and others.

OASA / *Italy 1930–1932*

Designed and produced by the Aliprandi brothers, the Oasa had Ladetto's 173cc ohv engines and also 246cc and 346cc JAP single-cylinder ohv engines.

OB / *Austria 1904–1907*

Made at Vienna by Messrs. Opel & Beyschlag who imported Opel cars into the Austro-Hungarian Empire, the OB motorcycles had their own 2 hp single-cylinder and 3·5 hp V-twin power units and shaft drive.

OBERLE / *Germany 1927–1929*

Villiers-engined 147cc and 172cc two-stroke machines, designed by the racing motorcyclist Eugen Oberle.

OCMA (DEVIL) / *Italy 1953–1957*

These are the 123cc to 244cc two and four-

stroke machines which have already been mentioned under Devil.

OCRA / *Germany 1923–1925*

Ottomar Cramer, who built Lloyd motorcycles, was also designer/manufacturer of the 137cc Ocra bicycle attachment engines and of 293cc and 346cc sv and ohv motorcycles.

OD / *Germany 1927–1935*

The blue-grey machines produced by the Willy Ostner factory at Dresden were of good and sturdy design. Most models had 347, 497, 597 and 996cc ioe and ohv MAG engines; only some special racing versions including the 996cc 55 hp V-twin ohv sidecar racer ridden by works rider Arno Zaspel had JAP power units. The big production 996cc MAG-engined version was the only German machine of the late 1920s and early 1930s with a reverse gear. Among the machines made were also 497cc racing models

with the MAG ohv racing D50 engine and from 1931 onwards a MAG-engined 846cc V-twin with the Le Vack-designed sv engine. There were also 198cc and 246cc models with Bark two-stroke engines and frames made from cast alloy. After the mid-1930s OD concentrated on three-wheelers, which were also made after 1945, when Ostner lived in West Germany. OD racing men besides Zaspel included Franz Heck, Ernst Bocktenk and Willi Zwolle.

996cc OD (ioe MAG V-twin) 1930

498cc OD (ioe MAG) 1931

498cc OD (ohv MAG production racer) 1932

498cc OD (ohv MAG Model 'Sport') 1934

ODA/*Germany 1925–1926*

Simple and cheaply built 293cc motorcycles with the JAP sv engine.

OEC/*England 1901–1954*

The name came from Osborn Engineering Company. Frederick Osborn built his first machines with Minerva and MMC engines. After an interruption of some years, his son John Osborn resumed manufacture in 1920, after the Blackburne factory decided to concentrate on producing proprietary engines only. That was the birth of the OEC-Blackburne, which later became just OEC. Fred Wood was also connected with the factory; he was a clever technician and invented among other things the duplex steering on OEC machines. There were 348cc and 547cc singles and 998cc V-twins with sv engines in the range of models in 1922–1923, among them a big 998cc sidecar version with a steering wheel instead of handlebars, which was also available with a 1096cc V-twin Blackburne engine. Very sporting was a 348cc ohv single. OEC also built many frames for record-breaking V-twins, among them the frame for Claude Temple's 996cc Hubert Hagens-designed British-Anzani ohc power unit. This was a double-loop frame with Harley-Davidson-type bottom-link forks.

Another OEC design was the duplex steering frame, used in 1930 by Joe Wright with a supercharged 85 bhp 996cc V-twin ohv JAP engine, when he reached a speed of 137·3 mph. This machine was fitted with a Powerplus supercharger. Another interesting frame was built in 1928, when the factory was on the verge of building the unorthodox Tinkler design in quantities. The Tinkler, first seen in the 1927 TT practice, had a fully enclosed 497cc flat single-cylinder engine with watercooling. The OEC production range included after 1925 347cc and 497cc Atlanta single-cylinder ohc engines with the camshafts driven by two pairs of bevel gears and a vertical shaft. Other models had Villiers two-stroke engines from 147cc to 342cc and JAP as well as Blackburne engines from 173cc to 998cc, including 678cc, 746cc and 998cc V-twins with sv and ohv engines. Villiers-engined machines and 498cc special Speedway versions which had been made from 1929 onwards again came into production after 1945. Among the models built in the second half of the 1930s were 248cc and 498cc, afterwards also 347cc singles and 998cc V-twins with JAP and Matchless ohv engines. Only the big version had an sv engine. The range included also the unorthodox Atlanta-Duo model with a 498cc ohv JAP and 746cc V-twin sv JAP engine. A 498cc ohv Speedway JAP engine was fitted to post-war speedway models. Road-going OEC machines had besides Villiers engines also the Brookhouse-built Indian 246cc sv unit-design single-cylinder engine.

346cc OEC (ohv Blackburne racing model) 1924

496cc OEC (ohv Matchless engine, Duplex steering) 1937

347cc OEC (ohv Matchless engine) 1938

986cc OEC (sv V-twin Blackburne 'Taxi') 1923

OFRAN / *Germany 1923–1925*
Concentrated on the production of a single model with its own 425cc two-stroke three-port engine.

OGAR / *Czechoslovakia 1934–1950*
Closely connected with a big accessory firm, Ogar was building superb 246cc two-stroke machines of very sporting appearance. Concentrating on this one model, they developed it from year to year. They built also a few water-cooled versions for the works riders, who competed successfully in races and in trials. There were also a few Ogar-built 498cc speedway machines with ohv JAP and also their own ohv power units. The black-green machines designed by František Bartuška were very popular among younger riders, and some leading racing men including Jan Lucak, František Fiala, Lada Steiner, Vašek Liška, Jiři Plichta and Anton Mikl rode them too. The speedway machines were ridden by Lucak and Hugo Rosák; afterwards by Šimek, Špinka and Němeček. After 1945 and nationalisation, Ogar designer Vincenz Sklenář created a new and modern 348cc ohc single with unit-design engine, telefork and plunger-type rear suspension. It never went into quantity production. The new Ogar was really a 346cc twin-cylinder two-stroke, designed on lines of the 246cc Jawa by Jawa designers. It had for some time the Ogar tank transfer, but became eventually the forerunner of all today's twins made by the big Czechoslovakian factory.

OGE / *Germany 1921–1924*
This was a 118cc two-stroke bicycle engine, designed by Oskar Giebel.

OGSTON / *England 1911–1913*
Name used during a short period for Wilkinson-TMC motorcycles.

OHB / *Germany 1927–1928*
Designed by Otto Hoffmann, this was an English-looking 490cc single with the JAP sv engine. Small scale production.

OK (OK-SUPREME) / *England 1899–1939*
Early OK motorcycles had De Dion, Minerva, Precision and Green engines. After WWI, the range used the company's own 292cc (70mm × 76mm bore/stroke) two-stroke and Blackburne 247cc and 347cc sv and ohv engines. There were also 348cc machines with the oilcooled Bradshaw engine and also JAP-engined versions from 246cc to 496cc. The 248cc racing models were famous; the young Walter Handley rode Blackburne-engined racers in 1922. From the mid-1920s onwards, JAP engines powered the 248cc racing models. Ridden by Frank Longmann, Alec Bennett, C. T. Ashby, Joe Sarkis, Rudolf Runtsch, Vic Anstice and others, they won many races. New Jones-designed 248cc long-stroke engines replaced the proprietary racing engines in the early 1930s, and 348cc ohc engines were added to the range of machines, which still relied on JAP engines up to 498cc. There was also a special grass-track version with a 348cc JAP ohv engine, still available in limited numbers after the war until the death of John Humphries, the son of one of the founders of OK, the late Ernest Humphries. Among the last OK-Supreme models were ohv JAP-engined high-camshaft versions with 248cc, 348cc and 498cc single-cylinder engines.

293cc OK (sv JAP) 1926

346cc OK (ohv Bradshaw oilcooled) 1926

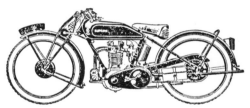
248cc OK-Supreme (ohv JAP) 1928

348cc OK-Supreme (ohc racing engine) 1936

248cc OK-Supreme (ohc) 1936

346cc Ogar (TS twin) 1948

OLIVA/*Italy 1920–1925*
The Oliva brothers built 120cc bicycle engines, afterwards a 173cc two-stroke motorcycle with the French Train engine.

OLIVERIO/*Italy 1929–1932*
Assembled motorcycles with 346cc and 496cc Sturmey-Archer ohv engines.

OLIVOS/*England 1920–1921*
Blackburne-engined 496cc sv singles in spring frames of the company's own design and limited manufacture.

OLLEARO/*Italy 1923–1952*
With the exception of early 131cc two-strokes, Ollearo became known as a producer of heavy motorcycles with unit-design 173cc to 499cc single-cylinder ohv engines and with shaft drive to the rear wheel. The 173cc models had two-stroke engines as well as ohv versions. They were probably the first shaft-driven, four-speed, unit-design 173cc models built commercially. After 1945, a 45cc bicycle engine with 1·25 bhp at 4500 rpm was made, followed by slightly modernised pre-war 173cc, 246cc, 346cc and 496cc singles. Neftali Ollearo, the founder of the factory, never showed interest in racing; his machines were destined to serve exclusively as good touring motorcycles.

OLMO/*Italy 1951–1961*
Produced lightweights, including mopeds, with 38cc Mosquito and 48cc two-strokes of various makes.

OLYMPIC/*England 1903–1923*
MMC engines with 2·75 hp powered the first Olympic motorcycles. After a long interruption, new 1919 models had 269cc Verus and afterwards 261cc Orbit two-stroke engines. Frank H. Parkyn's factory supplied frames to other companies, also fitted Villiers, JAP and Blackburne engines and produced under the New Courier trade mark cheap versions of Olympic machines.

OLYMPIQUE/*France 1922–1958*
For many years Zurcher proprietary engines (two and four-stroke) and also JAP engines powered these Courbevoie-built machines. Most models had 98cc, 173cc and 346cc. After 1945 the range consisted of two-strokes from 98cc to 173cc and also of a Zurcher-engined 230cc model. There were also AMC-engined 123cc, 173cc and 248cc ohv and partly ohc singles and a 123cc scooter with a two-stroke engine. Like Thomann, Armor, La Francaise and other companies, Olympique was part of the Aleyon group.

OLYMPUS-KING/*Japan 1956–1960*
Built on English lines, most models had 123cc two-stroke and 346cc ohv single-cylinder engines.

OM/*Germany 1923–1925*
These machines had 173cc ohv, 346cc and 490cc JAP sv and ohv engines. The total production was small.

OMA/*Italy 1952–1955*
Built 173cc unit-design ohv and ohc singles with three-speed gearboxes.

OMB/*Italy 1933–1934*
Modern Angelo Blatto-designed 174cc ohv single-cylinder machines. Blatto was also connected with the machines produced by the Ladetto & Blatto concern.

OMC/*Italy 1933–1935*
This Giovanni Ladetto-designed 174cc machine was built by the Officine Meccaniche Calabresi. The engine was an ohv single.

OMC/*England 1930*
An offshoot of Vale Onslow's S.O.S. firm. Very small production of 175cc Villiers trials machines.

OMEA/*Italy 1950–1953*
Interesting machine with a cast alloy frame designed by Carlo Bottari. There was a leading link fork and swinging arm rear suspension. The engine was a 124cc two-stroke with 5·4 bhp at 5400 rpm.

OMEGA/*England 1909*
Designed by A. J. Dorsett of Diamond fame, the old Omega had a horizontal 1·5 hp engine.

170cc Omega (TS Model 'Junior') 1923

346cc Omega (ohv JAP) 1926

OMEGA/*England 1919–1927*
When Premier in Coventry closed down, factory manager W. J. Green founded the Omega works. The first models had 269cc Villiers and 499cc Blackburne engines. Other models included Omega's own 170cc and 348cc two-stroke engines as well as JAP, Blackburne, Bradshaw and Barr & Stroud engines up to 678cc.

OMEGA/*Japan 1960s*
These were Kawasaki machines renamed for the American market.

OMER/*Italy 1968–*
Sporting lightweights with 49cc FB-Minarelli two-stroke engines.

348cc Ollearo (ohv shaft-drive) 1935

OMN/*Italy 1924–1925*
Villiers-engined 147cc and 172cc two-strokes, built in limited numbers.

OMNIA/*Germany 1931–1933*
Cheap two-strokes with 98cc and 147cc Villiers and 198cc Bark engines, built by the Imperia motorcycle works at Bad Godesberg.

OMT/*Italy 1949–1953*
Identical machines—248cc ohc vertical twins —to the MT.

ONAWAY/*England 1904–1908*
Unconventional design with low triangular frames, bucket seats and Kelecom 5 hp V-twins or the Berkley vertical-twin power unit.

OPEL/*Germany 1901–1930*
There were different periods when the big Opel car factory at Rüsselsheim, now owned by General Motors, built motorcycles too. The earliest models had 1·75 hp–2 hp and bigger versions 2·25 hp–2·75 hp single cylinder engines in open as well as in closed tubular frames. Production seems to have stopped around 1907 and was resumed soon after WWI. Leading link forks were used in 1906–1907. The next motor-cycle engine, designed in 1914 but built after 1918, was a four-stroke sv bicycle attachment engine of about 123cc, which was fitted on the left side of the rear wheel. Opel, then a leading bicycle manufacturer, also supplied complete machines with strengthened frames and tanks which looked like fire extinguishers. There were also complete motorcycles with 148cc ioe engines and two-speed gearboxes from 1922 to 1925.

From 1926–1927 there was a 498cc single with an 84mm bore and 90mm stroke sv engine. 1928 saw the production of designer Ernst Neumann's Opel frames made from pressed steel, identical to the original Neander products. Opel built

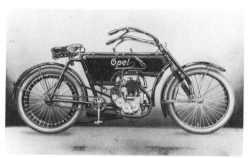

2¾ hp Opel (sv) 1905

204cc Opel (ohv watercooled track-racing machine) 1922

140cc Opel (sv rear-engine) 1921

148cc Opel (sv) 1924

498cc Opel (ohv 'Motoclub') 1928

498cc Opel (sv 'Motoclub') 1928

them under licence at the former Elite-Diamant car factory, after they stopped building Diamant motorcycles and Elite cars. The new models, known as Motoclub, had 499cc sv and ohv engines with 16 bhp and 22 bhp respectively. These models were the last motorcycles made by this famous car factory. There were two interesting non-production Opel machines, ridden from 1922 to 1924 by Fritz von Opel and Philipp Karrer. One was a watercooled track-racing machine with a 204cc ohv engine, rearward facing exhaust port and a big outside flywheel. And a 1928 Motoclub with a 499cc ohv engine was tested — also by Fritz von Opel — with six rockets, three on each side of the rear wheel. The experiment was soon dropped.

OPRA / *Italy 1927–1929*
Designed by two famous designers, Pietro Remor and Carlo Gianini, the OPRA was an aircooled 490cc four-cylinder in-line ohc racing machine with the power unit mounted transversely. In later years it formed the basic design for the famous Rondine 4, which in 1937 became the first watercooled and supercharged 498cc Gilera Four and the forerunner of the latest aircooled Gilera and MV Agusta four-cylinder works racing models.

OR / *Italy 1928–1931*
Produced bicycle engines and 173cc motorcycles which were equipped with their own sv and ohv engines.

ORBIT / *England 1913–1924*
The versatile Dorsett also designed Orbit motorcycles, first with 346cc sv engines, and after 1919 261cc two-strokes. Although there was only a small output from the works, models with various Barr & Stroud, Bradshaw and Blackburne engines were added.

OREOL / *France 1903–WWI*
Pioneer motorcycle producer, whose rider Cissac broke many records on a 333cc single-cylinder model. Oreol also built V-twins with Zedel, Moto-Rêve and other engines.

ORI / *Germany 1923–1925*
Lightweight machines with 145cc two-stroke engines.

ORIAL / *France 1919–1926*
Was closely connected with the French MAG branch factory at Lyon and fitted MAG 346cc and 496cc ioe and ohv single-cylinder and V-twin engines into their own frames.

2½ hp Orient (sv Aster engine) 1901

ORIAL / *Germany 1929–1931*
This name came into being when the marriage between Triumph (TEC) in Coventry and Triumph (TWN) in Nuremberg was dissolved. The Germans had until then used mainly Coventry-made engines and parts. Now they fitted Swiss MAG engines and renamed the machines Orial for export into certain countries.

Afterwards they changed to TWN, which stood for Triumph Werke Nürnberg.

ORIENT / *America 1900–c1906*
Excellent design by Harry Metz, who fitted 2·25 hp and 2·5 hp engines into strong modified bicycle frames.

ORIGAN / *France 1933–early 1950s*
Lightweights with two-stroke engines (mainly Aubier-Dunne) from 98cc to 174cc.

ORIGINAL-KRIEGER / *Germany 1925–1926*
After the original KG design was sold to Cito and via Cito to Allright, the Krieger brothers left and founded a new company, producing first their 498cc models. After Allright intervention, they had to stop and used 346cc Blackburne sv engines in the slightly modified KG frames.

ORION / *Czechoslovakia 1902–1933*
Vilém Michl, the designer-manufacturer, built in the early years superb singles and V-twins with his own engines. He was assisted in the works by his sons, especially Zdeněk Michl who created many interesting designs after WWI. There was

348cc Orial (ohv MAG) 1929 (German)

347cc Orial (ioe MAG) 1924 (France)

241

a good 346cc two-stroke single as well as a 594cc double-piston two-stroke single. From 1927 onwards they made 496cc and 598cc sv singles and also a 496cc ohv machine. With Z. Michl, Václav Liška, Jarda Melzer etc. Orion machines gained many successes in sporting events.

ORIONE / *Italy 1923–1928*
Guido Carpi produced very fast 123cc and 173cc two-strokes with three-port deflector-type engines. Nello Pagani, Raffaele Alberti and Martino Soffientini were among the successful racing riders.

497cc Orion (ohv) 1929

347cc Orion (TS) 1923

4½ hp Orion (sv V-twin Model 'W') 1908

ORIONETTE/*Germany 1921–1925*
Built a range of good 129cc, 137cc, 148cc and
346cc two-stroke machines with mainly unit-
design engines and two or three-speed gearboxes. The design department, headed by Engel-
bert Zaschka, also produced some interesting
unorthodox designs. Among them was a 'combined' two and four-stroke with a valve in the
crankcase. Only few of these 'overhead two-
strokes' were actually made.

ORIX/*Italy 1949–1954*
Designed by Amedeo Prina, Orix built Ilo-
engined 173cc two-strokes as well as a variety of
123cc and 173cc two-stroke scooters.

ORMONDE/*England 1900–c1906*
Once a well-known make. Fitted 2·25 hp and
2·75 hp Kelecom as well as 3·5 hp Antoine
engines.

ORTLOFF/*Germany 1924–1926*
Lightweights with 185cc and 198cc Gruhn sv
engines.

ORTONA/*England 1904–1906*
A 3·5 hp single-cylinder machine was the only
model built by this factory.

ORUK/*Germany 1922–1924*
Interesting design. Oruk means without belt and
chain (ohne Riemen und Kette). The engine was
— not unlike the Opel of that period — a 189cc
sv single, mounted outside the rear wheel with a
direct shaft drive. It was not a great commercial
success and Oruk was taken over by the Schüttoff works.

OSA/*Poland 1958–*
Made by WFM (Warszawska Fabrica Moto-
cyklowa), a leading motorcycle factory, the OSA
was a scooter with 123cc to 173cc two-stroke
engines and a nice appearance.

OSA-LIBERTY/*France 1926–1932*
Assembled good motorcycles with JAP licence-
built 346cc and 490cc sv and ohv engines. Manufacturer of the power units was the French Staub
factory. Small 173cc and 246cc two-stroke
engines were the company's own design and
manufacture.

OSCAR/*England 1953–1955*
The only product of this short-lived English
make was a scooter with 122cc and 197cc Villiers
two-stroke engines.

346cc Orionette (TS) 1925

246cc Orionette (TS Prototype with ohv) 1925

189cc Oruk (ohv rear-engine) 1923

OSCAR / *Italy 1965–1982*
Franco-Morini-engined 49cc and 84cc lightweights of sporting appearance.

OSCHA / *Germany 1924–1925*
Watercooled 496cc flat twins with opposing cylinders. The sv engine was designed by Otto Schaaf. Only a small number were actually built.

OSMOND / *England 1911–1924*
A company belonging to James in Birmingham. Built machines with 485cc Precision single-cylinder engines, and after 1918 small 102cc and 110cc machines resembling mopeds with Simplex two-stroke motors. The last model had a 239cc two-stroke engine of Osmond's design and manufacture.

OSSA / *Spain 1951—1980s*
Makers of excellent two-strokes designed by Eduardo Giro, usually of 250cc, but also the 500cc twin 'Yankee'. Sales of trail bikes in America, and trials models in Britain were good in the 1960s. At home, Ossa were strong in road racing and competed in Grand Prix with an advanced alloy monocoque-framed 250cc disc valve single. Santiago Herrero was third in the 1969 TT and world championship, but was killed in the 1970 TT. Sales fell in the USA in the 1970s and in 1984 the factory passed into the hands of a 'workers' co-operative' with inevitable results.

230cc Ossa (TS 'Sport') 1966

250cc Ossa Explorer 1976

OTTO / *Germany 1921–1937*
These were really Flottweg machines with the Otto trade mark. The Otto works produced

244cc Ossa (TS 'Sixdays') 1973

246cc Ossa (TS 'Enduro America') 1973

Flottweg machines; the Otto name was used mainly in the late 1920s, when the factory built machines with 293cc and 198cc sv JAP engines.

OTTOLENGHI / *Italy 1928–1932*
Concentrated on the production of well-made sporting 174cc ohv machines with a variety of engines, including Piazza, Ladetto & Blatto and JAP. The JAP-powered versions had 246cc and 346cc ohv engines.

OVERDALE / *England 1921–1922*
The word England is not exact in this case, because the Overdale was offered by a Glasgow company, but the factory was in the Midlands, where the simple frame was fitted with a 269cc Villiers engine.

OVERSEAS / *England 1909–1915*
Built exclusively motorcycles for British Colonies. They had very strong and heavy frames. The engines were sv V-twins with 842cc.

P

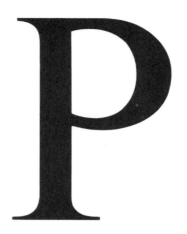

PA / *Belgium 1921–1929*
For many years a leading make in Belgian races, the Praillet-designed machines were of typical English design. Equipped with 174cc, 247cc and 347cc sv and ohv Blackburne engines, they were occasionally ridden by Blackburne's British works riders, which included Paddy Johnston and Ernie Remington. From 1925 onwards, PA built their own 245cc two-stroke and 345cc ohv engines and also fitted after 1927 348cc and 490cc JAP and MAG sv and ohv engines.

PACER / *England 1914*
This short-lived motorcycle was built on the Island of Guernsey. The engine used was a 116cc single, made by JES.

PAFFRATH / *Germany 1923–1926*
Very interesting and unusual machines, designed by Paul Paffrath. For a description see MW. In 1949 Paffrath designed and built the Eilenriede bicycle attachment power units.

PAGLIANTI / *Italy 1958–1966*
Built 49cc mopeds and 75cc miniscooters with two-stroke engines.

PALLION / *England 1905–1914*
Assembled machines with various engines made by Minerva, Fafnir, JAP and Villiers.

PALOMA / *France early 1950s to late 1960s*
A fully enclosed three-speed scooter with a 70cc engine was among the first products. Other models included 74cc and 123cc scooters, lightweights and also 49cc and 58cc mopeds etc. with Lavalette and René Gillet two-strokes.

PAMAG / *Germany 1952–1953*
When Anker stopped production of motor-

cycles, Pamag took over and built 123cc, 174cc and 197cc two-strokes with Sachs and Ilo engines.

PAN / *Germany 1924–1925*
Equipped with an unusual leaf-sprung fork, these motorcycles were driven by 346cc ohv Kühne engines.

PANDA / *Italy 1980–*
Assembler of trial machines with German Sachs engines of 79cc capacity.

PANDRA / *Japan early 1950s to early 1960s*
Ceased production in the early 1960s.

PANNI / *Hungary 1959–1962*
Miniscooters with 48cc two-stroke power-units built by the state-owned Czepel works.

246cc Pannonia (TS twin) 1974

PANNONIA / *Hungary 1951–1970s*
Also made by the Czepel works, the Pannonia motorcycles had a certain similarity with Jawa products. The 247cc two-stroke was built with one and two cylinders and was also exported to European countries.

PANTHER (P&M) / *England 1900—1967*
Yorkshiremen Joah Phelon and Harry Rainer patented the use of the cylinder and crankcase of an engine as a stressed member of a motorcycle frame in 1900, and licensed the idea to Humber of Coventry who used it extensively for their motor cycles and forecars. In 1903, Rainer died in a road accident and Phelon took Richard Moore, who had designed a two-speed gear using two primary chains and clutches, into partnership. The company now became P&M, making motorcycles with Moore's gear and chain drive and their own 500cc side-valve engine at Cleckheaton. The machine was developed year by year and, in 1914, was adopted by the Royal Flying Corps (later the RAF) as their standard despatch riders' machine.

Post war, production resumed, with minor improvements and a 555cc engine for some models. For 1924, there was a proper four-speed gearbox, and the P&M Panther, with a new ohv

499cc Panther P&M (ohv Model TT) 1925

246cc Panther P&M (ohv transverse V-twin Model 'Panthette') 1928

500cc engine designed by Granville Bradshaw. This very sporting machine proved a ready seller and Tommy Bullus finished fourth on a virtually

245

Royal Automobile Club patrolman on a P&M, 1920s

645cc Panther ohv with Viceroy sidecar 1964

standard model in the 1925 Senior TT. Unfortunately, another Bradshaw design, the 1926 250cc transverse V twin engined Panthette was disastrously inept and came close to ruining the company on the very eve of the depression of the early 1930s.

Production continued with small Villiers-engined two strokes and with 500cc and 600cc Slopers. Frank Leach designed conventional framed 250cc and 350cc ohv models in 1932. The 250cc, in a special deal with London retailer Pride & Clarke, was sold as the Red Panther for less than £30! After 1945, the 600cc Sloper, now known as the model 100, gained Dowty air spring telescopic forks, which were also fitted to the 250cc and 350cc ohv Frank Leach designs. These were available additionally in trials trim as the Stroud. Villiers-engined 200cc and 250cc singles were introduced; later the Villiers 250cc and 325cc twins were used. The 600cc was supplemented by the 650cc model 120. Involvements with the importing of Terrot mopeds and scooters caused financial difficulties, as did an unsuccessful scooter, the Panther Princess, at a time when, in any case, the British market was declining. The last 650cc Slopers — still with engines as a stressed frame member — were made in 1967.

PANTHER / *Germany 1933–mid-1970s*
Built in pre-war days mofas with 73cc and 98cc Sachs and Ilo two-strokes, after the war a wide range of 32cc and 48cc mopeds as well as motorcycles from 98cc to 174cc with Sachs engines. When Panther offered motorcycles in England during the 1950s, they had to be renamed Leopard, as there was already a Panther motorcycle factory in the UK.

PAQUE / *Germany 1921–1925*
The first product was a 140cc bicycle engine. Motorcycles had 147cc and 197cc ohv engines, which were also built as proprietary engines for Busse, Zürtz, Ammon and other factories. The last Paqué models had their own 497cc sv single-cylinder engines and there were also a few 198cc ohc engines built.

PARAGON / *England 1919–1923*
Produced a single model, a 348cc three-port deflector-type, only. The engine had 76mm bore and 79mm stroke and an Albion two-speed gearbox.

PARAMOUNT-DUO / *England 1926–1927*
Unusual design without top tube, with two bucket seats, a fully enclosed engine and rear wheel half enclosed by panels. This design was offered with 490cc and 990cc sv JAP or Blackburne engine, neither model succeeded in gaining many customers.

PARILLA/*Italy 1946–1967*
Giovanni Parilla's first design, a 248cc single-cylinder ohc machine, created quite a sensation, a 1947 racing version of it even a greater one. It was a beautiful design; unfortunately never as fast as Guzzi's production racer, the Albatross. Luigi Ciai and others rode the Parilla, but the best racing model was in Germany, where it was developed by Roland Schnell and its rider Hermann Gablenz. Schnell also built a 348cc version and developed improved frames for both models. The normal model had 17 bhp at 7250 rpm, racing versions around 30 bhp. These had two overhead camshafts and Electron crankcases. The first production model was a 247cc two-stroke of unit design, followed by 98cc and 123cc two-stroke versions. There was also a 123cc two-stroke scooter with a three-speed gearbox and fully enclosed. The following models had 248cc and 348cc vertical-twin ohv engines. Two very fast 123cc models had a two-stroke engine and a double-ohc engine with a telescopic fork and a swinging-arm rear suspension. The last one, a racing machine, developed 13·5 bhp at 10,000 rpm. Less hot machines were 148cc and 158cc two-strokes; a range of 173cc double-ohc sports machines with engines which were also supplied to the German Victoria works; an improved 347cc vertical-twin and a 98cc version; and the Slughi, with an enclosure which was nearly complete but also sporting. Engines fitted were a 98cc two-stroke with 50mm bore and 50mm stroke and a similar ohv version of 97·7cc with 52mm bore and 46mm stroke. Other Parillas included the Oscar scooter with a 158cc flat two-cylinder, two-stroke engine and a range of 48cc mopeds and sporting motorcycles up to 247cc. These included the 99cc Olympia, a Slughi design with an open engine which was either a 99cc ohv or a 123cc two-stroke unit. A special version called Impala, was made exclusively for the US.

98cc Parilla (ohv 'Slughi') 1958

PARVUS/*Italy 1921–1926*
Was among the first Italian producers of bicycle engines. In this case they were 104cc two-strokes. Motorcycles, made from 1923, had 123cc two-stroke engines.

PASCO/*Australia 1919–1922*
Built partly on American lines, these motorcycles had English 548cc single-cylinder and 746cc V-twin sv engines made by JAP.

PASCO-JAP/*Australia 1919–1922*
Produced V-twins with 496cc and 990cc JAP and MAG engines and English components.

PASQUET/*France 1932–WWII*
Aubier-Dunne 98cc and 123cc engines in motorcycles made in limited quantities.

PASSONI/*Italy 1902–1904*
Pioneer of the motorcycle trade. Used own 2 hp engines in strengthened bicycle frames.

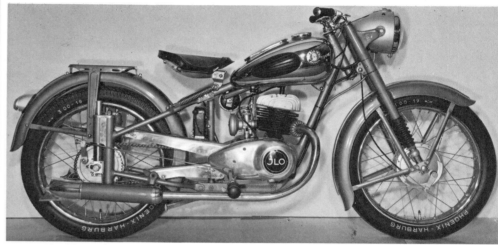
173cc Patria (TS Ilo) 1950

PATRIA/*Germany 1925–1950*
The first models had 248cc and 348cc Roconova single-cylinder ohc engines, designed by Johannes Rössig, but from 1927 to 1949 only mopeds were made. 98cc and 123cc Sachs and 98cc Imme engines powered post-war Patria motorcycles, which were of good design. Hans A. May, the owner of the Patria works, died suddenly in 1950 and the factory closed down.

PATRIARCA/*Italy 1925–1933*
Well-designed 124cc, 174cc and eventually 248cc singles, designed by Gustav Patriarca, who was one of Italy's better designers. Most models had ohv heads and the two or three-speed gearboxes in unit with the engine.

173cc Patriarca (ohv) 1927

PAUVERT/*France 1933–WWII*
Assembler of two-stroke machines with 98cc to 198cc. Limited production.

PAWA/*Germany 1922–1923*
Very unorthodox motorcycle designed by Kurt Passow. They had an unusually long wheelbase, a complete fairing from steering head to the centre of the rear wheel, partly enclosed front wheel, a bucket seat but a completely open chain to the rear wheel. The 226cc two-stroke engine had 60mm bore and 80mm stroke; a valve regulated the incoming mixture, but neither the engine or the frame parts were properly developed. The whole machine was more a designer's dream than a good commercial proposition and production ceased in 1923.

PAWI/*Germany 1922–1924*
Made by a small car factory at Berlin, Pawi motorcycles were built in small numbers only. They were powered by the well-known 493cc sv flat-twin proprietary BMW engine with 68mm bore stroke.

PAX/*England 1920–1922*
Orthodox motorcycles with 348cc and 499cc Blackburne single-cylinder sv engines. The bigger model had a 3-speed Sturmey-Archer gearbox and a Senspray carburettor. The cost was £120.

PDC/*England 1903–1906*
Made by the old Imperial Company, these machines had Coronet 2hp, 2·75 hp and 3·5 hp proprietary engines.

PE/*Germany 1923–1924*
Lightweights with own 132cc three-port, deflector-type, two-stroke engines.

PEARSON/*England 1903–1904*
Equipped with 3 hp Aster engines, the Pearson is now a forgotten make.

PEARSON & COX/*England 1912*
The only steam-driven motorcycle ever offered to the British public. Though not many were sold, the Pearson & Cox definitely reached production. One, with a sectioned engine, is in the Science Museum, London.

PEBOK/*England 1903–1909*
Was among leading English motorcycle producers. The 2·25 hp, 2·75 hp and 3·5 hp engines were of their own design and manufacture.

PECO/*England 1913–1915*
Supplied 349cc proprietary two-stroke engines and also complete motorcycles, when Calthorpe bought the Peco works at Birmingham.

PEERLESS/*England 1902–c1908*
These machines were identical with Bradburys built at Oldham. They had 2 hp and 2·5 hp engines, built like the frames under Birch patents.

PEERLESS/*England 1913–1914*
Small assembler, who fitted 292cc and 499cc Veloce (later Velocette) engines. The producer — International Mfg. Co. Ltd. — may have been a branch of Veloce Ltd.

PEERLESS/*America 1913–1916*
Strong 4 hp, 5 hp and 8 hp motorcycles with own ioe single-cylinder and V-twin engines, double-loop frames, telescopic fork and shaft drive. The factory was also connected with the four-cylinder Champion machines, made at the St. Louis works. The Peerless was built at Boston.

PEGASO/*Italy 1956–1964*
Lightweight with 48cc ohv engines, built in large numbers. Producer was the SIM (Societa Italiana Motori), a company with many ex-Motom employees.

PEM/*America 1910–1915*
This motorcycle manufacturer was well known in the United States in the period before the First World War. It produced a single-cylinder 4 hp motorcycle with its own ohv engine.

PENNINGTON/*England 1897*
Regarded in some circles as a pioneer, the American 'inventor' E. J. Pennington was really a businessman who made promises to keep shareholders happy. His design had two horizontal and totally uncooled cylinders arranged behind the rear wheel spindle and driving directly on the cranks of that wheel. The machine had a kind of flywheel built into the wheel. By invitation of Harry John Lawson, Pennington arrived in England in 1896 and built two of his machines at the Coventry-based Humber Company, which was controlled by Lawson and his associates. Pennington reportedly took £100,000 for his design, which proved to be a complete failure. Only the two machines were actually built when Pennington bought a return ticket to America, instead of keeping his promise to motorise good old England.

PER/*Germany 1924–1926*
Kurt Passow, who created the unlucky Pawa, also built the 308cc Per. Compared with the Pawa, the Per was a much improved design. He again put the power unit behind a steel cover and used additional steel plates for covering most other parts. Again a bucket seat was used and everything done to make riding comfortable. The original 308cc engine was superseded by a more powerful 342cc unit with 12 bhp, but it was no use. The whole design was not really de-

344cc Per (TS) 1925

veloped as it should have been. According to the designer, the two-stroke engine could run on anything, including crude oil, benzol, spirit etc. The smaller model had a two-speed gearbox and belt drive; the bigger version two or three-speed gearboxes and — if required — chain drive to the rear wheel.

PERFECTA/*Switzerland 1946–1950*
Fitted French AMC ohv engines of 123cc, 148cc and 173cc into modern frames.

PERIPOLI/*Italy 1957–1980*
Producer of the Giulietta who also has a big output of 47cc and 49cc mofas, mopeds and similar lightweight models. Engines used included the German Zündapp.

PERLEX/*Germany 1924–1926*
One of the many small producers of the mid-1920s. Fitted 197cc sv Gruhn engines into simple frames.

PERKS & BIRCH/*England 1899–1901*
This was a 222cc sv single-cylinder engine, built into a driving wheel as a complete unit. These wheels were fitted to two and three-wheeled vehicles. The design was eventually taken over by the Singer factory.

PERMO/*Germany 1952–1954*
Post-war mopeds with 32cc Victoria two-stroke engines.

PERNOD/*France c1900*
Very much like the Birch design, the 1 hp Pernod engine was fitted to a separate wheel which could be bought and attached as a 'pusher' to existing bicycles.

PERPEDES/*Austria 1922–1926*
Yet another bicycle attachment engine. In this case the 110cc two-stroke had to be fitted above the rear wheel directly to the bicycle. Drive was by belt.

PERSCH/*Austria 1922–1925*
Built 110cc bicycle engines at a factory near the Puch works at Graz. Frames for Persch engines (strengthened bicycles with special attachments) were built by Krammer of Vienna.

PERUGINA/*Italy 1953–1962*
Menicucci built very nice 158cc and 173cc two-stroked and ohv machines and after 1956 248cc versions. He was also the man behind BMP motorcycles. The range also included 123cc versions and a fast 173cc ohc single.

PERUN/*Czechoslovakia 1904–1924*
Built 3·5 hp single-cylinder and 4·5 hp V-twin motorcycles probably with Fafnir engines. After 1918 manufacture concentrated on 1·4 hp bicycle engines.

PETA/*Czechoslovakia 1921–1924*
Lightweight motorcycles and scooters with 170cc two-stroke engines, built in small numbers.

PETERS/*Germany 1924*
Lightweights equipped with 143cc DKW two-stroke engines. These machines were only built in small numbers.

PETERS / *England 1921—1925*

One of the few motorcycles made in the Ísle of Man, from an address in Ramsey. The Mk I had Peters' own 350cc two-stroke engine as a stressed frame member, with a strong steel fuel tank and a large diameter saddle tube as the other components. There was cantilever rear springing and belt drive with a variable engine pulley. The belt tension was maintained by rear wheel movement controlled by foot pedals! The Mk II Peters dispersed with the stressed member frame, though the general appearance remained the same. The machine used Blackburne four-stroke and Villiers two-stroke engines, a three-speed Jardine gearbox and all-chain drive. Sales were never large.

PEUGEOT / *France 1899—*

Lion Peugeot, famous pioneers of both cars and motorcycles, were an offshoot of the giant Peugeot Frères conglomerate. As well as their own motorcycles, they sold V twin proprietary engines to several firms, notably Vindec, DOT, and Norton. Rem Fowler's win for Norton in the 1907 twin-cylinder TT was with a Peugeot engine. Peugeo raced themselves — curiously, their machines were still using atmospheric inlet valves as late as 1912 — and were early users of the distinctive Truffault swinging-arm front forks. In 1913, they revealed 500cc vertical twin racing motorcycles with double overhead camshafts, designed by the famous Ernest Henry who had pioneered the double overhead camshaft engine in the Peugeot Grand Prix car of 1912. Though the cycle parts appear primitive in today's eyes, the engines — with unit construction gearbox — were of a sophistication not to be seen elsewhere for years to come. Both before and after the war, these twins won many races and broke records on the continent. In 1923 they were redesigned by Tony Antoniescu with sohc valve gear, neat four speed gearboxes and more modern

Pierre Péan on his works Peugeot, single ohc, 1924

173cc Peugeot (TS) 1927

cycle parts. Again, they were very successful, though, when ridden in the 1924 Senior TT by Pean, Richard and Gillard, they made no impression. The post-WWI range of road bikes had 300cc, 350cc and 750cc V twin engines; in 1921, a single-cylinder 270cc two-stroke was added.

During the late 1920s, Peugeot made various other two-strokes, and a sporting ohv single of 350cc. However the trend in France was towards ultra lightweight 'Velomoteurs' of 100cc, which could be ridden by anybody without a licence or payment of tax. Peugeot, naturally enough, followed this mood, which came to dominate the French industry in the 1930s and, in the course of time, abandoned all their previous sporting pretensions. After WWII, they were still France's largest manufacturer, with 50cc mopeds, 100cc and 125cc two-strokes, and 250cc and 350cc two-stroke twins. They also made several different models of scooters. In common with most French firms, production declined in the 1970s and, despite a brief undercover tie up with Gilera in Italy, production now consists only of 50cc mopeds.

PG / *Italy 1927–1931*

Produced 123cc and 173cc ohv machines, gave up the smaller versions in 1929 and concentrated on different models of the bigger PG, designed by Giuseppe Parena.

PHÄNOMEN / *Germany 1903–1940*

Produced in early years Fafnir-engined singles and V-twins, afterwards three-wheelers called

Champoneau on a racing Peugeot V-twin, 1904

Phänomobil, and cars. Motorcycle manufacture was resumed in 1930 with motorised bicycles which had 74cc Sachs engines and afterwards with 98cc and 123cc Sachs-engined lightweights, designed by Rudi Albert. These Ahoj models used rubber suspension both for the fork and for the saddle.

PHÄNOMEN / *Germany 1950–1956*
Identical model range to the Meister and Mammut. Engines fitted were from 98cc to 197cc, made by Sachs and Ilo.

PHANTOM / *Germany 1921–1928*
A manufacturer of touring motorcycles, Phantom built own 148cc, 198cc and 246cc sv engines and also fitted from 1926 onward JAP sv engines from 173cc to 490cc.

246cc Phantom (sv) 1923

PHILLIPS / *England 1954–1964*
Built mofas and mopeds with 48cc two-stroke engines. Part of the big Raleigh group of companies.

PHOENIX / *England 1900–1908*
A factory founded by former racing cyclist and motorcyclist, J. V. Hooydonk. Excellent design with 211cc and 345cc Minerva engines. Built also engines of the company's own design.

2½ hp Phoenix (sv) 1903

PHOENIX / *England 1955–1964*
The Eric Barrett-designed scooters had Villiers-engines from 147cc to 323cc. Barrett built also a range of mainly JAP-engined ohv racing machines from 248cc to 498cc, which he rode in many races, including the TT.

PHOENIX / *Germany 1933–1939*
Made by RMW of Neheim-Ruhr, the Phoenix range was identical to that range of models. It included Bark-engined 198cc and 246cc two-strokes and sv, ohv and even ohc models from 346cc to 498cc with Sturmey-Archer, Moser, Bark, Küchen and MAG engines. The company tried to re-enter motorcycle manufacture with its own 246cc two-strokes after 1945, but few were made.

PIAGGIO / *Italy 1946–*
World-famous producer of Vespa scooters, which are still in production with 121cc, 145cc and 198cc two-stroke engines. Also a wide range of 49cc mofas, mopeds etc. is in production. Piaggio at Genoa also owns the Gilera motorcycle works at Arcore near Milan.

PIANA / *Italy 1923–1931*
The first machines designed by Gualtiero Piana had 147cc Villiers engines, afterwards models with 247cc Villiers and 346cc and 490cc JAP sv and ohv engines followed. 248cc JAP-engined models were superseded from 1927 onward by Piana's own 248cc ohv motors in complete and very sporting machines.

PIATTI / *Belgium 1955–1958*
Designed by an Italian, the 123cc scooter was actually built in England and sold by a Belgian company. Piatti designed afterwards 248cc two-stroke engines for Associated Motor Cycles Ltd. in London. They failed to find many customers for this product.

PIAZZA / *Italy 1924–1934*
Small 124cc two-stroke bicycle engines were Antonio Piazza's first creations. Complete 174cc sv and ohv motorcycles followed and a 496cc ohv JAP-engined machine was added during the 1930s. While they were made in limited numbers only, 173cc Piazza ohv engines were popular and were also used by other Italian motorcycle producers.

PIERCE (ARROW) / *America 1909–1913*

Interesting design, in which a wide-diameter tube formed the tank. There were single-cylinder and 4 hp four-cylinder models with air-cooling and the cylinders in line. This model was offered for $400 and had, like the single cylinder version, shaft drive to the rear wheel. Pierce-Arrow was also a manufacturer of expensive motor cars.

PIERTON / *France 1922–1925*
Assembler, whose motorcycles had Aubier Dunne, Train, Villiers, Blackburne and JAP engines from 98cc to 498cc.

PILOT / *England 1903–1915*
Well-known factory. Produced 318cc two-strokes and fitted also Precision and JAP engines from 174cc to 598cc.

PIMPH / *Germany 1924–1926*
Assembled motorcycles with 490cc sv and ohv JAP engines and V-twin MAG power units as well.

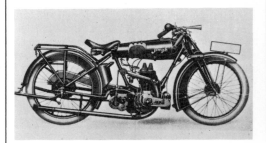

490cc Pimph (sv JAP) 1926

PIOLA / *Italy 1919–1921*
Flat twins with opposing cylinders. The 620cc sv machines were made in small numbers only.

PIRATE / *America 1911–1915*
Ambitious factory which built ioe singles and V-twins with 3 hp, 6 hp and 8 hp. Most models had pedalling gears.

948cc Pirate (ioe V-twin) 1911

PIROTTA / *Italy 1949–1955*
Built 49cc bicycle engines designed by Gianfranco Viviani, afterwards also two-stroke and ohv motorcycles up to 158cc.

PITTY / *East Germany 1955–late 1960s*
Scooter with 147cc MZ two-stroke engines, built in large numbers.

PLANET / *England 1919–1920*
Fitted 269cc Villiers engines and 293cc to 546cc Union and Blackburne engines into open frames.

PLANETA / *Russia 1976–*
The Planeta 'Sport' is a 344cc single-cylinder two-stroke, built on lines similar to Jawa/ČZ designs. It has 32 bhp at 6800 rpm.

PLASSON / *France 1921–1924*
Lightweight machines of primitive design. Plasson fitted two-stroke and also 197cc sv engines of its own manufacture.

PMC / *England 1908–1915*
The name stood for Premier Motorcycle Company, but was not the Coventry based Premier. PMC of Birmingham was somehow connected with Wall (Roc) and Rex and produced motorcycles and three-wheelers under names like Warwick, Rex-JAP. etc. with JAP engines from 393cc to 996cc.

PMZ / *Russia 1931–WWII*
One of the oldest motorcycle factories in Russia. The company originally produced bicycle engines, and subsequently progressed to 746cc and 996cc motorcycles with BMW-like flat twin sv engines, and V-twin engines reminiscent of the Harley-Davidson design. These were used by the Russian Army.

PO / *Italy 1921–1923*
Built a variety of 346cc single-cylinder two-strokes, designed by Pagni.

POINARD / *France 1951–1956*
Built motorcycles and scooters with 123cc to 248cc Aubier-Dunne, Ydral and four-stroke AMC ohv engines.

POINTER / *Japan 1946–1962*
Two-strokes from 123cc to 247cc with own engines. Was a big factory.

POLENGHI / *Italy 1950–1955*
Mopeds, mofas and similar 48cc vehicles.

POLET / *Italy 1923–1924*
Made 481cc singles with own ioe engines.

PONNY / *Germany 1924–1926*
Lightweights with mainly 142cc and 172cc DKW two-stroke engines.

PONY / *Germany 1924–1926*
German Pony with one 'n', but with 185cc sv engines.

PONY / *Spain 1952–1954*
Assembled machines with Hispano-Villiers 123cc two-stroke engines.

PONY-MONARK / *Japan 1951–early 1960s*
Produced 147cc ohv and 123cc to 247cc two-stroke motorcycles.

POPE *USA 1911—1918*
Made by a branch of a famous car factory with 500cc single and 1000cc V twins, these were excellent sporting machines, some with plunger rear springing.

499cc Pope (ohv) 1913

998cc Pope (ohv V-twin) 1914

POPET / *Japan 1957–early 1960s*
Miniscooter with 47cc two-stroke engines.

POPMANLEE / *Japan late 1950s to late 1960s*
Motorcycles with 124cc to 174cc and scooters with 49cc and 79cc two-stroke engines.

PORTLAND / *England 1910–1911*
This was the make of a big dealer in London, Maudes Motor Mart. Engines fitted were 498cc JAP and Peugeot.

POSDAM / *Italy 1926–1929*
The Alberto Da Milano-designed machines had 123cc, 147cc and 173cc ioe single-cylinder engines and with the exception of the 173cc machine, belt drive to the rear wheel. The biggest model had chain drive.

POSTLER / *Germany 1920–1924*
Designed by Walter Postler, who was a well-known racing-car driver, the first products were scooters with own 252cc ioe engines. After 1923 he built also a 246cc ohv machine with his own single-cylinder engine.

POTTHOFF / *Germany 1924–1926*
Built in limited quantities 185cc ohv machines with English Norman proprietary engines.

POUNCY / *England 1930–1938*
Built a range of Villiers-engined two-strokes, which included 147cc, 247cc and 346cc single-cylinder versions. The quarter-litre machine was also supplied with flat-top piston engines. From 1935 onwards, OEC rear suspension was available on all Pouncy models.

POUSTKA / *Czechoslovakia 1924–1934*
Made from English components, the Poustka had 147cc, 247cc and 346cc Villiers two-stroke engines. Like the Pouncy, it was a hand-made machine built in limited quantities.

POWELL / *England 1921–1926*
The first Powell with its 547cc Blackburne sv engine was a design which did not attract many customers. The factory also built 168cc, 198cc and 245cc two-strokes with their own engines.

POWERFUL / *England 1903–c1906*
French 2·25 hp Buchet and English MMC engines powered these machines.

2¼ hp Powerful (sv Buchet engine) 1903

P&P / *England 1922–1930*

Ealing Poppe, whose father owned the White & Poppe engine factory, designed these well-made sporting motorcycles. He made the first serious attempt to reduce engine noise and at the same time to keep the machine and the rider clean by introducing the superbly silenced and fully enclosed Silent Three, with a Barr & Stroud sleeve-valve power unit. Other models had JAP engines from 248cc to 996cc, which were actually made by the Montgomery works for P&P, which stood for Packmann & Poppe of Coventry. When a fire destroyed Montgomery's in 1925 P&P machines were not available for some time.

PRAGA / *Czechoslovakia 1929–1935*

Well-known car factory which merged with the Breitfeld-Daněk machine works and also took over the J. F. Koch-designed 499cc BD motorcycle. This single-cylinder ohc machine had 84mm bore and 90mm stroke. A 346cc ohc Praga was built in 1932 with 70mm bore and 90mm stroke. This time the fork and frame were made from pressed steel and the unit-design engine had shaft drive to the rear wheel.

PRECISION *England 1912—1919*

Frank Baker worked for many years in the US motor cycle industry before returning to England to set up the very successful Precision proprietary engine manufacturing company. Like JAP before and Blackburne after him, Baker discovered that making his own motorcycle upset the customers who were buying his engines, so Precision motorcycles, mainly of 500cc, were sold exclusively in Australia, a country without a large domestic motorcycle manufacturing industry.

PRECISION / *England 1902–1906*

No connection with F. E. Baker's Precision works. Produced motorcycles with mainly 211cc Minerva engines.

PREMIER / *England 1908–1920*

Once a great name in the British motorcycle industry, Premier in Coventry built big V-twins with outside flywheels, afterwards mainly singles with 348cc, 445cc and 490cc engines of Premier's own manufacture. After a reorganisation in November 1914, the name was changed to Coventry-Premier. The last design was a 322cc two-stroke vertical twin arranged lengthwise in the frame. It never went into quantity production, and there were no Premier motorcycles built in England after 1915. The factory, founded by Messrs. Hillmann, Herbert and Cooper, was really controlled by the Rotherham family, which in 1910 founded a branch in Germany. It was headed by Basil Jones, who raced Premiers

348cc Praga (dohc shaft-drive) 1932

in the TT races and who eventually became a brother-in-law of Geoffrey Rotherham, who controlled in the 1920s and early 1930s yet another Premier factory. Coventry-Premier produced three-wheeled and even four-wheeled light cars when it was absorbed in the early 1920s by Singer.

PREMIER / *Germany 1910–1913*

This was the Nuremberg-based branch of Premier in Coventry. Real owner was the machine factory J. C. Braun, but Basil Jones controlled production which consisted of a 346cc single-cylinder sv machine, and also bicycles and prams. Bad economic situation forced a transfer of the factory over the border into the Austro-Hungarian Empire, to Eger which in 1918 became part of Czechoslovakia.

PREMIER / *Czechoslovakia 1913–1933*

This was the most active period of Premier, although real motorcycle production did not start until 1923. Earlier they had only the 346cc sv single and the manufacture of a few experimental light cars, as in England. Production at Eger commenced with a 269cc two-stroke, based on the English Triumph Baby. It had a round tank at first and was built for nearly ten years. Other models included JAP-engined 348cc and 498cc sv and ohv singles. From 1927 onwards, Premier's own engines of the same size were fitted, a 746cc V-twin sv engine added. New in 1929 was a 498cc longstroke ohv sloping engine. The factory, at that time the leading motorcycle producer in the country, was headed by Geoffrey Rotherham. Chief designer was Hans Baumann, but the longstroke was created by Otto Lausmann. The factory had a racing department,

348cc Premier (sv) 1913 (German)

498cc Premier (sv) 1930 (Czechoslovakia)

where they used JAP engines, until the long-stroke came into service. The JAP racing motors were of 348cc, 490cc, 746cc and 998cc; the leading riders Alois Kraus, Václav Lischka, Karl Tauber, Mila Stipek, Ernst Haubner etc.

498cc Premier (ohv Model 'Longstroke') 1930 (Czechoslovakia)

PREMO/*England 1908–1915*
One of the names under which Premier (PMC) of Birmingham traded their motorcycles.

PREMOLI/*Italy 1935–WWII*
Racing motorcyclist Guido Premoli built 498cc motorcycles of sporting appearance with four-valve Python (Rudge) and OMB engines. In addition, he created 174cc singles with his own ohc engines which he raced himself.

PRESTER (JONGHI)/*France 1926–late 1950s*
Produced a wide range of models from 98cc to 496cc with Aubier-Dunne and Chaise engines. A merger with Jonghi in 1936 led to new models which included the famous Remondini-designed 174cc, 248cc and 348cc double-ohc racing machines. After the war, production concentrated on models from 98cc to 248cc and included beautiful 123cc ohv machines, 248cc two-strokes and also a nice 123cc scooter.

PRESTO/*Germany 1901–1940*
Was a well-known car factory, but little known as producer of motorcycles. In early years they had Zedel, Minerva and Fafnir engines; after WWI the 197cc Alba sv engine was fitted, but production of Presto motorcycles was never large. During the 1930s Presto produced mopeds with 74cc and 98cc Sachs two-stroke engines.

PRIDE & CLARKE/*England 1938–1940*
Lightweight, offered by a famous London-based motorcycle dealer. It had a 63cc two-stroke engine.

PRIM/*England 1906–1907*
Money's Prim machines had a wide diameter petrol tank which formed the top part of the frame. The engine was a Belgian 5 hp V-twin, made by Sarolea of Liège.

PRINA/*Italy 1949–1954*
Offered under the Orix trade mark, Prina's motorcycles and scooters had 123cc, 147cc and 173cc two-stroke engines made by Ilo of Germany.

PRINCEPS/*England 1903–1907*
Once a well-known producer of singles and V-twins with the factory's own engines.

PRINETTI & STUCCHI/*Italy 1898–1911*
Famous pioneer who built bicycles, three and four-wheeled vehicles and afterwards motorcycles with engines designed by Carlo Leidi. Ettore Bugatti, whose Bugatti cars are still regarded as masterpieces, spent his first years in the trade with Prinetti & Stucchi. The first motorcycles had 2 hp engines, but there were also bigger models built.

PRIOR/*Germany 1904*
A German make unknown in Germany. Prior motorcycles were Hercules products renamed for sale in Britain, where there was already a Hercules factory owned by a British company.

PRIORY/*England 1919–1926*
Assembler of two-stroke motorcycles with 269cc Arden, 292cc Union and 147cc to 247cc Villiers engines.

PROGRESS/*Germany 1901–1914*
One of the leading makes in the early years of motorcycle production in Germany. Fitted Zedel and Fafnir proprietary singles and V-twins. Afterwards models with their own 532cc single-cylinder and 698cc V-twin engines came onto the market.

PROGRESS/*England 1902–1908*
The English Progress was a well-known motorcycle. Minerva, MMC, Antoine and other engines were fitted into strong frames.

PROGRESS/*Germany 1951–1957*
Another Progress, but this was a Sachs-engined 98cc, 147cc, 173cc and 198cc scooter.

3½ hp Progress (sv) 1905 (German)

PROMOT/*Poland late 1960s–early 1970s*
Trials and moto-cross machines with 123cc Puch two-stroke engines.

PROPUL/*France 1923–1926*
Limited assembly of motorcycles with 246cc, 346cc and 498cc single-cylinder sv and ohv engines made by JAP, MAG and Blackburne. Built also a 98cc two-stroke.

PSW/*Germany 1924–1929*
Produced interesting 247cc two-strokes with inlet and exhaust ports in front of the cylinder, built a range of JAP and Blackburne-engined racing machines from 248cc to 490cc with single-cylinder ohv engines, and even minicars with 98cc engines for children.

PUCH / *Austria*—

Johann Puch's factory at Graz, Austria, started by making bicycles in 1899 and rapidly expanded over the next decade, producing cars, lorries and even railway locomotives by 1914. The sturdy, conventional four-strokes, singles and V twins of between 300cc and 800cc were therefore only a minor part of Puch's output. During WWI Puch concentrated on armament manufacture, but after it, eventually decided to concentrate on bicycles and motorcycles. For the latter, a design by Giovanni Marcellino for a 175cc 'split single' two-stroke engine of 175cc was chosen and, though the design was to be altered and updated continuously, this engine configuration remained in use for the next 50 odd years. It powered the original Puch 'Harlette', a spindly affair characterized by the British magazine 'The Motor Cycle' as a 'motorised bicycle', but it did have a two-speed gear and clutch, in the rear hub. Almost from the start, Puch raced in the 175cc and later in the 250cc class, using an auxiliary charging pump and, on later models, water cooling. The 250cc Puch's finest hour was the 1931 German Grand Prix, when Elvetio Toricelli won the 250cc class beating the

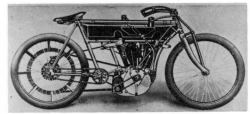

9 hp Puch (sv V-twin works racing-machine) 1907

2¾ hp Puch (sv Model A) 1904

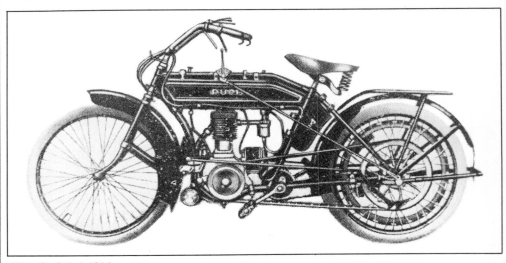

398cc Puch (sv) 1914

496cc Puch (TS twin-cylinder, double-piston) 1932

792cc Puch (sv transverse flat-four) 1936

246cc Puch (TS double-piston) 1932

348cc Puch (TS double piston GS Trials) 1938

works New Imperial, Rudge and Excelsior teams, and convincing DKW that the 'blown' split single was their future salvation in racing. Unfortunately, Puch were badly hit by the depression of the early 1930s and withdrew from racing.

Split single two-strokes were Puch's strong point in the 1930s, although a flat four-cylinder four-stroke model was introduced in 1936. Manufacture of this was dropped after WWII, though the split singles continued to be made in various capacities. In the 1960s, however, new, more orthodox, two-stroke engines appeared in the 50cc to 125cc capacities, while production diversified into small scooters, off road machines and mopeds. Puch had long since had a reputation in ISDT-type events, and the new models were just as successful — and in moto-cross as well, with new 250cc designs.

In the late 1970s Puch began to use two-stroke and four-stroke Rotax engines for competition models, but more and more the 50cc class beckoned with ready sales of small motorcycles and

246cc Puch (TS double-piston Model 'SGS') 1966

49cc Puch (TS Model M50 Racing) 1974

49cc Puch (TS Monza G.P.) 1982

498cc Puch (Enduro ohc Rotax engine) 1982

mopeds. The Puch Maxi moped was a world best seller in the early 1980s. However, Puch were no more proof against the decline of the motor cycle market than the other European motor cycle manufacturers, and sales fell off badly in the late 1980s. In 1991 Puch were taken over by the Italian company Piaggio and now only make mopeds.

PUMA / *Argentine 1954–early 1960s*
Mopeds and lightweights with 98cc two-stroke engines.

P&S / *England 1919–1921*
Identical with Pearson models, but the last versions built had the name changed to P&S (Pearson & Sopwith). They were actually made by Excelsior of Birmingham, owned by the Walker family.

PV / *England 1910–1925*
This London-based make fitted a variety of proprietary engines into sturdy spring-frames of their own design. JAP supplied mainly sv engines from 293cc to 996cc, Villiers two-strokes from 247cc to 347cc, while Barr & Stroud supplied 346cc sleeve-valve and Bradshaw 348cc oilcooled ohv engines.

PZI / *Poland 1936–1937*
Small producer of motorcycles with own 598cc single-cylinder and 1196cc V-twin engines. Most were supplied to the Polish army.

976cc PV (sv V-twin JAP) 1923

QUADRANT / *England 1901–1929*
Superbly made W. L. Lloyd-designed motorcycles. The first models had 211cc Minerva engines, but from 1903 onwards, the Birmingham works also produced engines of their own design. They included 374cc two-strokes; 498cc, 554cc, 654cc and even 780cc singles and 1130cc V-twins with sv engines as well as a 498cc ohv version. There was also a 654cc version with ioe valves, while other models had splash lubrication. Tom Silver, one of the great English pioneers, rode these machines successfully in sporting events for many years.

2 hp Quadrant with spring fork 1905

QUAGLIOTTI / *Italy 1902–1907*
Producer of 2 hp and 3 hp single-cylinder and of 5 hp V-twin machines. Carlo Quagliotti was regarded as one of the leading designer-manufacturer pioneers in the country.

QUIRKS / *Australia 1913–1915*
Built 496cc side-valve flat-twins on a small scale. The frames were of double-loop variety.

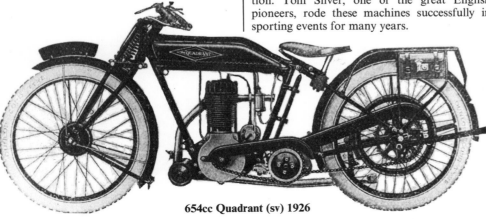

654cc Quadrant (sv) 1926

R

RABBIT / *Japan 1946–1968*
A very popular scooter with own 90cc, 123cc and 199cc two-stroke engines.

RABENEICK / *Germany 1933–1958*
Produced in pre-war days mopeds with 74cc Sachs engines, after 1945 38cc and 48cc mofas and mopeds and a range of motorcycles with 98, 123, 147, 173, 244 and 247cc Ilo and Sachs engines. The machines were of excellent design and good finish. The works were bought by Fichtel & Sachs and now recondition car clutches.

248cc Rabeneick (ohv shaft-drive Prototype) 1955

RACER / *France 1953–1956*
Small factory which produced bicycle engines and lightweight motorcycles with own 49cc and 74cc two-stroke engines.

246cc Radco (TS) 1923

269cc Radco (TS) 1915

490cc Radco (ohv JAP) 1928

RADCO / *England 1913–1932*
Excellent 211cc and 247cc two-strokes with outside flywheels, afterwards 247cc ohv models with Radco's own engines and Villiers-engined 145cc and 198cc two-strokes. JAP-engined versions had 293cc and 490cc sv and 248cc and 490cc ohv motors. All had one cylinder, but the 490cc ohv machine was built in three versions: Touring, Sport and Super-Sport.

RADEX / *Germany 1951–late 1950s*
This name was used for some post-war machines built by the Express motorcycle factory. *See also* Express.

RADIOLA / *France 1933–1939*
These were bicycle attachments with a capacity of 98cc.

RADIOR / *France 1904–1960*
Old established factory. Fitted Peugeot and Antoine engines and during the 1920s their own 98cc to 247cc two-strokes as well as JAP and Chaise engines from 247cc to 498cc. Most Chaise-engined models were of unit design, some had ohv, others ohc. After 1945, most engines were supplied by the associated Nervor works, by AMC and NSU. The German factory also supplied 48cc and 98cc two-strokes for mopeds, lightweights etc. while Radior production included ohv models up to 248cc and also some interesting two-stroke vertical twins of the same capacity.

490cc Radior (ohv JAP) 1929

175cc Radior (ohv AMC engine) 1952

RADMILL / *England 1912–1914*
Assembled motorcycles with 269cc Villiers and 346cc Precision two-stroke engines. If required other Precision engines could also be supplied.

RADVAN / *Czechoslovakia 1909–1926*
See also Meteor. After 1924 Radvan supplied under his own name 145cc and 174cc DKW-engined two-strokes.

RAGLAN / *England 1909–1913*
Built motorcycles with 292cc, 347cc and 496cc Precision sv engines, watercooled 490cc Green-Precision singles and also with their own power units.

RALEIGH / *England 1899—1970s*
Raleigh were famous bicycle makers, who also produced proprietary Sturmey Archer gearboxes and later, engines. Their first motor cycles, unashamed copies of the Werner Motocyclette, gave way in 1902 to a more orthodox model, notable for using Bowden cable controls. Production of this ceased in 1905 and Raleigh did not re-enter the motor-

3 hp Raleigh No. 2 aircooled 1905

3½ hp Raleigh watercooled 'Raleighette' 1905

173cc Raleigh (sv) 1924

cycle scene until 1919, when a new 650cc flat twin appeared, followed by a wide range of singles and twins designed by William Comery. These worthy (but rather dull) machines did very well in trials in the 1920s under publicity chief Hugh Gibson, a particular star being the brilliant lady rider Marjorie Cottle. In later years, Raleigh strove for a more sporting image, hiring 'Wizard' O'Donovan (of Brooklands and Norton fame) to design TT racers, which, though promising, never really justified their considerable cost. In the depressed early 1930s Raleigh decided that bicycles were more profitable, and motorcycle production ended in 1933.

Raleigh re-entered the market again 25 years later with a Sturmey Archer-engined moped, but soon found it cheaper to import a range of machines with automatic transmission — the Mobylette, built in France by Motobécame. A small wheeled version was the Raleigh Wisp. The Raleigh Roma was a 75cc (Bianchi) scooter.

In the late 1970s, Raleigh again decided that bicycles were a better bet — they by now owned many other famous names and they gave up the moped market.

RAMBLER / *America 1903–WWI*
Made 4 hp singles and 6 hp V-twins.

RAMBLER / *England 1937–1961*
This was the trade mark for some Norman models — especially the Villiers-engined 197cc two-stroke — in certain foreign countries.

RANZANI / *Italy 1923–1931*
Interesting make, because the Ranzani had not only 175cc sv engines from the German Heros factory, but also 170cc ohv engines from Norman in England, a proprietary engine factory which was not connected with Norman motorcycles. The last Ranzani motorcycles had their own unit-design ohv 173cc engines.

RAS / *Italy 1932–1936*
Made by Fusi, for many years FN Importer to Italy, the RAS had mainly JAP ohv engines from 173cc to 490cc, and some frame parts made by the FN works. A nice 248cc ohc single of their own design and manufacture was built in 1935. It was the last RAS model; after 1936, all machines used the Fusi tank transfer.

RASSER / *France 1922–1923*
Unusual design with rivetted pressed steel frame and 98cc two-stroke engine.

RATIER / *France 1955–1962*
Produced in the late 1920s small cars and was successor to the CMR and CEMEC works, which after 1945 built BMW-like motorcycles

496cc Ratier (ohv transverse flat-twin) 1958

with parts which were partly made in France by BMW for the German army during the war, and partly after the war in French factories. The first models were 746cc sv flat twins. Ratier built mainly 494cc and 597cc ohv models of pure French design and manufacture.

RATINGIA / *Germany 1923–1925*
Lightweights with 170cc and 195cc sv engines.

RAVAT / *France 1898–late 1950s*
Produced a range of models to 498cc including two-strokes of 98cc and 173cc.

RAY / *England 1919–1920*
Limited production of motorcycles with own 331cc two-stroke engines.

RAY / *England 1922–1925*
W. H. Raven designed the beautiful 193cc sv monobloc Ray, which weighed only 130 lb with a saddle height of 24 in. Another model with a Cohen-designed 172cc Villiers-Jardine engine was added in 1924, after the factory moved from Nottingham to Leicester.

RAYNAL / *England 1914–1953*
Early models had the 269cc Villiers two-stroke engine; during the mid-1930s and after 1945 the machines had 98cc Villiers engines.

READING-STANDARD / *America 1903–1922*
A leading make of the period and together with Indian, Harley-Davidson, Super-X, Henderson, ACE and Cleveland a very popular one. The production included 499cc singles and V-twins

990cc Reading-Standard (sv V-twin) 1917

990cc Reading-Standard (ohc V-twin works-racer) 1921

with 990cc and 1170cc. Most had sv engines, some racing versions ohv and even ohc power units, but the ohc engines were used by works riders only and were not for sale.

READY / *England 1920–1922*
Assembled machines of simple design. Engines used were JAP 293cc and 346cc sv units. Built later the 147cc Villiers-engined Rebro.

READY / *Belgium 1924–1939*
Originally known as Ready-Courtrai, the Ready motorcycles were of typical English design. Most

engines came from England: Villiers, JAP, Blackburne and Python. The exception was the Swiss MAG. Models built had 173cc to 498cc.

REAL / *Germany 1981–*
New producer of various light machines which includes a 79cc enduro model called 'Nevada'.

REBRO / *England 1922–1928*
Of simple design, the Rebro, priced at £37, had a 147cc Villiers engine. After Rebro closed, Ready took over production of this model, but only very few such machines actually appeared.

RECORD / *Germany 1922–1924*
Equipped machines of simple design with their own 147cc two-stroke engines.

REDDIS / *Spain 1957–1960*
Small producer of 124cc two-stroke machines with Hispano-Villiers engines.

REDRUP / *England 1919–1922*
Created by a former aircraft-engine designer Charles Redrup, these machines had a 304cc radial three-cylinder sv engine of simple and practical appearance. Although offered also by two other makes — Beaumont and British Radial — the actual production of the engine was limited. Redrup also built a six-cylinder prototype by putting two such engines together. It was a smooth machine, but not a good commercial proposition.

RED STAR / *Belgium 1902*
Built at Antwerp and fitted with a 211cc Minerva engine.

REFORM / *Austria 1903–1905*
Monarch in Birmingham, better known as the Excelsior works, supplied 2·25 hp sv engines for the Vienna-based Austrian manufacturer.

REGAL / *England 1909–1915*
Excellent machines of sound design. The range included 349cc two-strokes with Peco engines, 346cc and 492cc sv and ohv singles with air-cooled Precision and watercooled Green-Precision engines, while a 602cc twin was also made by Precision.

REGENT / *England 1920–1921*
Small manufacturer, who fitted 688cc Coventry-Victor flat twin sv engines into heavy frames of own design and manufacture.

REGINA / *England 1903–1915*
Early models had Minerva, MMC and Fafnir engines. Production stopped in 1907, but was resumed just before WWI, when the factory fitted its own 292cc two-stroke engines into orthodox frames. This machine was made at Ilford in Essex; at the same time identical machines were offered from an address in Derby.

REGINA / *France 1905–WWI*
Early French machines with Zurcher, Buchet and Peugeot proprietary engines.

REGNIS / *Australia 1919–1923*
Built by the Singer importers at Melbourne, the Regnis housed a 746cc ioe V-twin engine of Swiss MAG (Motosacoche) manufacture.

REH / *Germany 1948–1953*
The Richard Engelbrecht-designed Reh was made in small numbers and was of good design and quality. The engines fitted were of Ilo manufacture and had 173cc, 198cc, 244cc and 248cc.

REITER / *Italy 1927–1929*
Despite the German name, the Reiter was a sporting Italian machine, made mainly from Using English components Timone and Fresia built these at Turin. The engines used were the 247cc sv and ohv Blackburne and the oilcooled 348cc ohv Bradshaw, the so-called 'oilboiler'.

RELIANCE / *America 1912–1915*
One of the smaller US works, Reliance built 4·5 hp single cylinder machines with ioe engines.

REMUS / *England 1920–1922*
Concentrated on the assembly of 211cc two-strokes engines built by Radco of Birmingham.

RENÉ-GILLET / *France 1898–1957*
Excellent heavy machines used by the French armed forces and the police. This concerned mainly the 748cc and 996cc V-twins with sv engines, which were run with sidecars attached. Another popular model was the 346cc single-

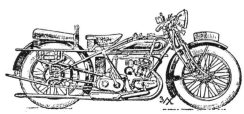

346cc René-Gillet (sv) 1928

248cc René-Gillet (TS) 1952

cylinder sv model. Improved versions of the big V-twins were built after the war, while main production switched to two-strokes of 48cc, 123cc and 246cc. All engines were of own design and manufacture. Never regarded as a very sporting make, René-Gillet machines were known as 'unbreakable' touring machines.

RENNER-ORIGINAL/*Germany 1924–1932*
Designed by Carl Ostner, brother of the manufacturer of OD motorcycles, Renner-Original concentrated on 346cc single-cylinder and 678cc V-twin machines with sv JAP engines. On request, they supplied also other JAP power units and also German Kühne and Küchen engines.

346cc Renner-Original (sv JAP) 1927

RENNSTEIG/*Germany 1925–1930*
Arms factory which took over the production of Original-Krieger machines and fitted 198cc to 497cc Blackburne engines into typical KG (Krieger-Gnädig) double-loop frames.

REPUBLIC/*Czechoslovakia 1899–1908*
Made by the Laurin & Klement factory (now Skoda) in the old Austro-Hungarian Empire, these machines were identical to Laurin & Klement products.

REVERE/*England 1915–1922*
Small two-strokes with 269cc Villiers engines with frames, built by Sparkbrook for Whitehouse & Co., the Revere manufacturer.

REVOLUTION/*England 1904–1906*
This was a conventional 2·75 hp single with power units made by NRCC.

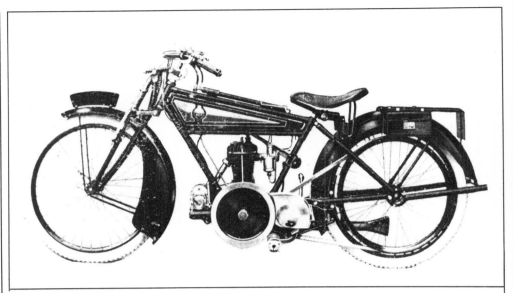

346cc Rex (sv Blackburne) 1922

3¼ hp Rex (sv) 1905

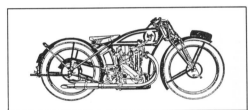

346cc Rex-Acme (ohv MAG) 1928

REX (REX ACME) / *England 1900—1933*
Under two energetic brothers, Harold and Billy Williamson, Rex of Coventry became one of the leading motorcycle manufacturers in England. From the start, they made their own single-cylinder and V twin engines with characteristic square finning and were amongst the first to fit spring front forks, with a telescopic action. Rex were prominent in all sorts of competition and their lady rider Muriel Hind won considerable publicity for them in long-distance trials and speed hill climbs. In 1908 Rex entered into an agreement with Premier in Birmingham to build proprietary engined models under the name Rex-JAP.

Later in 1911 the Williamson brothers left the company after a board room argument, and George Hemingway took over, continuing to expand Rex company until WWI. During it Rex were engaged in war work, and made only a batch of 50 V twins for Russia and a few sidecar outfits for the Daily Mail's distribution fleet. Post war, Rex at first offered advanced singles and twins with their own engines, but few of these were made and following their take-over of the smaller Acme company, they now began to use JAP and Blackburne engines. After the 1922 Lightweight TT rider Walter Handley (who had made fastest lap before crashing) quarrelled violently with Ernie Humphries, his boss at OK Motor Cycles. He was signed up

on the spot by Hemmingway, starting a partnership that was to make motorcycle racing history. Between 1923 and 1927, Handley won three TTs and made five fastest TT laps for Rex Acme, as well as scoring Grand Prix victories and innumerable other wins and places. His career, though brief, raised him to a level comparable to, later, Stanley Woods, Geoff Duke and Mike Hailwood, simply the best in the world in their time.

In the 1920s, Rex Acme offered a wide range of machines, with Villiers two-strokes, JAP, Blackburne and MAG singles and twins. They also produced some oddities, such as an Aza two-stroke engined 175cc model and another 175cc ohv machine with what they claimed was their own engine, but which, in fact, was an AKD. They sold TT replica models and genuine racing machines that were very successful and earned Rex Acme a sporting reputation second to none.

However, the survival rate of 'vintage' Rex Acmes is low, and overall sales were probably not high enough. The company showed signs of faltering when Handley left in 1929, and they collapsed in the depression of 1930. They were bought by the Mills Fulford sidecar manufacturing concern, but a re-launch of the Rex Acme name in 1932 was not a success, and they and Mills Fulford disappeared forever in 1933.

REX / *Germany 1923–1925*
Produced 283cc two-stroke machines in a small factory near Nuremberg.

REX / *Germany 1948–1964*
Built bicycle attachment engines with 31cc, 34cc and 40cc, afterwards a large number of mofas, mopeds and lightweights with 48cc two-stroke power units.

REX / *Sweden 1908–*
The first machines had Swiss Motosacoche engines. In 1908 Rex built their own 2·5 hp V-twin engines. Later there were Villiers and JAP-engined models from 147cc to 746cc. After WWI Sachs, Ilo, Husqvarna and other two-stroke engines from 48cc to 248cc were fitted.

REX JAP / *England 1908–1915*
Made by the Premier company for Rex to use JAP engines in Rex running gear. The Williamson brothers (see Rex) wanted to expand Rex engine production facilities, but other directors did not. This confrontation led to boardroom conflict and eventually the Williamsons' resigned.

REYNOLDS-RUNABOUT / *England 1919–1922*
Fully enclosed scooter-like machines with small wheels and a very low centre of gravity. Engines used were the 269cc Liberty two-stroke and the 346cc sv JAP.

269cc Reynolds-Runabout (TS Liberty-engine) 1921

REYNOLDS-SPECIAL / *England 1930–1933*
Made by Albert Reynolds, who founded in 1938 the AER motorcycle works and who for many years was closely connected with Scott, the Reynolds-Specials were actually modified and improved 498cc and 598cc two-stroke, twin-cylinder watercooled Scotts.

R&F / *Germany 1924–1926*
Another German 348cc ohv machine, but in this case the engine was R&F's own design and manu-facture.

RHONSON / *France 1952–1958*
Built the 49cc Rhonsonette mopeds and other small machines and also 123cc two-stroke motorcycles.

RHONY-X / *France 1924–1932*
Built during the years a wide range of models. These included 185cc and 246cc two-strokes, in the late 1920s and 1930s also 98cc versions as well as JAP and Chaise-engined sv and ohv models up to 498cc. Some of the Chaise engines were ohc unit-design models.

RIBI / *Germany 1923–1925*
A Berlin-based manufacturer of 196cc and 248cc ohv single-cylinder machines with their own engines.

RICHARD / *France 1901–1904*
Car and motorcycle manufacturer, whose motor-cycles had engines made by Peugeot and other proprietary engine manufacturers.

RICKMAN / *England 1959–*
Experienced and successful producer of chassis kits, which are now produced for Honda 900cc, Suzuki GS 1000 as well as Kawasaki Z1, Z900 and Z1000 engines, i.e. four-cylinder versions. Rickman exports such kits to many countries, especially the USA.

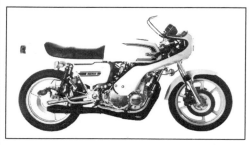

903cc Rickman (ohc four-cylinder Kawasaki engine) 1977

RIEJU / *Spain 1952*
Makers of two-stroke and four-stroke motorcycles and scooters of between 125cc and 175cc. Latterly have specialized in 50cc and 75cc lightweights.

RIGAT / *Italy 1912–1914*
Produced motorcycles with 487cc single-cylinder Fafnir engines.

RIKUO / *Japan 1953–1962*
Took a good look at other designs before they built a new model. The results were 996cc and 1198cc V-twins with a Harley-Davidson look

and 248cc and 348cc ohv singles with a **BMW** appearance.

RILEY / *England 1901–c1908*
The Riley brothers were pioneer makers of two- and three-wheeled vehicles, using De Dion engines and then their own, before turning to cars. Percy Riley was the first designer to use mechanically operated inlet valves and patented 'overlap' valve timing.

RINNE / *Germany 1924–1932*
Concentrated on 124cc, 174cc and 248cc two-stroke engines. Complete machines were made in limited numbers with a horizontal cylinder. Racing versions were ridden by Max Hucke, Lücke and Rannacher and it was Hucke who built Rinne frames.

RIP / *England 1905–1908*
Peugeot, Stevens and White & Poppe engines drove these early machines, which had spring frames.

RIVIERRE / *France c1903*
Had a Megola-like engine, ie a 1·75 hp radial engine built into the rear wheel, but designer Gaston Rivierre offered also stronger engines up to 20 hp, built on similar lines. They were really two-strokes with the opposite cylinder working as a kind of scavenging pump for the intake of the mixture.

RIWINA / *Germany 1924–1925*
Assembler who built his machines at Bielefeld, then a centre of the German bicycle industry. The engine was a 142cc two-stroke, made by DKW. Other power units were also fitted.

RIXE / *Germany 1934–1985*
Pre war, Rixe made Sachs-engined motorised bicy-cles, and, post war, continued with Sachs two-strokes from 50cc up to 250cc. In the 1970s, production was almost entirely of 50cc models, but Rixe's last offering was a water-cooled 80cc sports model with five gears.

RIZZATO / *Italy 1972–1979*
Small factory that used 125cc Minarelli engines in sports machines, mostly trials models.

R&K / *Czechoslovakia 1924–1926*
Equipped lightweight motorcycles with 147cc and 172cc Villiers two-stroke engines. Kroboth later designed and built cars and — in Germany after the war — scooters.

RMW / *Germany 1925–1955*
The first machines built had their own 132cc and 148cc two-stroke engines. Later ones also had 198cc versions with 62mm bore and 66mm stroke. Four-stroke models used a variety of proprietary engines up to 498cc. Among them were Sturmey-Archer, MAG, JAP, Küchen, Moser and Bark products. RMW took over the Phoenix motorcycle works, used for some time screwed-together frames and had after 1945 a comparatively small production.

ROA / *Spain 1952–early 1960s*
Built motorcycles and three-wheeled transport vehicles with Hispano-Villiers engines with capacities up to 325cc.

ROBAKO / *Germany 1924–1926*
One of the many Berlin-based motorcycle assemblers of the 1920s. Fitted 129cc Bekamo and 132cc MGF two-stroke engines.

ROC / *England 1904–1915*
Designed by one of the great pioneers, A. W. Wall. The works, based at Guildford and afterwards at Birmingham, were financed by the famous author Conan-Doyle. Roc motorcycles had unusually long wheelbases with Precision and Roc engines of 2 hp, 2·5 hp and 3·5 hp; most of them were V-twins. The versatile A. W. Wall designed during the years many different and often unorthodox vehicles and other products. They included different kinds of gearboxes, three-wheelers with motorcycle engines and car-like bodies, bicycle attachment engines etc.

ROCHESTER / *France 1923–1929*
Concentrated on lightweight machines with engines up to 174cc.

ROCHET / *France 1902–c1908*
Was among the first producers of motorcycles with two-speed gears. The single-cylinder 1·75 hp ioe engine was of their own manufacture.

ROCKET / *Italy 1953–1958*
For its period an ultra-modern flat-twin ohv machine of 198cc only. The opposing cylinders were transverse-mounted and in unit with the engine. Drive to the rear wheel was by shaft. Made by IMN of Naples, the Rocket was an expensive, probably over ambitious design.

ROCKSON / *England 1920–1923*
Assembler who used 269cc Villiers two-strokes and 346cc Blackburne sv engines.

ROCO / *Germany 1922–1925*
Beautiful lightweight machines with 110cc, afterwards also 147cc two-stroke engines. Unconfirmed sources claim the engines were supplied by Cockerell. Among the owners of the Roco works were the famous designer and racing motorist Johannes Rössig and the Rosner brothers, also well-known racing men. The Roco had a triangular double-loop frame and a very low saddle position.

ROCONOVA / *Germany 1924–1926*
Designed by Johannes Rössig, who raced Douglas and Victoria machines, the Roconovas were the first 248cc and 348cc ohc singles built commercially in Germany. Racing versions of the quarter-litre machine won many races. Among the riders were Rössig, Thevis, Zadek, Count Bismarck, Perl, Nakonzer, Elsner, Pohle and others. Roconova also supplied engines to other factories including TX and Patria.

248cc Roconova (ohc) 1925

ROÉS / *France 1932–1934*
Lightweight machines with 98cc and 123cc two-stroke engines.

ROESSLER & JAUERNIGG / *Czechoslovakia 1902–1907*
Another make born in the old Austro-Hungarian Empire, in a town called Aussig. The Fehers-designed singles and V-twins were of excellent quality. Some models had rear suspension. The engines were of 2, 2·75 and 4 hp.

RÖHR / *Germany 1952–1958*
Scooters made by an agricultural-machine factory with 197cc Ilo engines.

ROLAND / *Germany 1904–1907*
Roland, Allright, Tiger, Vindec-Special etc. were all trade marks used by the Köln-Lindenthaler Motorenwerke AG at Cologne. Like the others, early Roland machines had Kelecom, FN and other engines built under licence. These engines were singles of 2·25 and 2·75 hp and V-twins of 5 hp. Roland motorcycles were also made available equipped with Truffault swinging-arm forks.

2¾ hp Roland (sv Truffault fork) 1905

ROLAND / *Germany 1923–1924*
Small producer of two-strokes with 132cc Bekamo and 145cc DKW engines.

ROLEO / *France 1924–1939*
See CP Roleo.

ROLFE / *England 1911–1914*
Ambitious factory which built good motorcycles with 498cc single-cylinder and 746cc V-twin sv JAP engines.

ROMEO / *Italy 1969–1975*
A make of the younger Italian generation. Romeo concentrates on 49cc two-stroke machines with Minarelli engines.

ROMP / *England 1913–1914*
Short-lived 499cc sv single with Precision engine.

RONDINE / *Italy 1923–1928*
Prinelli's two-stroke Rondine lightweights with 98cc Train engines had no connection with Rondine racing Fours.

RONDINE / *Italy 1934–1935*
Designed by Carlo Gianini and Piero Remor, the Rondine was a supercharged, watercooled 499cc four-cylinder racing machine. Its production by the Compagnia Nazionale Aeronautica at Rome was financed by Count Bonmartini. He also entered a team in races. His top riders: Piero Taruffi and Amilcare Rosetti. The design was bought by Gilera in 1936 and raced until after the war under that trade mark.

RONDINE / *Italy 1951–1954*
These Rondines, designed by Martino Siccomario, had 124cc and 147cc Sachs two-stroke engines.

RONDINE/*Italy 1968–early 1970s*
Yet another Rondine, designed by former MV-Agusta racing-team member Alfredo Copeta. His moto-cross and racing version had 48cc two-stroke engines.

ROND-SACHS/*The Netherlands 1971–1975*
Concentrated on the production of 49cc and 123cc moto-cross machines with Sachs two-stroke engines. The bigger had 22 bhp at 9300 rpm.

ROSENGART/*France 1922–1923*
Rosengart, where they built the old Austin 7 under licence like Dixi-BMW in Germany, was earlier connected with a lightweight motorcycle. It had a 98cc Train two-stroke engine, and did not become a world-beater.

ROSELLI/*Italy 1899–1910*
Probably the most famous pioneer of the Italian motorcycle industry, Emanuel di A. Rosselli produced first his 1 hp Lilliput, a bicycle with the engine in front of the pedalling gear. His next models included a 1·75 hp lady's motor-cycle and a 258cc (2·5 hp) machine. Rosselli also produced cars.

ROSSI/*Italy 1950–1955*
The Parma-built machines had 123cc Sachs engines and proved the excellent design with successes in trials.

ROSSI/*Italy 1929*
With its frame made from aluminium alloy the 348cc 90 degree V-twin was a technically interesting but commercially not very successful design. Paolo Rossi, the designer, had insufficient resources to market this motorcycle on a bigger scale.

ROTARY/*Japan early 1950s–1961*
Modern two-strokes with 124cc, built by one of Japan's bigger factories.

ROTER TEUFEL/*Germany 1923–1925*
Berlin had many producers of two-strokes, but only few factories which built four-stroke motorcycles. This was one of them. The machines had 170cc sv engines.

ROTTER/*Germany 1924–1925*
Before the First World War, the Rotter factory had been used to build the Weltrad. For a time in the mid 1920s they fitted DKW engines into simple frames.

ROULETTE/*England 1918–1919*
Assembled machines with 269cc Villiers two-stroke, three-port, deflector-type engines.

ROUSSEY/*France 1948–1956*
Concentrated on lightweights, including 48cc bicycle engines as well as motorcycles and scooters with 123cc and 174cc power units.

ROVA-KENT/*Australia 1913–1914*
Unit-design 496cc single-cylinder machine with its own four-valve ohv engine.

ROVER/*England 1902–1925*
Equipped with orthodox diamond frames, Rover motorcycles were known for their sound design and excellent workmanship. In pre-1914 days they had an excellent 496cc sv single, which was also built after 1918. The engine had 85mm bore and 88mm stroke. There were also JAP-engined models, including 676cc V-twins. The last Rover models built had 248cc and 348cc ohv single-cylinder engines of own design and manufacture.

ROVENA /*Spain 1960s*
Rovena were actually made by Sanglas, being so named because of Sanglas' involvement with single-cylinder four-strokes. The first Rovenas used 250cc and 325cc two-stroke twin engines from Hispano Villiers, later, there were 50cc and 100cc Zundapp-engined models and a 250cc sports model (Hispano Villiers), credited with a 90mph top speed. Sanglas' success with police contracts led to them winding-up the manufacture of Rovenas in 1968.

ROVETTA/*Italy 1900–1906*
Once a well-known factory, Rovetta already produced in 1904 watercooled machines with their own 2·55 hp engines.

ROVIN/*France 1920–1934*
Raoul de Rovin was a very versatile man. He built motorcycles from 98cc to 499cc with two-stroke engines and also JAP and MAG sv and ohv engines. He built three-wheelers and very fast small sports and racing cars with JAP racing engines, which he successfully drove in races. He raced also Delage GP cars, bought in 1929 the San-Sou-Pap motorcycle factory and built after 1945 very neat small cars.

ROVLANTE/*France 1929–1935*
Built 98cc and 124cc two-stroke machines.

ROYAL/*America 1901–c1908*
Typical American design with the 445cc cylinder sloping rearward and the petrol tank above the rear wheel of a strengthened bicycle frame.

ROYAL/*Switzerland 1900–1908*
Was one of the first motorcycle producers in the country. The 1·5 hp and 2 hp engines were of Zedel manufacture.

ROYAL/*Italy 1923–1928*
Built by the Santogastino brothers at Milan, the little machine had their own 132cc two-stroke engine. In addition, they built a limited number of JAP-engined 346cc and 490cc sv and ohv machines.

ROYAL-AJAX/*England 1901–c1908*
Single-cylinder machines with 2·5 hp—probably MMC—engines.

ROYAL-EAGLE/*England 1901–1939*
This name on the tank of Coventry-Eagle machines was available until 1910.

ROYAL-ENFIELD/*India late 1950s*
Was originally a branch of Royal-Enfield (England) and concentrated on 173cc and other small machines with Villiers engines. When Royal-Enfield stopped motorcycle production in England, the Madras branch — Enfield India Ltd. — took over some designs and production equipment. This included the 346cc Bullet, which since 1976 is also exported to Europe, although the basic design is outdated.

346cc Enfield India

ROYAL ENFIELD / *England 1901—1970*
Bicycle makers Royal Enfield experimented with De Dion engines and, in 1901, produced a motorcycle with a Minerva engine over the front wheel and driving the rear wheel by a crossed belt. However, no motor cycles were made between 1904 and 1911. Then, Royal Enfield offered a single-speed model with 425cc MAG V twin engine, revising it the same year to include the RE two-speed gear, which worked by selecting either one of

223cc Royal Enfield (TS) 1923

346cc Royal Enfield (ohv Model 352) 1926

two different ratios of primary chain drive. In 1912, there was a much larger 770cc JAP engined V twin, also with two speed gear and with a patented 'cush drive' in the rear hub. In 1913, an improved MAG engine, again of 425cc, with overhead inlet valves was fitted to the smaller model and, in 1914, a 225cc two-stroke was introduced. After WWI, the small twin was phased out and, until 1924, only the two-stroke and an 8hp JAP V twin sidecar model

496cc Royal Enfield (sv Model 501) 1929

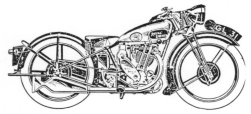

496cc Royal Enfield (ohv Model GL 31) 1931

348cc Royal Enfield (ohv Model Bullet) 1938

692cc Royal Enfield (ohv twin Model Super Meteor) 1959

692cc Royal Enfield (ohv twin Model Airflow Meteor) 1960

were offered.

In 1924 engine designer E O (Ted) Pardoe joined Royal Enfield and a year later so did development engineer Tony Wilson-Jones. Both men saw long service, Pardoe staying with RE until the mid-1950s and Wilson-Jones virtually until the end. So did Major Frank Smith who was first joint managing director from 1914 to 1933 and then sole managing director until his death in 1963. This continuity at the the top explains why RE designs showed consistent evolvement over long periods.

With Pardoe's arrival, Royal Enfield began to develop their own engines, which, by the late 1920s, powered the whole range. Though their designs were generally conservative, RE were not afraid to experiment. In the 1930s they tried four-valve and three-valve cylinder heads, while the 150cc two-stroke 'Cycar' of 1932 featured a pressed steel frame that doubled as the enclosing bodywork. They also offered a 150cc ohv ultra-lightweight to take advantage of 1933 tax concessions. The mainstay of the range, however, were the sporting ohv Bullets 250cc, 350cc and 500cc.

RE a luxurious 1140cc side-valve V twin model, in theory for export only until 1938, but in fact available to special order. Export also provided the company with yet another model. Just before WWII, Royal Enfield had made a 125cc copy of a DKW two-stroke, specifically for export to Holland. During the war this was supplied to the British Army as the 'Flying Flea', and it remained in the post-war range, uprated later to 150cc, until the early 1950s.

Post war, Royal Enfield were quick to specify telescopic forks, and in 1949 swinging arm rear suspension. There were new 250cc and 350cc Bullets, and in 1949, a brand-new 500cc vertical twin. Later, in 1953, this was to be joined by the 700cc Meteor twin (later developed into the Constellation. In the same decade, Johnny Brittain re-established the Royal Enfield name on the trials scenes, winning many major events and proving the value of rear suspension. A major innovation was the 1957 unit construction 250cc Crusader that was to become hugely popular later as the sporting Continental GT. RE also investigated streamlining and offered fully aerodynamic Airflow fairings.

When Frank Smith died in 1963, the company was sold to the E & H P Smith engineering group. An unfortunate excursion into racing with a 250cc two stroke is best forgotten. Happier memories are of the 250cc Villiers-engined Turbo Twin made from 1964. A rapid decline in British sales after 1965 led to the drastic pruning of the range, the last new model being the 736cc Interceptor twin, and production of the once popular 250cc models ceasing in 1967. Thereafter, only the Interceptor twin was made, almost entirely for export to the USA. The original Redditch factory was sold, the twins being made by new owners NVT, at Bradford-on-Avon. An involvement with Floyd Clymer's Indian company and with the Rickman brothers was a mere sideshow.

ROYAL-MOTO / *France 1923–1933*
Built a wide range of lightweight machines with 98cc, 174cc and 244cc Massardin two-strokes and also four-strokes with 246cc to 498cc sv and ohv engines.

ROYAL NORD / *Belgium 1950–early 1960s*
Produced 48cc mofas, mopeds etc. and also motorcycles to 248cc with Villiers, Maico, Sachs and other engines.

ROYAL-RUBY / *England 1909–1933*
Excellent machines which before WWI already had fully enclosed rear wheel chains. Most models had the company's own sv engines, including 349cc and 375cc single-cylinder versions. The JAP-engined 976cc V-twin had leaf springs on both sides. Double-loop frames and saddle tanks were introduced in 1927, when the factory fitted 172cc to 346cc Villiers engines and 248cc and 348cc JAP ohv engines. The factory also built three-wheelers with motorcycle engines.

ROYAL SCOT / *Scotland 1922–1924*
The tank transfer was probably the only thing really made at the Glasgow Royal Scot works. The frame was built at the Glasgow Victoria motorcycle works for Royal Scot and the 348cc sleeve-valve engine was made in the nearby Barr & Stroud factory; most other parts and accessories were bought in England from specialised factories.

ROYAL SOVEREIGN / *England c1902*
Unorthodox machines with 211cc Minerva engines.

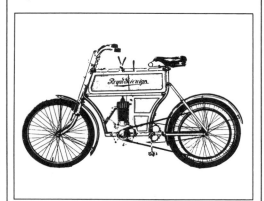

2¼ hp Royal-Sovereign (sv) 1903

ROYAL STANDARD / *Switzerland 1928–1932*
Pauchand's design was a vertical 398cc twin-cylinder unit-design machine, with a Zurcher engine built exclusively for this make. The design was ahead of its time.

ROYAL SUPER / *Italy 1923–1928*
Identical with the 132cc Royal two-stroke models.

ROYAL WELLINGTON / *England c1901*
Strengthened bicycle frames with 211cc Minerva engines.

R&P / *England 1902–c1906*
Was among the first commercially-built motorcycles in England. Most machines had 346cc single-cylinder engines with their own engine fitted in what is now the standard centre position, developed by the Werner brothers in France.

RS / *Germany 1924–1925*
Unusual two-stroke, whose 380cc vertical-twin unit-design engine had a crank-pin rotary valve. The design was probably not fully developed when it was sold to another firm, and never appeared on the market.

RS / *Germany 1925–1928*
This was the successor to the above RS, but with an orthodox engine, the old 493cc BMW flat-twin. Still a mystery, because BMW stopped producing that engine in 1922. Such engines were probably still in stock with some dealers.

RUBINELLI / *Italy 1921–1927*
Built 122cc and 172cc two-strokes and also supplied these engines to other small motorcycle assemblers.

RUCHE / *France 1952–1954*
A short-lived producer of 123cc and 173cc two-stroke machines.

RUD / *Germany 1927–1930*
Assembled motorcycles in small numbers with Kühne, MAG and JAP engines from 348cc to 748cc.

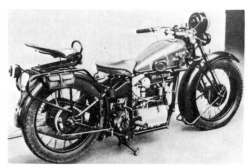

398cc Royal Standard (ohc twin) 1932

RUDGE / *England 1911—1940*

Though famous for their bicycles, Rudge resisted making motorcycles until their single-cylinder 500cc inlet-over-exhaust-valve engine and direct belt drive model of 1911. That year, Rudge rider Victor Surridge broke records at Brooklands, including 'the hour' at over 65mph. The company entered the 1911 TT in force, but, after Surridge was killed in practice, the team withdrew. They returned in 1913, when Ray Abbot finished second, while in 1914, Cyril Pullin won the only two-day Senior TT ever staged. By then, Rudge had proven their expanding-pulley belt-drive Multi gear and were making a 750cc multi-gear single for sidecar use.

Post war, the 500cc Multi was very popular, until belt drive began to lose favour. A 1000cc V twin was generally unsatisfactory, but served to introduce chain drive and Rudge's own four-speed gearbox. For 1924, there were new four-valve ohv 350cc and 500cc singles with four speeds and chain drive, such was the demand that only the 500cc model could be made. A tentative return to the Senior TT in 1926 revealed cycle part shortcomings, especially those of the rim brakes, and for 1927 there was another design.

A vigorous racing programme ensued, strongly supported by managing director J V Pugh with George Hack as designer and development engineer. This produced excellent results. In 1928 and 1929 rider Graham Walker won the Ulster Grand Prix, gaining Rudge a reputation that lasted until the end. Along with Walker, Ernie Nott and Tyrell Smith also won many other races in those years, 1930 being Rudge's greatest year, when Walter Handley won the Senior TT and with Walker second. In addition, with brand-new Junior machines, with four valves radically disposed, Rudge were 1-2-3 in this class.

Thereafter things went sadly wrong, Rudge were hit far harder than most of their competitors by the depression of the early 1930s — not helped by some catastrophic business decisions by J V Pugh. A 1-2-4 finish in the 1931 Lightweight TT was not enough. Rudge did their best to retrieve the situation, offering 250cc, 350cc and 500cc engines to other makers as 'Pythons', which sold well, but by 1933, they were in receivership and J V Pugh had left the company.

499cc Rudge-Whitworth (ioe Multi-gear) 1914

499cc Rudge-Whitworth (ohv four-valve Model Standard) 1926

499cc Rudge-Whitworth (ohv Ulster) 1929

499cc Rudge-Whitworth (ohv four-valve Model Sport) 1926

Production continued, however; Rudges even finished 1-2-3 in the 1934 Lightweight TT. In 1936 the company was sold to the electrical and electronics company EMI, and though sales were small, development of road bikes continued. two-valve 250cc proved briefly popular. In 1938 EMI moved the factory from Coventy to Hayes in Middlesex and in 1939 a Villiers-engined autocycle joined the range. However, with the outbreak of war, though a 250 machine was scheduled for acceptance by the British Army, production ceased after only 200 had been made. The Hayes factory was now devoted to making vitally needed radar equipment. The Autocycle was sold to Norman cycles, and the Rudge name acquired by Raleigh.

Post war, Rudge spares were privately manufac-

499cc Rudge-Whitworth (ohv four-valve Model Special) 1931

tured from original jigs and patterns, and an attempt was made to revive the marque, using AMC cycle parts. There was even a 1000cc V twin prototype. But effectively Rudge had disappeared for ever.

RUEDER / *Germany late 1910s to early 1920s*
Assembler who used 348cc Kühne ohv engines in orthodox frames.

RULLIERS / *Czechoslovakia 1924–1929*
Two-stroke motorcycles with 147cc, 172cc and 346cc Villiers engines.

RUMI / *Italy 1949–late 1950s*
Designed by Dr. Rumi at Bergamo, these were excellent 124cc twin-cylinder two-stroke machines with forward-facing horizontal cylinders and sporting appearance. The cylinders each had 42mm bore and 45mm stroke. The production sport model had a top speed of 80 mph, racing versions were even faster. Rumi also built scooters and introduced a range of very unorthodox V-twin ohc machines with 98cc, 124cc and 174cc, which never came into quantity production. There was in the mid-1950s also a Salmaggi-designed 248cc twin-cylinder double ohc racing machine, which was never fully developed and never ran in a big race. Rumi's heyday was around 1952 with the small Bees.

499cc Rudge-Whitworth (ohv four-valve Model Ulster) 1935

123cc Rumi (TS flat-twin) 1952

173cc Rumi (ohv v-twin) 1960

RUNGE / *Germany 1923–1926*
A small company which built 197cc sv machines on a limited scale.

RUPP / *Germany 1928–1932*
Produced two models. One was a 198cc ohv machine with its own engine, the other with a 498cc ohc single-cylinder three-valve Küchen power plant.

499cc Rudge-Whitworth (ohv four-valve Model Ulster) 1938

RUSH/ *Belgium 1922–1934*
Became well-known when the manufacturer-rider Van Geert won the 250cc class at the 1924 Monza GP. His machine had a 248cc Blackburne ohv engine. He also built 348cc single-cylinder ohv models. He built his own engines after 1927, when the range included 397cc, 497cc and 597cc sv and ohv models.

RUSPA/ *Italy 1926–1929*
Built 124cc two-strokes and 174cc two-stroke and ohv machines. A 347cc single with chain-driven ohc was built in very small numbers only.

RUSSELL/ *England 1913*
Limited production of 172cc and 492cc ohv machines.

RUT/ *Germany 1923–1924*
Two-strokes of simple design with 124cc and an outside flywheel.

RUTER/ *Spain 1957–1960*
Assembled machines with 95cc and 124cc two-stroke engines, supplied to the factory by Hispano-Villiers.

RUWISCH/ *Germany 1948–1949*
Miniscooter with 38cc Victoria bicycle engines.

RWC/ *Austria 1949–late 1950s*
Lightweight motorcycles made by a bicycle factory. The engine was a 98cc Rotax-Sachs.

RW SCOUT/ *England 1920–1922*
Made by R. Wheaterell of London, was an assembled machine with 269cc Villiers and 318cc Dalm two-stroke engines, but Blackburne 346cc sv and ohv engines could also be fitted.

SACI/ *Brazil 1959–late 1960s*
Scooter made with 174cc two-stroke engines.

SADEM/ *France 1951–1954*
Lightweight machines with engines up to 98cc.

SADRIAN/ *Spain 1956–1963*
Producer of three-wheelers, who also built Hispano-Villiers-engined 123cc to 198cc two-stroke motorcycles.

SAGITTA/ *Czechoslovakia 1928–1930*
Limited assembly of machines with 247cc Villiers engines.

SALIRA/ *Belgium 1955–early 1960s*
Assembler who used 98cc to 197cc Villiers engines, among others.

SALTLEY/ *England 1919–1924*
Also an assembler, whose machines had 269cc Villiers, 347cc Vulcanus and 497cc sv Blackburne engines.

SALVE/ *Italy 1925–1926*
The only model had a 496cc unit-design sv engine.

SANCHOC/ *France 1922–1924*
Built two-strokes from 98cc to 246cc and sv machines up to 346cc.

SAN CHRISTOPHORO/ *Italy 1951–1954*
One of the small Italian producers of 124cc two-stroke machines. The Simonetta had 54mm bore/stroke and 6 bhp at 4800 rpm.

SANGLAS / *Spain 1942—1982*
Exclusively makers of single-cylinder four-strokes, widely used by the Spanish police and army. Sanglas began with a 350cc model of extremely advanced design with telescopic forks, unit engine and four-speed gearbox. A 500cc model for police use appeared in 1956. Later 500cc and 400cc models had electric starting. Sanglas were taken over by Yamaha in 1978, and a model fitted with the MS400 twin engine was launched. By 1982, however, even the name Sanglas had disappeared.

connected with Yamaha, the factory supplies a 391cc vertical ohv twin with the 27 bhp engine from the Japanese factory.

SAN-SOU-PAP/ *France 1923–1936*
The name stands for 'without any valves', but this was correct only until the factory built Train-engined 98cc to 248cc two-strokes, and commenced manufacture of 248cc to 498cc sv and ohv singles with JAP and MAG power-units. San-Sou-Pap became part of the Rovin works in 1929.

SANTAMARIA/ *Italy 1951–1963*
Mofas, mopeds, etc. with 49, 69, 98, 123 and 147cc Zündapp, Sachs and Ilo-engines.

SAN YANG/ *Taiwan 1962–*
Assembled and built partly under licence various Honda models in Taiwan.

SANYO/ *Japan 1958–1962*
Sporting machines, singles with Sanyo's own 248cc ohv engines.

SAR / *Italy 1920–1925*
Based on the design of the Elect, the 498cc SAR was a nice flat-twin sv and ohv machine. Another model had the oilcooled 346cc Bradshaw ohv engine, which had 68mm bore and 96mm stroke with automatic lubrication.

348cc SAR (ohv Bradshaw engine) 1924

SAR / *Germany 1923–1930*
The Raetsch-designed SAR engines were three-port two-strokes with 122cc, 147cc and 198cc.

SARACEN / *England 1967–1973*
Concentrated on the manufacture of Sachs-engined 123cc, 188cc and trials machines, and on 244cc Mickmar-engined moto-cross versions.

SARCO (SARCO-RELIANCE) / *England 1920–1923*
Concentrated on a 261cc two-stroke single with 68mm bore × 72mm stroke and a Burman two-speed gearbox.

SARENKA / *Poland 1961–*
A 123cc two-stroke, built by the well-known Polish WSK factory.

SARKANA-SWAIGSNE / *Latvia 1958–*
Supplies 49cc mofas, mopeds and similar means of transport.

SAROLEA / *Belgium 1898–1957*
Was among the first producers of motorcycles and of proprietary single-cylinder and V-twin engines. Became famous during the 1920s with with English-looking 346cc and 496cc sv and ohv singles. They built in the 1930s 124cc, 147cc and 174cc two-strokes and 596cc ohv models. The works rider 'Grizzly' (Gilbert de Ridder) rode after 1935 348cc and 498cc machines with their own ohc racing engines. Other well-known Sarolea riders were Gregoire, Claessens, Tom, Vidal, Stobart; Poncin of Luxembourg; Stěpan of Czechoslovakia; Dirtl, Gayer, Runtsch, Benesch and Trella of Austria; Arcangeli and Colombo of Italy and others. After the war, there was a production co-operative created with other Belgian factories, and Sarolea's production concentrated on two-strokes from 49cc to 248cc.

SARTORIUS / *Germany 1924–1926*
Limited production of 195cc sv and 348cc Kühne ohv engined singles.

SATAN / *Czechoslovakia 1929*
This was a machine with its own sloping 548cc sv engine. Small production.

SATURN / *Germany 1921–1927*
Made by the Steudel car and boat-engine works, Saturn motorcycles had 246cc two-stroke, 348cc ohv and 497cc V-twin sv engines. There was also a 149cc bicycle sv engine and a prototype of a shaft-driven version of the 497cc V-twin, built at a Steudel branch factory at Leipzig.

SATURN / *England 1925–1926*
Produced a small number of 346cc singles with own two-stroke engines.

SAUND / *India 1970–*
Originally a 98cc two-stroke DKW (Zweirad Union) design, the Sound—built with many parts made in India—is still influenced by the German design. The 98cc engine has 9·7 bhp at 6800 rpm.

SBD / *Germany 1923–1924*
Munich-built motorcycles with the 293cc Bosch-Douglas flat-twin engine with opposing sv cylinders.

SCARAB / *Italy 1967—1985*
Scarabs, in effect, were Ancilotti motorcycles under a different name, like Ancilotti, they used various makes of small capacity two-stroke German and Italian engines. The range was mostly 50cc and 125cc and styled in off-road fashion. The marque did not survive Ancilotti's demise.

496cc Sarolea (ohv) 1927

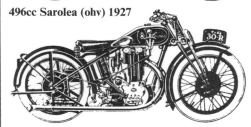

496cc Sarolea (ohv racing model) 1930

at 8000 rpm. Good design, excellent finish.

SCARABEO / *Italy 1968–*
A division of Aprilia, concentrating on smaller motorcycles and mopeds with mostly 50cc and 125cc Sachs or Hiro two-stroke engines. Off-road styling as trials and moto-cross machinery.

SCHEIBERT / *Austria 1911–1913*
Motorcycles with strengthened frames and a 197cc sv engine mounted above the front wheel.

SCHICKEL / *America 1912–1915*
Interesting design with a cast light-alloy frame which included the petrol tank. Its engine was a 648cc two-stroke single.

198cc Schliha (TS with ohv) 1930

SHIFTY / *Italy 1979–*
Big assembled machines with 903 and 1049cc four-cylinder ohc (dohc) engines, supplied partially by Abarth.

SCHLIHA / *Germany 1924–1933*
Was one of the many unorthodox two-stroke designs built during the 1920s and early 1930s in Berlin. Designed by Heinrich Schlüpmann, Schliha motorcycles were ohv singles from 129cc to 596cc.

347cc Sarolea (ohv sport model) 1931

596cc Sarolea (ohv) 1932

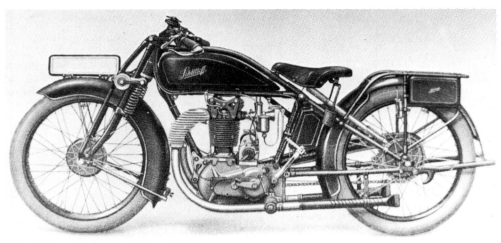

347cc Schottoff (ohv Model Sport) 1927

SCHLIMME / *Germany 1924–1925*
Assembled machines with 142cc and 173cc DKW two-stroke engines.

SCHMIDT / *Germany 1921–1924*
Produced bicycle engines and 196cc lightweight motorcycles. The sv engines were of Schmidt's own design and manufacture.

SCHNEIDER / *Germany 1924–1926*
Another assembler, who fitted 142cc, 173cc and 206cc DKW engines.

SCHNELL-HOREX / *Germany 1952–1954*
Designed by racing motorcyclist Roland Schnell, who built these racing machines with 248cc, 348cc and 498cc single-cylinder gear-driven ohc engines in conjunction with the Horex works, the Schnell-Horex was made in limited numbers only and proved especially formidable in the 350cc size. Among the riders besides Schnell were Hermann Gablenz, H. P. Müller, Robert Zeller, Georg Braun, Erwin Aldinger, Fritz Kläger and others.

SCHROFF-RECORD / *Germany 1923–1925*
Simple 148cc three-port two-strokes with sloping engines.

SCHUNK / *Germany 1924–1926*
Little 198cc ohv machines with own unit-design engines and belt-drive.

SCHÜRHOFF / *Germany 1949–1953*
Producer of mofas, mopeds etc. with 49cc Sachs, Ilo and Zündapp engines and of lightweights with screwed triangular frames and 123cc to 173cc Ilo two-stroke engines.

SCHÜTT / *Germany 1933–1934*
Equipped with frames made from Duralumin, the Paul Schütt-designed 196cc two-strokes had a transverse-mounted engine of his design.

SCHÜTTOFF / *Germany 1924–1933*
Made by a machine factory, Schüttoff motorcycles had 246cc sv, afterwards 346cc sv and ohv as well as 496cc sv and ohv single-cylinder engines. From 1930 onwards, they also fitted 198cc and 298cc DKW two-stroke power units. In 1932 Schüttoff became part of the DKW works. The 348cc ohv models were very successful from 1925 to 1929. With a works team consisting of the riders Ihle, Lohse, A. Müller, E. Hirth etc. they won many races, while Josef Mittenzwei gained success in trials with a 498cc sidecar outfit.

SCHWALBE / *Germany 1922–1924*
Lightweight motorcycles with 124cc and 198cc flat-twin engines. The smaller version was also delivered as a bicycle attachment engine. Producer of these machines, the Spiegler brothers, afterwards built Spiegler motorcycles at their Aalen factory.

SCHWALBE / *Switzerland 1901–1905*
The Rugg-designed Schwalbe had a strengthened bicycle frame and a 2·75 hp Zedel engine.

124cc Schürhoff (TS Ilo engine) 1953

SCHWEPPE / *Germany 1949–1950*
A scooter with swinging arms on both sides and 143cc to 184cc Ilo engines, which eventually became the Pirol scooter.

SCK / *Germany 1924–1925*
Assembler, who fitted 348cc and 498cc sv and ohv JAP and MAG engines into own frames. Production was on a small scale.

SCOOTAVIA / *France 1951–1956*
Luxurious scooters with 173cc ohv AMC single-cylinder engines.

SCORPION / *England mid 1960s*
Motorcycles with pressed steel frames and 197cc and 246cc Villiers two-stroke engines.

SCOTO / *France 1949–early 1950s*
Miniscooter with 39cc Mosquito engines.

SCOTT / *England 1909—late 1960s*
Few designs have inspired such devotion from admirers as the Scott. Yorkshire engineer Alfred Scott developed a twin-cylinder two-stroke engine small and powerful enough to use in a motorcycle and built six prototypes in 1908. Production began the next year. Early Scotts had air-cooled cylinders and water-cooled heads, but the water cooling was soon extended to the cylinders. There was a triangulated frame of straight tubes, with telescopic front forks, a two-speed gear, which selected one or ther other of two different ratio primary chain drives, and a kickstarter — the world's first. Chain final drive was used from the start. Petrol was carried in an oval drum beneath the saddle. Scotts did well in trials and racing — four fastest laps in the Senior TT between 1911 and 1914 and wins in 1912 and 1913.

Alfred Scott left the company late in 1918 to devote his time to an unorthodox three-wheeler, the Scott Sociable, and the designer throughout the 1920s was Harry Shackleton. The Scott gained more powerful engines of 498cc and 596cc, a more orthodox fuel tank and a three-speed gearbox. But sales, hitherto respectable, plunged disastrously in the depressed early 1930s. Most machines built

486cc Scott (TS watercooled twin) 1914

498cc Scott (TS watercooled twin) 1925

595cc Scott (TS watercooled twin 'Flying Squirrel') 1926

498cc Scott (TS watercooled twin 'TT') 1929

498cc Scott (TS watercooled twin 'TT Prototype') 1930

996cc Scott (TS watercooled three-cylinder) 1935

596cc Scott (TS watercooled twin) 1948

after that were made from components held in stock, the company becoming involved in more general engineering. However, in the mid-1930s, new designer Bill Cull became involved in developing a three cylinder in line two-stroke, first of 750cc then of 1000cc, of which six were made.

Post war, production resumed with what was virtually a pre-war model, but with new brakes and Dowty air-sprung telescopic forks. In 1950, the company was sold to Matt Holder, who moved it from Shipley to Birmingham. He modernised the Scott's appearance with a new spring frame, a shapely petrol tanbk and a dualseat, but the 1930s-style engine and three-speed gearbox were retained. However, though a small, steady demand existed, production came to an end when Birmingham city development forced Holder to move his engineering business in the late 1960s. He also developed a 350cc air-cooled two-stroke twin, which was raced but never went into production.

SCOTT-CYC-AUTO / *England 1934–1950*
Early and typical English moped with Scott-built 98cc two-stroke engine.

SCOUT / *England 1912–1913*
Produced motorcycles with 498cc Precision single-cylinder sv engines.

SCYLLA / *France 1931–1937*
Lightweight machines with 98cc and 123cc Aubier-Dunne two-stroke engines.

SEAL / *England 1914–1921*
Very unorthodox motorcycle with a 996cc V-twin JAP sv engine, without handlebar and without saddle. It had a steering wheel in the attached sidecar.

SEARS / *America 1912–1916*
Made for Sears, Roebuck & Co. at Chicago, these machines had 9 to 10 hp V-twin engines produced by Spake. *See also* Allstate.

SEEGARD / *Germany 1924–1925*
Built singles with their own sv 146cc and 197cc engines.

SEELEY / *England 1966—1992*
Colin Seeley took over production of the AJS 7R and Matchless G.50 racing engines from AMC and built successful racing motorcycles with his own frames and fittings. Production ceased when they became uncompetitive, but later was resumed by Mick Rutter for Classic racing. Rutter's products were marketed as replicas, though very close in specification to the originals.

SEILING/*Italy 1938–1939*
After MAS motorcycle manufacturer Alberico Seilig left that make, he produced 247cc and 347cc sv singles with his own unit-design engines and rear suspension.

346cc Seiling (sv) 1938

SEITH/*Germany 1949–1950*
Mini-vehicles for children with 38cc Victoria two-stroke engines.

SENIOR/*Italy 1913–1914*
Sporting machines with 296cc and 330cc single-cylinder and 499cc V-twin engines supplied by Moser of Switzerland.

SERTUM/*Italy 1931–1951*
Precision instruments were the first products made by Fausto Alberti's Milan factory. The first motorcycle was a 174cc sv machine, which was followed by a 120cc two-stroke. Other models were 174cc ioe and ohv and 246cc sv and ohv versions. A 498cc unit-design sv vertical-twin with a four-speed gearbox was built in the mid-1930s. There were also 248cc ohv machines and the 174cc models were replaced by 198cc machines. 120cc, 248cc and 498cc models were also built after the war, when the 498cc vertical twin was dropped and a 498cc sv single took its place. Until 1950, when a new 125cc two-stroke single appeared on the market, all Sertum machines were of strong and heavy design. They competed in many trials with such riders as Grieco, Fornasari, Ventura and several others, but never in bigger races. In 1949–1950 the factory moved to new, modern and much bigger buildings, but two years later Sertum — despite a first class reputation for quality and finish — had to close down.

496cc Sertum (sv twin) 1938

SERVETTA/*Spain 1973–*
Originally producers of 50cc lightweights, they now make and export Lambretta scooters under licence.

SERVICE/*England c1900–1912*
A sales organisation which sold under their own name motorcycles actually built by Connaught and Wartnaby & Draper.

SESSA/*Italy 1950–1956*
Small assembler of motorcycles with 147cc Ilo engines.

SETTER/*Spain 1954–1956*
Lightweight machines with their own 60cc engines.

SEWÜT/*Germany 1924–1926*
DWK-engined 142cc, 173cc and 206cc two-strokes, built in limited numbers.

SFM/*Poland 1956–1964*
While most motorcycles built in eastern countries are two-strokes, the machine built by SFM at Szeczin was a modern ohv design with 248cc and 348cc single-cylinder engines. It was called Junak.

S-FORTIS/*Czechoslovakia 1929–1931*
Produced a single model only, a 598cc ohv single with engine supplied by Sarolea. Few were actually made.

SFW/*Germany 1924–1926*
After Nordstern went bankrupt, SFW took over the manufacture of the 2·5 hp two-stroke machine.

S&G/*Germany 1926–1932*
A Nuremberg machine factory which produced 346cc ohv single-cylinder engines for the Hecker factory. They had much in common with similar AJS motors of that period. When S&G (Scharrer & Gross) built complete motorcycles, the range consisted of 346cc, 496cc and 596cc sv and 496cc ohv single-cylinder models. The factory also built three-wheeled delivery vehicles with motorcycle engines. The last motorcycles made had 172cc and 198cc two-stroke engines.

SGS/*England 1927–1931*
The name stood for Syd Gleave Special, after the well-known racing motorcyclist who won the 1933 Lightweight TT on a four-valve 248cc ohv Excelsior Mechanical Marvel. His motorcycles had Villiers engines from 147cc and JAP ohv motors from 248cc to 490cc.

SH/*Germany 1925–1928*
Identical to the RS motorcycles.

SHARRATT/*England 1920–1930*
Assembler of good machines with JAP engines from 293cc to 996cc V-twins. After 1924 a reduced production only. Also fitted Villiers and MAG engines, but the last Sharratt motorcycles had 346cc sv and ohv JAP engines.

SHAW/*America 1909–1923*
Produced two single-cylinder 2·5 hp and 3·5 hp models, which had clutchless sv engines of own manufacture.

SHAW/*England 1904–1922*
Early machines had Kelecom and Minerva engines. After a long interruption, this company supplied American 115cc bicycle attachment engines made by Shaw Mfg. Co. at Galesburg, Kansas.

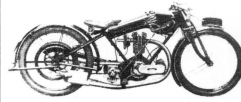

346cc Sheffield-Henderson (ohv Blackburne racer) 1922

SHEFFIELD-HENDERSON/*England 1919–1923*
A sidecar factory which produced 348cc ohv and 498cc sv machines with single-cylinder Blackburne engines.

SHIN MEIWA/*Japan early 1950s to early 1960s*
Scooter-like machines with pressed steel frames and flat 89cc, 123cc and 153cc two-stroke engines.

496cc S&G (sv) 1930

SHL / *Poland 1935–*
Probably the oldest Polish motorcycle factory. Produced in the 1930s Villiers-engined 123cc machines and after 1945 a range of 123cc, 147cc and 174cc two-stroke machines.

SHOWA / *Japan early 1950s to 1960*
Manufacturer of 49cc mopeds and of motorcycles from 123cc to 247cc with their own two-stroke engines. In addition there was also a 173cc ohv machine.

SIAMT / *Italy 1907–1914*
Designed by Luigi Semeria, the Siamt was an excellent machine and very successful in races. The range included 260cc, 262cc and 344cc singles and 494cc, 688cc and 731cc V-twins.

SIAT / *Italy 1924–1926*
Once a popular bicycle engine with 75cc capacity. The Turin-built Siat was a lightweight with two-stroke and ohv engines from 98cc to 198cc.

SIC / *France 1921–1925*
Assembler who fitted 98cc to 346cc proprietary engines made by Aubier-Dunne, Zurcher and Train.

SICRAF / *France 1947–1953*
Paul Vallée not only produced motorcycles, mofas, scooters, three-wheelers etc. with 49cc to 246cc Ydral and AMC engines, but was also the owner of F-1 racing cars.

SIEG / *Germany 1922–1930*
Designed by H. Jüngst, the Sieg was supplied with a wide range of engines from 110cc to 598cc. These engines were made by DKW, Cockerell, Ilo, Bober, Alba, Hansa, Villiers, JAP, MAG and especially Blackburne.

SIEGFRIED / *Germany 1925*
Lightweights with 142cc DKW engines.

SIGNORELLI / *Italy 1928–1930*
One of the many Italian producers of 173cc two-strokes in the late 1920s.

SILK / *England 1974—early 1980s*
George Silk fitted a modified vintage Scott engine and Velocette four-speed gearbox into a special frame. There was a commercial demand for replicas, but difficulty in obtaining engines led to the design and manufacture of a special 700cc unit of Silk's own. About 150 such machines were made.

SILVA / *England 1919–1920*
One of the first scooters built in England. The ohv engine had 117cc.

SILVER PIDGEON / *Japan early 1950s to 1965*
Made by the Mitsubishi group, the Silver Pidgeon was a mass-produced scooter with 87cc two-stroke and 192cc ohv engines.

SILVER PRINCE / *England 1919–1924*
Was one of the many small motorcycle assemblers of the early 1920s. Engines used were the 148cc, 248cc and 269cc Villiers and the 346cc Blackburne.

SILVER STAR / *Japan 1953–1958*
Lightweights with own 123cc and 147cc ohv engines.

SIM / *Italy 1953–1955*
Produced unconventional scooters with 123cc and 147cc Puch engines. Also 147cc two-stroke machines with shaft drive to the rear wheel.

SIMARD / *France 1951–1954*
Lambretta-like scooters with 174cc Ydral engines.

SIMONCELLI / *Italy 1927–1935*
Concentrated on the production of 174cc machines, first with Train two-stroke and then with sv and ohv JAP engines. In 1934 the Simoncelli company had already introduced a good rear suspension.

SIMONETTA / *Italy 1951–1954*
This was a 124cc two-stroke machine, built at the San Christoforo works.

SIMONINI / *Italy 1970—1983*
Enzo Simonini produced excellent off-road machines with Sachs engines before selling out to Fornetti Impianti of Maranello in 1975. A superb 125cc roadster appeared in 1979 with full fairing, cast wheels, Brembo disc brakes and a 90mph top speed. Unfortunately, Fornetti Impianti, in turn, sold the company and its fortunes declined sharply under the new management, ending in failure.

SIMPLEX / *Holland 1902–1968*
Was for many years Holland's leading motorcycle factory. Fitted Minerva, Fafnir and MAG engines from 2 hp to 6 hp; from the mid-1920s also 346cc ohv Blackburne, 498cc sv Blackburne and 348cc ohv Bradshaw engines with oilcooling into strong frames. Other engines fitted were the 98cc and 148cc Villiers and the 98cc Sachs; during the late 1930s also the 60cc Sachs and the 124cc Villiers. In the years after the war, there was a close connection with Juncker and Gazelle. Leading-link forks and duplex frames were used in 1911, 9 hp V-twins with ioe Motosacoche engines were built in 1921, triangular frames were used in the mid-1920s and a 246cc single built in 1935 which had a watercooled Villiers two-stroke power unit.

SIMPLEX / *England 1919–1922*
Producer of 105cc 1 hp two-stroke bicycle attachment engines.

SIMPLEX / *Italy 1921–1950*
Luigi Pellini built beautiful little 124cc auxiliary engines and from 1927 onwards 149cc ohv machines with their own unit-design engines, followed by 174cc models. Improved 'Ala d'Oro' versions with engines which had fully enclosed valve gears and other modern design features were built in 1930. The range included also a 210cc and from 1934 a 496cc ohv with four-speed gearboxes. After 1945 models from 148cc to

498cc Sieg (ohv V-twin MAG engine) 1928

173cc Simplex (ohv) 1929 (I)

248cc based on pre-war designs were built in limited numbers.

SIMPLEX / *America late 1930s to late 1960s*
Lightweight machines for short distances, fitted with American 198cc industrial four-stroke sv engines.

198cc Simplex (TS Clinton Industrial engine) 1966 (USA)

SIMSON / *East Germany 1950—*
Originally called AWO, this one-time car factory made 250cc ohv models with shaft drive until 1960, changing the name to Simson along the way. Thereafter, it concentrated on smaller 50cc x 75cc two-stroke roadsters and mopeds. Were particularly successful in the ISDT and similar events. As with MZ, with whom they have commercial ties, Simson made strenuous efforts to export, but ran into difficulties with German re-unification.

49cc Simson (TS model Enduro) 1982

SINGER / *England 1900–1915*
The first products were three-wheelers, followed by Perks & Birch-licenced motorwheels, which

with their 208cc engines were fitted into bicycles. In later years a wide range of Singer motorcycles of sturdy conventional design appeared on the market. Included were watercooled singles and 346cc two-strokes, but the best sellers were sv models of 299cc, 499cc and 535cc. They had some monobloc engines and a variety of gearboxes. Everything was of Singer's own design and manufacture. Singer bought Premier of Coventry in the early 1920s, but was by then a car manufacturer only.

SIPHAX / *France 1951–1956*
Small factory which produced 98cc two-strokes with a horizontal cylinder. The engines were of AMC manufacture.

SIROCCO / *Czechoslovakia 1925–1928*
Designed by Gustav Heinz, the Sirocco was built on English lines and also had English Villiers engines from 147cc to 346cc.

SIRRAH / *England 1922–1925*
The Sirrah, designed by Harris, was available with a wide range of engines. These included the 211cc Wisemann and 292cc Union two-strokes and 248cc, 348cc and 490cc sv and ohv Blackburne and JAP engines. Wisemann at Birmingham—manufacturer of the Sirrah—produced also the Verus motorcycles. The Sirrah (Harris in reverse) was a cheaper version of the Verus. There was also a 996cc Sirrah model with the V-twin sv JAP engine.

SIS / *Portugal 1950–*
Bicycle producer J. Simones Costa became the Portuguese importer of Sachs two-stroke engines and founded his own motorcycle factory. His machines are fitted with 49cc and 98cc Sachs power units.

SISSY / *Austria 1957–1960*
Unorthodox miniscooter with 98cc and 123cc Rotax two-stroke engines. Produced by the old-established Lohner works.

SITTA / *Germany 1950–1955*
Scooters with 119cc and 123cc Ilo engines, 49cc mopeds and also Ilo-engined motorcycles from 123cc to 247cc.

SJK / *Japan 1956–early 1960s*
Built a variety of mopeds and motorcycles from 49cc to 249cc with their own two-stroke engines, but like several other manufacturers failed during the slump in the Japanese motorcycle industry.

SKF / *Russia 1961–1965*
Russian Jawa-like 348cc double-ohc racing twins, destined for official works riders only.

SKO / *Czechoslovakia 1924–1926*
Designed by František Skopec, the SKO had a 498cc single-cylinder two-stroke deflector-type three-port engine.

SKOOTAMOTA
See ABC Skootamota

SL / *England 1924–1925*
Produced in limited numbers a 345cc single-cylinder machine with two inlet valves and one exhaust valve.

SLADE-JAP / *England 1920–1923*
A machine with a 346cc sv JAP engine. Small production.

SLANEY / *England 1921–1922*
Only one model was made by H. H. Timbrell's factory. It had a 688cc flat-twin Coventry-Victor sv engine.

SLAVIA / *Czechoslovakia 1899–1908*
The Slavia was built in the Austro-Hungarian Empire by the Czech Laurin & Klement factory. The name Slavia was also used by the Laurin & Klement machines built under licence in Germany.

173cc Sitta (TS Ilo engine) 1953

SLINGER / *England 1900–1901*
Extremely unorthodox motorcycle with three wheels in line. The two small front wheels, one of which was directly driven by chain from the watercooled 3·5 hp single-cylinder De Dion Bouton engine, had a common frame; the rear part was more or less an orthodox bicycle frame.

SM / *Poland 1935*
Had a 346cc single-cylinder ohv unit-design engine with shaft drive to the rear wheel. Was built in small numbers only.

SMART / *Austria 1925–1932*
Assembled motorcycles with sv and ohv JAP engines of 346cc, 498cc and 596cc.

SMART / *France 1922–1927*
Lightweight motorcycles with 198cc sv engines of own manufacture.

346cc Smart (sv JAP engine) 1928

SMS / *England 1913–1914*
Unorthodox 211cc two-stroke with a patented inlet port arrangement.

SMW / *Germany 1923–1933*
Built two types of motorcycles with flat-twin engines. One had the 293cc Bosch Douglas, built under licence, the other the 493cc BMW, as found in the Victoria and other makes. New models appeared in 1928, when chief designer Karl Rühmer designed 198cc two-strokes with Villiers engines and 198cc as well as 498cc singles with sv and ohv Blackburne and Sturmey-Archer engines.

S&N / *Germany 1901–1908*
Big machine factory which also built Erika typewriters. The motorcycles were called Germania, and for a short period Slavia. They were made under Laurin & Klement licence, and were partly directly imported from the then famous L&K factory at Jungbunzlau.

SNOB / *Germany 1921–1925*
Was the leading four-stroke lightweight machine in Germany during the early 1920s. Production versions had 154cc ioe single-cylinder engines, while works racing models had ohv engines. Designed by Karl Döpfner.

SOCOVEL / *Belgium 1947–1955*
The first 123cc Socovel was a quite orthodox two-stroke lightweight. Less orthodox were the following Villiers-engined 123cc and 197cc machines with completely enclosed engines and pressed steel frames. They had a triangular shape, plunger-type rear suspension and teleforks. The next model was a 98cc Autocycle, followed by entirely new 246cc two-strokes with Jawa engines

and Jawa-like frames. There was also a 346cc Jawa-engined twin. Other versions had Ilo, Sachs and also Coventry-Victor 296cc flat-twin engines; the last ones with opposing cylinders and transverse-mounted.

SOK / *Sweden 1925–1928*
Concentrated on a 346cc ohv machine with mainly JAP engines.

SOKOL / *Poland 1936–1939*
The Sokol was a 598cc sloper, not unlike earlier BSA models, with own sv engine. Production of this motorcycle was destined for the army.

49cc Solo (TS model 40) 1982

SOLO / *Germany 1949–*
Produces a variety of mofas and mopeds with their own 49cc two-stroke engines. There are also watercooled versions and an Electro-mofa.

SOS / *England 1927–1939*
Villiers engines always played an important part in the production of these machines. A few 490cc JAP-engined machines were made in earlier years but most models had 147cc to 347cc Villiers two-strokes. Among the models was a 172cc road-racing and a 172cc speedway machine. Earlier versions had three-port, deflector-type motors, later ones the flat-top Villiers. There were also watercooled 249cc versions and models with the 346cc Villiers Longstroke.

SOUPLEX / *Belgium 1947–1953*
Produced 123cc two-strokes with Villiers engines and afterwards 296cc sv twin-cylinder machines with transverse-mounted horizontal Coventry-Victor engines.

SOUTHEY / *England 1905–1925*
This was a small company which built its own motorcycles as well as frames for other motorcycle assemblers. The company's own machines had 246cc, 249cc and 346cc engines. The first ones were made by Villiers and the last one was a side-valve Blackburne.

SOYER / *France 1920–1935*
The first models had 247cc engines, and a lady's version had a frame without a top tube. Afterwards 98cc and 174cc two-strokes sv as well as ohv models from 248cc to 498cc with Chaise, Sturmey-Archer and JAP engines were made. The two-stroke engines were of their own manufacture. A Soyer with C. J. Williams in the saddle won the 1930 French Grand Prix. The engine used was a 498cc Sturmey-Archer ohv single.

SPA-JAP / *England 1921–1923*
Small assembler, whose machines had 246cc and 293cc sv JAP engines.

SPAKE / *America 1911–1914*
Produced strong and heavy 550cc single-cylinder and 980cc V-twin models with own ioe engines. The engines also sold to other manufacturers.

SPARK / *England 1921–1923*
Made by Sparkbrook, the Spark was a utility model with the 269cc Villiers engine.

SPARK / *England 1903–1904*
This much older Spark had a 2 hp engine and a patented surface carburettor.

SPARKBROOK / *England 1912–1925*
A well-known manufacturer who fitted in the early years 746cc and 980cc V-twin JAP engines and after WWI a 269cc two-stroke Villiers. There were also 247cc and 346cc models with the two-strokes from Wolverhampton as well as 346cc singles with the JAP sv engine, the sleeve-valve Barr & Stroud and the oilcooled Bradshaw.

SPARTA / *The Netherlands 1931–*
Bicycle factory, which produced 49cc machines with attachment engines, and afterwards models with 98cc Sachs and Villiers engines. There were

244cc Sparta (TS twin Ilo engine) 1954

also 74cc Sachs-engined and eventually 198cc Villiers-engined motorcycles. During the late 1930s, 120cc and 123cc two-strokes with Ilo and

Sachs engines were added. Improved versions with 123cc to 198cc Villiers engines came after 1945; a 246cc two-stroke with a Victoria double-port engine was added in 1951. The Dutch factory also built a machine with the 244cc Ilo vertical two-stroke twin, but concentrated since the early 1960s on 49cc mopeds.

SPARTAN / *England 1920–1922*
Small production of 349cc single-cylinder two-stroke motorcyles with Broler three-part deflector-type engines.

SPARTON / *Wales 1976—1980s*
A co-operation between Spondon Engineering and Barton Engineering to build racing two-strokes designed by Barry Hart. Success with a simple air-cooled three-cylinder 500cc model led Sparton to over-reach themselves with the Phoenix, a vastly more complicated 'square four'.

SPAVIERO / *Italy 1955*
A 100cc ohv twin model, the Sparrow, offered for only one season by the Chiorda factory. Very few were made.

SPECIAL-MONNERET / *France 1952–1958*
Georges Monneret, famous French racing motorcyclist, produced in Paris his own lightweight motorcycles of sporting appearance. The engines were 49cc VAP and Sachs.

SPEED / *France 1951–1956*
This was a scooter with 60cc, 115cc and 124cc engines, manufactured by a branch of the former Mors car works.

SPEED-KING-JAP / *England 1913–1914*
These motorcycles were made to a low price for a chain store. They were equipped with 293cc JAP sv engines.

SPHINX / *Belgium 1923–1926*
Made from mainly English components, the Sphinx had 346cc and 490cc sv and ohv engines made by JAP in London.

SPIEGLER / *Germany 1923–1932*
This make was the successor to the Schwalbe machines, also built by the Spiegler works at Aalen. The unusual frames, made from pressed steel and tubes with the tank forming the backbone of the frame, housed 346cc, 498cc and 598cc single-cylinder sv and ohv engines, made by JAP, MAG and at the works. A 198cc JAP-engined ohv single was introduced in 1929.

SPIESS / *Germany 1903–1905*
Assembler who bought his 2 to 2·75 hp engines from the Minerva, Zedel and Fafnir factories.

SPINDLER / *Germany 1922–1925*
Bekamo-engined 149cc two-strokes, built in limited numbers.

SPIRIDITIS / *Latvia early 1950s–*
These machines, built by the Sarkana-Swaigsne motorcycle works, had 123cc and 246cc two-stroke engines. According to unconfirmed information, the Riga factory now produces 49cc machines, mainly mopeds.

SPRING / *Belgium 1910–1940*
The first model was a four-cylinder with a frame which was sprung both front and back. New models which appeared after 1920 had transverse-mounted V-twin engines with 496cc, 746cc and 996cc. The last one was equipped with a reverse gear.

498cc Spiegler (ohv) 1929

SPRITE / *England 1965—1971*
Frank Hipkin made trials and moto-cross machines, latterly with his own copies of Husqvarna two-stroke engines. An over-ambitious American venture ended the company.

STABIL / *Belgium 1931–1933*
Limited production of 98cc and 123cc machines with Villiers engines.

STADION / *Czechoslovakia 1958–1966*
Moped factory, which used 49cc engines supplied by Jawa.

STAFFETT / *Norway 1953–early 1960s*
Another moped producer fitting 49cc engines.

STAG / *England 1912–1914*
The factory was at Sherwood Forest, Nottingham. Used Precision engines from 4·5 to 6 hp.

STAHL / *America 1910–1914*
Built at Philadelphia, the Stahl motorcycles had 4·5 hp single-cylinder and 7 hp V-twin engines.

STANDARD / *Germany 1922–1924*
One of the many workshops which built motorcycles in the early 1920s. These had simple frames and simple 132cc and 148cc three-port two-stroke engines.

498cc Spiegler (sv) 1928

347cc Standard (ohv racing JAP) 1929

STANDARD/*Germany*/*Switzerland 1925–early 1950s*

This was a very successful make. Wilhelm Gutbrod, who founded the factory, had been with the Klotz works until 1925. The first models had 248cc and 348cc ohv JAP engines, but he soon switched to Swiss MAG proprietary engines from 347cc to 998cc with ioe and partly ohv engines. Works racing models in 1929 had 347cc and 497cc Marchant-designed MAG ohc engines. A few 998cc racing V-twins with ohv JAP racing engines were also built. 1930 saw the introduction of 198cc and 248cc ohv singles with their own engines; 1931 the 498cc production racer with the then new ohv MAG racing engine. Brough-licence forks were used from 1929 onwards on many models, including the Rex models of the mid-1930s with Standard's own 348cc engine. Standard built Josef Ganz-designed small cars and mainly 198cc and 248cc two-strokes during the late 1930s. In the 1920s

497cc Standard (ohv MAG engine) 1931

198cc Standard (ohv JAP-Licence engine) 1932

846cc Standard (sv V-twin MAG engine) 1935

Wilhelm Gutbrod had bought the Swiss Zehnder factory and continued manufacture of these good lightweight machines; he also owned another Swiss factory where he built bigger machines, among them a beautiful 846cc V-twin with the MAG sv engine. There were Swiss versions of the popular 497cc MAG-engined ohv singles. There were attempts after 1945 to re-enter motorcycle production with modern two-strokes up to 248cc and there were also prototypes of various ohv models; unfortunately, few Standard machines were built in the early post-war period. Wilhelm Gutbrod died soon after the war and his sons concentrated on the production of Gutbrod cars and on agricultural machinery. Now they produce lawn mowers among other things. Connected with Standard motorcycles were such famous racing men as A. F. Dom (who was also an excellent designer), Karl Gall, Paul Rüttchen, Hermann Lang, Franz Ecker, Konrad Dürr. With first class design, quality workmanship and excellent finish, Standard motorcycles were among the best built between the wars.

STANGER / *England 1921–1923*

Interesting design, as the 538cc Stanger had a 70mm bore × 70mm stroke V-twin two-stroke engine and was probably the very first half-litre motorcycle with such an engine conception. It also had a spring frame and was offered for £95 in 1923. The engine with its big outside flywheel had a tendency to overheat, and the plugs to become fouled with oil.

STANLEY / *England c1902*

Made by a well-known bicycle factory, Stanley motorcycles had 2·5 hp power-units and friction drive to the rear wheel. The production was taken over by Singer.

STAR / *England 1898–1914*

Big factory with wide interests. Produced first three-wheelers and then motorcycles with De Dion engines. There was also a co-operation with Griffon of France. The last motorcycles built by Star were JAP-engined 625cc singles and 770cc V-twins. Star was also a well-known manufacturer of cars.

STAR / *Germany 1895–c1900*

According to unconfirmed information, Star built motorcycles under Werner licence with the 1·5 hp engines above the front wheel. This may have been around 1898 or possibly 1895, but this is doubtful.

STAR / *Germany 1920–1922*

Flat-twins designed by H. F. Günther which

eventually became the first D-Rad motorcycles. The 393cc engines with opposing cylinders were of the company's own design and manufacture. The first D-Rad versions were identical to the Star machines.

STAR / *England 1919–1921*

This was a small assembly plant for motorcycles with 269cc Villiers engines.

STAR-GEM / *Belgium 1930–1933*

Built small machines of 98cc and 123cc with their own and also Sachs two-stroke engines.

STEFFEY/*America c1902–1910*

Supplied 1·25 and 3 hp single-cylinder machines with aircooled and watercooled engines of their own manufacturer.

STEIDINGER / *Germany 1925–1927*

Lightweight machines with triangular frames. The two-stroke engines had 199cc.

STELLA / *Belgium 1921–1936*

The Stella range included frames made from tubes as well as from pressed steel. Engines were 98cc two-strokes and 346cc and 490cc sv and ohv singles made in France by Staub under JAP licence.

STELLAR / *England 1912–1914*

Interesting design of a vertical-twin two-stroke machine with its own watercooled 784cc engine and shaft drive to the rear wheel.

STERLING / *France 1952–1954*

Scooter with a fully enclosed 123cc Ydral two-stroke engine.

614cc Sterna (sv watercooled flat-twin; Designer J. Pässler) 1922

STERNA / *Germany 1922–1924*

This watercooled 614cc sv flat-twin with opposing cylinders was nearly identical to Aristos and Menos motorcycles.

STERVA/*France 1953–1956*
Another French scooter of the early 1950s. Engines used were the 98cc and 123cc Sabb.

STERZI/*Italy 1948–early 1960s*
Well-designed lightweight machines from the 47cc ohv Pony to 174cc ohv models. Among them were 123cc and 158cc two-stroke versions in a variety of models.

STEVENS/*England 1934–1937*
The Stevens brothers, founders of AJS, who lost that factory in 1931 to the Colliers brothers in London, re-entered the motorcycle market with 248cc, 348cc and 498cc single-cylinder ohv models. They also supplied AJW with 498cc proprietary engines. Stevens motorcycles were of typical English design and were supplied for use in trials with upswept exhaust pipes.

496cc Stevens (ohv 'Sport') 1937

STICHERLING/*Germany 1923–1926*
DKW-engined 145cc, 173cc and 206cc two-strokes, built by a small factory.

STIMULA/*France 1902–WWI*
Built motorcycles with Minerva, Buchet, Peugeot and also 346cc and 492cc sv and ohv engines of their own.

STOCK/*Germany 1924–1933*
The first Stock, a 119cc two-stroke, was made under Evans licence. Entirely new Heuss-designed 173cc, 198cc, 246cc and 298cc models appeared in 1929. Of advanced design with own unit-design three-port two-stroke engines, shaft drive to the rear wheel and double-loop frames.

119cc Stock (TS Evans-Licence) 1925

STOEWER/*Germany 1904–1905*
Was a well-known car factory which built three-wheelers first and then for a short period Fafnir-engined 2·75 hp motorcycles.

STOLCO/*Germany 1922–1924*
Lightweight machines with Grade-built 144cc two-stroke motors.

STROLCH/*Germany 1950–1958*
Gassmann-designed scooters with 98cc, 147cc, 173cc and 198cc Sachs engines. After a short period they were renamed Progress.

STRUCO/*Germany 1922–1925*
Built 147cc two-strokes and also 198cc models with their own sv engines.

748cc Stuart (TS watercooled twin, shaft-drive) 1912

STUART/*England 1911–1912*
This factory also built Stellar motorcycles. The Stuart was a single-cylinder 298cc two-stroke.

STUCCHI/*Italy 1901–1927*
Ettore Bugatti, Carlo Leidi and Adalberto Garelli were among famous technicians which were working for this once-famous firm, which built three-wheelers, motorcycles and four-wheeled vehicles. See also Prinetti & Stucchi.

246cc Stock (TS shaft-drive) 1931

STURM/*Germany 1923–1925*
These were assembled motorcycles equipped with 147cc Alba engines.

STYLSON/*France 1919–WWII*
Assembled motorcycles with JAP and STAUB (JAP licence) engines up to 996cc. Some Staub engines were modified to unit-design with shaft drive to the rear wheel. Other versions had the V-engine transverse-mounted. The company competed officially in races and Pierre Amort won many sidecar events with a 996cc JAP-engined racing machine.

STYRIA/*Austria 1905–1908*
The machines produced by this early Austrian factory had 2 hp single-cylinder and 5 hp V-twin Fafnir proprietary engines.

SUDBRACK/*Germany 1949–1951*
Bicycle factory with 98cc and 123cc motorcycles. The machines were equipped with two-stroke engines of Ilo manufacture.

SUDBROOK/*England 1919–1920*
This short-lived company assembled machines which were equipped with 269cc two-stroke Villiers engines.

SUECIA/*Sweden 1928–1940*
Built 248cc, 348cc and 490cc machines with JAP engines. There were also Sùecia two-stroke models up to 248cc, actually made by Sparta of The Netherlands.

SULKY/*France 1954–1957*
Built by Motobloc, the Sulky miniscooter had AMC two-stroke engines of 98cc, 117cc and 124cc.

SUMITA / *Japan 1951–1955*
Producer of 123cc and 148cc motorcycles with their own ohv engines.

SUN / *England 1911–1961*
Belonging to the Parkes family and now to the Raleigh group, Sun produced bicycles and accessories before they entered motorcycle production with 346cc singles, which had Villiers ioe engines. After 1918 the range included 269cc and eventually 247cc models with Vitesse rotary-valve two-stroke engines as well as Villiers-engined models from 147cc to 247cc. Others had 346cc Blackburne and 246cc to 746cc sv and ohv JAP engines. There was no motorcycle manufacture during the second half of the 1930s. After 1945 production was resumed; now all models had Villiers two-stroke engines, including a scooter called Sunwasp. Engines used were from 98cc to 225cc.

SUNBEAM / *England 1912—1957*
Sunbeam motor cycles were first made by the famous bicycle makers John Marston of Wolverhampton. After WWI, the company was sold to Nobel Industries (later ICI), who allowed Sunbeam considerable autonomy. In 1936 ICI sold the name and precious little else to the Collier brothers London-based AMC. Finally the name was purchased by BSA.

From 1912 to 1936, Sunbeam designs were by the highly respected J.E. Greenwood. Marston (and ICI) Sunbeams were famous for their superb black enamel finish, their sporting performance and, on many models, their all-enclosed chain drive. Though before 1914 they made a 350cc

SUNBEAM

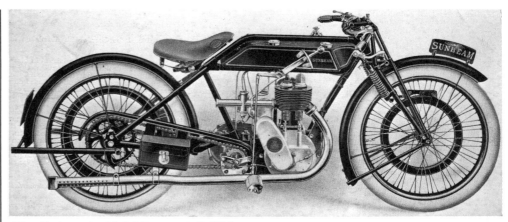

492cc Sunbeam (sv Model 'Longstroke') 1924

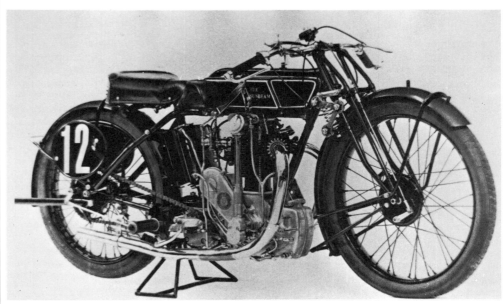

497cc Sunbeam (ohc works racing Model) 1925

493cc Sunbeam (ohv Model TT 90) 1927

493cc Sunbeam (ohv Model TT 90) 1929

497cc Sunbeam (hc Model Sports) 1939

single cylinder model and later several proprietary-engined V twins, Sunbeam's early reputation was founded on their 500cc side-valve singles, one of which, ridden by H.R. Davies, was second in the 1914 Senior TT. T.C. de la Hay won in 1920, and Alec Bennett in 1923. Thereafter, Sunbeam raced ohv models (an ohc version in 1925 was not successful) and Charlie Dodson won the 1928 and 1929 Senior TTs. Racing ended with the depression of the early 1930s, when Sunbeam sales declined badly.

When AMC took over and moved production to London, they produced new 250cc, 350cc and 500cc models with Collier-designed high camshaft ohv engines, seen at the 1938 Show. These scarcely had a chance to prove themselves, being killed off by the outbreak of war in 1939. During the war, the name was sold to BSA. The post-war Sunbeam S7 was designed by Ehrling Poppe, once partner in P & P Motor Cycles, who leaned heavily on the 1939

BMW for many of its features and styling. The twin-cylinder 500cc all-alloy ohc engine was rubber mounted in line with the frame, with unit four-speed gearbox, shaft drive and worm and wheel final transmission. With its four-inch tyres there was nothing sporting about the S8, but it was a refined and pleasant touring machine. Unfortunately it sold better abroad than at home, and even the S8 a sports model with lighter looking front forks, tyres and brakes did not sell in the quantities

746cc Super-X (ioe V-twin) 1927

for which BSA had hoped. Reluctantly, BSA ended Sunbeam production in 1957 and thereafter used the name on bicycles. There was a so called BSA-Sunbeam scooter, but it had absolutely nothing in common with the great name that it bore.

497cc Sunbeam (ohc twin Model 8) 1950

SUPER-X / *America 1924–1930*
Made by the Schwinn company of Chicago, the 746cc and 996cc Super-X machines were really successors to the American-X. All models had V-twin ioe engines and were of excellent design.

746cc Super-X (ioe V-twin) 1930

SUZUKI / *Japan 1952–*
Suzuki were old established and successful makers of textile machinery, who, in 1952, took advantage of the demand in Japan for cheap transport and produced a simple motorised bicycle. Three years

later — after, in common with so many other concerns, a close study of a DKW RT 125 two-stroke — Suzuki produced their first real motor cycle. This was the 125cc two-stroke Colleda, which was raced somewhat half-heartedly at Asama Plains in 1955 and then not again until 1959. The following year, Suzuki unexpectedly entered the TT with 125cc twin-cylinder two-strokes, in 1961, it raced 125cc and 250cc twins. Performance in both classes was dire, but Suzuki had an ace up their sleeve.

In 1961, the East German MZ company were enjoying an extraordinarily successful season in the 125cc class. In a truly cloak and dagger operation, worthy of any thriller, Suzuki persuaded rider-technician Ernst Degner (and his family) to defect to them and to hand over MZ's secrets. With Degner's assistance, Suzuki won the newly-instituted 50cc world championship in 1962 and the 50cc and 125cc titles the next year. They won the 50cc title again in 1964, 1966 and 1967 and the 125cc title again in 1965 before withdrawing from Grand Prix racing. However success in the 250cc clas always eluded them, despite investing heavily in an advanced 'square four' racer, campaigned in 1964 and 1965.

Suzuki were even more successful in moto cross, using single-cylinder two-strokes in the late 1960s and 1970s. Joel Robert won the 250cc world title in 1970, 1971 and 1972 and Roger De Coster the 500cc title five times between 1971 and 1976. Meanwhile, the company sold 50cc, 125cc and 250cc two-strokes for the road, which became ever more sophisticated from crude beginnings. A landmark was the T20 Super Six (six speed) two-stroke twin of 1965. The aircooled 500cc twin T500 Cobra followed in 1967, in 1971, the very impressive three-cylinder water-cooled GT750 was launched. As its designation implied, it was of 750cc. Its transverse engine allegedly making 70 horsepower. This was a truly awesome power output for the time, giving breathtaking performances, though this was scarcely matched by the GT750's brakes and handling. Suzuki followed this

up with smaller aircooled triples — the 380cc, GT380 and 550cc GT550.

The export market to the USA was very important to Suzuki, and, claiming to be the world's largest maker of two-stroke motor cycles, they were extremely conscious of the growing threat from US anti-pollution. They now made a major error in staking a great deal on Wankel engine technology. In 1970 they had taken out a Wankel development licence from NSU, and in 1974 revealed what they hoped would be the motor cycle of the future — the (nominally 500cc) rotary-engined RE5.

The RE5 was not a positively bad motor cycle, but it was not a good one and for all its novelty, it did not sell. The engine looked messy, bulky and was too high in the frame. The bike was heavy, it guzzled petrol and performance was far from impressive, while its one-off technology made it extremely expensive to service and maintain. The machine lasted for only two disappointing seasons before Suzuki hastily rushed into production a close copy of Kawasaki's Z1000, reduced to 750cc as the Suzuki GS.750. This was followed by the GS.1000. Fortunately, both sold well and Suzuki settled into a new generation of four-stroke fours and twins.

Though they had abandoned Grand Prix racing, the company raced the T500 two-stroke twin at Daytona from 1968 on. In that year Ron Grant was fifth on his TR500 and in 1969 he was second. In Europe, Jack Findley had successes on a TR500, including victories in the 1971 Ulster Grand Prix and the 1978 Senior TT with a later water-cooled version.

The TR750, a racing version of the road going GT750, was very impressive, but despite a claimed 115hp, failed to score at Daytona, destroying chains and rear tyres faster than they could be replaced. With the 500cc RG500 square four, Suzuki re-entered Grand Prix racing, which they have successfully supported ever since. Through the period, they also maintained a range of road machines from 50cc upwards in production.

In 1985 Suzuki claimed to have made a design breakthrough with the new 750cc transverse four-cylinder GSX-R. The innovation, so Suzuki claimed, was improved oil-cooling — the oil was circulated around the inside of the engine castings by a separate pump. Though, in fact, this was not a new idea, it was well applied, eliminating bulky, heavy water cooling. Only in 1991 did Suzuki find it necessary to resort to water-cooling for their new GSX-R750 in the face of stricter noise legislation.

Like other Japanese manufacturers, Suzuki offer a wide and varied range of models for all purposes and tastes, from 50cc upwards. Some of these are only available in certain markets rather than worldwide, which, again, reflects the custom of the Japanese industry generally.

1067cc Suzuki (four-cylinder, four-valve, dohc) 1982

986cc Suzuki (four-cylinder, four-valve, dohc) 1982

Suzuki GSX-R750 1985.

SUZY / *France 1932–1933*
Made by a small factory, the Suzy had a fully enclosed 498cc ohc Chaise unit-design engine.

SWALLOW / *England 1946–1951*
The Swallow Gadabout scooter was designed by Frank Rainbow and had 125cc and 197cc Villiers engines. Swallow, who also made sidecars, were an early offshoot of SS — (later Jaguar).

SWASTIKA / *Australia 1913–1916*
There was, during the twenties, a Swastika bicycle factory in Germany, but this at Adelaide built motorcycles with no German connections. Using English components this machine had a sv engine of 746cc.

SWIFT / *England 1898–1915*
Famous pioneer who built De Dion-engined three-wheelers and motorcycles with shaft drive for Starley. The Coventry-based factory also built cars. The Swift motorcycles had White & Poppe as well as their own 492cc and 768cc V-twin engines. Commercially and technically Swift was closely connected with the Ariel works at Birmingham, then headed by Charles Sangster.

SWM / *Italy 1971–1985*
SWM were extremely successful in the 1970s, making 125cc Sachs and 250cc Rotax engines for off-road motor cycles. They over-reached themselves by acquiring the Gori company, however, and foundered in the face of the market downturn of the early 1980s.

SYMPLEX / *England 1913–1922*
Simple machines with 311cc Dalm two-stroke engines. Designer was J. J. Allen.

SYPHAX / *France early 1950s*
Built nice lightweights with flat 98cc single-cylinder AMC two-stroke engines and bigger two-stroke models with vertical Aubier-Dunne engines. These had 123cc and 174cc. Other versions housed ohv AMC engines with 123cc and 174cc.

399cc Suzuki (two-cylinder, four-valve, dohc) 1982

281

T

TANDON / *England 1948—1957*
A range of simple Villiers-engined lightweights of 125cc, 200cc and 225cc, later, Villiers 250cc and 325cc twins were used.

TAPELLA-FUCHS / *Italy c1957*
Concentrated on mopeds and used 49cc Fuchs two-stroke engines exclusively.

TAS / *Germany 1924—1931*
A bicycle factory which was closely connected with the French Gnome & Rhône works. The result was the use of 173cc and 248cc two-stroke and of 346cc and 498cc four-stroke sv and ohv engines made by the G&R works in TAS frames. When they broke that connection the German factory used Swiss MAG 347cc and 497cc ioe and ohv single-cylinder engines.

TAURA / *Italy 1927—1930*
Giulio Doglioli's motorcycles relied on English JAP and Blackburne engines. The range included first 173cc sv versions only, but in the next years models up to 490cc were built. Most of them had the 490cc ohv double-port JAP engine. A three-wheeler for invalids was also built.

TAURUS / *Italy 1933—1966*
The first models were 173cc two-strokes and a 173cc ohv version. Modern 346cc and 496cc ohc singles with unit-design four-speed gearboxes were built in 1934. New pre-war models were also 246cc and 498cc ohv singles, which had rear suspension, but the top design was without doubt the 1938 498cc double-ohc single. Unfortunately Taurus could not afford competing officially in races, but it was a superb design which needed only more development to become a first-class racing machine. The production version had 34 bhp at 6000 rpm and a top speed of 108 mph.

A 248cc single-ohc model built after 1945 had 14 bhp at 7000 rpm. After the war, production included 49cc engines, 158cc two-stroke machines and a beautiful 199cc ohv unit-design machine, while the older 248cc ohc single was superseded by a quite tame 248cc ohv version. New also was a 173cc ohv model.

119cc Tautz (TS) 1922

TAUTZ / *Germany 1921—1923*
One of the first German scooters built. It had a 118cc DKW two-stroke engine.

TAVERNIER / *France 1921—1923*
Assembler, who built a range of machines with Zurcher, JAP and Blackburne engines.

TECNOMOTO / *Italy 1968—1977*
Makers of small moto cross and enduro models, who switched to the manufacture of children's motor cycles. Tecnomoto was sold to a British company in 1977, but did not survive.

TECO / *Germany 1920—1926*
Built mainly 198cc machines with sv, ioe and ohv engines of Alba manufacture although the crankcase bore the name Teco. The last model, had a 346cc Kühne ohv engine.

TEDDY / *France 1922—1924*
Lightweight machines with 203cc sv engines.

TEE-BEE / *England 1908—1911*
Assembled machines with their own and also 293cc JAP sv engines.

TEHUELCHE / *Argentina 1958—1962*
75cc ohv machine of Italian design, built with many parts imported from Italy.

TEMPLE / *England 1924—1928*
The Temple was part of the OEC range of models. Claude Temple was a well-known rider and breaker of records as well as a technician. He broke many records on 996cc V-twins, which had Hubert Hagens-designed ohc Anzani engines. This 1923 machine developed 58 hp. Production versions had 496cc four-valve ohv Vulpine and 347cc and 497cc ohc Atlanta engines. From 1927 onwards the OEC also had duplex steering.

TEMPO / *Germany 1924—1927*
Built 197cc single-cylinder two-strokes and also 297cc sv machines in limited numbers with very strong frames.

TEMPO / *Norway 1949—*
Built a range of lightweights with 49cc and 123cc two-stroke engines. Among the engines used were the Villiers, Ilo, CZ and Sachs.

TERRA / *Germany 1922—1924*
Simple two-strokes of own design and manufacture. They had 127cc, 143cc and 172cc.

TERROT / *France 1901—early 1960s*
This was for many years the factory with the largest motorcycle production in France. Terrot in Dijon was also a well-known make in races during the 1920s. Late in that decade they bought

238cc Terrot (TS Sport) 1923

348cc Terrot (ohv) 1930

498cc Terrot (ohv) 1952

In the meantime they built motorcycles on English lines, including 98cc, 174cc and 246cc two-strokes and sv and ohv models from 246cc to 746cc. The last ones were V-twins. Used Blackburne, JAP and mainly their own engines, of which in pre-war days the 246cc ohv singles were extremely popular. There was also in the late 1920s a Blackburne-engined 174cc ohv racing model. A 498cc works racing model, built in 1937, had a transverse-mounted ohv V-twin engine. After 1945, Terrot built a range of modern ohv singles up to 498cc and also two-strokes, including scooters of advanced design. Famous Terrot riders in the period between the wars: Rolland, Perrotin, Coulon, Fraichard, Durant, Boetsch, Simo, Riha, J. and H. Tichy, Zukal, Raab and others.

TERROT / *Czechoslovakia 1933–1935*
A branch factory of Terrot-Dijon built a 346cc sv model in Czechoslovakia.

TESTI / *Italy 1951—1983*
Testi built a vast range of proprietary-engined lightweight motor cycles and mopeds, using Sachs, Franco Massimi, Demm and Minarelli engines. At different times, Testis were sold in Germany as Horex, and elsewhere as Gitanes, though there was no direct connection with those companies. Like so

90cc Testi (TS) 1965

many other small and quite vigorous companies, Testi did not have the resources to survive the depression of the early 1980s.

TETGE / *Germany 1923–1926*
Produced on a limited scale 148cc and 172cc sv singles and also machines with MAG 597cc V-twins.

TGM / *Italy 1974—*
Makers of trials and moto-cross models, with Hella, Danth and Villa two-stroke engines. Sammy Miller acted as a design consultant. Though not owned by Cagiva, TGM have had a 'working relationship' with them in recent years.

THIEM / *America 1903–1914*
Built like other American factories of that period 550cc ioe single-cylinder and 890cc as well as 996cc V-twin machines of advanced design. Some had two-speed gearboxes.

THOMANN / *France 1912–1939*
Built two-strokes from 98cc to 248cc and was another factory which belonged to the Alcyon group from the mid-1920s onward.

THOMAS / *England 1904*
Assembler who built a limited number of motorcycles with various engines including Minerva and Sarolea engines.

THOMAS / *America 1907–1908*
Made in a branch of the Thomas car works, the motorcycles had 3 hp single-cylinder engines with a sloping cylinder and belt drive to the rear wheel. The price: $175.

THOR / *America 1903–1916*
Produced proprietary engines for various factories, including Indian at Springfield. The Aurora Automatic Machinery Co. later built

6 hp Thor (ioe V-twin) 1915

complete V-twin motorcycles with 6 hp and 9 hp ioe engines, which had an excellent reputation among riders.

THOROUGH / *England 1903*
Another small assembler of motorcycles. These had MMC and Coronet engines.

THREE-SPIRES / *England 1931–1932*
Made by Coventry Bicycles Ltd, these little 147cc two-stroke machines were offered for £18.18s.

THUMANN / *Germany 1925–1926*
Although a comparatively small factory, Thumann built their own 246cc and 346cc sv engines.

THUNDER / *Italy 1952–1954*
Very up-to-date but expensive design of a 127cc vertical twin unit-design ohv machine with telefork, swinging-arm rear suspension, the dynamo incorporated in the crankcase, four-speed gearbox etc. The price was 285.000 lire, ie approximately 100.000 lire higher than normal 124cc two-strokes.

TICKLE / *England 1967–1973*
Producer of 348cc and 499cc 'Manx' Norton single-cylinder double-ohc racing machines, after the Norton works decided to drop the manufacture of this model. Tickle also produced the necessary spares and parts when the original parts were no longer available.

TIGER / *America 1915–1916*
Attempted to produce a lightweight machine in the USA. The Fredricksen-designed Tiger had a 241cc two-stroke engine.

TIKA / *Germany 1921–1924*
Assembled machines with 145cc and 197cc Herko sv engines.

TILBROOK / *Australia 1950–1953*
Designed by Rex Tilbrook, these Villiers-engined 123cc and 198cc two-strokes were of advanced design, but failed to stay in the trade. A 123cc racing model was successful in Australian road events.

TILSTON / *England 1919*
Short-lived producer, whose machines had 225cc Precision two-stroke engines.

TITAN / *Austria 1927–1933*
The first product of this factory was the 144cc two-stroke, two-cylinder Austro-Motorette; the second design by Karl Schüber was the 346cc two-stroke Titan. This was probably the first commercially built two-stroke engine with the incoming mixture controlled by membranes. The aircooled engine had 75mm bore and 77mm stroke and 10 hp. Another model had first the 490cc sv JAP and later a Blackburne sv engine.

346cc Titan (TS Model Touring) 1928

TITAN / *San Marino 1975–*
Moto-cross machines with 49cc two-stroke engines built in the smallest European republic by a small factory.

TIZ-AM / *Russia 1931–1940*
Heavy 596cc single-cylinder sv machines built at the Taganrog factory.

TM / *Italy 1968–*
Makers of moto-cross and trials machines with 50cc and 125cc proprietary engines, usually water-cooled. In 1987, they offerred an 80cc road racer with disc valve induction and six-speed gearbox.

TOHATSU / *Japan 1935–1966*
Was one of the leading Japanese motorcycle factories. Built two-strokes from 48cc to 248cc with rotary valves, including very fast 124cc two-cylinder racing versions.

TOMASELLI / *Italy 1931–1939*
Assembled sporting motorcycles with 173cc to 490cc sv and ohv JAP engines. The production was small.

TOMMASI / *Italy 1926–1927*
Produced 123cc and 246cc two-stroke machines with engines supplied by Della Ferrera. The bigger model had two 123cc power units coupled.

TOMOS / *Yugoslavia 1956–*
Leading motorcycle factory in Yugoslavia, which concentrated for many years on a variety of 49cc machines including mofas, mopeds and other lightweights. There were also racing machines. Bigger machines were added more recently, among them modern 87cc and 174cc single-cylinder versions with 18 bhp at 7000 rpm and sports models with 22 bhp at 8200 rpm. There is now also a branch factory at Epe in The Netherlands.

TOREADOR / *England 1924–1926*
Closely connected with Granville Bradshaw, designer of the oilcooled Bradshaw engines, Bert Houlding's factory produced not only 348cc ohv models, but also the rare 348cc Bradshaw ohc version, of which only very few were actually built. The Toreador range included models with 346cc and 490cc JAP and 496cc MAG ohv engines.

346cc Toreador (ohv oilcooled Bradshaw engine) 1926

TORNAX / *Germany 1925–1955, 1982–84*
Superbly built motorcycles with a variety of proprietary engines. These included JAP sv and ohv engines from 346cc to 996cc, Columbus vertical twin-cylinder 598cc and 798cc ohc engines and also 496cc and 596cc single-cylinder ohv versions made by the same factory. After 1945, Tornax production concentrated on two-stroke machines up to 248cc with mainly Ilo engines. A few 247cc models with the Küchen-designed Opti vertical twin-cylinder ohc engine were built as well. Tornax produced in the mid-1930s a nice sports car with the DKW two-stroke engine and built also many racing machines; the last one was a 124cc ohc single in 1952 which had a Küchen-designed engine.

The Tornax name was revived in 1982 by a com-

pany in Frankfurt who used it on a range of small Franco Morini engined lightweights, but the revival was short lived.

548cc Tornax (sv JAP engine) 1927

596cc Tornax ohv Columbus engine Model Superior) 1934

80cc Tornax (TS RX-80, Morini engine) 1982

TORPADO / *Italy 1950–*
Lightweight machines with 38cc Mosquito and 48cc and 74cc Minarelli two-stroke engines.

TORPEDO / *Czechoslovakia 1903–1912*
When Czechoslovakia was still part of the Austro-Hungarian Empire, the Torpedo was one of the best machines. Designed by František Trojan, it was built entirely at the Kolin factory. Not only the ioe engines but even carburettors were made there. Single-cylinder Torpedo engines had 3·5 hp and 4 hp, V-twin versions 6 hp and 8 hp.

TORPEDO / *Germany 1901–1907*
Assembled motorcycles with single-cylinder and V-twin Zedel and Fafnir engines.

TORPEDO / *England 1910–1920*
Another Torpedo bicycle factory which built strong frames with 294cc, 346cc and 499cc single-cylinder and V-twin Precision engines.

TORPEDO / *Germany 1928–1956*
Well-known bicycle factory which concentrated on 198cc machines with Blackburne sv engines and later with mainly Sachs and Ilo two-strokes.

TORROT / *Spain 1960—*
Originally an offshoot of the French Terrot company one of the few surviving small Spanish factories, who make motorcycles, mopeds and trail bikes with 50cc Sachs engines.

TOWNEND / *England 1901–1904*
Pioneer who fitted 2 hp and 2·5 hp engines into heavy bicycle frames.

TOYOMOTOR / *Japan 1957–early 1960s*
Built 246cc two-stroke twins, which had much in common with German Adler motorcycles.

TRAFALGAR / *England 1902–1905*
Pioneer motorcycle producer, who used MMC and Minerva engines and was also involved in the manufacture of wicker sidecars.

TRAFFORD / *England 1919–1922*
Assembled on a small scale motorcycles with 269cc Villiers engines.

TRAGATSCH / *Czechoslovakia 1946–1949*
This racing shop, owned by the author of this book, built track-racing machines with 348cc and 498cc JAP ohv engines. Long-track versions had a rear suspension which could be regulated to give various degrees of movement. Top rider: Hugo Rosak.

TRAIN / *France 1913–1939*
Was for many years a supplier of engines to other factories, many of which found their way to Italy, where the 173cc two-stroke versions became especially popular. Complete Train machines had two-strokes from 98cc to 346cc and sv and ohv engines from 246cc to 995cc. Among them were 746cc and 995cc V-twins. Also a 124cc racing two-stroke was built and most versions were available with watercooling.

346cc Train (ohv) 1931

The twin-carburettor racing engine had 6 hp at 5000 rpm and a top speed of 63 mph. 1930 saw the introduction of a 496cc four-in-line ohc engine which had shaft drive and — like most Train models at that period — a unit design.

TRANS-AMA / *Italy 1979–*
Concentrates on moto-cross and trial machines with two-stroke engines of 49·6, 80, 124·8, 244 and 321·5cc capacity.

TREBLOC / *England 1922–1925*
Lightweight machines with own 63cc engines.

TREMO / *Germany 1925–1928*
Singles with their own 308cc sv and ohv unit-design engines. Production on a limited scale.

TRENT / *England 1902–c1906*
Produced strengthened bicycles with 207cc power units.

TRESPEDI / *Italy 1926–1930*
Built good 173cc and 246cc two-stroke machines with their own engines, which were of the three-port deflector-type.

TRIANON / *Germany 1922–1926*
Bicycle producer who built only one motorcycle model, with their own 232cc two-stroke engines.

TRIBUNE / *America 1903–WWI*
As far as we know these machines had Aster and later Thor engines.

TRIPLE-H / *England 1921–1923*
The name came from the three founders of this make: Hobbis, Hobbis and Horrell. The machine was a simple 246cc two-stroke with a John Morris engine.

TRIPLETTE / *England 1923–1925*
Made at a low price, the Triplette was a simple machine with a 147cc Villiers motor.

TRIPOL / *Czechoslovakia 1925–1926*
Bicycle factory which built 246cc two-stroke Villiers-engined machines in limited numbers.

TRIUMPH / *America 1912*
There was a small branch Triumph factory at Detroit, where they built machines with parts from the 548cc sv single. After WWII, Triumph had HQs at Baltimore and Pasadena.

TRIUMPH / *England 1902—*
German immigrants Siegried Bettmann and Maurice Schulte started building bicycles in Coventry in 1887, in 1902 they fitted a Minerva engine into one and a new make of motorcycle was born. Improved Minerva, Fafnir and JAP engined models followed, but in 1905 Charles Hathaway was engaged to design a new 300cc side-valve engine to be manufactured by Triumph themselves. Hathaway also designed front forks with a peculiar fore-and-aft movement, which were used by Triumph for many years. Production rose to 500 machines in 1906; in 1907 the engine capacity was raised to 450cc and then to 475cc.

Success followed quickly. Jack Marshall was second in the first TT in 1907 and won the second in 1908. These results, plus the addition of a 'free engine' clutch in the rear hub, meant sales of 3000 Triumphs in 1909. For 1910, engine capacity was raised further to a full 500cc. In 1913, the Baby Tri-

499cc Triumph (ohv four-valve Model Ricardo) 1923

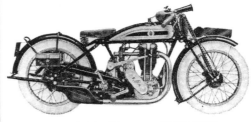

496cc Triumph (ohv Horsmann T.T.) 1927

148cc Triumph (ohv) 1935

246cc Triumph (ohv Model Tiger 70) 1938

497cc Triumph (ohv twin, Model 'Grand Prix') 1947

497cc Triumph (ohv twin, Model 'Tiger Daytona Sports') 1964

umph, a 225cc two-stroke, was introduced, while late in 1914 came the 550cc sv model H, with three-speed Sturmey Archer gearbox and chain and belt drive. Over 30,000 of these were supplied to the British Army between 1914 and 1918. In 1920 the model H became the SD (Spring Drive), with all chain transmission, while 1921 saw a new ohv model, the four-valve Ricardo. This was conceived as a racing machine, but was more successful as a sports model for the road.

Maurice Schulte left in 1922 to be succeeded by Colonel Claude Holbrook, who steered the company into car manufacture — not, as it turned out, the wisest of moves. The little two-stroke was enlarged to 250cc and given a kickstarter and clutch, but was killed off in 1925 to make room for production of the sensationally successful Model P, which at less than £43 was the cheapest-ever 500cc motor cycle in the world. Production of the P was soon up to 1000 per week.

The demands of the car programme and depressed trading conditions after 1930 meant stagnation in the motorcycle side of the business. Even the arrival of designer Vale Page in 1932 — he was responsible for the 650cc 6/1 vertical twin of 1933 and new 250cc, 350cc and 500cc ohv singles — could not arrest Triumph's decline. In 1936, entrepreneur Jack Sangster bought the Triumph motorcycle side for a song and installed Edward Turner as general manager. Turner, an all round genius if there ever was one, first redesigned and restyled the range of ohv singles as the Tiger 70, 80 and 90, which were soon best sellers. He then produced the 500cc Triumph Speed Twin (and the later Tiger 100), which broke new ground and inspired nearly 50 years of development of a basic theme.

It was Turner's conviction that the Speed Twin would sell in the USA but he had to wait until th eend of WWII to vindicate his belief. In 1949, US sales escalated with the 650cc Thunderbird, while, for those looking for smaller models, there were 350cc and 500cc twins, plus the single-cylinder 150cc Terrier, which developed into the long-running 200cc Tiger cub.

In 1951 Sangster sold Triumph to BSA, but both companies retained their automony until Turner's retirement in 1964. Unfortunately, both BSA and Triumph were thereafter managed by men from outside the industry who, by and large, showed a lamentable ignorance of its peculiar problems. Even brilliant designs, such as the 750cc in line three-cylinder model manufactured with slight styling differences, as both the Triumph Trident and the BSA Rocket Three, could not save BSA at a time when the competition in the USA from the Japanese motorcycle industry was at its sharpest. A series of appalling blunders led BSA into bankruptcy in 1973. A rescue operation of Triumph by Dennis Poore's Norton Villiers group was mounted with government aid, but the plan did not work, and resulted in a sit-in at the Meridan Triumph factory and the formation of a 'workers' co-operative.

This ill-conceived and ill-managed venture absorbed millions of tax-payers' money, only to founder finally in 1983.

All interests in Triumph were purchased by successful builder and entrepreneur John Bloor, who licensed production of the 750cc T140 Bonneville to Racing Spares' Les Harris. After considerable preparation, production began in 1985 at Newton Abbot, Devon, but, despite a motorcycle that was vastly improved in detail and quality control, the firm lasted only until March 1988. Meanwhile at a purpose-built factory at Hinckley, Bloor invested millions in the design, tooling, testing and manufacture of a new generation of Triumph motor cycles. These were revealed at the Cologne Show at the end of 1990 under the names Daytona, Trophy and Trident — but there was nothing at all traditional about these 750cc three- and 1000cc four-cylinder water-cooled models. They were in every respect worthy products of the 1990s with performance to match. It remains to be seen whether as many fervently hope, Triumph has now been re-established as a viable motorcycle concern.

749cc Triumph (in-line three-cylinder dohc) Daytona 1991.

740cc Triumph (ohv trans. three Trophy) 1974

646 Triumph (ohv twin Trophy TR6) 1964

TRIUMPH (ORIAL-TWN)/*Germany 1903–57*
Built for a long period nearly identical machines to English Triumph, including a 269cc, afterwards 248cc Baby-type two-stroke, called 'Knirps'. After the break with Triumph in Coventry, the German factory used their own

885cc Triumph (in-line three cylinder dohc) Trophy 1991.

TROPFEN/*Germany 1923–1924*
An airship firm which built very unorthodox 248cc and 308cc two-stroke motorcycles. Everything—engine, frame, wheels and all—was enclosed in an airship-shaped shell. The whole thing was so unusual that nobody bought it.

TRUMP (TRUMP-JAP)/*England 1906–1923*
Two leading racing men, F. A. McNab and Colonel Stewart, were among the owners of this ambitious factory, which built a couple of very fast racing machines. Together with Mrs. Stewart —who eventually became the famous Gwenda Hawkes of racing car fame—they broke many records. Trump motorcycles were not only built with 248cc to 996cc JAP engines, but also with 269cc Peco two-strokes and the big 996cc V-twin ohv engine made by British Anzani.

TSUBASA/*Japan 1950s*
Built a range of 246cc machines with their own ohv engines.

TUK/*Germany 1921–1922*
Narrow-angle 397cc sv V-twins with comparatively short and high single-loop frames, built by a small company.

TÜRKHEIMER/*Italy 1902–1905*
The designer, a leading Milan-based motorcycle importer who imported the first Hildebrand & Wolfmüller motorcycles into Italy in 1896, fitted 1·25 hp engines into his own machines.

TWM/*Italy 1979–*
This producer concentrates on competition machines, especially trial and moto-cross versions with 123, 173 and 244cc engines.

TX/*Germany 1924–1926*
One of the most unorthodox machines ever built, the TX had a tube of wide diameter which acted as a tank and replaced the steering head too. The tank cap was in front of the steering and the front fork, which had a leaf spring, was made from pressed steel. The 132cc and 174cc two-stroke Bekamo-licence engines had forced induction by using a second piston as a pump in the bottom of the crankcase. A few 248cc ohc racing machines with Roconova engines were also built. Designer was Kurt Pohle.

TYLER/*England 1913–1923*
Built lightweight motorcycles with 198cc Precision, 269cc Villiers and also with own 269cc two-stroke engines.

TYPHOON/*Sweden 1949–1951*
Designed by the famous Folke Mannerstedt, this machine was a 198cc two-stroke of advanced design.

TYPHOON/*The Netherlands 1955–early 1960s*
Well-known manufacturer of mofas, mopeds etc. with 49cc two-stroke engines.

U

UDE / *Germany 1924–1925*
A small producer of a 249cc two-stroke machine with a deflector-type three-port engine.

ULTIMA / *France 1908–1958*
Built a range of machines with Zurcher, Aubier-Dunne, JAP and other engines. Among them were 248cc and 348cc single-cylinder and 498cc V-twin sv machines. After WWII, the factory concentrated on two-strokes up to 198cc, among which was a very successful 124cc model with a horizontal cylinder. Ultima built new 498cc twin-cylinder double-ohc racing machines with horizontally-mounted cylinders in 1951, but the promising design was never fully developed.

UNIBUS / *England 1920–1922*
The Boultbee-designed Unibus was one of the best scooters made after WWI. It had a 269cc two-stroke engine and 16 inch × 2·5 inch tyres. With the exception of the handlebar, everything was fully enclosed. The pressed steel chassis was made on car lines and leaf suspension was used.

UNION / *Sweden 1943–1952*
Sporting single-cylinder machines with 348cc and 498cc JAP ohv engines.

UNIVERSAL / *Switzerland 1928–1964*
Famous factory which produced Helvetia motorcycles with 170cc PA engines before they built Universal machines. These had a variety of proprietary engines including JAP, Python, Anzani, Ilo and others with capacities up to 998cc. Among them were racing versions with big V-twin JAP ohv engines of 55 bhp and Python-engined 248cc racing machines. V-twins with their own 676cc and 990cc sv engines were made for the Swiss Army. The outstanding model after the war was a 578cc flat-twin with the ohv engine transverse-mounted and with shaft drive to the rear wheel. The engine was of Universal's own design and manufacture. The same was true of a 248cc ohv single, which came on the market in 1956. Like the bigger twin, it too had a unit-design engine and shaft drive. A licence was sold to the German Rabeneick factory, but this factory never went into quantity production. Famous riders such as Kirsch, Franconi, Alfter, Bianchi, and H. Taveri raced the machines between the wars.

UNIVERSELLE (UNIVERSAL) / *Germany 1925–1929*
Designed by Erich Landgrebe and made by a cigarette machine factory, the little ioe four-stroke machines originally had 183cc unit-design engines with big outside flywheels. Improved versions with 197cc and 247cc followed. Universelle built also delivery three-wheelers.

URAL / *Russia 1979–*
This is the export version of the 650cc Dnjepr transverse-mounted ohv flat-twin sidecar machine. Basically a BMW-like design, the M 66 Ural develops 32 bhp at 4500 rpm.

678cc Universal (ohv transverse flat-twin, shaft-drive) 1955

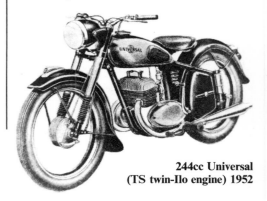
244cc Universal (TS twin-Ilo engine) 1952

996cc Universal (ohv V-twin JAP) 1937

URANIA / *Germany 1934–1939*
Assembled 98cc and 123cc two-stroke machines with Sachs and Ilo engines.

UT / *Germany 1922–1959*
Built on English lines, UT motorcycles were assembled machines with Bekamo, Blackburne, JAP, Küchen and Bark engines in pre-war days, while Sachs and Ilo engines played the most important part after 1945. The first 247cc two-strokes built in the mid-1920s had flat single-cylinder engines and triangular frames; the biggest models had 598cc single-cylinder JAP and Blackburne ohv engines. The two-strokes which were built after the war had 122cc, 173cc, 197cc and 244cc engines. The last one was a vertical twin with an Ilo engine. Some 246cc twins with the Küchen-designed Opti ohc engine were also built. The factory had a successful racing department in the 1920s with Frenzen, Kohfink, Blind and other good riders.

UTILIA / *France 1929–1936*
Was a well-known producer of two-strokes from 98cc to 498cc and of sv and ohv machines with JAP, LMP and Chaise engines. The two-stroke engines came from the Sachs, Duten and Train factories; some were also built by Utilia.

VAGA / *Italy 1925–1935*
Produced 124cc two-strokes, afterwards 174cc machines with JAP and Blackburne sv and ohv as well as CF ohc engines. The last models, 348cc ohv versions, had Sturmey-Archer engines.

VAL / *England 1913–1914*
Sidecar producer which built JAP-engined 488cc sv machines in limited quantities.

VALENTI / *Italy 1979–*
A company making moto-cross and enduro models, with 125cc and 250cc proprietary two-stroke engines.

VALIANT / *America late 1960s*
Produced Simplex lightweight machines with modified 124cc Clinton lawn-mower engines.

VAN VEEN / *Germany 1978–1981*
The Dutch Van Veen OCR 1000, built in a German factory, was a 498cc 100 bhp Wankel-engined, water/oilcooled luxury motorcycle, built with the French-licence motor in limited numbers. Van Veen also built the successful 49cc Kreidler-Van Veen racing machines.

VAP / *France early 1950s to early 1960s*
VAP was a mass-producer of 49cc mopeds, mofas etc. and was closely connected with Alcyon, Rhonson, Lucer and other factories.

VAREL / *Germany 1952–1953*
Mopeds and miniscooters with own 43cc engines and scooters with 99cc Mota two-stroke engines.

VASCO / *England 1921–1923*
Only a single model was made by this small factory. It had 261cc Orbit engines; when Orbit went out of business, Vasco switched over to 349cc Broler engines. Both were single-cylinder two-strokes.

VASSENA / *Italy 1926–1929*
Designed by Pietro Vassena, these machines had 124cc two-stroke engines with a horizontal cylinder.

VATERLAND / *Germany 1933–1939*
A bicycle factory which built lightweight machines with 98cc and 120cc Sachs engines and closed just before the outbreak of war.

VECCHIETTI / *Italy 1954–1957*
Moped producer who used 49cc two-stroke engines made by Victoria in Germany.

VELAMOS / *Czechoslovakia 1927–1930*
Like the Sirocco, the Velamos was made by Gustav Heinz. While the Sirocco had Villiers engines, the Velamos had its own two-stroke engines with 246cc, 346cc and 496cc. All were singles with three ports and deflector-type pistons. In races they were ridden by Kliwar, Zwesper and Heinz. Velamos still exists as a nationalised bicycle factory.

VELOCETTE / *England 1904—1968*
Two brothers, Percy and Eugene Goodman made several earlier forays into motorcycle design and construction before Velocette was established, with Percy Goodman's neat and advanced 206cc two-stroke of 1913. Sales were brisk, and even better post-war with 220cc, followed by 250cc,

models. Velocette two-strokes did well in trials, speed hill climbs and even the TT. However, the firm's fortunes were really established by Percy Goodman's 350cc ohc model K of 1925. A poor showing in that year's TT led to a redesigned engine and a win by Alex Bennett in 1926. It was the first of six victories, and guaranteed a volume of orders that forced a move into larger premises. Harold Willis joined the company in 1927 as rider and development engineer, contributing the positive stop foot change and experimenting with rear springing and supercharging. Before his untimely death in 1939, he designed the remarkable blown 'Roarer' twin.

Riders of KTT production racers won five Manx Grand Prix between 1929 and 1938 and in 1930 filled the first six places! The 1939 KTT was given swinging-arm rear suspension, such as had been used on the factory bikes since 1936. Stanley Woods won the 1938 and 1939 Junior TTs and was second in the 1937 and 1938 Senior races.

249cc Velocette (TS) 1924

348cc Velocette (Mk. 8, KTT Racing ohc) 1950

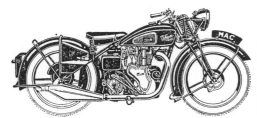

349cc Velocette (hc Model 'MAC') 1935

348cc Velocette (ohc Model 'KTS') 1936

348cc Velocette (ohc Model 'KTT' racer) 1929

Road-going KTS and KSS ohc models sold well in the 1930s, and there was a 250cc two stroke in the range until 1939. Popular, too, were the push rod 'high camshaft' series, the 250cc MOV and 350cc MAC of 1933 and the 500cc MSS of 1935.

Post war, Velocette won the 1949 and 1950 350cc world championships, made a few VIII KTTs and sold the KSS until 1947. Their main gamble, however, was on the remarkable LE model, with its water-cooled transverse horizontally-opposed twin-cylinder 150cc (later 192cc) side-valve engine, shaft drive and wonderfully clean pressed steel chassis-cum-bodywork. Unfortunately, it never sold in large enough numbers, though it was popular with the police, being superbly reliable and so silent as to be ideal for patrol duties. Variants were the fibre glass bodied Vogue and the 200cc ohv air-cooled Valiant, a sporting model with a conventional tubular frame, but these, too, were badly received. These disappointments stimulated development of the push-rod models, which, much modernised, became the 350cc Viper and 500cc Venom, also sold as Clubman production racing versions.

In 1961 a Venom Clubman, with an Avon fairing and megaphone exhaust but otherwise standard, averaged 100.05mph at the Montlhery track in France for 24 hours. The attempt was sponsored by the French Velocette importer and involved four French and four British riders. Viper and Venom Clubman racers did very well in production racing in the 1950s and 1960s, selling to the sort of rider who for a couple of generations had bought the KTS model for the road. The ultimate development was the Thruxton Velocette Venom of 1964, equally at home on road or race-track, and of stunning appearance — and performance. But several bad decisions, including the manufacture of a truly awful scooter with a flat twin two-stroke engine and shaft drive, weakened the fragile company and the relatively small sales of the Thruxton could not starve off inevitable liquidation in 1968.

149cc Velocette (sv transverse watercooled flat-twin) 1948

VELOX/*Czechoslovakia 1923–1926*
Designed by racing motorcyclist Hynek Vohanka, Velox lightweights had 147cc Villiers and afterwards 123cc and 174cc Bekamo two-stroke engines.

VELOSOLEX / *France 1945—1991*
A 50cc moped with friction drive to the front wheel. Probably the largest production ever of a single model.

VENUS / *England 1920–1922*
Was one of the many machines built during the early 1920s in England. Only a single model with the 318cc Dalm engine was in production.

VENUS/*Germany 1920–1922*
Scooter with 98cc, 147cc and 174cc Sachs engines, made by a small factory.

VERGA/*Italy 1951–1954*
Small two-strokes with 73cc and frames with swinging-arm rear suspension.

VERLOR/*France 1930–1938*
Aubier-Dunne and Stainless-engined 98cc and 124cc two-stroke machines.

VEROS/*Italy 1922–1924*
Blackburne-engined 346cc sv and ohv machines built by Verus in England were renamed Veros when exported to racing motorcyclist Oreste Garanzini, who represented this make in Italy. One of the design differences was the fully enclosed rear chain on the Veros sv models.

346cc Veros (sv Blackburne engine) 1925

VERUS/*England 1919–1925*
Made by Wisemann in Birmingham, Verus motorcycles had their own 211cc and 269cc two-stroke engines and also 246cc to 996cc four-strokes made by Blackburne and JAP. Wisemann built also Sirrah and Weaver motorcycles.

VESPA/*Italy 1946–*
Piaggio, producer of the famous Vespa scooters, still supplies 121cc, 145cc and 198cc versions and also produced earlier models with other power units. The factory, which took over the Gilera works at Arcore in 1970, produces also a variety of 49cc mopeds and similar lightweights.

VESUV/*Germany 1924–1926*
A small make. Had an open frame and its own 246cc two-stroke engine.

VIATKA/*Russia 1958–*
Leading scooter in the USSR. The engine is a 148cc two-stroke.

VIBERTI/*Italy 1955–late 1960s*
Built Victoria-engined 47cc mofas, mopeds and similar machines. Motorcycles made by this factory had 123cc ohv engines.

VICTA/*England 1912–1913*
Built 499cc single-cylinder motorcycles with Precision proprietary engines.

VICTORIA/*Scotland 1902–1926*
The Victoria motorcycle for many years was Scotland's leading make, being built at Glasgow (Dennistoun) and never in England. Typically English was the whole design and most of the components. Villiers, JAP, Blackburne and Coventry-Victor engines from 127cc to 688cc were mounted in Scottish frames, which were of excellent quality. There was never a connection between this factory and the German-built motorcycles of the same name.

VICTORIA/*Germany 1899–1966*
Founded in 1886 by Max Frankenburger and Max Ottenstein as a bicycle factory, Victoria built their first motorcycles 13 years later and fitted Zedel and Fafnir engines into their frames. After WWI, production concentrated on 493cc machines with two horizontally opposed cylinders in the popular sv proprietary engine built by BMW. When the Munich factory decided to produce complete motorcycles, Victoria of Nuremberg engaged the former BMW designer Martin Stolle, who designed new ohv engines which were built for Victoria at the Sedlbauer factory at Munich. After a while Victoria bought the engine factory and continued building ohv 498cc and afterwards 598cc ohv flat-twins. Successor to Stolle after 1924 was Gustav Steinlein, who designed in 1925 the first supercharged racing machines with 498cc flat-twin engines in Germany, which in 1926 broke the German speed record with nearly 104 mph. New single-cylinder models were introduced in 1928. The engines were of Sturmey-Archer manufacture and had from 198cc to 499cc; a 348cc ohv version was built by Horex (Columbus) under Sturmey-Archer licence for Victoria. Racing versions of this and 499cc machines as well as 598cc flat-twins were officially raced by the

346cc Victoria (ohv transverse V-twin, shaft-drive) 1955 (D)

works, where they had excellent riders with Kurt Füglein, Othmar Mühlbacher, Josef Möritz, Adolf Brudes, Hans Escoffier, Albert Richter, Josef Alt, H. P. Müller, Karl Bodmer, Eugen Grohmann, Georg Dotterweich and others. Among models built during the 1930s were two-strokes from 98cc to 198cc and new Stolle-designed 497cc vertical ioe and ohv twins with triangular pressed steel frames and completely enclosed unit-design engines. Richard Küchen and Albert Roder were Victoria designers in the 1930s. After 1945 production concentrated first on two-strokes from 38cc—a bicycle attachment—to 248cc. The first new four-stroke came into production in 1953. Also designed by Küchen, it had a transverse-mounted 348cc ohv V-twin unit-design engine with shaft drive to the rear wheel, telescopic fork and plunger-type rear suspension. New also were scooters, 38cc and 48cc mopeds, and the 198cc Swing, a very modern motorcycle with the engine and rear wheel on a swinging arm. Designed by Norbert Riedel, it was costly to produce. The last new model had a 173cc ohv engine, made by Parilla in Italy. Victoria supplied to the Italians in exchange small 49cc two-stroke moped motors. Soon afterwards the Zweirad-Union was founded and Victoria became part of it. While motorcycle manufacture stopped immediately, production of mopeds etc. under the Victoria trade mark continued for some time.

4½ hp Victoria (ioe Fafnir engine) 1904 (D)

493cc Victoria (sv flat-twin BMW engine) 1920 (D)

VICTORY / *Italy 1950–1955*
Produced lightweight machines with 98cc and 123cc Villiers engines.

VILLA / *Italy 1968*
Brothers Francesco and Walter Villa were famous road racers and two-stroke technicians, who worked and rode successfully for Montesa, Mondial and Aermacchi—Harley Davidson. Francesco Villa designed and made very successful 125cc road race machines in the 1970s, and also moto-cross and trail models of between 50cc and 250cc. Villa later concentrated on very advanced water-cooled moto-cross models.

VILLOF / *Spain 1951–early 1960s*
Produced motorcycles with Hispano Villiers two-strokes and own engines from 75cc to 123cc.

496cc Victoria (ohv flat-twin engine) 1923 (D)

496cc Victoria (ohv twin-cylinder Model 'KR 9') 1937 (D)

VINCENT (VINCENT-HRD) / *England 1928–1956*
Philip Vincent bought in 1928 the manufacturing rights of HRD, the make founded in 1924 by Howard R. Davies, the well-known racing motorcyclist. He continued using 346cc, 498cc and 598cc sv and ohv JAP engines, but equipped the new models with a rear suspension of his own design. Entirely new 497cc high-camshaft ohv engines of his own design and manufacture came into production in 1935 and machines with this engine were priced from £79.10s. to £98 for the TT Replica racing model. Late in 1936 appeared

the first 998cc Vincent with its V-twin high-camshaft engine, rear-wheel springing and twin brakes in each wheel. The cylinders were set at 47 degrees and were nearly identical to those used on the 497cc Meteor single. After the war, Vincent concentrated on improved versions of this big twin such as the Black Knight, the Black Prince and the very fast Black Lightning, a racing version of the 84mm bore × 90mm stroke 100 bhp engine, which broke many speed records in the hands of George Brown, Roland Free, René Milhoux and others. Free reached 156·71 mph with his special machine, running on alcohol fuel. In 1950 Vincent also brought back

996cc Vincent (hc V-twin Model 'Rapide') 1954

996cc Vincent (hc V-twin Model 'Black Knight') 1955

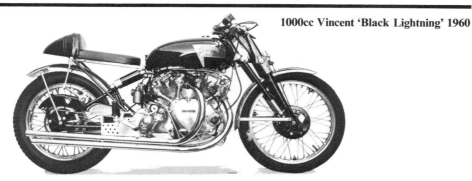

1000cc Vincent 'Black Lightning' 1960

499cc singles, which were almost the twins without the rear cylinder. A racing version, the Grey Flash, was built but did not win many road races. John Surtees rode them successfully. The 998cc twins won many races, including the Clubmans TT and among the riders were Phil Heath, Dennis Lashmar, Cliff Horn, Jock Daniels, Joe Davis and others. The last works riders competed in 1937 races. Phil Vincent's big twins had gained a world-wide reputation and there were times when demand was much bigger than supply. But they were expensive in production and when motorcycle sales went down in the late 1950s the situation became very difficult. The manufacture of the Firefly bicycle engine and co-operation with NSU of Germany could not put off the end of the Vincent.

VINCO / *England 1903–1905*
Small firm which built motorcycles with 211cc Minerva engines.

VINDEC / *England 1902–1929*
These machines were made by Brown Bros. Ltd., the famous supplier of parts and accessories. The range included 172cc and 224cc two-strokes and 490cc JAP-engined sv machines; the last model built had the 293cc JAP sv engine.

VINDEC-SPECIAL (VS) / *England 1903–1914*
Was really a machine built for the English market by Allright at Cologne in Germany and identical to Allright models in those far-off days. The South British Trading Co. in London was the importer. Most versions had V-twin engines, made by FN, Minerva, Fafnir etc. There were Truffault-designed swinging-arm front forks from 1905 onwards. After 1909 the machines were renamed VS to avoid confusion with the Brown brothers' Vindec motorcycles.

VIPER / *England 1919–1922*
Limited production of machines with 293cc sv JAP engines in open frames.

VIRATELLE / *France 1907–1924*
Built many models with proprietary engines, some of them unusual. The last one was a 686cc V-twin sv machine with a very long wheelbase.

VIS / *Germany 1923–1925*
Very interesting design. There was the comparatively orthodox 249cc two-stroke Vis-Simplex single with a forward inclined engine, but there was also the Vis-Duplex with a 496cc opposed twin-cylinder two-stroke engine, built in line

with the duplex cradle frame. This engine suffered from overheating of the rear cylinder and was built in limited numbers only.

VITTORIA / *Italy 1931–1972*
Carnielli's machines had 98cc Sachs, 173cc and 248cc JAP, 346cc and 496cc Küchen and 499cc four-valve Python ohv engines. Most models built since the war—including delivery three-wheelers—had two-stroke engines up to 98cc.

VOLLBLUT / *Germany 1925–1927*
Assembler of sporting motorcycles with 248cc and 348cc ohv Blackburne engines.

VOMO / *Germany 1922–1931*
Moped-like machines with 1 hp and 1·75 hp two-stroke engines.

VORAN / *Germany 1921–1924*
Yet another small motorcycle, a typical lightweight with a 143cc two-stroke deflector-type three-port motor.

174cc Voskhod (own TS engine) 1981

VOSKHOD / *Russia late 1940s–*
These are the mass-produced Russian 174cc two-strokes. Now with 10·5 bhp at 5500 rpm, they are of quite modern conception, having originally been very similar to DKW and Jawa designs.

VULCAAN / *The Netherlands 1911–1927*
Was closely connected with Zedel, the proprietary engine factory. Built 264cc and 299cc sv singles and also a range of sv V-twins, of which some were Vulcaan's own power units, probably built with some Zedel parts.

VULCAN / *Czechoslovakia 1904–1924*
See also Perun motorcycles, built by Zdarsky. The successor Ružička concentrated on the manufacture of spare parts after WWI.

VULCAN / *England 1922–1924*
Like other English firms, this one concentrated on 248cc two-strokes and on 293cc sv machines with JAP engines.

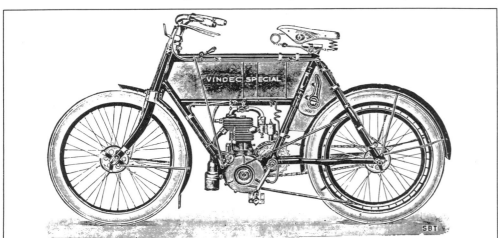

2¾ hp Vindec-Special (sv FN engine) 1903

W

WACKWITZ / *Germany 1920–1922*
These 108cc engines were bicycle attachments or complete with strengthened bicycle frames.

WADDINGTON / *England 1902–1906*
Single-cylinder motorcycles with a variety of engines which included Minerva and MMC.

WADDON-EHRLICH / *England 1981—1983*
Built Rotax-engined racing two-strokes, on one of which Irishman Con Law won the 1982 250cc TT at over 105mph. However, Dr Erhlich left later that year to make his own 250cc and 350cc Rotax-engined EMC racing machines.

248cc Waddon-Ehrlich (two-cylinder Rotax) 1981

WAG / *England 1924–1925*
One of the very few makes which produced 496cc V-twin machines with two-stroke engines. The actual production was limited.

WAGNER / *Czechoslovakia 1930–1935*
Offered motorcycles from 98cc to 499cc with two-stroke as well as sv, ohv and ohc engines.

WAGNER / *America 1901–1914*
One of the pioneers of the American motorcycle industry. This firm built 1·5, 2 and 2·5 hp machines equipped with own and Thor engines.

WAKEFIELD / *England c1902*
One of the factories fitting Minerva and MMC engines above the pedalling gear of bicycles.

WALBA / *Germany 1949–1952*
Ilo-engined scooters from 98cc to 173cc, designed by W. Baibaschewski.

WALLIS / *England 1925–1926*
Technically interesting 348cc and 498cc machines with hub-steering, not dissimilar to the Ner-a-car. The engines used were mainly JAP ohv engines. Wallis, a superb technician, was also the designer of Comerford-Wallis speedway frames.

346cc Wallis (ohv Blackburne engine) 1926

WALMET / *Germany 1924–1926*
Limited production of 246cc two-strokes with own engines and 346cc models with Kühne ohv power units.

WALTER / *Germany 1903–1942*
Assembler whose first machines had Fafnir engines. From the 1920s to the mid-1930s Villiers two-strokes from 172cc to 347cc were fitted into excellent frames of modern design. After 1935 production concentrated on mopeds with 98cc Sachs and Ilo engines.

WALTER / *Czechoslovakia 1923–1926*
The factory, still headed by Josef Walter, designed in 1917 a 746cc flat-twin machine. It never went into production when Josef Zubatý, the designer, left. The Itar factory took over manufacture after the war in 1922, when Walter director Plocek had a new 746cc on the drawing board. This was a transverse-mounted ohv V-twin machine and was built—like the Itar—mainly for the Czech army. The factory, now also building cars and aircraft engines, also produced a few enlarged 998cc racing machines, which proved very fast. Demand for cars and aircraft engines increased, and that was the end of the motorcycle manufacture at the Jinonice Walter factory. Successful Walter riders: Vašek Liška, Bohumil Turek, Stanislav Chaloupka, Jaroslav Knapp.

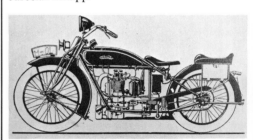

746cc Walter (ohv transverse V-twin) 1923 (CS)

WALTER / *Czechoslovakia 1900–1949*
Josef Walter built first-class single-cylinder and V-twin motorcycles with his own engines, afterwards also three-wheelers with modified motorcycle power units. In 1922 he left the Walter works and founded a new Walter factory for the manufacture of gears, sprockets etc. There he designed—in conjunction with his sons Jaroslav and Jan—new 496cc sv singles in 1926. In 1938 Jaroslav Walter created superb 248cc ohv racing engines and soon afterwards an even better ohc version, which after the war gained many racing successes on road and track. In 1947 a new 348cc ohc racing single was added which —together with the 248cc ohc engine—was taken over in 1949 by the big CZ factory, when Jaroslav Walter joined the Strakonice works. Successful Walter riders: Václav Hovorka, Jan

Lucak, Vojta Diviš, Jan Horak, Václav Stanislav, Eman Hajek, Jarda Kost, Peter Kopal, Lada Steiner and others.

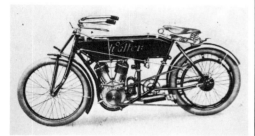

4½ hp Walter (sv V-twin Model 'B') 1906 (CS)

WANDERER / *Germany 1902–1929*
Was a well-known manufacturer of high-class motorcycles. Built 327cc and 387cc singles and 408cc and 616cc V-twins with own sv engines. Many of them were used by the Germans during WWI. After the war, Wanderer built a nice 184cc ohv single with a horizontal cylinder and a range of 708cc and 749cc ohv V-twins with unit-design engines, some with 8 valves. A new 498cc ohv single with unit-design engine, shaft drive and pressed steel frame, designed by Alexander Novikoff, was built in 1927. In 1929 this design, complete with all drawings and production equipment, was sold to Jawa at Prague, then a new company. That was practically the end of Wanderer motorcycle production, although they signed an agreement with NSU and produced during the 1930s motorised bicycles. Wanderer was a successful make in races during the 1920s. The top riders were Schuster, Urban, Kohlrausch, Ebert.

4½ hp Wanderer (sv V-twin) 1923

WARD / *England 1915–1916*
Two-strokes with 298cc engines. The war prevented production on a bigger scale.

WARDILL / *England 1924–1926*
Unorthodox two-stroke machines with a patented 346cc engine, which was not fully developed when it was put on the market.

WARRIOR / *England 1921–1923*
Concentrated on one model with the 247cc Villiers engine.

WASSELL / *England 1970–1975*
Built excellent 123cc trials and moto-cross machines with German Sachs two-stroke engines; the untimely death of W. E. Wassell led to the demise of motorcycle production by this well-known accessories factory.

WATNEY / *England 1922–1923*
Assembler who fitted 269cc Villiers, 293cc sv JAP and 346cc sv Blackburne engines.

WAVERLEY / *England 1921–1923*
Another assembler whose Harry Cox-designed motorcycles had 269cc Peco two-strokes and 346cc and 496cc Blackburne sv engines.

WD / *England 1911–1913*
Modern 496cc single-cylinder machines with own ioe power units.

WEARWELL / *England 1901–c1906*
One of the first factories producing motorcycles in England. The company also built Wolfruna and Wolf machines as well as frames for other factories and assemblers. The first engines used for Wearwell machines had 2·5 and 3·25 hp and were a product of the Stevens brothers.

WEATHERELL / *England 1922–1923*
Concentrated on sporting Blackburne-engined 349cc ohv machines, but also supplied 248cc versions and a machine with an ohv 676cc V-twin Blackburne engine.

WEAVER / *England 1922–1925*
The original model had a 142cc ohv single-cylinder engine, other versions used 147cc Villiers and AZA two-stroke engines.

WEBER-MAG / *Germany 1926–1927*
Assembled motorcycles with MAG engines of 346cc, 498cc and 746cc. All had ioe engines.

WEBER & REICHMANN / *Czechoslovakia 1923–1926*
Produced 142cc and 172cc machines with pressed steel frames under DKW licence. The engines were supplied directly by DKW.

WECOOB / *Germany 1925–1930*
Built a variety of motorcycles. With 142cc Rinne two-stroke engines, 172cc to 347cc Villiers motors and also 348cc to 996cc JAP power units. Despite the large number of models, actual production was small.

WEE McGREGOR / *England 1922–1925*
Made at Coventry Bicycles Ltd. by former Hobart employees, this was a 170cc two-stroke machine, with the engine capacity later increased to 202cc.

WEGRO / *Germany 1922–1923*
Very unorthodox — and not very good — Passow-designed 452cc vertical two-stroke twin with a very long wheelbase and disc wheels.

WEISS / *Germany 1925–1928*
Munich-built 198cc unit-design ohv machines with belt-drive to the rear wheel and two-speed gearboxes.

WELA / *Germany 1925–1927*
Assembled 348cc single with the Gnädig-designed Kühne ohv engine.

WELLER / *England 1902–1905*
Pioneer factory, which also produced cars. The motorcycles had their own 1·75 and 2·25 hp single-cylinder power units.

WELS / *Germany 1925–1926*
These machines had a BMW-like frame with 348cc Kühne ohv and 490cc JAP ohv engines fitted.

346cc Wels (ohv Kühne engine) 1925

WELT-RAD / *Germany 1901–1907*
A bicycle factory and motorcycle pioneer which fitted its own 3·5 hp single-cylinder and 6 hp V-twin engines into strong frames.

WERNER / *France 1897–1908*
The Werner brothers, Russians living in Paris, were important and innovative motorcycling pioneers. Their 1897 Motocyclette, with its engine over the front wheel, was the first popular motorcycle to be produced. In 1901, they moved the engine to a position ahead of the pedalling gear, such a machine won the Paris-Vienna race of 1901 and set a new fashion. In 1904 there was a side-by-side vertical twin engine. The Werners licensed

217cc Werner (sv) 1901

manufacturing rights to many other firms, including Britain's Harry Lawson. The company was still thriving when first one and then the other brother died and, without their enterprise, the company soon followed.

WERNER-MAG / *Austria 1928–1930*
Designed by Konstantin Leschan, Werner-MAG motorcycles used 498cc double-port single-cylinder ohv engines from the Swiss engine factory. Other models of 746cc and 996cc capacity had MAG ioe V-twin power units.

WERNO / *Germany 1921–1924*
The Werner Noel-designed ohv singles had their own 154cc and 197cc engines.

WESPE / *Austria 1937–1938*
Designed by Thos. G. Harbourn, who for many years imported English Triumph motorcycles into Austria, the 123cc Wespe had an unlucky life. Just when it entered quantity production, Hitler entered Austria, Nazi industrial dictatorship meant the end of a nice lightweight.

WESTFALIA / *Germany 1901–1906*
Zedel, De Dion and Fafnir supplied most of the 1·75 and 2·5 hp engines fitted to these early motorcycles.

WESTFIELD / *England c1903*
Assembler who fitted 2·75 hp MMC power-units.

WESTOVIAN / *England 1914–1916*
Had a big model range with TDC, Villiers, Precision and JAP engines from 197cc to 498cc.

WFM / *Poland 1947–*
Well-known make which concentrated on the production of well-designed 123cc, 147cc and 173cc two-strokes.

W&G / *England 1927–1928*
A transverse-mounted 490cc two-stroke twin with the cylinders facing slightly forward, not unlike the big DKW twin of that period. But while the DKW was a success, the W&G soon disappeared.

WHEATCROFT / *England 1924*
Was the successor to the New Era and had 318cc Dalm two-stroke and 546cc Blackburne sv engines.

WHIPPET / *England 1903–c1906*
This factory had many patents for engines and motorcycles and produced 1·75, 2·25, 2·5 and 3 hp machines. Early models used Aster and FN engines.

WHIPPET / *England 1920–1921*
Scooter of advanced design with 180cc ohv engines and 16-inch wheels.

WHIPPET / *England 1957–1959*
Unusual lightweight, which really was a combination scooter and moped. It had ohv engines of 49cc, 61cc and 64cc.

WHIRLWIND / *England 1901–1903*
Made by the Dorman Engineering Co., the factory which in 1925–1927 built Granville Bradshaw's 348cc oilboilers, ie oilcooled ohv proprietary engines. Among earlier products was a 1·5 hp bicycle engine and complete motorcycles with 2 and 2·5 hp.

WHITE & POPPE / *England 1902–1922*
Built V-twin motorcycles and in 1906 a 489cc

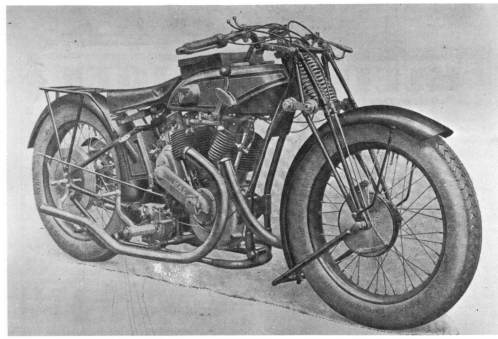

996cc Werner-MAG (ioe V-twin MAG) 1928

vertical twin, which was available with water-cooling too. The factory produced also proprietary engines for motorcycles and cars, which included at that time the 493cc Ariel engines and after 1918 a 347cc two-stroke.

WHITLEY / *England 1902–c1906*
Another manufacturer of proprietary engines, whose own motorcycles had 2·75 and 3·5 hp single-cylinder engines.

2¾ **hp Whitley (ioe) 1903**

WHITWOOD / *England 1934–1936*
Offered with 248cc, 348cc and 490cc ohv JAP engines, the OEC-built Whitwood-Monocar was a motorcycle with a car-like body; not unlike the Mauser Einspurauto of ten years earlier. It was an unusual vehicle which did not find many customers.

WHIZZER / *America 1947–1954*
Moped-like means of transport, of quite unusual appearance. The engine was a 199cc sv unit.

WIGA / *Germany 1928–1932*
Made by a small factory, the Wiga was of good design and while production stopped in the early 1930s, there was a prototype of a new JAP-engined model with rear suspension made in 1938. The range included Küchen and JAP-engined models of 198cc, 93cc, 348cc and 498cc. The ohc Küchen engines had three valves.

WIGAN-BARLOW / *England 1921*
Small production of motorcycles with 293cc sv JAP and 346cc Barr & Stroud sleeve-valve engines.

WIKRO / *Germany 1924–1926*
The first machines had 346cc Precision engines while newer versions were powered by 347cc and 497cc Blackburne sv engines.

WILBEE / *England 1902–c1906*
Advanced design with 2 hp Minerva engines and good frames made from BSA parts.

WILHELMINA / *The Netherlands 1903–1915*
A motorcycle importer, who built a range of machines in earlier years, but had the biggest output just before WWI with a 2·5 hp single-cylinder Precision-engined model.

WILIER / *Italy 1962–c1970*
Concentrated on 49cc mopeds and lightweight machines.

WILKIN / *England 1919–1923*
Was using 499cc sv Blackburne engines in spring frames, but had a small output only. A 346cc model with an identical frame was also built.

WILKINSON-ANTOINE / *England 1903–1906*
Built in England 2·25 and 2·75 hp machines with Belgian Antoine single-cylinder power-units.

WILKINSON / *England 1909–1916*
The Wilkinson Sword Company made the luxurious 680cc air-cooled in line four-cylinder TAC (Touring Autocycle), with separate gearbox and shaft drive, until 1911 and thereafter the 850cc (and later 1000cc) water-cooled TMC (Touring Motor Cycle). Early in 1914, Wilkinson sold their motorcycling interests to the Ogston Motor Co, who continued to make an improved TMC until 1916. The engine was later used in a light car, the Ogston Deemster.

844cc **Wilkinson-TMC (ioe aircooled four-cylinder) 1911**

WILLIAMS / *America 1912–1920*
Unusual design with a rotating single-cylinder engine built into the rear wheel.

WILLIAMSON / *England 1912–1920*
Excellent air and watercooled 996cc flat twins with opposing cylinders. The engines were made by Douglas exclusively for Williamson. Machines built after 1919 had 770cc V-twin sv JAP engines.

WILLOW / *England 1920*
Another early scooter which was not a success. The engine used was the 269cc Villiers two-stroke.

WIMMER / *Germany 1921–1939*
A still existing factory. Built during the years 134cc bicycle engines, then 137cc and 172cc single-cylinder ohv unit-design motorcycles with watercooling. The last ones proved very successful in races with such riders as Kolm, Kolmsperger, Gmelch and others. From 1928 onwards aircooled 198cc and 247cc models, afterwards also 299cc and 497cc versions were made. During the 1930s there was also a 346cc ohv trials version and a 198cc two-stroke, both with Bark engines. No Wimmer motorcycles were made after the war.

173cc **Wimmer (ohv watercooled) 1925**

247cc **Wimmer (ohv) 1931**

346cc **Wimmer (ohv Model GS) 1936**

WIN / *England 1908–1914*
Built a two-model range with 499cc and 599cc Precision single-cylinder sv engines.

WINCO / *England 1920–1922*
Assembled motorcycles with 261cc Orbit two-stroke engines.

WINDHOFF / *Germany 1924–1933*
Built radiators before entering motorcycle production with superb watercooled 122cc and 173cc two-strokes. These had Bekamo-type horizontal-cylinder engines with a second

297

scavenging) piston at the bottom of the crank-case. They were very successful in races. A sensational Windhoff appeared on the market in 1927: an oilcooled 746cc four-cylinder unit-design ohc engine as the centre of the whole machine. There was no real frame; everything was bolted onto the power unit. Shaft drive was another feature. A 996cc model built on similar lines was in prototype stage, but never built in quantities. Instead, a BMW-like 996cc Windhoff was built. It had a twin-cylinder sv engine trans-verse-mounted, shaft-drive and was, like the smaller Four, without a real frame. The last Windhoffs were the most conventional, using 198cc and 298cc Villiers-licence two-stroke engines. The Berlin-based factory also supplied these power units to other motorcycle manu-facturers. Successful Windhoff riders: Erich Tennigkeit, Walter Ebstein, Karl Wittig, Richard Scholz.

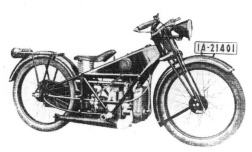

173cc Windhoff (TS watercooled Bekamo-Licence engine) 1926

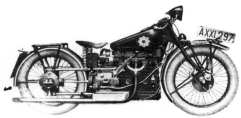

746cc Windhoff (ohc oilcooled four-cylinder engine) 1928

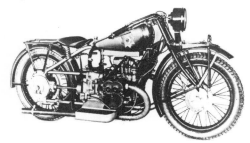

996cc Windhoff (sv transverse flat-twin, shaft-drive) 1929

WITTALL / *England 1919–1923*
Assembled machines with 269cc Villiers engines.

WITTEKIND / *Germany 1952–1954*
Moped producer who fitted 40cc Komet engines.

WITTLER / *Germany 1924–1953*
Produced during the 1920s a 249cc two-stroke machine with its own engine. After 1949 pro-duction of 49cc mopeds with Sachs and Zündapp engines was resumed and there was also a 124cc lightweight with the Sachs engine.

248cc Wittler (TS) 1925

WIZARD / *Wales 1920–1922*
Build in Wales, this machine had the Wall-designed 269cc Liberty two-stroke power-unit.

WK / *Germany 1920–1922*
This was a 249cc sv engine built into a wheel which could be attached to any bicycle.

WKB / *Austria 1923–1924*
Another bicycle engine. Designed by Hermann Medinger, it had 183cc and was a two-stroke three-port engine.

WMB / *Germany 1924–1926*
Lightweight machines with own 1·8 hp sv engines. Small production.

WOLF / *England 1901–1939*
Besides Wolf motorcycles also built the Wear-well and Wolfruna at the Wolverhampton works. In the early years Moto-Rêve engines were used; all Wolf machines had proprietary power units, among them Blackburne and JAP engines up to 678cc. From 1928, Villiers two-strokes up to 248cc were used including deflector-less flat-top versions of 123cc and 248cc.

247cc Wolf (TS Villiers engine) 1936

WOTAN / *Germany 1923–1925*
Like many others of that period, the Wotan was a simple 170cc two-stroke with a three-port engine.

WOOLER / *England 1911–1955*
John Wooler was a designer with many brilliant ideas and all his creations were very unconven-tional. His first 344cc two-stroke had a flat single cylinder and a double-ended piston, using the bottom part for pre-compression inside the crankcase. The machine had both wheels sprung by plunger suspension and was of advanced design throughout. Similar frames were used for 346cc and 496cc twins with horizontally opposed cylinders or over-head-valves on the *side* of the cylinder heads. A 611cc single, the only vertical engine known to be made by John Wooler, was built in 1926 as a prototype, but never in quan-tities. After WWII he built a variety of 498cc four-cylinder machines with opposing cylinders transverse-mounted, shaft drive, spring frames etc. These beautiful ohv machines were actually built in very small numbers for sale; the last one was priced at £292.4s1d.

346cc Wooler (sv flat-twin) 1921

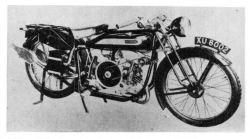

499cc Wooler (semi-ohv flat-twin) 1924

WSE / *Germany 1924–1925*
Small producer of 249cc sv machines, who also supplied the engines to other assemblers.

WSK / *Poland 1946–*
Leading Polish motorcycle factory. Produces modern 123cc and 173cc two-strokes of sporting appearance. A 240cc version was also built in the Swidnik works.

WSM / *Germany 1919–1923*
Built 496cc Stolle-designed flat twins with

opposing cylinders and with ohv for Victoria until that company bought the whole WSM (Sedlbauer) factory at Munich. Earlier machines had 493cc BMW-made flat twin sv engines, but the manufacture of complete Sedlbauer motorcycles was never on a large scale.

WUCO / *Germany 1925*
Lightweights with own 174cc sv engines. JAP-engined 248cc, 348cc and 490cc models were also made.

WURRING / *Germany 1921–1959*
Known for their excellent frames, Wurring motorcycles had a variety of proprietary engines. Among them were DKW, Villiers, Küchen, Kühne, Columbus, Bark, Sachs, Ilo and other makes with capacities from 142cc to 596cc. The last ones were 244cc Ilo vertical two-stroke twins. *See also* AWD.

Württembergia

WÜRTTEMBERGIA / *Germany 1925–1933*
Made by a big agricultural machine factory, these machines always had 198cc to 596cc sv and ohv engines made by Blackburne. Good design and workmanship.

W&W / *Austria 1925–1927*
The Josef Wild-designed machines had 498cc single-cylinder MAG ioe engines while 746cc and 996cc V-twins — also MAGs — could be supplied on order.

XY

XL / *England 1921–1923*
Strong machines with double loop frames and 490cc JAP and 538cc Blackburne single-cylinder sv engines.

XL-ALL / *England 1902–c1906*
Built 2 and 4hp V-twins with their own engines which — according to the producer could run on one cylinder if for any reason the second one fell out. Early models were lightweights and had the cylinders set at 90 degrees. The frames were of the loop bicycle type and had a long wheelbase.

X-TRA / *England 1920–1922*
This was really a three-wheeler with a 346cc single-cylinder Villiers engine. It had two front wheels and a body which was not unsimilar to a sidecar of the early 1920s.

YALE / *America 1902–1915*
Was a well-known machine in the USA; especially the big 950cc V-twin with two-speed gearbox and chain drive to the rear wheel. The price in 1915: $260.

YAMAGUCHI / *Japan 1941–1964*
Once a leading factory, Yamaguchi concentrated on a variety of 49cc models including mofas, mopeds etc. and also built 123cc two-strokes with vertical twin-cylinder engines. The range included trials machines. When the factory closed, Hodaka took over the works.

247cc Yamaha (TS Model DT) 1974

YAMAHA / *Japan 1954—*
Yamaha were — and still are — world-famous makers of musical instruments, hence their logo of three crossed tuning forks. Surplus capacity in the foundry that cast their piano frames led them into light engineering and motorcycle manufacture. The original Yamaha YA1 of 1954 was an improved copy of a 125cc DKW RT125 two-stroke, while the 250cc YD1 of 1957 was an equally improved copy of the Adler MB250 twin two-stroke. Both sold well, and special versions were raced in Japan.

In 1959 Yamaha introduced the tubular framed YDS1, a 250cc twin with five speed gearbox that was to be the basis for their development of 250cc and 350cc two-strokes for the next 20 odd years. Th next year, they set up two racing divisions, one for development of machines for private customers and the other for the factory's own Grand Prix entries. The customer TD series were comparatively ineffectual until the TD1C of 1967, which was enormously successful. Thereafter, especially with the water-cooled TR and TZ models, Yamaha achieved a total domination of the 250cc and 350cc classes. The Grand Prix models, which were successfully raced between 1960 and 1968, were the most effective two-strokes ever seen until that time, and raced on level terms in the 250cc class with Honda, and in the 125cc with Honda and Suzuki.

The bare statistics — five TT wins and seven second places, and five world championships and seven second places — scarcely conveys the influence exerted by Yamaha on motorcycle racing in the 1960s. More than any other manufacturer, they were responsible for the development of the modern racing two-stroke still being used today. Similarly, they undoubtedly led the world in the 1960s and 1970s in the quality and performance of two-stroke road machines of between 50cc and 350cc. Consequently, it was with some reluctance that they acknowledged in the early 1970s that US

981cc Yamaha (ohc V-twin TR-1) 1982

743cc Yamaha (ohc two-cylinder) 1974

552cc Yamaha (watercooled dohc V-twin XZ550) 1982

386cc Yamaha (XS400 ohc twin) 1982

anti-pollution laws forced the development of four-stroke engines. In fact, having taken the decision, Yamaha applied their efforts just as vigorously to development of the four-stroke as they had previously to the two-stroke. Starting with a 650cc twin in 1972, they rapidly developed a full range of four strokes, which included single-cylinder engines, twins, threes and, of course, fours, many of which had shaft-drive transmission. Gradually, the range of two-strokes was reduced in number; they are confined to the smaller capacities, though the super-sporting 350cc RD350 two-stroke is still available in Europe.

It would be fair to say that next to Honda, and sometimes ahead of them, Yamaha have been technically the most advanced of the Japanese motorcycle manufacturers. They offer a huge range of models from 50cc to 1200cc in every category conceivable — almost bewilderingly so — but, in fact, reflecting the fact that market needs vary considerably from country to country.

YOUNG / *England 1919–1923*
Made by the producers of Mohawk motorcycles, the Young was a 269cc bicycle engine, which could be mounted above the rear wheel. A new 130cc two-stroke version was introduced in 1923, but production of it went to the Waltham Engineering Co. Ltd.

YVEL / *France 1921–1924*
Lightweight machines of 174cc and 233cc with their own sv engines.

490cc York (sv JAP engine) 1929

ZANELLA / *Argentina 1958–late 1960s*

Built on Italian lines, the Zanella was a sporting two-stroke design, which used partly Italian components. The machines were of 49cc, 98cc and 123cc.

123cc Zanella (TS) 1963

ZEDEL / *France 1902–1915*

While the Swiss parent company Zürcher & Lüthi concentrated on the manufacture of proprietary engines, the French branch supplied complete machines with 2, 2·25, 2·5, 2·75, and 3·5 hp single-cylinder and V-twin engines.

ZEGEMO / *Germany 1924–1925*

When some partners of the Zetge factory left, they founded the Zegemo works. Designed by Hans Knipp, the Zegemo was a 248cc two-stroke with the rare Baumi engine.

ZEHNDER / *Switzerland 1923–1939*

The 110 Zehnder called Zehnderli, was a very popular lightweight. It had a two-stroke engine with a horizontal cylinder, not unlike the German Cockerell. Zehnder's racing versions had 123cc engines with watercooling. There were 148cc models and from 1929 onwards a 248cc two-stroke single with a vertical cylinder, which was also built as a sports model. In the early 1930s the factory was bought by Wilhelm Gutbrod,

owner of the German Standard motorcycle works, who continued the production of Zehnder machines in Switzerland. Otto Zehnder won many races in the 125cc and 250cc class. The quarter-litre racing models also had watercooled engines. Other leading riders were Graf, Wiedmer, and Liechti. After 1945 there were to be new Zehnder motorcycles; a design was ready for production when the designer, Robert Zehnder, died suddenly. Price for the complete 110cc 2·2 hp Zehnder in 1929: Fr. 885, in 1937: Fr. 700.

110cc Zehnder (TS flat-single) 1926

ZEHNER / *Germany 1924–1926*

The Zehner was a 197cc sv machine, designed by Otto Dehne. Made by a small manufacturer, comparatively few machines reached the market.

ZENIT / *Italy 1954–1956*

Assembled machines with French 123cc and 174cc AMC ohv engines.

ZENITH / *England 1904—1950*

Freddie Barnes established Zenith at Weybridge to build a strange machine with centre hub steering and Fafnir engine, known as Tooley's patent Bicar. This metamorphosised into the Zenette, which had a sprung sub frame, and from 1908, Barnes' patent Gradua infinitely variable gear. This used an engine pulley with flanges that moved in and out under control of a hand wheel, the belt tension being maintained by a linked mechanism that moved the rear wheel back and forwards in the frame. Applied to 500cc, 750cc and 1000cc JAP-

348cc Zenith (ohv JAP engine) 1929

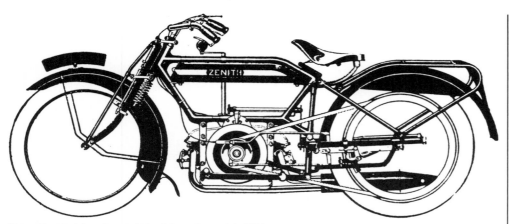

496cc Zenith (ohv oilcooled Bradshaw flat-twin) 1922

engined motor cycles of otherwise conventional construction, the system was enormously successful and gained Zenith a great reputation.

Post WWI, Zenith continued with the Gradua gear, until belt drive became discredited. Granville Bradshaw was briefly associated with Zenith after Sopwith's ABC company collapsed, introducing his flat twin 500cc oil-cooled engine in a 1922 Zenith model. However, later Zeniths were entirely orthodox machines, mainly using single-cylinder and V twin JAP engines and later small Villiers four-strokes. Zenith gained quite a reputation in the late 1920s for racing and record breaking successes with 1000cc JAP engines, but in late 1930 Barnes lost control and the company was sold to London dealer Writers. Limited production continued in the 1930s and even after WWII, but the great days were over. Using old stocks of JAP engines, Zenith lasted until 1950.

1096cc Zenith (sv V-twin JAP) 1936

ZEPHYR / England 1922–1923
Bicycle engines which were also available as complete lightweight machines. The two-stroke engine had 131cc and was of the deflector-type three-port variety.

ZETA / Italy 1948–1954
Very ordinary and primitive scooter-like vehicles with 48cc and 60cc proprietary engines, built by Cucciolo, Ducati and other producers of similar small power units. The Zeta had very small wheels.

ZETGE / Germany 1922–1925
Built well-designed two-strokes with 142cc and 173cc DKW engines as well as with 147cc to 173cc engines of Zetge (Gehlich) design and manufacture.

ZEUGNER / Germany 1903–1906
Pioneer assembler, who fitted Fafnir, Zedel, Minerva, FN, Peugeot and other proprietary engines.

ZEUS / Czechoslovakia 1902–1912
The Christian Linser-designed Zeus machines, actually made when Czechoslovakia was still part of the Austro-Hungarian Empire, were among the leading singles and V-twins built. The range included 3 and 3·5 hp singles and 4 and 4·5 hp V-twins. Zeus machines were also sold under the Linser trade mark.

ZEUS / Germany 1925–1927
Equipped with double-loop frames, German Zeus motorcycles had 348cc and 498cc Küchen three-valve ohc engines.

ZIEJANÜ / Germany 1924–1926
Built 211cc and 246cc two-strokes, while a 449cc single-cylinder two-stroke never went into production. Instead the factory assembled motorcycles with 348cc and 498cc sv and ohv JAP engines.

ZIRO / Germany 1919–1924
Designed by Albert Roder, who eventually became chief designer at the NSU works, the 148cc and 346cc Ziro were excellent two-strokes with a rotary valve in the crankcase. After Ziro closed down, Roder was with Ermag, Zündapp and Victoria before he eventually joined the firm of NSU.

ZUNDAPP / Germany 1921–1985
Zundapp, part of a giant engineering conglomerate, were at one time one of Europe's largest motorcycle manufacturers. Their involvement began in 1921, with a remarkably frank copy of the successful British 211cc Levis two-stroke, and continued in this vein until 1926, Levis models being copied in every detail without the least acknowledgement! Thereafter Zundapp began to produce two-strokes of their own design. In response to the depression of the early 1930s, the company called in Richard Kuchen, who designed a range of transverse horizontally opposed engines, gearboxes that used chains and sprockets, shaft drive and characteristic pressed steel frames. There were side-valve twins of 400cc and 500cc and a four-cylinder of 600cc, which were immediately successful.

Later development centred on the 597cc KS600 flat twin, while, from 1939 to 1945, the company's efforts were devoted to the production of the 750cc KS750 sidecar outfit with sidecar wheel drive and reverse gears. Post-war motorcycle production resumed in 1947, with a 200cc two-stroke. The KS600 was re-introduced, to be replaced in 1951 by the KS601 with a new ohv design. This was highly successful in the ISDT and similar events through the 1950s. Zundapp also introduced a clip-on engine for bicycles, the 50cc Combimot,

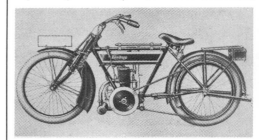

211cc Zündapp (TS Model Z22) 1921

249cc Zündapp (TS Model K 249) 1927

298cc Zündapp (TS Model Z 300) 1929

later to become a moped — the Combinette.

There were other larger two-strokes and, in 1953, the 150cc and later 200cc Bella scooter was introduced. It was to be one of Zundapp's most successful products, lasting until 1964 in various forms. However, though exports were still good in the 1950s, the German market was shrinking.

In the 1960s Zundapps of 50cc, 75cc and 100cc put up some remarkable performances in the ISDT

598cc Zündapp (ohv transverse flat-twin Model KS 601) 1950

and other important events, and production consisted of largely such smaller two-strokes. A 50cc Zundapp with streamlining, broke world's records at Monza in 1965 including the hour at over 101mph! Zundapp now moved increasingly towards 50cc Sports machines and mopeds, and entered the 1950s with only two capacities, 175cc and 50cc. Sales plunged disastrously, so a water-cooled 80cc sports model was introduced in 1981. Zundapp raced in the 80cc class, and won the world championship in 1983, 1984 and 1985, but such success did not save the company, which went into liquidation on the eve of the 1985 Cologne Show. In 1986, it was sold lock, stock and barrel to the People's Republic China.

123cc Zündapp (TS Model KS 125 Sport) 1971

78cc Zündapp (TS model K-80) 1982

797cc Zündapp (sv transverse flat-four) 1936

746cc Zündapp (ohv transverse flat-twin army Model KS 750) 1941

ZÜRTZ-REKORD / *Germany 1922–1926*
Interesting design with a wide top tube, which served also as tank. The Zürtz brothers used a variety of engines including 142cc and 173cc DKW two-strokes, the rare 198cc ohv Paqué and also the 249cc Columbus with ohv, as used by the first Horex. A small number had 346cc and 490cc sv and ohv JAP engines.

ZWEIRAD-UNION / *Germany 1958–1974*
Originally a combination of the DKW, Express and Victoria works with the HQ at the Nuremberg Victoria factory. Hercules was added in 1966 and eventually taken over by the big Fichtel & Sachs group of companies.

ZWERG / *Germany 1924–1925*
Lightweights with own 147cc and 187cc two-stroke deflector-type engines.

ZWI / *Israel 1952–1955*
Only motorcycle factory in Israel. Founded by former Hungarian racing rider Stefan Ausländer, it built exclusively 123cc two-stroke machines with JAP and Villiérs engines.

ZZR / *Poland 1960–*
Concentrates on the manufacture of 49cc two-stroke machines, which are being sold under the Komar trade mark.

THE SPEED RECORDS

THE FIRST official world speed record for motorcycles was established on April 14, 1920, at Daytona, by Ernie Walker, riding a 994cc Indian V-twin. The motorcycle was by then sufficiently reliable to achieve such feats, and new records were set regularly in the period up to the outbreak of the Second World War. The 1930s were great years. Bert le Vack set a speed record in 1929 on a Brough-Superior. But less than a month later, Ernst Henne of Germany set a new record on a 733cc BMW. This happened near Munich, and a fight began for the record, with Henne taking on all comers. Claude Temple had retired from competition, but continued designing. Joe Wright set a new record riding a Temple-OEC with a supercharged 996cc JAP V-twin in 1930 at Arpajon. Again, in less than a month, Henne and his BMW took the record back.

Next, Joe Wright's intention was to get the record back to England before the Olympia motorcycle show opened in November, 1930. He went to Cork, in Ireland, with the Temple-OEC and a Zenith with a nearly identical engine. His first run was so fast that the only photographer present left the scene in a hurry to dispatch the picture to his agency, but technical trouble prevented the return run, and another try on the Zenith was successful.

When the Olympia show opened, there on the OEC stand was a machine labelled 'the fastest motorcycle in the world'. There had been no photograph of the Zenith; OEC must have known that it had not been their machine which broke the record, but J. A. Prestwich (JAP) reasoned that the engines were almost identical anyway, and they had sponsored the attempt. OEC gave them better sales publicity, as the Zenith factory was having financial difficulties. It was a while before the controversy died down.

In 1932, 1934, 1935 and 1936 Henne broke his own records. Then Eric Fernihough, a lone Englishman who bought and tuned his own machines, broke the record in Hungary using a Brough-Superior frame and a 996cc supercharged JAP. Piero Taruffi held the record next, with a supercharged and watercooled Gilera four.

Eric Fernihough was killed in a 1938 attempt, when his machine went into a wobble at about 180 mph. There were no new record holders until 1951, when William Hertz reached 180 mph near

THE FASTEST MEN ON TWO WHEELS

Date:	Course:	Driver:	Motorcycle:	ccm:	(km/h)	mph)
1920	Daytona (USA)	Ernie Walker	Indian	994	167.670	104.12
1923	Brooklands (GB)	Claude Temple	British-Anzani	996	174.580	108.41
1924	Arpajon (F)	Bert Le Vack	Brough-Superior	998	191.590	118.98
1926	Arpajon (F)	Claude Temple	OEC-Temple	996	195.330	121.30
1928	Arpajon (F)	O. M. Baldwin	Zenith-JAP	996	200.560	124.55
1929	Arpajon (F)	Bert Le Vack	Brough-Superior	998	207.330	128.75
1930	Arpajon (F)	Joe Wright	OEC-Temple	994	220.990	137.23
1930	Ingolstadt (D)	Ernst Henne	BMW	735	221.540	137.58
1930	Cork (Irl)	Joe Wright	Zenith–JAP	998	242.590	150.65
1932	Tat (H)	Ernst Henne	BMW	735	244.400	151.77
1934	Gyon (H)	Ernst Henne	BMW	735	246.069	152.81
1935	Frankfurt-Ab. (D)	Ernst Henne	BMW	735	256.046	159.01
1936	Frankfurt-Ab. (D)	Ernst Henne	BMW	495	272.006	168.92
1937	Gyon (H)	Eric Fernihough	Brough-Superior-JAP	995	273.244	169.68
1937	Brescia (I)	Piero Tarffi	Gilera	492	274.181	170.27
1937	Frankfurt-Ab. (D)	Ernst Henne	BMW	495	279.503	173.57
1951	Ingolstadt (D)	Wilhelm Herz	NSU	499	290.322	180.29
1955	Christchurch (NZ)	Russell Wright	Vincent-HRD	998	297.640	184.83
1956	Bonneville (USA)	Wilhelm Herz	NSU	499	338.092	211.40
1962	Bonneville (USA)	Bill Johnson	Triumph	649	361.410	224.57
1966	Bonneville (USA)	Bob Leppan	Triumph Spec.	1298	395.280	245.60
1970	Bonneville (USA)	Don Vesco	Yamaha	700	405.25	251.66
1970	Bonneville (USA)	Cal Rayborn	Harley-Davidson	1480	410.37	254.84
1970	Bonneville (USA)	Cal Rayborn	Harley-Davidson	1480	426.40	265.49
1978	Bonneville (USA)	Don Vesco	Kawasaki	2030(T)	509.757	318.598

Successful machines have included the supercharged NSU ridden by Wilhelm Herz in 1956 (left), Bob Leppan's Triumph-powered Gyronaut of 1967 (below), and Don Vesco's turbo-charged Yamaha (inset) in 1975.

Munich. Next, Russel Wright set a new record near Christchurch, New Zealand, riding a tuned 998cc Vincent-HRD.

In 1956, the German NSU factory sent Herz to the USA. The new venue was Bonneville, where the salt flats permitted higher speeds than anywhere in Europe. Herz had two record machines, one of which was a 499cc super-charged dohc twin in a streamlined shell. At Bonneville, he reached 211·4 mph, with Johnny Allen slightly in front at 214·5 mph. Allen's machine was powered by a 650cc Triumph twin engine but his US record was unratified. In 1962 Bill Johnson, on a Triumph-engined 649cc, reached 224·57 mph. Two similar engines powered Robert Leppan's 'projectile' when he reached 245·6 mph at Bonneville in 1966. Just four years later he was beaten by Cal Rayborn whose 1480cc Harley-Davidson reached 265·6 mph. This record stood until 1975 when Don Vesco reached 302·92 mph on his improved 1496cc Yamaha Streamliner. In 1978, riding a turbo-charged Kawasaki with two 1015cc engines, he raised the record to 318·6 mph.

THE LEADING MODELS.... FROM THE GOLDEN AGE TO THE PRESENT

The 1920's

Marque:	Country:	Cyl:	Bore:	Stroke:	CCM:	HP:	2 or 4 Stroke:	Engine:
A.J.S.	GB	1	74	81	349	2¾	sv	Own
		2 V	74	93	799	4–7	sv	
Albertus	D	1	60	75	212	3	2	Löwy
Alecto	GB	1	76	76	344	3½	2	Own
Allon	GB	1	70	76	292	2½	2	Own
Ardie	D	1	72	75	305	3	2	Own
Ariel	GB	1	60	88	249	2½	sv	Blackburne
		1	92	100	662	4½	sv	Own
		2 V	73	95	796	6–7	ioe	MAG
		2 V	82	94	994	8	ioe	MAG
BAT	GB	1	70	90	347	2¾	sv	JAP
		2 V	70	88	676	5	sv	JAP
		2 V	85.5	85	986	8	sv	JAP
Beardmore	GB	1	70	90	347	2¾	sv	Precision
		1	81	96	494	3½	sv	Precision
		1	89	96	598	4½	sv	Precision
Bekamo	D	1	50	66	129	2½	2	Own
BMW	D	1	68	68	249	2½	ohv	Own
		2	68	68	493	6.5	sv	Own
		2	68	68	493	16	ohv	Own
Bianchi	I	2 V	70	78	600	—	sv	Own
Bradbury	GB	1	74.5	80	349	2¾	sv	Own
		1	89	89	554	4	sv	Own
		2 V	74.5	86	749	6	sv	Own
Brough	GB	2 F	70	64.5	496	3½	ohv	Own
		2 F	70	90	692	5–6	sv	Own
Brough-Superior	GB	2 V	72	91	742	6	ioe	MAG
		2 V	85.5	86	976	8	sv	JAP
		2 V	90	77.5	984	8	ohv	JAP
B.S.A.	GB	1	72	85.5	349	2¾	sv	Own
		1	80	98	493	3½	sv	Own
		1	85	98	557	4¼	sv	Own
		2 V	76	85	770	6	sv	Own
		2 V	80	98	985	8	sv	Own
Burney	GB	1	81	96	495	3½	sv	Own
Calthorpe	GB	1	67	69	247	2½	2	Peco
Campion	GB	1	70	76	293	2¾	sv	JAP
		1	71	88	347	2¾	sv	JAP
		2 V	85.5	85	976	8	sv	JAP
Cedos	GB	1	62	70	211	2¼	2	Own
		1	67	70	247	2¾	2	Own
Chater Lea	GB	1	70	70	269	2½	2	Own
		1	71	88	349	2¾	sv	Blackburne
		1	85	96	545	4¼	sv	Own
		2 V	85.5	85	976	8	sv	Own
Clément	F	2 V	54	75	345	3	sv	Own
		2 V	64	77	496	3½	sv	Own
Cleveland	USA	1	70	70	269	3½	2	Own
Clyno	GB	1	70	70	269	2½	2	Own
		2 V	76	102	925	8	sv	Own
Connaught	GB	1	73	70	293	2½	2	Own
		1	76	77	348	2¾	2	Own
Cotton	GB	1	70	70	269	2½	2	Villiers
		1	60	88	248	2½	sv	Blackburne
		1	71	88	348	2¾	sv	Blackburne
		1	71	88	348	2¾	ohv	Blackburne
Coventry-Eagle	GB	1	55	60	147	1¾	2	Villiers
		1	71	88	348	2¾	sv	Blackburne
		2 V	85	85	998	8	sv	JAP
Coventry-Mascot	GB	1	70	90.6	349	2¾	sleeve	Barr & Stroud
Coventry-Victor	GB	2 F	75	78	688	6	sv	Own
D-Rad	D	1	82	94	496	10	sv	Own
Diamond	GB	1	55	62	147	1¾	2	Villiers
		1	70	90.6	349	2¾	sleeve	Barr & Stroud
Dolf	D	1	62	66	199	3	2	
Dot	GB	1	60	70	198	2¼	2	
		1	70	70	269	2¾	2	Villiers
		1	70	76	293	2¾	sv	JAP
		2 V	85	85	986	8	sv	JAP

Marque:	Country:	Cyl:	Bore:	Stroke:	CCM:	HP:	2 or 4 Stroke:	Engine
Douglas	GB	2 F	60.8	60	348	$2\frac{3}{4}$	sv	Own
		2 F	68	68	496	$3\frac{1}{2}$	sv	Own
		2 F	74.5	68	595	4	sv	Own
		2 F	83	68	733	6	ohv	Own
Dunelt	GB	1	85	88	499	$3\frac{1}{2}$	2	Own
Duzmo	GB	1	89	79	497	$3\frac{1}{2}$	ohv	Own
Economic	GB	2 F	52.5	38.5	163	$1\frac{3}{4}$	2	Own
Excelsior	GB	1	55	62	147	$1\frac{3}{4}$	2	Villiers
		1	67	70	247	$2\frac{1}{2}$	2	Villiers
		1	71	88	348	$2\frac{3}{4}$	sv	Blackburne
		2 V	76	85	770	6	sv	JAP
		2 V	85.5	85	976	8	sv	JAP
F.N.	B	1	65	86	285	$2\frac{3}{4}$	sv	Own
		1	74	80.5	348	$2\frac{3}{4}$	sv	Own
		4	52	88	749	8	sv	Own
Francis-Barnett	GB	1	70	76	293	$2\frac{3}{4}$	sv	JAP
		1	70	90	346	$2\frac{3}{4}$	sv	JAP
Garelli	I	1	50	89	348	$2\frac{3}{4}$	2	Own 2-Piston
Gnome & Rhone	F	1	85	88	499	$3\frac{1}{2}$	sv	Own
		1	85	88	499	$3\frac{1}{2}$	ohv	Own
Hanfland	D	1	55	65	149	3	2	Own
Harley-Davidson	USA	2 F	69	76	584	5	sv	Own
		2 V	84	88.9	989	9	ioe	Own
		2 V	87	101	1208	12	ioe	Own
H.E.C.	GB	1	67	70	247	$2\frac{1}{4}$	2	Villiers
Henderson	USA	4	68.3	88.9	1303	$11\frac{1}{2}$	sv	Own
Henley	GB	1	68	96	348	$2\frac{3}{4}$	ohv	Bradshaw
Hobart	GB	1	60	88	248	$2\frac{1}{2}$	sv	Blackburne
		1	71	88	348	$2\frac{3}{4}$	sv	Blackburne
Humber	GB	1	75	79	348	$2\frac{3}{4}$	sv	Own
		2 F	75	68	600	$4\frac{1}{2}$	sv	Own
Indian	USA	2 V	70	78	596	4	sv	Own
		2 V	79	100	998	7–8	sv	Own
		2 V	82	112	1204	10	sv	Own
Invicta	GB	1	70	90	346	$2\frac{3}{4}$	sv	JAP
Ivy	GB	1	75	79	348	$2\frac{3}{4}$	2	Own
James	GB	1	73	83.5	349	$2\frac{3}{4}$	sv	Own
		2 V	64	77	499	$3\frac{1}{2}$	sv	Own
		2 V	73	89.5	749	7	sv	Own
J.E.S.	GB	1	60	60	169	$1\frac{1}{2}$	2	Own
J.N.U.	GB	1	73	76	318	$2\frac{3}{4}$	2	Dalm
K.G.	D	1	80	99	497	4	ohv	Own
Lea Francis	GB	2 V	64	77	497	$3\frac{1}{2}$	ioe	MAG
		2 V	64	92	592	5	ioe	MAG
Levis	GB	1	62	70	211	2.1	2	Own
Lutéce	F	2	75	113	997	7	sv	Own
Mabeco	D	2 V	70	78	600	11	sv	Simens & Halske
Mars	D	2 F	80	95	956	7.3	sv	Maybach
Martinsyde	GB	1	70	90	437	$2\frac{3}{4}$	eoi	Own
		2 V	70	88	678	6	eoi	Own
Massey	GB	1	71	88	348	$2\frac{3}{4}$	sv	Blackburne
Matchless	GB	1	71	88	348	$2\frac{3}{4}$	sv	Blackburne
		2 V	85	85	980	8	sv	JAP
		2 V	82	94	993	8	ioe	MAG
McKenzie	GB	1	60	60	170	$1\frac{1}{2}$	2	Own
Metro-Tyler	GB	1	70	70	269	$2\frac{1}{2}$	2	Own
Megola	D	5	52	60	640	6.5–14	sv	Own Radial
M.F.Z.	D	1	64	77	249	3	2	Own
Mohawk	GB	1	70	70	269	$2\frac{1}{2}$	2	Villiers
Moto-Rêve	CH	1	61	85	248	$2\frac{1}{2}$	ohv	Own
Motosacoche	CH	2 V	54	75	345	3	ioe	MAG
		2 V	64	77	496	4	ioe	MAG
		2 V	72	91	750	6	ioe	MAG
New Comet	GB	1	70	76	293	$2\frac{1}{2}$	2	Climax
New Gerrard	GB	1	70	90.5	384	$2\frac{3}{4}$	Sleeve	Barr & Stroud
New Hudson	GB	1	62	70	211	$1\frac{3}{4}$	2	Own
		1	70	90	346	$2\frac{3}{4}$	sv	Own
		1	79.5	100	498	$3\frac{1}{2}$	sv	Own
		1	87	100	596	4	sv	Own
New Imperial	GB	1	70	76	293	$2\frac{1}{2}$	sv	JAP
		1	70	90	348	$2\frac{3}{4}$	sv	JAP
		2 V	85.5	85	976	8	sv	JAP
Nimbus	DK	4	60	66	746	7	ioe	Own
Norton	GB	1	79	100	490	$3\frac{1}{2}$	sv	Own
		1	79	100	490	$3\frac{1}{2}$	ohv	Own
		1	82	120	633	4	sv	Own
N.S.U.	D	1	58	72	190	$1\frac{1}{2}$	ioe	Own
		1	73	78	326	$2\frac{1}{2}$	ioe	Own
		1	85	88	499	$3\frac{1}{2}$	ioe	Own
		2 V	58	75	396	3	ioe	Own
		2 V	63	80	499	$3\frac{1}{2}$	ioe	Own
		2 V	72.5	90	749	6–14	ioe	Own
		2 V	75	94	931	$6\frac{1}{2}$	ioe	Own
		2 V	80	99	998	8–17	ioe	Own
N.U.T.	GB	2 V	64.5	76	499	$3\frac{1}{2}$	sv	Own
		2 V	64.5	76	499	$3\frac{1}{2}$	ohv	Own
		2 V	70	88	676	$4\frac{1}{2}$	sv	Own
O.E.C.	GB	1	71	88	348	$2\frac{3}{4}$	sv	Blackburne
		1	85	96.8	549	4	sv	Blackburne
		2 V	85	88	998	8	sv	Blackburne
O.K.	GB	1	70	70	269	$2\frac{1}{2}$	2	Villiers
		1	60	88	248	$2\frac{1}{2}$		Blackburne
Olympic	GB	1	68	72	261	$2\frac{1}{2}$	2	Orbit
Omega	GB	1	60	60	170	$1\frac{1}{2}$	2	Own
		1	71	88	348	$2\frac{3}{4}$	2	Own
Paragon	GB	1	76	79	349	$2\frac{3}{4}$	2	Own
Peugeot	F	1	52	52	110	1	2	Own
Puch	A	1	36×2	60	123	1	2	Own

The 1920's
continued

Marque:	Country:	Cyl:	Bore:	Stroke:	CCM:	HP:	2 or 4 Stroke:	Engine:
P. & M. (Panther)	GB	1	84. 1	100	555	5	sv	Own
P. & P.	GB	1	70	90. 5	349	2¾	Sleeve	Barr & Stroud
Quadrant	GB	1	79	100	490	3½	sv	Own
		1	87	110	654	4½	ioe	Own
Radco	GB	1	67	70	247	2½	2	Own
Raleigh	GB	1	71	88	348	2¾	sv	Own
		2 F	77	75	698	5–6	sv	Own
Ray	GB	1	60	70	198	1½	sv	Own
Reading-Standard	USA	2 V	85. 7	101. 6	1170	10	sv	Own
Ready	GB	1	70	76	293	2¾	sv	JAP
Rex-Acme	GB	1	70	90. 5	349	2¾	Sleeve	Barr & Stroud
		1	85	95	550	4	sv	JAP
		1	60	88	248	2½	ohv	Blackburne
Rover	GB	1	63	80	249	2½	ohv	Own
		2 V	70	88	678	5	sv	JAP
Royal Enfield	GB	1	64	70	225	2. 5	sv	Own
		2 V	85. 5	85	976	8	sv	JAP
Rudge	GB	1	85	88	499	3½	ioe	Own
		2 V	85	88	998	7–9	ioe	Own
R. & H.	GB	1	55	62	147	1¼	2	Villiers
Sarolea	B	1	85	97	553	4	sv	Own
Scott	GB	2	70	63. 5	487	3. 5	2	Own
		2	73	63. 5	532	3¾	2	Own
Sparkbrook	GB	1	67	70	247	2½	2	Villiers
Sun	GB	1	70	70	269	2½	2	Vitesse
		1	71	88	348	2¾	sv	Blackburne
Sunbeam	GB	1	70	90	347	2¾	sv	Own
		1	77	105. 5	492	3½	sv	Own
		1	85	88	499	3½	sv	Own
		1	85	105. 5	599	4½	sv	Own
		2 V	85. 5	85	976	6–8	sv	JAP
Stanger	GB	2 V	70	70	538	4	2	Own
Triumph	D	1	70	72	277	2½	2	Own
Triumph	GB	1	67. 2	70	249	2¼	2	Own
		1	80. 9	97	499	3½	ohv	Own
		1	85	97	550	4	sv	Own
Trump	GB	1	70	90	348	2¾	sv	JAP
		2 V	76	85	748	6	sv	JAP
Velocette	GB	1	62	73	220	1¾	2	Own
		1	63	80	247	2½	2	Own
Victoria	GB	1	79	70	347	2¾	2	Villiers
Victoria	D	2 F	70. 5	64	499	6. 5	ohv	Own
Vindec	GB	1	70	76	293	2½	sv	JAP
		2 V	85. 5	85	976	8	sv	JAP
Vis-Duplex	D	2 F	63	80	498	3½	2	Own
Wanderer	D	1	65	76	251	2	sv	Own
		2 V	65	76	502	4	sv	Own
		2 V	70	80	615	4	sv	Own
		2 V	71	94	749	6	ohv	Own
Weaver	GB	1	56	61	149	1¼	ohv	Own
Wee McGregor	GB	1	60	60	170	1¼	2	Own
Wolf	GB	1	71	88	348	2¾	sv	Blackburne
Wooler	GB	2 F	60	60. 5	345	2¾	ioe	Own
Zenith	GB	1	70	76	293	2¾	sv	JAP
		1	70	90	348	2¾	sv	JAP
		2 F	68	68	496	3½	ohv	Bradshaw
		2 V	70	88	678	5	sv	JAP
		2 V	85. 5	85	976	8	sv	JAP
Zündapp	D	1	62	70	211	2¼	2	Own

The 1930's

Marque:	Model:	Country:	Cyl:	Bore:	Stroke:	CCM:	2 or 4 Stroke:	Engine:
A.J.S.	S 4	GB	1	74	93	399	sv	Own
	S 5		1	74	81	349	sv	Own
	S 6		1	74	81	349	ohv	Own
	S 8		1	84	90	498	ohv	Own
	S 2		2 V	84	90	996	sv	Own
A.J.W.	B. Fox	GB	1	57. 1	67	172	2	Villiers
	Flying Fox		1	70	90. 5	348	ohv	Python
	Flying Foy		1	85	88	499	ohv	Python
	680		2 V	70	88	675	ohv	JAP
	8–55		2 V	80	90	996	ohv	JAP
A.K.D.	70 Merkur	GB	1	60	61	172	ohv	Own
	40 Polar		1	76	77	348	sv	Own
Allegro	Supersp.	CH	1	57	67	172	2	Villiers
	Grand Sport		1	79	101	498	ohv	Sturmey-Archer
Ardie	Jubilee	D	1	85. 7	85	490	sv	JAP
	Silberpfeil		1	85. 7	85	490	ohv	JAP
	750		2 V	70	97	743	sv	JAP
Ariel	L 1 F	GB	1	65	75	248	ohv	Own
	V F		1	81. 8	95	497	ohv	Own
	S B		1	86. 4	95	557	sv	Own
	4 F		4 Sq	51	61	497	ohc	Own
Austria		A	1	70	90	346	2	Villiers
Bianchi		I	1	59. 5	62. 5	174	ohv	Own
BMW	R 2	D	1	63	64	198	ohv	Own
	R 52		2 F	63	78	486	sv	Own
	R 57		2 F	68	68	494	ohv	Own
	R 62		2 F	78	78	745	sv	Own
	R 63		2 F	83	68	735	ohv	Own
Brough-Superior	500	GB	2 V	62. 5	80	492	ohv	JAP
	680		2 V	70	88	676	ohv	JAP
	SS 80		2 V	85	85. 7	998	sv	JAP
	SS 100		2 V	80	99	998	ohv	JAP
BSA	B 1	GB	1	63	80	249	sv	Own

Marque:	Model:	Country:	Cyl:	Bore:	Stroke:	CCM:	2 or 4 Stroke:	Engine
	B 3		1	63	80	249	ohv	Own
	L 5		1	72	85.5	349	sv	Own
	L 6		1	72	85.5	349	ohv	Own
	S 7		1	80	98	493	sv	Own
	S 9		1	80	98	493	ohv	Own
	E 11		2 V	76	85	770	sv	Own
	G 12		2 V	80	98	986	sv	Own
Condor	312	CH	1	72	85	348	ioe	MAG
	322		1	82	94	498	ioe	MAG
	GP 572		1	82	94	498	ohv	MAG
Calthorpe	Ivory	GB	1	74	81	348	ohv	Own
Coventry-Eagle	G 22	GB	1	67	67	196	2	Villiers
	G 45		1	70	90	348	sv	Sturmey–Archer
	G 44		1	71	88	348	ohv	Sturmey–Archer
	G 54		1	79	101	496	ohv	Sturmey–Archer
	G 55		1	85.7	85	490	ohv	JAP
	F 130		2 V	85.5	85	996	sv	JAP
Diamond		GB	1	67	70	247	2	Villiers
Delta-Gnom		A	1	71	88	348	ohv	Sturmey–Archer
			1	82	94	496	ohv	Own
			2 V	85.5	85	996	sv	JAP
DKW	VR	D	1	63	64	198	2	Own
	300		1	74	68	296	2	Own
	500		2	68	68	494	2	Own
Dollar		F	1	66	70	239	ohv	Chaise
			1	75	79	349	ohv	Chaise
			1	89	79	492	ohv	Chaise
Douglas	B	GB	2 F	60.8	60	347	sv	Own
	D		2 F	68	82	595	sv	Own
	G		2 F	68	82	595	ohv	Own
D-Rad	R9	D	1	82	94	496	sv	Own
	R10		1	82	94	496	ohv	Own
Dresch	E	F	1	76	77	348	sv	Own
	C		2	64	77	495	sv	Own
Dunelt	J2	GB	1	65.5	88	298	sv	Sturmey–Archer
	J4		1	71	88	348	ohv	Sturmey–Archer
	J5		1	79	101	496	ohv	Sturmey–Archer
	J7		1	86.8	101	598	sv	Sturmey–Archer
Elfa	T200	D	1	63	64	198	2	Windhoff
	LS300		1	68	64	294	2	Kühne
	LS350		1	70	90	346	ohv	Küchen
	LS500		1	79	100	492	sv	Küchen
Elite (E.O.)	Sport	D	1	86	86	496	ohv	Küchen
Excelsior	A 4	GB	1	61	67	196	2	Villiers
	A 9		1	62.5	90	248	ohv	JAP
	A 12		1	85.7	85	490	ohv	JAP
FN		B	1	74	80.5	348	sv	Own
			1	85	87	495	sv	Own
			1	85	87	495	ohv	Own
Francis-Barnett	Hawk	GB	1	61	67	196	2	Villiers
	18 Falcon		1	61	67	196	2	Villiers-DP
Frera	Sport	I	1	53	79	174	sv	Own
	Sport		1	63	79	247	sv	Own
	Sport		1	71	88	347	sv	Own
	Spinta		1	84.5	88	497	ohv	Own
Garelli	314	I	1	50	82	348	2	Own 2 Piston
	315		1	50	89	349	2	Own 2 Piston
Gilera	Sixdays	I	1	84	90	498	ohv	Own
Gillet Herstal	Welttur	B	1	79.5	70	348	2	Own
	SS		1	70	90	348	ohv	Own
	T		1	84	90	498	sv	Own
	Rekord		1	84	90	498	ohv	Own
Gnome Rhone	Touring	F	1	69	82	306	sv	Own
	CM 1 GS		1	73	82	344	ohv	Own
	GS 500		1	85	88	497	sv	Own
	V2		2 F	68	68	495	sv	Own
Harley-Davidson	C	USA	1	70.6	101.6	493	sv	Own
	D		2 V	69.8	96.8	743	sv	Own
	V		2 V	86.9	101.6	1208	sv	Own
Henderson	De Luxe	USA	4	58.8	89	1301	ioe	Own
Horex	S 200	D	1	57	78	198	ohv	Columbus
	T 500		1	80	99	496	sv	Columbus
	S 500		1	79	101	496	ohv	Columbus-S.A.
	T 600		1	80	118	596	sv	Columbus
Hulla	Bremen	D	1	60	68	196	2	DKW
Husqvarna		S	1	64.5	76	248	sv	Own
			1	62.5	80	248	ohv	JAP
			1	79	101	496	ohv	Sturmey–Archer
Imperia	Ulster	D	1	70	88	346	ohv	Python
	Grand Sport		1	85	88	498	ohv	Python
	Sport		1	80	94	498	ohv	MAG
	Berggeist		1	90	94	598	ioe	MAG
	Rheingold		1	70	88	676	ohv	JAP
James	C 10	GB	1	57.5	67	172	2	Villiers
	C 4		1	73.5	83.5	348	ohv	Own
	C3		1	85	88	498	ohv	Python
	C 2		2 V	64	77.5	497	ohv	Own
Jawa		CS	1	58	65	173	2	Lic. Villiers
			1	63	80	246	2	Lic. DKW
			1	84	90	499	ohv	Lic. Wanderer
Keller	O 1	CH	1	79	81	397	sv	Own
Koehler-Escoffier	KG 35	F	1	72	85	347	ohv	MAG
	K 50		1	80	99	498	ohc	Own
Levis	Z	GB	1	67	70	247	2	Own
	A 2		1	70	90	346	ohv	Own
Magnat-Debon	LMP	F	1	57	68	174	2	Own
	MOSSE		1	59	90	246	ohv	Own
	CSS		1	85.5	85	490	ohv	JAP

Marque:	Model:	Country:	Cyl:	Bore:	Stroke:	CCM:	2 or 4 Stroke:	Engine:
Mammut	2 T	D	1	61	67	196	2	Villiers
	4 T		1	56.3	79	198	sv	Blackburne
MAS	119 L	I	1	60	61.5	173.8	ohv	Own
	125/3		1	85	61.5	348	ohv	Own
Matchless	R 7	GB	1	62.5	80	246	sv	Own
	D		1	69	93	347	sv	Own
	C/S		1	85.5	85.5	495	ohv	Own
	X/3		2 V	85.5	85.5	990	sv	Own
	S. Arrow		2 V	54	86	398	sv	Own
	S. Hawk		4 V	50.8	73	593	ohc	Own
Miller-Balsamo	Erretre	I	1	57	67	172	ohv	Own
	TT-Replica		1	85	88	498	ohv	Python
La Mondiale	LT	B	1	75	68	308	2	Own
	ZS		1	75	79	349	2	Own
	GS		1	70	90	346	ohv	JAP
	GSSS		1	85.7	85	490	ohv	JAP
Monet-Goyon	AT	F	1	67	70	247	2	Villiers
			1	72	85	348	ioe	MAG
			1	82	94	498	ohv	MAG
Montgomery		GB	1	62.5	80	248	ohv	JAP
			1	70	90	348	ohv	JAP
			1	85.7	85	490	sv	JAP
			2 V	70	88	676	sv	JAP
Moser	STD	CH	1	60	61	174	ohv	Own
			1	74	81	348	ohv	Own
			1	79	100	498	ohv	Own
			1	85	106	598	ohv	Own
Motobécane (Motoconfort)	B1	F	1	46	60	99.6	2	Own
	B2		1	56	70	172	2	Own
	B4		1	70	90	346	ohv	Own
	B7		4	54	81.7	749	ohc	Own
	B 75		4	54	54.5	499	ohc	Own
Moto Guzzi		I	1	68	68	248	ohc	Own
			1	88	82	499	ioe	Own
			1	88	82	499	ohc	Own
Motosacoche	316	CH	1	72	85	347	ioe	Own (MAG)
	317		1	72	85	347	ohv	Own (MAG)
	417		1	82	94	498	sv	Own (MAG)
	714		2 V	72	91	746	ioe	Own (MAG)
MT	H 29	A	1	79	70	342	2	Villiers
	N.O.		1	85.7	85	490	sv	JAP
	TSP 4		1	79	101	496	ohv	Sturmey-Archer
	2 29 B		2 V	70	97	746	sv	JAP
New Hudson	31	GB	1	70	90	346	sv	Own
	33		1	70	90	346	ohv	Own
	3		1	79.5	100	496	ohv	Own
	1		1	83.5	100	547	sv	Own
New Imperial	Leinster	GB	1	62.5	80	248	ohv	Own
	10 Prince		1	70	90	348	ohv	Own
	11 Prince		1	86	86	499	ohv	Own
Norton	JE	GB	1	71	88	348	ohv	Own
	CJ		1	71	88	348	ohc	Own
	16H		1	79	100	490	sv	Own
	18		1	79	100	490	ohv	Own
	CS		1	79	100	490	ohc	Own
	19		1	79	120	588	ohv	Own
	Big Four		1	82	120	633	sv	Own
NSU	Pony	D	1	45	40	63	2	Own
	175Z		1	59	64	174	2	Own
	201 Z		1	63	64	198	2	Own
	251 TS		1	63	80	247	ioe	Own
	351 TS		1	71	88	346	ohv	Own
	501 TS		1	80	99	494	sv	Own
	500 SS		1	80	99	494	ohc	Own
OEC		GB	1	70	90	346	sv	JAP
			1	85.7	85	490	ohv	JAP
	Flying Squad		2 V	80	90	994	ohv	JAP
OK-Supreme	N	GB	1	85.7	85	490	sv	JAP
	A		1	70	64.5	248	ohc	Own
	M		2 V	70	97	749	sv	JAP
Peugeot	P 109	F	1	54	76	174	sv	Own
	P 107		1	72	85	348	sv	Own
	P 105		1	72	85	348	ohv	Own
P. & M.-Panther	50	GB	1	84	90	498	ohv	Own
	90 Redwing		1	79	100	490	ohv	Own
	25		1	65	70	247	2	Villiers
Praga	350	CS	1	70	90	346	ohc	Own
	500		1	84	90	499	ohc	Own
Premier	A 1	CS	1	70	70	269	2	Own
	S2		1	71	88	346	sv	Own
	S3		1	85	88	499	sv	Own
	SL		1	75.5	110	494	ohv	Own
	S6		2 V	76	82	744	sv	Own
Puch	250	A	1	45×2	78	248	2	Own
	500Z		2	45×2	78	496	2	Own
Radco	L	GB	1	55	62	147	2	Villiers
	P		1	67	70	247	2	Own
Raleigh	MO	GB	1	65.6	88	298	sv	Own-S.A.
	MT		1	71	88	348	ohv	Own-S.A.
	MH		1	79	101	496	ohv	Own-S.A.
Ready		B	1	70	90	346	sv	JAP
			1	85.7	85	490	ohv	JAP
René-Gillet	H	F	1	70	90	346	sv	Own
	G		2 V	70	97.7	749	sv	Own
	J		2 V	80	97.7	981	sv	Own
Rhony'X	VM	F	1	46	60	100	2	Own
	H3		1	70	90	346	sv	Own

Marque:	Model:	Country:	Cyl:	Bore:	Stroke:	CCM:	2 or 4 Stroke:	Engine:
RMW	H5		1	83	90	490	sv	Own
	200	D	1	62	66	198	2	Own
			1	71	88	348	sv	Sturmey-Archer
			1	82	96	498	ioe	MAG
			1	82	96	496	ohv	MAG
Royal-Enfield	C	GB	1	70	90	346	sv	Own
	CO		1	70	90	346	ohv	Own
	HA		1	85.5	85	498	sv	Own
	JA		1	85.5	85	498	ohv	Own
	H		1	80.5	99.25	570	sv	Own
	K		2 V	85.5	85	976	sv	Own
Rudge-Whitworth	250	GB	1	62.5	81	249	ohv	Own
	350		1	70	90.5	349	ohv	Own
	500 Spec.		1	85	88	499	ohv	Own
Sarolea	A	B	1	75	79	347	sv	Own
	S		1	80.5	97	494	ohv	Own
Schliha		D	1	69.3	70	193	2	Own
			1	82.4	86	349	2	Own
			1	102.5	86	498	2	Own
Schüttoff	200	D	1	60	68	192	2	DKW
			1	74	68	296	2	DKW
			1	72	85	346	ohv	Own
			1	80	99	494	sv	Own
			1	80	99	494	ohv	Own
Scott	Squirrel	GB	1	73	71.4	298	2	Own
	Fl. Squirell		2	68.25	68.25	498	2	Own
	Fl. Squirell		2	74.6	68.25	596	2	Own
	TT Replica		2	66.6	71.4	498	2	Own
	TT Replica		2	73	71.4	596	2	Own
SMW	S IV		1	61	67	196	2	Villiers
	S III		1	81	96.8	498	ohv	Blackburne
Soyer	500 Block F		1	80	91	498	ohc	Own
	500 S Sport		1	80	91	498	ohc	Own
Standard	DS 250	D	1	62.5	80	249	ohv	Own
	CT 350		1	72	84	342	ioe	MAG
	CS 500		1	82	94	498	ohv	MAG
	Rennsport		1	82	94	498	ohv	MAG
	BT 1000		2 V	82	94	997	ioe	MAG
Stock	Extra		1	55	50	119	2	Own
	Kardan 200		1	66	58	197	2	Own
	GR 300		1	74	68	292	2	Own
Sunbeam	10	GB	1	74	80	344	ohv	Own
	Lion Longstroke		1	77	105.5	492	sv	Own
	9 (90) TT		1	80	98	493	ohv	Own
Super-X	Touring	USA	2 V	76	83	752	ioe	Own
Terrot	LPP	F	1	57	68	174	2	Own
	FST		1	67	70	247	2	Own
	OSSE		1	59	90	246	ohv	Own
	NSSL		1	85.5	85	490	ohv	JAP
	V		2 V	70	88	676	sv	JAP
Titan	Spezial	A	1	75	77	340	2	Own
	500		1	81	96.8	498	sv	Blackburne
Train	M-5	F	1	64	54	173	2	Own
			1	76	76	344	2	Own
			1	76	76	344	ohv	Own
Triumph	X	GB	1	59.5	62.5	74	2	Own
	WO		1	63	80	249	ohv	Own
	WL		1	72	85.5	348	sv	Own
	NT		1	84	89	493	ohv	Own
	ND		1	84	99	548	sv	Own
Triumph (TWN)	SK 200	D	1	59	72	197	2	Own
	T 350		1	72	85	346	ioe	MAG
	SST 500		1	82	94	498	ohv	MAG
	RR		V 2	72	91	741	ioe	MAG
Universal		CH	1	70	90	348	sv	JAP
			1	85.7	85	490	ohv	JAP
U.T.		D	1	60	68	193	2	Bark
			1	70	90	348	ohv	JAP
			1	85.7	104	599	ohv	JAP
Velocette	GTP	GB	1	63	80	249	2	Own
	KTP		1	74	81	348	ohc	Own
	KTT		1	74	81	348	ohc	Own
Victoria	KR 20	D	1	60	88	248	sv	Sturmey-Archer
	KR 35		1	71	87	348	ohv	Sturmey-Archer
	KR 50		1	79	101	492	ohv	Sturmey-Archer
	KR 6		2 F	77	64	596	ohv	Own
Wimmer	GG 25	D	1	67	71	247	ohv	Own
	GG 50		1	84	90	499	sv	Bark
Wolf	Utility	GB	1	61	67	196	2	Villiers
Württembergia	BL 200	D	1	56.3	79	196	sv	Blackburne
	SS 350		1	71	88	348	ohv	Blackburne
	RL 600		1	85	105	596	sv	Blackburne
Zündapp	S 200		1	60	70	198	2	Own
	S 300		1	68	82.5	298	2	Own
	S 500		1	85	88	499	ohv	Python

The post-war period

Marque:	Model:	Country:	Cyl:	Bore:	Stroke:	CCM:	2 or 4 Stroke:	Engine:	Bhp:
Adler	M 100	D	1	50	50	98	2	Own	3.8
	M 150		1	54	59	147	2	Own	8.4
	M 250		2	54	54	247	2	Own	16
Aermacchi	125	I	1 F	52	58	123	2	Own	5
Aero-Caproni	Capriolo	I	1	47	43	75	ohv	Own	3.5
A.J.S.	16 M	GB	1	69	93	347	ohv	Own	15.2
	18		1	82.5	93	498	ohv	Own	21.1

Marque:	Model:	Country:	Cyl:	Bore:	Stroke	CCM:	2 or 4 Stroke:	Engine:	Bhp:
	7R Boys Racer		1	75.5	78	349	ohc	Own	30
Alpino	Sport	I	1	53.5	55	123	2	Own	6.5
Ardie	BD 175	D	1	60	61	172	2	Own	9
	B 252		1	66	72	244	2	Own	13
Aeriel	NG	GB	1	72	85	347	ohv	Own	14.2
	VG		1	81.8	95	497	ohv	Own	22
	VH Red Hunter		1	81.8	95	497	ohv	Own	24.6
	VB		1	86.4	102	598	sv	Own	15.5
	4G Square Four		4 Sq	65×4	75	997	ohv	Own	34.5
Astoria	Sport	I	1	56	60	148	2	Own	6.3
B (Motobi)	115	I	1	52	54	115	2	Own	5.2
	200	I	2 F	48	54	196	2	Own	9
Bauer		D	1	68	68	246	ohv	Own	16
Benelli	Sport Leoncino	I	1	54	54	123	2	Own	6.5
	Leonessa		2	53	56	247	ohv	Own	16
Beta	Sport	I	1	57	62	158	2	Own	7.5
Bianchi	Freccia Celeste	I	1	52	58	123	2	Own	7.5
BMW	R 25/2	D	1	68	68	245	ohv	Own	12
	R 51/3		2	68	68	494	ohv	Own	24
	R 67/2		2	72	73	590	ohv	Own	28
	R 68		2	72	73	590	ohv	Own	35
Bonvicini	BM 160	I	1	58	66	174	2	Ilo	6.5
Borghi	Olympia	I	1	52	58	123	2	BSA	5.5
BSA	C 10	GB	1	63	80	249	sv	Own	8
	C 11		1	63	80	249	ohv	Own	11
	B 31		1	71	88	348	ohv	Own	17
	B 33		Z	85	88	499	ohv	Own	23
	M 20		1	82	94	496	sv	Own	13
	M 21		1	82	112	591	sv	Own	15
	M 33		1	95	88	499	ohv	Own	23
	A 7		2	66	72.6	498	ohv	Own	27.4
	A 10 GF		2	70	84	646	ohv	Own	35.5
Bücker	TZ 200	D	1	62	66	198	2	Ilo	11
	Ilona II		2	52	58	246	2	Ilo	15.1
Carnielli	75	I	1	46	44	73	2	Vittoria	3
Ceccato		I	1	54	54	123	2	Own	5.5
Cimatti	SS	I	1	57	62	158	2	Own	7
C.M.		I	1	52	58	123	2	Own	4.5
			2	52	58	246	2	Own	8.5
Condor	25 De Luxe	CH	1	63	72	225	2	Villiers	10
	Racer		2	58	66	348	2	Own	14
	580 Ralye		2 F	70	75.2	577	sv	Own	20
	750 Touriste		2 F	78	78	748	sv	Own	25
Cotton	Vulcan	GB	1	79	72	197	2	Villiers	7.6
	Herald		2	50	63.5	249	2	Villiers	8.5
	Messenger		2	57	63.5	324	2	Villiers	—
CZ		CS	1	52	58	124	2	Own	5.6
			1	57	58	148	2	Own	6.5
			1	60	61	173	2	Own	6.5
			1	65	75	247	2	Own	9
Delta Gnom	Luxus	A	1	52	58	123	2	Rotax	5.8
DKW	RT 125	D	1	52	58	123	2	Own	4.75
	RT 200		1	62	64	192	2	Own	8.5
	RT 250		1	70	64	244	2	Own	11.5
	RT 350		2	62	58	348	2	Own	18
Douglas	Standard Mk. III	GB	2 F	60.8	60	348	ohv	Own	20
Dot	200 SCH	GB	1	59	72	197	2	Villiers	7.6
	250 SCH		1	66	72	246	2	Villiers	8.5
Dürkopp	MD 150	D	1	53	60	150	2	Own	7.5
	MD 200		1	61	64	198	2	Own	10.2
Ducati	48	I	1	39	40	48	ohv	Own	1.5
EMW	R 35/3	DDR	1	72	84	340	ohv	Own	14
Excelsior	Autobyk	GB	1	50	50	98	2	Brockhouse	2.2
	Consort	1	47	57	98	98	2	Villiers	2.8
	Condor		1	50	62	123	2	Villiers	5
	Courier		1	55	62	148	2	Villiers	6.5
	Roadsmaster		1	59	72	197	2	Villiers	8.5
	Talisman		2	50	62	244	2	Villiers	12.8
Express	SL 107	D	1	48	54	98	2	Sachs	3.1
	Radex 200		1	62	66	197	2	Ilo	11.2
	Radex 252		2	52	58	244	2	Ilo	15.1
F.B.M.	Gabbiano	I	1 F	52	58	122	2	Own	4.75
F.B.-Mondial	200	I	1	62	66	198	ohc	Own	12
Farrari	Tourismo	I	1	54	54	124	2	Own	6
FN	22	B	1	45×2	55	173	2	BP	8.3
	13250		1	63	80	249	ohv	Own	11
	13350		1	74	80	344	sv	Own	10
	13350		1	74	80	344	ohv	Own	13
	13450		1	84.5	80	444	ohv	Own	18
	20		2	63	80	498	ohc	Own	22
Franchi		I	1	57	58	147	2	Sachs	6.5
Francis-Barnett	66	GB	1	50	62	122	2	Villiers	5
	62		1	59	72	197	2	Villiers	8.4
	68		1	63	72	225	2	Villiers	9.7
	80		1	66	73	249	2	Villiers	12.8
Fusi	250	I	1	68	68	248	ohc	Own	13
Galbusera	Lusso	I	1	57	58	147	2	Sachs	6
Ganna	Sport	I	1	40×2	59.6	148	2	Puch	6.5
Gilera	150 S	I	1	60	54	152	ohv	Own	6.5
	Nettuno S		1	68	68	248	ohv	Own	14
	B 300		2	60	54	306	ohv	Own	13
	Saturno		1	84	90	498	ohv	Own	22
Gillet (Herstal)	150 S	B	1	55	60	143	2	Own	6.5
	175 S		1	57	68	172	2	Own	8
	200 Belgica		1	61	68	194	2	Own	9
	250 S		1	65	72	248	2	Own	9
	250 Milan		1	65	72	248	ohv	Own	11
	300 S		1	70	76	292	ohv	Own	13

Marque:	Model:	Country:	Cyl:	Bore:	Stroke:	CCM:	2 or 4 Stroke:	Engine:	Bhp:
	500 S		1	77	105	488	ohv	Own	17
Gitan	Turbine	I	1	52	58	158	ohv	Own	7.5
Göricke	200 S	D	1	62	66	198	2	Ilo	11
Greeves	20 DB	GB	1	59	72	197	2	Villiers	9
	25 DC		2	50	63.5	249	2	Villiers	13.2
Guazzoni	150 SS	I	1	56	62	148	2	Own	8
	250 T		1	68	68	246	2	Own	9
Harley-Davidson	XLH	USA	2 V	76	97	833	ohv	Own	
	FLF		2 V	87.3	100.8	1213	ohv	Own	
Hecker	K 175	D	1	58	66	173	2	Ilo	8.5
	K 250 Z		2	52	58	246	2	Ilo	15.1
Hercules	313	D	1	57	58	147	2	Sachs	6.5
	315		1	65	75	248	2	Ilo	11.2
Hoffman	250	D	1	65	75	248	2	Ilo	12.8
	Gouverneur		2 F	47	58	248	ohv	Own	13.4
Horex	Regina	D	1	69	91.5	342	ohv	Columbus	19
	Regina		1	74.5	91.5	399	ohv	Columbus	21.2
Honda	Benly C 92	JAP	1	44	41	124	ohc	Own	11.5
	Dream C72		2	54	54	247	ohc	Own	20
Husqvarna	30	S	1	55	50	120	2	Own	6
	281		1	60	61.5	174	2	Own	7
Iso	200	I	1	44×2	64	199	2	Own	10.5
Itom	Alba MT 34	I	1	39	40	48	2	Own	0.7
Ifa	BK 350	DDR	2 F	58	65	343	2	Own	15
James	Captain	GB	1	59	72.8	199	2	Villiers	9
	Commando		1	66	72.8	249	2	Villiers	12.8
Jawa	250	CS	1	65	75	248	2	Own	9
	350		2	58	65	348	2	Own	12
	500		2	65	73.6	498	ohc	Own	26
Kreidler	K 50	D	1	38	44	50	2	Own	2.2
KTM	R 100	A	1	48	54	98	2	Rotax	3
	125 T		1	54	54	123	2	Rotax	6.1
Laverda	75 Sport	I	1	46	45	75	ohv	Own	3.2
Leprotto	Tourismo	I	1	46×2	60	198	2	Own	10.5
Maico	Fanal	D	1	61	59.5	174	2	Own	9.2
	M 200 T		1	65	59.5	197	2	Own	11
	M 250 S		1	67	70	246	2	Own	13.2
	Taifun		2	61	59.5	348	2	Own	18.2
	Taifun		2	65	59.5	394	2	Own	21.2
Mammut	257 S	D	1	57	58	147	2	Own	6.5
Mars	Stella	D	1	58	62	174	2	Sachs	9.5
MAS	Zenith	I	1	62	57.5	174	ohv	Own	7.5
Matchless	G3L	GB	1	69	93	347	ohv	Own	16.6
	G80		1	82.5	93	498	ohv	Own	23.5
	G9		2	66	72.8	498	ohv	Own	30
Miller Balsamo	175 Sport	I	1	58	66	174	2	Own	6.5
	250 Jupiter		1	62.5	81	249	ohv	Own	16
Mival	125S	I	1	52	58	123	2	Own	6.
M.M.	AS	I	1	64	77	247	ohc	Own	
	CT		1	76	77	349	ohc	Own	
Monark	M88B	S	1	57	58	148	2	Sachs	6.5
	M550		2	52	58	244	2	Ilo	15.1
Morini	125 Sport	I	1	52	58	123	2	Own	7.5
Motobécane	D45S	F	1	51	60	122	sv	Own	4.3
	Z54C		1	52	58	124	ohv	Own	5.4
	Z2C		1	56	71	174	ohv	Own	8.5
	L4C		2 V	56	71	348	ohv	Own	
Moto-Guzzi	65	I	1	42	46	65	2	Own	2
	Galetto		1	62	53	158	ohv	Own	5
	Airone Tour.		1 F	70	64	249	ohv	Own	9.5
	Falcone		1 F	88	82	498	ohv	Own	23
Motom	Delfino	I	1	62	54	158	ohv	Own	7.5.
M.V.-Agusta	125 T	I	1	53	56	123	2	Own	6
	150 S		1	56	60	149	2	Own	8
	500 Sport		4	54	54	497	ohc	Own	45
Norton	16H	GB	1	79	100	490	sv	Own	12
	18		1	79	100	490	ohv	Own	20
	Intern. 40		1	71	88	348	ohc	Own	24
	Intern. 30		1	79	100	490	ohc	Own	29.5
	Manx 40		1	71	88	348	ohc	Own	27
	Manx 30		1	79.6	100	499	ohc	Own	33
NSU	Fox	D	1	50	50	98	ohv	Own	5.2
	2 T Fox		1	52	58	123	2	Own	5.4
	2 T Lux		1	62	66	197	2	Own	8.6
	Max		1	69	66	247	ohc	Own	17
	Consul		1	80	99	497	ohv	Own	22
Omea	125 C	I	1	56.5	50	124	2	Own	5.4
Orix	175 GS	I	1	66	58	173	2	Ilo	8.6
Panther (P. & M.)	60	GB	1	60	88	248	ohv	Own	11
	70		1	71	88	348	ohv	Own	18
	100		1	87	100	499	ohv	Own	26
Panther	KS 175	D	1	58	62	173	2	Sachs	9
Parilla	125 Sport	I	1	54	54	124	2	Own	7
	250 Boxer		1	65	75	249	2	Own	9
	Fox		1	59.8	62	174	ohv	Own	9
	Fox SS		1	59.8	62	174	ohc	Own	12
	Veltro Twin		2	62	58	349	ohv	Own	16
Peugeot	55 TA	F	1	51	60	124	2	Own	4.5
	176 GS		1	60	60	174	2	Own	10
	256 TC4		2	51	60	248	2	Own	13
Puch	125 SVS	A	1	38 × 2	55	124	2	Own	8
	175 SVS		1	42 × 2	62	172	2	Own	12.3
	250 SGS		1	45 × 2	78	248	2	Own	16.5
Rabeneick	F 250/1	D	1	65	75	247	2	Ilo	12.8
Rondine	SS	I	1	53	56	124	2	Own	5.8
Royal Enfield	Re 2	GB	1	53.8	55	123	2	Own	4.5
	Ensign		1	56	60	148	2	Own	8
	Clipper		1	64	77	248	ohv	Own	11.2

Marque:	Model:	Country:	Cyl:	Bore:	Stroke:	CCM:	2 or 4 Stroke:	Engine:	Bhp:
	Bullet		1	70	90	348	ohv	Own	18.3
	Bullet		1	84	90	498	ohv	Own	25.4
	500 Twin		2	64	77	496	ohv	Own	25.4
	Meteor		2	70	90	692	ohv	Own	36.5
Rumi	Sport	I	2 F	42	45	124	2	Own	8.5
RWC	T 98	A	1	48	54	98	2	Rotax	2.3
Sarolea	Carena	B	1	60	70	198	2	Own	7.5
	Vedette		1	75	79	349	ohv	Own	15
	Continental		1	75	90	398	sv	Own	10.5
	Atlantic		2	63	80	498	ohv	Own	26
	Atlantic Major		2	70	78	599	ohc	Own	30
Sitta	250	D	2	52	58	244	2	Ilo	15
Sparta	125	NL	1	50	60	122	2	Villiers	5
	250		1	67	70	247	2	Villiers	10.3
Sunbeam	S7 & S8	GB	2	70	63.5	487	ohc	Own	25.4
Taurus	B8	I	1	65	60	199	ohv	Own	13.8
Terrot	ETD	F	1	52	58	123	ohv	Own	5.5
	OSSD		1	68	68	247	ohv	Own	11
	RGST		1	84	90	499	ohv	Own	22
Thunder	Twin	I	2	43	44	127	ohv	Own	5.5
Tornax	K 125 H	D	1	52	58	123	2	Ilo	5.9
	KTV 200		1	62	66	197	2	Ilo	11
	Z 250		2	52	58	244	2	Ilo	15.1
Triumph (TWN)	BDG 125	D	1	35.5 × 2	62	123	2	Own	6.5
	BDG 250		1	45 × 2	78	246	2	Own	11
	Boss		1	53 × 2	78	344	2	Own	16
Triumph	T 15 Terrier	GB	1	51	58.5	149	ohv	Own	8
	T 20 Tiger Cub		1	63	64	199	ohv	Own	10
	T 5 Speed Twin		2	63	80	498	ohv	Own	27
	T 100 Tiger		2	63	80	498	ohv	Own	34
	T 6 Thunderbird		2	71	82	649	ohv	Own	34
	T 110 Tiger		2	71	82	649	ohv	Own	42
Universal	Junior	CH	1	67	70	247	ohv	Own	14
	Meteor		2 F	72	71	578	ohv	Own	30
U.T.	KTN 125	D	1	52	58	123	2	Ilo	5.9
	TS 250		1	65	75	248	2	Ilo	12.8
Velocette	Le II	GB	2 F	50	49	198	sv	Own	8
	MAC		1	68	96	349	ohv	Own	14.3
	KSS Mk II		1	74	81	348	ohc	Own	
	MSS		1	86	86	499	ohv	Own	39
Victoria	Bifix	D	1	51	60	123	2	Own	5
	KR 25		1	67	70	247	2	Own	10.5
	KR 26 Aero		1	67	70	247	2	Own	14
	Bergmeister-Sport		2 V	64	54	345	hc	Own	21
Vincent HRD	Comet	GB	1	84	90	499	hc	Own	28.4
	Rapide		2 V	84	90	998	hc	Own	45
	Black Shadow		2 V	84	90	998	hc	Own	55
	Black Lightning		2 V	84	90	998	hc	Own	70
Zündapp	Norma Luxus	D	1	60	70	198	2	Own	8.3
	Elastic 200		1	60	70	198	2	Own	9.5
	Elastic 250		1	67	70	236	2	Own	13
	KS 601 Sport		2 F	75	85	597	ohv	Own	32

The sixties and seventies

Marque:	Model:	Country:	Cyl:	Bore:	Stroke:	Ccm:	2 or 4 Stroke:	Engine:	Bhp:
Ancillotti	Cross	I	1	40	39.5	49	2	Sachs	11
	Cross		1	54	54	123	2	,,	24
	Cross		1	71.5	61	245	2	,,	32
Aspes	Cross	I	1	54	54	123	2	Own	24
	Hopi		1	54	54	123	2	Own	21
Avello	Nebraska	E	1	38	43	49	2	Puch	5
	Cobra		1	48	39.7	72	2	Puch	10
Benelli	125	I	1	56	49	120	2	Own	15.4
	125 Enduro		1	56	49	120	2	Own	15.4
	125 2C		2	52.5	44	124	2	Own	16
	250 2C		2	56	47	232	2	Own	30
	250 Quattro		4	44	38	231	4 ohc	Own	26.6
	500 Quattro		4	56	50.6	498	4 ohc	Own	55
	750 Sei		6	56	50.6	748	4 ohc	Own	75
Beta	125 SG	I	1	54	54	124	2	Own	20
	250 GS		1	70	64.5	249	2	Own	34
	250 CR		1	70	64.5	249	2	Ilo	36
BMW	R 60/7		2	73.5	70.6	599	4 ohv	Own	40
	R 75/7		2	82	70.6	745	4 ohv	Own	50
	R 100/7		2	94	70.6	980	4 ohv	Own	60
	R 100 S		2	94	70.6	980	4 ohv	Own	65
Bultaco	Mercurio GT 175	E	1	61.15	60	176.2	2	Own	12.5
	Metralla GT 250		1	72	60	244	2	Own	22.7
	Alpina 250		1	71	60	237.6	2	Own	14.1
	Alpina 350		1	83.2	60	326	2	Own	21.6
	Sherpa Trials		1	54.2	51.5	119	2	Own	9.12
	Sherpa Trials		1	71	60	237	2	Own	14.1
	Sherpa Trials		1	83.2	60	326	2	Own	18.5
	Pursang MC		1	51.5	60	124	2	Own	24.5
	Pursang MC		1	72	60	244	2	Own	34.3
	Pursang MC		1	85	64	363	2	Own	40.2
CCM	MC 500	GB	1	84	90	498	4 ohv	Own	45
CZ	125	CS	1	52	58	123	2	Own	11
	175		1	58	65	172	2	Own	15
	175 Enduro		1	62	57	172	2	Own	16
	250 Enduro		1	70	64	246	2	Own	20
	250 Twin		2	52	58	246	2	Own	17
	350 Twin		2	58	64	343	2	Own	21
	Moto Cross 125		1	55	52	123	2	Own	21
	Moto Cross 250		1	70	64	246	2	Own	34

Marque:	Model:	Country:	Cyl:	Bore:	Stroke:	CCM:	2 or 4 Stroke:	Engine:	Bhp:
	Moto Cross 400		1	82	72	381	2	Own	42
DKW	MC 125	D	1	54	54	122	2	Sachs	24
	GS 250		1	71.5	61	245	2		32
Dnéiper	M 10	USSR	2	78	68	649	4 ohv	Own	34
Ducati	125 ISDT	I	1	54	54	123.7	2	Own	22
	350 GTL		2	71.8	43.2	349.6	4 ohc	Own	27
	500 GTL		2	78	52	496	4 ohc	Own	40
	500 S. Desmo		2	78	52	496	4 ohc	Own	50
	750 Super Sport		2 V	80	74.4	748	4 ohc	Own	68
	GT 860		2 V	86	74.4	864	4 ohc	Own	65
	900 Super Sport		2 V	86	74.4	864	4 ohc	Own	72
Fantic	Caballero Reg.	I	1	55	52	123.5	2	Own	21.5
	Caballero Cross		1	55	52	123.5	2	Own	26
Garelli	50 RSL Electr.	I	1	40	39.5	49.6	2	Own	6.3
Gilera	150 Strada	I	1	60	54	152.6	4 ohv	Own	14.2
Gori	Codice 50	I	1	40	39.5	49	2	Sachs	6.5
	Moto Cross		1	54	54	123	2	,,	22
	Competizione		1	71.5	61	245	2	,,	33
Greeves	250 MX	GB	1	70	64	246	2	Own	28.5
	380 MX		1	82	72	380	2	Own	44
Harley-Davidson	SX 125	USA	1	56	50	123	2	Own	12
	SX 175		1	61	59.6	174	2	Own	17
	SX 250		1	71.8	59.6	243	2	Own	20
	SS 250		1	71.8	59.6	243	2	Own	19
	XLH (XLCH)		2 V	80	97	975	4 ohv	Own	65
	FX (FXE)		2 V	87.3	100.8	1207	4 ohv	Own	66
	Electra Glide		2 V	87.3	100.8	1207	4 ohv	Own	66
Hercules	K 50 Sprint	D	1	38	44	49	2	Sachs	6.25
	K 50 Ultra		1	38	44	49	2	,,	6.25
	K 125 S		1	54	54	122	2	,,	17
	125 GS		1	54	54	122	2	,,	22
	175 GS		1	60	61	173	2	,,	26
	250 GS		1	71.5	61	245	2	,,	32
	Wankel 3 Chamber					294		,,	27
Honda	ST 70 (Dax)	J	1	47	41.4	72	4 ohc	Own	5.2
	CB 125 S		1	56.5	49.5	124	4 ohc	Own	14
	CB 125 disc		2	44	41	124	4 ohc	Own	15
	CB 200 disc		2	55.5	41	198	4 ohc	Own	17
	CJ 250 T		2	56	50.6	249	4 ohc	Own	27
	CJ 360 T		2	67	50.6	356	4 ohc	Own	34
	CB 500 T		2	70	64.8	498	4 2×ohc	Own	42
	CB 400		4	51	50	408	4 ohc	Own	37
	CB 500		4	56	50.6	499	4 ohc	Own	48
	CB 550		4	58.5	50.6	539	4 ohc	Own	50
	CB 750		4	61	63	736	4 ohc	Own	63
	GL Gold Wing		4 F	72	61.4	999	4 2×ohc	Own	82
	TL 125 S		1	56.5	49.5	124	4 ohc	Own	9
	CR 125 Elsinore		1	56	50	123	2	Own	24
Indian	ME 125	USA	1	55	52	123.5	2	Own	19
Jawa	23	CS	1	38	44	49.9	2	Own	4
	634		2	58	65	343	2	Own	26
	GS 175		1	62	57.5	174	2	Own	22.5
	GS 250		1	70	64	246	2	Own	28.5
	GS 350		1	78	72	344	2	Own	35
	GS 370		1	80	72	362	2	Own	36
Kawasaki	KH 125	J	1	56	50.6	124	2	Own	
	KX 125 M/C		1	56	50.6	124	2	Own	22
	KX 250 M/C		1	40	64.9	249	2	Own	34
	KX 400 M/C		1	82	76	401	2	Own	42
	KE 125		1	56	50.6	124	2	Own	13
	KT 250 Trials		1	69.5	64.9	246	2	Own	16
	KH 250		3	45	52.3	249	2	Own	28
	KH 400		3	57	52.3	400	2	Own	40
	KH 500		3	60	58.8	498	2	Own	52
	City Bike		1	46	44	73	2	Own	4.2
	Z 200		1			198	4 ohc	Own	
	Z 400		2	64	62	398	4 ohc	Own	36
	Z 750		2	78	78	745	4 ohc	Own	51
	Z 650		4	62	54	652	4 2×ohc	Own	64
	Z 1000		4	70	66	1015	4 2×ohc	Own	85
Kreidler	Florett RSL	D	1	40	39.7	49.8	2	Own	6.25
KTM	GP 50 RS Comet	A	1	38	44	49	2	Sachs	6.25
	GP 125 RS Comet		1	54	54	122	2	,,	17
	MC 125		1	54	54	124	2	,,	26
	MC 250+GS 250		1	71	62	246	2	,,	34
	MC 400+GS 400		1	81	69	356	2	Own	42
	GS 125		1	54	54	124	2	Own	24
	GS 175		1	63.5	54	172	2	Own	27
Laverda	H 125 TR	I	1	55	52	124	2	Own	24
	H 250 Tr		1	68	68	247	2	Own	27
	500 Twin		2	72	61	497	4 2×ohc	Own	46
	750 SF 3		2	80	74	744	4 ohc	Own	50
	1000		3	75	74	980	4 2×ohc	Own	78
Maico	MD 50	D	1	38	44	49	2	Own	6.3
	MD 125		1	54	54	124	2	Own	16
	MD 250		1	76	54	245	2	Own	27
	GS 125		1	54	54	124	2	Own	21
	GS 250		1	67	70	247	2	Own	36
	GS 400		1	77	83	386	2	Own	43
	GS 450		1	82	83	438	2	Own	47
Malanca	125 E2C	I	2	43	43	124	2	Own	15
	125 E2C Sport		2	43	43	124	2	Own	18
	150 GT		2	46	46	149	2	Own	20
Mondial	Touring	I	1	55	52	123	2	Own	9
	Regolaritá		1	54	54	124	2	Own	12
Montesa	Enduro 250	E	1	70	64	246.3	2	Own	27
	Cota 123		1	54	54	123	2	Own	13
	Cota 247		1	72.5	60	247	2	Own	20

Marque:	Model:	Country:	Cyl:	Bore:	Stroke:	CCM:	2 or 4 Stroke:	Engine:	Bhp:
	Cappra 125 Reg.		1	54	54	123	2	Own	24
	Cappra 250 VB		1	70	64	246	2	Own	36
Morbidelli	Competizione	I	2	44	41	124.6	2	Own	35
Morini	Corsarino ZZ50	I	1	41	37	49	4 ohv	Own	4.5
	125 T		1	59	45	123	4 ohv	Own	14
	3 1/2 V		2 V	62	57	344	4 ohv	Own	35
	3 1/2 Sport VS		2 V	62	57	344	4 ohv	Own	39
Motobécane	125 LT	F	2	43	43	125	2	Own	16
	350		3	53	52.8	349.5	2	Own	38
Moto Guzzi	250 TS	I	2	56	47	231	2		25
	350 GTS		4	50	44	345	4 ohc	Own	38
	400 GTS		4	50	51	397	4 ohc	Own	40
	Falcone Sahara		1	88	82	499	4 ohv	Own	27
	750 T		2 V	82	70	748	4 ohv	Own	70
	850 T 3		2 V	73	78	844	4 ohv	Own	68
	850 T 3 California		2 V	73	78	844	4 ohv	Own	68
	V 1000-Convert		2 V	88	78	949	4 ohv	Own	71
	850 Le Mans		2 V	73	78	844	4 ohv	Own	81
Mototrans-Ducati	350 Road	E	1	76	75	340	4 ohc	Own	28
Münch-4	1200 TSS-E	D	4	78.5	66.5	1278	4 ohc	NSU	104
MV Agusta	125 Sport	I	1	53	56	123.5	4 ohv	Own	12
	350 Sport		2	63	56	349	4 ohv	Own	35
	800 S		4	67	56	790	4 2×ohc	Own	82
	900 S		4	70	58	893	4 2×ohc	Own	95
MZ	150 TS	DDR	1	56	58	143	2	Own	11.5
	250 TS		1	69	65	249	2	Own	19
Norton	Commando	GB	2	77	89	828	4 ohv	Own	51
Ossa	250 S.Pion.	E	1	72	60	244	2	Own	27
	350 S.Pion.		1	77	65	302	2	Own	30
	GS 250 Desert		1	72	60	244	2	Own	32
	350 MAR Trial		1	77	65	302	2	Own	18
Planeta (Jupiter)	Sport	SU	1	76	75	355	2	Own	32
Puch	M 50 Jet	A	1	40	39.7	49	2	Own	6.25
	M 125 GS		1	54	54	124	2	Rotax	23
	M 175 GS		1	62	57.5	174	2	Rotax	28
	M 250 GS		1	74	57.5	247	2	Rotax	32
	MC 250 Replica		1	70	64	246	2	Puch	43.5
	MC 50 Super		1	40	39.7	49	2	Puch	11.2
Rickmann	Kawasaki CR	GB	4	66	66	903	4 ohc	Kawa	82
Sanglas	400 F	E	1	82	79	422	4 ohv	Own	24
	500 S		1	89.5	79	496	4 ohv	Own	27
Seeley	Honda-750	GB	4	61	63	736	4 ohc	Honda	67
Simonini	Long Range R	I	1	54	54	123	2	Sachs	21
	H.R.Cross		1	54	54	123	2	Sachs	24
Suzuki	TS 125	J	1	56	50	123	2	Own	13
	TS 250		1	70	64	246	2	Own	18.7
	RM 125		1	56	50	123	2	Own	25
	RM 250		1	67	70	247	2	Own	36
	RM 350		1	77	80	372	2	Own	42
	GT 125		2	43	43	124	2	Own	14.2
	GT 185		2	49	49	184	2	Own	15
	GT 250		2	54	54	247	2	Own	26
	GT 380		3	54	54	371	2	Own	33
	GT 500		2	70	64	429	2	Own	38
	GT 550		3	61	62	539	2	Own	48
	GT 750		3	70	64	738	2	Own	63
	RE 5-Rotary					497	Ro.	Wankel	63
	GS 400		2	65	60	398	4 2×ohc	Own	36
	GS 750		4	65	56.4	738	4 2×ohc	Own	63
SWM	Silver Vase	I	1	40	39.7	49	2	Sachs	10
	Cross		1	40	39.7	49	2	,,	11
	Silver Vase		1	48	54	97	2	,,	19.5
	,,		1	54	54	123	2	,,	24
	,,		1	60	61	173	2	,,	28
	,,		1	72	61	248	2	,,	34
	,,		1	73	61	255	2	,,	35
Testi	Easy Raider	I	1	52	55	123	2	Minarelli	9
	Corsa 2000		1	52	55	123	2	,,	16
Triumph	Bonneville	GB	2	76	82	744	4 ohv	Own	53
	Trident		3	67	70	741	4 ohv	Own	64
Villa	Enduro 125 F	I	1	54	54	123	2	Morini	16
	Reg. + Cross		1	54	54	123	2		22
	Reg. + Cross		1	85	78	442	2	Own	42
Voskhod	175	SU	1	62	58	174	2	Own	10.5
WSK	M 06 B3	Pl	1	52	58	123	2	Own	7.3
	M 21 W2		1	61	59.5	174	2	Own	14
Yamaha	RD 50 DX	J	1	40	39.7	49	2	Own	6.26
	RS 100 DX		1	52	45.6	97	2	Own	10.5
	RD 200		2	52	46	195	2	Own	22
	RD 250		2	52	54	247	2	Own	27
	RD 400		2	64	62	398	2	Own	43
	YZ 125		1	56	50	123	2	Own	24
	YZ 250 Moto-Cross		1	70	64	246	2	Own	34
	YZ 400 ,, ,,		1	85	70	397	2	Own	41
	TZ 250 Racer		2	54	54	247	2	Own	46
	TZ 350 ,,		2	64	54	347	2	Own	54
	XT 500		1	87	84	499	4 ohc	Own	27
	XS 500		2	73	59.6	498	4 2×ohc	Own	48.5
	XS 650		2	75	74	653	4 ohc	Own	51
	XS 750		3	68	68.6	748	4 2×ohc	Own	60
	TZ 750 Racer		4	66.4	54	747	2	Own	90
Zündapp	KS 50 Sport	D	1	39	41.8	49.9	2	Own	6.25
	KS 50 Super–Sport		1	39	41.8	49.9	2	Own	6.25
	KS 50 W/c		1	39	41.8	49.9	2	Own	6.25
	KS 125 Sport		1	54	54	123	2	Own	17
	KS 175		1	62	54	163	2	Own	17
	KS 350		2	62	57	344	2	Own	27
	GS 125		1	54	54	123	2	Own	18

Marque:	Model:	Country:	Cyl.:	Bore:	Stroke:	CCM:	2 or 4 Stroke:	Engine:	Bhp:
Accossato	Cross-Unitrac	I	1	54	54	124	2	Own	31
Ancillotti	CH 125	I	1	54	54	124	2	Own	24.5
Aspes	Yuma monoscocca	I	1	54	53.8	124	2	Own	17
Bajaj	Chetak	IND	1	57	57	145	2	Own	6.3
Benelli	125 T	I	2	42.5	44	124	2	Own	18
	Sport		2	42.5	44	124	2	Own	18
	250 2CE		2	56	47	231.4	2	Own	32
	124		2	45.5	38	123.5	4 ohc	Own	16
	304		4	44	38	231.1	4 ohc	Own	27
	354 T (Sport)		4	50	44	346	4 ohv	Own	27
	654 Sport		4	60	53.4	605	4 ohc	Own	50
	900 Sei		6	60	53.4	906	4 ohc	Own	80
Bimota	HB 2	I	4	64.5	69	901.8	4 dohc	Honda	95
	SB 3		4	70	64.8	997	4 dohc	Suzuki	90
	KB 2		4	58	52.4	553.8	4 dohc	Kawasaki	54
	KB 1		4	70	66	1015	4 dohc	Kawasaki	81
BMW	R 45	D	2	70	61.5	473	2 ohv	Own	35
	R 65 (LS)		2	82	61.5	650	4 ohv	Own	50
	R 80 G/S		2	84.8	70.6	797	4 ohv	Own	50
	R 100		2	94	70.6	980	4 ohv	Own	67
	R 100 (CS, RT, RS)		2	94	70.6	980	4 ohv	Own	70
BSA	Tracker 125/6	GB	1	56	50	123	2	—	—
	Tracker 175/6		1	66	50	171	2	—	—
Bultaco	Sherpa T 125	E	1	54.2	51.5	119	2	Own	10
	Sherpa T 200		1	61	60	175	2	Own	10
	Sherpa T 250 (Alpina)		1	71	60	238	2	Own	10
	Sherpa T 350		1	83.2	60	326	2	Own	17
	Alpina 350		1	83.2	64	348	2	Own	17
	Frontera 250 GS		1	70	64	246	2	Own	17
	Frontera 370 GS		1	85	64	363	2	Own	27
Cagiva	SST 125	I	1	56	50.6	123	2	Own	10
	SST 250/Chopper		1	72	59.6	243	2	Own	10
	SST 350/Chopper		1	80	68	325	2	Own	27
	SX 125 (RX 125)		1	56	50.6	124	2	Own	17
	SX 250		1	72	59.6	243	2	Own	17
	SX 350		1	80	68	325	2	Own	27
	RX 250		1	72	81	249	2	Own	15
CAN-AM	125	CDN	1	54	54	123	2	Rotax	—
	175		1	62	57.5	173	2	Rotax	—
	250		1	72	61	248	2	Rotax	—
	400		1	84	72	399	2	Rotax	—
	Sonic 500		1	89	79.4	494	4 ohc	Rotax	40
Dnjepr	MT 12	USSR	2	78	68	650	4 ohv	Own	37
Ducati	Pantah 350 XL	I	2	66	51	349	4 ohc/Desmo	Own	40
	Pantah 600 TL		2	80	58	583	4 ohc/Desmo	Own	58
	900 S2		2	86	74.4	863.9	4 ohc/Desmo	Own	70
Egli	CBX	CH	6	64.5	53.4	1047	4 dohc	Own	100
	CBX		6	67	53.4	1129	4 dohc	Own	113
Enfield	Bullet 350 S/L	IND	1	70	90	346	4 ohv	Own	17
Fantic	RSX 80	I	1	47.5	45	79.7	2	Own	6.5
	Trial 80 Exp.		1	47.5	42	74.4	2	Own	8
	Cross-Comp.		1	47.5	45	79.74	2	Own	17.5
	RSX 125		1	55.2	52	124.4	2	Own	16
	Strada 125		1	55.2	52	124.4	2	Own	18.6
	Trial 125		1	55.2	52	124.4	2	Own	12
	Trial 200		1	62	52	156.9	2	Own	14.5
	Trial 240 Prof.		1	69	56.5	212	2	Own	18
Gilera	TG 1 (GR 1)	I	1	57	48	122	2	Own	14.5
	T 4		1	66	58	198	4 ohv	Own	17
Godier-Genoud	1000 GG 03	F	4	69.4	66	998	4 dohc	Kawasaki	102
	750 GG 07		4	66	54	738	4 dohc	Kawasaki	75
Harley-Davidson	Sportster/Roadster	USA	2	81	96.8	998	4 ohv	Own	55
	Other models (FXE, FXR, FXRS, FXS, FXWG, FXB-Sturgis, FLH, FLHC, FLT, FLTC)		2	88.8	108	1338	4 ohv	Own	67
Hercules	K 125	D	1	54	54	122	2	Sachs	12.5
Hesketh	V 1000	GB	2	95	70	992.3	4 ohc	Own	—
Honda	CR 80R	J	1	49.5	41.4	79	2	Own	—
	CR 124R		1	55.5	50.7	122	2	Own	—
	CR 250R		1	66	72	246	2	Own	—
	CR 480R		1	89	76	472	2	Own	—
	MTX80		1	45	49.5	78.7	2	Own	8.4
	CB 125 Twin		2	44	41	124	4 ohc	Own	10
	CB 250 N E.-Sport		2	62	41.4	245	4 ohc	Own	17
	CB 250 RS		1	74	57.8	249	4 ohc	Own	17
	CL 250 S		1	74	57.8	249	4 ohc	Own	17
	VT 250 F		2	60	44	248	4 dohc	Own	35
	XL 250 S (R)		1	74	57.8	249	4 ohc	Own	17
	CB 400 N E.-Sport		2	70.5	50.6	395	4 ohc	Own	—
	CM 400 T		2	70.5	50.6	395	4 ohc	Own	27
	FT 500		1	89	80	498	4 ohc	Own	27
	CB 500		4	56	50.6	498	4 ohc	Own	48
	CX 500 (CX 500 Euro, C)		2	78	52	497	4 ohv	Own	27
	CX 500 Turbo		2	78	52	497	4 ohv (T)	Own	82
	GL 500 DX Silver Wing		2	78	52	497	4 ohv	Own	27
	XL 500 R (XL 500 S)		1	89	80	498	4 ohc	Own	27
	XR 500 R		1	89	80	498	4 ohc	Own	35
	CBX 550 F (F II)		4	59.2	52	572	4 dohc	Own	60
	CB 650 (650 C, 650 SC)		4	59.8	55.8	626	4 ohc	Own	50
	CB 750 K (C, F, F 2)		4	62	62	748	4 dohc	Own	79
	VF 750 Custom (Sport)		4	70	48.6	748	4 dohc	Own	81.6
	CB 900 F (CB 900 F2)		4	64.5	69	901	4 dohc	Own	95
	CBX Pro Link		6	64.5	53.4	1047	4 dohc	Own	100
	CB 1100 R (F)		4	70	69	1062	4 dohc	Own	115
	GL 1100 Interstate (flat)		4	75	61.4	1085	4 ohc	Own	83
Horex	Rebell 80 N	D	1	46	48	79.8	2	Sachs	8.1
	Rebell 80 T (TC, L)		1	46	48	79.8	2	Sachs	8.5

Marque:	Model:	Country:	Cyl.:	Bore:	Stroke:	CCM:	2 or 4 Stroke:	Engine:	Bhp:
	80 TR		1	46	48	79.8	2	Sachs	7
Husqvarna	125 WR	S	1	55	52	123	2	Own	15
	250 WR		1	68.5	64.5	240	2	Own	16
	430 WR		1	86	74	430	2	Own	17
	Military Automatic		1	69.5	64.5	245	2	Own	24
	420 A E Automatic		1	86	71	412	2	Own	17
Isch	Planeta	USSR	1	76	75	346	2	Own	20
	Jupiter		2	—	—	347	2	Own	27
Italjet	Casual 350	I	1	83.7	60	329	2	Own	26
Jawa (Čezet)	350	CS	2	58	65	343.4	2	Own	18
Kawasaki	KE 125	J	1	56	50.6	123	2	Own	10
	KX 125		1	56	50.6	123	2	Own	32
	KE 175 (KDX 175)		1	62.5	57	173	2	Own	17
	Z 250 J		2	55	52.4	248	4 ohc	Own	17
	Z 250 A		2	55	52.4	248	4 ohc	Own	27
	Z 250 C (Z 250 LTD)		1	70	64	246	4 ohc	Own	17
	KL 250 (KLX 250)		1	70	64	246	4 ohc	Own	17
	KX 250		1	70	64.9	249	2	Own	42.5
	Z 400 J		4	52	47	399	4 dohc	Own	27
	Z 440 H (Z 440 LTD)		2	67.5	62	443	4 ohc	Own	27
	Z 550 LTD (Z 550 B)		4	58	52.4	553	4 dohc	Own	50
	GP Z 550		4	58	52.4	553	4 dohc	Own	62
	Z 650 F		4	62	54	647	4 dohc	Own	67
	Z 750 LTD		2	78	78	745	4 dohc	Own	49
	Z 750 LTD		4	66	54	738	4 dohc	Own	74
	Z 750		4	66	54	738	4 dohc	Own	77
	Z 750 GT		4	66	54	738	4 dohc	Own	78
	Z 750 GP		4	66	54	738	4 dohc	Own	80
	Z 750 Turbo		4	66	54	738	4 dohc (T)	Own	110
Kawasaki	Z 1000 J	J	4	69.4	66	998	4 dohc	Own	98
	Z 1000 LTD		4	69.4	66	998	4 dohc	Own	95
	Z 1100 ST		4	72.5	66	1089	4 dohc	Own	97
	Z 1100 FI GP		4	72.5	66	1089	4 dohc	Own	100
	Z 1300		6	62	71	1277	4 dohc	Own	99
Kramer	ER 125	D	1	54	54	124	2	Own	10
	EX 125		1	54	54	124	2	Own	30
	ER 250 (Gritti Rep.)		1	72	61	248	2	Own	17
	EX 250		1	72	61	248	2	Own	42
	ER 500		1	84	72	406	2	Own	27
	EX 500		1	84	73	406	2	Own	50
KTM	GS 125	A	1	54	54	124	2	Own	10
	GS 250		1	76	54	246	2	Own	17
	GS 420		1	85	54	420	2	Own	17
	GS 500		1	89	81	503.5	4 ohc	Rotax	45
Laverda	125 SLZ Custom	I	1	54	54	123.6	2	Zündapp	16.5
	500 (500 SFC)		2	72	61	497	4 dohc	Own	45
	1000 Jota (RGS 1000)		3	75	74	981	4 dohc	Own	85
	1200 TS		3	80	74	1116	4 dohc	Own	86
Maico	MD 250 wk	D	1	76	54	245	2	Own	27
	MC 250 (GSE 240)		1	67	70	247	2	Own	40
	MC 400 (GSE 400)		1	77	83	386	2	Own	47
	MC 490 (GSE 490)		1	86.5	83	488	2	Own	53
Malaguti	Cavalone	I	1	47	46	79.8	2	F. Morini	7
Malanca	E 2C Sport	I	2	43	43	124	2	Own	17
	E 2C Sport w/c		2	43	43	124	2	Own	24
MF	650 R	F	2	77	70	652	4	Citroen	52
Montesa	Cota 123	E	1	54	54	123.7	2	Own	7
	Cota 200		1	64	54	173.7	2	Own	10
	Cota 248		1	69	64	239.3	2	Own	12
	Trail 348		1	83.4	64	349.4	2	Own	16
	Enduro 360 H7		1	83.4	64	349.4	2	Own	27
Morini	125 T	I	1	59	45	123	4 ohv	Own	9
	Amex 250 J		2	59	44	240	4 ohv	Own	23
	3-1/2 Sport (V)		2	62	57	344	4 ohv	Own	27
	500 T/S		2	69	64	479	4 ohv	Own	42
	500 Camel		2	69	64	479	4 ohv	Own	38
	500 Turbo		2	69	64	479	4 ohv	Own	75
Motobécane	Enduro 80	F	1	43	48	78	2	Own	7.4
	125 LT 3		2	43	43	124.8	2	Own	16
Motobi	253	I	4	44	38	231	4 ohc	Own	26
Moto Guzzi	V-35 II (Imola, 35C)	I	2	66	50.6	346.2	4 ohv	Own	35
	V-50 III (Monza, 50C)		2	74	57	490.3	4 ohv	Own	49
	V-65 (V 65 SP)		2	80	64	643	4 ohv	Own	52
	850—T 4		2	83	78	844	4 ohv	Own	68.5
	850 Le Mans—III		2	85	78	844	4 ohv	Own	76
	V-1000 I Convert (G 5, California II, SP)		2	88	78	949	4 ohv	Own	61
	V 1000 Le Mans—II		2	88	78	949	4 ohv	Own	82
MZ	123	DDR	1	52	58	123	2	Own	10
	ETZ 250		1	69	65	243	2	Own	17
Ossa	250 Desert	E	1	72	60	244	2	Own	16
	T 250 Copa		1	72	60	244	2	Own	27
Peugeot	TXE 125	F	1	57	48	123	2	Own	14
Planeta	Sport 350	USSR	1	76	75	346	2	Own	32
Puch	GS 80 W	A	1	50	40	78.5	2	Own	21
	GS 125 F3		1	54	54	123.7	2	Rotax	29
	GS 250 F3		1	72	61	248.4	2	Rotax	38
	GS 366 F3		1	84	66	365.8	2	Rotax	40
	GS 504 F4 T U.H.S.		1	90	79	502.6	4 ohc	Rotax	45
	MC 250 U.H.S.		1	72	61	248.4	2	Rotax	40
	MC 500 U.H.S.		1	91	72	468.3	2	Rotax	47
Sanglas	400 Y	E	2	69	52.4	391	4 ohv	Yamaha	27
	500 S 2		1	85.5	79	496	4 ohv	Own	27
Suzuki	DR 125 S	J	1	57	48.8	124	2	Own	9.5
	GSX 250 E		2	60	44.2	249	4 dohc	Own	17
	GNX 250 E		1	72	61.2	249	4 ohc	Own	17
	DR 250		1	72	61.2	249	4 ohc	Own	17
	GN 400 TD (400 L)		1	88	65.2	396	4 ohc	Own	27

Marque:	Model:	Country:	Cyl.:	Bore:	Stroke:	CCM:	2 or 4 Stroke:	Engine:	Bhp:
	GS 400 T (GSX 400 L & E)		2	65	60	395	4 dohc	Own	27
	GSX 400 F Katana		4	53	45.2	394	4 dohc	Own	42
	GS 450 L (GS 450 T)		2	71	56.6	448	4 dohc	Own	42
	DR 500 S		1	88	82	495	4 ohc	Own	27
	GS 550 T (GS 550 M Katana)		4	56	55.8	543	4 dohc	Own	50
	GS 650 G Katana		4	62	55.8	665	4 dohc	Own	73
	GSX 750 E		4	67	53	742	4 dohc	Own	80
	GSX 750 S Katana		4	67	53	742	4 dohc	Own	82
	GSX 1100 E		4	72	66	1074	4 dohc	Own	100
	Bimota SB 3 D		4	70	64.8	986	4 dohc	Suzuki	90
SWM	XN 500 Enduro	I	1	89	81	502.3	4 ohc	Rotax	45
	RS 125 TL (RS-GS, GTS)		1	54	54	124	2	Own	10
	RS 175 GS		1	62	57.5	174	2	Own	15
	RS 250 GS		1	72	61	248	2	Own	17
	RS 320 TL		1	76	61	277	2	Own	15
	RS 280 GS		1	76	61	277	2	Own	25
	RS 370 GS		1	84	71	393	2	Own	17
Tornax	TS 80	D	1	47	46	79.8	2	F. Morini	7
	RX 80 Enduro		1	47	46	79.8	2	F. Morini	7
Triumph	TR 6 Thunderbird	GB	2	76	71.5	649	4 ohv-twin	Own	42
	TR 7 RV Tiger		2	76	82	744	4 ohv-twin	Own	46
	TR 7 Tiger Trial		2	76	82	744	4 ohv-twin	Own	42
	T 140 Bonneville		2	76	82	744	4 ohv-twin	Own	49
WSK	125 KOS	PL	1	52	58	123	2	Own	7.3
	175 Perkoz		1	61	59.5	174	2	Own	14
Yamaha	DT 125 LC	J	1	56	50	123	2	Own	16.2
	DT 175 MX		1	66	50	169	2	Own	16
	SR 350 Spec.		1	73.5	56.5	238	4 ohc	Own	17
	RD 250		2	54	54	248	2	Own	27
	DT 250 MX		1	70	64	244	2	Own	16
	XT 250		1	75	56.5	249	4 ohc	Own	17
	RD 350		2	64	54	347	2	Own	46
	XS 400 (XS 400 Spec.)		2	69	52.4	386	4 ohc	Own	27
	SR 500 G/S (XT 500)		1	87	84	499	4 ohc	Own	27
	XJ 550		4	57	51.8	528	4 dohc	Own	50
	XZ 550 LC		2	80	55	552	4 dohc	Own	50
	XJ 650		4	63	52.4	653	4 dohc	Own	50
	XJ 650 Turbo		4	65	52.4	653	4 dohc	Own	85
	XS 650		2	75	74	653	4 ohc	Own	50
	XS 650 Spec.		2	75	74	657	4 ohc	Own	48
	XJ 750 Seca		4	65	56.4	748	4 ohc	Own	81
	XV 750 Special		2	83	69.2	749	4 ohc	Own	50
	XS 850		3	71.5	68.6	826	4 dohc	Own	79
	TR 1		2	95	69.2	981	4 dohc	Own	69
	XS 1100 (XS 1100 S)		4	71.5	68.6	1101	4 dohc	Own	95
Zündapp	KS 175	D	1	62	54	163	2	Own	18

GLOSSARY

Acceleration
The time in which the motorcycle attains a given speed from the state of rest.

Advanced ignition
Term used to describe the setting of the ignition-timing of the engine so that the spark occurs at the plug points before the piston reaches the top of its stroke.

Air cooling
Term referring to the method of dispersing the heat produced in the cylinder (cylinders) of the engine.

Air intake
The port through which the air-supply to the carburettor is drawn.

Automatic inlet valves
Inlet valves which open at-mospherically, without any mechanical control. Used on early engines.

Ball joint
A joint in which a ball on the end of a rod or lever moves in a socket provided in another member, thus providing for movement in different directions.

Balloon tyres
Tyres of large cross-section, containing air of relatively low-pressure. Used in the late twenties mainly.

Beaded-edge tyres
Outer cover of pneumatic tyres which has a hard edge or beading to fit into a channel at each side of the wheel rim. Had its heyday in pre-war years.

Belt-drive
Made from leather or some other flexible material, belts were used for the power transmission from engine or gear-box to the rearwheel of motorcycles. Lightweight machines had such drive until the early thirties. Bicycle-engines often had belt-drive to the frontwheel also.

Benzole
Motor fuel, derived from the distillation of coal-tar. Was used together with petrol in road-racing, after the use of alcohol-fuel was disallowed by the FIM.

Bevel drive
Usually, gear which ac-tuates overhead camshaft. Sometimes used in shaft-drive systems, or to actuate magnetos.

Bhp
Brake horsepower (the brake horsepower available at the engine flywheel).

Bialbero
Two overhead camshafts (double-ohc)

Big end
Name given to the lower part of the connecting-rod at its point of attachment to the crank-pin.

Blower
Better known as a super-charger; means of forced induction.

Bore
Visually, the diameter of the cylinder, measured in millimetres (mm).

Bottom dead centre
Description of the position of the piston when it reaches the lowest point in its travel within the cylinder and is about to begin its up-ward journey.

Camshaft
The shaft or spindle, with or upon which the cam rotates. The cams are some-times formed in one piece with the camshaft.

Capacity
Cylinder capacities of engines are expressed in cubic centimetres (cc). A thousand cubic centimetres equals one litre. A 500cc machine is therefore a half-litre motorcycle.

Carburettor
A device for converting the engine fuel into a vapour and mixing it with the necessary amount of air to form an explosive mixture.

Cardan shaft
Replaces on many machines the chain as a drive from the gearbox to the rear wheel.

Chain drive
Term used generally to denote the transmission of power from one sprocket-wheel to another by means of a chain. Chain drive is used mainly for driving the rear wheel; also used for transmitting the power from engine to the gearbox to the magneto or the over-head camshaft.

Charge
The volume of fuel vapour and air which is sucked into the cylinder of an engine by the induction stroke of the piston.

Combustion chamber
Space above the piston in the cylinder in which the explosive charge is com-pressed and ignited.

Compression
The reduction in volume of a mass of material due to externally-applied pressure. The term is used to denote the compression of the cylinder by the action of the piston. This compression is usually defined in terms of lbs per square inch.

Connecting rod
A light metal bar connec-ting the under-side of the

piston to the crankshaft. It is provided with bearings on each side.

Contact breaker
A mechanical device which constantly breaks and restores a low-tension cir-cuit in order to create igni-tion from the spark plug.

Crankcase
The metal casing which surrounds and encloses the crankshaft and its assembly.

Crankpin
The shorter part of the crankshaft which receives the downward thrust from the piston.

Crankshaft
The main revolving shaft of the engine which converts the up and down move-ments of the pistons into rotary motion.

Cubic centimetre
A metric system measure of the volume or capacity of the engine.

Cylinder
The cylindrical metal chamber in which com-bustion takes place. This explosion converts the fuel into power.

Diesel engine
A type of engine first devised in 1892 by Dr Rudolf Diesel. In such engines, a charge of air is drawn into the cylinder by

the piston and then highly compressed. The compres-sion effected is so high, that the air becomes hot enough to ignite a charge of fueld which is injected into the cylinder-head just at the end of the compression stroke. Ignition follows, and the piston is driven downwards again by the expansion of the burning mixture.

Dry-sump lubrication
A system of engine lubrication in which two oil-pumps are used. One of the pumps feeds oil from a reservoir around the engine bearings under pressure, the other pump removes surplus oil from the sump and returns it to the oil reservoir.

Duralumin
Name given to a class of aluminium alloys containing aluminium, copper magnesium and manganese in varying proportions.

Dynamometer
An instrument which measures the brake horse power of an engine.

Exhaust
The conduit through which the exhaust gases from the cylinder are expelled into the air.

Exhaust gases
The products of the combustion taking place within the cylinder. Exhaust gases are normally composed of carbon dioxide, carbon monoxide, steam, nitrogen, together with varying amounts of oil-vapour, and traces of unburnt fuel and hydro-carbon gases.

Exhaust stroke
The upward stroke of the piston which pushes out through the raised exhaust valve the burnt charge within the cylinder.

Exhaust valve
The cylinder valve of the engine which is made to open once for every two revolutions of the flywheel in order to permit the escape of the combusted mixture.

Expansion
The increase in volume of a material which occurs when it is heated. The power developed by the ignition of the fuel mixture within the cylinder is mainly due to the heat generated during the rapid chemical combination of the constituents of the vapour.

Fins
Metal ribs which are formed on the exterior of air-cooled cylinders and in adjacent positions. Their object it to present as great a surface as possible to the cooling action of the air.

Float
The light hollow metal box which, forming part of the carburettor, regulates the supply of petrol to the float chamber.

Float chamber
The metal case or cylinder in which the carburettor float is housed and which serves as a reservoir for the supply of petrol to the jet or other vapourising device of the carburettor.

Flywheel
A heavy steel or cast-iron wheel mounted on the main shaft of the engine, the purpose of which is to balance the intermittent power impulses given to the crankshaft by the pistons. The flywheel gives the character of steady-running to the engine.

Four-stroke cycle
This is the engine cylce which has four successive piston movements, for induction, compression, power and exhaust.

Friction drive
A form of friction gear, once used on some motor-cycles. This form of gear dispenses with the ordinary type of gearbox-clutch assembly and substitutes for it an arrangement of friction discs making variable contact with the flywheel from which the drive is taken.

Gasket
The gasket is a washer made up of various packing materials such as thick paper, thin rubber, asbestos, oiled fabric etc. which is placed between two metal faces in order to produce a gas-tight joint.

Gate change
Term referring to the method of changing gears by a hand lever on old motorcycles, the gear-lever being moved into various postions in the gate.

Gearbox
Train of pinion wheels arranged in a metal casing. Various combinations of the wheels can be engaged, thereby enabling engine power to be transmitted from the crankshaft to the road-wheels in varying ratios.

Gear ratio
The ratio between the input and the output speeds of a train of gear wheels. Applied to motorcylce practice, the term denotes the ratio of engine revolutions to the number of road-wheel revolutions.

Gudgeon pin
A steel rod which passes horizontally through the piston on its underside and which serves to connect the small end of the connecting rod to the piston, thus enabling power to be transmitted to the crankshaft.

Horizontal engine
Engine which has its cylinders placed horizontally.

Horsepower
The conventional unit of motor power. One horse-power represents the power required to raise 33,0000lb by 1 foot in 1 minute. Many other local systems have been used in the past.

Indicated horsepower
The power expended by the burning fuel mixture in driving the piston down-wards. So-called because an instrument termed and 'Indicator' can be used to measure or indicate the downward pressure on the piston. Indicated horse-power does not account for the power lost by friction within the engine. Hence it does not represent the external power-output of the engine.

Induction pipe
The metal pipe or conduit which conveys the explosive mixture from the carburettor to the cylinders of the engine.

Inlet valve
The valve which admits the mixture of fuel vapour and air into the cylinder at regular intervals, the valve being operated by means of a cam.

Kilometre
A metric measure of length origination in Europe. One kilometre equals a thousand metres.

Leaf springs
Name given to springs which consist of a number of thin leaves or strips of spring steel clamped together. Such springs were used up to the thirties on some front forks and also on some rear-suspensions.

Litre
The metric unit of volume, which is used to indicate the cylinder capacities of engines. One litre equals 1000cc.

Little end
The upper end and bearing of the connecting-rod at its point of connection to the gudgeon-pin of the piston.

Magneto
A special form of dynamo comprising an armature which revolves between the poles of one or more permanent magnets. It is employed in many machines as a generator of high-tension current for ignition purposes.

Manifold
A term which denotes a short passage or chamber through which gases may flow, as for instance the exhaust manifold of a motorcycle engine, through which the gases flow from the exhaust ports of the cylinders. The term mani-fold is also used for the mixture-inlet, or induction pipe assembly.

Mechanical efficiency
The ratio of the brake horsepower of an engine to the actual horsepower obtained from it under running conditions. The mechanical efficiency of an engine is governed by varying factors, including the speed at which it runs.

Metre
The fundamental unit of length in the metric system of measurements. Equals 39.3707 inches.

Mile
The unit of road measure-ments which originated in Britain. One mile equals 1760 yards or 1.6 kilometres.

Near-side
The left-hand side of a motorcycle as seen from the driving position.

Otto cycle
The four-stroke cycle of operations which produces the power within the cylinder of an internal combustion engine. It is called after Dr Nicholas Otto (1833-1891) who introduced it in his 'silent' gas-engine in 1876.

Overall length
Applied to a motorcycle, this is the total length, ie the distance between the fore-most projection and the farthest point at the rear.

Over-heating
Refers to the point at which the internal temperature of the cylinder produces inadequate lubrication between piston and cylinder, together with other unwanted effects. Overheating often occurs in modern two-stroke racing machines.

Petrol
Highly-inflammable, colourless liquid, obtained by the distillation and refinement of crude petroleum. It is a mixture of a large number of hydro-carbon liquids.

Petroleum
The naturally-occuring mineral oil from which commercial petrol is distilled.

Pinking
Characteristic light tapping sound which is generally in evidence when the engine is under heavy load or when it is accelerating. Occurs mainly when the ignition is too far advanced or the petrol used is of low octane.

Planetary gear
A form of gearing, common in change-speed mechanisms in which small pinion-wheels revolve sun-and-planet-wise, around a large central wheel. Used on some older designs.

Plunger
This term usually denotes a small piston provided with a hand-operating stem and knob, which is used as a forcer of liquids in small pumps, including suspension units.

Poppet valve
Ordinary type of valve employed in four-stroke motorcycle engines.

Port
A passage or opening leading to the interior of the cylinder through which the gases are drawn or expelled. Thus the terms inlet port, transfer port and exhaust port of a cylinder.

Power
Term which should be dis-tinguished from force, as the two are not synony-mous. Power is best described as the rate at which work is performed. This power is divided by time.

Push rods
Steel rods which operate overhead valves, being themselves actuated by revolving cams below.

Retarded ignition
Term used to denote the setting of the ignition-timing of the engine, so that the spark occurs at the plug points after the piston has reached the top of its stroke and has begun again its downward journey.

Revolution indicator
Instrument for registering the number of revolutions per minute of a wheel or shaft. They work on principles similar to those of an ordinary speedometer.

Rocker
Pivoted lever having a rocking motion by means of which it conveys movement from one point to another. Used mainly in valve mechanisms.

Rotary valve
A special form of valve which is driven off the cam-shaft by means of a spiral screw. It is usually mounted in the normal side-valve position and by its communication successively between the cylinder and the exhaust pipe. The rotary valve is silent in operation.

rpm
Recognised abbreviation for 'revolution per minute'

Scavenging
Term used to describe the clearing out of the products of combustion from the cylinder during the exhaust stroke of the piston. In some engines special devices are fitted to effect the maxi-mum degree of scavenging.

Seizing
The act of two rubbing surfaces binding together owing to the frictional heat generated having locally melted the parts and causing them to become welded together. Seizures occur mainly between cylinders and pistons in highly stressed two-stroke racing machines.

Side-valve
Any type of valve set in the side of the engine. Seldom used in modern motorcycle engines.

Silencer
Device fitted to the exhaust system of an engine where-by the pressure of the exhaust gases is con-siderably reduced before they reach the outer air. By this means, the noise of the escaping gases is con-siderably reduced. Silencers generally utilise expansion chambers in which the exhaust gases can dissipate a good deal of their energy before gaining access to the external air. The design of expansion chambers if of particular importance to the efficiency of two-stroke engines.

Slide valve
A type of engine valve, in which the entry and exit of the cylinder gases is controlled by two concentric slinding sleeves placed between the piston and the cylinder.

Spray lubrication
Simplest and oldest system of engine lubrication, in which oil contained in the crank-chamber is, by the rotation of the crankshaft, thrown up and distributed in the form of a spray over the lower parts of the engine. Known also as splash lubrication.

Stroke
Distance which the piston travels during its upward and downward movement in the cylinder. The stroke is always measured in millimetres.

Suction stroke
Downward stroke of the piston which sucks or draws the mixture of fuel vapour and air into the cylinder through the inlet valve.

Supercharger
A device which forces more fuel vapour and air into the cylinder than could be taken into it normally by the induction strike of the piston. The use of any engines with superchargers or any other kind of forced induction is now not permitted in road races.

Tappet
A steel rod which transmits the lifting motion of the valve cams to the valves, so that they are regularly opened.

Tappet clearance
Minute space provided between the end of the valve stem and its tappet in order to allow for the expansion of the valve stem when heated.

Thermal efficiency
Ration of heat converted into work to the total amount of heat produced by the engine.

Throttle
Valve which contains the entry of the gaseous mixture into the cylinder or cylinders.

Titanium
Hard, light metal with a high melting-point. Comparatively costly.

Top dead centre
Position of the piston when it reaches the top of its travels within the cylinder and is about to begin its downward journey.

Torque
A twisting effect. The turning tendency of a shaft. Torque is supplied to the crankshaft by the down-ward movement of the piston.

Transmission shaft
Shaft which transmits power from the gearbox to the rear-wheel.

Tube ignition
Early system of firing the explosive mixture by means of a small platinum tube which was heated to red-ness. Now obsolete.

Two-stroke
Engine cycle in which the power impulse on the piston occurs as every alternate stroke, the engine combining compression of the mixture with an explosion at every revolution of the crank-shaft. The two-stroke engine eliminates the use of valves and timing gears.

Universal joint
Joint between two rotating shafts which permits the side-to-side movement of one shaft without severing the power connection between them.

V-engine
Engine whose cylinders are set opposite one another in the shape of a letter V.

Wheelbase
Term used to denote the distance between the centres of the front and rear wheels.

Worm gear
A form of gearing comprising a gear-wheel whose teeth mesh with a worm of endless screw.

Yard
Measure of distance, originating from Britain. One yard equals 3 feet (36 inches) or 0.91 of a metre.